AUTOBIOGRAPHY

Nineteenth-Century British Autobiographies
Series Editors: Linda H. Peterson and Janice Carlisle

AUTOBIOGRAPHY

Harriet Martineau

edited by Linda H. Peterson

Nineteenth-Century British Autobiographies

Library and Archives Canada Cataloguing in Publication

Martineau, Harriet, 1802–1876.
    Autobiography / Harriet Martineau ; edited by Linda H. Peterson.

(Nineteenth-century British autobiographies)
Includes bibliographical references.

ISBN-13: 978-1-55111-555-9
ISBN-10: 1-55111-555-7

    1. Martineau, Harriet, 1802–1876. 2. Women authors, English—19th century—Biography. 3. Women social reformers—Great Britain—Biography. 4. Women intellectuals—Great Britain—Biography. I. Peterson, Linda H. II. Title. III. Series.

PR4984.M5Z46 2006   828'.809   C2006-906126-2

Advisory editor for this volume: Michel W. Pharand

Broadview Press is an independent, international publishing house, incorporated in 1985. Broadview believes in shared ownership, both with its employees and with the general public; since the year 2000 Broadview shares have traded publicly on the Toronto Venture Exchange under the symbol BDP.

We welcome comments and suggestions regarding any aspect of our publications–please feel free to contact us at the addresses below or at broadview@broadviewpress.com / www.broadviewpress.com

North America
PO Box 1243, Peterborough, Ontario, Canada K9J 7H5
Tel: (705) 743-8990; Fax: (705) 743-8353
email: customerservice@broadviewpress.com
PO Box 1015, 3576 California Road, Orchard Park, NY, USA 14127

UK, Ireland, and continental Europe
NBN International
Estover Road
Plymouth PL6 7PY UK
Tel: 44 (0) 1752 202 300
Fax: 44 (0) 1752 202 330
email: enquiries@nbninternational.com

Australia and New Zealand
UNIREPS, University of New South Wales
Sydney, NSW, 2052
Australia
Tel: 61 2 9664 0999; Fax: 61 2 9664 5420
email: info.press@unsw.edu.au

PRINTED IN CANADA

Contents

Acknowledgements

I am grateful to two past editors of Martineau's letters—Valerie Sanders (*Selected Letters*, Clarendon Press, 1990) and Elisabeth Sanders Arbuckle (*Harriet Martineau's Letters to Fanny Wedgwood*, Stanford University Press, 1983)—as well as to a current editor, Deborah Anna Logan (*The Collected Letters of Harriet Martineau*, Pickering & Chatto, forthcoming 2007). Their editions have helped me identify and annotate references to Martineau's family, friends, and professional acquaintances; Professors Sanders and Logan have additionally responded to queries, provided me with useful references, and encouraged this project. I am also grateful to members of the Martineau Society who volunteered aid and passed on suggestions; to Lori Misura, reference librarian, and Angus Trumble, curator of paintings, at the Yale Center for British Art for their help with British engravers, painters, and paintings; to Julia Gaunce, Barbara Conolly, Judith Earnshaw, Anne Hodgetts, Tara Lowes, Marjorie Mather, and Michel Pharand at Broadview, for timely advice and careful editing; and to Maria Frawley, Joanne Shattock, Linda Hughes, Janice Carlisle, and other Victorianists who have read sections of this edition, or listened to my thoughts on this important Victorian autobiography.

Introduction

When Harriet Martineau wrote her autobiography in 1855, she thought she was dying. She had consulted an eminent London physician, Dr. Peter Latham, who diagnosed a fatal heart condition, and after hearing his opinion that "the substance of the heart has deteriorated, so that 'it is too feeble for its work'" (628), she set her house in order. She made a new will, arranged for her servants' futures, visited family and friends, and completed a life history that she had begun in 1843 during another "fatal" illness.

Writing an autobiography hardly seems, to us moderns, commensurate with arranging financial affairs or saying a last farewell to friends. Yet Martineau thought it her "duty" to record her life experiences. In the introduction to her *Autobiography*, written at her home, The Knoll, in the Lake District, she explains this conviction: "I have always enjoyed, and derived profit from, reading those of other persons, from the most meagre to the fullest: and certain qualities of my own mind,—a strong consciousness and a clear memory in regard to my early feelings,—have seemed to indicate to me the duty of recording my own experience" (34). This rationale for life writing—conventional in its emphasis on instruction and pleasure for the reader, a clear memory and strong sense of self for the writer—almost obscures the remarkable nature of her autobiographical act. For Martineau had lived an extraordinary life—becoming a literary journalist when her family's fortune collapsed, publishing a best-selling series by the age of thirty, overcoming a hearing disability to become a "literary lion" in London society, traveling to America and writing two founding texts of sociological method, exploring north Africa and the Middle East to observe non-European societies, and commenting publicly on economics, politics, history, and religion in an era when women supposedly maintained their place in the sphere of domesticity.

Like her life, Martineau's *Autobiography* is remarkable in the history of women's literature. Most nineteenth-century women writers allowed their memoirs to be assembled by a family member or literary friend after their deaths—as in "Biographical Notice of the Author" (1818) by Jane Austen's brother Henry, the "Memoir" (1837) of Felicia Hemans by her sister Mrs. Hughes, or *The Life of Charlotte Brontë* (1857) by friend and fellow-novelist Elizabeth Gaskell. Harriet Martineau told her own story. (Indeed, she told it more than once, even writing the third-person obituary that appeared in the *Daily News* on June 29, 1876, two days after her death.)

By interdicting the publication of her letters and asking friends to burn private correspondence, Martineau in effect prevented others from shaping her life story, and thus she maintained the power to tell it her own way.

That way includes, generically speaking, several ways. The *Autobiography* is hybrid in form and engages multiple genres of life writing: the *bildungsroman*, or account of a young person's educational and intellectual development; the spiritual autobiography, or account of religious beliefs and (de)conversion; a disabilities memoir, or testimony to overcoming physical handicaps and illness; and the professional artist's life, a nineteenth-century genre increasingly important with the rise of the man and woman of letters. Martineau treats these strands as inter-related: she suggests, for example, that her unusual education prepared her for a life of professional journalism, and she insists that she wrote books to share knowledge with others that had been important to her own development. Nonetheless, we might analyze these generic strands separately to understand Martineau's purposes and to place her *Autobiography* within a broad context of British life writing.

Autobiography as *Bildungsroman*

Bildung—a German term signifying intellectual, moral, and spiritual development—is not a word that appears in Martineau's *Autobiography*, but the concept underlies its narrative. In the first section, Martineau testifies to her parents' determination to provide their children with an excellent education: "They pinched themselves in luxuries to provide their girls, as well as their boys, with masters and schooling" (51). Throughout, her *Autobiography* illustrates a principle articulated in her treatise, *Household Education* (1849): that education is the privilege and duty of every person, not just of the young, and that the goal of both individuals and nations should be "to bring out and strengthen *all* the powers of every human being."[1] In the final section, Martineau testifies to her own continuing education, as well as to the intellectual advancement of the human race: "It is my belief that we can in no way but by sound knowledge of Man learn, fully and truly, ... I believe that this science is fairly initiated; and it follows of course that I anticipate for the race amelioration and progression at a perpetually accelerated rate" (645). For Martineau, as for other Victorians, education was the key to personal development.

---

[1]   See "Old and Young at School," in *Household Education* (Philadelphia: Lea and Blanchard, 1849), p. 13.

The specifics of Martineau's education, however, included opportunities unavailable to most nineteenth-century women. As a child, she was taught at home by parents, elder siblings, and private tutors, receiving lessons in Latin from her eldest brother Thomas, in French from her eldest sister Elizabeth, and in writing and arithmetic from her brother Henry. She also took music lessons from the cathedral organist, Dr. John Beckwith. Then, by a lucky twist of provincial religion and politics, Harriet and her sister Rachel were sent to a local grammar school run by the Rev. Isaac Perry, a clergyman-schoolmaster in Norwich, the town where Martineau grew up. Perry had changed his religious affiliation from Presbyterianism to Unitarianism—and consequently lost most of his students. The Unitarian families decided to support him by sending their daughters to his once all-male school. And thus, at the age of eleven, began "that delectable schooling" which Martineau recalled "with clear satisfaction and pleasure" (73) and which provided a basis for her career as a professional writer.

At Perry's grammar school, Martineau studied French with a native French tutor, Latin from the Eton grammar, and rhetoric from a system of Perry's own devising, based loosely on the neo-classical *Principles of Rhetoric* of Hugh Blair (1785). As Harriet recalls, "There was the Proposition, to begin with: then the Reason, and the Rule; then the Example, ancient and modern; then the Confirmation; and finally, the Conclusion" (75). She was thrilled to learn the secrets of composition. "It was a capital way of introducing some order into the chaos of girls' thoughts," she remarks (75), and she attributed her highly successful career as a professional woman of letters to this instruction. Remembering her induction into the mysteries of rhetoric, she comments: "I got credit by my themes. Mr. Perry told me so, in 1834, when I had just completed the publication of my Political Economy Tales, and when I had the pleasure of making my acknowledgments to him as my master in composition, and probably the cause of my mind being turned so decidedly in that direction" (76).

Although Martineau attributes her professional success to her schoolmaster, in a larger sense we might credit Dissenting academies for their emphasis on civic rhetoric—that is, on rhetoric as a vehicle for participation in the public sphere. As Thomas Miller has shown in *The Formation of College English: Rhetoric and Belles Lettres in the British Cultural Provinces* (1998), Dissenting academies of the eighteenth and early nineteenth centuries—in contrast to Oxford and Cambridge Universities—emphasized training in neo-classical rhetoric. They did so because their constituents, excluded from elite institutions and denied full participation in British political life, needed to make their views and voices heard.[1] Miller traces the rise of Dissenting rhetoric, and its engagement with the public sphere, through the work of Unitarian schoolmasters such as Joseph Priestley and John Aikin (father of the poet, Anna Laetitia Barbauld) at Warrington Academy and of Rochement Barbauld at Palgrave School. Both these academies were familiar to the Martineau family—Harriet's uncle having studied at Warrington, her father at Palgrave under the tutelage of Anna Barbauld. Harriet's training in rhetoric and composition, while perhaps unusual for a girl, was nonetheless consistent with her family's educational tradition and with the enlightened views of Unitarians on women's education. The Norwich school of Harriet's teacher, Isaac Perry, may not have achieved the distinguished reputation of Warrington and Palgrave, but it nonetheless continued the Dissenting practice of educating its pupils for participation in the public sphere.

More personally, Martineau's rhetorical training gave her the confidence to explore serious subjects rationally and systematically. Although her comment that composition "was a capital way of introducing some order into the chaos of girls' thoughts" may sound sexist, in fact it speaks to the empowerment of women. By learning to treat a subject systematically, to analyze it logically and reassemble its parts in a "theme," Martineau gained the ability to take on difficult religious, philosophical, and political questions. The *Autobiography* testifies to her success in doing so—from her discussion of the theological problem of God's foreknowledge and man's free will (Period I), to her redaction and illustration of the principles of political economy (Period III), to her analysis of American social institutions, including slavery (Period IV), to her exploration of Auguste Comte's then-groundbreaking philosophy and her adoption of materialist "laws" to interpret herself and her world (Period VI). In sum, the story of her educational progress, told in Period II, merges seamlessly with the account of her religious, psychological, and professional development in the remainder of her *Autobiography*.

Autobiography as Spiritual Quest

In writing her life history, Martineau produced one of the great spiritual autobiographies of the nineteenth century. The Martineaus were

[1]   Thomas Miller, "Liberal Education in the Dissenting Academies," in *The Formation of College English: Rhetoric and Belles Lettres in the British Cultural Provinces* (Carbondale, Il: Southern Illinois UP, 1998), pp. 98–99.

French Huguenots who immigrated to England in 1685 when the Revocation of the Edict of Nantes took away their civil liberties, and they were proud of their heritage of Protestant dissent. The family attended the famous Octagon Chapel in Norwich and participated in regional and national Unitarian assemblies. Harriet became a leading writer for the Unitarian periodical, *The Monthly Repository*; her brother James, a prominent Unitarian minister, theologian, and professor at Manchester New College. When she diverged from her Unitarian roots in the 1840s and 50s and embraced a scientific, or "positive," philosophy, many family members were dismayed. Eventually, her loss of faith caused a breach with James, who reviewed her agnostic *Letters on the Laws of Man's Nature and Development* (1851) harshly, publicly regretting that his sister had forsaken her faith and followed Henry Atkinson, her co-author, "in the infection of his blind arrogance and scorn."[1]

Although her *Autobiography* records a de-conversion from Unitarian Christianity to agnostic materialism rather than a conversion to religious belief, it nonetheless reproduces the quest for spiritual truth fundamental to English autobiography from John Bunyan's *Grace Abounding* (1666) and Philip Doddridge's *Rise and Progress of Religion in the Soul* (1745) to John Henry Newman's *Apologia pro vita sua* (1865) and Edmund Gosse's *Father and Son* (1907). Like these works, Martineau's *Autobiography* traces a search for an adequate hermeneutics, an authoritative system for interpreting her life experiences and comprehending their meaning. Martineau found this interpretive framework in Auguste Comte's *Philosophie Positive*, which she read in 1851, translated in 1852, and published in abbreviated form in 1853. According to Comte, each human being and humankind as a whole passes through three stages of development: "the theological, or fictitious; the metaphysical, or abstract; and the scientific, or positive."[2] These stages fit Martineau's sense of her own development—perhaps unsurprisingly, given that she had immersed herself in Comte's work just before she began writing her *Autobiography*.

Martineau organizes her account according to the Comtian model, moving from an early religious period (1802–19) through what she calls

---

[1]   "Mesmeric Atheism," *Prospective Review* 7 (June 1851), 224–62; see R.K. Webb, *Harriet Martineau: A Radical Victorian* (New York: Columbia UP, 1960) for an excellent discussion of Martineau's Unitarian roots and her adult divergence from the family religion.

[2]   Harriet Martineau, trans., *The Positive Philosophy of Auguste Comte*, 2 vols. (London: John Chapman, 1853), I, 3. According to Comte, "the phases of the mind of man correspond to the epochs of the mind of the race. Each of us is aware, if he looks back upon his own history, that he was a theologian in his childhood, a metaphysician in his youth, and a natural philosopher in his manhood."

a "metaphysical fog" (1819–39) to a final positivistic stage of thought (1839–55). Each stage encompasses roughly two books of the total six, with Period V representing a transitional state between metaphysical confusion and her final positivistic stance.[1] Explained this abstractly, Martineau's approach to life writing may sound routine (or dull). But her quest for spiritual and intellectual truth was intense, and her method, in the *Autobiography* as in her other books, relies on illustration and lively anecdote. Martineau is a superb storyteller.

To explain her early religiosity, for example, she recalls that as an infant in delicate health, she had been sent to convalesce in a rural farmhouse, where her nurse was "a Methodist or melancholy Calvinist of some sort" (41). This stay produced a humorous effect and a lasting personality trait:

> I came home the absurdist little preacher of my years. . . . I used to nod my head emphatically, and say, 'Never ky for tyfles:' "Dooty fust, and pleasure afterwards,' and so forth: and I sometimes got courage to edge up to strangers, and ask them to give me—'a maxim.' Almost before I could join letters, I got some sheets of paper, and folded them into a little square book, and wrote, in double lines, two or three in a page, my beloved maxims. (41)

If Martineau rid herself of the habit of asking strangers for maxims, she did not eliminate her religiosity (or, for that matter, her fondness for maxims). She read her Bible regularly, even in old age after she had renounced the Christian faith; she wrote devotional prayers and exercises for personal use and for publication; and she maintained a deep interest in religious issues and church affairs. In retrospect, she acknowledged "the good of those old superstitions": "I don't know what I should have done without my faith; for I was an unhealthy and most unhappy child, and had no other resource" (529).

It was the theological question of foreknowledge and free will, "how, if God foreknew every thing, we could be blamed or rewarded for our conduct" (63), that propelled Martineau out of her religious phase and into metaphysical speculation. In her teens, she puzzled over this conundrum, basic to Christian doctrine, and she discovered the principles of

---

[1]   For a fuller analysis of Comte's influence on the structure of Martineau's *Autobiography*, see Linda H. Peterson, *Victorian Autobiography: The Tradition of Self-Interpretation* (New Haven: Yale UP, 1986), pp. 135–55.

necessarianism. Like determinists, necessarians believed that all action is determined by antecedent causes, but unlike determinists, they believed that an individual's own decisions and efforts significantly contribute to such antecedent causes. Thus, all our actions may be determined by prior causes, but our own actions also influence the chain of cause and effect. As the American Unitarian William E. Channing explained, the knowledge that men's "endeavours to promote their happiness will have a certain and necessary effect, and that no well-judged effort of their will be lost, will encourage them to exert themselves with redoubled vigor."[1]

Martineau describes her discovery of necessarianism in the language of conversion: "a new vigour pervaded my whole life, a new light spread through my mind, and I began to experience a steady growth in self-command, courage, and consequent integrity and disinterestedness" (106). This beneficial change recalls the effects of religious conversion on Bunyan, Doddridge, and their heirs. In her *Autobiography*, however, necessarian philosophy replaces the Bible as the principal guide to action. At first it coexists with Christian beliefs; later, those beliefs fall away as Martineau discovers scientific method, materialist philosophy, and Comtian positivism. Although she acknowledges that her life "began in winter" and "had no spring," she concludes that she is "satisfied in a higher sense than that in which the Necessarian is always satisfied" (151). Indeed, she characterizes herself as "a free rover on the broad, bright breezy common of the universe" (110).

The story of Martineau's shift from Unitarianism to positivism occupies much of Period VI, in which she explains her philosophical position carefully and quotes letters to Henry Atkinson, her collaborator on the *Letters on the Laws of Man's Nature and Development* (1851), to illustrate her calmness in the face of family storm and public controversy. Some modern readers may find these sections overly long and elaborate; indeed, Martineau's temporal proximity to the controversy causes her to rely more on documentation than memory. But it is important to note that Martineau responds, in this final section, to the common assumption that "there are no atheists on the brink of the grave" (in modern terms, "no atheists in foxholes"). She expresses her agnosticism (as it would later be called) quietly and with special authority, in that she has received a fatal diagnosis and speaks *de facto* from her deathbed. In spiritual autobiography, the deathbed testimony holds special status as an utterance of truth in the face of eternity.

---

[1]   Quoted in Webb, p. 83.

Martineau's final utterance includes the human race as well as herself. She notes that "successive mythologies" have arisen and then declined. She declares that the last, Christianity, "is now not only sinking to the horizon, but paling in the dawn of a brighter time. The dawn is unmistakable. ... The last of the mythologies is about to vanish before the flood of a brighter light" (647). If we today find these pronouncements conventional rather than *avant garde*, it may be because we have completed the historical trajectory that she predicted 150 years ago, moving away from Christianity to a common, if not necessarily "brighter," era of science.

Autobiography as Disability Memoir

From infancy through adult life, Martineau suffered from serious physical infirmities. As a newborn infant, she nearly "starved to death" because the milk of her wetnurse was inadequate and gave her diarrhea (39). In her mid-teens, she suffered from a severe hearing impairment, which left her deaf and forced her to use a "trumpet" to carry on conversation (114–15). Her health was bad until she was nearly thirty: "never was poor mortal cursed with a more beggarly nervous system" (40). Just when she seemed to recover her health in her mid-thirties, she was struck with an incapacitating gynecological condition, diagnosed as a prolapse of the uterus and polypous tumors, for which no medical cure was possible. Martineau spent over five years in bed or on a couch "in the sickroom," "an exile of years from fresh air, exercise, and change of scene" (450). After a successful trial of mesmerism, she recovered her health, moved to the Lake District, and spent another decade actively engaged in authorship—until the gynecological condition recurred and caused (or aggravated) the heart condition that she believed would be fatal.

Martineau actively sought remedies for her disabilities—if not in traditional medicine, than in experimental practices. When she found a remedy, she shared it with others by writing a book, pamphlet, or series of magazine articles. When no remedy could be found, she wrote anyway, advising those similarly afflicted of the best psychological or practical means of coping with disability. Martineau thus participates in what Maria Frawley has called the "culture of invalidism," a nineteenth-century phenomenon that recognized the subjective experience and important social role of the invalid.[1] Martineau felt that disability authorized her to

---

[1]   Maria H. Frawley, *Invalidism and Identity in Nineteenth-Century Britain* (Chicago: U of Chicago P, 2004), pp. 1–5.

speak and that she had a duty to do so: "I have felt myself qualified to say more in the way of exhortation and remonstrance to deaf people than could be said by any one who had not only never been deaf, but had never shared the selfish and morbid feelings which are the ordinary attendant curses of suffering" (115). In speaking out, her *Autobiography* engages the medical debates of her day and anticipates the modern disability memoir (an autobiographical genre that acknowledges rather than hides handicaps, and defines identity through disability).

Martineau had previously contributed to popular medical literature. Her "Letter to the Deaf" (1834) advises deaf children and their parents about the best means of education and social management. *Life in the Sickroom* (1844), written to "unknown comrades in suffering," describes the experience of long-term illness and advises friends about effective (as opposed to deleterious) ways to intervene. "Six Letters of Mesmerism" (1844), published in the *Athæneum*, explain her treatment and cure by this innovative hypnotic practice and advocate its wider use. Her later *Health, Husbandry, and Handicraft* (1861), a collection of journalism written after an extensive correspondence with Florence Nightingale, includes essays on public health and on issues specific to professions (e.g., "The Baker: His Health" or "The Governess: Her Health").

In the *Autobiography* Martineau discusses her disabilities as they aid or impair her personal development. Trev Broughton has argued that the entire narrative is framed by "the liminal view from the Sick Room,"[1] but it is more accurate to say that this view dominates in specific sections that focus on illness and invalidism. Clearly marked in the Table of Contents, these carry such subheads as "Ill health and terrors" (I, I), "Deafness" (II, ii), "Faults and miseries" (II, iii), and "Morbid conditions as a matter of study" (V, I).

In recounting childhood illnesses and adolescent deafness, Martineau focuses on the proper medical treatment or social practices that might have spared her undue distress. She questions the common nineteenth-century practice of sending infants to a wetnurse, and argues that it may have caused "my bad health during my whole childhood and youth" (39). She describes her loss of hearing and inability to participate in conversation, "very noticeable, very inconvenient, and excessively painful to myself" (81). She advises those with "a growing infirmity" to "face the truth," and explains how family and friends often "aggravate [the

---

[1]   Trev Lynn Broughton, "Making the Most of Martyrdom: Harriet Martineau, Autobiography and Death," *Literature & History* 2 (Autumn 1993), 30.

infirmity] terribly by their way of treating it" (83). Most significantly, she speaks against the Christian "Worship of Suffering," the belief that "it [is] a duty and a privilege to dwell on the morbid conditions of human life" (432). She admits, but deeply regrets, that in her religious phase she turned her "imagination far too much on bodily suffering, and on the peculiar glory attending fortitude in that direction" (63), even dreaming of an early death. In these sections Martineau seeks, to quote Shelagh Hunter, to transform "personal loss to public service in a particularly intimate way."[1]

In recounting her adult illness, Martineau similarly deprecates the Christian tendency to glorify suffering, but she more controversially advocates mesmerism, an experimental hypnotic treatment disapproved by some Christians and unsanctioned by the medical establishment.[2] About this illness and treatment, Martineau is both explicit and coy. The *Autobiography* explains her mesmerism in detail, but never describes the gynecological condition it was meant to cure. Martineau simply states that, like her deafness, her ill health was "largely ascribable to disobedience to the laws of nature": "It was unquestionably the result of excessive anxiety of mind,—of the extreme tension of nerves under which I had been living for some years" (434). Yet her condition involved a *physical* problem: uterine tumors which were visible upon medical examination and about which her brother-in-law, Dr. T. M. Greenhow, had published a pamphlet, "Medical Report of The Case of Miss H— M—," in 1845. Today, we would most likely associate the problem with hormonal imbalance, not "excessive anxiety of mind."

Why was Martineau both reticent and explicit? Certainly, Victorian decorum accounts for some of the reticence. She was shocked and irritated by her brother-in-law's publication of her medical history, including graphic details of her vagina, tumors, and menstrual patterns—"not in a Medical Journal, where nobody but the profession would ever have seen it, and where I should never have heard of it,—but in a shilling pamphlet,—not even written in Latin,—but open to all the world" (467), and she avoided repeating his indiscretion. Certainly, she wrote explicitly of her mesmeristic treatment to counter the spurious documents that had circulated about

---

[1] Shelagh Hunter, *Harriet Martineau: The Poetics of Moralism* (Brookfield, VT: Scolar Press, 1995), p. 192.

[2] For an example of Christian disapproval, see Charlotte Elizabeth Tonna's *Mesmerism: A Letter to Miss Martineau* (Philadelphia: William S. Martien, 1847), which calls the practice "diabolical"; for the medical controversy over mesmerism, see Maria H. Frawley's edition of *Life in the Sick-Room* (Peterborough, ON: Broadview Press, 2003), Appendix C.

herself and her maid Jane Arrowsmith, who had served as her mesmeristic assistant. In a sense, Period V, section iii, "Recovery," sets the public record straight. But we might also see Martineau's decision about what to discuss and what to leave unsaid as a strategy for assuming control, for "tak[ing] my case into my own hands" (83). Just as she decided to "take a firm stand" (83) in her deafness, so she decided to take charge of a disease that the medical establishment had pronounced "incurable" (463). By attributing its causes to "extreme tension of nerves," aggravated by responsibility for three aging family members and a domineering mother (434), Martineau could enact self-help and engage her illness in an active mode. As Margaret Oliphant for *Blackwood's Edinburgh Magazine* noted in a discussion of the medical controversy, "It seems extremely unreasonable that a sick person should not be permitted to cure herself or achieve a cure in any way that is practicable. Any treatment in the world which made a sufferer well, and restored an invalid to active life, must have had an excellent claim upon the belief of that invalid, if on no one else."[1] Martineau's *Autobiography* testifies to her belief in the mesmerism that had "cured" her and restored her to active professional life.

Autobiography as Professional Author's Life

If Martineau's *Autobiography* incorporates features of the *bildungsroman*, spiritual autobiography, and disability memoir, it also—and most importantly—presents the life of a professional woman of letters. Several early episodes hint that young Harriet is destined for a writerly career: her childish delight in assembling books of maxims, her passion for reading Milton's *Paradise Lost*, her retreat into solitude with the newspaper or a book when her deafness makes communal life difficult. Even Martineau's disability marks her for authorship within contemporary myths of literary genius. In an 1832 review of Walter Scott's life, "The Characteristics of the Genius of Scott," Martineau suggested that one "characteristic" of Scott's literary genius was early "vicissitude," his "ill health" and "lameness in childhood," which caused the growth of "compassion" and "genius of a benignant character."[2] She, too, had this characteristic.

Whether it was nature or nurture, whether "genius" made Martineau a writer or whether her rhetorical education "trained" her

---

[1] *Blackwood's Edinburgh Magazine* (April 1877), 492. This review is included in Appendix C.
[2] The two-part review essay on Scott's life and work originally appeared in *Tait's Edinburgh Magazine* in 1832–33, just after Scott's death; it was reprinted as the lead essay in Harriet Martineau's *Miscellanies* 2 vols. (Boston: Hilliard, Gray, 1836); for the quotations, see I, 10.

for the profession, she wanted to have her literary abilities confirmed. From various anecdotes in the *Autobiography*, it seems clear that external validation, especially by respected men of letters, was crucial to her decision to take up her professional pen. The account of publishing her first essay includes, for example, not only Robert Aspland's acceptance of her anonymous submission to the *Monthly Repository*, but also his request "to hear more from V. of Norwich" (111). It includes W. J. Fox's statement, as incoming editor of the periodical, "that he wished for my assistance from the moment when he, as editor, discovered from the office books that I was the writer of certain papers which had fixed his attention" (125). Martineau notes, too, her beloved eldest brother's reading of the anonymous article, his praise for the "new hand" at the magazine, and his sanction of her exchange of domestic life for an authorial career: "Leave it to other women to make shirts and darn stockings; and do you devote yourself to this" (112). Further confirmation of her abilities came when Martineau submitted, again anonymously, three essays for a Unitarian competition—and won all three prizes (134–35).

Perhaps Martineau was unusual in needing—and receiving—so much encouragement and validation. But once she devoted herself to authorship, she proceeded in an utterly professional manner. Her first publications demonstrate her knowledge of the publishing market and its special niches for women writers. Her essays and reviews for the Unitarian *Monthly Repository* provided an apprenticeship in journalism; an independently-financed book, *Devotional Exercises for Use of Young Persons* (1823), gave her direct experience with booksellers, printers, and advertisers; and her tracts and short stories for a religious publisher, Houlston and Son, included payment for copyright and practice in didactic narrative.[1] Together, these three forms of publication taught Martineau the ins and outs of the nineteenth-century literary marketplace. She discusses them in detail in Period III, giving pride of place to her work for the *Monthly Repository* and praising its editor, W. J. Fox, for his mentorship: "His editorial correspondence with me was unquestionably the occasion,

---

[1] *Devotional Exercises for the Use of Young Persons* (London: Rowland Hunter, 1823). In producing this book, Martineau negotiated with S. Wilkins, a Norwich "Bookseller, Printer, Stationer, and Binder," to print and bind the sheets and with the London bookseller Rowland Hunter to sell the volumes either directly or in response to advertisements placed in the *Monthly Repository*. She kept the accounts of this early publication, which now reside in the Birmingham University Library and are microfilmed as *Women, Emancipation and Literature: The Papers of Harriet Martineau* (Wiltshire: Adam Matthew Publications, 1991), reel 10.

and in great measure the cause, of the greatest intellectual progress I ever made before the age of thirty" (125).

Martineau's most extended discussion of authorship focuses on the *Illustrations of Political Economy* (1832–34), the ground-breaking series of twenty-four pamphlets that brought her lasting fame and financial independence. In the early 1830s, the era of the First Reform Act, no publisher would believe that the reading public wanted pamphlets about what Carlyle called "the dismal science": the classical economic theories of Adam Smith, David Ricardo, James Mill, and Thomas Malthus. Yet Martineau believed that her "Political Economy Series" would sell (137–38), and that the middle and working classes, as well as politicians, needed to understand political economy not in abstract theory but as it affected everyday life:

> I thought of the multitudes who needed it,—and especially of the poor,—to assist them in managing their own welfare. I thought too of my own conscious power of doing this very thing. Here was the thing wanting to be done, and I wanting to do it[.] (145)

Martineau tells her tale of obstacles encountered, humiliating rejections, ceaseless hard work, and ultimate vindication with drama and verve— ending Period III with the astonishing success of her first pamphlet, *Life in the Wilds*, which sold over 5000 copies in the first week of publication and sent her to London as a full-fledged professional writer and "literary lion."

The formula Martineau uses for her *Illustrations of Political Economy*— public need, personal desire—runs through her account of authorship. In 1829, as a young woman considering "literary pursuits," she vowed to "write on subjects of universal concern as to inform some minds and stir up others."[1] In 1855, as she wrote her own obituary for the London *Daily News*, she emphasized her ability to "popularize" and "sympathize in other people's views," while "keep[ing] a firm grasp on her own."[2] The *Illustrations of Political Economy* provided an unprecedented opportunity to turn her "need for utterance" into positive influence in the public sphere.[3] After its success, she continued to use her rhetorical skills to

---

[1]   This document originally appeared in the *Memorials* volume of Martineau's *Autobiography* (London: Smith, Elder, 1877), III, 32–34; it is reprinted in Appendix B.

[2]   See Appendix B.

[3]   The phrase comes from her obituary, where she states: "Her stimulus in all she wrote, from first to last, was simply the need for utterance"; see Appendix B.

address important public issues: American slavery and the abolitionist movement in *Society in America* (1837), *Retrospect of Western Travel* (1838), and *The Martyr Age of the United States* (1839); religion and philosophy in *Eastern Life* (1848), *Letters on the Laws of Man's Nature and Development* (1851), and *The Positive Philosophy of Auguste Comte* (1853); modern British history and empire in *A History of England During the Thirty Years' Peace, 1861–1846* (1849) and *British Rule in India* (1857); and the pressing social and political questions of the moment in her editorials for the *Daily News* during the 1850s and 60s.

In writing for the public sphere, Martineau fulfilled the purpose of her Dissenting education. By influencing political reform, she believed that she was breaking new ground for women writers. In a letter to Richard Hengst Horne in 1844 about the *Illustrations*, she commented:

> The Amer[ica]ns told me that every tale of mine, & every manifestation of opinion was followed by something perceptible in Govt or Parlt. I laughed at first; but, on thinking, it seemed to be true.— Whence Guizot had his informa[tion] I know not. ... but he said, before coming over, that mine was a new case;—that in all history there was no preceding case of a woman having solid political influence otherwise than through some clever man[.][1]

Influence in the public sphere, influence on society and government— these goals were primary to Martineau's career. In achieving them, she advanced the cause of women, opening the way for women to pursue careers as essayists and journalists, not just as poets or novelists. As she noted, "The progression or emancipation of any class usually, if not always, takes place through the efforts of individuals of that class."[2]

Martineau wrote on women's issues throughout her career. Her first published articles, "Female Writers on Practical Divinity" and "On Female Education," reviewed the work of leading women authors, particularly Hannah More and Anna Barbauld, and presented a rationale for women's education.[3] In mid-career, her *Society in America* (1837) chastised Americans for failing to fully enact the principles of their

---

[1] Letter of 4 June 1844, Aitken, GA Misc., Harry Ransom Research Library, University of Texas.

[2] Harriet Martineau, *Society in America* (London: Saunders and Otley, 1837), III, 150.

[3] "Female Writers on Practical Divinity," *Monthly Repository* 17 (November 1822), 593–96, and (December 1822), 746–50; "On Female Education," *Monthly Repository* 18 (February 1823), 77–81.

constitution and thus sanctioning the "political non-existence of women."[1] *Household Education* (1849) included a strong argument that "everything possible should be done to improve the quality of the mind of every human being" and a rebuttal of the commonplace belief that women could not learn Greek, mathematics, or "studies of an abstract nature."[2] In later life, Martineau supported the Married Women's Property Bill and wrote an editorial in the *Daily News* (25 March 1853) advocating its passage; she published "What Women are Educated For" in *Once a Week* (10 August 1861) and "Middle-Class Education in England: Girls" in the *Cornhill Magazine* (November 1864); and she joined other Englishwomen in the campaign to repeal the Contagious Diseases Act (which violated women's civil liberties by giving police and medical officers authority to arrest and examine women suspected of prostitution). In response to the shock of American women that she should involve herself in this last campaign, Martineau replied: "I am told that this is discreditable work for woman, especially for an *old* woman. But it has always been esteemed our especial function as women, to mount guard over society and social life,—the spring of national existence,—and to keep them pure; and who so fit as an old woman?"[3]

Despite her lifelong attention to women's issues, the *Autobiography* does not dwell on the plight—or progress—of the woman writer. Except for an early snub from a cousin and a setback in 1829 when her mother refused to allow her to stay in London to "undertake proof-correcting and other literary drudgery" (130), Martineau pursued her career systematically, viewing herself as "a professional son"[4]. She asked and received the frequent aid of brothers, uncles, cousins, and friends. In her *Autobiography* she praises her family, male and female members alike, for their support, and thanks her mother for being "a great support to me" (203). Martineau overcame many obstacles on the path to professional success, but gender does not rank high among them.

Perhaps Martineau's downplaying of gender reflects a decision to show a woman writer's success through effective action rather than ideological pronouncement. As Valerie Pichanick has observed,

---

1   *Society in America* (London: Sanders & Otley, 1837), I, 148–54.

2   *Household Education* (London: Edward Moxon, 1849), 240–41. See Gayle Graham Yates, ed. *Harriet Martineau on Women* (New Brunswick, NJ: Rutgers UP, 1985) for selections from Martineau's writing on women's issues.

3   Letter to Maria Weston Chapman, included in *Memorials, Autobiography*, III, 438.

4   Letter to her mother, included in *Memorials, Autobiography*, III, 91.

Martineau "opposed female acquiescence to the limits which had been set on women's social role and political position,"[1] yet she also disliked literary women who aired their personal complaints or paraded their "gross and palpable vanities" (269). As Martineau wrote in *Household Education*, "Every woman ought to have that justice done to her faculties that she may possess herself in all the strength and clearness of an exercised and enlightened mind, and may have at her command, for her subsistence, as much intellectual power and as many resources as education can furnish her with."[2] With education and opportunity, she had "by thirty years of age, ascertained [her] career, found occupation, and achieved independence" (151), and that was evidence enough of a woman writer's achievement. As she affirms at the conclusion to Period III: "Any one to whom that happens by thirty years of age may be satisfied; and I was so" (151).

---

[1]   Valerie Kossew Pichanick, *Harriet Martineau: The Woman and Her Work, 1802–1876* (Ann Arbor: U of Michigan P, 1980), p. 97.

[2]   *Household Education*, 245.

Harriet Martineau: A Brief Chronology

1802 Born in Norwich on June 12 to Thomas and Elizabeth Rankin Martineau.

1822 Publishes "Female Writers on Practical Divinity" in the *Monthly Repository*.

1823 Publishes *Devotional Exercises for the Use of Young Persons*.

1826 Death of Thomas Martineau, Harriet's father.

1827 Publishes *The Rioters; or, A Tale of Bad Times*, her first industrial tale.

1829 Suffers financially from collapse of family business and investments.

1827–32 Reviews regularly for the *Monthly Repository*.

1832–34 Publishes *Illustrations of Political Economy*, the series that made her famous.

1832 Moves to London to work on the *Illustrations* at closer proximity to her sources.

1833–34 Publishes *Illustrations of Taxation* and *Poor Laws and Paupers Illustrated*.

1834 Travels to America, where she tours for two years and becomes committed to the abolitionist cause.

1837 Publishes *Society in America*.

1838–39 Publishes *Retrospect of Western Travel*, a popular version of her American tour, and *The Martyr Age of the United States*, an account of the abolitionist movement.

1839 Publishes *Deerbrook*, a novel.

1839 Becomes ill while traveling in Europe and returns to England, settling in Tynemouth for five years as an invalid.

1841 Publishes *The Hour and the Man*, the story of the Haitian revolutionary Toussaint L'Ouverture, and *The Playfellow*, four children's tales.

1844 Publishes *Life in the Sick-Room*.

1844 Experiments with mesmerism and writes of her cure in "Letters on Mesmerism," published in *The Athenæum*.

1845 Moves to the Lake District and builds her own home, The Knoll, where she lives until her death.

1846 Travels to Egypt and the Middle East.

1848 Publishes *Eastern Life, Past and Present*.

1849 Publishes *Household Education.*
1849–50 Publishes *A History of England During the Thirty Years' Peace.*
1851 Co-authors, with Henry G. Atkinson, *Letters on the Laws of Man's Nature and Development,* a book taken to be a declaration of atheism.
1852 Travels to Ireland and writes *Letters from Ireland* for the London *Daily News.*
1852–66 Writes regularly for the London *Daily News.*
1852–53 Translates and abridges *The Positive Philosophy of Auguste Comte.*
1855 Diagnosed with a fatal heart condition; writes and prints her *Autobiography* for distribution after her death.
1857 Publishes *British Rule in India.*
1866 Signs petition to Parliament on Women's suffrage.
1869 Publishes *Biographical Sketches,* a collection of obituaries originally written for the *Daily News.*
1876 Dies on June 27 at her home in the Lake District.
1877 *Autobiography* published, with *Memorials* edited by Maria Chapman.

A Note on the Text

This edition of Harriet Martineau's *Autobiography* follows the original English edition (London: Smith, Elder, 1877) and reproduces volumes I and II precisely, including spelling and punctuation. When Martineau composed her autobiography, she believed that she was dying and might not live to complete the entire narrative. But she lived on, and as her life story reached its conclusion in March, 1855, she decided to have it printed in two volumes, overseeing the production process and storing the bound volumes for release after her death. For a projected third volume, the *Memorials*, she asked her American friend, Maria Weston Chapman, to "render the last services to me" and turned over an "immense mass of journals, memoranda, letters, papers, and manuscript studies of her whole life."[1] That final volume was published, along with the *Autobiography*, in 1877.

Only the text of the autobiography *per se* is included in this edition. Given space constraints, I have omitted the appendices to the first edition, which included an obituary of Miss Mary Berry for the London *Daily News* of November 28, 1852; a "Memorial against Prosecution for Opinion," sent to the governor of Massachusetts on behalf of Abner Kneeland, who was tried for blasphemy; "A Month at Sea," an account of Martineau's trans-Atlantic voyage; and various correspondence about a government pension. Instead of these appendices, I have included important autobiographical selections from the *Memorials* (see Appendix B). I have also included most of the topical "running heads" published in the first edition. Like other Victorian books, Martineau's *Autobiography* included a consistent running head on the left ("Autobiography") and topical running heads on the right (e.g., "First Appearance in Print" or "Method of Composition"). The latter are useful not only as indices of content, but also as interpretive signals (e.g., "Hap-hazard Phrenology" or "Desideratum in Philosophy").

Martineau was a swift, accurate writer. If the published *Autobiography* is representative of her work, she was also a careful, accurate proofreader. I have found very few errors in the 1877 English edition (except for a missing comma or two, or a missing mark to close a quotation, silently

---

[1] Maria Weston Chapman, "Introduction" to the *Memorials*, *Harriet Martineau's Autobiography* (London: Smith, Elder, 1877), III, 4.

corrected). The first American edition (Boston: James W. Osgood, 1877) reproduces the three-volume English edition, including the "Memorials," in two volumes, but it is less reliable, with more typographical errors and inconsistent Americanization of spelling.

Throughout this Broadview edition, I have annotated references to persons, places, books, periodicals, and historical events that are not self-explanatory and that might be unfamiliar to readers in the twenty-first century. For public figures, such annotations have been relatively straightforward. For many private figures, however, Martineau gives no name or adopts the nineteenth-century convention of initials (e.g., "Mrs. A—" or "J.S."). When her letters suggest a possible identification, I have included it; when no person mentioned in her letters or the *Memorials* seems likely, I have omitted a footnote so as not to burden the reader with too many "unidentifieds."

HARRIET MARTINEAU'S

AUTOBIOGRAPHY

WITH MEMORIALS
BY
MARIA WESTON CHAPMAN

'Etiam capillus unus habet umbram suam.'—PROVERB.

'And this dear freedom hath begotten me this peace,
that I mourn not that end which must be,
nor spend one wish to have one minute added
to the uncertain date of my years.'—BACON.

WITH PORTRAITS AND ILLUSTRATIONS

IN THREE VOLUMES

VOL. I

LONDON

SMITH, ELDER, & CO., 15 WATERLOO PLACE
1877

CONTENTS

OF

THE FIRST VOLUME

PERIOD IV

TO THIRTY-SEVEN YEARS OLD

CONTENTS

OF

THE SECOND VOLUME

PERIOD IV

ILLUSTRATIONS TO VOL. I

ILLUSTRATIONS TO VOL. II

INTRODUCTION

TO

HARRIET MARTINEAU'S AUTOBIOGRAPHY

AMBLESIDE,[1] March, 1855.

FROM MY YOUTH UPWARDS I have felt that it was one of the duties of my life to write my autobiography. I have always enjoyed, and derived profit from, reading those of other persons, from the most meagre to the fullest: and certain qualities of my own mind,—a strong consciousness and a clear memory in regard to my early feelings,—have seemed to indicate to me the duty of recording my own experience. When my life became evidently a somewhat remarkable one, the obligation presented itself more strongly to my conscience: and when I made up my mind to interdict the publication of my private letters, the duty became unquestionable. For thirteen or fourteen years it has been more or less a weight on my mind that the thing was not done. Twice in my life I made a beginning; once in 1831, and again about ten years later, during my long illness at Tynemouth:[2] but both attempts stopped short at an early period, answering no other purpose than preserving some facts of my childhood which I might otherwise have forgotten. Of late years, I have often said to my most intimate friends that I felt as if I could not die in peace till this work was done; and there has been no lack of encouragement and instigation on their part: but, while I was in health, there was always so much to do that was immediately wanted, that, as usually happens in such cases, that which was not immediately necessary was deferred. At the beginning of this last winter, however, I had hopes of being able to unite my political work with this; and on New Year's Day I said to myself that the year must not close without my having recorded the story of my life. I was probably strengthened in this purpose by having for some time past felt that my energies were declining, and that I had no longer a right to depend on

---

[1]   The village in the Lake District where Martineau built a house with her literary profits after recovering from a debilitating illness. She discusses her house-building in Period VI, sec. i-ii.

[2]   The seaside town in Northumberland where Martineau moved in 1841 to place herself under the care of her sister Elizabeth's husband, Dr. Thomas Greenhow. When Greenhow and another physician, Sir Charles Clarke, decided that her uterine tumors were untreatable, Martineau turned to mesmerism for a cure. See Period V, sec. i and iii.

34

being able to do whatever I chose. Two or three weeks more settled the business. Feeling very unwell, I went to London to obtain a medical opinion in regard to my health. Two able physicians informed me that I had a mortal disease,[1] which might spare me some considerable space of life, but which might, as likely as not, destroy me at any moment. No doubt could remain after this as to what my next employment should be: and as soon after my return home as I had settled my business with my Executor, I began this autobiography. I thought it best to rewrite the early portion, that the whole might be offered from one point of view, and in a consistent spirit. Without any personal desire about living a few months or weeks more or less, I rather hope that I may be able to finish my story with my own hands. If not, it will be done by another, from materials of more or less value. But one part which ought to be done by myself is the statement of my reasons for so serious a step as forbidding the publication of my private correspondence; and I therefore stop at the Third Period of my Memoir, to write this Introduction, to the following passages of which I request the reader's earnest attention.

I admit, at the outset, that it is rather a piece of self-denial in me to interdict the publication of my letters.[2] I have no solicitude about fame, and no fear of my reputation of any sort being injured by the publication of any thing I have ever put upon paper. My opinions and feelings have been remarkably open to the world; and my position has been such as to impose no reserves on a disposition naturally open and communicative; so that if any body might acquiesce in the publication of correspondence, it should be myself. Moreover, I am disposed to think that what my friends tell me is true; that it would be rather an advantage to me than the contrary to be known by my private letters All these considerations point out to me that I am therefore precisely the person to bear emphatic practical testimony on behalf of the principle of the privacy of epistolary intercourse; and therefore it is that I do hereby bear that testimony.

Epistolary correspondence is written speech; and the *onus* rests with those who publish it to show why the laws of honour which are uncontested in regard to conversation may be violated when the conversation is written instead of spoken. The plea is of the utility of such material

---

[1]   An "uncurably diseased" heart, according to Dr. Thomas Watson, but Martineau's symptoms suggest also a regrowth of the tumors that had earlier afflicted her.

[2]   As Martineau explains, she believed that letters to friends and family represent "private" conversation and should not be transmitted to the "public" realm; nonetheless, most of her letters reveal a mingling of public and domestic matters, and many of her correspondents disregarded her wishes.

for biographical purposes; but who would admit that plea in regard to fireside conversation? The most valuable conversation, and that which best illustrates character, is that which passes between two friends, with their feet on the fender, on winter nights, or in a summer ramble: but what would be thought of the traitor who should supply such material for biographical or other purposes? How could human beings ever open their hearts and minds to each other, if there were no privacy guaranteed by principles and feelings of honour? Yet has this security lapsed from that half of human conversation which is written instead of spoken. Whether there is still time to restore it, I know not: but I have done my part towards an attempted restoration by a stringent provision in my Will against any public use whatever being made of my letters, unless I should myself authorize the publication of some, which will, in that case, be of some public interest, and not confidential letters. Most of my friends have burnt my letters,—partly because they knew my desire thus to enforce my assertion of the principle, and partly because it was less painful to destroy them while I was still among them than to escape the importunities of hunters of material after my death. Several eminent persons of this century have taken stringent precautions against the same mischief; and very many more, I fear, have taken the more painful precaution of writing no letters which any body would care to have. Seventy years ago, Dr. Johnson[1] said in conversation 'It is now become so much the fashion to publish letters, that, in order to avoid it, I put as little into mine as I can.' Nobody will question the hardship and mischief of a practice which acts upon epistolary correspondence as the spy system under a despotism acts upon speech: and when we find that a half a dozen of the greatest minds of our time have deprived themselves and their friends of their freedom of epistolary speech for the same reason, it does seem to be time that those qualified to bear testimony against such an infringement on personal liberty should speak out.

'But,' say unscrupulous book-makers and readers, 'there are many eminent persons who are so far from feeling as you do that they have themselves prepared for the publication of their letters. There was Doddridge:—he left a copy of every letter and note that he ever wrote, for this very purpose. There was Madame D'Arblay:—on her death-bed, and in extreme old age, she revised and had copies made of all the letters she received and wrote when in the height of her fame as Fanny

---

[1]   Samuel Johnson (1709–84), famous for his *Dictionary* and for the aphorisms recorded by James Boswell in *The Life of Samuel Johnson* (1791).

Burney,—preparing for publication the smooth compliments and monstrous flatteries written by hands that had long become dust. There was Southey:[1]—he too kept copies, or left directions, by which he arranged the method of making his private letters to his friends property to his heirs. These, and many more, were of a different way of thinking from you.' —They were indeed: and my answer is,—what were the letters worth, as letters, when these arrangements became known? What would fireside conversation be worth, as confidential talk, if it was known that the speaker meant to make it a newspaper article the next day? And when Doddridge's friends, and Southey's, heard that what they had taken for conversational out-pouring on paper was so much literary production, to appear hereafter in a book,—what was the worth of those much-prized letters then? Would the correspondents not as soon have received a page of a dissertation, or the proof of a review article? Surely the only word necessary as to this part of the question is a word of protest against every body, or every eminent person, being deprived of epistolary liberty because there have been some among their predecessors or contemporaries who did not know how to use it, or happen to value it.

We are recommended, again, to 'leave the matter to the discretion of survivors.' I, for my part, have too much regard for my Executors to bequeath to them any such troublesome office as withstanding the remonstrances of any number of persons who may have a mind to see my letters, or of asserting a principle which it is my business to assert for myself. If they were to publish my letters, they would do what I believe to be wrong: and if they refused to publish them, they might be subject to importunity or censure which I have no right to devolve upon them. And why are we to leave this particular piece of testamentary duty to the discretion of survivors, when we are abundantly exhorted, in the case of every other, to do our own testamentary duty ourselves,—betimes, carefully and conscientiously?

Then comes the profit argument,—the plea of how much the world would have lost without the publication of the letters of A. B. and C. This is true, in a way. The question is whether the world has not lost more by the injury to epistolary freedom than it has gained by reading the letters of nonconsenting letter-writers. There will always be plenty of consenting and willing letter-writers: let society have their letters. But there should be no others,—at least till privacy is altogether abolished as an unsocial

---

[1]   Philip Doddridge (1702–51), Nonconformist theologian; Frances Burney [Madame D'Arblay] (1752–1840), novelist; Robert Southey (1771–1843), poet laureate and historian.

privilege. This grossly utilitarian view does not yet prevail; and I do not think it ever will. Meantime, I claim the sanction of every principle of integrity, and every feeling of honour and delicacy, on behalf of my practice. I claim, over and above these, the sanction of the law.—Law reflects the principles of morals; and in this case the mirror presents a clear image of the right and the duty. The law vests the right of publication of private letters solely in the writer, no one else having any such right during the author's life, or after his death, except by his express permission. On the knowledge of this provision I have acted, in my arrangements about my own correspondence; and I trust that others, hitherto unaccustomed to the grave consideration of the subject, will feel, in justice to myself and others who act with me, that there can be no wrong, no moral inexpediency, in the exercise of a right thus expressly protected by the Law. If, by what I have done, I have fixed attention upon the morality of the case, this will be a greater social benefit than the publication of any letters written by me, or by persons far wiser and more accomplished than myself.

I have only to say further, in the way of introduction, a word or two as to my descent and parentage. On occasion of the Revocation of the Edict of Nantes, in 1688,[1] a surgeon of the name of Martineau, and a family of the name of Pierre, crossed the Channel, and settled with other Huguenot refugees, in England. My ancestor married a young lady of the Pierre family, and settled in Norwich,[2] where his descendants afforded a succession of surgeons up to my own day. My eminent uncle, Mr. Philip Meadows Martineau, and my eldest brother, who died before the age of thirty, were the last Norwich surgeons of the name.—My grandfather, who was one of the honourable series, died at the age of forty-two, of a fever caught among his poor patients. He left a large family, of whom my father was the youngest. When established as a Norwich manufacturer, my father married Elizabeth Rankin, the eldest daughter of a sugar-refiner at Newcastle upon Tyne.[3] My father and mother had eight children, of whom I was the sixth: and I was born on the 12th of June, 1802.[4]

---

[1] This act of Louis XIV revoked many of the religious, political, and civil rights of French Protestants and spurred their mass migration to England, the Netherlands, and America.

[2] The cathedral city and commercial center of Norfolk, East Anglia.

[3] Harriet's father Thomas Martineau (1764–1826) was a manufacturer of bombazine, a fine twilled cloth of silk and cotton or worsted wool, often dyed black and used for mourning dresses. Her mother Elizabeth Rankin (1771–1848) was the daughter of Robert Rankin, a sugar refiner and merchant.

[4] There were eight children in the Martineau family: Elizabeth (b. 1794), Thomas (b. 1795), Henry (b. 1797), Robert (b. 1798), Rachel (b. 1800), Harriet (b. 1802), James (b. 1805), and Ellen (b. 1811).

HARRIET MARTINEAU'S AUTOBIOGRAPHY

FIRST PERIOD

TO EIGHT YEARS OLD

SECTION I

MY first recollections are of some infantine impressions which were in abeyance for a long course of years, and then revived in an inexplicable way,—as by a flash of lightning over a far horizon in the night. There is no doubt of the genuineness of the remembrance, as the facts could not have been told me by any one else. I remember standing on the threshold of a cottage, holding fast by the doorpost, and putting my foot down, in repeated attempts to reach the ground. Having accomplished the step, I toddled (I remember the uncertain feeling) to a tree before the door, and tried to clasp and get round it; but the rough bark hurt my hands. At night of the same day, in bed, I was disconcerted by the coarse feel of the sheets,—so much less smooth and cold than those at home; and I was alarmed by the creaking of the bedstead when I moved. It was a turn-up bedstead in a cottage, or small farm-house at Carleton,[1] where I was sent for my health, being a delicate child. My mother's account of things was that I was all but starved to death in the first weeks of my life,—the wetnurse being very poor, and holding on to her good place after her milk was going or gone. The discovery was made when I was three months old, and when I was fast sinking under diarrhœa. My bad health during my whole childhood and youth, and even my deafness,[2] was always ascribed by my mother to this. However it might be about that, my health certainly was very bad till I was nearer thirty than twenty

---

[1] A village southwest of Norwich, the city where the Martineaus lived. It was common, if debated, practice in middle-class families to hire a wetnurse.

[2] Martineau describes her growing deafness in Period II, sec. ii, which became perceptible at age twelve and pronounced by age sixteen. As an adult she used a trumpet or, as she calls it, a "caoutchouc tube" in conversation to amplify the speaker's voice.

years of age; and never was poor mortal cursed with a more beggarly nervous system. The long years of indigestion by day and night-mare terrors are mournful to think of now.—Milk has radically disagreed with me, all my life: but when I was a child, it was a thing unheard of for children not to be fed on milk: so, till I was old enough to have tea at breakfast, I went on having a horrid lump at my throat for hours of every morning, and the most terrific oppressions in the night. Sometimes the dim light of the windows in the night seemed to advance till it pressed upon my eyeballs, and then the windows would seem to recede to an infinite distance. If I laid my hand under my head on the pillow, the hand seemed to vanish almost to a point, while the head grew as big as a mountain. Sometimes I was panic struck at the head of the stairs, and was sure I could never get down; and I could never cross the yard to the garden without flying and panting, and fearing to look behind, because a wild beast was after me. The starlight sky was the worst; it was always coming down, to stifle and crush me, and rest upon my head. I do not remember any dread of thieves or ghosts in particular; but things as I actually saw them were dreadful to me; and it now appears to me that I had scarcely any respite from the terror. My fear of persons was as great as any other. To the best of my belief, the first person I was ever not afraid of was Aunt Kentish,[1] who won my heart and my confidence when I was sixteen. My heart was ready enough to flow out; and it often did: but I always repented of such expansion, the next time I dreaded to meet a human face.—It now occurs to me, and it may be worth while to note it,—what the extremest terror of all was about. We were often sent to walk on the Castle Hill at Norwich.[2] In the wide area below, the residents were wont to expose their feather-beds, and to beat them with a stick. That sound,—a dull shock,—used to make my heart stand still: and it was no use my standing at the rails above, and seeing the process. The striking of the blow and the arrival of the sound did not correspond; and this made matters worse. I hated that walk; and I believe for that reason. My parents knew nothing of all this. It never occurred to me to speak of anything I felt most: and I doubt whether they ever had the slightest idea of my miseries. It seems to me now that a little closer observation would have shown them the causes of the bad health and

---

[1] Harriet's mother's sister-in-law Mrs. Robert Rankin, Jr., née Ann Cole (1780–1840), with whom Harriet spent fifteen months in Bristol in 1818–19; see Period II, sec. iii.

[2] The site of a Norman castle, built just after the Conquest (1066) by Henry I and later surrounded by gardens with walking paths.

fitful temper which gave them so much anxiety on my account; and I am sure that a little more of the cheerful tenderness which was in those days thought bad for children, would have saved me from my worst faults, and from a world of suffering.

My hostess and nurse at the above-mentioned cottage was a Mrs. Merton, who was, as was her husband, a Methodist or melancholy Calvinist of some sort. The family story about me was that I came home the absurdest little preacher of my years (between two and three) that ever was. I used to nod my head emphatically, and say 'Never ky for tyfles:' 'Dooty fust, and pleasure afterwards,' and so forth: and I sometimes got courage to edge up to strangers, and ask them to give me—'a maxim.' Almost before I could join letters, I got some sheets of paper, and folded them into a little square book, and wrote, in double lines, two or three in a page, my beloved maxims. I believe this was my first effort at book-making. It was probably what I picked up at Carleton that made me so intensely religious as I certainly was from a very early age. The religion was of a bad sort enough, as might be expected from the urgency of my needs; but I doubt whether I could have got through without it. I pampered my vain-glorious propensities by dreams of divine favor, to make up for my utter deficiency of self-respect: and I got rid of other-wise incessant remorse by a most convenient confession and repentance, which relieved my nerves without at all, I suspect, improving my conduct.

To revert to my earliest recollections:—I certainly could hardly walk alone when our nursemaid took us,—including my sister Elizabeth, who was eight years older than myself,—an unusual walk; through a lane, (afterwards called by us the 'Spinner's Lane') where some Miss Taskers, acquaintances of Elizabeth's and her seniors, were lodging, in a cottage which had a fir grove behind it. Somebody set me down at the foot of a fir, where I was distressed by the slight rising of the ground at the root, and by the long grass, which seemed a terrible entanglement. I looked up the tree, and was scared at its height, and at that of so many others. I was comforted with a fir-cone; and then one of the Miss Taskers caught me up in her arms and kissed me; and I was too frightened to cry till we got away.—I was not more than two years old when an impression of touch occurred to me which remains vivid to this day. It seems indeed as if impressions of touch were at that age more striking than those from the other senses. I say this from observation of others besides myself; for my own case is peculiar in that matter. Sight, hearing and touch were perfectly good in early childhood; but I never had the sense of smell; and that of taste was therefore exceedingly imperfect.—On the occasion I refer to, I was carried down a flight of steep back stairs, and Rachel (a year and half older than I) clung to the nursemaid's gown, and Elizabeth was going before, (still quite a little girl) when I put down my finger ends to feel a flat velvet button on the top of Rachel's bonnet. The rapture of the sensation was really monstrous, as I remember it now. Those were our mourning bonnets for a near relation; and this marks the date, proving me to have been only two years old.

I was under three when my brother James was born. That day was another of the distinct impressions which flashed upon me in after years. I found myself within the door of the best bedroom,—an impressive place from being seldom used, from its having a dark, polished floor, and from the awful large gay figures of the chintz bed hangings. That day the curtains were drawn, the window blinds were down, and an unknown old woman, in a mob cap, was at the fire, with a bundle of flannel in her arms. She beckoned to me, and I tried to go, though it seemed impossible to cross the slippery floor. I seem to hear now the pattering of my feet. When I arrived at her knee, the nurse pushed out with her foot a tiny chair, used as a footstool, made me sit down on it, laid the bundle of flannel across my knees, and opened it so that I saw the little red face of the baby. I then found out that there was somebody in the bed,—seeing a nightcap on the pillow. This was on the 21st of April, 1805. I have a distinct recollection of some incidents of that summer. My mother did not recover well from her confinement, and was sent to the sea, at Yarmouth.[1] On our arrival there, my father took me along the old jetty,—little knowing what terror I suffered. I remember the strong grasp of his large hand being some comfort; but there were holes in the planking of the jetty quite big enough to let my foot through; and they disclosed the horrible sight of waves flowing and receding below, and great tufts of green weeds swaying to and fro. I remember the sitting-room at our lodgings, and my mother's dress as she sat picking shrimps, and letting me try to help her.—Of all my many fancies, perhaps none was so terrible as a dream that I had at four years old. The impression is as fresh as possible now; but I cannot at all understand what the fright was about. I know nothing more strange than this power of re-entering, as it were, into the narrow mind of an infant, so as to compare it with that of maturity; and therefore it may be worth while to record that piece of precious nonsense,—my dream at four years old. I imagine I

---

[1]   Town east of Norwich on the North Sea coast, now called Great Yarmouth.

was learning my letters then from cards, where each letter had its picture,—as a stag for S. I dreamed that we children were taking our walk with our nursemaid out of St. Austin's Gate (the nearest bit of country to our house). Out of the public-house there came a stag, with prodigious antlers. Passing the pump, it crossed the road to us, and made a polite bow, with its head on one side, and with a scrape of one foot, after which it pointed with its foot to the public-house, and spoke to me, inviting me in. The maid declined, and turned to go home. Then came the terrible part. By the time we were at our own door it was dusk, and we went up the steps in the dark; but in the kitchen it was bright sunshine. My mother was standing at the dresser, breaking sugar; and she lifted me up, and set me in the sun, and gave me a bit of sugar. Such was the dream which froze me with horror! Who shall say why?—But my panics were really unaccountable. They were a matter of pure sensation, without any intellectual justification whatever, even of the wildest kind. A magic-lantern was exhibited to us on Christmas-day, and once or twice in the year besides. I used to see it cleaned by daylight, and to handle all its parts,—understanding its whole structure; yet, such was my terror of the white circle on the wall, and of the moving slides, that, to speak the plain truth, the first apparition always brought on bowel-complaint; and, at the age of thirteen, when I was pretending to take care of little children during the exhibition, I could never look at it without having the back of a chair to grasp, or hurting myself, to carry off the intolerable sensation. My bitter shame may be conceived; but then, I was always in a state of shame about something or other. I was afraid to walk in the town, for some years, if I remember right, for fear of meeting two people. One was an unknown old lady who very properly rebuked me one day for turning her off the very narrow pavement of London Lane, telling me, in an awful way, that little people should make way for their elders. The other was an unknown farmer, in whose field we had been gleaning (among other trespassers) before the shocks were carried. This man left the field after us, and followed us into the city,—no doubt, as I thought, to tell the Mayor, and send the constable after us. I wonder how long it was before I left off expecting that constable. There were certain little imps, however, more alarming still. Our house was in a narrow street; and all its windows, except two or three at the back, looked eastwards. It had no sun in the front rooms, except before breakfast in summer. One summer morning, I went into the drawing-room, which was not much used in those days, and saw a sight which made me hide my face in a chair, and scream with terror. The drops of the lustres[1] on the mantle-piece, on which the sun was shining, were some-how set in motion, and the prismatic colours danced vehemently on the walls. I thought they were alive,—imps of some sort; and I never dared go into that room alone in the morning, from that time forward. I am afraid I must own that my heart has beat, all my life long, at the dancing of prismatic colours on the wall.

I was getting some comfort, however, from religion by this time. The Sundays began to be marked days, and pleasantly marked, on the whole. I do not know why crocuses were particularly associated with Sunday at that time; but probably my mother might have walked in the garden with us, some early spring Sunday. My idea of Heaven was of a place gay with yellow and lilac crocuses. My love of gay colours was very strong. When I was sent with the keys to a certain bureau in my mother's room, to fetch miniatures of my father and grandfather, to be shown to visitors, I used to stay an unconscionable time, though dread-ing punishment for it, but utterly unable to resist the fascination of a certain watch-ribbon kept in a drawer there. This ribbon had a pattern in floss silk, gay and beautifully shaded; and I used to look at it till I was sent for, to be questioned as to what I had been about. The young wild parsley and other weeds in the hedges used to make me sick with their luscious green in spring. One crimson and purple sunrise I well remem-ber, when James could hardly walk alone, and I could not therefore have been more than five. I awoke very early, that summer morning, and saw the maid sound asleep in her bed, and 'the baby' in his crib. The room was at the top of the house; and some rising ground beyond the city could be seen over the opposite roofs. I crept out of bed, saw James's pink toes showing themselves invitingly through the rails of his crib, and gently pinched them, to wake him. With a world of trouble I got him over the side, and helped him to the window, and upon a chair there. I wickedly opened the window, and the cool air blew in; and yet the maid did not wake. Our arms were smutted with the blacks on the window-sill, and our bare feet were corded with the impression of the rush-bottomed chair; but we were not found out. The sky was gorgeous, and I talked very religiously to the child. I remember the mood, and the pleasure of expressing it, but nothing of what I said.

I must have been a remarkably religious child, for the only support and pleasure I remember having from a very early age was from that

[1] Glass pendants that hang from a chandelier or candelabra.

source. I was just seven when the grand event of my childhood took place,—a journey to Newcastle[1] to spend the summer (my mother and four of her children) at my grandfather's; and I am certain that I cared more for religion before and during that summer than for anything else. It was after our return, when Ann Turner, daughter of the Unitarian Minister there, was with us, that my piety first took a practical character; but it was familiar to me as an indulgence long before. While I was afraid of everybody I saw, I was not in the least afraid of God. Being usually very unhappy, I was constantly longing for heaven, and seriously, and very frequently planning suicide in order to get there. I was sure that suicide would not stand in the way of my getting there. I knew it was considered a crime; but I did not feel it so. I had a devouring passion for justice;—justice, first to my own precious self, and then to other oppressed people. Justice was precisely what was least understood in our house, in regard to servants and children. Now and then I desperately poured out my complaints; but in general I brooded over my injuries, and those of others who dared not speak; and then the temptation to suicide was very strong. No doubt, there was much vindictiveness in it. I gloated over the thought that I would make somebody care about me in some sort of way at last: and, as to my reception in the other world, I felt sure that God could not be very angry with me for making haste to him when nobody else cared for me, and so many people plagued me. One day I went to the kitchen to get the great carving knife, to cut my throat; but the servants were at dinner, and this put it off for that time. By degrees, the design dwindled down into running away. I used to lean out of the window, and look up and down the street, and wonder how far I could go without being caught. I had no doubt at all that if I once got into a farm-house, and wore a woollen petticoat, and milked the cows, I should be safe, and that nobody would inquire about me any more.—It is evident enough that my temper must have been very bad. It seems to me now that it was downright devilish, except for a placability which used to annoy me sadly. My temper might have been early made a thoroughly good one, by the slightest indulgence shown to my natural affections, and any rational dealing with my faults: but I was almost the youngest of a large family, and subject, not only to the rule of severity to which all were liable, but also to the rough and contemptuous treatment of the elder children, who meant no harm,

---

[1]   Newcastle-upon-Tyne, where Martineau's mother was born and her maternal grandfather, Robert Rankin, a sugar refiner, still lived.

but injured me irreparably. I had no self-respect, and an unbounded need of approbation and affection. My capacity for jealousy was something frightful. When we were little more than infants, Mr. Thomas Watson, son of my father's partner, one day came into the yard, took Rachel up in his arms, gave her some grapes off the vine, and carried her home, across the street, to give her Gay's Fables,[1] bound in red and gold. I stood with a bursting heart, beating my hoop, and hating every body in the world. I always hated Gay's Fables, and for long could not abide a red book. Nobody dreamed of all this; and the 'taking down' system was pursued with me as with the rest, issuing in the assumed doggedness and wilfulness which made me desperately disagreeable during my youth, to every body at home. The least word or tone of kindness melted me instantly, in spite of the strongest predeterminations to be hard and offensive. Two occasions stand out especially in my memory, as indeed almost the only instances of the enjoyment of tenderness manifested to myself individually.

When I was four or five years old, we were taken to a lecture of Mr. Drummond's, for the sake, no doubt, of the pretty shows we were to see,—the chief of which was the Phantasmagoria[2] of which we had heard, as a fine sort of magic-lantern. I did not like the darkness, to begin with; and when Minerva appeared, in a red dress, at first extremely small, and then approaching, till her owl seemed coming directly upon me, it was so like my nightmare dreams that I shrieked aloud. I remember my own shriek. A pretty lady who sat next us, took me on her lap, and let me hide my face in her bosom, and held me fast. How intensely I loved her, without at all knowing who she was! From that time we knew her, and she filled a large space in my life; and above forty years after, I had the honour of having her for my guest in my own house. She was Mrs. Lewis Cooper, then the very young mother of two girls of the ages of Rachel and myself, of whom I shall have to say more presently.—The other occasion was when I had a terrible ear-ache one Sunday. The rest went to chapel in the afternoon; and my pain grew worse. Instead of going into the kitchen to the cook, I wandered into a lumber room at the top of the house. I laid my aching ear against

---

[1] John Gay, *Fables* (London, 1816), a collection of animal fables, including "The Lion, the Fox, and the Geese" and "The Butterfly and the Snail."

[2] The "Phantasmagoria," begun in the 1790s, projected ghost shows from a hidden lantern onto smoke. Robert Hare's invention of the oxy-hydrogen blow-lamp (1802) and Thomas Drummond's of the signal light (1826), which used calcium oxide to produce "limelight," allowed its development into large-scale entertainment.

the cold iron screw of a bedstead, and howled with pain; but nobody came to me. At last, I heard the family come home from chapel. I heard them go into the parlor, one after another, and I knew they were sitting round the fire in the dusk. I stole down to the door, and stood on the mat, and heard them talking and laughing merrily. I stole in, thinking they would not observe me, and got into a dark corner. Presently my mother called to me, and asked what I was doing there. Then I burst out,—that my ear ached so I did not know *what* to do! Then she and my father both called me tenderly, and she took me on her lap, and laid the ear on her warm bosom. I was afraid of spoiling her starched muslin handkerchief with the tears which *would* come; but I was very happy, and wished that I need never move again. Then of course came remorse for all my naughtiness; but I was always suffering that, though never, I believe, in my whole childhood, being known to own myself wrong. I must have been an intolerable child; but I need not have been so.

I was certainly fond of going to chapel before that Newcastle era which divided my childhood into two equal portions: but my besetting troubles followed me even there. My passion for justice was baulked there, as much as any where. The duties preached were those of inferiors to superiors, while the *per contra* was not insisted on with any equality of treatment at all. Parents were to bring up their children 'in the nurture and admonition of the Lord,' and to pay servants due wages; but not a word was ever preached about the justice due from the stronger to the weaker. I used to thirst to hear some notice of the oppression which servants and children had (as I supposed universally) to endure, in regard to their feelings, while duly clothed, fed, and taught: but nothing of the sort ever came; but instead, a doctrine of passive obedience which only made me remorseful and miserable. I was abundantly obedient in act; for I never dreamed of being otherwise; but the interior rebellion kept my conscience in a state of perpetual torture. As far as I remember, my conscience was never of the least use to me; for I always concluded myself wrong about every thing, while pretending entire complacency and assurance. My moral discernment was almost wholly obscured by fear and mortification.—Another misery at chapel was that I could not attend to the service, nor refrain from indulging in the most absurd vain-glorious dreams, which I was ashamed of, all the while. The Octagon Chapel at Norwich[1] has some curious

---

[1]   Designed by Thomas Ivory and built in 1755, the eight-sided chapel was first a Presbyterian, later a Unitarian meeting house within easy walking distance of the Martineau home.

windows in the roof;—not skylights, but letting in light indirectly. I used to sit staring up at those windows, and looking for angels to come for me, and take me to heaven, in sight of all the congregation,—the end of the world being sure to happen while we were at chapel. I was thinking of this, and of the hymns, the whole of the time, it now seems to me. It was very shocking to me that I could not pray at chapel. I believe that I never did in my life. I prayed abundantly when I was alone; but it was impossible to me to do it in any other way; and the hypocrisy of appearing to do so was a long and sore trouble to me.— All this is very painful; but I really remember little that was not painful at that time of my life.—To be sure, there was Nurse Ayton, who used to come, one or two days in the week, to sew. She was kind to me, and I was fond of her. She told us long stories about her family; and she taught me to sew. She certainly held the family impression of my abil- ities,—that I was a dull, unobservant, slow, awkward child. In teaching me to sew, she used to say (and I quite acquiesced) that 'slow and sure' was the maxim for me, and 'quick and well' was the maxim for Rachel. I was not jealous about this,—it seemed to me so undeniable. On one occasion only I thought Nurse Ayton unkind. The back of a rickety old nursing-chair came off when I was playing on it; and I was sure she could save me from being scolded by sewing it on again. I insisted that she could sew *anything*. This made my mother laugh when she came up; and so I forgave nurse: and I believe that was our only quarrel.

My first political interest was the death of Nelson.[1] I was then four years old. My father came in from the counting-house at an unusual hour, and told my mother, who cried heartily. I certainly had some conception of a battle, and of a great man being a public loss. It always rent my heart-strings (to the last day of her life,) to see and hear my mother cry; and in this case it was clearly connected with the death of a great man. I had my own notions of Bonaparte too. One day, at dessert, when my father was talking anxiously to my mother about the expected invasion, for which preparations were made all along the Norfolk coast, I saw them exchange a glance, because I was standing staring, twitching my pinafore with terror. My father called me to him, and took me on his knee, and I said 'But, papa, what will you do if Boney comes?' 'What will I do?' said he, cheerfully, 'Why, I will ask him to take a glass of Port

---

[1] Horatio, Viscount Nelson (1758–1805), was victorious but mortally wounded at the battle of Trafalgar in 1805. Napoleon Bonaparte (1769–1821) was finally defeated ten years later by Arthur Wellesley (1769–1852), later the Duke of Wellington, at Waterloo.

with me,'—helping himself to a glass as he spoke. That wise reply was of immense service to me. From the moment I knew that 'Boney' was a creature who could take a glass of wine, I dreaded him no more. Such was my induction into the department of foreign affairs. As to social matters,—my passion for justice was cruelly crossed, from the earliest time I can remember, by the imposition of passive obedience and silence on servants and tradespeople, who met with a rather old-fashioned treatment in our house. We children were enough in the kitchen to know how the maids avenged themselves for scoldings in the parlor, before the family and visitors, to which they must not reply; and for being forbidden to wear white gowns, silk gowns, or any thing but what strict housewives approved. One of my chief miseries was being sent with insulting messages to the maids,—e.g., to 'bid them not be so like carthorses overhead,' and the like. On the one hand, it was a fearful sin to alter a message; and, on the other, it was impossible to give such an one as that: so I used to linger and delay to the last moment, and then deliver something civil, with all imaginable sheepishness, so that the maids used to look at one another and laugh. Yet, one of my most heartfelt sins was towards a servant who was really a friend of my mother's and infinitely respected, and a good deal loved, by us children,—Susan Ormsby, who came to live with us just before James was born, and staid till that memorable Newcastle journey, above four years afterwards. When she was waiting at dinner one day, I stuck my knife upright, in listening to something, so that the point cut her arm. I saw her afterwards washing it at the pump; and she shook her head at me in tender reproach. My heart was bursting; but I dared not tell her how sorry I was. I never got over it, or was happy with her again; and when we were to part, the night before our journey, and she was kissing us with tears, it was in dumb grief and indignation that I heard her tell my mother that children do not feel things as grown people do, and that they could not think of any thing else when they were going a journey.

One more fact takes its place before that journey,—the awakening of a love of money in me. I suspect I have had a very narrow escape of being an eminent miser. A little more, or a little less difficulty, or another mode of getting money would easily have made me a miser. The first step, as far as I remember, was when we played cards, one winter evening, at our uncle Martineau's,[1] when I was told that I had won twopence. The pavement hardly seemed solid when we walked

---

[1] Most likely, Philip Meadows Martineau (1752–1829), the eminent Norwich surgeon.

home,—so elated was I. I remember equal delight when Mrs. Meadows
Taylor[1] gave us children twopence when we expected only a halfpenny,
to buy string for a top: but in this last case it was not the true *amor
nummi*, as in the other. The same avarice was excited in the same way,
a few years later, when I won eighteen-pence at cards on a visit. The
very sight of silver and copper was transporting to me, without any
thought of its use. I stood and looked long at money, as it lay in my
hand. Yet, I do not remember that this passion ever interfered with my
giving away money, though it certainly did with my spending it otherwise. I certainly was very close, all my childhood and youth. I may as
well mention here that I made rules and kept them, in regard to my
expenditure, from the time I had an allowance. I believe we gave away
something out of our first allowance of a penny a week. When we had
twopence, I gave away half. The next advance was to half-a-guinea a
quarter, to buy gloves and sashes: then to ten pounds a year (with help)
for clothes; then fifteen, and finally twenty, without avowed help. I
sewed indefatigably all those years,—being in truth excessively fond of
sewing, with the amusement of either gossiping, or learning poetry by
heart, from a book, lying open under my work. I never had the slightest difficulty in learning any amount of verse; and I knew enough to
have furnished me for a wandering reciter,—if there had been such a
calling in our time,—as I used to wish there was. While thus busy, I
made literally all my clothes, as I grew up, except stays and shoes. I plat-
ted bonnets at one time, knitted stockings as I read aloud, covered silk
shoes for dances, and made all my garments. Thus I squeezed something out of the smaller allowance, and out of the fifteen pounds, I never
spent more than twelve in dress; and never more than fifteen pounds
out of the twenty. The rest I gave away, except a little which I spent in
books. The amount of time spent in sewing now appears frightful; but
it was the way in those days, among people like ourselves. There was
some saving in our practice of reading aloud, and in mine of learning
poetry in such mass: but the censorious gossip which was the bane of
our youth drove prose and verse out of the field, and wasted more of
our precious youthful powers and dispositions than any repentance and
amendment in after life could repair. This sort of occupation, the sewing
however, was less unfitting than might now appear, considering that the
fortunes of manufacturers, like my father, were placed in jeopardy by

---

[1]   Wife of Samuel Taylor, of Bonham, Norfolk, and mother of Emily Taylor (1795–1872),
   Martineau's second cousin and close friend.

the war, and that there was barely a chance for my father ever being able to provide fortunes for his daughters. He and my mother exercised every kind of self-denial to bring us up qualified to take care of ourselves. They pinched themselves in luxuries to provide their girls, as well as their boys, with masters and schooling; and they brought us up to an industry like their own;—the boys in study and business, and the girls in study and household cares. Thus was I saved from being a literary lady who could not sew; and when, in after years, I have been insulted by admiration at not being helpless in regard to household employments, I have been wont to explain, for my mother's sake, that I could make shirts and puddings, and iron and mend, and get my bread by my needle, if necessary,—(as it once was necessary, for a few months), before I won a better place and occupation with my pen.

SECTION II

BUT it is time to set out on the second period of my childhood,— beginning with that memorable Newcastle journey. That period was memorable, not only from the enlarging of a child's ideas which ensues upon a first long journey, but because I date from it my becoming what is commonly called 'a responsible being.' On my return home I began to take moral charge of myself. I had before, and from my earliest recollections, been subject to a haunting, wretched, useless remorse; but from the time of our return from Newcastle, bringing Ann Turner[1] with us, I became practically religious with all my strength. Ann was, I think, fourteen when I was seven; and that she made herself my friend at all was a great thing for me; and it fell out all the more easily for her tendencies being exclusively religious, while I was only waiting for some influence to determine my life in that direction.

Travelling was no easy matter in those days. My mother, our dear, pretty, gentle aunt Margaret,[2] sister Elizabeth, aged fifteen, Rachel, myself, and little James, aged four, and in nankeen frocks, were all

---

[1]   Ann Turner, sister of Henry Turner (1793–1822), a Unitarian minister in Newcastle-upon-Tyne who had married Harriet's cousin Catherine Rankin (1797–1894).

[2]   Margaret Lee (1756–1840), sister of Harriet's father.

crammed into a post-chaise, for a journey of three or four days. Almost every incident of those days is still fresh: but I will report only one, which is curious from showing how little aware we children were of our own value. I really think, if I had once conceived that any body cared for me, nearly all the sins and sorrows of my anxious childhood would have been spared me; and I remember well that it was Ann Turner who first conveyed the cheering truth to me. She asked me why my mother sat sewing so diligently for us children, and sat up at night to mend my stockings, if she did not care for me; and I was convinced at once;—only too happy to believe it, and being unable to resist such evidence as the stocking-mending at night, when we children were asleep. Well: on our second day's journey, we stopped at Burleigh House,[1] and the three elders of the party went in, to see the picture gallery.—Children were excluded; so we three little ones were left to play among the haymakers on the lawn. After what seemed a long time, it suddenly struck us that the elders must have forgotten us, and gone on to Newcastle without us. I, for my part, was entirely persuaded that we should never be missed, or remembered more by any body; and we set up a terrible lamentation. A good-natured haymaker, a sunburnt woman whose dialect we could not understand, took us in hand, and led us to the great door, where we were soon comforted by my mother's appearance. I remember wondering why she and aunt Margaret laughed aside when they led us back to the chaise.

Of course it was difficult to amuse little children so cooped up for so long. There was a little quiet romping, I remember, and a great deal of story telling by dear aunty: but the finest device was setting us to guess what we should find standing in the middle of grandpapa's garden. As it was something we had never seen or known about, there was no end to the guessing. When we arrived at the gates of the Forth, (my grandfather's house) the old folks and their daughters came out to meet us, all tearful and agitated: and I, loathing myself for the selfishness, *could not* wait, but called out,—'I want to see what that thing is in the garden.' After an enlightening hint, and without any rebuke, our youngest aunt took me by the hand, and led me to face the mystery. I could make nothing of it when I saw it. It was a large, heavy, stone sundial. That dial is worth this much mention, for it was of immeasurable value to me. I

---

[1] Burleigh (or Burghley) House, in Stamford, Lincolnshire, was built between 1565 and 1587 by William Cecil, lord high treasurer to Queen Elizabeth I, and landscaped by Capability Brown in the eighteenth century. It holds one of the most extensive private collections of fine art in England.

could see its face only by raising myself on tiptoe on its step: and there, with my eyes on a level with the plate, did I watch and ponder, day by day, painfully forming my first clear conceptions of Time, amidst a bright confusion of notions of day and night, and of the seasons, and of the weather. I loved that dial with a sort of superstition; and when, nearly forty years after, I built a house for myself at Ambleside, my strong wish was to have this very dial for the platform below the terrace: but it was not to be had. It had been once removed already,—when the railway cut through the old garden; and the stone mass was too heavy, and far too much fractured and crumbled for a second removal. So a dear friend set up for me a beautiful new dial; and I can only hope that it may possibly render as great a service to some child of a future generation as my grandfather's did for me.

It seems to me now that I seldom asked questions in those days. I went on for years together in a puzzle, for want of its ever occurring to me to ask questions. For instance, no accounts of a spring-gun[1] answered to my conception of it;—that it was a pea-green musket, used only in spring! This absurdity at length lay by unnoticed in my mind till I was twenty! Even so! At that age, I was staying at Birmingham; and we were returning from a country walk in the dusk of the evening, when my host warned us not to cross a little wood, for fear of spring-guns; and he found and showed us the wire of one. I was truly confounded when the sense of the old mistake, dormant in my mind till now, came upon me. Thus it was with a piece of mystification imposed on me by my grandfather's barber in 1809. One morning, while the shaving-pot was heating, the barber took me on his knee, and pretended to tell me why he was late that morning. Had I ever heard of a falling star? Yes, I had. Well: a star had fallen in the night; and it fell in the Forth lane, which it completely blocked up, beside Mr. Somebody's orchard. It was quite round, and of the beautifullest and clearest crystal. 'Was it there still?' O yes,—or most of it: but some of the crystal was shivered off, and people were carrying it away when he arrived at the spot. He had to go round by Something Street; and it was that which made him late. 'Would there be any left by the time we went for our walk?' He hoped there might. I got through my lessons in a fever of eagerness that morning, and engaged the nurse maid to take us through that lane. There was the orchard, with the apple-tree stretching over the wall: but not a single spike of the crystal was left.

---

[1]   A gun that discharges on contact, by means of a wire attached to the trigger; used to detract trespassers and poachers.

I thought it odd; but it never occurred to me to doubt the story, or to speak to any body about it, except the barber. I lay in wait for him the next morning; and very sorry he professed to be;—so sorry that he had not just picked up some crystals for me while there were so many; but no doubt I should come in the way of a fallen star myself, some day. We kept this up till October, when we bade him good bye: and my early notions of astronomy were cruelly bewildered by that man's rhodomontade. I dare not say how many years it was before I got quite clear of it.

There is little to say of the rest of that absence from home. There was a naughty boy staying at my grandfather's, who caused us to be insulted by imputations of stealing the green fruit, and to be shut out of the garden, where we had never dreamed of touching a gooseberry: and he led little James into mischief; and then canted and made his own part good. Our hearts swelled under the injuries he caused us. Then, we were injudiciously fed, and my nightmare miseries were intolerable. The best event was that my theological life began to take form. I had a prodigious awe of clergymen and ministers, and a strong yearning towards them for notice. No doubt there was much vanity in this; but it was also one investment of the religious sentiment, as I know by my being at times conscious of a remnant of the feeling now, while radically convinced that the intellectual and moral judgment of priests of all persuasions is inferior to that of any other order of men. The first of the order who took any direct notice of me was, as far as I know, good Mr. Turner of Newcastle, my mother's pastor and friend before her marriage. At Newcastle, we usually went to tea at his house on Sunday evenings; and it was then that we began the excellent practice of writing recollections of one of the sermons of the day. When the minister preaches what children can understand, this practice is of the highest use in fixing their attention, and in disclosing to their parents the character and imperfections of their ideas on the most important class of subjects. On occasion of our first attempt,—Rachel's and mine,—I felt very triumphant before hand. I remembered the text; and it seemed to me that my head was full of thoughts from the sermon. I scrawled over the whole of a large slate, and was not a little mortified when I found that all I had written came into seven or eight lines of my mother's handwriting. I made sure that I had not been cheated, and then fell into discouragement at finding that my grand 'sermon' came to nothing more. However, my attempt was approved; I was allowed to 'sit up to supper,' and the Sunday practice was begun which continued till I grew too deaf to keep up my attention successfully. For some years of that long period, our success was small, because Mr. Madge's,[1] (our minister's) sermons conveyed few clear ideas to children, though much sweet and solemn impression. Dr. Carpenter's[2] were the best I ever listened to for the purpose:—so good that I have known him carry a 'recollection' written by a cousin of mine at the age of sixteen, to Mrs. Carpenter, as a curiosity,—not a single sentence of his sermon being altogether absent from the hearer's version of it.— Another religious impression that we children brought from Newcastle is very charming to me still. Our gentle, delicate aunt Mary,[3] whom I remember so well in her white gown, with her pink colour, thin silky brown hair, and tender manner towards us, used to get us round her knees as she sat in the window-seat at the Forth, where the westerly sun shone in, and teach us to sing Milton's hymn 'Let us with a gladsome mind.' It is the very hymn for children, set to its own simple tune; and I always, to this day, hear aunt Mary's weak, earnest voice in it. That was the gentle hymn. The woe-breathing one was the German Evening Hymn. The heroic one, which never failed to rouse my whole being, was 'Awake, my soul; stretch every nerve,' sung to Artaxerxes.[4]— In those days, we learned Mrs. Barbauld's Prose Hymns[5] by heart; and there were parts of them which I dearly loved: but other parts made me shiver with awe. I did not know what 'shaking bogs' were, and was alarmed at that mysterious being 'Child of Mortality.'[6] On the whole,

---

[1] The Rev. Thomas Madge (1786–1870), minister at the Octagon Chapel, Norwich, from 1811–25.

[2] The Rev. Lant Carpenter (1780–1840), minister at Lewin's Mead Chapel, Bristol, when Harriet attended her aunt Kentish's school there.

[3] Mary Rankin (bap. 1783), an unmarried aunt who lived at Newcastle.

[4] John Milton's hymn, written when he was fifteen years old, begins: "Let us with a gladsome mind / Praise the Lord, for He is kind; / For His mercies shall endure, / Ever faithful, ever sure." The German evening hymn ("Nun ruhen alle Waelder"), written by Paul Gerhardt (1607–76), has been translated, "Now rest beneath night's shadow," "The duteous day now closeth," or "Now all the woods are sleeping." The morning hymn might be one written by Thomas Ken ("Awake, my soul, and with the sun / Thy daily stage of duty run; / Shake off dull sloth and joyful rise / To pay thy morning sacrifice.") or one by Philip Doddridge ("Awake, my soul, stretch every nerve, / And press with vigor on; / A heavenly race demands thy zeal, / And an immortal crown"). Artaxerxes is the hymn tune.

[5] Anna Laetitia Barbauld (1743–1825), poet, essayist, educator, and author of many children's books, including *Hymns in Prose for Children* (1781), which she wrote at Palgrave School while Harriet's father Thomas was in attendance.

[6] The first phrase appears in Hymn IX, which includes a catalogue of flowers and where they grow: "on steep rocks, where no man can climb; in shaking bogs, and deep forests, and desert islands"; the second in Hymn X, which begins, "CHILD of mortality, whence comest thou? why is thy countenance sad, and why are thine eyes red with weeping?"

however, religion was a great comfort and pleasure to me; and I studied the New Testament very heartily and profitably, from the time that
Ann Turner went south with us, and encouraged me to confession and
morning and nightly prayer.

———

SECOND PERIOD

TO THE AGE OF SEVENTEEN

SECTION I

I THINK it could not have been long after that time that I took up a project which was of extraordinary use to me. My mind, considered dull and unobservant and unwieldy by my family, was desperately methodical. Every thing must be made tabular that would at all admit of it. Thus, I adopted in an immense hurry Dr. Franklin's youthful and absurd plan of pricking down his day's virtues and vices under heads.[1] I found at once the difficulty of mapping out moral qualities, and had to give it up,—as I presume he had to. But I tried after something quite as foolish, and with immense perseverance. I thought it would be a fine thing to distribute scripture instructions under the heads of the virtues and vices, so as to have encouragement or rebuke always ready at hand. So I made (as on so many other occasions) a paper book, ruled and duly headed. With the Old Testament, I got on very well; but I was amazed at the difficulty with the New. I knew it to be of so much more value and importance than the Old, that I could not account for the small number of cut and dry commands. I twisted meanings and wordings, and made figurative things into precepts, at an unconscionable rate, before I would give up: but, after rivalling any old puritan preacher in my free use of scripture, I was obliged to own that I could not construct the system I wanted. Thus it was that I made out that great step in the process of thought and knowledge,—that whereas Judaism was a preceptive religion, Christianity was mainly a religion of principles,— or assumed to be so.

---

[1] In his *Autobiography* Benjamin Franklin (1706–90) describes a plan for improving his character by creating a weekly chart of thirteen desirable virtues (temperance, industry, frugality, chastity, etc.) and marking a black spot for any he failed to practice on a given day. Over the course of several weeks, Franklin saw the lessening of the black spots and had the "pleasure of seeing on my pages the progress I made in virtue, by clearing successively my lines of their spots."

For many years past, my amazement has been continually on the increase that Unitarians can conceive that they are giving their children a Christian education in making their religious training what it is.[1] Our family certainly insisted very strongly, and quite sincerely, on being Christians, while despising and pitying the orthodox as much as they could be despised and pitied in return; while yet, it must have been from wonderful slovenliness of thought, as well as ignorance, that we could have taken Unitarianism to be Christianity, in any genuine sense,—in any sense which could justify separate Christian worship. In our particular case, family pride and affection were implicated in our dissent. It was not the dissent that was to be wondered at, but its having degenerated into Unitarianism. Our French name indicates our origin. The first Martineaus that we know of were expatriated Huguenots, who came over from Normandy on the Revocation of the Edict of Nantes. They were, of course, Calvinists,—so fully admitting the Christian religion to be a scheme of redemption as to deserve, without limitation or perversion, the title of Christians. But their descendants passed by degrees, with the congregations to which they belonged, out of Calvinism into the pseudo-Christianity of Arianism[2] first, and then of Unitarianism, under the guidance of pastors whose natural sense revolted from the essential points of the Christian doctrine, while they had not learning enough, biblical, ecclesiastical, historical or philosophical, to discover that what they gave up was truly essential, and that the name of Christianity was a mere sham when applied to what they retained. One evening when I was a child, I entered the parlor when our Unitarian minister, Mr. Madge, was convicting of error (and what he called idiotcy) an orthodox schoolmaster who happened to be our visitor. 'Look here,' said Mr. Madge, seizing three wine-glasses, and placing them in a row: 'here is the Father,—here's the Son,—and here's the Holy Ghost; do you mean to tell me that those three glasses can be in any case one? 'Tis mere nonsense.' And so were we

---

[1]   By the mid-1840's Martineau abandoned the Unitarianism of her family, and with the publication of her agnostic *Letters on the Laws of Man's Nature and Development* (1851), co-authored with Henry Atkinson, her brother James, a prominent Unitarian clergyman, published an attack, "Mesmeric Atheism," in the *Prospective Review*. James's review caused a permanent breach between them.

[2]   The original Arians were followers of Arius, a 4th-century Alexandrian Christian who taught that the Father and Son were distinct and divine, but not equal beings—a doctrine condemned as heresy in 325 A.D. In eighteenth-century England, Arianism was a halfway house between orthodox Trinitarian belief in the Father, Son, and Holy Spirit as one God, coequal, coeternal and indivisible, and Unitarian belief in the singular personality of God, with Christ as the highest, holiest, but non-divine human being.

children taught that it was 'mere nonsense.' I certainly wondered exceedingly that so vast a majority of the people of Norwich could accept such nonsense, and so very few see through it as the Unitarians of the city: but there was no one to suggest to me that there might be more in the matter than we saw, or than even our minister was aware of. This was pernicious enough: but far worse was the practice, necessarily universal among Unitarians, of taking any liberties they please with the revelation they profess to receive. It is true, the Scriptures are very properly declared by them to be not the revelation itself, but the record of it: but it is only through the record that the revelation can be obtained—at least by Protestants: and any tamperings with the record are operations upon the revelation itself. To appreciate the full effect of such a procedure, it is only necessary to look at what the Unitarians were doing in the days of my youth. They were issuing an Improved Version, in which considerable portions were set aside (printed in a different type) as spurious. It is true, those portions flatly contradicted some other portions in regard to dates and other facts; but the shallow scholarship of the Unitarians made its own choice what to receive and what to reject, without perceiving that such a process was wholly incompatible with the conception of the Scriptures being the record of a divine revelation at all. Having begun to cut away and alter, there was no reason for stopping; and every Unitarian was at liberty to make the Scriptures mean what suited his own views. Mr. Belsham's Exposition of the Epistles[1] is a remarkable phenomenon in this way. To get rid of some difficulties about heaven and hell, the end of the world, salvation and perdition, &c., he devised a set of figurative meanings which he applied with immense perseverance, and a poetical ingenuity remarkable in so thoroughly prosaic a man; and all the while, it never seems to have occurred to him that that could hardly be a revelation designed for the rescue of the human race from perdition, the explanation of which required all this ingenuity at the hand of a Belsham, after eighteen centuries. I was as deeply-interested a reader of those big volumes as any Unitarian in England; and their ingenuity gratified some of my faculties exceedingly; but there was throughout a haunting sense of unreality which made me uneasy,—a consciousness that this kind of solemn amusement was no fitting treatment of the burdensome troubles of conscience, and the moral irritations which made the misery of my life. This theological dissipation, and the music and poetry of psalms and hymns, charmed away my woes for the hour; but they were not the solid consolation I needed.

---

[1]   Thomas Belsham's *New Translation and Exposition of the Epistles of Paul* (London, 1824).

So, to work I went in my own way, again and again studying the New Testament, —making 'Harmonies,' poring over the geography, greedily gathering up every thing I could find in the way of commentary and elucidation, and gladly working myself into an enthusiasm with the moral beauty and spiritual promises I found in the Sacred Writings. I certainly never believed, more or less, in the 'essential doctrines' of Christianity, which represent God as the predestinator of men to sin and perdition, and Christ as their rescuer from that doom. I never was more or less beguiled by the trickery of language by which the perdition of man is made out to be justice, and his redemption to be mercy. I never suffered more or less from fear of hell. The Unitarianism of my parents saved me from that. But nothing could save me from the perplexity of finding so much of indisputable statement of those doctrines in the New Testament, nor from a covert sense that it was taking a monstrous liberty with the Gospel to pick and choose what made me happy, and reject what I did not like or could not receive. When I now find myself wondering at Unitarians who do so,—who accept heaven and reject hell,—who get rid somehow of the reign of Christ and the apostles on earth, and derive somehow a sanction of their fancy of a heaven in the stars, peopled with old acquaintances, and furnished for favourite pursuits, I try to recal the long series of years during which I did the same thing, with far more, certainly, of complacency than of misgiving. I try to remember how late on in life I have said that I confidently reckoned on entering the train of Socrates in the next world, and getting some of his secrets out of Pythagoras, besides making friendship with all the Christian worthies I especially inclined to. When I now see the comrades of my early days comfortably appropriating all the Christian promises, without troubling themselves with the clearly-specified condition,—of faith in Christ as a Redeemer,—I remind myself that this is just what I did for more than the first half of my life. The marvel remains how they now, and I then, could possibly wonder at the stationary or declining fortunes of their sect,—so evidently as Unitarianism is a mere clinging, from association and habit, to the old privilege of faith in a divine revelation, under an actual forfeiture of all its essential conditions.

My religious belief, up to the age of twenty, was briefly this. I believed in a God, milder and more beneficent and passionless than the God of the orthodox, inasmuch as he would not doom any of his creatures to eternal torment. I did not at any time, I think, believe in the Devil, but understood the Scriptures to speak of Sin under that name, and of eternal detriment under the name of eternal punishment. I believed in inestimable and eternal rewards of holiness; but I am confident that I never in my life did a right thing, or abstained from a wrong one from any consideration of reward or punishment. To the best of my recollection, I always feared sin and remorse extremely, and punishment not at all; but, on the contrary, desired punishment or any thing else that would give me the one good that I pined for in vain,—ease of conscience. The doctrine of forgiveness on repentance never availed me much, because forgiveness for the past was nothing without safety in the future; and my sins were not curable, I felt, by any single remission of their consequences,—if such remission were possible. If I prayed and wept, and might hope that I was pardoned at night, it was small comfort, because I knew I should be in a state of remorse again before the next noon. I do not remember the time when the forgiveness clause in the Lord's Prayer was not a perplexity and a stumbling-block to me. I did not care about being let off from penalty. I wanted to be at ease in conscience; and that could only be by growing good, whereas I hated and despised myself every day. My belief in Christ was that he was the purest of all beings, under God; and his sufferings for the sake of mankind made him as sublime in my view and my affections as any being could possibly be. The Holy Ghost was a mere fiction to me. I took all the miracles for facts, and contrived to worship the letter of the Scriptures long after I had, as desired, given up portions as 'spurious,' 'interpolations' and so forth. I believed in a future life as a continuation of the present, and not as a new method of existence; and, from the time when I saw that the resurrection of the body and the immortality of the soul could not both be true, I adhered to the former,—after St. Paul. I was uncomfortably disturbed that Christianity had done so little for the redemption of the race: but the perplexity was not so serious as it would have been if I had believed in the perdition of the majority of men; and, for the rest, I contrived to fix my view pretty exclusively on Christendom itself,— which Christians in general find a grand resource in their difficulties. In this way, and by the help of public worship, and of sacred music, and Milton, and the Pilgrim's Progress, I found religion my best resource, even in its first inconsistent and unsatisfactory form, till I wrought my way to something better, as I shall tell by and by.

When I was seven years old,—the winter after our return from Newcastle,—I was kept from chapel one Sunday afternoon by some ailment or other. When the house door closed behind the chapel-goers, I looked at the books on the table. The ugliest-looking of them was turned down open; and my turning it up was one of the leading incidents of my life. That plain, clumsy, calf-bound volume was 'Paradise

Lost;' and the common blueish paper, with its old-fashioned type, became as a scroll out of heaven to me. The first thing I saw was 'Argument,' which I took to mean a dispute, and supposed to be stupid enough: but there was something about Satan cleaving Chaos, which made me turn to the poetry; and my mental destiny was fixed for the next seven years. That volume was henceforth never to be found but by asking me for it, till a young acquaintance made me a present of a little Milton of my own. In a few months, I believe there was hardly a line in Paradise Lost that I could not have instantly turned to. I sent myself to sleep by repeating it: and when my curtains were drawn back in the morning, descriptions of heavenly light rushed into my memory. I think this must have been my first experience of moral relief through intellectual resource. I am sure I must have been somewhat happier from that time forward; though one fact of which I am perfectly certain shows that the improvement must have been little enough. From the time when Ann Turner and her religious training of me put me, as it were, into my own moral charge, I was ashamed of my habit of misery,—and especially of crying. I tried for a long course of years,— I should think from about eight to fourteen,—to pass a single day without crying.[1] I was a persevering child; and I know I tried hard: but I failed. I gave up at last; and during all those years, I never did pass a day without crying. Of course, my temper and habit of mind must have been excessively bad. I have no doubt I was an insufferable child for gloom, obstinacy and crossness, Still, when I remember my own plac-ability,—my weakness of yielding every thing to the first word or tone of tenderness, I cannot but believe that there was grievous mistake in the case, and that even a little more sympathy and moral support would have spared me and others a hideous amount of fault and suffering.

How I found my way out we shall see hereafter: meantime, one small incident, which occurred when I was eleven years old, may foreshadow my release. Our eldest brother, Thomas, was seven years older than myself. He was silent and reserved generally, and somewhat strict to us younger ones, to whom he taught our Latin grammar. We revered and loved him intensely, in the midst of our awe of him: but once in my childhood I made him laugh against his will, by a pun in my Latin lesson (which was a great triumph) and once I ventured to confide to him a real difficulty,—without result. I found myself by his side during a

---

[1]   In a semi-autobiographical didactic tract for the Evangelical publisher Houlston, *Christmas Day; or, The Friends: A Tale* (1826), Martineau wrote about this difficulty and her attempt to overcome it by turning to Christian principles and practice.

summer evening walk, when something gave me courage to ask him—
(the man of eighteen!)—the question which I had long been secretly
revolving:—how, if God foreknew everything, we could be blamed or
rewarded for our conduct, which was thus absolutely settled for us
beforehand. He considered for a moment, and then told me, in a kind
voice, that this was a thing which I could not understand at present, nor
for a long time to come. I dared not remonstrate; but I was disappointed:
and I felt that if I could feel the difficulty, I had a right to the solution.
No doubt, this refusal of a reply helped to fix the question in my mind.

I have said that by this time I had begun to take moral or spiritual
charge of myself. I did try hard to improve; but I fear I made little
progress. Every night, I reviewed the thoughts and actions of the day,
and tried to repent; but I could seldom comfort myself about any
amendment. All the while, however, circumstances were doing for me
what I could not do for myself,—as I have since found to be incessantly
happening. The first great wholesome discipline of my life set in (unrec-
ognized as such) when I was about eight years old. The kind lady who
took me upon her lap at Mr. Drummond's lecture had two little girls,
just the ages of Rachel and myself: and, after that incident, we children
became acquainted, and very soon, (when the family came to live close
beside us in Magdalen Street) as intimate as possible. I remember being
at their house in the Market Place when I was seven years old; and little
E. could not stand, nor even sit, to see the magic-lantern, but was held
in her papa's arms, because she was so very lame. Before the year was
out, she lost her leg.[1] Being a quiet-tempered child, and the limb being
exceedingly wasted by disease, she probably did not suffer very much
under the operation. However that might be, she met the occasion with
great courage, and went through it with remarkable composure, so that
she was the talk of the whole city. I was naturally very deeply impressed
by the affair. It turned my imagination far too much on bodily suffering, and on the peculiar glory attending fortitude in that direction. I am
sure that my nervous system was seriously injured, and especially that
my subsequent deafness was partly occasioned by the exciting and vain-
glorious dreams that I indulged for many years after my friend E. lost
her leg. All manner of deaths at the stake and on the scaffold, I went
through in imagination, in the low sense in which St. Theresa[2] craved

---

[1]   Dr. Philip Meadows Martineau, Harriet's uncle, performed the amputation on Emily
       Cooper, her friend.
[2]   St. Theresa of Avila, Spain (1515–82), mystic and founder of the reformed Carmelites (the
       Discalced, or Barefoot, Carmelites).

martyrdom; and night after night, I lay bathed in cold perspiration till I sank into the sleep of exhaustion. All this is detestable to think of now; but it is a duty to relate the truth, because parents are apt to know far too little of what is passing in their children's imaginations, unless they win the confidence of the little creatures about that on which they are shyest of all,—their aspirations. The good side of this wretched extravagance of mine was that it occasioned or strengthened a power of patience under pain and privation which was not to be looked for in a child so sensitive and irritable by nature. Fortitude was in truth my favorite virtue; and the power of bearing quietly a very unusual amount of bodily pain in childhood was the poor recompense I enjoyed for the enormous detriment I suffered from the turn my imagination had taken.

This, however, is not the discipline I referred to as arising from my companionship with E. In such a case as hers, all the world acquiesces in the parents' view and method of action: and in that case the parents made a sad mistake. They enormously increased their daughter's suffering from her infirmity by covering up the fact in an unnatural silence. E.'s lameness was never mentioned, nor recognized in any way, within my remembrance, till she, full late, did it herself. It was taken for granted that she was like other children; and the delusion was kept up in play-hours at my expense. I might almost say that from the time E. and I grew intimate, I never more had any play. Now, I was fond of play,—given to romp; and I really wonder now when I look back upon the many long years during which I stood, with cold feet and a longing mind, with E. leaning on my arm, looking on while other children were at play. It was a terrible uneasiness to me to go walks with her,—shy child as I was,— fancying every body in the streets staring at us, on account of E.'s extreme difficulty in walking. But the long self-denial which I never thought of refusing or grumbling at, must have been morally good for me, if I may judge by the pain caused by two incidents;—pain which seems to me now to swallow up all that issued from mere privation.— The fatigue of walking with E. was very great, from her extreme need of support, and from its being always on the same side. I was never very strong; and when growing fast, I was found to be growing sadly crooked, from E.'s constant tugging at one arm. I cannot at all understand how my mother could put it upon me to tell E.'s mother that I must not walk with her, because it made me crooked: but this ungracious message I was compelled to carry; and it cost me more pain than long years of privation of play. The hint was instantly taken; but I suffered the shame and regret over again every time that I saw E. assigned to any one else; and

I had infinitely rather have grown crooked than have escaped it by such a struggle.—The other incident was this. We children were to have a birthday party; and my father gave us the rare and precious liberty to play hide-and-seek in the warehouse, among the packing-cases and pigeon-holes where the bombasines were stored.[1] For weeks I had counted the days and hours till this birthday and this play; but E. could not play hide-and-seek; and there we stood, looking at the rest,—I being cold and fidgety, and at last uncontrollably worried at the thought that the hours were passing away, and I had not had one bit of play. I did the fatal thing which has been a thorn in my mind ever since. I asked E. if she would much mind having some one else with her for a minute while I hid once,—just once. O no,—she did not mind; so I sent somebody else to her, and ran off, with a feeling of self-detestation which is fresh at this day. I had no presence-of-mind for the game,—was caught in a minute; and came back to E. damaged in self-respect, for the whole remaining course of our friendship. However, I owe her a great deal; and she and her misfortune were among the most favourable influences I had the benefit of after taking myself in hand for self-government. I have much pleasure in adding that nothing could be finer than her temper in after life, when she had taken her own case in hand, and put an end, as far as it lay with her to do so, to the silence about her infirmity. After I wrote my 'Letter to the Deaf,' we seemed to be brought nearer together by our companionship in infirmity. Years after that, when I had written 'The Crofton Boys,'[2] and was uneasy lest my evident knowledge of such a case should jar upon her feelings,—always so tenderly considered,—I wrote her a confession of my uneasiness, and had in reply a most charming letter,—free, cheerful, magnanimous;—such a letter as has encouraged me to write as I have now done.

The year 1811 was a marked one to me,—first, by my being sent into the country for my health, for the whole summer and autumn; and next, for the birth of the best-beloved member of my family,—my sister Ellen.—It was not a genuine country life in a farm-house, that summer, but a most constrained and conventional one, in the abode of a rich lawyer,—a cousin of my father's,[3] who sent a daughter of his to our

---

[1] Harriet's father Thomas Martineau manufactured bombazine, a fine twilled cloth of silk and cotton or worsted wool.

[2] Martineau published her "Letter to the Deaf," about her own disability, in 1834 in *Tait's Magazine*, and *The Crofton Boys* in the *Playfellow* series, 1841–43.

[3] Unidentified, but most likely Harriet was sent to the house of Samuel Taylor of Bonham, Norfolk; his daughter Emily, seven years older than Harriet, became a close friend.

house for the advantage of city masters, in exchange for me, who went for health. I was not, on the whole, happy there:—indeed, it is pretty clear by this time that I was not happy anywhere. The old fancy for running away came back strongly upon me, and I was on the very point of attempting it when a few words of concession and kindness upset my purpose, as usual. I detested the governess,—and with abundant reason. The very first day, she shut me up and punished me because I, a town-bred child, did not know what a copse was. 'Near yonder copse,' &c. She insisted that every body must know what a copse is, and that therefore I was obstinate and a liar. After such a beginning, it will be easily conceived that our relations could not be cordial or profitable. She presently showed herself jealous of my being in advance of her pupils in school-room knowledge; and she daily outraged my sense of justice, expressly, and in the most purpose-like manner. She was thoroughly vulgar; and in a few weeks she was sent away.—One annoyance that I remember at that place was (what now appears very strange) the whispers I overheard about myself, as I sat on a little stool in a corner of the dining-room, reading. My hostess, who might have said anything in her ordinary voice without my attending to her, used to whisper to her morning visitors about my wonderful love of reading,—that I never heard anything that was said while I sat reading, and that I had written a wonderful sermon. All the while, she pretended to disguise it, winking and nudging, and saying 'We never hear any thing when we are reading.' 'We have written a sermon which is really quite wonderful at our age,' &c. &c. I wished that sermon at Jericho a hundred times; for in truth, I was heartily ashamed of it. It was merely a narrative of St. Paul's adventures, out of the Acts; and I knew it was no more a sermon than a string of parables out of the Gospels would have been.

There were some sweet country pleasures that summer. I never see chestnuts bursting from their sheaths, and lying shining among the autumn leaves, without remembering the old Manor-house where we children picked up chestnuts in the avenue, while my hostess made her call at the house. I have always loved orchards and apple-gatherings since, and blossomy lanes. The truth is, my remembrances of that summer may be found in 'Deerbrook,'[1] though I now finally, (as often before,) declare that the characters are not real. More or less suggestion from real characters there certainly is; but there is not one, except the hero, (who is not English,) that any person is justified in pointing out

---

[1]　Martineau's novel of 1839.

as 'from the life.' Of the scenery too, there is more from Great Marlow[1] than from that bleak Norfolk district; but the fresh country impressions are certainly derived from the latter. It was there that I had that precious morsel of experience which I have elsewhere detailed;[2] —the first putting my hand in among the operations of Nature, to modify them. After a morning walk, we children brought in some wild strawberry roots, to plant in our gardens. My plant was sadly withered by the time we got home; and it was then hot noon,—the soil of my garden was warm and parched, and there seemed no chance for my root. I planted it, grieved over its flabby leaves, watered it, got a little child's chair, which I put over it for shelter, and stopped up the holes in the chair with grass. When I went at sunset to look at it, the plant was perfectly fresh; and after that, it grew very well. My surprise and pleasure must have been very great, by my remembering such a trifle so long; and I am persuaded that I looked upon Nature with other eyes from the moment that I found I had power to modify her processes.

In November came the news which I had been told to expect. My sister Rachel had been with us in the country for a fortnight; and we knew that there was to be a baby at home before we went back; and I remember pressing so earnestly, by letter, to know the baby's name as to get a rebuff. I was told to wait till there was a baby. At last, the carrier brought us a letter one evening which told us that we had a little sister. I still longed to know the name, but dared not ask again. Our host saw what was in my mind. He went over to Norwich a day or two after, and on his return told me that he hoped I should like the baby's name now she had got one,—'Beersheba.' I did not know whether to believe him or not; and I had set my mind on 'Rose.' 'Ellen,' however, satisfied me very well. Homesick before, I now grew downright ill with longing. I was sure that all old troubles were wholly my fault, and fully resolved that there should be no more. Now, as so often afterwards, (as often as I left home) I was destined to disappointment. I scarcely felt myself at home before the well-remembered bickerings began;—not with me, but from the boys being troublesome, James being naughty; and our eldest sister angry and scolding. I then and there resolved that I would look for my happiness to the new little sister, and that she should never want for the tenderness which I had never found. This resolution turned out more of a prophecy than such decisions, born of a momentary emotion, usually do. That child

---

[1]   Great Marlow, Buckinghamshire, a picturesque town north of London on the Thames River.

[2]   *Household Education*, p. 152. [Martineau's note]

was henceforth a new life to me. I did lavish love and tenderness on her; and I could almost say that she has never caused me a moment's pain but by her own sorrows. There has been much suffering in her life; and in it I have suffered with her: but such sympathetic pain is bliss in comparison with such feelings as she has *not* excited in me during our close friendship of above forty years. When I first saw her it was as she was lifted out of her crib, at a fortnight old, asleep, to be shown to my late hostess, who had brought Rachel and me home. The passionate fondness I felt for her from that moment has been unlike any thing else I have felt in life,—though I have made idols of not a few nephews and nieces. But she was a pursuit to me, no less than an attachment. I remember telling a young lady at the Gate-House Concert, (a weekly undress concert) the next night, that I should now see the growth of a human mind from the very beginning. I told her this because I was very communicative to all who showed me sympathy in any degree. Years after, I found that she was so struck by such a speech from a child of nine that she had repeated it till it had spread all over the city, and people said somebody had put it into my head; but it was perfectly genuine. My curiosity *was* intense; and all my spare minutes were spent in the nursery, watching,— literally watching,—the baby. This was a great stimulus to me in my lessons, to which I gave my whole power, in order to get leisure the sooner. That was the time when I took it into my head to cut up the Bible into a rule of life, as I have already told; and it was in the nursery chiefly that I did it,—sitting on a stool opposite the nursemaid and baby, and getting up from my notes to devour the child with kisses. There were bitter moments and hours,—as when she was vaccinated or had her little illnesses. My heart then felt bursting, and I went to my room, and locked the door, and prayed long and desperately. I knew then what the Puritans meant by 'wrestling in prayer.'—One abiding anxiety which pressed upon me for two years or more was lest this child should be dumb: and if not, what an awful amount of labour was before the little creature! I had no other idea than that she must learn to speak at all as I had now to learn French,—each word by an express effort: and if I, at ten and eleven, found my vocabulary so hard, how could this infant learn the whole English language? The dread went off in amazement when I found that she sported new words every day, without much teaching at first, and then without any. I was as happy to see her spared the labour as amused at her use of words in her pretty prattle.

For nearly two years after our return from that country visit, Rachel and I were taught at home. Our eldest brother taught Latin, and the

next brother, Henry, writing and arithmetic: and our sister, French, reading and exercises. We did not get on well, except with the Latin. Our
sister expected too much from us, both morally and intellectually; and
she had not been herself carried on so far as to have much resource as
a teacher. We owed to her however a thorough grounding in our
French grammar (especially the verbs) which was of excellent service
to us afterwards at school, as was a similar grounding in the Latin grammar, obtained from our brother. As for Henry, he made our lessons in
arithmetic, &c. his funny time of day; and sorely did his practical jokes
and ludicrous severity afflict us. He meant no harm; but he was too
young to play schoolmaster; and we improved less than we should have
done under less head-ache and heart-ache from his droll system of
torture. I should say, on their behalf, that I, for one, must have seemed
a most unpromising pupil,—my wits were so completely scattered by
fear and shyness. I could never give a definition, for want of presence
of mind. I lost my place in class for every thing but lessons that could
be prepared beforehand. I was always saying what I did not mean. The
worst waste of time, energy, money and expectation was about my
music. Nature made me a musician in every sense. I was never known
to sing out of tune. I believe all who knew me when I was twenty
would give a good account of my playing. There was no music that I
ever attempted that I did not understand, and that I could not
execute,—under the one indispensable condition, that nobody heard
me. Much money was spent in instruction; and I dislike thinking of the
amount of time lost in copying music. My mother loved music, and, I
know, looked to me for much gratification in this way which she never
had. My deafness put an end to all expectation of the kind at last; but
long before that, my music was a misery to me,—while yet in another
sense, my dearest pleasure. My master was Mr. Beckwith,[1] organist of
Norwich Cathedral;—an admirable musician; but of so irritable a
temper as to be the worst of masters to a shy girl like me. It was known
that he had been dismissed from one house or more for rapping his
pupils' knuckles; and that he had been compelled to apologize for insufferable scolding. Neither of these things happened at our house; but
really I wondered sometimes that they did not,—so very badly did I
play and sing when he was at my elbow. My fingers stuck together as

---

[1] Either Dr. John Christmas Beckwith, who died in 1809, or, more likely, his son John
Charles Beckwith, who succeeded his father as organist at Norwich Cathedral in 1809
and died in 1819.

in cramp, and my voice was as husky as if I had had cotton-wool in my throat. Now and then he complimented my ear; but he oftener told me that I had no more mind than the music-book,—no more feeling than the lid of the piano,—no more heart than the chimney-piece; and that it was no manner of use trying to teach me any thing. All this while, if the room-door happened to be open without my observing it when I was singing Handel by myself, my mother would be found dropping tears over her work, and I used myself, as I may now own, to feel fairly transported. Heaven opened before me at the sound of my own voice when I believed myself alone;—that voice which my singing-master assuredly never heard. It was in his case that I first fully and suddenly learned the extent of the mischief caused by my shyness. He came twice a week. On those days it was an effort to rise in the morning,—to enter upon a day of misery; and nothing could have carried me through the morning but the thought of the evening, when he would be gone,— out of my way for three days, or even four. The hours grew heavier: my heart fluttered more and more: I could not eat my dinner; and his impatient loud knock was worse to me than sitting down in the dentist's chair. Two days per week of such feelings, strengthened by the bliss of the evenings after he was gone, might account for the catastrophe, which however did not shock me the less for that. Mr. Beckwith grew more and more cross, thinner and thinner, so that his hair and beard looked blacker and blacker, as the holidays approached, when he was wont to leave home for a week or two. One day when somebody was dining with us, and I sat beside my father at the bottom of the table, he said to my mother, 'By the way, my dear, there is a piece of news which will not surprise you much, I fancy. Poor John Beckwith is gone. He died yesterday.' Once more, that name made my heart jump into my mouth; but this time, it was with a dreadful joy. While the rest went on very quietly saying how ill he had looked for some time, and 'who would have thought he would never come back?'—and discussing how Mrs. B. and the children were provided for, and wondering who would be organist at the Cathedral, my spirits were dancing in secret rapture. The worst of my besetting terrors was over for ever! All days of the week would henceforth be alike, as far as that knock at the door was concerned. Of course, my remorse at this glee was great; and thus it was that I learned how morally injured I was by the debasing fear I was wholly unable to surmount.

Next to fear, laziness was my worst enemy. I was idle about brushing my hair,—late in the morning,—much afflicted to have to go down

to the apple-closet in winter; and even about my lessons I was indolent. I learned any thing by heart very easily, and I therefore did it well:
but I was shamefully lazy about using the dictionary, and went on, in
full anticipation of rebuke, translating *la rosée* the rose, *tomber* to bury,
and so on. This shows that there must have been plenty of provocation
on my side, whatever mistakes there may have been on that of my
teachers. I was sick and weary of the eternal 'Telemachus,'[1] and could
not go through the labours of the dictionary for a book I cared so little
about. This difficulty soon came to an end; for in 1813 Rachel and I
went to a good day-school for two years, where our time was thoroughly well spent; and there we enjoyed the acquisition of knowledge
so much as not to care for the requisite toil.

Before entering on that grand new period, I may as well advert to a
few noticeable points.—I was certainly familiar with the idea of death
before that time. The death of Nelson, when I was four years old, was
probably the earliest association in my mind of mournful feelings with
death. When I was eight or nine, an aunt died whom I had been in the
constant habit of seeing. She was old-fashioned in her dress, and peculiar in her manners. Her lean arms were visible between the elbow-
ruffles and the long mits she wore; and she usually had an apron on, and
a muslin handkerchief crossed on her bosom. She fell into absent-fits
which puzzled and awed us children: but we heard her so highly praised
(as she richly deserved) that she was a very impressive personage to us.
One morning when I came down, I found the servants at breakfast
unusually early: they looked very gloomy; bade me make no noise; but
would not explain what it was all about. The shutters were half-closed;
and when my mother came down, she looked so altered by her weeping that I hardly knew whether it was she. She called us to her, and told
us that aunt Martineau[2] had died very suddenly, of a disease of the heart.
The whispers which were not meant for us somehow reached our ears
all that week. We heard how my father and mother had been sent for
in the middle of the night by the terrified servants, and how they had
heard our poor uncle's voice of mourning before they had reached the
house; and how she looked in her coffin, and all about the funeral: and
we were old enough to be moved by the sermon in her praise at chapel,

---

[1]   The *Aventures de Télémaque, fils d'Ulysse* [*Adventures of Telemachus, the son of Ulysses*] (1699)
      by François de Salignac de La Mothe-Fénelon.
[2]   Elizabeth Martineau, née Humphrey, wife of Dr. Philips Meadows Martineau, died in
      1810; he married Mrs. Ann Dorothy Clarke in 1811, and their daughter Frances Anne was
      born in 1812.

and especially by the anthem composed for the occasion, with the words from Job,—'When the ear heard her then it blessed her,'[1] &c. My uncle's gloomy face and unpowdered hair were awful to us; and, during the single year of his widowhood, he occasionally took us children with him in the carriage, when he went to visit country patients. These drives came to an end with the year of widowhood; but he gave us something infinitely better than any other gift or pleasure in his second wife, whose only child was destined to fill a large space in our hearts and our lives.—Soon after that funeral, I somehow learned that our globe swims in space, and that there is sky all round it. I told this to James; and we made a grand scheme which we never for a moment doubted about executing. We had each a little garden, under the north wall of our garden. The soil was less than two feet deep; and below it was a mass of rubbish,—broken bricks, flints, pottery, &c. We did not know this; and our plan was to dig completely through the globe, till we came out at the other side. I fully expected to do this, and had an idea of an extremely deep hole, the darkness of which at the bottom would be lighted up by the passage of stars, slowly traversing the hole. When we found our little spades would not dig through the globe, nor even through the brickbats, we altered our scheme. We lengthened the hole to our own length, having an extreme desire to know what dying was like. We lay down alternately in this grave, and shut our eyes, and fancied ourselves dead, and told one another our feelings when we came out again. As far as I can remember, we fully believed that we now knew all about it.

A prominent event of my childhood happened in 1812, when we went to Cromer[2] for the sake of the baby's health. I had seen the sea, as I mentioned, when under three years old, as it swayed under the old jetty at Yarmouth: and I had seen it again at Tynemouth,[3] when I was seven: but now it was like a wholly new spectacle; and I doubt whether I ever received a stronger impression than when, from the rising ground above Cromer, we caught sight of the sparkling expanse. At Tynemouth, that singular incident took place which I have elsewhere narrated,[4]— that I was shown the sea, immediately below my feet, at the foot of the very slope on which I was standing, and could not see it. The rest of the party must have thought me crazy or telling a lie; but the distress of

---

[1]   Job 29:11 (KJV): 'When the ear heard me, then it blessed me.'
[2]   Seaside resort north of Norwich on the North Sea coast.
[3]   I.e., during her visit to Newcastle upon Tyne, described in Period I, sec. ii.
[4]   Letters on the Laws of Man's Nature and Development, p. 161. [Martineau's note]

being unable to see what I had so earnestly expected, was real enough; and so was the amazement when I at last perceived the fluctuating tide. All this had gone out of my mind when we went to Cromer; and the spectacle seemed a wholly new one. That was a marvellous month that the nursemaid and we children spent there. When we were not down on the sands, or on the cliffs, I was always perched on a bank in the garden whence I could see that straight blue line, or those sparkles which had such a charm for me. It was much that I was happy for a whole month; but I also obtained many new ideas, and much development;—the last chiefly, I think, in a religious direction.

In the preceding year another instance had occurred,—a most mortifying one to me,—of that strange inability to see what one is looking for (no doubt because one looks wrongly) of which the Tynemouth sea-gazing was a strong illustration.[1] When the great comet of 1811 was attracting all eyes, my star-gazing was just as ineffectual. Night after night, the whole family of us went up to the long windows at the top of my father's warehouse; and the exclamations on all hands about the comet perfectly exasperated me, —because I could not see it! 'Why, there it is!' 'It is as big as a saucer.' 'It is as big as a cheese-plate.' 'Nonsense;—you might as well pretend not to see the moon.' Such were the mortifying comments on my grudging admission that I could not see the comet. And I never did see it. Such is the fact; and philosophers may make of it what they may,— remembering that I was then nine years old, and with remarkably good eyes.

SECTION II

I WAS eleven when that delectable schooling began which I always recur to with clear satisfaction and pleasure. There was much talk in 1813 among the Norwich Unitarians of the conversion of an orthodox dissenting minister, the Rev. Isaac Perry, to Unitarianism. Mr. Perry had been minister of the Cherry Lane Chapel, and kept a large and flourishing boys' school. Of course, he lost his pulpit, and the chief part of his school. As a preacher he was wofully dull; and he was far too simple

---

[1]   Letters on the Laws of Man's Nature and Development, p. 161. [Martineau's note]

and gullible for a boys' schoolmaster. The wonder was that his school kept up so long, considering how completely he was at the mercy of naughty boys. But he was made to be a girls' schoolmaster. Gentlemanly, honourable, well provided for his work, and extremely fond of it, he was a true blessing to the children who were under him.—Rachel and I certainly had some preconception of our approaching change, when my father and mother were considering it; for we flew to an upper window one day to catch a sight of this Mr. Perry and our minister, Mr. Madge, before they turned the corner.[1] That was my first sight of the black coat and grey pantaloons, and powdered hair, and pointing and see-sawing fore-finger, which I afterwards became so familiar with.

We were horribly nervous, the first day we went to school. It was a very large vaulted room, white-washed, and with a platform for the master and his desk; and below, rows of desks and benches, of wood painted red, and carved all over with idle boys' devices. Some good many boys remained for a time; but the girls had the front row of desks, and could see nothing of the boys but by looking behind them. The thorough way in which the boys did their lessons, however, spread its influence over us, and we worked as heartily as if we had worked together. I remember being somewhat oppressed by the length of the first morning,—from nine till twelve,—and dreading a similar strain in the afternoon, and twice every day: but in a very few days, I got into all the pleasure of it, and a new state of happiness had fairly set in. I have never since felt more deeply and thoroughly the sense of progression than I now began to do. As far as I remember, we never failed in our lessons, more or less. Our making even a mistake was very rare: and yet we got on fast. This shows how good the teaching must have been. We learned Latin from the old Eton grammar,[2] which I therefore, and against all reason, cling to,—remembering when we recited all that Latin, prose and verse, which occupied us four hours. Two other girls, besides Rachel and myself, formed the class; and we certainly attained a capability of enjoying some of the classics, even before the two years were over. Cicero, Virgil, and a little of Horace were our main reading then: and afterwards I took great delight in Tacitus. I believe it was a genuine understanding

---

[1] Thomas Madge (1786–1870), from 1811 co-pastor, from 1812–25 sole pastor of the Octagon Chapel, which the Martineaus attended.

[2] *A Short Introduction to the Latin Tongue* (1758). The Eton grammar was so familiar that it inspired parodies, including *The Comic Latin Grammar: A New and Facetious Introduction to the Latin Tongue* by the *Punch* humorists Gilbert à Beckett and John Leech (London: Charles Tilt, 1840).

and pleasure, because I got into the habit of thinking in Latin, and had something of the same pleasure in sending myself to sleep with Latin as with English poetry. Moreover, we stood the test of verse-making, in which I do not remember that we ever got any disgrace, while we certainly obtained, now and then, considerable praise. When Mr. Perry was gone, and we were put under Mr. Banfather,[1] one of the masters at the Grammar School, for Latin, Mr. B. one day took a little book out of his pocket, and translated from it a passage which he desired us to turn into Latin verse. My version was precisely the same as the original, except one word (*annosa* for *antiqua*) and the passage was from the Eneid. Tests like these seem to show that we really were well taught, and that our attainment was sound, as far as it went. Quite as much care was bestowed on our French, the grammar of which we learned thoroughly, while the pronunciation was scarcely so barbarous as in most schools during the war, as there was a French lady engaged for the greater part of the time. Mr. Perry prided himself, I believe, on his process of composition being exceedingly methodical; and he enjoyed above every thing initiating us into the mystery. The method and mystery were more appropriate in our lessons in school than in his sermons in chapel;—at least, the sermons were fearfully dull; whereas the lessons were highly interesting and profitable. The only interest we could feel in his preaching was when he first brought the familiar fore-finger into play, and then built up his subject on the scaffolding which we knew so well. There was the Proposition, to begin with: then the Reason, and the Rule; then the Example, ancient and modern; then the Confirmation; and finally, the Conclusion.[2] This may be a curious method, (not altogether apostolic) of preaching the gospel; but it was a capital way of introducing some order into the chaos of girls' thoughts. One piece of our experience which I remember is highly illustrative of this. In a fit of poetic furor one day we asked leave

---

[1] The Rev. Henry Banfather was, like Isaac Perry, a clergyman and schoolmaster.

[2] Although Martineau calls Perry's method "curious," it was in fact common in nineteenth-century classrooms. In their rhetorics, Hugh Blair (1785), David Booth (1831), and William and Robert Chambers (1843) in Britain and William Russell (1823), Alexander Jamieson (1826), and Richard Parker (1832) in America introduced students to a similar method of composition. Parker's *Progressive Exercises in English Composition*, under "Complex Themes," gives these parts: 1. The Proposition, or Narrative; 2. The Reason; 3. The Confirmation; 4. The Simile, or Comparison; 5. The Example "where we bring instances from history to corroborate the truth of our theme"; 6. The Testimony; and 7. The Conclusion. Perry's method, which Martineau learned, has only five parts, but "the Example, ancient and modern," indicates that he was drawing on the same pedagogical tradition of classical rhetoric.

for once to choose our own subject for a theme,—the whole class having agreed before-hand what the subject should be. Of course, leave was granted; and we blurted out that we wanted to write 'on Music.' Mr. Perry pointed out that this was not definite enough to be called a subject. It might be on the Uses of Psalmody, or on the effect of melody in certain situations, or of martial music, or of patriotic songs, &c. &c.: but he feared there would be some vagueness if so large a subject were taken, without circumscription. However, we were bent on our own way, and he wisely let us have it. The result may easily be foreseen. We were all floating away on our own clouds, and what a space we drifted over may be imagined. We came up to Mr. P.'s desk all elate with the consciousness of our sensibility and eloquence; and we left it prodigiously crest-fallen. As one theme after another was read, no two agreeing even so far as the Proposition, our folly became more and more apparent; and the master's few, mild, respectful words at the end were not necessary to impress the lesson we had gained. Up went the fore-finger, with 'You perceive, ladies' . . . . and we saw it all; and thenceforth we were thankful to be guided, or dictated to, in the choice of our topics. Composition was my favourite exercise; and I got credit by my themes, I believe. Mr. Perry told me so, in 1834, when I had just completed the publication of my Political Economy Tales,[1] and when I had the pleasure of making my acknowledgments to him as my master in composition, and probably the cause of my mind being turned so decidedly in that direction. That was a gratifying meeting, after my old master and I had lost sight of one another for so many years. It was our last. If I remember right, we met on the eve of my sailing for America; and he was dead before my return.

Next to Composition, I think arithmetic was my favourite study. My pleasure in the working of numbers is something inexplicable to me,—as much as any pleasure of sensation. I used to spend my play hours in covering my slate with sums, washing them out, and covering the slate again. The fact is, however, that we had no lessons that were not pleasant. That was the season of my entrance upon an intellectual life. In an intellectual life I found then, as I have found since, refuge from moral suffering, and an always unexhausted spring of moral strength and enjoyment.

Even then, and in that happy school, I found the need of a refuge from trouble. Even there, under the care of our just and kind master, I found my passion for justice liable to disappointment as elsewhere. Some of our school-fellows brought a trumpery charge, out of school,

---

[1]   The *Illustrations of Political Economy* (1832–34) made Martineau famous; see Period IV, sec. i.

against Rachel and me; and our dismay was great at finding that Mrs. Perry, and therefore, no doubt, Mr. Perry believed us capable of a dirty trick. We could not establish our innocence; and we had to bear the knowledge that we were considered guilty of the offence in the first place, and of telling a lie to conceal it in the next. How vehemently I used to determine that I would never, in all my life, believe people to be guilty of any offence, where disproof was impossible, and they asserted their innocence.—Another incident made a great impression on me. It happened before the boys took their final departure; and it helped to make me very glad when we girls (to the number of sixteen) were left to ourselves.

Mr. Perry was one day called out, to a visitor who was sure to detain him for some time. On such occasions, the school was left in charge of the usher, whose desk was at the farther end of the great room. On this partic-ular day, the boys would not let the girls learn their lessons. Somehow, they got the most absurd masks within the sphere of our vision; and they said things that we could not help laughing at, and made soft bow-wows, cooings, bleatings, &c., like a juvenile House of Commons, but so as not to be heard by the distant usher. While we girls laughed, we were really angry, because we wanted to learn our lessons. It was proposed by some-body, and carried unanimously, that complaint should be made to the usher. I believe I was the youngest; and I know I was asked by the rest to convey the complaint. Quite innocently I did what I was asked. The consequence,—truly appalling to me,—was that coming up the school-room again was like running the gauntlet. O! that hiss! 'S-s-s—tell-tale—tell-tale!' greeted me all the way up: but there was worse at the end. The girls who had sent me said I was served quite right, and they would have nothing to do with a tell-tale. Even Rachel went against me. And was I really that horrible thing called a tell-tale? I never meant it; yet not the less was it even so! When Mr. Perry came back, the usher's voice was heard from the lower regions—'Sir!' and then came the whole story, with the names of all the boys in the first class. Mr. Perry was generally the mildest of men; but when he went into a rage, he did the thing thoroughly. He became as white as his powdered hair, and the ominous fore-finger shook: and never more than on this occasion. J.D., as being usually 'correct,' was sentenced to learn only thirty lines of Greek, after school. (He died not long after, much beloved.) W.D., his brother, less 'correct' in character, had fifty. Several more had from thirty to fifty; and R.S. (now, I believe, the leading innkeeper in old Norwich)— 'R.S., always foremost in mischief, must now meet the consequences. R.S. shall learn SEVENTY lines of

Greek before he goes home.' How glad should I have been to learn any thing within the compass of human knowledge to buy off those boys! They probably thought I enjoyed seeing them punished. But I was almost as horror-struck at their fate as at finding that one could be a delinquent, all in a moment, with the most harmless intentions.

An incident which occurred before Mr. Perry's departure from Norwich startled me at the time, and perhaps startles me even more now, as showing how ineffectual the conscience becomes when the moral nature of a child is too much depressed.—All was going on perfectly well at school, as far as we knew, when Mr. Perry one day called, and requested a private interview with my father or mother. My mother and he were talking so long in the drawing-room, that dinner was delayed above half-an-hour, during which time I was growing sick with apprehension. I had no doubt whatever that we had done something wrong, and that Mr. Perry had come to complain of us. This was always my way,—so accustomed was I to censure, and to stiffen myself under it, right or wrong; so that all clear sense of right and wrong was lost. I believe that, at bottom, I always concluded myself wrong. In this case it made no difference that I had no conception what it was all about. When my mother appeared, she was very grave: the mood spread, and the dinner was silent and gloomy, —father, brothers and all. My mother had in her heart a little of the old-fashioned liking for scenes: and now we had one, —memorable enough to me! 'My dear,' said she to my father, when the dessert was on the table, and the servant was gone, 'Mr. Perry has been here.' 'So I find, my love.' 'He had some very important things to say. He had something to say about—Rachel—and—Harriet.' I had been picking at the fringe of my doily; and now my heart sank, and I felt quite faint. 'Ah! here it comes,' thought I, expecting to hear of some grand delinquency. My mother went on, very solemnly. 'Mr. Perry says that he has never had a fault to find with Rachel and Harriet; and that if he had a school full of such girls, he should be the happiest man alive.' The revulsion was tremendous. I cried desperately, I remember, amidst the rush of congratulations. But what a moral state it was, when my conscience was of no more use to me than this! The story carries its own moral.

What Mr. Perry came to say was, however, dismal enough. He was no man of the world; and his wife was no manager: and they were in debt and difficulty. Their friends paid their debts (my father taking a generous share) and they removed to Ipswich.[1] It was the bitterest of

---

[1]   A Suffolk town, approximately 40 miles south of Norwich.

my young griefs, I believe,—their departure. Our two years' schooling seemed like a lifetime to look back upon: and to this day it fills a disproportionate space in the retrospect of my existence,—so inestimable was its importance. When we had to bid our good master farewell, I was deputed to utter the thanks and good wishes of the pupils: but I could not get on for tears, and he accepted our grief as his best tribute. He went round, and shook hands with us all, with gracious and solemn words, and sent us home passionately mourning.—Though this seemed like the close of one period of my life, it was in fact the opening of its chief phase,—of that intellectual existence which my life has continued to be, more than any thing else, through its whole course.

After his departure, and before I was sent to Bristol, our mode of life was this. We had lessons in Latin and French, and I in music, from masters; and we read aloud in family a good deal of history, biography, and critical literature. The immense quantity of needlework and music-copying that I did remains a marvel to me; and so does the extraordinary bodily indolence. The difficulty I had in getting up in the morning, the detestation of the daily walk, and of all visiting, and of every break in the monotony that I have always loved, seem scarcely credible to me now,—active as my habits have since become. My health was bad, however, and my mind ill at ease. It was a depressed and wrangling life; and I have no doubt I was as disagreeable as possible. The great calamity of my deafness was now opening upon me; and that would have been quite enough for youthful fortitude, without the constant indigestion, languor and muscular weakness which made life a burden to me. My religion was a partial comfort to me; and books and music were a great resource: but they left a large margin over for wretchedness. My beloved hour of the day was when the cloth was drawn, and I stole away from the dessert, and read Shakspere by firelight in winter in the drawing-room. My mother was kind enough to allow this breach of good family manners; and again at a subsequent time when I took to newspaper reading very heartily. I have often thanked her for this forbearance since. I was conscious of my bad manners in keeping the newspaper on my chair all dinner-time, and stealing away with it as soon as grace was said; and of sticking to my Shakspere, happen what might, till the tea was poured out: but I could not forego those indulgences, and I went on to enjoy them uneasily. Our newspaper was the Globe,[1] in its best days, when, without ever mentioning Political Economy,

[1] *The Globe*, founded in 1803 as a trade journal, increasingly came to adopt a Whig perspective and became an important forum for discussions of political economy, according to Stephen Koss, *The Rise and Fall of the Political Press in Britain* (London: Hamish Hamilton, 1981).

it taught it, and viewed public affairs in its light. This was not quite my first attraction to political economy (which I did not know by name till five or six years later;) for I remember when at Mr. Perry's fastening upon the part of our geography book (I forget what it was) which treated of the National Debt, and the various departments of the Funds. This was fixed in my memory by the unintelligible raillery of my brothers and other companions, who would ask me with mock deference to inform them of the state of the Debt, or would set me, as a forfeit at Christmas Games, to make every person present understand the operation of the Sinking Fund. I now recal Mr. Malthus's amusement,[1] twenty years later, when I told him I was sick of his name before I was fifteen. His work was talked about then, as it has been ever since, very eloquently and forcibly, by persons who never saw so much as the outside of the book. It seems to me that I heard and read an enormous deal against him and his supposed doctrines; whereas when, at a later time, I came to inquire, I could never find any body who had read his book. In a poor little struggling Unitarian periodical, the Monthly Repository, in which I made my first appearance in print, a youth, named Thomas Noon Talfourd,[2] was about this time making his first attempts at authorship. Among his earliest papers, I believe, was one 'On the System of Malthus,' which had nothing in fact to do with the real Malthus and his system, but was a sentimental vindication of long engagements. It was prodigiously admired by very young people: not by me, for it was rather too luscious for my taste,—but by some of my family, who read it, and lived on it for awhile: but it served to mislead me about Malthus, and helped to sicken me of his name, as I told him long afterwards. In spite of this, however, I was all the while becoming a political economist without knowing it, and, at the same time, a sort of walking Concordance of Milton and Shakspere.

The first distinct recognition of my being deaf, more or less, was when I was at Mr. Perry's,—when I was about twelve years old. It was a very slight, scarcely-perceptible hardness of hearing at that time; and the recognition was merely this;—that in that great vaulted school-room before-mentioned, where there was a large space between the class and

[1] Thomas Malthus (1766–1834), historian, political economist, and author of *An Essay on the Principle of Population* (1793), whose lessons Martineau would illustrate in her political economy tales.

[2] Thomas Noon Talfourd (1795–1854), author best known for his blank verse tragedies and as a friend of Samuel Coleridge, Robert Browning, and Charles Dickens, who dedicated *Pickwick Papers* to him. Martineau's first essay, "Female Writers on Practical Divinity," appeared in the *Monthly Repository* in November, 1822.

the master's desk or the fire, I was excused from taking places in class, and desired to sit always at the top, because it was somewhat nearer the master, whom I could not always hear further off. When Mr. Perry changed his abode, and we were in a smaller school-room, I again took places with the rest. I remember no other difficulty about hearing at that time. I certainly heard perfectly well at chapel, and all public speaking (I remember Wilberforce[1] in our vast St. Andrew's Hall) and general conversation everywhere: but before I was sixteen, it had become very noticeable, very inconvenient, and excessively painful to myself. I did once think of writing down the whole dreary story of the loss of a main sense, like hearing; and I would not now shrink from inflicting the pain of it on others, and on myself, if any adequate benefit could be obtained by it. But, really, I do not see that there could. It is true,—the sufferers rarely receive the comfort of adequate, or even intelligent sympathy: but there is no saying that an elaborate account of the woe would create the sympathy, for practical purposes. Perhaps what I have said in the 'Letter to the Deaf,' which I published in 1834, will serve as well as anything I could say here to those who are able to sympathise at all; and I will therefore offer no elaborate description of the daily and hourly trials which attend the gradual exclusion from the world of sound.

Some suggestions and conclusions, however, it is right to offer.—I have never seen a deaf child's education well managed at home, or at an ordinary school. It does not seem to be ever considered by parents and teachers how much more is learned by oral intercourse than in any other way; and, for want of this consideration, they find too late, and to their consternation, that the deaf pupil turns out deficient in sense, in manners, and in the knowledge of things so ordinary that they seem to be matters of instinct rather than of information. Too often, also, the deaf are sly and tricky, selfish and egotistical; and the dislike which attends them is the sin of the parent's ignorance visited upon the children. These worst cases are of those who are deaf from the outset, or from a very early age; and in as far as I was exempt from them, it was chiefly because my education was considerably advanced before my hearing began to go. In such a case as mine, the usual evil (far less serious) is that the sufferer is inquisitive,—*will* know everything that is said, and becomes a bore to all the world. From this I was saved (or it helped to save me) by a kind word from my eldest brother. (From how much would a few

---

[1]   William Wilberforce (1759–1833), Evangelical M.P. who led the movement to abolish the slave trade.

more such words have saved me?) He had dined in company with an elderly single lady,—a sort of provincial blue-stocking in her time,—who was growing deaf, rapidly, and so sorely against her will that she tried to ignore the fact to the last possible moment. At that dinner-party, this lady sat next her old acquaintance, William Taylor of Norwich,[1] who never knew very well how to deal with ladies (except, to his honour be it spoken, his blind mother;) and Miss N—teased him to tell her all that every body said till he grew quite testy and rude. My brother told me, with tenderness in his voice, that he thought of me while blushing, as every body present did, for Miss N—; and that he hoped that if ever I should grow as deaf as she, I should never be seen making myself so irksome and absurd. This helped me to a resolution which I made and never broke, —never to ask what was said. Amidst remonstrance, kind and testy, and every sort of provocation, I have adhered to this resolution,—confident in its soundness. I think now, as I have thought always, that it is impossible for the deaf to divine what is worth asking for and what is not; and that one's friends may always be trusted, if left unmolested, to tell one whatever is essential, or really worth hearing.

One important truth about the case of persons deficient in a sense I have never seen noticed; and I much doubt whether ever occurs to any but the sufferers under that deficiency. We sufferers meet with abundance of compassion for our privations: but the privation is, (judging by my own experience) a very inferior evil to the fatigue imposed by the obstruction. In my case, to be sure, the deficiency of three senses out of five renders the instance a very strong one: but the merely blind or deaf must feel something of the laboriousness of life which I have found it most difficult to deal with. People in general have only to sit still in the midst of Nature, to be amused and *diverted* (in the strict sense of the word,—*distracted*, in the French sense) so as to find 'change of work as good as rest:' but I have had, for the main part of my life, to go in search of impressions and influences, as the alternative from abstract or unrelieved thought, in an intellectual view, and from brooding, in a moral view. The fatigue belonging to either alternative may easily be conceived, when once suggested: and considerate persons will at once see what large allowance must in fairness be made for faults of temper, irritability or weakness of nerves, narrowness of mind, and imperfection of sympathy, in sufferers so worn with toil of body and mind as I, for one, have been.

---

[1]   William Taylor (1765–1836), author and critic who belonged to the Unitarian community in Norwich. He was an enthusiast for German poetry, his most important work being his *Historic Survey of German Poetry* (1828–30).

I have sustained, from this cause, fatigue which might spread over double my length of life; and in this I have met with no sympathy till I asked for it by an explanation of the case. From this labour there is, it must be remembered, no holiday, except in sleep. Life is a long, hard, unrelieved working-day to us, who hear, or see, only by express effort, or have to make other senses serve the turn of that which is lost. When three out of five are deficient, the difficulty of cheerful living is great, and the terms of life are truly hard.—If I have made myself understood about this, I hope the explanation may secure sympathy for many who cannot be relieved from their burden, but may be cheered under it.

Another suggestion that I would make is that those who hear should not insist on managing the case of the deaf for them. As much sympathy as you please; but no overbearing interference in a case which you cannot possibly judge of. The fact is,—the family of a person who has a growing infirmity are reluctant to face the truth; and they are apt to inflict frightful pain on the sufferer to relieve their own weakness and uneasiness. I believe my family would have made almost any sacrifice to save me from my misfortune; but not the less did they aggravate it terribly by their way of treating it. First, and for long, they insisted that it was all my own fault,—that I was so absent,—that I never cared to attend to any thing that was said,—that I ought to listen this way, or that, or the other; and even (while my heart was breaking) they told me that 'none are so deaf as those that won't hear.' When it became too bad for this, they blamed me for not doing what I was sorely tempted to do,—inquiring of them about every thing that was said, and not managing in *their* way, which would have made all right. This was hard discipline; but it was most useful to me in the end. It showed me that I must take my case into my own hands; and with me, dependent as I was upon the opinion of others, this was redemption from probable destruction. Instead of drifting helplessly as hitherto, I gathered myself up for a gallant breasting of my destiny; and in time I reached the rocks where I could take a firm stand. I felt that here was an enterprise; and the spirit of enterprise was roused in me; animating me to sure success, with many sinkings and much lapse by the way. While about it, I took my temper in hand,—in this way. I was young enough for vows,—was, indeed, at the very age of vows;—and I made a vow of patience about this infirmity,—that I would smile in every moment of anguish from it; and that I would never lose temper at any consequences from it,— from losing public worship (then the greatest conceivable privation) to the spoiling of my cap-borders by the use of the trumpet I foresaw I must arrive at. With such a temper as mine was then, an infliction so worrying, so unintermitting, so mortifying, so isolating as loss of hearing must 'kill or cure.' In time, it acted with me as a cure, (in comparison with what my temper was in my youth:) but it took a long time to effect the cure, and it was so far from being evident, or even at all perceptible when I was fifteen, that my parents were determined by medical advice to send me from home for a considerable time, in hope of improving my health, nerves and temper by a complete and prolonged change of scene and objects.

Before entering upon that new chapter of my life, however, I must say another word about this matter of treatment of personal infirmity. We had a distant relation, in her young womanhood when I was a child, who, living in the country, came into Norwich sometimes on market days, and occasionally called at our house. She had become deaf in infancy,—very very deaf; and her misfortune had been mismanaged. Truth to speak, she was far from agreeable: but it was less for that than on account of the trouble of her deafness that she was spoken of as I used to hear, long before I ever dreamed of being deaf myself. When it was announced by any child at the window that — — was passing, there was an exclamation of annoyance; and if she came up the steps, it grew into lamentation. 'What *shall* we do?' 'We shall be as hoarse as ravens all day.' 'We shall be completely worn out,' and so forth. Sometimes she was wished well at Jericho. When I was growing deaf, all this came back upon me; and one of my self-questionings was— 'Shall I put people to flight as — — does? Shall I be dreaded and disliked in that way all my life?' The lot did indeed seem at times too hard to be borne. Yet here am I now, on the borders of the grave, at the end of a busy life, confident that this same deafness is about the best thing that ever happened to me;—the best, in a selfish view, as the grandest impulse to self-mastery; and the best in a higher view, as my most peculiar opportunity of helping others, who suffer the same misfortune without equal stimulus to surmount the false shame, and other unspeakable miseries which attend it.

By this time, the battle of Waterloo had been fought.[1] I suppose most children were politicians during the war. I was a great one. I remember Mr. Perry's extreme amusement at my breaking through my shyness, one day, and stopping him as he was leaving the school-room, to ask, with

---

[1] In 1815. The original edition of the *Autobiography* indicated Martineau's age and the historical date in the running heads.

much agitation, whether he believed in the claims of one of the many Louis XVII.'s who have turned up in my time. It must be considered that my mother remembered the first French Revolution. Her sympathies were with the royal family; and the poor little Dauphin was an object of romantic interest to all English children who knew anything of the story at all. The pretence that he was found set thousands of imaginations on fire, whenever it was raised; and among many other wonderful effects, it emboldened me to speak to Mr. Perry about other things than lessons. Since the present war (of 1854) broke out,[1] it has amused me to find myself so like my old self of forty years before, in regard to telling the servants the news. In the old days, I used to fly into the kitchen, and tell my father's servants how sure 'Boney' was to be caught,—how impossible it was that he should escape,—how his army was being driven back through the Pyrenees,—or how he had driven back the allies here or there. Then, I wanted sympathy, and liked the importance and the sensation of carrying news. Now, the way has been to summon my own servants after the evening post, and bid them get the map, or come with me to the globe, and explain to them the state of the war, and give them the latest news,—probably with some of the old associations lingering in my mind; but certainly with the dominant desire to give these intelligent girls an interest in the interests of freedom, and a clear knowledge of the position and duties of England in regard to the war. I remember my father's bringing in the news of some of the Peninsular victories, and what his face was like when he told my mother of the increase of the Income-tax to ten per cent., and again, of the removal of the Income-tax. I remember the proclamation of peace in 1814, and our all going to see the illuminations; those abominable transparencies, among the rest, which represented Bonaparte (always in green coat, white breeches and boots) as carried to hell by devils, pitchforked in the fiery lake by the same attendants, or haunted by the Duc d'Enghien.[2] I well remember the awful moment when Mr. Drummond (of the chemical lectures)[3] looked in at the back door (on his way from

---

[1]   The Crimean War, 1853–56.

[2]   Louis Antoine Henri, Duc d'Enghien (1772–1804), was shot at dawn in the moat of the Chateau of Vincennes after a sham trial; the execution was widely viewed as an atrocity because the Duke had not committed any crime (except being born a Bourbon). In his final will and testament, Napoleon stated: "I had the Duke of Enghien arrested and judged because it was necessary for the safety, the interests, and the honor of the French people. . . . I would do the same again."

[3]   Thomas Drummond; see Period I, p. 46, n. 2.

the counting-house) and telling my mother that 'Boney' had escaped
from Elba, and was actually in France.[1] This impressed me more than
the subsequent hot Midsummer morning when somebody (I forget
whether father or brother) burst in with the news of the Waterloo
slaughter. It was the slaughter that was uppermost with us, I believe,
though we never had a relative, nor, as far as I know, even an acquaintance, in either army or navy.

I was more impressed still with the disappointment about the effects
of the peace, at the end of the first year of it. The country was overrun
with disbanded soldiers, and robbery and murder were frightfully
frequent and desperate. The Workhouse Boards were under a pressure
of pauperism which they could not have managed if the Guardians had
been better informed than they were in those days; and one of my political panics (of which I underwent a constant succession) was that the
country would become bankrupt through its poor-law. Another panic
was about revolution,—our idea of revolution being, of course, of guil-
lotines in the streets, and all that sort of thing. Those were Cobbett's
grand days, and the days of Castlereagh and Sidmouth spy-systems and
conspiracies.[2] Our pastor was a great radical; and he used to show us the
caricatures of the day (Hone's, I think) in which Castlereagh was always
flogging Irishmen, and Canning spouting froth, and the Regent insulting his wife, and the hungry, haggard multitude praying for vengeance
on the Court and the Ministers;[3] and every Sunday night, after supper,
when he and two or three other bachelor friends were with us, the talk
was of the absolute certainty of a dire revolution. When, on my return
from Bristol in 1819, I then turned to say what my conscience bade me

---

[1]   In 1814 Napoleon was forced to abdicate by the coalition allies (led by Prince Klemens
      von Metternich of Austria and the English "Iron Duke," Arthur Wellesley) and was
      banished to the island of Elba; he escaped ten months later, returned to France to regain
      power, and was defeated in 1815 at Waterloo.
[2]   William Cobbett (1763–1835) was a political Radical imprisoned for his attack on flog-
      ging in the army; he was the first to publish the Parliamentary debates, later taken over
      by Hansard. Robert Stewart, Viscount Castlereagh, was foreign secretary from 1812–22,
      and played a leading role in the Congress of Vienna after Waterloo. Disliked by many for
      his conservative policies, Shelley wrote in *The Mask of Anarchy*: "I met Murder on the
      way—/He had a mask like Castlereagh." Henry Addington (1759–1844), Lord Sidmouth,
      was home secretary from 1812–21, and set up a network to spy on political radicals.
[3]   William Hone (1780–1842) wrote political satires and pamphlets, many illustrated. In this
      period Castlereagh was known for his advocacy of flogging for military discipline; George
      Canning (1770–1827), foreign secretary in 1808–09 and an opponent of Castlereagh, was
      ambassador to Lisbon and an opponent of political reform; and the Prince Regent (later
      George IV) was separated from his wife, Caroline of Brunswick, who had moved to Italy.

say, and what I had been led to see by a dear aunt, that it was wrong to catch up and believe and spread reports injurious to the royal family, who could not reply to slander like other people, I was met by a shout of derision first, and then by a serious reprimand for my immorality in making more allowance for royal sinners than for others. Between my dread of this worldliness, and my sense that they had a worse chance than other people, and my further feeling that respect should be shown them on account of their function first, and their defenseless position after-wards, I was in what the Americans would call 'a fix.' The conscientious uncertainty I was in was a real difficulty and trouble to me; and this prob-ably helped to fix my attention upon the principles of politics and the characteristics of parties, with an earnestness not very common at that age. Still,—how astonished should I have been if any one had then fore-told to me that, of all the people in England, I should be the one to write the 'History of the Peace!'[1]

One important consequence of the peace was the interest with which foreigners were suddenly invested, in the homes of the middle classes, where the rising generation had seen no foreigners except old émigrés,—powdered old Frenchmen, and ladies with outlandish bonnets and high-heeled shoes. About this time there came to Norwich a foreigner who excited an unaccountable interest in our house,—considering what exceedingly proper people we were, and how sharp a look-out we kept on the morals of our neighbors. It was poor Polidori,[2] well known after-wards as Lord Byron's physician, as the author of 'the Vampire,' and as having committed suicide under gambling difficulties. When we knew him, he was a handsome, harum-scarum young man,—taken up by William Taylor as William Taylor did take up harum-scarum young men,—and so introduced into the best society the place afforded, while his being a Catholic, or passing for such, insured him a welcome in some of the most aristocratic of the county houses. He was a foolish rattle,—with no sense, scarcely any knowledge, and no principle; but we took for granted in him much that he had not, and admired whatever he had. For his part, he was an avowed admirer of our eldest sister (who however escaped fancy-free;) and he was forever at our house. We younger ones romanced amazingly about him,—drew his remarkable profile on the backs of all our letters, dreamed of him, listened to all his marvelous stories,

---

[1] *A History of England during the Thirty Years' Peace, 1816–1846* (London: Charles Knight, 1849–50).

[2] John Polidori (1795–1821), best known as Martineau describes him, but also the uncle of Dante and Christina Rossetti.

and, when he got a concussion of the brain by driving his gig against a tree in Lord Stafford's park,[1] were inconsolable. If he had (happily) died then, he would have remained a hero in our imaginations. The few following years (which were very possibly all the wilder for that concussion of the brain) disabused every body of all expectation of good from him; but yet when he died, frantic under gaming debts, the shock was great, and the impression, on my mind at least, deep and lasting. My eldest sister, then in a happy home of her own, was shocked and concerned; but we younger ones felt it far more. I was then in the height of my religious fanaticism; and I remember putting away all doubts about the theological propriety of what I was doing, for the sake of the relief of praying for his soul. Many times a day, and with my whole heart, did I pray for his soul.

SECTION III

As I HAVE said, it was the state of my health and temper which caused me to be sent from home when I was in my sixteenth year. So many causes of unhappiness had arisen, and my temper was so thoroughly ajar, that nothing else would have done any effectual good. Every thing was a misery to me, and was therefore done with a bad grace; and hence had sprung up a habit of domestic criticism which ought never to have been allowed, in regard to any one member of the family, and least of all towards one of the youngest, and certainly the most suffering of all. My mother received and administered a check now and then, which did good for the time: but the family habit was strong; and it was a wise measure to institute an entire change. Two or three anecdotes will suffice to give an idea of what had to be surmounted.

I was too shy ever to ask to be taught any thing,—except, indeed, of good-natured strangers. I have mentioned that we were well practiced in some matters of domestic management. We could sew, iron, make sweets, gingerbread and pastry, and keep order generally throughout the house. But I did not know,—what nobody can know without being

---

[1]   Lord Stafford's park, surrounding Costessey Hall in Norfolk, about five miles northwest of the city of Norwich, was a well-wooded park of 900 acres, watered by a stream, and bounded on the north by the river Wensum. In the nineteenth century, the park contained some of the finest forest trees in the county, and was famous for its sylvan beauty.

taught,—how to purchase stores, or to set out a table, or to deal with the butcher and fish monger. It is inconceivable what a trouble this was to me for many years. I was always in terror at that great mountain of duty before me, and wondering what was to become of me if my mother left home, or if I should marry. Never once did it occur to me to go to my mother, and ask to be taught: and it was not pride but fear which so incapacitated me. I liked that sort of occupation, and had great pleasure in doing what I could do in that way; insomuch that I have sometimes felt myself what General F. called his wife,[1]—'a good housemaid spoilt.' My 'Guides to Service,' ('The Maid-of-all-work,' 'Housemaid,' 'Lady's Maid,' and 'Dress-maker,') written twenty years afterwards, may show something of this.[2] Meantime, never was poor creature more dismally awkward than I was when domestic eyes were upon me: and this made me a most vexatious member of the family. I remember once upsetting a basin of moist sugar into a giblet pie. (I remember nothing else quite so bad.) I never could find any thing I was sent for, though I could lay my hands in the dark on any thing I myself wanted. On one occasion, when a workwoman was making mourning in the midst of us, I was desired to take the keys, and fetch a set of cravats for marking, out of a certain drawer. My heart sank at the order, and already the inevitable sentence rung in my ears,—that I was more trouble than I was worth; which I sincerely believed. The drawer was large, and crammed. I could not see one thing from another; and in no way could I see any cravats. Slowly and fearfully I came back to say so. Of course, I was sent again, and desired not to come back without them. That time, and again the next, I took every thing out of the drawer; and still found no cravats. My eldest sister tried next; and great was my consolation when she returned crest-fallen,—having found no cravats. My mother snatched the keys, under a strong sense of the hardship of having to do every thing herself, when Rachel suggested another place where they might have been put. Then they were found; and my heart was swelling with vindictive pleasure when my mother, by a few noble words, turned the tide of feeling completely. In the presence of the workwoman, she laid her hand on my arm, kissed me, and said, 'And now, my dear, I have to beg your pardon.' I answered only by tears; but the words supported me for long after.

---

[1]   General Henry Edward Fox (1755–1811) or possibly Charles Richard Fox (1796–1873), son of Lord Holland and Elizabeth Vassall Webster, whom Martineau mentions again in Period IV, sec. ii.

[2]   *The Guide to Service* (London: Charles Knight, 1838–39), intended to train young men and women for domestic service.

I look back upon another scene with horror at my own audacity, and wonder that my family could endure me at all. At Mr. Perry's, one of our school-fellows was a clever, mischievous girl,—so clever, and so much older than myself as to have great influence over me when she chose to try her power, though I disapproved her ways very heartily. She one day asked me, in a corner, in a mysterious sort of way, whether I did not perceive that Rachel was the favourite at home, and treated with manifest partiality. Every body else, she said, observed it. This had never distinctly occurred to me. Rachel was handy and useful, and not paralysed by fear, as I was; and, very naturally, our busy mother resorted to her for help, and put trust in her about matters of business, not noticing the growth of an equally natural habit in Rachel of quizzing or snubbing me, as the elder ones did. From the day of this mischievous speech of my school-fellow, I was on the watch, and with the usual result to the jealous. Months,—perhaps a year or two—passed on while I was brooding over this, without a word to any one; and then came the explosion, one winter evening after tea, when my eldest sister was absent, and my mother, Rachel and I were sitting at work. Rachel criticized something that I said, in which I happened to be right. After once defending myself, I sat silent. My mother remarked on my 'obstinacy,' saying that I was 'not a bit convinced.' I replied that nothing convincing had been said. My mother declared that she agreed with Rachel, and that I ought to yield. Then I passed the verge, and got wrong. A sudden force of daring entering my mind, I said, in the most provoking way possible, that this was nothing new, as she always did agree with Rachel against me. My mother put down her work, and asked me what I meant by that. I looked her full in the face, and said that what I meant was that every thing that Rachel said and did was right, and every thing that I said and did was wrong. Rachel burst into an insulting laugh, and was sharply bidden to 'be quiet.' I saw by this that I had gained some ground; and this was made clearer by my mother sternly desiring me to practise my music. I saw that she wanted to gain time. The question now was how I should get through. My hands were clammy and tremulous: my fingers stuck to each other; my eyes were dim, and there was a roaring in my ears. I could easily have fainted; and it might have done no harm if I had. But I made a tremendous effort to appear calm. I opened the piano, lighted a candle with a steady hand, began, and derived strength from the first chords. I believe I never played better in my life. Then the question was—how was I ever to leave off? On I went for what seemed to me an immense time, till my mother sternly called to me to leave off and go to bed. With my candle in my hand, I said 'Good-night.'

My mother laid down her work, and said, 'Harriet, I am more displeased with you to-night than ever I have been in your life.' Thought I, 'I don't care: I have got it out, and it is all true.' 'Go and say your prayers,' my mother continued; 'and ask God to forgive you for your conduct to-night; for I don't know that I can. Go to your prayers.' Thought I,— 'No, I shan't.' And I did not: and that was the only night from my infancy to mature womanhood that I did not pray. I detected misgiving in my mother's forced manner; and I triumphed. If the right was on my side (as I entirely believed) the power was on hers; and what the next morning was to be I could not conceive. I slept little, and went down sick with dread. Not a word was said, however, then or ever, of the scene of the preceding night; but henceforth, a most scrupulous impartiality between Rachel and me was shown. If the occasion had been better used still,—if my mother had but bethought herself of saying to me, 'My child, I never dreamed that these terrible thoughts were in your mind. I am your mother. Why do you not tell me every thing that makes you unhappy?' I believe this would have wrought in a moment that cure which it took years to effect, amidst reserve and silence.

It has been a difficulty with me all my life (and its being a difficulty shows some deep-seated fault in me) how to reconcile sincerity with peace and good manners in such matters as other people's little mistakes of fact. As an example of what I mean, a school-fellow spelled Shakspere as I spell it here. Mr. Perry put in an *a*, observing that the name was never spelt in print without an *a*. I ventured to doubt this; but he repeated his assertion. At afternoon school, I showed him a volume of the edition we had at home, which proved him wrong. He received the correction with so indifferent a grace that I was puzzled as to whether I had done right or wrong,—whether sincerity required me to set my master right before the face of his scholars. Of course, if I had been older, I should have done it more privately. But this is a specimen of the difficulties of that class that I have struggled with almost ever since. The difficulty was immensely increased by the family habit of requiring an answer from me, and calling me obstinate if the reply was not an unconditional yielding. I have always wondered to see the ease and success with which very good people humour and manage the aged, the sick and the weak, and sometimes every body about them. I could never attempt this; for it always seemed to me such contemptuous treatment of those whom I was at the moment respecting more than ever, on account of their weakness. But I was always quite in the opposite extreme;—far too solemn, too rigid, and prone to exaggeration of differences and to obstinacy at the same time. It was actually not till I was near forty that I saw how the matter should really be,—saw it through a perfect example of an union of absolute sincerity with all possible cheerfulness, sweetness, modesty and deference for all, in proportion to their claims. I have never attained righteous good-manners, to this day; but I have understood what they are since the beauties of J.S.'s character and manners were revealed to me under circumstances of remarkable trial.

While organised, it seems to me, for sincerity, and being generally truthful, except for the exaggeration which is apt to beset persons of repressed faculties, I feel compelled to state here (what belongs to this part of my life) that towards one person I was habitually untruthful, from fear. To my mother I would in my childhood assert or deny any thing that would bring me through most easily. I remember denying various harmless things,—playing a game at battledore, for one; and often without any apparent reason: and this was so exclusively to one person that, though there was remonstrance and punishment, I believe I was never regarded as a liar in the family. It seems now all very strange: but it was a temporary and very brief phase. When I left home, all temptation to untruth ceased, and there was henceforth nothing more than the habit of exaggeration and strong expression to struggle with.

Before I went to Bristol, I was the prey of three griefs,—prominent among many. I cannot help laughing while I write them. They were my bad hand-writing, my deafness, and the state of my hair. Such a trio of miseries! I was the first of my family who failed in the matter of hand-writing; and why I did remains unexplained. I am sure I tried hard; but I wrote a vulgar, cramped, untidy scrawl till I was past twenty,—till authorship made me forget manner in matter, and gave freedom to my hand. After that, I did very well, being praised by compositors for legibleness first, and in course of time, for other qualities. But it was a severe mortification while it lasted; and many bitter tears I shed over the reflections that my awkward hand called forth. It was a terrible penance to me to write letters home from Bristol; and the day of the week when it was to be done was very like the Beckwith music-lesson days. If any one had told me then how many reams of paper I should cover in the course of my life, life would have seemed a sort of purgatory to me.—As to my deafness, I got no relief about that at Bristol. It was worse when I returned in weak health.—The third misery, which really plagued me seriously, was cured presently after I left home. I made my dear aunt Kentish the depositary of my confidence in all matters; and this, of course, among the rest. She induced me to consult a friend of hers, who had remarkably beautiful hair; and then it came out that I had been combing overmuch, and that there was nothing the matter with my hair, if I would be content with brushing it. So that grief was annihilated, and there was an end of one of those trifles which 'make up the sum of human things.'[1]

I did not understand the facts about my leaving home till I had been absent some months; and when I did, I was deeply and effectually moved by my mother's consideration for my feelings. We had somehow been brought up in a supreme contempt of boarding-schools: and I was therefore truly amazed when my mother sounded me, in the spring of 1817, about going for a year or two to a Miss Somebody's school at Yarmouth. She talked of the sea, of the pleasantness of change, and of how happy L.T——, an excessively silly girl of our acquaintance, was there: but I made such a joke of L. and her studies, and of the attainments of the young ladies, as we had heard of them, that my mother gave up the notion of a scheme which never could have answered. It would have been ruin to a temper like mine at that crisis to have sent me among silly and ignorant people, to have my 'manners formed,' after the most ordinary boarding school fashion. My mother did much better in sending me among people so superior to myself as to improve me morally and intellectually, though the experiment failed in regard to health. A brother of my mother's had been unfortunate in business at Bristol, and had not health to retrieve his affairs; and his able and accomplished wife, and clever young daughters opened a school.[2] Of the daughters, one was within a few weeks of my own age; and we have been intimate friends from that time (the beginning of 1818) till this hour. Another was two years younger; another, two years older; while the eldest had reached womanhood. Of these clever cousins we had heard much, for many years, without having seen any of them. At the opening of the year 1818, a letter arrived from my aunt to my mother, saying that it was time the young people should be becoming acquainted; that her girls were all occupied in the school, for the routine of which Rachel was somewhat too old; but that if Harriet would go, and spend some time with them, and take the run of the school, she would be a welcome guest, &c. &c. This

---

[1]   A quotation from "Sensibility" by Hannah More (1745–1833): "Since trifles make the sum of human things, / And half our misery from our foibles springs."

[2]   The brother was Robert Rankin, Jr., who had lost over £4000. His wife, née Ann Cole (1780–1840), known as "Aunt Kentish," was Harriet's favorite. The daughter mentioned in the next sentence was Isabella Rankin, who later went out as a governess to Lady and Sir Isaac Goldsmid, but suffered from ill health and sought various cures, including a rest trip to Switzerland (see Period IV, sec. iv) and mesmerism.

pleased me much, and I heard with joy that I was to go when my father took his next journey to Bristol,—early in February. My notion was of a stay of a few weeks; and I was rather taken aback when my mother spoke of my absence as likely to last a year or more. It never entered my head that I was going to a boarding-school; and when I discovered, long after, that the Bristol family understood that I was, I was not (as I once might have been) angry at having been tricked into it, but profoundly contrite for the temper which made such management necessary, and touched by the trouble my mother took to spare my silly pride, and consider my troublesome feelings.

I was, on the whole, happy during the fifteen months I spent at Bristol, though home-sickness spoiled the last half of the time. My home affections seem to have been all the stronger for having been repressed and baulked. Certainly, I passionately loved my family, each and all, from the very hour that parted us; and I was physically ill with expectation when their letters became due;—letters which I could hardly read when they came, between my dread of something wrong, and the beating heart and swimming eyes with which I received letters in those days. There were some family anxieties during the latter part of the time; and there was one grand event,—the engagement of my eldest sister, who had virtually ceased to belong to us by the time I returned home.

I found my cousins even more wonderfully clever than I had expected; and they must have been somewhat surprised at my striking inferiority in knowledge, and in the power of acquiring it. I still think that I never met with a family to compare with theirs for power of acquisition, or effective use of knowledge. They would learn a new language at odd minutes; get through a tough philosophical book by taking turns in the court for air; write down an entire lecture or sermon, without missing a sentence; get round the piano after a concert, and play and sing over every new piece that had been performed. Ability like this was a novel spectacle to me; and it gave me the pure pleasure of unmixed admiration; for I was certainly not conscious of any ability whatever at that time. I had no great deal to do in the school, being older than every girl there but one; and I believe I got no particular credit in such classes as I did join. For one thing, my deafness was now bad enough to be a disadvantage; but it was a worse disqualification that my memory, always obedient to my own command, was otherwise disobedient. I could remember whatever I had learned in my own way, but was quite unable to answer in class, like far younger girls, about any thing just communicated. My chief intellectual improvement during that important period was derived from private study. I read some analytical books, on logic and rhetoric, with singular satisfaction; and I lost nothing afterwards that I obtained in this way. I read a good deal of History too, and revelled in poetry,—a new world of which was opened to me by my cousins. The love of natural scenery was a good deal developed in me by the beauty around Bristol. One circumstance makes me think that I had become rather suddenly awakened to it not long before, —though my delight in the sea at Cromer dated some years earlier. Mr. Perry tried upon us the reading of L'Allegro and Il Penseroso; and it failed utterly. I did not feel any thing whatever, though I supposed I understood what I heard. Not long after he was gone, I read both pieces in the nursery, one day; and straightway went into a transport, as if I had discovered myself in possession of a new sense. Thus it was again now, when I was transferred from flat, bleak Norfolk to the fine scenery about Bristol. Even the humble beauty of our most frequent walk, by the Logwood Mills, was charming to me,—the clear running water, with its weedy channel, and the meadow walk on the brink: and about Leigh woods, Kingsweston, and the Downs, my rapture knew no bounds.[1]

Far more important, however, was the growth of kindly affections in me at this time, caused by the free and full tenderness of my dear aunt Kentish, and of all my other relations then surrounding me. My heart warmed and opened, and my habitual fear began to melt away. I have since been told that, on the day of my arrival, when some of the schoolgirls asked my cousin M. what I was like, (as she came out of the parlour where I was) she said that I looked as if I was cross; but that she knew I was not; and that I looked unhappy. When I left Bristol, I was as pale as a ghost, and as thin as possible; and still very frowning and repulsive-looking; but yet with a comparatively open countenance. The counteracting influence to dear aunt Kentish's was one which visited me very strongly at the same time,—that of a timid superstition. She was herself, then and always, very religious; but she had a remarkable faculty of making her religion suggest and sanction whatever she liked: and, as she liked whatever was pure, amiable, unselfish and unspoiling, this tendency did her no harm. Matters were otherwise with me. My religion too took the character of my mind; and it was harsh, severe and mournful accordingly. There was a great furor among the Bristol Unitarians at that time

---

[1]   Many of these places in or near Bristol, on the Avon River, have been swallowed by subsequent urbanization, except for part of Clifton Downs and Leigh Woods, on the Avon Gorge north of the city, which is now a National Trust property.

about Dr. Carpenter, who had recently become their pastor. He was a very devoted Minister, and a very earnest pietist: superficial in his knowledge, scanty in ability, narrow in his conceptions, and thoroughly priestly in his temper. He was exactly the dissenting minister to be worshipped by his people, (and especially by the young) and to be spoiled by that worship. He was worshipped by the young, and by none more than by me; and his power was unbounded while his pupils continued young: but, as his instructions and his scholars were not bound together by any bond of essential Christian doctrine, every thing fell to pieces as soon as the merely personal influence was withdrawn. A more extraordinary diversity of religious opinion than existed among his pupils when they became men and women could not be seen. They might be found at the extremes of catholicism and atheism, and every where between. As for me, his devout and devoted Catechumen, he made me desperately superstitious,—living wholly in and for religion, and fiercely fanatical about it. I returned home raving about my pastor and teacher, remembering every word he had ever spoken to me,—with his instructions burnt in, as it were, upon my heart and conscience, and with an abominable spiritual rigidity and a truly respectable force of conscience casually mingled together, so as to procure for me the no less curiously mingled ridicule and respect of my family. My little sister, then learning to sew on her stool at my mother's knee, has since told me what she perceived, with the penetrating eyes and heart of childhood. Whenever I left the room, my mother and elder sisters used to begin to quiz my fanaticism,—which was indeed quizzical enough; but the little one saw a sort of respect for me underlying the mockery, which gave her her first clear sense of moral obligation, and the nature of obedience to it.

The results of the Bristol experiment were thus good on the whole. My health was rather worse than better, through wear and tear of nerves,—home-sickness, religious emotions, overmuch study (so my aunt said, against my conviction) and medical mismanagement. I had learned a good deal, and had got into a good way of learning more. My domestic affections were regenerated; and I had become sincerely and heartily religious, with some improvement in temper in consequence, and not a little in courage, hope and conscientiousness. The fanaticism was a stage which I should probably have had to pass through at any rate,—and by the same phase of pastor-worship,—whoever the pastor might have been.

THIRD PERIOD

TO THE AGE OF THIRTY

SECTION I

I RETURNED home in April, 1819, and continued to reside in Norwich till November, 1832. These thirteen years, extending from my entering upon womanhood to my complete establishment in an independent position, as to occupation and the management of my own life, seem to form a marked period of themselves; and I shall treat them in that way.

My eldest sister's marriage in 1820 made young women at once of Rachel and myself. It was on all accounts a happy event, though we dreaded excessively the loss of her from home, which she eminently graced. But never did woman grow in grace more remarkably than she did by her marriage. When she had found her own heart, it proved a truly noble one; and the generosity, sweetness, and wisdom of her whole conduct towards her own children showed that her mistakes in her treatment of us were merely the crudities of inexperience. I may say, once for all, that her home at Newcastle was ever open to us, and that all possible kindness from her hospitable husband and herself was always at our command, without hindrance or difficulty, till my recovery from a hopeless illness, in 1844, by Mesmerism,[1] proved too much for the natural prejudice of a surgeon and a surgeon's wife, and caused, by the help of the ill-offices of another relation, a family breach, as absurd as it was lamentable. My sister was then under the early symptoms of her last illness; and matters might have ended more happily if she had been in her usual state of health and nerve, as they certainly would if advantage had not been taken of her natural irritation against Mesmerism to gratify in another jealousies to which she was herself far superior. My own certainty of this, and my grateful remembrance of the long course of years during which I enjoyed her friendship and

---

[1] A form of hypnotism introduced by the Austrian physician, Franz Anton Mesmer (1734–1815), used on Martineau by the English phrenomesmerist Spencer Timothy Hall, and disbelieved as medical treatment by her brother-in-law, Dr. Thomas Greenhow (1792–1881), who was treating her for polypous uterine tumors.

generosity, and her cordial sympathy in my aims and successes, incline me
to pass over her final alienation, and dwell upon the affectionate intercourse
we enjoyed, at frequent intervals, for twenty years from her marriage day.

Our revered and beloved eldest brother[1] had, by this time, settled in
Norwich as a surgeon, in partnership with our uncle, Mr. P.M.
Martineau, the most eminent provincial surgeon of his day,—in some
departments, if not altogether. My brother's health was delicate, and we
were to lose him by death in five years. One of the sweetest recollections of my life is that I had the honour and blessing of his intimate
friendship, which grew and deepened from my sister's marriage to the
time of his own death. My mother, too, took me into her confidence
more and more as my mind opened, and, I may add, as my deafness
increased, and bespoke for me her motherly sympathy. For some years,
indeed, there was a genuine and cordial friendship between my mother
and me, which was a benefit to me in all manner of ways; and, from the
time when I began to have literary enterprises, (and quite as much before
I obtained success as after) I was sustained by her trustful, generous, self-
denying sympathy and maternal appreciation. After a time, when she was
fretted by cares and infirmities, I became as nervous in regard to her as
ever, (even to the entire breaking down of my health;) but during the
whole period of which I am now treating,—(and it is a very large space
in my life)—there were no limitations to our mutual confidence.

One other relation which reached its highest point, and had begun to
decline, during this period was one which I must abstain from discussing.
The briefest possible notice will be the best method of treatment. All who
have ever known me are aware that the strongest passion I have ever entertained was in regard to my youngest brother,[2] who has certainly filled the
largest space in the life of my affections of any person whatever. Now, the
fact,—the painful fact,—in the history of human affections is that, of all
natural relations, the least satisfactory is the fraternal. Brothers are to sisters
what sisters can never be to brothers as objects of engrossing and devoted
affection. The law of their frames is answerable for this: and that other
law—of equity—which sisters are bound to obey, requires that they should
not render their account of their disappointments where there can be no
fair reply. Under the same law, sisters are bound to remember that they

[1]   Thomas Martineau (1795–1824).
[2]   James Martineau (1805–1900) trained as an engineer but became a prominent Unitarian
      theologian. When Harriet published *Letters on the Laws of Man's Nature and Development*
      (1851) with Henry Atkinson, James published a negative review that caused a permanent
      rupture in their relationship.

cannot be certain of their own fitness to render an account of their own disappointments, or to form an estimate of the share of blame which may be due to themselves on the score of unreasonable expectations. These general considerations decide me to pass over one of the main relations and influences of my life in a few brief and unsatisfactory lines, though I might tell a very particular tale. If I could see a more truthful, just, and satisfactory method of treating the topic, I should most gladly adopt it.— As for the other members of our numerous family, I am thankful and rejoiced to bear testimony that they have given all possible encouragement to the labours of my life; and that they have been the foremost of all the world to appreciate and rejoice in my successes, and to respect that independence of judgment and action on my part which must often have given them pain, and which would have overpowered any generosity less deeply rooted in principle and affection than theirs.

When I was young, it was not thought proper for young ladies to study very conspicuously; and especially with pen in hand. Young ladies (at least in provincial towns) were expected to sit down in the parlour to sew,— during which reading aloud was permitted,—or to practice their music; but so as to be fit to receive callers, without any signs of blue-stockingism which could be reported abroad. Jane Austen herself, the Queen of novelists, the immortal creator of Anne Elliott, Mr. Knightley, and a score or two more of unrivalled intimate friends of the whole public, was compelled by the feelings of her family to cover up her manuscripts with a large piece of muslin work, kept on the table for the purpose, whenever any genteel people came in. So it was with other young ladies, for some time after Jane Austen was in her grave; and thus my first studies in philosophy were carried on with great care and reserve. I was at the work table regularly after breakfast,—making my own clothes, or the shirts of the household, or about some fancy work: I went out walking with the rest,—before dinner in winter, and after tea in summer: and if ever I shut myself into my own room for an hour of solitude, I knew it was at the risk of being sent for to join the sewing-circle, or to read aloud,—I being the reader, on account of my growing deafness. But I won time for what my heart was set upon, nevertheless,—either in the early morning, or late at night. I had a strange passion for translating, in those days; and a good preparation it proved for the subsequent work of my life. Now, it was meeting James at seven in the morning to read Lowth's Prelections in the Latin,[1]

---

[1]   *De sacra poesi Hebraeorum: praelectiones academicae Oxonii habitae a Roberto Lowth* (1753), published in English as *Lectures on the Sacred Poetry of the Hebrews.*

after having been busy since five about something else, in my own room. Now it was translating Tacitus, in order to try what was the utmost compression of style that I could attain.—About this I may mention an incident while it occurs. We had all grown up with a great reverence for Mrs. Barbauld (which she fully deserved from much wiser people than ourselves) and, reflectively, for Dr. Aikin, her brother,—also able in his way, and far more industrious, but without her genius. Among a multitude of other labours, Dr. Aikin had translated the Agricola of Tacitus.[1] I went into such an enthusiasm over the original, and especially over the celebrated concluding passage, that I thought I would translate it, and correct it by Dr. Aikin's, which I could procure from our public library. I did it, and found my own translation unquestionably the best of the two. I had spent an infinity of pains over it,—word by word; and I am confident I was not wrong in my judgment. I stood pained and mortified before my desk, I remember, thinking how strange and small a matter was human achievement, if Dr. Aikin's fame was to be taken as a testimony of literary desert. I had beaten him whom I had taken for my master. I need not point out that, in the first place, Dr. Aikin's fame did not hang on this particular work; nor that, in the second place, I had exaggerated his fame by our sectarian estimate of him. I give the incident as a curious little piece of personal experience, and one which helped to make me like literary labour more for its own sake, and less for its rewards, than I might otherwise have done.—Well: to return to my translating propensities. Our cousin J.M.L.,[2] then studying for his profession in Norwich, used to read Italian with Rachel and me,—also before breakfast. We made some considerable progress, through the usual course of prose authors and poets; and out of this grew a fit which Rachel and I at one time took, in concert with our companions and neighbours, the C.'s, to translate Petrarch. Nothing could be better as an exercise in composition than translating Petrarch sonnets into English of the same limits. It was putting ourselves under compulsion to do with the Italian what I had set myself voluntarily to do with the Latin author. I believe we really succeeded pretty well; and I am sure that all these exercises were a singularly apt preparation for my after work.

---

[1] Anna Laetitia Barbauld (1743–1824) and her brother, John Aikin (1747–1822), were poets, essayists, and educators who often collaborated on political writing. Tacitus' *Agricola* was a laudatory account of the Roman general Gnaeus Julius Agricola (40–93 A.D.), who served as *tribunus militum* in Britain during the period of Boadicea's rebellion (c. 61 A.D.) and later became governor of Britain; the work includes information about the geography and ancient history of East Anglia, where the Martineaus lived.

[2] James Martineau Lee, son of her father's sister Mrs. Margaret Lee (1756–1840).

At the same time, I went on studying Blair's Rhetoric[1] (for want of a better guide) and inclining mightily to every kind of book or process which could improve my literary skill,— really as if I had foreseen how I was to spend my life.

These were not, however, my most precious or serious studies. I studied the Bible incessantly and immensely; both by daily reading of chapters, after the approved but mischievous method, and by getting hold of all commentaries and works of elucidation that I could lay my hands on. A work of Dr. Carpenter's, begun but never finished, called 'Notes and Observations on the Gospel History,'[2] which his catechumens used in class, first put me on this track of study,—the results of which appeared some years afterwards in my 'Traditions of Palestine.'[3] It was while reading Mr. Kenrick's translation from the German of 'Helon's Pilgrimage to Jerusalem,'[4] with which I was thoroughly bewitched, that I conceived, and communicated to James, the audacious idea of giving a somewhat resembling account of the Jews and their country, under the immediate expectation of the Messiah, and even in his presence, while carefully abstaining from permitting more than his shadow to pass over the scene. This idea I cherished till I found courage, under a new inspiration some years after, to execute it: and so pleasant was the original suggestion, and so congenial the subject altogether, that even now, at the distance of a quarter of a century, I regard that little volume with a stronger affection than any other of my works but one;—that one being 'Eastern Life.'[5]

Dr. Carpenter was inclined also to the study of philosophy, and wrote on it,—on mental and moral philosophy; and this was enough, putting all predisposition out of the question, to determine me to the study. He was of the Locke and Hartley school altogether, as his articles on 'Mental

---

1   Hugh Blair's *Lectures on Rhetoric and Belles Lettres* (1784), then the standard guide to rhetoric and composition.

2   The full title was *Systematic Education, or, Elementary Instruction in the Various Departments of Literature and Science: with practical rules for studying each branch of useful knowledge*, by the Rev. W. Shepherd, the Rev. J. Joyce, and the Rev. Lant Carpenter (London: Longman, Hurst, Rees, Orme, and Brown, 1815).

3   *Traditions of Palestine: Times of the Saviour* (London: Longman, Rees, Orme, Brown and Green, 1830).

4   John Kenrick (1788–1877), a historian, philologist, and principal of the Unitarian Manchester College, translated Friedrich Strauss's *Helon's Pilgrimage to Jerusalem: A Picture of Judaism in the Century which Preceded the Advent of our Saviour* into English (London, J. Mawman, 1824) after spending a sabbatical year in Germany in 1819.

5   *Eastern Life, Present and Past,* 3 vols. (London: Edward Moxon, 1848).

and Moral Philosophy,' in Rees's Cyclopedia, and his work on 'Systematic Education' show.[1] He used to speak of Hartley as one who had the intellectual qualities of the seraphic order combined with the affections of the cherubic; and it was no wonder if Hartley became my idol when I was mistress of my own course of study. I must clear myself from all charge of having ever entertained his doctrine of Vibrations. I do not believe that Dr. Carpenter himself could have prevailed with me so far as that. But neither did Hartley prevail with Dr. Carpenter so far as that. The edition of Hartley that I used was Dr. Priestley's,—that which gives the philosophy of Association, cleared from the incumbence of the Vibration theory. That book I studied with a fervor and perseverance which made it perhaps the most important book in the world to me, except the bible; and there really is in it, amidst its monstrous deficiencies and absurdities, so much that is philosophically true, as well as holy, elevating and charming, that its influence might very well spread into all the events and experience of life, and chasten the habits and feelings, as it did in my case during a long series of years. So far from feeling, as Dr. Channing[2] and other good men have done, that the influence of that philosophy is necessarily, in all cases, debasing, I am confident at this moment that the spirit of the men, Locke and Hartley, redeems much of the fault of their doctrine in its operation on young minds; and moreover, that the conscientious accuracy with which they apply their doctrine to the moral conduct of the smallest particulars of human life (Hartley particularly) forms a far better discipline, and produces a much more exalting effect on the minds of students than the vague metaphysical imaginations,—as various and irreconcilable as the minds that give them forth, which Dr. Channing and his spiritual school adopted (or believed that they adopted) as a 'spiritual philosophy.' I know this,—that while I read the Germans, Americans and English who are the received exponents of that philosophy with a general and extremely vague sense of elevation and beauty as the highest emotion produced, I cannot at this hour look at the portrait of Hartley prefixed to his work, or glance at his strange Scholia,—which

---

[1]   Like many other Unitarians, including Joseph Priestley, Lant Carpenter embraced the analytic philosophy of John Locke (1632–1704) and the associationist theory of David Hartley (1705–57), as in his *Principles of Education, Intellectual, Moral, and Physical* (London, Hurst, Bees, Orme, and Brown, 1820). Priestley's edition was *Hartley's Theory of the Human Mind, on the Principle of the Association of Ideas; with Essays Relating to the Subject of It* (London: J. Johnson, 1775).

[2]   William Ellery Channing (1780–1842), American Unitarian whom Martineau visited during her American travels.

I could almost repeat, word for word,—without a strong revival of the old mood of earnest desire of self-discipline, and devotion to duty which I derived from them in my youth. While the one school has little advantage over the other in the abstract department of their philosophy, the disciples of Hartley have infinitely the advantage over the dreaming school in their master's presentment of the concrete department of fact and of action. Compelled as I have since been to relinquish both as philosophy, I am bound to avow, (and enjoy the avowal) that I owe to Hartley the strongest and best stimulus and discipline of the highest affections and most important habits that it is perhaps possible, (or was possible for me) to derive from any book.—The study of Priestley's character and works (natural to me because he was the great apostle of Unitarianism) necessarily led me to the study of the Scotch school of philosophy,[1] which I took the liberty to enjoy in its own way, in spite of Priestley's contempt of it. I never believed in it, because it was really inconceivable to me how anybody should; and I was moreover entirely wrong in not perceiving that the Scotch philosophers had got hold of a fragment of sound truth which the other school had missed,—in their postulate of a fundamental complete faculty, which could serve as a basis of the mind's operations,—whereas Hartley lays down simply the principle of association, and a capacity for pleasure and pain. I ought to have perceived that the Scotch proposition of Common Sense would answer much better for purposes of interpretation, if I had not yet knowledge enough to show me that it was much nearer the fact of the case. I did not perceive this, but talked as flippantly as Priestley, with far less right to do so. At the same time, I surrendered myself, to a considerable extent, to the charm of Dugald Stewart's writings,—having no doubt that Priestley, if then living, would have done so too. About Beattie and Reid I was pert enough, from a genuine feeling of the unsatisfactoriness of their writings; but the truth of detail scattered through Dugald Stewart's elegant elucidations, the gentle and happy spirit, and the beautiful style, charmed me so much that I must have been among his most affectionate disciples, if I had not been fortified against his seductions by my devotion to Hartley.

It appears to me now that, though my prevailing weakness in study is excessive sympathy, intellectual as well as moral, with my author, I even then felt something of the need which long after became all-powerful in me, of a clear distinction between the knowable and the

---

[1]   Including Adam Smith (1723–90), Thomas Reid (1710–96), James Beattie (1735–1803), and Dugald Stewart (1753–1828).

unknowable,—of some available indication of an indisputable point of view, whence one's contemplation of human nature, as of every thing else in the universe, should make its range. It may be that I am carrying back too far in my life this sense of need. When I consider how contentedly I went on, during the whole of this third period, floating and floundering among metaphysical imaginations, and giving forth inbred conceptions as truths of fact, I am disposed to think it probable that I am casting back the light of a later time among the mists of an earlier, and supposing myself sooner capable than I really was of practically distinguishing between a conception and a conviction. But there can be no mistake about the time and manner of my laying hold of a genuine conviction in a genuine manner, as I will presently tell. It would no doubt have been a fine thing for me,—an event which would have elevated my whole after-life,— if a teacher had been at hand to show me the boundary line between the knowable and the unknowable, as I see it now, and to indicate to me that the purely human view of the universe, derived solely from within, and proceeding on the supposition that Man and his affairs and his world are the centre and crown of the universe, could not possibly be the true one. But, in the absence of such a teacher,—in my inability to see the real scope and final operation of the discovery of Copernicus and Galileo,—and the ultimate connexion of physical and moral science,—it was the next best thing, perhaps, to obtain by my own forces, and for my own use, the grand conviction which henceforth gave to my life whatever it has had of steadiness, consistency, and progressiveness.

I have told how, when I was eleven years old, I put a question to my brother about the old difficulty of foreknowledge and freewill,—the reconciliation of God's power and benevolence,—and how I was baulked of an answer. That question had been in my mind ever since; and I was not driven from entertaining it by Milton's account of its being a favourite controversy in hell,[1] nor even by a rebuke administered to one of our family by Mr. Turner of Newcastle,[2] who disapproved inquiry into what he took for granted to be an unknowable thing. To me it seemed, turn it which way I would, to be certainly a knowable thing,—so closely as it presses on human morality,—to say nothing of man's religion and internal peace. Its being reconcilable with theology is quite another affair. I

---

[1] In *Paradise Lost*, Book II, ll. 557–61.
[2] Henry Turner (1793–1822), Unitarian minister of the Rankin family in Newcastle, Martineau's mother's birthplace.

tried long to satisfy myself with the ordinary subterfuge;—with declaring myself satisfied that good comes out of evil, and a kind of good which could accrue in no other way: but this would not do. I wrote religious poetry upon it, and wrought myself up to it in talk: but it would not do. This was no solution; and it was unworthy of a rational being to pretend to think it so. I tried acquiescence and dismissal of the subject; but that would not do, because it brought after it a clear admission of the failure of the scheme of creation in the first place, and of the Christian scheme in the next. The time I am now speaking of was, of course, prior to my study of Priestley and of Hartley, or I should have known that there was a recognised doctrine of Necessity.[1]

One summer afternoon, when my brother James (then my oracle) was sitting with my mother and me, telling us some of his experiences after his first session at the York College (the Unitarian college) I seized upon some intimation that he dropped about this same doctrine of Necessity. I uttered the difficulty which had lain in my mind for so many years; and he just informed me that there was, or was held to be, a solution in that direction, and advised me to make it out for myself. I did so. From that time the question possessed me. Now that I had got leave, as it were, to apply the Necessarian solution, I did it incessantly. I fairly laid hold of the conception of general laws, while still far from being prepared to let go the notion of a special Providence. Though at times almost overwhelmed by the vastness of the view opened to me, and by the prodigious change requisite in my moral views and self-management, the revolution was safely gone through. My laboring brain and beating heart grew quiet, and something more like peace than I had ever yet known settled down upon my anxious mind. Being aware of my weakness of undue sympathy with authors whom I read with any moral interest, I resolved to read nothing on this question till I had thought it out; and I kept to my resolve. When I was wholly satisfied, and could use my new method of interpretation in all cases that occurred with readiness and ease, I read every book that I could hear of on the subject of the Will; and I need not add that I derived confirmation from all I read on both sides. I am bound to add that the moral

---

[1]   The doctrine, as advanced by Necessarians, held that all action is determined by antecedent causes and that one's own actions contribute to those causes; in moral terms, as William Ellery Channing wrote, "the apprehension that [men's] endeavors to promote their own happiness will have a certain and necessary effect, and that no well-judged effort of theirs will be lost, instead of disposing them to remit their labour, will encourage them to exert themselves with redoubled vigor."

effect of this process was most salutary and cheering. From the time when I became convinced of the certainty of the action of laws, of the true importance of good influences and good habits, of the firmness, in short, of the ground I was treading, and of the security of the results which I should take the right means to attain, a new vigour pervaded my whole life, a new light spread through my mind, and I began to experience a steady growth in self-command, courage, and consequent integrity and disinterestedness. I was feeble and selfish enough at best; but yet, I was like a new creature in the strength of a sound conviction. Life also was like something fresh and wonderfully interesting, now that I held in my hand this key whereby to interpret some of the most conspicuous of its mysteries.

That great event in my life seems very remote; and I have been hearing more or less of the free-will difficulty ever since; and yet it appears to me, now as then, that none but Necessarians at all understand the Necessarian doctrine. This is merely saying in other words that its truth is so irresistible that, when once understood, it is adopted as a matter of course. Some, no doubt, say of the doctrine that every body can prove it, but nobody believes it; an assertion so far from true as not to be worth contesting, if I may judge by my own intercourses. Certainly, all the best minds I know are among the Necessarians;—all indeed which are qualified to discuss the subject at all. Moreover, all the world is practically Necessarian. All human action proceeds on the supposition that all the workings of the universe are governed by laws which cannot be broken by human will. In fact, the mistake of the majority in this matter is usually in supposing an interference between the will and the action of Man. The very smallest amount of science is enough to enable any rational person to see that the constitution and action of the human faculty of Will are determined by influences beyond the control of the possessor of the faculty: and when this very plain fact is denied in words it is usually because the denier is thinking of something else,—not of the faculty of willing, but of executing the volition. It is not my business here to argue out a question which has been settled in my own mind for the greater part of my life; but I have said thus much in explanation of the great importance of the conviction to me. For above thirty years I have seen more and more clearly how awful, and how irremediable except by the spread of a true philosophy, are the evils which arise from that monstrous remnant of old superstition,—the supposition of a self-determining power, independent of laws, in the human will; and I can truly say that if I have had the blessing of any available strength under sorrow, perplexity, sickness and toil, during a life which has been any thing but easy, it is owing to my repose upon eternal and irreversible laws, working in every department of the universe, without any interference from any random will, human or divine.—As to the ordinary objection to the doctrine,—that it is good for endurance but bad for action, —besides the obvious reply that every doctrine is to be accepted or rejected for its truth or falsehood, and not because mere human beings fancy its tendency to be good or bad, —I am bound to reply from my own experience that the allegation is not true. My life has been (whatever else) a very busy one; and this conviction, of the invariable action of fixed laws, has certainly been the main-spring of my activity. When it is considered that, according to the Necessarian doctrine, no action fails to produce effects, and no effort can be lost, there seems every reason for the conclusion which I have no doubt is the fact, that true Necessarians must be the most diligent and confident of all workers. The indolent dreamers whom I happen to know are those who find an excuse for their idleness in the doctrine of free-will, which certainly leaves but scanty encouragement to exertion of any sort: and at the same time, the noblest activity that I ever witness, the most cheerful and self-denying toil, is on the part of those who hold the Necessarian doctrine as a vital conviction.

As to the effect of that conviction on my religion, in those days of my fanaticism and afterwards, I had better give some account of it here, though it will lead me on to a date beyond the limits of this third period of my life.—In the first place, it appeared to me when I was twenty, as it appears to me now, that the New Testament proceeds on the ground of necessarian, rather than free-will doctrine. The prayer for daily bread is there, it is true; but the Lord's prayer is compiled from very ancient materials of the theocratic age. The fatalistic element of the Essene doctrine strongly pervades the doctrine and morality of Christ and the apostles; and its curious union with the doctrine of a special providence is possible only under the theocratic supposition which is the basis of the whole faith.—As for me, I seized upon the necessarian element with eagerness, as enabling me to hold to my cherished faith; and I presently perceived, and took instant advantage of the discovery, that the practice of prayer, as prevailing throughout Christendom, is wholly unauthorized by the New Testament. Christian prayer, as prevailing at this day, answers precisely to the description of that pharisaic prayer which Christ reprobated. His own method of praying, the prayer he gave to his disciples, and their practice, were all wholly unlike any thing now understood by Christian prayer, in protestant as well as catholic countries. I changed my method accordingly,—gradually, perhaps, but beginning immediately and decidedly. Not knowing what was good for me, and being sure that every external thing would come to pass just the same, whether I liked it or not, I ceased to desire, and therefore to pray for, any thing external,—whether 'daily bread,' or health, or life for myself or others, or any thing whatever but spiritual good. There I for a long time drew the line. Many years after I had outgrown the child-ishness of wishing for I knew not what,—of praying for what might be either good or evil,—I continued to pray for spiritual benefits. I can hardly say for spiritual aid; for I took the necessarian view of even the higher form of prayer,—that it brought about, or might bring about, its own accomplishment by the spiritual dispositions which it excited and cherished. This view is so far from simple, and so irreconcilable with the notion of a revelation of a scheme of salvation, that it is clear that the one or the other view must soon give way. The process in my case was this. A long series of grave misfortunes brought me to the conviction that there is no saying beforehand what the external condi-tions of internal peace really are. I found myself now and then in the loftiest moods of cheerfulness when in the midst of circumstances which I had most dreaded, and the converse; and thus I grew to be, generally speaking, really and truly careless as to what became of me. I had cast off the torment of fear, except in occasional weak moments. This experience presently extended to my spiritual affairs. I found myself best, according to all trustworthy tests of goodness, when I cared least about the matter. I continued my practice of nightly examination of my hourly conduct; and the evidence grew wonderfully strong that moral advancement came out of good influences rather than self-management; and that even so much self-reference as was involved in 'working out one's own salvation with fear and trembling' was demor-alizing. Thus I arrived,—after long years,—at the same point of ease or resignation about my spiritual as my temporal affairs, and felt that (to use a broad expression uttered by somebody) it was better to take the chance of being damned than be always quacking one's self in the fear of it. (Not that I had any literal notion of being damned,—any more than any other born and bred Unitarian.) What I could not desire for myself, I could not think of stipulating for others; and thus, in regard to petition, my prayers became simply an aspiration,—'Thy will be done!' But still, the department of praise remained. I need hardly say that I soon drew back in shame from offering to a Divine being a homage which would be offensive to an earthly one: and when this practice was over, my devotions consisted in aspiration,—very frequent and heart-felt,—under all circumstances and influences, and much as I meditate now, almost hourly, on the mysteries of life and the universe, and the great science and art of human duty. In proportion as the taint of fear and desire and self-regard fell off, and the meditation had fact instead of passion for its subject, the aspiration became freer and sweeter, till at length, when the selfish superstition had wholly gone out of it, it spread its charm through every change of every waking hour,—and does now, when life itself is expiring.

As to the effect that all this had on my belief in Christianity,—it did not prevent my holding on in that pseudo-acceptance of it which my Unitarian breeding rendered easy. It was a grand discovery to me when I somewhere met with the indication, (since become a rather favourite topic with Unitarian preachers) that the fact of the miracles has noth-ing whatever to do with the quality of the doctrine. When miracles are appealed to by the Orthodox as a proof of, not only the supernatural origin, but the divine quality of the doctrine, the obvious answer is that devils may work miracles, and the doctrine may therefore be from hell. Such was the argument in Christ's time; and such is it now among a good many protestants,—horrifying the Catholics and High-Churchmen of our time as much as it horrified the evangelists of old. The use to which it is turned by many who still call themselves Unitarians, and to which it was applied by me is,—the holding to Christianity in a manner as a revelation, after surrendering belief in the miracles. I suppose the majority of Unitarians still accept all the mira-cles (except the Miraculous Conception, of course)—even to the with-ering away of the fig-tree. Some hold to the resurrection, while giving up all the rest; and not a few do as I did,—say that the interior evidence of a divine origin of that doctrine is enough, and that no amount of miracles could strengthen their faith. It is clear however that a Christianity which never was received as a scheme of salvation,—which never was regarded as essential to salvation, —which might be treated, in respect to its records, at the will and pleasure of each believer, — which is next declared to be independent of its external evidences, because those evidences are found to be untenable,—and which is finally subjected in its doctrines, as in its letter, to the interpretation of each individual,—must cease to be a faith, and become a matter of spec-ulation, of spiritual convenience, and of intellectual and moral taste, till it declines to the rank of a mere fact in the history of mankind. These are the gradations through which I passed. It took many years to travel through them; and I lingered long in the stages of speculation and taste, intellectual and moral. But at length I recognized the monstrous super-stition in its true character of a great fact in the history of the race, and found myself, with the last link of my chain snapped,—a free rover on the broad, bright breezy common of the universe.

SECTION II

At this time,—(I think it must have been in 1821,)[1] was my first appear-ance in print. I had some early aspirations after authorship,—judging by an anecdote which hangs in my memory, though I believe I never thought about it, more or less, while undergoing that preparation which I have described in my account of my studies and translations. When I was assorting and tabulating scripture texts, in the way I described some way back, I one day told my mother, in a moment of confidence, that I hoped it might be printed, and make a book, and then I should be an authoress. My mother, pleased, I believe, with the aspiration, told my eldest sister; and she, in an unfortunate moment of contempt, twitted me with my conceit in fancying I could be an authoress; whereupon I instantly resolved 'never to tell any body any thing again.' How this reso-lution was kept it is rather amusing now to consider, seeing that of all people in the world, I have perhaps the fewest reserves. The ambition seems to have disappeared from that time; and when I did attempt to write, it was at the suggestion of another, and against my own judgment and inclination. My brother James, then my idolized companion, discov-ered how wretched I was when he left me for his college, after the vaca-tion; and he told me that I must not permit myself to be so miserable. He advised me to take refuge, on each occasion, in a new pursuit; and on that particular occasion, in an attempt at authorship. I said, as usual, that I would if he would: to which he answered that it would never do for him, a young student, to rush into print before the eyes of his tutors; but he desired me to write something that was in my head, and try my chance

---

[1] Her first publication, "Female Writers on Practical Divinity," appeared in the *Monthly Repository* 17 (Nov. 1822), 593–96.

with it in the 'Monthly Repository,'—the poor little Unitarian periodical in which I have mentioned that Talfourd tried his young powers.[1]
What James desired, I always did, as of course; and after he had left me to
my widowhood soon after six o'clock, one bright September morning,
I was at my desk before seven, beginning a letter to the Editor of the
'Monthly Repository,'—that editor being the formidable prime minister of his sect,—Rev. Robert Aspland. I suppose I must tell what that first
paper was, though I had much rather not; for I am so heartily ashamed
of the whole business as never to have looked at the article since the first
flutter of it went off. It was on Female Writers on Practical Divinity. I
wrote away, in my abominable scrawl of those days, on foolscap paper,
feeling mightily like a fool all the time. I told no one, and carried my
expensive packet to the post-office myself, to pay the postage. I took the
letter V for my signature,—I cannot at all remember why. The time was
very near the end of the month: I had no definite expectation that I
should ever hear any thing of my paper; and certainly did not suppose it
could be in the forthcoming number. That number was sent in before
service-time on a Sunday morning. My heart may have been beating
when I laid hands on it; but it thumped prodigiously when I saw my article there, and, in the Notices to Correspondents, a request to hear more
from V. of Norwich. There is certainly something entirely peculiar in the
sensation of seeing one'sself in print for the first time:—the lines burn
themselves in upon the brain in a way of which black ink is incapable, in
any other mode. So I felt that day, when I went about with my secret.—
I have said what my eldest brother was to us,—in what reverence we held
him. He was just married, and he and his bride asked me to return from
chapel with them to tea. After tea he said, 'Come now, we have had plenty
of talk; I will read you something;' and he held out his hand for the new
'Repository.' After glancing at it, he exclaimed, 'They have got a new
hand here. Listen.' After a paragraph, he repeated, 'Ah! this is a new hand;
they have had nothing so good as this for a long while.' (It would be
impossible to convey to any who do not know the 'Monthly Repository'
of that day, how very small a compliment this was.) I was silent, of course.
At the end of the first column, he exclaimed about the style, looking at
me in some wonder at my being as still as a mouse. Next (and well I

---

[1]   When she and Thomas Noon Talfourd (1795–1854) first published in the *MR*, the periodical was edited by Robert Aspland (1782–1845); William Johnson Fox (1786–1864)
succeeded as editor from 1828 to 1836. The *MR* also published Robert Browning's first
dramatic monologues, "Porphyria's Lover" and "Johannes Agricola in Meditation," under
the rubric "Madhouse Cells," in 1836.

remember his tone, and thrill to it still) his words were—'What a fine sentence that is! Why, do you not think so?' I mumbled out, sillily enough, that it did not seem any thing particular. 'Then,' said he, 'you were not listening. I will read it again. There now!' As he still got nothing out of me, he turned round upon me, as we sat side by side on the sofa, with 'Harriet, what is the matter with you? I never knew you so slow to praise any thing before.' I replied, in utter confusion,—'I never could baffle any body. The truth is, that paper is mine.' He made no reply; read on in silence, and spoke no more till I was on my feet to come away. He then laid his hand on my shoulder, and said gravely (calling me 'dear' for the first time) 'Now, dear, leave it to other women to make shirts and darn stockings; and do you devote yourself to this.' I went home in a sort of dream, so that the squares of the pavement seemed to float before my eyes. That evening made me an authoress.

It was not all so glorious, however. I immediately after began to write my first work,—'Devotional Exercises,'[1] of which I now remember nothing. But I remember my brother's anxious doubting looks, in which I discerned some disappointment, as he read the M.S. I remember his gentle hints about precision and arrangement of ideas, given with the utmost care not to discourage me; and I understood the significance of his praise of the concluding essay (in a letter from Madeira, where he was closing his precious life)—praise of the definiteness of object in that essay, which, as he observed, furnished the key to his doubts about the rest of the book, and which he conveyed only from an anxious desire that I should work my way up to the high reputation which he felt I was destined to attain. This just and gentle treatment, contrasting with the early discouragements which had confused my own judgment, affected me inexpressibly. I took these hints to heart in trying my hand at a sort of theologico-metaphysical novel, which I entered upon with a notion of enlightening the world through the same kind of interest as was then excited by Mr. Ward's novel, 'Tremaine,'[2] which was making a prodigious noise, and which perfectly enchanted me, except by its bad philosophy. I mightily enjoyed the prospect of this work, as did my mother; and I was flattered by finding that Rachel had

---

[1]   *Devotional Exercises: Consisting of Reflections and Prayers, for the Use of Young Persons* (London: Rowland Hunter, 1823) was self-financed, with its pages printed in Norwich and advertisements placed in the *Monthly Repository* for sales in London. Martineau took the concept and title from Charles Wellbeloved's *Devotional Exercises for the Use of Young Persons* (1801), which had promised but not produced a second volume.

[2]   R[obert] Plumer Ward, *Tremaine; or, The Man of Refinement* (London: H. Colburn, 1835).

higher expectations from it than even my own. But, at the end of half a volume, I became aware that it was excessively dull, and I stopped. Many years afterwards I burned it; and this is the only piece of my work but two (and a review) in my whole career that never was published.

Already I found that it would not do to copy what I wrote; and here (at the outset of this novel) I discontinued the practice for ever,—thus saving an immense amount of time which I humbly think is wasted by other authors. The prevalent doctrine about revision and copying, and especially Miss Edgeworth's account of her method of writing,—scribbling first, then submitting her manuscript to her father, and copying and altering many times over till, (if I remember right) no one paragraph of her 'Leonora' stood at last as it did at first,—made me suppose copying and alteration to be indispensable.[1] But I immediately found that there was no use in copying if I did not alter; and that, if ever I did alter, I had to change back again; and I, once for all, committed myself to a single copy. I believe the only writings I ever copied were 'Devotional Exercises,' and my first tale;—a trumpery story called 'Christmas Day.'[2] It seemed clear to me that distinctness and precision must be lost if alterations were made in a different state of mind from that which suggested the first utterance; and I was delighted when, long afterwards, I met with Cobbett's advice;—to know first what you want to say, and then say it in the first words that occur to you.[3] The excellence of Cobbett's style, and the manifest falling off of Miss Edgeworth's after her father's death (so frankly avowed by herself) were strong confirmations of my own experience. I have since, more than once, weakly fallen into mannerism,—now metaphysically elliptical, —now poetically amplified, and even, in one instance, bordering on the Carlylish;[4] but through all this folly, as well as since having a style of my own,— (that is, finding expression by words as easy as breathing air)—I have always used the same method in writing. I have always made sure of what I meant to say, and then written it down without care or anxiety,—glancing at it again only to see if any words were omitted or

---

1   Maria Edgeworth (1768–1849) published *Leonora* in 1806; *Ormond*, considered a lesser novel, appeared in 1817, the year her father died.

2   *Christmas Day; or, The Friends: A Tale* (Wellington: Houlston, 1826); this didactic tale is autobiographical in its details of a father's death, a family's bankruptcy, and the protagonist's disability.

3   William Cobbett (1763–1835) founded the periodical *Cobbett's Political Register* in 1802, in which his famous *Rural Rides* appeared from 1821 on.

4   In the mannered, eccentric, and bombastic mode of the essayist Thomas Carlyle (1795–1881). Martineau called him "the greatest mannerist of the age."

repeated, and not altering a single phrase in a whole work. I mention this because I think I perceive that great mischief arises from the notion that botching in the second place will compensate for carelessness in the first. I think I perceive that confusion of thought, and cloudiness or affectation in style are produced or aggravated by faulty prepossessions in regard to the method of writing for the press. The mere saving of time and labour in my own case may be regarded as no inconsiderable addition to my term of life.—Some modifications of this doctrine there must of course be in accordance with the strength or weakness of the natural faculty of expression by language: but I speak as strongly as I have just done because I have no reason to believe that the natural aptitude was particularly strong in myself. I believe that such facility as I have enjoyed has been mainly owing to my unconscious preparatory discipline; and especially in the practice of translation from various languages, as above related. And, again, after seeing the manuscripts or proof-sheets of many of the chief authors of my own time, I am qualified to say that the most marked mannerists of their day are precisely those whose manuscripts show most erasures, and their proof-sheets most alterations.

SECTION III

I HAVE said that it was through a long train of calamities that I learned some valuable truths and habits. Those calamities were now coming fast upon me. In 1820, my deafness was suddenly encreased by what might be called an accident, which I do not wish to describe. I ought undoubtedly to have begun at that time to use a trumpet; but no one pressed it upon me; and I do not know that, if urged, I should have yielded; for I had abundance of that false shame which hinders nine deaf people out of ten from doing their duty in that particular. The redeeming quality of personal infirmity is that it brings its special duty with it; but this privilege waits long to be recognized. The special duty of the deaf is, in the first place, to spare other people as much fatigue as possible; and, in the next, to preserve their own natural capacity for sound, and habit of receiving it, and true memory of it, as long as possible. It was long before I saw, or fully admitted this to myself; and it was ten years from this time before

I began to use a trumpet. Thus, I have felt myself qualified to say more in the way of exhortation and remonstrance to deaf people than could be said by any one who had not only never been deaf, but had never shared the selfish and morbid feelings which are the ordinary attendant curses of suffering so absolutely peculiar as that of personal infirmity.

Next, our beloved brother, who had always shown a tendency to consumption, ruptured a blood-vessel in the lungs, and had to give up his practice and professional offices, and to go, first into Devonshire, and afterwards to Madeira, whence he never returned. He died at sea, on his way home. I went with him and his wife into Devonshire, for the spring of 1823; and it was my office to read aloud for many hours of every day, which I did with great satisfaction, and with inestimable profit from his comments and unsurpassed conversation. Before breakfast, and while he enjoyed his classical reading on the sofa, I rambled about the neighbour-hood of Torquay,—sometimes sketching, sometimes reading, sometimes studying the sea from the shelter of the caves, and, on the whole, learn-ing to see nature, under those grave circumstances, with new eyes. Soon after our return, their child was born; and never was infant more beloved. It was my great solace during the dreary season of dismantling that home which we had had so much delight in forming, and sending those from us who were the joy of our lives. It was then that I learned the lesson I spoke of,—of our peace of mind being, at least in times of crisis, inde-pendent of external circumstances. Day by day, I had been silently grow-ing more heartsick at the prospect of the parting; and I especially dreaded the night before, —the going to bed, with the thoughtful night before me, after seeing every thing packed, and knowing that the task of the coming day was the parting. Yet that night was one of the happiest of my life. It is easy to conceive what the process of thought was, and what the character of the religious emotion which so elevated me. The lesson was a sound one, whatever might be the virtue of the thoughts and feelings involved. The next day, all was over at length. I was the last who held the dear baby,—even to the moment of his being put into the carriage. The voyage was injurious to him; and it was probably the cause of his death, which took place soon after reaching Madeira. There was something peaceful, and very salutary in the next winter, though it could not reason-ably be called a very happy one. There was a close mutual reliance between my mother and myself,—my sister Rachel being absent, and our precious little Ellen, the family darling, at school. We kept up a close correspondence with our absent ones; and there were the beautiful Madeira letters always to look for. I remember reading Clarendon's

Rebellion[1] aloud to my mother in the evenings; and we took regular walks in all weathers. I had my own troubles and anxieties, however. A dream had passed before me since the visit of a student friend of my brother James's, which some words of my father's and mother's had strengthened into hope and trust. This hope was destined to be crushed for a time in two hearts by the evil offices of one who had much to answer for in what he did. This winter was part of the time of suspense. Under my somewhat heavy troubles my health had some time before begun to give way; and now I was suffering from digestive derangement which was not cured for four years after; and then only after severe and daily pain from chronic inflammation of the stomach. Still, with an ailing body, an anxious and often aching heart, and a mind which dreaded looking into the future, I regarded this winter of 1823–4 as a happy one:— the secret of which I believe to have been that I felt myself beloved at home, and enjoyed the keen relish of duties growing out of domestic love. At the end of the next June, my brother died. We were all prepared for the event, as far as preparation is ever possible; but my dear father, the most unselfish of men, who never spoke of his own feelings, and always considered other people's, never, we think, recovered from this grief. He was very quiet at the time; but his health began to go wrong, and his countenance to alter; and during the two remaining years of his life, he sustained a succession of cares which might have broken down a frame less predisposed for disease than his had become. In our remembrance of him there is no pain on the ground of any thing in his character. Humble, simple, upright, self-denying, affectionate to as many people as possible, and kindly to all, he gave no pain, and did all the good he could. He had not the advantage of an adequate education; but there was a natural shrewdness about him which partly compensated for the want. He was not the less, but the more, anxious to give his children the advantages which he had never received; and the whole family have always felt that they owe a boundless debt of gratitude to both their parents for the self-sacrificing efforts they made, through all the vicissitudes of the times, to fit their children in the best possible manner for independent action in life. My father's business, that of a Norwich manufacturer,[2] was subject to the fluctuations to which all manufacture was liable during the war, and to others of its own; and our parents' method was to have no reserves

---

[1]   Edward Hyde Clarendon's *The True Historical Narrative of the Rebellion and Civil Wars in England* (1702–04), written by a supporter of Charles I and lord chancellor after the Restoration of Charles II.

[2]   Thomas Martineau was a cloth manufacturer.

from their children, to let us know precisely the state of their affairs, and to hold out to us, in the light of this evidence, the probability that we might sooner or later have to work for our own living,—daughters as well as sons,—and that it was improbable that we should ever be rich. The time was approaching which was to prove the wisdom of their method. My father's business, never a very enriching one, had been for some time prosperous; and this year (1824) he indulged my brother James and myself with a journey;—a walking tour in Scotland, in the course of which we walked five hundred miles in a month. I am certainly of opinion now that that trip aggravated my stomach-complaint; and I only wonder it was no worse. I spent the next winter with my married sister, my sister-in-law, and other friends, and returned to Norwich in April, to undergo long months,—even years—of anxiety and grief.

In the reviews of my 'History of the Thirty Years' Peace,'[1] one chapter is noticed more emphatically than all the rest;—the chapter on the speculations, collapse, and crash of 1825 and 1826. If that chapter is written with some energy, it is no wonder; for our family fortunes were implicated in that desperate struggle, and its issue determined the whole course of life of the younger members of our family,—my own among the rest. One point on which my narrative in the History is emphatic is the hardship on the sober man of business of being involved in the destruction which overtook the speculator; and I had family and personal reasons for saying this. My father never speculated; but he was well nigh ruined during that calamitous season by the deterioration in value of his stock. His stock of manufactured goods was larger, of course, than it would have been in a time of less enterprise; and week by week its value declined, till, in the middle of the winter, when the banks were crashing down all over England, we began to contemplate absolute ruin. My father was evidently a dying man;—not from anxiety of mind, for his liver disease was found to be owing to obstruction caused by a prodigious gall-stone: but his illness was no doubt aggravated and rendered more harassing by his cares for his family. In the spring he was sent to Cheltenham,[2] whence he returned after some weeks with the impression of approaching death on his face. He altered his Will, mournfully reducing the portions left to his daughters to something which could barely be called an independence. Then, three weeks before his death,

---

[1]   *The History of England during the Thirty Years' Peace, 1816–1846* (London: Charles Knight, 1849–50).

[2]   A spa town in the Cotswold hills, known for the purgative powers of a spring discovered in 1718.

117

he wisely, and to our great relief, dismissed the whole subject. He told my brother Henry, his partner in the business, that he had done what he could while he could: that he was now a dying man, and could be of no further use in the struggle, and that he wished to keep his mind easy for his few remaining days: so he desired to see no more letters of business, and to hear no more details. For a few more days, he sunned himself on the grass-plat in the garden, in the warm June mornings: then could not leave the house; then could not come down stairs; and, towards the end of the month died quietly, with all his family round his bed.—As for my share in this family experience,—it was delightful to me that he took an affectionate pleasure in my poor little book,—of value to me now for that alone,—'Addresses, Prayers and Hymns, for the use of families and school.'[1] It was going through the press at that time; and great was my father's satisfaction; and high were his hopes, I believe, of what I should one day be and do. Otherwise, I have little comfort in thinking of his last illness. The old habit of fear came upon me, more irresistibly than ever, on the assembling of the family; and I mourn to think how I kept out of the way, whenever it was possible, and how little I said to my father of what was in my heart about him and my feelings towards him. The more easily his humility was satisfied with whatever share of good fell to him, the more richly he should have been ministered to. By me he was not,—owing to this unhappy shyness. My married sister,[2] who was an incomparable nurse, did the duty of others besides her own; and mine among the rest, while I was sorrowing and bitterly chiding myself in silence, and perhaps in apparent insensibility.

And now my own special trial was at hand. It is not necessary to go into detail about it. The news which got abroad that we had grown comparatively poor,—and the evident certainty that we were never likely to be rich, so wrought upon the mind of one friend as to break down the mischief which I have referred to as caused by ill-offices. My friend had believed me rich, was generous about making me a poor man's wife, and had been discouraged in more ways than one.[3] He

---

[1]   *Addresses, with Prayers and Original Hymns, for the Use of Families and Schools* (London: Rowland Hunter, 1826) was published anonymously. A second edition appeared in 1838 (London: Charles Fox, 1838).

[2]   Elizabeth, married to the surgeon Thomas Greenhow.

[3]   John Hugh Worthington, a fellow seminarian with James at Manchester New College at York, who first visited the Martineau family in August, 1823. Biographers speculate that it was James whose "ill-offices" delayed the engagement, though it may also have been James's concerns about Worthington's mental health.

now came to me, and we were soon virtually engaged. I was at first very anxious and unhappy. My veneration for his *morale* was such that I felt that I dared not undertake the charge of his happiness: and yet I dared not refuse, because I saw it would be his death blow. I was ill,— I was deaf,—I was in an entangled state of mind between conflicting duties and some lower considerations; and many a time did I wish, in my fear that I should fail, that I had never seen him. I am far from wishing that now;—now that the beauty of his goodness remains to me, clear of all painful regrets. But there was a fearful period to pass through. Just when I was growing happy, surmounting my fears and doubts, and enjoying his attachment, the consequences of his long struggle and suspense overtook him. He became suddenly insane; and after months of illness of body and mind, he died. The calamity was aggravated to me by the unaccountable insults I received from his family, whom I had never seen. Years afterwards, when his sister and I met, the mystery was explained. His family had been given to understand, by cautious insinuations, that I was actually engaged to another, while receiving my friend's addresses! There has never been any doubt in my mind that, considering what I was in those days, it was happiest for us both that our union was prevented by any means. I am, in truth, very thankful for not having married at all. I have never since been tempted, nor have suffered any thing at all in relation to that matter which is held to be all-important to woman,—love and marriage. Nothing, I mean, beyond occasional annoyance, presently disposed of. Every literary woman, no doubt, has plenty of importunity of that sort to deal with; but freedom of mind and coolness of manner dispose of it very easily: and since the time I have been speaking of, my mind has been wholly free from all idea of love affairs. My subsequent literary life in London was clear from all difficulty and embarrassment,—no doubt because I was evidently too busy, and too full of interests of other kinds to feel any awkwardness,—to say nothing of my being then thirty years of age; an age at which, if ever, a woman is certainly qualified to take care of herself. I can easily conceive how I might have been tempted,—how some deep springs in my nature might have been touched, then as earlier; but, as a matter of fact, they never were; and I consider the immunity a great blessing, under the liabilities of a moral condition such as mine in the olden time. If I had had a husband dependent on me for his happiness, the responsibility would have made me wretched. I had not faith enough in myself to endure avoidable responsibility. If my husband had not depended on me for his happiness,

I should have been jealous. So also with children. The care would have so overpowered the joy,—the love would have so exceeded the ordinary chances of life,—the fear on my part would have so impaired the freedom on theirs, that I rejoice not to have been involved in a relation for which I was, or believed myself unfit. The veneration in which I hold domestic life has always shown me that that life was not for those whose self-respect had been early broken down, or had never grown. Happily, the majority are free from this disability. Those who suffer under it had better be as I,—as my observation of married, as well as single life assures me. When I see what conjugal love is, in the extremely rare cases in which it is seen in its perfection, I feel that there is a power of attachment in me that has never been touched. When I am among little children, it frightens me to think what my idolatry of my own children would have been. But, through it all, I have ever been thankful to be alone. My strong will, combined with anxiety of conscience, makes me fit only to live alone; and my taste and liking are for living alone. The older I have grown, the more serious and irremediable have seemed to me the evils and disadvantages of married life, as it exists among us at this time: and I am provided with what it is the bane of single life in ordinary cases to want—substantial, laborious and serious occupation. My business in life has been to think and learn, and to speak out with absolute freedom what I have thought and learned. The freedom is itself a positive and never-failing enjoyment to me, after the bondage of my early life. My work and I have been fitted to each other, as is proved by the success of my work and my own happiness in it. The simplicity and independence of this vocation first suited my infirm and ill-developed nature, and then sufficed for my needs, together with family ties and domestic duties, such as I have been blessed with, and as every woman's heart requires. Thus, I am not only entirely satisfied with my lot, but think it the very best for me, —under my constitution and circumstances: and I long ago came to the conclusion that, without meddling with the case of the wives and mothers, I am probably the happiest single woman in England. Who could have believed, in that awful year 1826, that such would be my conclusion a quarter of a century afterwards!

My health gave way, more and more; and my suffering throughout the year 1827 from the pain which came on every evening was such as it is disagreeable to think of now. For pain of body and mind it was truly a terrible year, though it had its satisfactions, one of the chief of which was a long visit which I paid to my brother Robert and his wife (always a dear friend of mine to this day) at their home in Dudley.[1] I remember our walks in the grounds of Dudley Castle, and the organ-playing at home, after my brother's business hours, and the inexhaustible charm of the baby, as gleams amidst the darkness of that season. I found then the unequalled benefit of long solitary walks in such a case as mine. I had found it even at Norwich, in midwinter, when all was bleak on that exposed level country; and now, amidst the beauty which surrounds Dudley, there was no end of my walks or of my relish for them; and I always came home with a cheered and lightened heart. Such poetry as I wrote (I can't bear to think of it) I wrote in those days. The mournful pieces, and those which assume *not* to be mournful, which may be found in my 'Miscellanies' (published in America) may be referred to that period. And so may some dull and doleful prose writings, published by the solemn old Calvinistic publisher, Houlston, of Wellington in Shropshire.[2] An acquaintance of mine had some time before put me in the way of correspondence with Houlston; and he had accepted the first two little eightpenny stories I sent him. I remember the amusement and embarrassment of the first piece of pecuniary success. As soon as it was known in the house that the letter from Wellington contained five pounds, every body wanted, and continued to want all day, to borrow five pounds of me. After a pause, Houlston wrote to ask for another story of somewhat more substance and bulk. My 'Globe' newspaper readings suggested to me the subject of Machine-breaking as a good one,—some recent outrages of that sort having taken place: but I had not remotest idea that I was meditating writing on Political Economy, the very name of which was then either unknown to me, or conveyed no meaning. I wrote the little story called 'The Rioters;' and its success was such that some hosiers and lacemakers of Derby and Nottingham sent me a request to write a tale on the subject of Wages, which I did, calling it 'The Turn Out.' The success of both was such as to dispose Mr. Houlston to further dealings; and I wrote for him a good many tracts, which he sold for a penny, and for which he gave me a sovereign apiece. This seems to be the place in which to tell a fact or

---

1   Robert, Harriet's third brother, became a brass manufacturer in Birmingham after first settling in Dudley, a town ten miles south which was a center of iron manufacturing. Dudley Castle was a ruin from the 14th century.

2   Houlston and Son published many of Martineau's early didactic tales, including *Christmas Day; or, The Friends* (1826), *The Friends, A Continuation of Christmas Day* (1826), *Principle and Practice; or, The Orphan Family* (1827), *Sequel to Principle and Practice* (1831), *The Rioters; or, a Tale of Bad Times* (1827), and *The Turn-out; or, Patience is the Best Policy* (1829). She typically received £5–10 for these longer stories.

two about the use made of those early writings of mine, by the old man's sons and successors. Old Houlston died not very long afterwards, leaving among his papers, (I now remember,) a manuscript story of mine which I suppose lies there still;—about a good governess, called, I think, 'Caroline Shirley.' I mention this that, if that story should come out with my name after my death, it may be known to have been written somewhere about this time,—1827. Old Houlston died, on perfectly good terms with me, as far as I remember. The next thing I heard was (and I heard it from various quarters) that those little tracts of mine, and some of my larger tales, were selling and circulating as Mrs. Sherwood's,[1]—Houlston being her publisher. This was amusing; and I had no other objection to it than that it was not true. Next, certain friends and relations of my own who went to the Houlstons' shop in Paternoster Row,[2] and asked for any works by me, had foisted upon them any rubbish that was convenient, under pretence of its being mine. A dear old aunt was very mysterious and complimentary to me, one day, on her return from London, about 'Judith Potts;'[3] and was puzzled to find all her allusions lost upon me. At length, she produced a little story so entitled, which had been sold to her as mine over the Houlstons' counter, and, as she believed, by Mr. Houlston himself. This was rather too bad; for 'Judith Potts' was not altogether a work that one would wish to build one's fame on: but there was worse to come. Long years after, when such reputation as I have had was at its height, (when I was ill at Tynemouth, about 1842) there had been some machine breaking; and Messrs. Houlston and Stoneman (as the firm then stood) brought out afresh my poor little early story of 'The Rioters,'[4] with my name in the title-page for the first time, and not only with every external appearance of being fresh, but with interpolations and alterations which made it seem really so. For instance, 'His Majesty' was altered to 'Her Majesty.' By advice of my friends, I made known the trick far and wide; and I wrote to Messrs. Houlston and Stoneman, to inform them

---

[1] Mary Martha Sherwood (1775–1851), evangelical children's author, best known for *Little Henry and his Bearer* (1814) and *The History of the Fairchild Family* (1818). Because many of Houlston's tracts were published anonymously or with a reference to another tale ("by the author of"), there is no full bibliographic record of the short tracts Martineau sold to Houlston that may bear Mrs. Sherwood's name.

[2] Street near St. Paul's cathedral in the City of London known for its publishers and booksellers, many religious.

[3] *The History of Judith Potts*, by the author of "A Week at Christmas" (Wellington, Salop.: Houlston and Son, 1829).

[4] *The Rioters: A Tale*, by Harriet Martineau, 2nd edition (London: Houlston and Stoneman, 1842).

that I was aware of their fraudulent transaction, and that it was action-able. These caterers for the pious needs of the religious world replied with insults, having nothing better to offer. They pleaded my original permission to their father to use my name or not; which was a fact, but no excuse for the present use of it: and to the gravest part of the whole charge,—that of illegal alterations for the fraudulent purpose of concealing the date of the book, they made no reply whatever. I had reason to believe, however, that by the exertions of my friends, the trick was effectually exposed. As far as I remember, this is almost the only serious complaint I have had to make of any publisher, during my whole career.

Meantime, in 1827 I was on excellent terms with old Houlston, and writing for him a longer tale than I had yet tried my hand on. It was called 'Principle and Practice;' and it succeeded well enough to induce us to put forth a 'Sequel to Principle and Practice' three or four years after. These were all that I wrote for Houlston, as far as I remember, except a little book whose appearance made me stand aghast. A most excellent young servant of ours, who had become quite a friend of the household, went out to Madeira with my brother and his family, and confirmed our attachment to her by her invaluable services to them. Her history was a rather remarkable, and a very interesting one; and I wrote it in the form of four of Houlston's penny tracts. He threw them together, and made a little book of them; and the heroine, who would never have heard of them as tracts, was speedily put in possession of her Memoirs in the form of the little book called 'My Servant Rachel.'[1] An aunt of mine, calling on her one day, found her standing in the middle of the floor, and her husband reading the book over her shoulder. She was hurt at one anecdote,—which was certainly true, but which she had forgotten: but, as a whole, it could not but have been most gratify-ing to her. She ever after treated me with extreme kindness, and even tenderness; and we are hearty friends still, whenever we meet.—And here ends the chapter of my authorship in which Houlston, my first patron, was concerned.

It was in the autumn of 1827, I think, that a neighbour lent my sister Mrs. Marcet's 'Conversations on Political Economy.'[2] I took up the book, chiefly to see what Political Economy precisely was; and great was my surprise to find that I had been teaching it unawares, in my stories about

---

[1]   My Servant Rachel (London: Houlston, 1831).

[2]   Jane Marcet, Conversations on Political Economy in which the Elements of the Science are Familiarly Explained (London: Longman, 1816).

Machinery and Wages. It struck me at once that the principles of the whole science might be advantageously conveyed in the same way, — not by being smothered up in a story, but by being exhibited in their natural workings in selected passages of social life. It has always appeared very strange to me that so few people seem to have understood this. Students of all manner of physical sciences afterwards wanted me to 'illustrate' things of which social life (and therefore fiction) can afford no illustration. I used to say till I was tired that none but moral and political science admitted of the method at all; and I doubt whether many of those who talk about it understand the matter, to this day. In the 'Edinburgh Review' of my Political Economy series,[1]—a review otherwise as weak as it is kind,—there is the best appreciation of the principle of the work that I have seen anywhere;—a page or so[2] of perfect understanding of my view and purpose. That view and purpose date from my reading of Mrs. Marcet's Conversations. During that reading, groups of personages rose up from the pages, and a procession of action glided through its arguments, as afterwards from the pages of Adam Smith, and all the other Economists. I mentioned my notion, I remember, when we were sitting at work, one bright afternoon at home. Brother James nodded assent; my mother said 'do it;' and we went to tea, unconscious what a great thing we had done since dinner.

There was meantime much fiddle-faddling to be gone through, with such work as 'Principle and Practice' and the like. But a new educational period was about to open.— My complaint grew so serious, and was so unbearably painful, and, in truth, medically mismanaged at Norwich, that my family sent me to Newcastle, to my sister's, where her husband treated me successfully, and put me in the way of entire cure. It was a long and painful business; but the method succeeded; and, in the course of time, and by the unremitting care of my host and hostess, I was sent home in a condition to manage myself. It was some years before the stomach entirely recovered its tone; but it was thoroughly healthy from that time forward.

While I was at Newcastle, a spirited advertisement from the new editor of the 'Monthly Repository,' Mr. Fox,[3] met my eye, appealing for literary aid to those who were interested in its objects. I could not resist sending a practical reply; and I was gratified to learn, long afterwards, that

[1]   [William Empson], *Edinburgh Review* 57 (April 1833), 1–39.

[2]   *Edinburgh Review.* Vol. lvii., pp. 6 and 7. [Martineau's note]

[3]   William Johnson Fox (1786–1864), editor of the *MR* from 1828 to 1836 and Unitarian minister at South Place Chapel, Finsbury, London.

when my name was mentioned to Mr. Fox, before he issued his appeal, he had said that he wished for my assistance from the moment when he, as editor, discovered from the office books that I was the writer of certain papers which had fixed his attention: but that he could not specially invite my contributions while he had no funds which could enable him to offer due remuneration. His reply to my first letter was so cordial that I was animated to offer him extensive assistance; and if he had then no money to send me, he paid me in something more valuable—in a course of frank and generous criticism which was of the utmost benefit to me. His editorial correspondence with me was unquestionably the occasion, and in great measure the cause, of the greatest intellectual progress I ever made before the age of thirty. I sent him Essays, Reviews and poetry (or what I called such)—the best specimens of which may be found in the 'Miscellanies,' before mentioned.—The Diffusion Society was at that time the last novelty. A member of the Committee who overrated his own influence, invited me to write a Life of Howard the Philanthropist, which I did, with great satisfaction, and under the positive promise of thirty pounds for it. From time to time, tidings were sent to me of its being approved, and at length of its being actually in type. In the approaching crisis of my fortunes, when I humbly asked when I might expect any part of the payment, I could obtain no clear answer: and the end of the matter was that it was found that half-a-dozen or more Lives of Howard had been ordered in a similar manner, by different members of the Committee;[1] that my manuscript was found, after several years, at the bottom of a chest,—not only dirty, but marked and snipped,—its contents having been abundantly used without any acknowledgment,— as was afterwards admitted to me by some of the members who were especially interested in the prison question. I am far from regretting the issue now, because new materials have turned up which would have shamed that biography out of existence: but the case is worth mentioning, as an illustration of the way in which literary business is managed by corporate directories. I believe most people who ever had any connexion with the Diffusion Society have some similar story to tell.

While I was at Newcastle, a change, which turned out a very happy one, was made in our domestic arrangements. My cousin, James Martineau Lee, who had succeeded my brother as a surgeon at Norwich, having died

---

[1]   No edition of the *Life of Howard* published by the Society for the Diffusion of Useful Knowledge has been found. The SDUK later asked Martineau to write *Poor Laws and Paupers Illustrated*, for which she claimed she never was paid £100 owing her from Lord Brougham, one of its leading members. See Period IV, sec. i.

that year, his aged mother, —(my father's only surviving sister) came to live with us; and with us she remained till her death in 1840.[1] She was hardly settled with us when the last of our series of family misfortunes occurred. I call it a misfortune, because in common parlance it would be so treated; but I believe that my mother and all her other daughters would have joined heartily, if asked, in my conviction that it was one of the best things that ever happened to us. My mother and her daughters lost, at a stroke, nearly all they had in the world by the failure of the house,—the old manufactory,—in which their money was placed. We never recovered more than the merest pittance; and at the time, I, for one, was left destitute;—that is to say, with precisely one shilling in my purse. The effect upon me of this new 'calamity,' as people called it, was like that of a blister upon a dull, weary pain, or series of pains. I rather enjoyed it, even at the time; for there was scope for action; whereas, in the long, dreary series of preceding trials, there was nothing possible but endurance. In a very short time, my two sisters at home and I began to feel the blessing of a wholly new freedom. I, who had been obliged to write before breakfast, or in some private way, had henceforth liberty to do my own work in my own way; for we had lost our gentility. Many and many a time since have we said that, but for that loss of money, we might have lived on in the ordinary provincial method of ladies with small means, sewing, and economizing, and growing narrower every year: whereas, by being thrown, while it was yet time, on our own resources, we have worked hard and usefully, won friends, reputation and independence, seen the world abundantly, abroad and at home, and, in short, have truly lived instead of vegetated.

It was in June, 1829, that the old Norwich house failed. I had been spending a couple of days at a country town, where the meeting of the provincial Unitarian Association took place. Some of the members knew, on the last day, what had happened to us; but I heard it first in the streets of Norwich on my way to our own house. As well as I can remember, a pretty faithful account of the event is given in one of my Political Economy tales,—'Berkeley the Banker;' mixed up, however, with a good many facts about other persons and times. I need not give the story over again here, nor any part of it but what is concerned in the history of my own mind and my own work.—It was presently settled that my mother, my dear old aunt and I should live on in the family house. One sister

---

[1]   Margaret Lee, née Martineau (1756–1840) married James Lee, widower of her sister Sarah (1760–1802). Her son James Martineau Lee died in 1828, having succeeded in medical practice Thomas Martineau, Harriet's brother who died in 1824.

went forth to earn the independence which she achieved after busy and honourable years of successful exertion. The youngest was busy teaching and training the children, chiefly, of the family, till her marriage.[1]

The question was—what was *I* to do, with my deafness precluding both music and governessing. I devised a plan for guiding the studies of young people by correspondence, and sent out written proposals: but, while every body professed to approve the scheme, no pupil ever offered. I was ere long very glad of this; for the toil of the pen would have been great, with small results of any kind, in comparison to those which accrued from what I did write.—In the first place, I inquired about my 'Life of Howard,' and found, to my interior consternation, that there was no prospect in that quarter. Nobody knew that I was left with only one shilling, insomuch that I dreaded the arrival of a thirteenpenny letter, in those days of dear postage. The family supposed me to be well-supplied, through Houlston's recent payment for one of my little books: but that money had gone where all the rest was. The sale of a ball-dress brought me three pounds. That was something. I hoped, and not without reason, that my needle would bring me enough for my small expenses, for a time; and I did earn a good many pounds by fancy-work, in the course of the next year,—after which it ceased to be necessary. For two years, I lived on fifty pounds a year. My mother, always generous in money matters, would not hear of my paying my home expenses till she saw that I should be the happier for her allowing it: and then she assured me, and proved to me, that, as she had to keep house at all events, and as my habits were exceedingly frugal (taking no wine, &c.) thirty pounds a year would repay her for my residence. Twenty pounds more sufficed for clothes, postage and sundries: and thus did I live, as long as it was necessary, on fifty pounds a year.— I must mention here a gift which dropped in upon me at that time which gave me more pleasure than any money-gift that I ever received. Our rich relations made bountiful presents to my sisters, for their outfit on leaving home: but they supposed me in possession of the money they knew I had earned, and besides concluded that I could not want much, as I was to stay at home. My application about the Howard manuscript, however, came to the knowledge of a cousin of mine,[2]—

---

[1]   Rachel went out as a governess and eventually ran a girls' school in Liverpool; after governessing within the family and for the Nightingales, Ellen married Alfred Higginson, a Liverpool surgeon, in 1841.

[2]   Unidentified, but possibly Richard Martineau (1804–65), who became managing director of the Whitbred Brewery; see p. 134, n. 1 and p. 139, n. 5.

then and ever since, to this hour, a faithful friend to me; and he, divining the case, sent me ten pounds, in a manner so beautiful that his few lines filled me with joy. That happened on a Sunday morning; and I well remember what a happy morning it was. I had become too deaf now for public worship; and I went every fair Sunday morning over the wildest bit of country near Norwich,—a part of Mousehold,[1] which was a sweet breezy common, overlooking the old city in its most picturesque aspect. There I went that Sunday morning; and I remember well the freshness of the turf and the beauty of the tormentilla which bestarred it, in the light and warmth of that good cousin's kindness.

I now wrote to Mr. Fox, telling him of my changed circumstances, which would compel me to render less gratuitous service than hitherto to the 'Repository.' Mr. Fox replied by apologetically placing at my disposal the only sum at his command at that time,—fifteen pounds a year, for which I was to do as much reviewing as I thought proper. With this letter arrived a parcel of nine books for review or notice. Overwhelming as this was, few letters that I had ever received had given me more pleasure than this. Here was, in the first place, work; in the next, continued literary discipline under Mr. Fox; and lastly, this money would buy my clothes. So to work I went, with needle and pen. I had before begun to study German; and now, that study was my recreation; and I found a new inspiration in the world of German literature, which was just opening, widely and brightly, before my eager and awakened mind. It was truly *life* that I lived during those days of strong intellectual and moral effort.

After I had received about a dozen books, Mr. Fox asked me to send him two or three tales, such as his 'best readers' would not pass by. I was flattered by this request; but I had no idea that I could fulfil his wish, any more than I could refuse to try. Now was the time to carry out the notion I had formed on reading 'Helon's Pilgrimage to Jerusalem,'—as I related above. I wrote 'The Hope of the Hebrew' (the first of the 'Traditions of Palestine,') and two others, as unlike it and each other as I could make them:—viz, 'Solitude and Society,' and 'The Early Sowing,'—the Unitarian City Mission being at that time under deliberation.[2]

I carried these stories to London myself, and put them into Mr. Fox's own hands, —being kindly invited for a long stay at the house of an

---

[1]   A heath northeast of the city, within a mile of the Martineau house in Gurney Court, Magdalen Street.

[2]   "The Hope of the Hebrew" became the first tale in *Traditions of Palestine* (London, Longman, Rees, Orme, Brown, and Green, 1830); "Solitude and Society" and "The Earl Sowing" were included in Martineau's *Miscellanies* (Boston: Hilliard, Gray, and Company, 1836), II, 42–69.

uncle, in pursuit of my own objects. The Hebrew tale was put forth first; and the day after its appearance, such inquiries were made of Mr. Fox at a public dinner in regard to the authorship that I was at once determined to make a volume of them; and the 'Traditions of Palestine' appeared accordingly, in the next spring. Except that first story, the whole volume was written in a fortnight. By this little volume was my name first made known in literature. I still love the memory of the time when it was written, though there was little other encouragement than my own pleasure in writing, and in the literary discipline which I continued to enjoy under Mr. Fox's editorship. With him I always succeeded; but I failed in all other directions during that laborious winter and spring. I had no literary acquaintance or connexion what-ever; and I could not get any thing that I wrote even looked at; so that every thing went into the 'Repository' at last. I do not mean that any amount of literary connexion would necessarily have been of any serv-ice to me; for I do not believe that 'patronage,' 'introductions' and the like are of any avail, in a general way. I know this; —that I have always been anxious to extend to young or struggling authors the sort of aid which would have been so precious to me in that winter of 1829–1830, and that, in above twenty years, I have never succeeded but once. I obtained the publication of 'The Two Old Men's Tales,'—the first of Mrs. Marsh's novels:[1] but, from the time of my own success to this hour, every other attempt, of the scores I have made, to get a hearing for young or new aspirants has failed. My own heart was often very near sinking,—as were my bodily forces; and with reason. During the daylight hours of that winter, I was poring over fine fancy-work, by which alone I earned any money; and after tea, I went upstairs to my room, for my day's literary labour. The quantity I wrote, at prodigious expenditure of nerve, surprises me now,—after my long breaking-in to hard work. Every night that winter, I believe, I was writing till two, or even three in the morning,—obeying always the rule of the house,— of being present at the breakfast table as the clock struck eight. Many a time I was in such a state of nervous exhaustion and distress that I was obliged to walk to and fro in the room before I could put on paper the last line of a page, or the last half sentence of an essay or review. Yet was I very happy. The deep-felt sense of progress and expansion was delight-ful; and so was the exertion of all my faculties; and, not least, that of will

---

[1]   Anne Marsh, née Caldwell (1791–1874), published "The Deformed" and "The Admiral's Daughter" as *Two Old Men's Tales* (London: Saunders and Otley, 1834).

to overcome my obstructions, and force my way to that power of public speech of which I believed myself more or less worthy. The worst apprehension I felt,—far worse than that of disappointment, mortification and poverty,—was from the intense action of my mind. Such excitement as I was then sustaining and enjoying could not always last; and I dreaded the reaction, or the effects of its mere cessation. I was beginning, however, to learn that the future,—our intellectual and moral future,—had better be left to take care of itself, as long as the present is made the best use of; and I found, in due course, that each period of the mind's training has its own excitements, and that the less its condition is quacked, or made the subject of anticipation at all, the better for the mind's health. But my habit of anxiety was not yet broken. It was scarcely weakened. I have since found that persons who knew me only then, do not recognize me or my portraits now,—or at any time within the last twenty years. The frown of those old days, the rigid face, the sulky mouth, the forbidding countenance, which looked as if it had never had a smile upon it, told a melancholy story which came to an end long ago: but it was so far from its end then that it amazes me now to think what liberality and forbearance were requisite in the treatment of me by Mr. Fox and the friends I met at his house, and how capable they were of that liberality. My Sabbatarian strictness, and my prejudices on a hundred subjects must have been absurd and disagreeable enough to them: but their gentleness, respect and courtesy were such as I now remember with gratitude and pleasure. They saw that I was outgrowing my shell, and they had patience with me till I had rent it and cast it off; and if they were not equally ready with their sympathy when I had found freedom, but disposed to turn from me, in proportion as I was able to take care of myself, to do the same office for other incipient or struggling beings, this does not lessen my sense of obligation to them for the help and support they gave me in my season of intellectual and moral need.

My griefs deepened towards the close of that London visit. While failing in all my attempts to get my articles even looked at, proposals were made to me to remain in town, and undertake proof-correcting and other literary drudgery, on a salary which would, with my frugal habits, have supported me, while leaving time for literary effort on my own account. I rejoiced unspeakably in this opening, and wrote home in high satisfaction at the offer which would enable my young sister,— then only eighteen,—to remain at home, pursuing her studies in companionship with a beloved cousin of nearly her own age, and gaining something like maturity and self-reliance before going out into the cold dark sphere of governessing. But, to my disappointment,—I might almost say, horror,—my mother sent me peremptory orders to go home, and to fill the place which my poor young sister was to vacate. I rather wonder that, being seven and twenty years old, I did not assert my independence, and refuse to return,—so clear as was, in my eyes, the injustice of remanding me to a position of helplessness and dependence, when a career of action and independence was opening before me. If I had known what my young sister was thinking and feeling, I believe I should have taken my own way, for her sake: but I did not know all: the instinct and habit of old obedience prevailed, and I went home, with some resentment, but far more grief and desolation in my heart. My mother afterwards looked back with surprise upon the peremptoriness with which she had assumed the direction of my affairs; and she told me, (what I had suspected before) that my well-meaning hostess, who knew nothing of literature, and was always perplexing me with questions as to 'how much I should get' by each night's work, had advised my return home, to pursue,—not literature but needlework, by which, she wrote, I had proved that I could earn money, and in which career I should always have the encouragement and support of herself and her family. (Nothing could be more gracious than the acknowledgment of their mistake volunteered by this family at a subsequent time.) My mother was wont to be guided by them, whenever they offered their counsel; and this time it cost me very dear. I went down to Norwich, without prospect,—without any apparent chance of independence; but as fully resolved against being dependent as at any time before or after.

My mother received me very tenderly. She had no other idea at the moment than that she had been doing her best for my good; and I, for my part, could not trust myself to utter a word of what was swelling in my heart. I arrived worn and weary with a night journey; and my mother was so uneasy at my looks that she made me lie down on her bed after breakfast, and, as I could not sleep, came and sat by me for a talk.—My news was that the Central Unitarian Association had advertized for prize Essays, by which Unitarianism was to be presented to the notice of Catholics, Jews, and Mohammedans. The Catholic one was to be adjudicated on at the end of September (1830) and the other two in the following March. Three sub-committees were appointed for the examination of the manuscripts sent in, and for decision on them: and these sub-committees were composed of different members, to bar all suspicion of partiality. The essays were to be superscribed with a motto;

and the motto was to be repeated on a sealed envelope, containing the writer's name, which was not to be looked at till the prize was awarded; and then only in the case of the successful candidate. The prizes were, ten guineas for the Catholic, fifteen for the Jewish, and twenty for the Mohammedan essay. I told my mother, as she sat by the bedside, of this gleam of a prospect for me; and she replied that she thought it might be as well to try for one prize. My reply was 'If I try at all, it shall be for all.' The money reward was trifling, even in the eyes of one so poor and prospectless as I was; but I felt an earnest desire to ascertain whether I could write, as Mr. Fox and other personal friends said I could. I saw that it was a capital opportunity for a fair trial of my competency in comparison with others; and I believe it was no small consideration to me that I should thus, at all events, tide over many months before I need admit despair. My mother thought this rather desperate work; but she gave me her sympathy and encouragement during the whole period of suspense,—as did the dear old aunt who lived with us. No one else was to know; and my secret was perfectly kept. The day after my return, I began to collect my materials; and before the week was done, I had drawn out the scheme of my Essay, and had begun it. It was done within a month; and then had to be copied, lest any member of the sub-committee should know my hand. I discovered a poor school-boy who wrote a good hand; and I paid him a sovereign which I could ill spare for his work. The parcel was sent in a circuitous way to the office in London: and then, while waiting in suspense, I wrote the Tale called 'Five Years of Youth,'[1] which I have never looked at since, and have certainly no inclination to read. Messrs. Darton and Harvey gave me twenty pounds for this; and most welcome was such a sum at that time. It set me forward through the toil of the Mohammedan Essay, which I began in October, I think. The 'Monthly Repository' for October contained a notification that the sub-committee sitting on the first of the three occasions had adjudged the prize for the Catholic Essay to me; and the money was presently forwarded. That announcement arrived on a Sunday morning and again I had a charming walk over Mousehold, as in the year before, among the heather and the bright tormentilla.

Next day, I went to the Public Library, and brought home Sale's Koran.[2] A friend whom I met said 'What do you bore yourself with

---

[1]   *Five Years of Youth, or, Sense and Sentiment* (London: Harvey and Darton, 1831).

[2]   George Sale, trans., *The Koran, commonly called the Alcoran of Mohammed, tr. into English immediately from the original Arabic; with explanatory notes, taken from the most approved commentators. To which is prefixed a preliminary discourse.* (London: J. Wilcox, 1734).

that book for? You will never get through it.' He little guessed what I meant to get out of it, and out of Sale's preliminary Essay. It occurred to me that the apologue form[1] would suit the subject best; and I ventured upon it, though fearing that such daring might be fatal. One of the sub-committee, an eminent scholar, told me afterwards that it was this which mainly influenced his suffrage in my favour. In five weeks, the work was done: but my tribulation about its preparation lasted much longer; for the careless young usher who undertook the copying was not only idle but saucy; and it was doubtful to the last day whether the parcel could be in London by the first of March. Some severe threatening availed however; and that and the Jewish Essay, sent round by different hands (the hands of strangers to the whole scheme) done up in different shapes, and in different kinds of paper, and sealed with different wax and seals, were deposited at the office on the last day of February. The Jewish Essay was beautifully copied by a poor woman who wrote a clerk-like hand. The titles of the three Essays were—

'The Essential Faith of the Universal Church' (to Catholics).

'The Faith as Unfolded by Many Prophets' (to Mohammedans).

'The Faith as Manifested through Israel' (to Jews).

The last of these was grounded on Lessing's 'Hundred Thoughts on the Education of the Human Race,'[2] which had taken my fancy amazingly, in the course of my German studies,—fancy then being the faculty most concerned in my religious views. Though my mind was already largely prepared for this piece of work by study, and by having treated the theory in the 'Monthly Repository,' and though I enjoyed the task in a certain sense, it became very onerous before it was done. I was by that time nearly as thin as possible; and I dreamed of the destruction of Jerusalem, and saw the burning of the Temple, almost every night. I might well be exhausted by that great and portentous first of March; for the year had been one of tremendous labour. I think it was in that year that a prize was offered by some Unitarian authority or other for any Essay on Baptism, for which I competed, but came in only third. If that was the year, my work stood thus:—my literary work, I mean; for, in that season of poverty, I made and mended everything

---

[1]   A moral fable.

[2]   Gotthold Ephraim Lessing's *Die Erziehung des Menschengeschlechts (Education of the Human Race*, 1780) provided Martineau with the material for a four-part essay in the *MR* 4, N.S. (1830), 300–06, 367–73, 453–58, 511–17, later included in *Miscellanies*, 2: 296–343. She refers to the title as "Hundred Thoughts" because it was translated and condensed under that title in the *MR* 1 (1806), 412–20, 467–73.

I wore, —knitting stockings while reading aloud to my mother and aunt, and never sitting idle a minute. I may add that I made considerable progress in the study of German that year. My writings within the twelve months were as follows:
'Traditions of Palestine' (except the first tale).
'Five Years of Youth.'
Seven tracts for Houlston.
Essay on Baptism.
Three Theological Essays for prizes, and
Fifty-two articles for the 'Monthly Repository.'
By this time my mother was becoming aware of the necessity of my being a good deal in London, if I was to have any chance in the field of literature; and she consented to spare me for three months in the spring of every year. An arrangement was made for my boarding at the house of a cousin[1] for three months from the first of March; and up I went, little dreaming what would be happening, and how life would be opening before me, by that day twelvemonths. One of my objects in the first instance was improving myself in German. An admirable master brought me forward very rapidly, on extremely low terms, in consideration of my helping him with his English prefaces to some of his works. After a few weeks of hard work, writing and studying, I accepted an invitation to spend a few days with some old friends in Kent. There I refreshed myself among pretty scenery, fresh air, and pleasant drives with hospitable friends, and with the study of Faust at night, till a certain day, early in May, which was to prove very eventful to me. I returned on the outside of the coach, and got down, with my heavy bag, at my German master's door, where I took a lesson. It was very hot; and I dragged myself and my bag home, in great fatigue, and very hungry. Dinner was ordered up again by my hostess, and I sat an hour, eating my dinner, resting and talking. Then I was leaving the room, bonnet in hand, when a daughter of my hostess seemed to recollect something, and called after me to say, 'O, I forgot! I suppose' (she was a very slow and hesitating speaker)—'I suppose......you know......you know about......those prizes......those prize essays, you know.'
'No......not I! What do you mean?'
'O! well, we thought.........we thought you knew......'
'Well,—but what?'

---

[1]   Most likely, a child of Peter or John Martineau, brewers and sugar refiners in London. Several of their sons carried on this business.

'O? you have......why....... you have got all the prizes.'

'Why J! why did you not tell me so before?'

'O! I thought ......I thought you might know.'

'How should I,—just up from the country? But what do you know?'

'Why, only......only the Secretary of the Unitarian Association has been here,—with a message,—with the news from the Committee.'— It was even so.

The next day was the Unitarian May Meeting; and I had come up from Kent to attend it. I was shocked to hear, after the morning service, that, in reading the Report in the evening, the whole story of the Essays must be told, with the announcement of the result. I had reckoned for weeks on that meeting, at which Rammohun Roy was to be present, and where the speaking was expected to be particularly interesting; and I neither liked to stay away nor to encounter the telling of my story. Mr. and Mrs. Fox promised to put me into a quiet pew if I would go as soon as the gates were opened. I did so; but the Secretary came, among others, to be introduced, and to congratulate; and I knew when the dreaded moment was coming, amidst his reading of the Report, by a glance which he sent in my direction, to see if his wife, who sat next me, was keeping up my attention. I thought the story of all the measures and all the precautions taken by the various Committees the longest I had ever sat under, and the silence with which it was listened to the very deadest. I heard little indeed but the beating of my own heart. Then came the catastrophe, and the clapping and the 'Hear! Hear!' I knew that many of my family connexions must be present, who would be surprised and gratified. But there was one person more than I expected. I slipped out before the meeting was over, and in the vestibule was met by my young sister with open arms, and with an offer to go home with me for the night. She was in the midst of an uncomfortable brief experiment of governessing, a few miles from town, and had been kindly indulged with a permission to go to this meeting, too late to let me know. She had arrived late, and got into the gallery; and before she had been seated many minutes, heard my news, so strangely told! She went home with me; and, after we had written my mother the account of the day, we talked away nearly all the rest of that May night.—It was truly a great event to me,—the greatest since my brother's reception of my first attempt in print. I had now found that I could write, and I might rationally believe that authorship was my legitimate career.

Of course, I had no conception at that time of the thorough weakness and falseness of the views I had been conveying with so much pains and so much complacency. This last act in connexion with the Unitarian

body was a *bonâ fide* one; but all was prepared for that which ensued,—
a withdrawal from the body through those regions of metaphysical fog
in which most deserters from Unitarianism abide for the rest of their
time. The Catholic essay was ignorant and metaphysical, if my recollection of it is at all correct; and the other two mere fancy pieces: and I can
only say that if either Mohammedans or Jews have ever been converted
by them, such converts can hardly be rational enough to be worth having.
I had now plunged fairly into the spirit of my time,—that of self-analy-
sis, pathetic self-pity, typical interpretation of objective matters, and
scheme-making, in the name of God and Man. That such was the stage
then reached by my mind, in its struggles upward and onward, there is
outstanding proof in that series of papers called 'Sabbath Musings' which
may be found in the 'Monthly Repository' of 1831.[1] There are the papers:
and I hereby declare that I considered them my best production, and
expected they would outlive every thing else I had written or should
write. I was, in truth, satisfied that they were very fine writing, and
believed it for long after,—little aware that the time could ever come
when I should write them down, as I do now, to be morbid, fantastical,
and therefore unphilosophical and untrue. I cannot wonder that it did
not occur to the Unitarians (as far as they thought of me at all) that I was
really not of them, at the time that I had picked up their gauntlet, and
assumed their championship. If it did not occur to me, no wonder it did
not to them. But the clear-sighted among them might and should have
seen, by the evidence of those essays themselves, that I was one of those
merely nominal Christians who refuse whatever they see to be impossible, absurd or immoral in the scheme or the records of Christianity, and
pick out and appropriate what they like, or interpolate it with views,
desires and imaginations of their own. I had already ceased to be an
Unitarian in the technical sense. I was now one in the dreamy way of
metaphysical accommodation, and on the ground of dissent from every
other form of Christianity: the time was approaching when, if I called
myself so at all, it was only in the free-thinking sense. Then came a few
years during which I remonstrated with Unitarians in vain against being
claimed by them, which I considered even more injurious to them than
to me. They were unwilling, as they said, and as I saw, to recognize the
complete severance of the theological bond between us: and I was careful to assert, in every practicable way, that it was no doing of mine if they
were taunted by the orthodox with their sectarian fellowship with the

---

[1]   Reprinted in the *Miscellanies*, 1:122–67.

writer of 'Eastern Life.'[1] At length, I hope and believe my old co-religionists understand and admit that I disclaim their theology *in toto*, and that by no twisting of language or darkening of its meanings can I be made out to have any thing whatever in common with them about religious matters. I perceive that they do not at all understand my views or the grounds of them, or the road to them: but they will not deny that I understand theirs,—chosen expositor as I was of them in the year 1831; and they must take my word for it that there is nothing in common between their theology and my philosophy. Our stand-point is different; and all our views and estimates are different accordingly. Of course, I consider my stand-point the truer one; and my views and estimates the higher, wider, and more accurate, as I shall have occasion to show. I consider myself the best qualified of the two parties to judge of the relative value of the views of either, because I have the experience of both, while I see that they have no comprehension of mine: but the point on which we may and ought to agree is that my severance from their faith was complete and necessarily final when I wrote 'Eastern Life,' though many of them could not be brought to admit it, nor some (whom I asked) to assert it at the time. While I saw that many Unitarians resented as a slander the popular imputation that their sect is 'a harbourage for infidels,' I did not choose that they should have that said of them in my case: and it is clear that if they were unwilling to exchange a disownment with me, they could have no right to quarrel with that imputation in future.

SECTION IV

My prize-money enabled me to go to Dublin, to visit my brother James and his wife;[2] and I stayed there till September,—writing all the time, and pondering the scheme of my Political Economy Series. I sketched out my plan in a very small blue book which was afterwards begged of me as a relic by a friend who was much with me at that time. My own idea was that my stories should appear quarterly. My brother and the publishers urged their

---

[1]   *Eastern Life, Present and Past.* 3 vols. (London: Edward Moxon, 1848).
[2]   James married Helen Higginson (1808–74) in 1828, and became co-minister at the Presbyterian Eustace Street Chapel in Dublin; in 1832 he moved to Liverpool to become minister at the Paradise Street Chapel.

being monthly. The idea was overwhelming at first: and there were times when truly I was scared at other parts of the scheme than that. The whole business was the strongest act of will that I ever committed myself to; and my will was always a pretty strong one. I could never have even started my project but for my thorough, well-considered, steady conviction that the work was wanted,—was even craved by the popular mind. As the event proved me right, there is no occasion to go into the evidence which determined my judgment. I now believed that for two years I must support an almost unequalled amount of literary labour: that, owing to the nature of some of the subjects to be treated, my effort would probably be fatal to my reputation: that the chances of failure in a scheme of such extent, begun without money or interest, were most formidable; and that failure would be ruin. I staked my all upon this project, in fact, and with the belief that long, weary months must pass before I could even discern the probabilities of the issue; for the mere preparations must occupy months. In the first place,—in that autumn of 1831,—I strengthened myself in certain resolutions,[1] from which I promised myself that no power on earth should draw me away. I was resolved that, in the first place, the thing should be done. The people wanted the book; and they should have it. Next, I resolved to sustain my health under the suspense, if possible, by keeping up a mood of steady determination, and unfaltering hope. Next, I resolved never to lose my temper, in the whole course of the business. I knew I was right; and people who are aware that they are in the right need never lose temper. Lastly, I resolved to refuse, under any temptation whatever, to accept any loan from my kind mother and aunt. I felt that I could never get over causing them any pecuniary loss,—my mother having really nothing to spare, and my aunt having been abundantly generous to the family already. My own small remnant of property (which came to nothing after all) I determined to risk; and, when the scheme began to take form, I accepted small loans from two opulent friends, whom I was able presently to repay. They knew the risks as well as I; and they were men of business; and there was no reason for declining the timely aid, so freely and kindly granted. What those months of suspense were like, it is necessary now to tell.

I wrote to two or three publishers from Dublin, opening my scheme; but one after another declined having any thing to do with it, on the ground of the disturbed state of the public mind, which afforded no encouragement to put out new books. The bishops had recently thrown out the Reform Bill; and every body was watching the progress of the

---

[1]   See her private memorandum of 1829, Appendix B.

Cholera,—then regarded with as much horror as a plague of the middle ages.[1] The terrifying Order in Council[2] which froze men's hearts by its doleful commands and recommendations, was issued just at the same time with my poor proposals; and no wonder that I met only refusals. Messrs. Baldwin and Cradock,[3] however, requested me to take London on my way back to Norwich, that we might discuss the subject. I did so; and I took with me as a witness a lawyer cousin who told me long afterwards what an amusing scene it was to him. Messrs. Baldwin and Cradock sat superb in their arm-chairs, in their brown wigs, looking as cautious as possible, but relaxing visibly under the influence of my confidence. My cousin[4] said that, in their place, he should have felt my confidence a sufficient guarantee,—so fully as I assigned the grounds of it: and Messrs. Baldwin and Cradock seemed to be nearly of the same mind, though they brought out a long string of objections, beginning with my proposed title, and ending with the Reform Bill and the Cholera. They wanted to suppress the words Political Economy altogether: but I knew that science could not be smuggled in anonymously. I gave up the point for the time, feeling assured that they would find their smuggling scheme impracticable. 'Live and let live' was *their* title; and its inadequacy was vexatious enough, as showing their imperfect conception of the plan: but it was necessary to let them have their own way in the matter of preliminary advertising. They put out a sort of feeler in the form of an advertisement in some of the Diffusion Society's publications;[5] but an intimation so

---

[1]   The Reform Act of 1832 was fiercely opposed by the Tories and passed only after William IV created additional peers to enable its passage through the House of Lords; the Act abolished rotten and pocket boroughs, redistributed 143 seats in the House of Commons to large towns and industrial cities, and extended the vote to all male householders paying an annual rent of £10 or more. The cholera of 1831, first noticed in India in 1817, became a lethal epidemic when it reached England late in 1831; cholera epidemics occurred again in 1848 and 1853–54. One positive consequence was the sanitary reform movement, established in the 1830s and known for the *Report on the Sanitary Conditions of the Labouring Population of Great Britain* (1842), authored by Edwin Chadwick.

[2]   Issued by the sovereign in times of war or other emergencies when normal parliamentary procedure would be too slow to take necessary action.

[3]   Baldwin and Craddock, 47 Paternoster Row, London, were the regular publishers of the SDUK's didactic literature (see n. 5 below).

[4]   Richard Martineau (1804–65), with whom she stayed while pursuing a London publisher.

[5]   The Society for the Diffusion of Useful Knowledge (SDUK) operated from 1826 to 1848 and aimed to "impart useful information to all classes of the community." It was a secular version of the Society for the Promotion of Christian Knowledge (SPCK), founded in 1698 to distribute cheap religious tracts throughout the United Kingdom, and the Society for the Propagation of Christian Knowledge (SPCK), founded in 1701 to promote the work of the Anglican Church in the colonies.

vague and obscure attracted no notice. This melancholy fact Messrs. Baldwin and Cradock duly and dolefully announced to me. Still, they did not let go for some time; and I afterwards heard that they were so near becoming my publishers that they had actually engaged a stitcher[1] for my monthly numbers. Fortunately for me, as it turned out, but most discouragingly at the time, they withdrew, after a hesitation of many weeks. They had read and approved of a part of the manuscript of 'Life in the Wilds,'— my first number: but they went on doubting; and at last wrote to me that, considering the public excitement about the Reform Bill and the Cholera, they dared not venture.

Here was the whole work to begin again. I stifled my sighs, and swallowed my tears, and wrote to one publisher after another, receiving instant refusals from all, except Messrs. Whittaker.[2] They kept up the negotiation for a few posts, but at length joined the general chorus about the Reform Bill and the Cholera. They offered, however, to do their best for the work as mere publishers, on the usual terms of commission.[3] My mother and aunt re-urged my accepting a loan from them of money which they were willing to risk in such a cause: but of course I would not hear of this. Mr. Fox appeared at that time earnest in the project; and a letter from him came by the same post with Messrs. Whittakers' last, saying that booksellers might be found to share the risk; and he named one (who, like Baldwin and Cradock, afterwards failed) who would be likely to go halves with me in risk and profit. I did not much relish either the plan or the proposed publisher; but I was in no condition to refuse suggestions. I said to my mother, 'You know what a man of business would do in my case.'—'What?'—'Go up to town by the next mail, and see what is to be done.'—'My dear, you would not think of doing such a thing, alone, and in this weather!'—'I wish it.'—'Well, then, let us show Henry the letters after dinner, and see what he will say.'—As soon as the cloth was removed, and we had drawn round the fire, I showed my brother Henry the letters, with the same remark I had made to my mother. He sat looking into the fire for several minutes, while nobody spoke: and then he turned to me, and

---

[1]   To bind the printed pages into a booklet.

[2]   The London publisher Whittaker, Treacher, & Arnot.

[3]   In this arrangement, the author bears the financial risk of publication, pays the publisher a set cost or percentage of profits, and takes whatever profit or loss results. Although Martineau published her first book, *Devotional Exercises* (1823), this way, it was not considered a professional arrangement in the 1830s, when sale of copyright and half profits were the more common modes.

said oracularly 'Go!'—I sprang up,—sent to have my place taken by the early morning coach, tied up and dispatched borrowed books, and then ran to my room to pack. There I found a fire, and my trunk airing before it. All was finished an hour before tea time; and I was at leisure to read to my old ladies for the rest of the evening. On my mother observing that she could not have done it, my aunt patted me on the shoulder, and said that, at least, the back was fitted to the burden. This domestic sympathy was most supporting to me; but, at the same time, it rendered success more stringently necessary.

My scheme of going to London was not at all a wild one, unless the speed of the movement, and the state of the weather made it so. It was the beginning of December, foggy and sleety. I was always sure of a home in London, with or without notice; and without notice I presented myself at my cousin's door that dreary December Saturday night.[1] It was a great Brewery house, always kept open, and cooking daily going on, for the use of the partners. My kind cousin and his family were to leave home the next morning, for three weeks: but, as he observed, this would rather aid than hinder my purposes, as I went for work. I was really glad to be alone during those three eventful weeks,—feeling myself no intruder, all the while, and being under the care of attentive servants.

My first step on Monday was seeing the publisher mentioned by Mr. Fox. He shook his head; his wife smiled; and he begged to see the opening chapters, promising to return them, with a reply, in twenty-four hours. His reply was what was already burnt in upon my brain. He had 'no doubt of the excellence,—wished it success—but feared that the excitement of the public mind about the Reform Bill and the Cholera would afford it no chance,' &c., &c. I was growing as sick of the Reform Bill as poor King William himself. I need not detail, even if I could remember, the many applications I made in the course of the next few days. Suffice it that they were all unsuccessful, and for the same alleged reasons. Day after day, I came home weary with disappointment, and with trudging many miles through the clay of the streets, and the fog of the gloomiest December I ever saw. I came home only to work; for I must be ready with two first numbers in case of a publisher turning up any day. All the while, too, I was as determined as ever that my scheme should be fulfilled. Night after night, the Brewery clock struck twelve, while the pen was still pushing on in my trembling hand. I had prom-

---

[1]   Richard Martineau, Managing Director of Whitbred's Brewery, lived in Chiswell Street, near Liverpool Street railway station and the current Barbican Arts Centre.

ised to take one day's rest, and dine and sleep at the Foxes'. Then, for the
first time, I gave way, in spite of all my efforts. Some trifle having touched
my feelings before saying 'Good-night,' the sluices burst open, and I cried
all night. In the morning, Mr. Fox looked at me with great concern,
stepped into the next room, and brought a folded paper to the breakfast
table, saying 'Don't read this now. I can't bear it. These are what may be
called terms from my brother.' (A young bookseller who did not pretend
to have any business, at that time.)[1] 'I do not ask you even to consider
them; but they will enable you to tell publishers that you hold in your
hand terms offered by a publisher: and this may at least procure attention to your scheme.' These were, to the subsequent regret of half a score
of publishers, the terms on which my work was issued at last.

I immediately returned to town, and went straight to Whittakers'.
Mr. Whittaker looked bored, fidgeted, yawned, and then said, with
extreme rudeness, 'I have told you already that these are not times for
new enterprises.' 'Then,' said I, rising, 'it is now time for me to consider
the terms from another publisher which I hold in my hand.' 'O, indeed,
—really, Ma'am?' said he, reviving. 'Do me the favour to give me a short
time for consideration. Only twenty-four hours, Ma'am.' I refreshed his
memory about the particulars, and endeavoured to make him see why
the times were not unseasonable for this special work, though they
might be for light literature.

It was next necessary to look at the paper I had been carrying. I read
it with dismay. The very first stipulation was that the work should be
published by subscription: and, moreover, the subscription must be for
five hundred copies before the work began. Subscribers were to be
provided by both parties; and Charles Fox was to have half the profits,
besides the usual bookseller's commission and privileges. The agreement was to cease at the end of any five numbers, at the wish of either
party. As Charles Fox had neither money nor connexion, I felt that the
whole risk was thrown upon me; and that I should have all the peril, as
well as the toil, while Charles Fox would enjoy the greater part of the
proceeds, in case of success, and be just where he was before, in case of
failure. In fact, he never procured a single subscriber; and he told me
afterwards that he knew from the beginning that he never should. After
pondering this heart-sickening Memorandum, I looked with no small
anxiety for Whittakers' final reply. I seemed to see the dreaded words

---

[1] Charles Fox (1794–1864), younger brother of W.J. Fox, was a bookseller in Paternoster
Row, London, primarily of Unitarian materials and reprints from the *Monthly Repository*.

through the envelope; and there they were within. Mr. Whittaker expressed his 'regrets that the public mind being so engrossed with the Reform Bill and the approach of the Cholera,' &c., &c. The same story to the end! Even now, in this low depth of disappointment, there were lower depths to be explored. The fiercest trial was now at hand.

I remonstrated strongly with Mr. Fox about the subscription stipulation; but in vain. The mortification to my pride was not the worst part of it, though that was severe enough. I told him that I could not stoop to that method, if any other means were left; to which he replied 'You will stoop to conquer.'[1] But he had no consolation to offer under the far more serious anxiety which I strove to impress on his mind as my main objection to the scheme. Those persons from whom I might hope for pecuniary support were precisely those to whom I despaired of conveying any conception of my aim, or of the object and scope of my work. Those who would, I believed, support it were, precisely, persons who had never seen or heard of me, and whose support could not be solicited. My view was the true one, as I might prove by many pages of anecdote. Suffice it that, at the very time when certain members of parliament were eagerly inquiring about the announced work, the wife of one of them, a rich lady of my acquaintance, to whom a prospectus had been sent, returned it, telling me that she 'knew too well what she was about to buy a pig in a poke:'[2] and the husband of a cousin of mine, a literary man in his way, sent me, in return for the prospectus, a letter, enclosing two sovereigns, and a lecture against my rashness and presumption in supposing that I was adequate to such work as authorship, and offering the enclosed sum as his mite towards the subscription; but recommending rather a family subscription which might eke out my earnings by my needle.[3] I returned the two sovereigns, with a declaration that I wished for no subscribers but those who expected full value for their payment, and that I would depend upon my needle and upon charity when I found I could not do better, and not before. This gentleman apologised handsomely afterwards. The lady never did. It should be remembered that it is easy enough to laugh at these incidents now; but

---

[1] Echoing the title Oliver Goldsmith's 1773 play, *She Stoops to Conquer*, about a young woman who disguises herself to discover the character and intentions of a potential husband—not a particularly apt allusion for Martineau's endeavor.

[2] A "poke" is a bag; thus, a blind bargain, something bought sight unseen, without knowing its worth.

[3] Unidentified; possibly Francis Fletcher, husband of Marriott Martineau (1799–1883), and a minor writer.

that it was a very different matter then, when success seemed to be growing more and more questionable and difficult every day. I had no
resource, however, but to try the method I heartily disapproved and
abhorred. I drew up a Prospectus, in which I avoided all mention of a
subscription, in the hope that it might soon be dispensed with, but fully
explanatory of the nature and object of the work. To this I added in my
own handwriting an urgent appeal to all whom I could ask to be
subscribers. I went to Mr. Fox's, one foggy morning, to show him one
of these, and the advertisement intended for the next day's papers,
announcing the first of February as the day of publication: (for it was
now too late to open with the year). I found Mr. Fox in a mood as
gloomy as the day. He had seen Mr. James Mill, who had assured him
that my method of exemplification,—(the grand principle of the whole
scheme) could not possibly succeed; and Mr. Fox now required of me
to change my plan entirely, and issue my Political Economy in a didactic form![1] Of course, I refused. He started a multitude of objections,—
feared every thing, and hoped nothing. I saw, with anguish and no little
resentment, my last poor chance slipping from me. I commanded myself
while in his presence. The occasion was too serious to be misused. I said
to him 'I see you have taken fright. If you wish that your brother should
draw back, say so now. Here is the advertisement. Make up your mind
before it goes to press.' He replied, 'I do not wish altogether to draw
back.' 'Yes, you do,' said I: 'and I had rather you would say so at once. But
I tell you this——the people want this book, and they *shall* have it.' 'I
know that is your intention,' he replied: 'but I own I do not see how it
is to come to pass.'—'Nor I: but it *shall*. So, say that you have done with
it, and I will find other means.' 'I tell you, I do not wish altogether to
draw out of it; but I cannot think of my brother going on without decisive success at the outset.' 'What do you mean, precisely?' 'I mean that
he withdraws at the end of two numbers, unless the success of the work
is secured in a fortnight.' 'What do you mean by success being secured?'
'You must sell a thousand in a fortnight.' 'In a fortnight! That is unreasonable! Is this your ultimatum?' 'Yes.' 'We shall not sell a thousand in the
first fortnight: nevertheless, the work shall not stop at two numbers. It
shall go on to five, with or without your brother.' 'So I perceive you say.'
'What is to be done with this advertisement?' I inquired. 'Shall I send
it,—yes or no?' 'Yes: but remember Charles gives up at the end of two
numbers, unless you sell a thousand in the first fortnight.'

---

[1]   In a non-narrative form, using abstract principles or question-and-answer.

I set out to walk the four miles and a half to the Brewery. I could not afford to ride, more or less; but, weary already, I now felt almost too ill to walk at all. On the road, not far from Shoreditch,[1] I became too giddy to stand without support; and I leaned over some dirty palings, pretending to look at a cabbage bed, but saying to myself, as I stood with closed eyes, 'My book will do yet.' I moved on as soon as I could, apprehending that the passers-by took me to be drunk: but the pavement swam before my eyes so that I was glad enough to get to the Brewery. I tried to eat some dinner; but the vast rooms, the plate and the liveried servant were too touching a contrast to my present condition; and I was glad to go to work, to drown my disappointment in a flow of ideas. Perhaps the piece of work that I did may show that I succeeded. I wrote the Preface to my 'Illustrations of Political Economy' that evening; and I hardly think that any one would discover from it that I had that day sunk to the lowest point of discouragement about my scheme.—At eleven o'clock, I sent the servants to bed. I finished the Preface just after the Brewery clock had struck two. I was chilly and hungry: the lamp burned low, and the fire was small. I knew it would not do to go to bed, to dream over again the bitter disappointment of the morning. I began now, at last, to doubt whether my work would ever see the light. I thought of the multitudes who needed it,—and especially of the poor,—to assist them in managing their own welfare. I thought too of my own conscious power of doing this very thing. Here was the thing wanting to be done, and I wanting to do it; and the one person who had seemed best to understand the whole affair now urged me to give up either the whole scheme, or, what was worse, its main principle! It was an inferior consideration, but still, no small matter to me, that I had no hope or prospect of usefulness or independence if this project failed: and I did not feel that night that I could put my heart into any that might arise. As the fire crumbled, I put it together till nothing but dust and ashes remained; and when the lamp went out, I lighted the chamber candle; but at last it was necessary to go to bed; and at four o'clock I went, after crying for two hours, with my feet on the fender. I cried in bed till six, when I fell asleep; but I was at the breakfast table by half-past eight, and ready for the work of the day.

The work of the day was to prepare and send out my Circulars. After preparing enough for my family, I took into my confidence the before-

---

[1]   Finsbury, where W.J. Fox lived, is north of the city of London; Shoreditch, once a village on the old Roman road to London, was then as now part of urban London, north of Liverpool Street station and near Martineau's cousin's house.

mentioned cousin,—my benefactor and my host at that time. He was regarded by the whole clan as a prudent and experienced man of business; and I knew that his countenance would be of great value to me. That countenance he gave me, and some good suggestions, and no discouragement. —It was very disagreeable to have to appeal to monied relations whose very confidence and generosity would be a burden on my mind till I had redeemed my virtual pledges; while the slightest indulgence of a critical spirit by any of them must be exceedingly injurious to my enterprise. It was indeed not very long before I had warnings from various quarters that some of my relations were doing me 'more harm by their tongues than they could ever do good by their guineas.' This was true, as the censors themselves have since spontaneously and handsomely told me. I could not blame them much for saying what they thought of my rashness and conceit, while I cordially honour the candour of their subsequent confession: but their sayings were so much added to the enormous obstructions of the case. From my first act of appeal to my monied relations, however, I derived such singular solace that every incident remains fresh in my mind, and I may fairly indulge in going over it once more.

My oldest surviving uncle and his large family, living near Clapham,[1] had always been ready and kind in their sympathy; and I was now to find the worth of it more than ever in connexion with the greatest of my enterprises. On the next Sunday, I returned with them when they went home from Chapel. While at luncheon, my uncle told me that he understood I had some new plan, and he was anxious to know what it was. His daughters proposed that I should explain it after dinner, when their brothers would be present. After dinner, accordingly, I was called upon for my explanation, which I gave in a very detailed way. All were silent, waiting for my uncle to make his remark, the very words of which I distinctly remember, at the distance of nearly a quarter of a century. In his gentle and gracious manner he said, 'You are a better judge, my dear, than we of this scheme; but we know that your industry and energy are the pride of us all, and ought to have our support.' When we ladies went to the drawing-room, I knew there would be a consultation between my uncle and his sons: and so there was. At the close of the pleasant evening, he beckoned to me, and made me sit beside him on the sofa, and told me of the confidence of his family and himself that what I was doing would be very

---

[1]   David Martineau (1754–1841), of Stockwell Common, Clapham, had three living sons and six unmarried daughters (which should bring the total number of subscriptions to seventeen).

useful: that his daughters wished for each a copy of the Series, his sons two each; and that he himself must have five. 'And,' he concluded, 'as you will like to pay your printer immediately, you shall not wait for our money.' So saying, he slipped a packet of bank notes and gold into my hand, to the amount of payment for fourteen copies of the whole series! To complete the grace of his hospitality, he told me that he should go to town late the next morning, and would escort me; and he desired me to sleep as late as I liked. And I did sleep,—the whole night through, and awoke a new creature. Other members of the family did what they thought proper, in the course of the week; and then I had only to go home, and await the result.

I was rather afraid to show myself to my mother,—thin as I was, and yellow, and coughing with every breath; and she was panic-struck at the evident symptoms of liver-complaint which the first half-hour disclosed. I was indeed in wretched health; and during the month of April following, when I was writing 'Demerara,' I was particularly ill. I do not think I was ever well again till, at the close of 1833, I was entirely laid aside, and confined to my bed for a month, by inflammation of the liver. I am confident that that serious illness began with the toils and anxieties, and long walks in fog and mud, of two years before. My mother took my health in hand anxiously and most tenderly. In spite of my entreaties, she would never allow me to be wakened in the morning; and on Sundays, the day when Charles Fox's dispatches came by a manufacturer's parcel, my breakfast was sent up to me, and I was not allowed to rise till the middle of the day. For several weeks I dreaded the arrival of the publisher's weekly letter. He always wrote gloomily, and sometimes rudely. The subscription proceeded very little better than I had anticipated. From first to last, about three hundred copies were subscribed for: and before that number had been reached, the success of the work was such as to make the subscription a mere burden. It was a thoroughly vexatious part of the business altogether,— that subscription. A clever suggestion of mother's, at this time, had, I believe, much to do with the immediate success of the book. By her advice, I sent, by post, a copy of my Prospectus (without a word about subscription in it) to almost every member of both Houses of Parliament. There was nothing of puffery in this,—nothing that I had the least objection to do. It was merely informing our legislators that a book was coming out on their particular class of subjects.

I may as well mention in this place, that I had offered (I cannot at all remember when) one of my tales,—the one which now stands as

'Brooke and Brooke Farm,'—to the Diffusion Society, whence it had been returned. Absurd as were some of the stories afterwards set afloat about this transaction, there was thus much foundation for them. Mr. Knight,[1] then the publisher of the Society, sent me a note of cordial and generous encouragement; but a sub-committee, to whose judgment the manuscript was consigned, thought it 'dull,' and pronounced against its reception accordingly. I knew nothing about this sub-committee, or about the method employed, and had in fact forgotten, among so many failures, that particular one, when, long after, I found to my regret and surprise, that the gentlemen concerned had been supposing me offended and angry all the while, and somehow an accomplice in Lord Brougham's mockery of their decision. In vain I told them that I now thought them perfectly right to form and express their own judgment, and that I had never before heard who had been my judges. I fear the soreness remains in their minds to this day, though there never was any in mine. Lord Brougham's words travelled far and wide,[2] and were certainly anything but comfortable to the sub-committee. He said he should revive the torture for their sakes, as hanging was too good for them. He tore his hair over the tales, he added, unable to endure that the whole Society, 'instituted for the very purpose, should be driven out of the field by a little deaf woman at Norwich.'—As I have said, I cannot remember at what time I made my application; but I imagine it must have been during that eventful year 1831,—in which case the writing of that story must come into the estimate of the work of that year.

A cheering incident occurred during the interval of awaiting the effects of the Circular. Every body knows that the Gurneys are the great bankers of Norwich.[3] Richard Hanbury Gurney, at that time one of

---

[1] The publisher Charles Knight (1791–1873), of Ludgate Street, London, was known for his efforts to make educational literature available to the working classes at cheap prices; he later published Martineau's *History of England during the Thirty Years' Peace, 1816–1846* (1849–50), a book he had started but found himself unable to complete, and her *Introduction to the History of the Peace, from 1800 to 1815* (1851).

[2] Lord Brougham chided the SDUK for failing to accept her proposal for the *Illustrations of Political Economy*, saying that a deaf woman from Norwich was doing more good than any man in the country. In a letter to Macvey Napier (1777–1847), editor of the *Edinburgh Review*, he noted that her tales "are of the highest merit, and indeed are of very great importance … and she has the best feelings and, generally, the most current principles of any of our political economists" (quoted in Valerie Pichanick, *Harriet Martineau: The Woman and her Work, 1802–1876* [Ann Arbor: U of Michigan P, 1980], 68–69).

[3] Quaker family that included the Gurneys of Earlham Hall, Norfolk, and Richard Hanbury Gurney (1783–1854) of Thickthorn Hall, Nethersett, who was the senior partner in his family's Norwich bank and M.P. for Norwich in 1818–26 and 1830–32.

the Members for Norfolk, was in the firm; and he was considered to be one of the best-informed men in England on the subject of Currency. The head officer of the bank, Mr. Simon Martin, deserved the same reputation, and had it, among all who knew him. He sent for my brother Henry, who found him with my Circular before him. He said that he had a message to communicate to me from the firm: and the message was duly delivered, when Mr. Martin had satisfied himself that my brother conscientiously believed me adequate to my enterprise. Messrs. Gurney considered the scheme an important one, promising public benefit: they doubted whether it would be immediately appreciated: they knew that I could not afford to go on at a loss, but thought it a pity that a beneficial enterprise should fall to the ground for want of immediate support; and they therefore requested that, in case of discouragement in regard to the sale, I should apply to them before giving up. 'Before she gives up, let her come to us,' were their words: words which were as pleasant to me in the midst of my success as they could have been if I had needed the support so generously offered.

Meantime the weekly letter grew worse and worse. But on the Sunday preceding the day of publication came a bit of encouragement in the shape of a sentence in these, or nearly these words. 'I see no chance of the work succeeding unless the trade take it up better. We have only one considerable booksellers' order—from A and B for a hundred copies.' 'Why, there,' said my mother, 'is a hundred towards your thousand!' 'Ah, but,' said I, 'where are the other nine hundred to come from, in a fortnight?' The edition consisted of fifteen hundred.

To the best of my recollection, I waited ten days from the day of publication, before I had another line from the publisher. My mother, judging from his ill-humour, inferred that he had good news to tell; whereas I supposed the contrary. My mother was right; and I could now be amused at his last attempts to be discouraging in the midst of splendid success. At the end of those ten days, he sent with his letter a copy of my first number, desiring me to make with all speed any corrections I might wish to make, as he had scarcely any copies left. He added that the demand led him to propose that we should now print two thousand. A postscript informed me that since he wrote the above, he had found that we should want three thousand. A second postscript proposed four thousand, and a third five thousand. The letter was worth having, now it had come. There was immense relief in this; but I remember nothing like intoxication;—like any painful reaction whatever. I remember walking up and down the grassplat in the garden (I think it was on the tenth of February) feeling that my cares were over. And so they were. From that hour, I have never had any other anxiety about employment than what to choose, nor any real care about money. Eight or nine years after, I found myself entirely cut off by illness from the power of working, and then my relations and friends aided me in ways so generous as to make it easy for me to accept the assistance. But even then, I was never actually pinched for money; and, from the time that the power of working was restored, I was at once as prosperous as ever, and became more and more so till now, when illness has finally visited me in a condition of independence. I think I may date my release from pecuniary care from that tenth of February, 1832.

The entire periodical press, daily, weekly, and, as soon as possible, monthly, came out in my favour; and I was overwhelmed with newspapers and letters, containing every sort of flattery. The Diffusion Society wanted to have the Series now; and Mr. Hume offered, on behalf of a new society of which he was the head,[1] any price I would name for the purchase of the whole. I cannot precisely answer for the date of these and other applications; but, as far as I remember, there was, from the middle of February onwards, no remission of such applications, the meanest of which I should have clutched at a few weeks before. Members of Parliament sent down blue books through the post-office, to the astonishment of the postmaster, who one day sent word that I must send for my own share of the mail, for it could not be carried without a barrow;— an announcement which, spreading in the town, caused me to be stared at in the streets. Thus began *that* sort of experience. Half the hobbies of the House of Commons, and numberless notions of individuals, anonymous and other, were commended to me for treatment in my Series, with which some of them had no more to do than geometry or the atomic theory. I had not calculated on this additional labour, in the form of correspondence; and very weary I often was of it, in the midst of the amusement. One necessity arose out of it which soon became very clear,—that I must reside in London, for the sake of the extensive and varied information which I now found was at my service there, and which the public encouragement of my work made it my duty to avail myself of.

It seemed hard upon my kind mother and aunt that the first consequence of the success they buoyed me up in hoping for should be to take

---

[1]   Joseph Hume (1777–1855), Radical M.P., who had adopted the Utilitarian principles of the school of Bentham. He was then on the General Committee of the Society for the Diffusion of Useful Knowledge, and active in its affairs.

me to London, after all: but the events of the summer showed them the necessity of the removal. We treated it as for a time; and I felt that my mother would not endure a permanent separation. The matter ended in their joining me in a small house in London, before many months were over: and meantime, my mother stipulated for my being in the house of some family well known to her. I obtained lodgings in the house of a tailor in Conduit Street, whose excellent wife had been an acquaintance of ours from her childhood to her marriage.[1] There I arrived in November, 1832; and there I lodged till the following September, when I went, with my mother and aunt, into a house (No. 17) in Fludyer Street, Westminster,[2] where I resided till the breakdown of my health (which took place in 1839) removed me from London altogether.

Here I stop, thinking that the third period of my life may be considered as closing with the conquest of all difficulty about getting a hearing from the public for what I felt I had to say. Each period of my life has had its trials and heart-wearing difficulties, —except (as will be seen) the last; but in none had the pains and penalties of life a more intimate connexion with the formation of character than in the one which closes here. And now the summer of my life was bursting forth without any interval of spring. My life began with winter, burst suddenly into summer, and is now ending with autumn,—mild and sunny. I have had no spring: but that cannot be helped now. It was a moral disadvantage, as well as a great loss of happiness; but we all have our moral disadvantages to make the best of; and 'happiness' is *not*, as the poet says, 'our being's end and aim,'[3] but the result of one faculty among many, which must be occasionally overborne by others, if there is to be any effectual exercise of the whole being. So I am satisfied in a higher sense than that in which the Necessarian is always satisfied. I cannot but know that in my life there has been a great waste of precious time and material; but I had now, by thirty years of age, ascertained my career, found occupation, and achieved independence; and thus the rest of my life was provided with its duties and its interests. Any one to whom that happens by thirty years of age may be satisfied; and I was so.

---

[1]   6 Conduit Street, between Regent and New Bond Streets.

[2]   Fludyer Street ran parallel to, and just south of, Downing Street. It no longer exists, having been consumed in the building of the Foreign Office.

[3]   Alexander Pope (1688–1744), *Essay on Man*, Epistle iv (1734), 1–4:
      O Happiness! our being's end and aim!
      Good, pleasure, ease, content! whate'er thy name:
      That something still which prompts th' eternal sigh,
      For which we bear to live, or dare to die.

FOURTH PERIOD

TO THE AGE OF THIRTY-SEVEN

SECTION I

IT WAS a dark, foggy November morning when I arrived in London. My lodgings were up two pair of stairs; for I did not yet feel secure of my permanent success, and had no conception of what awaited me in regard to society. A respectable sitting room to the front, and a clean, small bedroom behind, seemed to me all that could possibly be desired,— seeing that I was to have them all to myself. To be sure, they did look very dark, that first morning of yellow fog; but it was seldom so dark again; and when the spring came on, and I moved down into the handsomer rooms on the first floor, I thought my lodgings really pleasant. In the summer mornings, when I made my coffee at seven o'clock, and sat down to my work, with the large windows open, the sun-blinds down, the street fresh watered, and the flower-girls' baskets visible from my seat, I wished for nothing better. The evening walks in the Parks, when London began to grow 'empty,' were one of my chief pleasures; and truly I know few things better than Kensington Gardens and the Serpentine in the evenings of August and September.[1] I had lived in a narrow street all my life, except during occasional visits; and I therefore did not now object to Conduit Street, though it *was* sometimes too noisy, or too foggy, or too plashy, or too hot. It is well that I did not then know the charms of a country residence; or, knowing them, never thought of them as attainable by me. I have long felt that nothing but the strongest call of duty could make me now live in a street; and if I allowed myself to give way to distress at the mysteries of human life, one of my greatest perplexities would be at so many people being obliged so to live. Now that I have dwelt for nine years in a field, where there is never any dust, never

---

[1]   The Serpentine, a serpent-shaped pool, divides Hyde Park (on the east) from Kensington Gardens (on the west) in London. Living on Conduit Street, Martineau was half a mile away, and her walk took her through the fashionable district of Mayfair where she would have passed the empty town houses of the wealthy, who spent summer months in the country.

any smoke, never any noise; where my visitors laugh at the idea of the house ever being cleaned, because it never gets dirty; where there is beauty to be seen from every window, and in bad weather it is a treat to stand in the porch and see it rain, I cannot but wonder at my former contentment. I have visited and gone over our old house in Magdalen Street, at Norwich,[1] within a few years; and I could not but wonder how my romantic days could ever have come on in such a place. There it stands,—a handsome, plain brick house, in a narrow street,—Norwich having nothing but narrow streets. There it is,—roomy and good-looking enough; but prosaic to the last degree. Except the vine on its back gable, there is not an element of naturalness or poetry about it. Yet there were my dreamy years passed. In my London lodging, a splendid vision was to open upon me;—one which I am glad to have enjoyed, because it *was* enjoyment; and because a diversified experience is good; and because I really gained much knowledge of human life and character from it. I became the fashion, and I might have been the 'lion' of several seasons, if I had chosen to permit it. I detested the idea, and absolutely put down the practice in my own case: but I saw as much of a very varied society as if I had allowed myself to be lionised, and with a more open mind than if I had not insisted on being treated simply as a lady or let alone. The change from my life in Norwich to my life in London was certainly prodigious, and such as I did not dream of when I exchanged the one for the other. Before we lost our money, and when I was a young lady 'just introduced,' my mother insisted on taking me to balls and parties, though that sort of visiting was the misery of my life. My deafness was terribly in the way, both because it made me shy, and because underbred people, like the card-players and dancers of a provincial town, are awkward in such a case. Very few people spoke to me; and I dare say I looked as if I did not wish to be spoken to. From the time when I went to London, all that was changed. People began with me as with a deaf person; and there was little more awkwardness about hearing, when they had once reconciled themselves to my trumpet. They came to me in good will, or they would not have come at all. They and I were not jumbled together by mere propinquity; we met purposely; and, if we continued our intercourse, it was through some sort of affinity. I now found what the real pleasures of social intercourse are, and was deeply sensible of its benefits: but it really does not appear to me that I

---

[1]   See p. 650 for a drawing of the house, shown with perhaps more front garden than actually existed.

was intoxicated with the pleasure, or that I over-rated the benefit. I think so because I always preferred my work to this sort of play. I think so because some sober friends,—two or three whom I could trust,—said, first, that I might and probably should say and do some foolish things, but that I should 'prove ultimately unspoilable;' and afterwards that I was not spoiled. I think so because I altered no plan or aim in life on account of any social distinction; and I think so, finally, because, while vividly remembering the seven years from 1832 to 1839, and feeling as gratefully and complacently as ever the kindness and attachment of friends, and the good-will of a multitude of acquaintances, I had no inclination to return to literary life in London after my recovery at Tynemouth,[1] and have for ten years rejoiced, without pause or doubt, in my seclusion and repose in my quiet valley.[2] There is an article of mine on 'Literary Lionism' in the London and Westminster Review of April, 1839, which was written when the subject was fresh in my thoughts and feelings. In consideration of this, and of my strong repugnance to detailing the incidents of my own reception in society, on entering the London world, while such an experience cannot be wholly passed over in an account of my life, I think the best way will be to cite that article,—omitting those passages only which are of a reviewing character. By this method, it will appear what my impressions were while in conflict with the practice of literary lionism; and I shall be spared the disgusting task of detailing old absurdities and dwelling on old flatteries, which had myself for their subject. Many of the stories which I could tell are comic enough; and a few are exceedingly interesting: but they would be all spoiled, to myself and every body else, by their relating to myself. The result on my own convictions and feelings is all that it is necessary to give; and that result can be given in no form so trustworthy as in the record penned at the time. It must be remembered that the article appeared in an anonymous form, or some appearance of conceit and bad taste may hang about even that form of disclosure.—The statement and treatment of the subject will however lead forward so far into my London life that I must fill up an intermediate space. I must give some account of my work before I proceed to treat of my play hours.

In meditating on my course of life at that time, and gathering together the evidences of what I was learning and doing, I am less disposed than

---

[1]   That is, after mesmerism relieved the debilitating side effects of her uterine tumors.
[2]   Ambleside, in the Lake District, is three-quarters of a mile above Lake Windermere in the vale of the Rothay.

I used to be to be impatient with my friends for their incessant rebukes and remonstrances about over-work. From the age of fifteen to the moment in which I am writing, I have been scolded in one form or another, for working too hard; and I wonder my friends did not find out thirty years ago that there is no use in their fault-finding. I am heartily sick of it, I own; and there may be some little malice in the satisfaction with which I find myself dying, after all, of a disease which nobody can possibly attribute to over-work. Though knowing all along that my friends were mistaken as to what was moderate and what immoderate work, in other cases than their own (and I have always left *them* free to judge and act for themselves) I have never denied that less toil and more leisure would be wholesome and agreeable to me. My pleas have been that I have had no power of choice, and that my critics misjudged the particular case. Almost every one of them has proceeded on the supposition that the labour of authorship involved immense 'excitement;' and I, who am the quietest of quiet bodies, when let alone in my business, have been warned against 'excitement' till I am fairly sick of the word. One comfort has always been that those who were witnesses of my work-a-day life always came round to an agreement with me that literary labour is not necessarily more hurtfully exciting than any other serious occupation. My mother, alarmed at a distance, and always expecting to hear of a brain fever, used to say, amidst the whirl of our London spring days, 'My dear, I envy your calmness.' And a very intimate friend, one of the strongest remonstrants, told me spontaneously, when I had got through a vast pressure of work in her country house, that she should never trouble me more on that head, as she saw that my authorship was the fulfillment of a natural function,—conducive to health of body and mind, instead of injurious to either. It would have saved me from much annoyance (kindly intended) if others had observed with the same good sense, and admitted conviction with equal candour. Authorship has never been with me a matter of choice. I have not done it for amusement, or for money, or for fame, or for any reason but because I could not help it. Things were pressing to be said; and there was more or less evidence that I was the person to say them. In such a case, it was always impossible to decline the duty for such reasons as that I should like more leisure, or more amusement, or more sleep, or more of any thing whatever. If my life *had* depended on more leisure and holiday, I could not have taken it. What wanted to be said must be said, for the sake of the many, whatever might be the consequences to the one worker concerned. Nor could the immediate task be put aside, from the remote consideration, for ever pressed upon me, of lengthening my life. The work called for to-day must not be refused for the possible sake of next month or next year. While feeling far less injured by toil than my friends took for granted I must be, I yet was always aware of the strong probability that my life would end as the lives of hard literary workers usually end,—in paralysis, with months or years of imbecility. Every one must recoil from the prospect of being thus burdensome to friends and attendants; and it certainly was a matter of keen satisfaction to me, when my present fatal disease was ascertained, that I was released from that liability, and should die of something else, far less formidable to witnesses and nurses.[1] Yet, the contemplation of such a probability in the future was no reason for declining the duty of the time; and I could not have written a volume the less if I had foreknown that, at a certain future day and hour, I should be struck down like Scott and Southey,[2] and many another faithful labourer in the field of literature.

One deep and steady conviction, obtained from my own experience and observation, largely qualified any apprehensions I might have, and was earnestly impressed by me upon my remonstrating friends; that enormous loss of strength, energy and time is occasioned by the way in which people go to work in literature, as if its labours were in all respects different from any other kind of toil. I am confident that intellectual industry and intellectual punctuality are as practicable as industry and punctuality in any other direction. I have seen vast misery of conscience and temper arise from the irresolution and delay caused by waiting for congenial moods, favourable circumstances, and so forth. I can speak, after long experience, without any doubt on this matter. I have suffered, like other writers, from indolence, irresolution, distaste to my work, absence of 'inspiration,' and all that: but I have also found that sitting down, however reluctantly, with the pen in my hand, I have never worked for one quarter of an hour without finding myself in full train; so that all the quarter hours, arguings, doubtings, and hesitation as to whether I should work or not which I gave way to in my inexperience, I now regard as so much waste, not only of time but, far worse, of energy. To the best of my belief, I never but once in my life left my work because I could not do it: and that single occasion was on the

---

[1]   The diagnosis was an "incurably diseased" heart.

[2]   The novelist Walter Scott took full responsibility for the bankruptcy of a book-selling firm in which he was a partner and worked heroically to pay off a £114,000 debt, shortening his life in the process. Poet laureate Robert Southey suffered from mental illness in his last years, during which he was nursed by his wife and fellow poet Caroline Bowles.

opening day of an illness. When once experience had taught me that I could work when I chose, and within a quarter of an hour of my determining to do so, I was relieved, in a great measure, from those embarrassments and depressions which I see afflicting many an author who waits for a mood instead of summoning it, and is the sport, instead of the master, of his own impressions and ideas. As far as the grosser physical influences are concerned, an author has his lot pretty much in his own hands, because it is in his power to shape his habits in accordance with the laws of nature: and an author who does not do this has no business with the lofty vocation. I am very far indeed from desiring to set up my own practices as an example for others; and I do not pretend that they are wholly rational, or the best possible; but, as the facts are clear,—that I have, without particular advantages of health and strength, done an unusual amount of work without fatal, perhaps without injurious consequences, and without the need of pernicious stimulants and peculiar habits,—it may be as well to explain what my methods were, that others may test them experimentally, if they choose.

As for my hours,—it has always been my practice to devote my best strength to my work; and the morning hours have therefore been sacred to it, from the beginning. I really do not know what it is to take any thing but the pen in hand, the first thing after breakfast, except of course, in travelling. I never pass a day without writing; and the writing is always done in the morning. There have been times when I have been obliged to 'work double tides,' and therefore to work at night: but it has never been a practice; and I have seldom written any thing more serious than letters by candlelight. In London, I boiled my coffee at seven or half-past, and went to work immediately till two, when it was necessary to be at liberty for visitors till four o'clock. It was impossible for me to make calls. I had an immense acquaintance, no carriage, and no time; and I therefore remained at home always from two till four, to receive all who came; and I called on nobody. I knew that I should be quizzed or blamed for giving myself airs: but I could not help that. I had engaged before I came to London to write a number of my Series every month for two years; and I could not have fulfilled my engagement and made morning visits too. Sydney Smith was one of the quizzers. He thought I might have managed the thing better, by 'sending round an inferior authoress in a carriage to drop the cards.'

When my last visitor departed, I ran out for an hour's walk, returning in time to dress and read the newspaper, before the carriage came,—somebody's carriage being always sent,—to take me out to dinner. An evening visit or two closed the day's engagements. I tried my best to get home by twelve or half-past, in order to answer the notes I was sure to find on my table, or to get a little reading before going to rest between one and two. A very refreshing kind of visit was (and it happened pretty often) when I walked to the country, or semi-country house of an intimate friend, and slept there,—returning before breakfast, or in time to sit down to my morning's work. After my mother and aunt joined me in London, I refused Sunday visiting altogether, and devoted that evening to my old ladies. So much for the times of working.

I was deeply impressed by something which an excellent clergyman told me one day, when there was nobody by to bring mischief on the head of the relater. This clergyman knew the literary world of his time so thoroughly that there was probably no author of any mark then living in England, with whom he was not more or less acquainted. It must be remembered that a new generation has now grown up. He told me that he had reason to believe that there was no author or authoress who was free from the habit of taking some pernicious stimulant; either strong green tea, or strong coffee at night, or wine or spirits or laudanum. The amount of opium taken, to relieve the wear and tear of authorship, was, he said, greater than most people had any conception of: and all literary workers took something. 'Why, I do not,' said I. 'Fresh air and cold water are my stimulants.'—'I believe you,' he replied. 'But you work in the morning; and there is much in that.' I then remembered that when, for a short time, I had to work at night (probably on one of the Poor-law tales, while my regular work occupied the mornings) a physician who called on me observed that I must not allow myself to be exhausted at the end of the day. He would not advise any alcoholic wine; but any light wine that I liked might do me good. 'You have a cupboard there at your right hand,' said he. 'Keep a bottle of hock and a wine-glass there, and help yourself when you feel you want it.'— 'No, thank you,' said I. 'If I took wine, it should not be when alone; nor would I help myself to a glass. I might take a little more and a little more, till my solitary glass might become a regular tippling habit. I shall avoid the temptation altogether.' Physicians should consider well before they give such advice to brain-worn workers.

As for the method, in regard to the Political Economy Tales, I am not sorry to have an opportunity of putting it on record. When I began, I furnished myself with all the standard works on the subject of what I then took to be a science. I had made a skeleton plan of the course, comprehending the four divisions, Production, Distribution, Exchange and Consumption:[1] and, in order to save my nerves from being over-whelmed with the thought of what I had undertaken, I resolved not to look beyond the department on which I was engaged. The subdivisions arranged themselves as naturally as the primary ones; and when any subject was episodical (as Slave Labour) I announced it as such. Having noted my own leading ideas on the topic before me, I took down my books, and read the treatment of that particular subject in each of them, making notes of reference on a separate sheet for each book, and restraining myself from glancing even in thought towards the scene and nature of my story till it should be suggested by my collective didactic materials. It was about a morning's work to gather hints by this read-ing. The next process, occupying an evening, when I had one to spare, or the next morning, was making the Summary of Principles which is found at the end of each number. This was the most laborious part of the work, and that which I certainly considered the most valuable. By this time, I perceived in what part of the world, and among what sort of people, the principles of my number appeared to operate the most manifestly. Such a scene I chose, be it where it might.

The next process was to embody each leading principle in a char-acter: and the mutual operation of these embodied principles supplied the action of the story. It was necessary to have some accessories,—some out-works to the scientific erection; but I limited these as much as possible; and I believe that in every instance, they really were rendered subordinate. An hour or two sufficed for the outline of my story. If the scene was foreign, or in any part of England with which I was not familiar, I sent to the library for books of travel or topography: and the collecting and noting down hints from these finished the second day's work. The third day's toil was the severest. I reduced my materials to chapters, making a copious table of contents for each chapter on a sepa-rate sheet, on which I noted down, not only the action of the person-ages and the features of the scene, but all the political economy which it was their business to convey, whether by exemplification or conver-sation,—so as to absorb all the materials provided. This was not always completed at one sitting, and it made me sometimes sick with fatigue: but it was usually done in one day. After that, all the rest was easy. I paged my paper; and then the story went off like a letter. I never could decide whether I most enjoyed writing the descriptions, the narrative,

---

[1]   In this division Martineau follows the structure of James Mill's *Elements of Political Economy* (London: Baldwin, Craddock, and Joy, 1821), which was one of her primary sources.

or the argumentative or expository conversations. I liked each best while I was about it.

As to the actual writing,—I did it as I write letters, and as I am writing this Memoir,—never altering the expression as it came fresh from my brain. On an average I wrote twelve pages a day,—on large letter paper (quarto,[1] I believe it is called) the page containing thirty-three lines. In spite of all precautions, interruptions occurred very often. The proof-correcting occupied some time; and so did sitting for five portraits in the year and half before I went to America. The correspondence threatened to become infinite. Many letters, particularly anonymous ones, required or deserved no answer: but there were others from operatives, young persons, and others which could be answered without much expenditure of thought, and wear and tear of interest: and I could not find in my heart to resist such clients. Till my mother joined me, I never failed to send her a bulky packet weekly; as much for my own satisfaction as for hers,—needing as I did to speak freely to some one of the wonderful scenes which life was now opening to me. Having no maid, I had a good deal of the business of common life upon my hands. On the conclusion of a number, I sometimes took two days' respite; employing it in visiting some country house for the day and night, and indulging in eight hours' sleep, instead of the five, or five and a half, with which I was otherwise obliged to be satisfied: but it happened more than once that I finished one number at two in the morning, and was at work upon another by nine. During the whole period of the writing of the three Series, —the Political Economy, Taxation, and Poor Laws[2]—I never remember but once sitting down to read whatever I pleased. That was a summer evening, when I was at home and my old ladies were out, and I had two hours to do what I liked with. I was about to go to the United States; and I sat down to study the geography and relations of the States of the American Union; and extremely interesting I found it,—so soon as I was hoping to travel through them.

The mode of scheming and constructing my stories having been explained, it remains to be seen whence the materials were drawn. A review of the sources of my material will involve some anecdotes which may be worth telling, if I may judge by my own interest, and

---

[1] Called *quarto* because it is the size obtained by folding a full sheet of printing paper into quarters. Quarto sizes range from 7⅝ x 6⅛ in. (pott quarto) to 15 x 11 in. (imperial quarto).

[2] *Illustrations of Political Economy*, 25 vols. (London: Charles Fox, 1832–34); *Poor Laws and Paupers*, 4 vols. (London: Charles Fox, 1833–34); and *Illustrations of Taxation*, 5 vols. (London: Charles Fox, 1834).

that which I witness in others, in the history of the composition of any well-known work.

If I remember right, I was busy about the twelfth number,—'French Wines and Politics,'—when I went to London, in November, 1832. That is, I had done with the department of Production, and was finishing that of Distribution. The first three numbers were written before the stir of success began: and the scenery was furnished by books of travel obtained from the Public Library, and of farming by the late Dr. Rigby of Norwich, —a friend of the late Lord Leicester, (when Mr. Coke).[1] The books of travel were Lichtenstein's South Africa for 'Life in the Wilds:' Edwards's (and others') 'West Indies' for 'Demerara:' and McCulloch's 'Highlands and Islands of Scotland' for the two Garveloch stories.[2] Mr. Cropper of Liverpool heard of the Series early enough to furnish me with some statistics of Slavery for 'Demerara;' and Mr. Hume in time to send me Blue Books on the Fisheries, for 'Ella of Garveloch.'[3]—My correspondence with Mr. Cropper deserves mention, in honour of that excellent and devoted man. About the time that the success of my scheme began to be apparent, there arrived in Norwich a person who presented himself as an anti-slavery agent. It was the well-known Elliott Cresson,[4] associated with the American

---

[1]   Both Dr. Edward Rigby (1747–1821) and his son Edward (1804–60) were Norwich surgeons specializing in obstetrics. The second Dr. Rigby became a famous London obstetrician. Thomas William Coke (1754–1842), made Earl of Leicester of Holkham in 1837, was an English agriculturist, known as "Coke of Norfolk." His Norfolk estate was initially poor and unproductive, but he obtained expert advice, introduced many improvements, and in a few years greatly increased the wheat harvest and improved the breed of cattle, sheep, and pigs of his farms. His farming techniques are considered the basis of modern agriculture.

[2]   Henry [Hinrich] Lichtenstein, *Travels in Southern Africa in the Years 1803, 1804, 1805 and 1806,* trans. Anne Plumptre (London: Henry Colburn, 1812–15); Bryan Edwards, *The History. Civil and Commercial, of the British Colonies in the West Indies* (London: J. Stockdale, 1793–94); and J.R. McCulloch, *Principles of Political Economy* (Edinburgh: Adam and Charles Black, 1824) and the *Universal Gazetteer: A Dictionary, Geographical, Statistical, and Historical* (London, 1832), either of which might have provided information for the Garveloch stories.

[3]   James Cropper (1773–1840), a Quaker philanthropist, worked to abolish slavery in the West Indies. Joseph Hume (1777–1855), M.P., began his career as a Tory but became a Radical after reading the work of James Mill and the philosophical reformers of the school of Bentham.

[4]   Elliott Cresson (1796–1854), a Philadelphia Quaker, advocated the colonization of American Negroes in Africa, established the first colony of liberated slaves in Liberia, and became president of the American Colonization Society, serving as a liaison between Southern slaveholders and Philadelphia colonizationists and going on a two-year mission to England to raise $100,000 for the ACS. His work was opposed by British and American abolitionists, including William Lloyd Garrison, once they learned that a majority of ACS members did not advocate manumission (granting freedom to slaves) but simply wished to reduce the numbers of free blacks in the country and thus help preserve the institution of slavery.

Colonization scheme, which he hoped to pass upon us innocent provincial Britons as the same thing as anti-slavery. Many even of the Quakers were taken in; and indeed there were none but experienced abolitionists, like the Croppers, who were qualified even to suspect,— much less to detect,—this agent of the slaveholders and his false pretences. Kind-hearted people, hearing from Mr. Cresson that a slave could be bought and settled blissfully in Liberia for seven pounds ten shillings, raised the ransom in their own families and among their neighbours, and thought all was right. Mr. Cresson obtained an intro-duction to my mother and me, and came to tea, and described what certainly interested us very much, and offered to furnish me with plenty of evidence of the productiveness of Liberia, and the capabilities of the scheme, with a view to my making it the scene and subject of one of my tales. I was willing, thinking it would make an admirable framework for one of my pieces of doctrine; and I promised, not to write a story, but to consider of it when the evidence should have arrived. The papers arrived; and my conclusion was,—not to write about Liberia. Some time after, I had a letter from Mr. Cropper, who was a perfect stranger to me, saying that Elliott Cresson was announcing every where from the platform in his public lectures that I had promised him to make the colony of Liberia one of my Illustrations of Political Economy: and it was the fact that the announcement was made in many places. Mr. Cropper offered to prove to me the unreliableness of Cresson's repre-sentations, and the true scope and aim of the Colonization scheme. He appealed to me not to publish in its favour till I had heard the other side; and offered to bear the expense of suppressing the whole edition, if the story was already printed. I had the pleasure of telling him by return of post that I had given no such promise to Mr. Cresson, and that I had not written, nor intended to write, any story about Liberia or American Colonization. Before I went to the United States, this agent of the slaveholders had exposed his true character by lecturing, all over England, in a libellous tone, against Garrison[1] and the true abolitionists of America. When I had begun to see into the character and policy of the enterprise, and before I had met a single abolitionist in America, I encountered Mr. Cresson, face to face, in the Senate Chamber at Washington. He was very obsequious; but I would have

---

[1]   William Lloyd Garrison (1805–79), an American abolitionist, advocated the "immediate and complete emancipation of all slaves." His anti-slavery newspaper, *The Liberator*, was founded in 1831 and adapted its motto from Tom Paine: "Our country is the world—our countrymen are mankind."

nothing to say to him. He was, I believe, the only acquaintance whom I ever 'cut.' It was out of this incident that grew the correspondence with Mr. Cropper which ended in his furnishing me with material for an object precisely the reverse of Elliott Cresson's.[1]

On five occasions in my life I have found myself obliged to write and publish what I entirely believed would be ruinous to my reputation and prosperity. In no one of the five cases has the result been what I anticipated. I find myself at the close of my life prosperous in name and fame, in my friendships and in my affairs. But it may be considered to have been a narrow escape in the first instance; for every thing was done that low-minded recklessness and malice could do to destroy my credit and influence by gross appeals to the prudery, timidity, and ignorance of the middle classes of England. My own innocence of intention, and my refusal to conceal what I thought and meant, carried me through: but there is no doubt that the circulation of my works was much and long restricted by the prejudices indecently and maliciously raised against me by Mr. Croker and Mr. Lockhart, in the Quarterly Review.[2] I mention these two names, because Messrs. Croker and Lockhart openly assumed the honour of the wit which they (if nobody else) saw in the deed; and there is no occasion to suppose any one else concerned in it. As there is, I believe, some lingering feeling still,—some doubt about my being once held in horror as a 'Malthusian,' I had better tell simply all I know of the matter.

When the course of my exposition brought me to the Population subject,[3] I, with my youthful and provincial mode of thought and feeling,—brought up too amidst the prudery which is found in its great force in our middle class,—could not but be sensible that I risked much

---

[1]   In "Demerara" Martineau opposes slavery on philosophical and financial grounds. Philosophically, she argues that "property is held by convention, not natural right; … as the agreement to hold a man in property never took place between the parties concerned, *i.e.,* is not conventional, Man has no right to hold Man in property."

[2]   In a review of the *Illustrations* written primarily by George Poulett Scrope for the *Quarterly Review*, 49 (April 1833), 136–52, John Wilson Croker (1780–1857), a Tory M.P. and regular contributor, and John Gibson Lockhart (1794–1854), the editor, interlarded nasty innuendoes about Martineau's lack of femininity and morality.

[3]   "Weal and Woe in Garveloch" introduced the topic of population control, using the theories of Thomas Malthus (1766–1834) from *An Essay on the Principle of Population, as It Affects the Future Improvement of Society* (1798). Malthus maintained that human populations reproduce geometrically whereas food supplies increase only arithmetically, and thus that famine, disease, war, and crime inevitably become "positive" checks on population. Malthusians suggested that "moral restraint" (postponement of marriage, sexual continence, birth control) might provide a fifth "preventive" (and less drastic) check.

in writing and publishing on a subject which was not universally treated in the pure, benevolent, and scientific spirit of Malthus himself. I felt that the subject was one of science, and therefore perfectly easy to treat in itself; but I was aware that some evil associations had gathered about it,—though I did not know what they were. While writing 'Weal and Woe in Garveloch,' the perspiration many a time streamed down my face, though I knew there was not a line in it which might not be read aloud in any family. The misery arose from my seeing how the simplest statements and reasoning might and probably would be perverted. I said nothing to any body; and, when the number was finished, I read it aloud to my mother and aunt. If there had been any opening whatever for doubt or dread, I was sure that these two ladies would have given me abundant warning and exhortation,—both from their very keen sense of propriety and their anxious affection for me. But they were as complacent and easy as they had been interested and attentive. I saw that all ought to be safe. But it was evidently very doubtful whether all would be safe. A few words in a letter from Mr. Fox put me on my guard. In the course of some remarks on the sequence of my topics, he wrote, 'As for the Population question, let no one interfere with you. Go straight through it, *or you'll catch it.*' I did go straight through it; and happily I had nearly done when a letter arrived from a literary woman, who had the impertinence to write to me now that I was growing famous, after having scarcely noticed me before, and (of all subjects) on this, though she tried to make her letter decent by putting in a few little matters besides. I will call her Mrs. Z.[1] as I have no desire to point out to notice one for whom I never had any respect or regard. She expressed, on the part of herself and others, an anxious desire to know how I should deal with the Population question; said that they did not know what to wish about my treating or omitting it;—desiring it for the sake of society, but dreading it for me; and she finished by inform- ing me that a Member of Parliament, who was a perfect stranger to me, had assured her that I already felt my difficulty; and that he and she awaited my decision with anxiety. Without seeing at the moment the whole drift of this letter, I was abundantly disgusted by it, and fully sensible of the importance of its being answered immediately, and in a way which should admit of no mistake. I knew my reply was wanted for show; and I sent one by return of post which was shown to some

---

[1]   Unidentified; as in other anecdotes that involve intrigue, Martineau disguises the names of the participants.

purpose. It stopped speculation in one dangerous quarter. I showed my letter to my mother and brother; and they emphatically approved it, though it was rather sharp. They thought, as I did, that some sharpness was well directed towards a lady who professed to have talked over difficulties of this nature, on my behalf, with an unknown Member of Parliament by her own fireside. My answer was this. I believe I am giving the very words; for the business impressed itself deeply on my mind. 'As for the questions you put about the principles of my Series,— if you believe the Population question to be, as you say, the most serious now agitating society, you can hardly suppose that I shall omit it, or that I can have been heedless of it in forming my plan. I consider it, as treated by Malthus, a strictly philosophical question. So treating it, I find no difficulty in it; and there can be no difficulty in it for those who approach it with a single mind. To such I address myself. If any others should come whispering to me what I need not listen to, I shall shift my trumpet, and take up my knitting.' I afterwards became acquainted with the Member of Parliament whom my undesired correspondent quoted; and I feel confident that his name was used very unwarrantably, for the convenience of the lady's prurient curiosity.—I also saw her. She called on me at my lodgings (to catch a couple of franks from a Member of Parliament) and she mentioned my letter,—obtaining no response from me. She was then a near neighbour and an acquaintance of an intimate friend of mine. One winter morning, I was surprised by a note from this friend, sent three miles by a special messenger, to say, 'Mrs. Z. purposes to visit you this morning. I conjure you to take my advice. On the subject which she will certainly introduce, be deaf, dumb, blind and stupid. I will explain hereafter.' The morning was so stormy that no Mrs. Anybody could come. My friend's explanation to me was this. Mrs. Z. had declared her anxiety to her, in a morning call, to obtain from me, for her own satisfaction and other people's, an avowal which might be reported as to the degree of my knowledge of the controversies which secretly agitated society on the true bearings of the Population question. All this was no concern of mine; and much of it was beyond my comprehension. The whole interference of Mrs. Z. and her friends (if indeed there was anybody concerned in it but herself) was odious and impertinent nonsense in my eyes; and the fussy lady ever found me, as well as my friend, ready to be as 'deaf, dumb, blind and stupid' as occasion might require. I rather suspect that Mrs. Z. herself was made a tool of for the purposes of Mr. Lockhart, who employed his then-existing intimacy with her to get materials for turning her into ridicule afterwards. The connexion of Mr. Lockhart with this business presently appeared.

In an evening party in the course of the winter, I was introduced to a lady whose name and connexions I had heard a good deal of. Instead of being so civil as might be anticipated from her eagerness for an introduction, she was singularly rude and violent, so as to make my hostess very uncomfortable. She called me 'cruel' and 'brutal,' and scolded me for my story 'Cousin Marshall.' I saw that she was talking at random, and asked her whether she had read the story. She had not. I good-humouredly, but decidedly, told her that when she had read it, we would discuss it, if she pleased; and that meantime we would drop it. She declared she would not read it for the world; but she presently followed me about, was kind and courteous, and finished by begging to be allowed to set me down at my lodgings. When I alighted, she requested leave to call. She did so, when my mother was with me for two or three weeks, and invited us to dine at her house in the country, on the first disengaged day. She called for us, and told us during our drive that she had resisted the strongest entreaties from Mr. Lockhart to be allowed to meet me that day. She had some misgiving, it appeared, which made her steadily refuse; but she invited Lady G——, a relative of Lockhart's, and an intimate friend of her own. Lady G. was as unwilling as Lockhart was eager to come; and very surly she looked when introduced. She sat within hearing of my host and me at dinner; and as soon as we returned to the drawing-room, she took her seat by me, with a totally changed manner, and conversed kindly and agreeably. I was wholly unaware what lay under all this: but the fact soon came out that the atrocious article in the Quarterly Review which was avowedly intended to 'destroy Miss Martineau,' was at that time actually printed; and Mr. Lockhart wanted to seize an opportunity which might be the last for meeting me, —all unsuspecting as I was, and trusting to his being a gentleman, on the strength of meeting him in that house. I was long afterwards informed that Lady G. went to him early the next day, (which was Sunday) and told him that he would repent of the article, if it was what he had represented to her; and I know from the printers that Mr. Lockhart went down at once to the office, and cut out 'all the worst passages of the review,' at great inconvenience and expense. What he could have cut out that was worse than what stands, it is not easy to conceive.

While all this was going on without my knowledge, warnings came to me from two quarters that something prodigious was about to happen. Mr. Croker had declared at a dinner party that he expected a revolution under the Whigs, and to lose his pension; and that he intended to lay by his pension while he could get it, and maintain himself by his pen; and that he had 'begun by tomahawking Miss Martineau in the Quarterly.'[1] An old gentleman present, Mr. Whishaw,[2] was disgusted at the announcement and at the manner of it, and, after consulting with a friend or two, called to tell me of this, and put me on my guard. On the same day, another friend called to tell me that my printers (who also printed the Quarterly) thought I ought to know that 'the filthiest thing that had passed through the press for a quarter of a century' was coming out against me in the Quarterly. I could not conceive what all this meant; and I do not half understand it now: but it was enough to perceive that the design was to discredit me by some sort of evil imputation. I saw at once what to do. I wrote to my brothers, telling them what I had heard, and earnestly desiring that they would not read the next Quarterly. I told them that the inevitable consequence of my brothers taking up my quarrels would be to close my career. I had entered upon it independently, and I would pursue it alone. From the moment that any of them stirred about my affairs, I would throw away my pen; for I would not be answerable for any mischief or trouble to them. I made it my particular request that we might all be able to say that they had not read the article. I believe I am, in fact, the only member of the family who ever read it.—The day before publication, which happened to be Good Friday, a friend called on me,—a clergyman who occasionally wrote for the Quarterly,—and produced the forthcoming number from under his cloak. 'Now,' said he, 'I am going to leave this with you. Do not tell me a word of what you think of it; but just mark all the lies in the margin: and I will call at the door for it, on my way home in the afternoon.' I did it; sat down to my work again (secure from visitors on a Good Friday) and then went out, walking and by omnibus, to dine in the country. I remember thinking in the omnibus that the feelings called forth by such usage are, after all, more pleasurable than painful; and again, when I went to bed, that the day had been a very happy one. The testing of one's power of endurance is pleasurable; and the testing of one's power of forgiveness is yet sweeter: and it is no small benefit to learn something more of one's faults and weaknesses than friends and sympathisers either will or can tell. The compassion that I felt on this occasion for the low-minded and foul-mouthed creatures who could use their education and position as gentlemen to 'destroy' a woman whom they

---

[1]   See the *Quarterly Review* 49 (April 1833), 136–52.

[2]   John Whishaw (1765–1840), lawyer and member of the exclusive London dining club, King of Clubs, which included Lord Brougham, Sydney Smith, and others in Martineau's circle.

knew to be innocent of even comprehending their imputations, was very painful: but, on the other hand, my first trial in the shape of hostile reviewing was over, and I stood unharmed, and somewhat enlightened and strengthened. I mentioned the review to nobody; and therefore nobody mentioned it to me. I heard, some years after, that one or two literary ladies had said that they, in my place, would have gone into the mountains or to the antipodes, and never have shown their faces again; and that there were inquiries in abundance of my friends how I stood it. But I gave no sign. The reply always was that I looked very well and happy,—just as usual.— The sequel of the story is that the writer of the original article, Mr. Poulett Scrope, requested a mutual friend to tell me that he was ready to acknowledge the political economy of the article to be his; but that he hoped he was too much of a gentleman to have stooped to ribaldry, or even jest; and that I must understand that he was not more or less responsible for any thing in the article which we could not discuss face to face with satisfaction. Messrs. Lockhart and Croker made no secret of the ribaldry being theirs. When the indignation of the literary world was strong in regard to this and other offenses of the same kind, and Mr. Lockhart found he had gone too far in my case, he spared no entreaties to the lady who made Lady G. meet me to invite him,—professing great admiration and goodwill, and declaring that I must know his insults to be mere joking. She was won upon at last, and came one day with her husband, to persuade me to go over to dinner to meet Mr. Lockhart. When I persisted in my refusal, she said, in some vexation,—'But what am I to say to Lockhart? —because I promised him.' I replied, 'I have nothing to do with what you say to Mr. Lockhart: but I will tell you that I will never knowingly meet Mr. Lockhart; and that, if I find myself in the same house with him, I will go out at one door of the drawing-room when he comes in at the other.' Her husband, hitherto silent, said, 'You are quite right. I would on no account allow you to be drawn in to an acquaintance with Lockhart at our house: and the only excuse I can offer for my wife's rashness is that she has never read that Quarterly article.' From other quarters I had friendly warnings that Lockhart had set his mind on making my acquaintance, in order to be able to say that I did not mind what he had done. He was the only person but two whose acquaintance I ever refused. I never saw him but once; and that was twenty years afterwards, when he wore a gloomy and painful expression of countenance, and walked listlessly along the street and the square, near his own house, swinging his cane. My companion told me who he was; and we walked along the other side of the street, having a good and unobserved view of him till he reached his own house.

The sorrows of his later years had then closed down upon him, and he was sinking under them: but the pity which I felt for him then was not more hearty, I believe, than that which filled my mind on that Good Friday, 1833, when he believed he had 'destroyed' me.

As for destroying me,—it was too late, for one thing. I had won my public before Croker took up his 'tomahawk.' The simple fact, in regard to the circulation of my Series, was that the sale increased largely after the appearance of the Quarterly review of it, and diminished markedly and immediately on the publication of the flattering article on it in the Edinburgh Review.[1] The Whigs were then falling into disrepute among the great body of the people; and every token of favour from Whig quarters was damaging to me, for a time. In the long run, there is no doubt that the Quarterly injured me seriously. For ten years there was seldom a number which had not some indecent jest about me,—some insulting introduction of my name. The wonder is what could be gained that was worth the trouble: but it certainly seems to me that this course of imputation originated some obscure dread of me and my works among timid and superficial readers. For one instance among many:—a lady, calling on a friend of mine, wondered at seeing books of mine on the table, within the children's reach;—they being 'improper books,' she had been told, —declared to be so by the Quarterly Review. My friend said 'Though I don't agree with you, I know what you are thinking of. You must carry this home, and read it,—taking down from the shelf the volume which contained the Garveloch stories. The visitor hesitated, but yielded, and a few days after, brought back the book, saying that this could not be the one, for it was so harmless that her husband had read it aloud to the young people in the evening. 'Well,' said my friend, 'try another.' The lady and her husband read the whole series through in this way, and never could find out the 'improper book.'

And what was all this for? I do not at all know. All that I know is that a more simple-minded, virtuous man, full of domestic affections, than Mr. Malthus, could not be found in all England; and that the desire of his heart and the aim of his work were that domestic virtue and happiness should be placed within the reach of all, as Nature intended them to be. He found, in his day, that a portion of the people were underfed; and that one consequence of this was a fearful mortality among infants; and another consequence, the growth of a recklessness among the destitute which

---

[1]   William Empson (1791–1852) wrote the more positive article for the *Edinburgh Review* (57 [April 1833], 1–39), though he was not without criticism of the series.

caused infanticide, corruption of morals, and, at best, marriage between pauper boys and girls, while multitudes of respectable men and women, who paid rates instead of consuming them, were unmarried at forty, or never married at all. Prudence as to the time of marriage, and to making due provision for it was, one would think, a harmless recommendation enough, under the circumstances. Such is the moral aspect of Malthus's work. As to its mathematical basis, there is no one, as I have heard Mr. Hallam say,[1] who could question it that might not as well dispute the multiplication table. As for whether Mr. Malthus's doctrine, while mathematically indisputable, and therefore assailable in itself only by ribaldry and corrupt misrepresentation, may not be attacking a difficulty at the wrong end,—that is a fair matter of opinion. In my opinion, recent experience shows that it does attack a difficulty at the wrong end. The repeal of the corn-laws, with the consequent improvement in agriculture, and the prodigious increase of emigration have extinguished all present apprehension and talk of 'surplus population,'—that great difficulty of forty or fifty years ago. And it should be remembered, as far as I am concerned in the controversy, that I advocated in my Series a free trade in corn, and exhibited the certainty of agricultural improvement, as a consequence; and urged a carefully conducted emigration; and, above all, education without limit. It was my business, in illustrating Political Economy, to exemplify Malthus's doctrine among the rest. It was that doctrine 'pure and simple,' as it came from his virtuous and benevolent mind, that I presented; and the presentment was accompanied by an earnest advocacy of the remedies which the great natural laws of Society put into our power,—freedom for bringing food to men, and freedom for men to go where food is plentiful; and enlightenment for all, that they may provide for themselves under the guidance of the best intelligence. Mr. Malthus, who did more for social ease and virtue than perhaps any other man of his time, was the 'best-abused man' of the age. I was aware of this; and I saw in him, when I afterwards knew him, one of the serenest and most cheerful men that society can produce. When I became intimate enough with the family to talk over such matters, I asked Mr. Malthus one day whether he had suffered in spirits from the abuse lavished on him. 'Only just at first,' he answered.— 'I wonder whether it ever kept you awake a minute.'—'Never after the first fortnight,' was his reply. The spectacle of the good man in

---

[1]   Henry Hallam (1777–1859), historian best known for his *Constitutional History of England* (1827), was also the father of Arthur Henry Hallam, in whose memory Tennyson wrote the elegy *In Memoriam*.

his daily life in contrast with the representations of him in the periodical literature of the time, impressed upon me, more forcibly than anything in my own experience, the everlasting fact that the reformers of morality, personal and social, are always subject at the outset to the imputation of immorality from those interested in the continuance of corruption.—I need only add that all suspicious speculation, in regard to my social doctrines, seems to have died out long ago. I was not ruined by this first risk, any more than by any subsequent enterprises; but I was probably never so near it as when my path of duty led me among the snares and pitfalls prepared for the innocent and defenseless by Messrs. Croker and Lockhart, behind the screen of the Quarterly Review.

The behaviour of the Edinburgh was widely different. From the time of my becoming acquainted with the literary Whigs who were paramount at that time, I had heard the name of William Empson on all hands: and it once or twice crossed my mind that it was odd that I never saw him. Once he left the room as I entered it unexpectedly: and another time, he ran in among us at dessert, at a dinner party, to deliver a message to the hostess, and was gone, without an introduction to me,—the only stranger in company. When his review of my Series in the Edinburgh was out, and he had ascertained that I had read it, he caused me to be informed that he had declined an introduction to me hitherto, because he wished to render impossible all allegations that I had been favourably reviewed by a personal friend: but that he was now only awaiting my permission to pay his respects to me. The review was, to be sure, extraordinarily laudatory; but the praise did not seem to me to be very rational and sound; while the nature of the criticism showed that all accordance between Mr. Empson and me on some important principles of social morals was wholly out of the question. His objection to the supposition that society could exist without capital punishment is one instance of what I mean; and his view of the morality or immorality of opinions (apart from the process of forming them) is another. But there was some literary criticism which I was thankful for; and there was such kindliness and generosity in the whole character of the man's mind;—his deeds of delicate goodness came to my knowledge so abundantly; and he bore so well certain mortifications about the review with which he had taken his best pains, that I was as ready as himself to be friends. And friends we were, for several years. We were never otherwise than perfectly friendly, though I could not help feeling that every year, and every experience, separated us more widely in regard to intellectual and moral sympathy. He was not, from the character of his mind, capable of having opinions; and he was, as is usual in such cases, disposed to be afraid of those who had. He was in a perpetual course of being swayed about by the companions of the day, on all matters but politics. There he was safe; for he was hedged in on every side by the dogmatic Whigs, who made him their chief dogmatist. He was full of literary knowledge;—an omnivorous reader with a weak intellectual digestion. He was not personally the wiser for his reading; but the profusion that he could pour out gave a certain charm to his conversation, and even to his articles, which had no other merit, except indeed that of a general kindliness of spirit. During my intercourse with him and his set, he married the only child of his old friend, Lord Jeffrey: and after the death of Mr. Napier, who succeeded Jeffrey in the editorship of the Edinburgh Review, Mr. Empson accepted the offer of it,—rather to the consternation of some of his best friends.[1] He had been wont to shake his head over the misfortunes of the review in Napier's time, saying that that gentleman had no literary faculty or cultivation whatever. When he himself assumed the management, people said we should now have nothing but literature. Both he and his predecessor, however, inserted (it was understood) as a matter of course, all articles sent by Whig Ministers, or by their underlings, however those articles might contradict each other even in the same number. All hope of real editorship, of political and moral consistency, was now over; and an unlooked-for failure in modesty and manners in good Mr. Empson spoiled the literary prospect; so that the review lost character and reputation quarter by quarter, while under his charge. His health had so far, and so fatally, failed before he became Editor, that he ought not to have gone into the enterprise; and so his oldest and best friends told him. But the temptation was strong; and, unfortunately, he could not resist it. Unfortunately, if indeed it is desirable that the Edinburgh Review should live,—which may be a question.[2] It is a great evil for such a publication to change its politics radically; and this must be done if the Edinburgh is to live; for Whiggism has become mere death in life,—a mere transitional state, now nearly worn out. When Mr. Empson's review of me appeared, however, the Whigs were new in office, Jeffrey's parliamentary career was an object of high hope to his party, and the Edinburgh was more regarded than the younger generation can now easily believe. Mr. Empson's work was therefore of some consequence to him, to me, and to the public. As I have said, the sale of my Series declined immediately,—under the popu-

---

[1]   Lord Francis Jeffrey (1773–1850) was editor of the *Edinburgh Review* from its founding in 1802 until 1829 when he became an M.P. Macvey Napier (1776–1847) succeeded him as editor in 1829, followed by William Empson in 1847.

[2]   The *Edinburgh Review* survived until 1929, almost a century after this period.

lar notion that I was to be a pet of the Whigs. As for ourselves, we met very pleasantly at dinner, at his old friend, Lady S.'s,[1] where nobody else was invited. Thence we all went together to an evening party; and I seldom entered a drawing-room afterwards without meeting my kind-hearted reviewer.—Such were the opposite histories of my first appearance in the Edinburgh and Quarterly Reviews.—I may as well add that I speak under no bias, in either case, of contributor or candidate interest; for I never wrote or desired to write for either review. I do not remember that I was ever asked; and I certainly never offered. I think I may trust my memory so far as to say this confidently.

To return to the subject of the materials furnished to me as I proceeded in my work. There were still three more numbers written in Norwich, besides those which I have mentioned. The Manchester operatives were eager to interest me in their controversies about Machinery and Wages; and it was from them that I received the bundles of documents which qualified me to write 'A Manchester Strike.'[2]

It was while I was about this number that the crisis of the Reform Bill happened. One May morning, I remember, the people of Norwich went out, by hundreds and thousands, to meet the mail. At that time, little Willie B——, the son of the Unitarian Minister at Norwich,[3] used to come every morning to say certain lessons to my mother, with whom he was a great favourite. On that morning, after breakfast, in came Willie, looking solemn and business-like, and stood before my mother with his arms by his sides, as if about to say a lesson, and said, 'Ma'am, papa sends you his regards, and the Ministry has resigned.' 'Well, Willie, what does that mean?' 'I don't know, Ma'am.' We, however, knew so well that, for once, and I believe for the only time in those busy years, I could not work. When my mother came in from ordering dinner, she found me sitting beside Willie, mending stockings. She expressed her amazement: and I told her, what pleased her highly, that I really could not write about twopenny galloons,[4] the topic of the morning, after hearing of Lord

---

1   Probably Lady Mary Shepherd (1777–1847), second wife of Sir Samuel Shepherd, who had been a friend of many artists, including David Garrick and Walter Scott. Lady Shepherd was herself the author of three philosophical treatises.

2   *A Manchester Strike* (London: Charles Fox, 1832), the seventh volume in the series.

3   William J. Bakewell was minister at the Octagon Chapel, Norwich, from 1827 to 1838.

4   Galloons, a thin band or braid used as trimming, appear in her tale, *A Manchester Strike*. The Whig Prime Minister, Lord Charles Grey (1765–1845), resigned when his Reform Bill passed in the House of Commons but was defeated in the House of Lords. He returned to office a few days later, in May 1832, when King William IV promised to create enough new peers to ensure passage of the Reform Act of 1832 by the House of Lords.

Grey's resignation. We went out early into the town, where the people were all in the streets, and the church bells were muffled and tolling. I do not remember a more exciting day. My publisher wrote a day or two afterwards, that the London booksellers need not have been afraid of the Reform Bill, any more than the Cholera, for that during this crisis, he had sold more of my books than ever. Every thing indeed justified my determination not to defer a work which was the more wanted the more critical became the affairs of the nation.

In spite of all I could say, the men of Manchester persisted that *my* hero was *their* hero, whose name however I had never heard. It gratified me to find that my doctrine was well received, and, I may say, cordially agreed in, even at that time, by the leaders of the genuine Manchester operatives; and they, for their part, were gratified by their great topics of interest being discussed by one whom they supposed to have 'spent all her life in a cotton-mill,' as one of their favourite Members of Parliament told me they did.—It occurs to me that my life ought indeed to be written by myself or some one else who can speak to its facts; for, if the reports afloat about me from time to time were to find their way into print after my death, it would appear the strangest life in the world. I have been assigned a humbler life than that of the Cotton-mill. A friend of mine heard a passenger in a stage-coach tell another that I was 'of very low origin,— having been a maid-of-all-work.' This was after the publication of my model number of the 'Guide to Service,' done at the request of the Poor-law Commissioners.[1] My reply to the request was that I would try, if the Maid-of-all-work might be my subject. I considered it a compliment, when I found I was supposed to have been relating my own experience. One aunt of mine heard my Series extolled (also in a coach) as wonderful for a young creature, seventeen and no more on her last birthday; and another aunt heard the same praise, in the same way, but on the opposite ground that I was wonderfully energetic for eighty-four! So many people heard that I was dreadfully conceited, and that my head was turned with success, that I began to think, in spite of very sober feelings and of abundant self-distrust, that the account must be true. A shopman at a printseller's was heard by a cousin of mine, after the publication of 'Vanderput and Snoek,' giving an impressive account of my residence in Holland: and, long after, Mr. Laing[2] made inquiries of a relation about

---

[1]   *The Guide to Service* (London: Charles Knight, 1838–39) was meant to train girls for domestic work.

[2]   Samuel Laing (1780–1868), author and traveler, published a *Journal of a Residence in Norway during the Years 1834, 1835, and 1836* (1836).

how long I had lived in Norway,—of which 'Feats on the Fiord' were supposed to be an evidence: but I had visited neither country when I wrote of them, and shall die without seeing Norway now. Every body believed at one time that I had sought Lord Brougham's patronage;— and this report I did not like at all. Another,—that he had written the chief part of the books,—was merely amusing. Another gave me some little trouble, in the midst of the amusement;—that I had been married for two years before the Series was finished, and that I concealed the fact for convenience. More than one of my own relations required the most express and serious assurance from me that this was not true before they would acquit me of an act of trickery so unlike me,—who never had any secrets. The husband thus assigned to me was a gentle- man whom I had then never heard of, and whom I never saw till some years afterwards, when he had long been a married man. After my Eastern journey in 1846, it was widely reported, and believed in Paris, that my party and I had quarrelled, as soon as we landed in France; and that I had gone on by myself, and travelled through those eastern coun- tries entirely alone. I could not conceive what could be the meaning of the compliments I received on my 'wonderful courage,' till I found how unwilling people were to credit that I had been well taken care of. My 'Eastern Life'[1] disabused all believers in this nonsense; and I hope this Memoir will discredit all the absurd reports which may yet be connected with my station and my doings in life, in the minds of those who know me only from rumour.

'Cousin Marshall,' which treats of the Poor-laws, was written and at press before Lord Brougham had devised his scheme of engaging me to illustrate the operation of the Poor-laws. I obtained my material, as to details, from a brother who was a Guardian, and from a lady who took an interest in workhouse management.[2] For 'Ireland' and 'Homes Abroad,' I obtained facts from Blue-books on Ireland and Colonization which were among the many by this time sent me by people who had 'hobbies.' These were all that I wrote at Norwich.

Five of my numbers had appeared before Lord Brougham saw any of them, or knew any thing about them. He was at Brougham in June, 1832, when Mr. Drummond, —the Thomas Drummond of sacred

---

[1] Before writing *Eastern Life, Present and Past* (1848), Martineau traveled for eight months with Mr. and Mrs. Richard Yates and Joseph Ewart, all of Liverpool, in Egypt, Palestine, Syria, and Lebanon.

[2] Robert Martineau (1798–1870), a nail and brass manufacturer, who was a Justice of the Peace in Birmingham and served as mayor in 1846.

memory in Ireland,[1]—sent him my numbers, up to 'Ella of Garveloch' (inclusive). A friend of both was at that time at Norwich, canvassing for the representation; and Lord Brougham wrote to him, with his customary vehemence, extolling me and my work, and desiring him to engage me to illustrate the poor-laws, in aid of the Commission then appointed to the work of poor-law inquiry. It was hardly right in me to listen to any invitation to further work. That I should have done so for any considerations of fame or money can never have been believed by any who knew what proposals and solicitations from all manner of editors and publishers I refused. It was the extreme need and difficulty of Poor-law reform that won me to the additional task. I had for many years been in a state of despair about national affairs, on account of this 'gangrene of the state,' as the French commissioners had reported it, 'which it was equally impossible to remove and to let alone.' When Lord Brougham wrote to his friend an account of the evidence which was actually obtained, and which would be placed at my disposal; and when he added that there was an apparent possibility of cure, declaring that his 'hopes would be doubled' if I could be induced to help the scheme, the temptation to over-work was irresistible. When I met Lord Brougham in town, he urged me strongly to promise six numbers within a year. I was steady in refusing to do more than four altogether: and truly that was quite enough, in addition to the thirty numbers of my own Series, (including the 'Illustrations of Taxation'). These thirty-four little volumes were produced in two years and a half,—the greater part of the time being one unceasing whirl of business and social excitement. After my settlement in London, Lord Brougham called on me to arrange the plan.[2] He informed me that the evidence would be all placed in my hands; and that my Illustrations would be published by the Diffusion Society. He then requested me to name my terms. I declined. He proceeded to assign the grounds of the estimate he was about to propose, telling me what his Society and others had given for various works, and why he considered mine worth more than some to which I likened it. Finally, he told me I ought not to have less than one hundred pounds apiece for my four numbers. He said that the Society would pay me seventy-five pounds on

---

[1]   Thomas Drummond (1797–1840), who invented the "limelight" and whose Phantasmagoria frightened Harriet as a child (see Period I, sec. i), served as Irish under-secretary during this period.

[2]   Henry Peter, Lord Brougham (1778–1868) was a moving force in the Society for the Diffusion of Useful Knowledge but not, as this passage makes clear, able to dictate the SDUK's terms.

the day of publication of each; and that he then and there guaranteed to me the remaining twenty-five pounds for each. If I did not receive it from the Society, I should from him. He afterwards told the Secretary of the Society and two personal friends of his and mine that these were the terms he had offered, and meant to see fulfilled. I supplied the works which, he declared, fully answered his expectations; and indeed he sent me earnest and repeated thanks for them. The Society fulfilled its engagements completely and punctually: but Lord Brougham did not fulfil his own, more or less. I never saw or heard any thing of the four times twenty-five pounds I was to receive to make up my four hundred pounds. I believe that he was reminded of his engagement, while I was in America, by those to whom he had avowed it: but I have never received any part of the money to this day. I never made direct application to him for it; partly because I never esteemed or liked him, or relished being implicated in business with him, after the first flutter was over, and I could judge of him for myself; and partly because such an amount of unfulfilled promises lay at his door, at the time of his enforced retirement from power, that I felt that my application would be, like other people's applications, as fruitless as it would be disagreeable. I do not repent doing those tales, because I hope and believe they were useful at a special crisis: but they never succeeded to any thing like the extent of my own Series; and it certainly appeared that all connexion with the Diffusion Society, and Lord Brougham, and the Whig government, was so much mere detriment to my usefulness and my influence.

I had better relate here all that I have to say about that batch of Tales. Lord Brougham sent me all the evidence as it was delivered in by the Commissioners of Inquiry into the operation of the Poor-laws. There can be no stronger proof of the strength of this evidence than the uniformity of the suggestions to which it gave rise in all the minds which were then intent on finding the remedy. I was requested to furnish my share of conclusions and suggestions. I did so, in the form of a programme of doctrine for my illustrations, some of which expose the evils of the old system, while others pourtray the features of its proposed successor.[1] My

---

[1]   The first two tales, *The Parish* and *The Hamlets*, cover the abuses and weaknesses of the Old Poor Law, under which Justices of the Peace managed a system of financial relief within parishes; the final two tales were *The Town* and *The Land's End*. The Poor Law Amendment Act of 1834, as it was officially known, restricted access to "outdoor relief," the common form of aid under the Old Poor Law, and required the poor to enter workhouses. Under the direction of the social reformer Edwin Chadwick (1800–90), the workhouses were designed to be "uninviting places of wholesome restraint" so that only the truly needy would apply for aid.

document actually crossed in the street one sent me by a Member of the government detailing the heads of the new Bill. I sat down to read it with no little emotion, and some apprehension; and the moment when, arriving at the end, I found that the government scheme and my own were identical, point by point, was not one to be easily forgotten. I never wrote any thing with more glee than 'The Hamlets,'— the number in which the proposed reform is exemplified: and the spirit of the work carried me through the great effort of writing that number and 'Cinnamon and Pearls' in one month,—during a country visit in glorious summer weather.

Soon after my Poor-law Tales began to appear, I received a message from Mr. Barnes, Editor-in-chief of the 'Times,'[1] intimating that the 'Times' was prepared to support my work, which would be a valuable auxiliary of the proposed reform. I returned no answer, not seeing that any was required from an author who had never had any thing to do with her reviewers, or made any interest in reviews. I said this to the friend who delivered the message, expressing at the same time my satisfaction that the government measure was to have the all-powerful support of the 'Times.' The Ministers were assured of the same support by the same potentate. How the other newspapers would go there was no saying, because the proposed reform was not a party measure; but, with the 'Times' on our side we felt pretty safe. It was on the seventeenth of April, 1834, that Lord Althorp introduced the Bill.[2] His speech, full of facts, earnest, and deeply impressive, produced a strong effect on the House; and the Ministers went home to bed with easy minds,—little imagining what awaited them at the breakfast table. It was no small vexation to me, on opening the 'Times' at breakfast on the eighteenth, to find a vehement and total condemnation of the New Poor-law. Every body in London was asking how it happened. I do not know, except in as far as I was told by some people who knew more of the management of the paper than the world in general. Their account was that the intention had really been, up to the preceding day, to support the measure; but that such reports arrived of the hostility of the country-justices,—a most important class of customers,—that a meeting of proprietors was held in the evening, when the question of supporting or opposing the measure was put to the vote. The policy of humouring the country-justices was

---

[1] Thomas Barnes (1785–1841) was editor of the *London Times* from 1817 to 1841.
[2] John Charles Spencer, Viscount Althorp and third Earl Spencer (1782–1845), was chancellor of the exchequer and leader of the House of Commons during the Whig ministry of Lord Grey. An ardent supporter of the Reform Act of 1832, he also devoted much attention to the Poor Law Bill.

carried by one vote. So went the story. Another anecdote, less openly spoken of, I believe to have been true. Lord Brougham wrote a note, I was told, to Lord Althorp, the same morning, urging him to timely attendance at the Cabinet Council, as it must be immediately decided whether Barnes, (who was not very favourably described,) and the 'Times' should be propitiated or defied. A letter or message arriving from Lord Althorp which rendered the sending the note unnecessary, Lord Brougham tore it up, and threw it into the waste-basket under the table. The fragments were by somebody or other abstracted from the basket, pasted together, and sent to Mr. Barnes, whose personal susceptibility was extreme. From that day began the baiting of Lord Brougham in the 'Times' which set every body inquiring what so fierce a persecution could mean; and the wonder ceased only when the undisciplined politician finally fell from his rank as a statesman, and forfeited the remains of his reputation within two years afterwards.[1] A searching domestic inquiry was instituted; but, up to the time of my being told the story, no discovery had been made of the mischief-maker who had picked up the scraps of the note.

After talking over the debate and the comment on it with my mother and aunt, that April morning, I went up to my study to work, and was presently interrupted by a note which surprised me so much that I carried it to my mother. It was from a lady with whom I had only a very slight acquaintance,—the wife of a Member of Parliament of high consideration. This lady invited me to take a drive with her that morning, and mentioned that she was going to buy plants at a nursery. My mother advised me to leave my work early, for once, and go, for the fresh air and the pleasure. My correspondent called for me, and, before we were off the stones, out came the reason of the invitation. Her husband was aghast at the course of the 'Times,' and had been into the City to buy the 'Morning Chronicle,'—then a far superior paper to what it has been since. He and a friend were now the proprietors of the 'Chronicle,' and no time was to be lost in finding writers who could and would support the New Poor-law. I was the first to be invited, because I was known to have been acquainted with the principles and provisions of

---

[1]   Martineau alludes to Lord Brougham's exclusion from the cabinet when, in 1835, the Whigs returned to power with Lord Melbourne as prime minister and Lord John Russell as home secretary. His animosity to Lord Durham (discussed in Period IV, sec. ii)—over Catholic emancipation, over Brougham's exclusion from the committee that drafted the Reform Act of 1832, and over Durham's governance of Canada—led Brougham to public behavior that exceeded the bounds of civility; King William's disgust with Brougham, then lord chancellor, was a factor in his dismissal of the Whig ministry in 1834.

the measure from the beginning. The invitation to me was to write 'leaders' on the New Poor-law, as long as such support should be wanted. I asked why the proprietor did not do it himself, and found that he was really so engaged in parliamentary committees as to be already over-worked. I declared myself over-worked too; but I was entreated to take a few hours for consideration. An answer was to be sent for at five o'clock. My mother and I talked the matter over. The inducements were very strong; for I could not but see that I was the person for the work: but my mother said it would kill me,—busy as I was at present. I believed that it would injure my own Series; and I therefore declined.—For many months afterwards, even for years, it was a distasteful task to read the 'Times' on the New Poor-law,—so venomous, so unscrupulous, so perti-nacious, so mischievous in intention, and so vicious in principle was its opposition to a reform which has saved the state. But, as the reform was strong enough to stand, this hostility has been eventually a very great benefit. Bad as was the spirit of the opposition, it assumed the name of humanity, and did some of the work of humanity. Every weak point of the measure was exposed, and every extravagance chastised. Its right-eousness and principled humanity were ignored; and every accidental pressure or inconvenience was made the most of. The faults of the old law were represented (as by Mr. Dickens in 'Oliver Twist') as those of the new,[1] and every effort was made to protract the exercise of irre-sponsible power by the country justices: but the measure was working, all the while, for the extinction of the law-made vices and miseries of the old system; and the process was aided by the stimulating vigilance of the 'Times,' which evoked at once the watchfulness and activity of offi-cials and the spirit of humanity in society,—both essential conditions of the true working of the new law.—My share in the punishment I could never understand. Neither my mother nor I mentioned to any person whatever the transaction of that morning: but in a few days appeared a venomous attack on the Member of Parliament who had bought the 'Chronicle,' in the course of which he was taunted with going to a young lady in Fludyer Street for direction in his political conduct. After that, there were many such allusions:—my friends were appealed to to

---

[1]   The opening chapters of *Oliver Twist* (1837–38) depict the cruel treatment of pauper chil-dren like Oliver, who was born in a workhouse. Especially scathing is Dickens's depiction of Bumble, the tyrannical "beadle" (overseer of the workhouse) who keeps the children on starvation diets and refuses Oliver's request for more food. As Martineau notes, this depiction might as easily represent the old system as the workhouse of the New Poor Law, which was overseen by Guardians, not parish officers like Bumble.

check my propensity to write about all things whatsoever,—the world having by this time quite books enough of mine: and the explanation given of the ill success and bad working of the Whig measures was that the Ministers came to me for them. This sort of treatment gave me no pain, because I was not acquainted with any body belonging to the 'Times,' and I was safe enough with the public by this time: but I thought it rather too much when Mr. Sterling, 'the Thunderer of the "Times," ' [1] and at that period editor-in-chief, obtained an invitation to meet me, after the publication of my books on America, alleging that he himself had never written a disrespectful word of me. My reply was that he was responsible, as editor, and that I used the only method of self-defence possible to a woman under a course of insult like that, in declining his acquaintance. Not long afterwards, when I was at Tynemouth, hopelessly ill, poor and helpless, the 'Times' abused and insulted me for privately refusing a pension. Again Mr. Sterling made a push for my acquaintance; and I repeated what I had said before: whereupon he declared that 'it cut him to the heart' that I should impute to him the ribaldry and coarse insults of scoundrels and ruffians who treated me as I had been treated in the 'Times.' I dare say what he said of his own feelings was true enough; but it will never do for responsible editors, like Sterling and Lockhart, to shirk their natural retribution for the sins of their publica-tions by laying the blame on some impalpable offender who, on his part, has very properly relied on their responsibility. It appears to me that social honesty and good faith can be preserved only by thus enforcing integrity in the matter of editorial responsibility.

A curious incident occurred, much to the delight of my Edinburgh reviewer, in connexion with that story,—'The Hamlets,'—which, as I have said, I enjoyed writing exceedingly. While I was preparing its doctrine and main facts, I went early one summer morning, with a sister, to the Exhibition at Somerset House, (as it was in those days). I stopped before a picture by Collins,—'Children at the Haunts of the Sea-fowl;' and, after a good study of it, I told my sister that I had before thought of laying the scene by the sea-side, and that this bewitching picture decided me. [2] The girl in the corner, in the red petticoat, was irresistible; and she should be my heroine. There should be a heroine,—a girl and

---

[1] Edward Sterling (1773–1847) was a lead writer ("thunderer") for the *Times*—as in, "We thundered out the other day an article on social and political reform."

[2] William Collins (1788–1847) was a landscape painter famous for his scenes of the sea, often peopled with children. This picture, exhibited at the Royal Academy in 1833, depicts two boys on a dangerous rocky ledge, with a girl below who has descended by a safer route.

a boy, instead of two boys. I did this, and, incited by old associations, described myself and a brother (in regard to character) in these two personages. Soon after, at a music-party, my hostess begged to introduce to me Mr. Collins the artist, who wished to make his acknowledgments for some special obligation he was under to me. This seemed odd, when I was hailing the opportunity for precisely the same reason. Mr. Collins begged to shake hands with me because I had helped him to his great success at the Academy that year. He explained that Mrs. Marcet[1] had paid him a visit when he had fully sketched, and actually begun his picture, and had said to him 'Before you go on with this, you ought to read Miss Martineau's description in 'Ella of Garveloch' of destroying the eagle's nest.' Mr. Collins did so, and in consequence altered his picture in almost every part; and now, in telling me the incident, he said that his chief discontent with his work was not having effaced the figure of the girl in the corner. He was reconciled to her, however, when I told him that the girl in the red petticoat was the heroine of the story I was then writing. This incident strikes me as a curious illustration of the way in which minds play into one another when their faculties of conception and suggestion are kindred, whatever may be their several modes of expression. One of my chief social pleasures was meeting Wilkie,[2] and planning pictures with him, after his old manner, though alas! he was now painting in his new. He had returned from Spain, with his portfolios filled with sketches of Spanish ladies, peasants and children; and he enjoyed showing these treasures of his, I remember, to my mother and me one day when we went by invitation to Kensington,[3] to see them. But his heart was, I am sure, in his old style. He used to watch his opportunity,—being very shy,—to get a bit of talk with me unheard, about what illustrations of my stories should be, saying that nothing would make him so happy, if he were but able, as to spend the rest of his painting-life in making a gallery from my Series. He told me which group or action he should select from each number, as far as then published, and dwelt particularly, I remember, on the one in 'Ireland,' which was Dora letting down her petticoat from her shoulders as she entered the cabin. I write this in full recollection of Wilkie's countenance, voice and words, but in total forgetfulness of my own story, Dora,

---

[1]   Jane Haldimand Marcet (1769–1858) wrote *Conversations on Political Economy* (1816), which presented economic theory in conversations between a pupil, Caroline, and her tutor, Mrs. B. Her work influenced Martineau's *Illustrations of Political Economy*.

[2]   David Wilkie (1785–1841), genre painter and friend of William Collins.

[3]   District south of Hyde Park and Kensington Gardens where many middle-class artists lived at mid-nineteenth century.

and the cabin. I have not the book at hand for reference, but I am sure I am reporting Wilkie truly. He told me that he thought the resemblance of our respective mind's-eyes was perfectly singular; and that, for aught he saw, each of us might, as well as not, have done the other's work, as far as the pictorial faculties were concerned.

I have one more little anecdote to tell about the heroine of 'The Hamlets.' I was closely questioned by Miss Berry,[1] one day when dining there, about the sources of my draughts of character,—especially of children,—and above all, of Harriet and Ben in 'The Hamlets.' I acknowledged that these last were more like myself and my brother than any body else. Whereupon the lively old lady exclaimed, loud enough to be heard by the whole party, 'My God! did you go out shrimping?' 'No,' I replied: 'nor were we workhouse children. What you asked me about was the characters.'

While these Poor-law tales were appearing, I received a letter from Mrs. Fry,[2] requesting an interview for purposes of importance, at any time and place I might appoint. I appointed a meeting in Newgate, at the hour on a Tuesday morning when Mrs. Fry was usually at that post of sublime duty. Wishing for a witness, as our interview was to be one of business, I took with me a clerical friend of mine as an appropriate person. After the usual services, Mrs. Fry led the way into the Matron's room, where we three sat down for our conference. Mrs. Fry's objects were two. The inferior one was to engage me to interest the government in her newly planned District Societies. The higher one was connected with the Poor-law reform then in preparation. She told me that her brother, J.J. Gurney, and other members of her family had become convinced by reading 'Cousin Marshall' and others of my tales that they had been for a long course of years unsuspectingly doing mischief where they meant to do good; that they were now convinced that the true way of benefiting the poor was

---

1   Mary Berry (1763–1852) was a minor dramatist, friend of Horace Walpole, and fashionable eighteenth-century woman of letters. She had published a *Comparative View of the Social Life of England and France, from the Restoration of Charles the Second, to the French Revolution* (1828). At her death, Martineau wrote her obituary for the London *Daily News* and included it as an appendix to the first volume of her *Autobiography*.

2   Elizabeth Fry (1780–1845)), a Quaker famous for her work in prison reform, came from the Gurney family of Norfolk, well known to the Martineaus (see Period III, sec. iv). In her day Fry's image was widely known through the painting, *Elizabeth Fry Reading to Prisoners at Newgate in 1816*; today, she appears on the £5 note. John Joseph Gurney (1788–1847), her younger brother, was a philanthropist and religious writer who also worked to reform prisons and abolish the slave trade. Richard Hanbury Gurney (1783–1854) was M.P. for Norwich in 1818–26 and 1830–32.

to reform the Poor-law system; and that they were fully sensible of the importance of the measure to be brought forward, some months hence, in parliament. Understanding that I was in the confidence of the government as to this measure, they desired to know whether I could honourably give them an insight into the principles on which it was to be founded. Their object in this request was good. They desired that their section of the House of Commons should have time and opportunity to consider the subject, which might not be attainable in the hurry of a busy session. On consideration, I had no scruple in communicating the principles, without, of course, any disclosure of the measures. Mrs. Fry noted them down, with cheerful thanks, and assurances that they would not be thrown away. They were not thrown away. That section of Members came well prepared for the hearing of the measure, and one and all unflinchingly supported it.

From the time of my settlement in London, there was no fear of any dearth of information on any subject which I wished to treat. Every party, and every body who desired to push any object, forwarded to me all the information they held. It was, in fact, rather ridiculous to see the onset on my acquaintances made by riders of hobbies. One acquaintance of mine told me, as I was going to his house to dinner, that three gentlemen had been at his office that morning;—one beseeching him to get me to write a number on the navigable rivers of Ireland; a second on (I think) the Hamiltonian (or other) system of Education; and a third, who was confident that the welfare of the nation depended on it, on the encouragement of flax-growing in the interior of Guiana. Among such applicants, the Socialists were sure to be found; and Mr. Owen[1] was presently at my ear, laying down the law in the way which he calls 'proof,' and really interesting me by the candour and cheerfulness, the benevolence and charming manners which would make him the most popular man in England if he could but distinguish between assertion and argument, and abstain from wearying his friends with his monotonous doctrine. If I remember right, it was after my anti-socialist story, 'For Each and for All,' that I became acquainted with Mr. Owen himself; but the material was supplied by his disciples,—for the chance of what use I might make of it: so that I was perfectly free to come out as their opponent. Mr. Owen was not at all offended at my doing so. Having still

---

[1]   Robert Owen (1771–1858), a Welsh-born manufacturer, became a pioneer in British and American socialism. In 1825 he founded the New Harmony Community, based on Owenite principles, in southern Indiana, but it failed by 1827 and cost him his fortune and his theory, its influence.

strong hopes of Prince Metternich[1] for a convert, he might well have hopes of me: and, believing Metternich to be, if the truth were known, a disciple of his, it is no wonder if I also was given out as being so. For many months, my pleasant visitor had that hope of me; and when he was obliged to give it up, it was with a kindly sigh. He was sure that I desired to perceive the truth; but I had got unfortunately bewildered. I was like the traveller who could not see the wood for the trees. I cannot recal that story, more or less; ('For Each and All;') but I know it must have contained the stereotyped doctrine of the Economists of that day.

What I witnessed in America considerably modified my views on the subject of Property; and from that time forward I saw social modifications taking place which have already altered the tone of leading Economists, and opened a prospect of further changes which will probably work out in time a totally new social state. If that should ever happen, it ought to be remembered that Robert Owen was the sole apostle of the principle in England at the beginning of our century. Now that the Economy of Association[2] is a fact acknowledged by some of our most important recent institutions,—as the London Clubs, our Model Lodging-houses, and dozens of new methods of Assurance, every one would willingly assign his due share of honour to Robert Owen, but for his unfortunate persistency in his other characteristic doctrine,—that Man is the creature of circumstances,—his notion of 'circumstances' being literally *surroundings*, no allowance, or a wholly insufficient allowance, being made for constitutional structure and differences. His certainty that we might make life a heaven, and his hallucination that we are going to do so immediately, under his guidance, have caused his wisdom to be overlooked in his absurdity, and his services to be too nearly forgotten in vexation and fatigue at his eccentricity. I own I became weary of him, while ashamed, every time I witnessed his fine

---

[1]   Prince Klemens von Metternich (1773–1859) was minister of Austrian foreign affairs from 1809 to 1848. After the Napoleonic wars, he became the restorer of the "Old Regime" and overseer of the reconstruction of Europe. Given his conservative politics, it is no wonder that Martineau doubts Metternich's conversion to Owenite socialism, but it is nonetheless true that Metternich invited Owen to visit him in 1818, and employed government clerks for recording the conversations and copying documents relating to Owen's "Social System." Metternich found much of use in Owen's organizational schemes, and the Prussian system of education is said to owe much of its discipline to Owen's principles.

[2]   "Economy of Association," a favorite Owenite phrase, included the systematizing of the details of subsistence, clothing, education, leisure and amusements, and the management of the mill, farm, dairy, etc., so that the administration of the social unit would be efficient and of high quality.

temper and manners, of having felt so. One compact that we made, three parts in earnest, seems to me, at this distance of time, excessively ludicrous. I saw that he was often wide of the mark, in his strictures on the religious world, through his ignorance of the Bible; and I told him so. He said he knew the Bible so well as to have been heartily sick of it in his early youth. He owned that he had never read it since. He promised to read the four Gospels carefully, if I would read 'Hamlet,' with a running commentary of Necessarian doctrine in my own mind. My share was the easier, inasmuch as I was as thoroughgoing a Necessarian as he could desire. I fulfilled my engagement, internally laughing all the while at what Shakspere would be thinking, if he could know what I was about. No doubt, Mr. Owen did his part too, like an honourable man; and no doubt with as much effect produced on him by this book as by every other, as a blind man in the presence of the sunrise, or a deaf one of an oratorio. Robert Owen is not the man to think differently of a book for having read it; and this from no want of candour, but simply from more than the usual human inability to see any thing but what he has made up his mind to see.

I cannot remember what put the scene and story of my twelfth number, 'French Wines and Politics,' into my head: but I recall some circumstances about that and the following number, 'The Charmed Sea,' which amused me extremely at the time. Among the very first of my visitors at my lodgings was Mrs. Marcet, whose 'Conversations' had revealed to me the curious fact that, in my early tales about Wages and Machinery,[1] I had been writing Political Economy without knowing it. Nothing could be more kindly and generous than her acknowledgment and enjoyment of what she called my 'honours.' The best of it was, she could never see the generosity on which her old friends complimented her, because, by her own account, there was no sort of rivalship between us. She had a great opinion of great people;—of people great by any distinction,—ability, office, birth and what not: and she innocently supposed her own taste to be universal. Her great pleasure in regard to me was to climb the two flights of stairs at my lodgings (asthma notwithstanding) to tell me of great people who were admiring, or at least reading, my Series. She brought me 'hommages' and all that sort of thing, from French savans, foreign ambassadors, and others; and, above all the rest was her satisfaction in telling me that the then new and popular sovereign, Louis Philippe, had ordered a copy of my Series for each member of his

---

[1]   *The Rioters* (1827) and *The Turn-Out* (1829), discussed in Period III, sec. iii.

family, and had desired M. Guizot to introduce a translation of it into the national schools.[1] This was confirmed, in due time, by the translator, who wrote to me for some particulars of my personal history, and announced a very large order for the work from M. Guizot. Before I received this letter, my twelfth number was written, and I think in the press. About the same time, I heard from some other quarter, (I forget what) that the Emperor of Russia had ordered a copy of the Series for every member of his family; and my French translator wrote to me, some time afterwards, that a great number of copies had been bought, by the Czar's order, for his schools in Russia. While my twelfth number was printing, I was writing the thirteenth, 'The Charmed Sea,'—that sea being the Baikal Lake, the scenery Siberian, and the personages exiled Poles. The Edinburgh Review charged me with relaxing my Political Economy for the sake of the fiction, in this case,—the reviewer having kept his article open for the appearance of the latest number obtainable before the publication of the review. There was some little mistake about this; the fact being that the bit of doctrine I had to deal with,—the origin of currency,—hardly admitted of any exemplification at all. Wherever the scene had been laid, the doctrine would have been equally impracticable in action, and must have been conveyed mainly by express explanation or colloquial commentary. If any action were practicable at all, it must be in some scene where the people were at the first remove from a state of barter: and the Poles in Siberia, among Mongolian neighbours, were perhaps as good for my purpose as any other personages. Marco Polo's account of the stamped leather currency he met with in his travels determined me in regard to Asiatic scenery, in the first place; and the poet Campbell's appeals to me in behalf of the Poles, before I left Norwich, and the visits of the venerable Niemcewicz, and other Poles and their friends, when I went to London, made me write of the Charmed Sea of Siberia.[2] My reviewer was right as to the want of the due subordination of other interests to that of the science; but he failed to perceive that that particular bit of science was abstract and uninteresting. I took the hint,

---

[1]   Louis Philippe (1773–1850), known as the Citizen King, was king of France from 1830 to 1848. François Guizot (1787–1874) was his minister of instruction from 1832 to 1837. In 1847, Guizot became premier.

[2]   Thomas Campbell (1777–1844), a Scottish poet known for his ballads and war songs, was a political supporter of Polish liberation. Julian Ursin Niemcewicz (1758–1841) was a Polish poet famous for his *Historical Songs of the Poles* (1816), a series about heroes of Poland's golden age; he had been Kosciuszko's aide-de-camp during the insurrection of 1794, after which he fled to America; he was driven into exile again in 1831 after the unsuccessful resistance to the Russian annexation of Poland.

however; and from that time I was on my guard against making my Series a vehicle for any of the 'causes' of the time. I saw that if my Edinburgh reviewer could not perceive that some portions of doctrine were more susceptible of exemplification than others, such discrimination was not to be expected of the whole public; and I must afford no occasion for being supposed to be forsaking my main object for such temporary interests as came in my way.—Meantime, the incidents occurred which amused my friends and myself so much, in connexion with these two numbers. On the day of publication of the twelfth, Mrs. Marcet climbed my stair-case, and appeared, more breathless than ever, at a somewhat early hour,—as soon as my door was open to visitors. She was in a state of distress and vexation. 'I thought I had told you,' said she, in the midst of her panting,—'but I suppose you did not hear me:—I thought I had told you that the King of the French read all your stories, and made all his family read them: and now you have been writing about Egalité; and they will never read you again.' I told her I had heard her very well; but it was not convenient to me to alter my story, for no better reason than that. It was from history, and not from private communication, that I drew my materials; and I had no doubt that Louis Philippe and his family thought of his father very much as I did. My good friend could not see how I could hope to be presented at the Tuileries after this: and I could only say that it had never entered my head to wish it. I tried to turn the conversation to account by impressing on my anxious friend the hopelessness of all attempts to induce me to alter my stories from such considerations as she urged. I wrote with a view to the people, and especially the most suffering of them; and the crowned heads must, for once, take their chance for their feelings. A month after, I was subjected to similar reproaches about the Emperor of Russia. He was, in truth, highly offended. He ordered every copy of my Series to be delivered up, and then burnt or deported; and I was immediately forbidden the empire. His example was followed in Austria; and thus, I was personally excluded, before my Series was half done, from two of the three greatest countries in Europe, and in disfavour with the third,—supposing I wished to go there. My friends, Mr. and Mrs. F—,[1] invited me to go to the south of Europe with them on the conclusion of my work: and our plan was nearly settled when reasons appeared for my going to America instead.

---

[1]   Probably Mr. and Mrs. Fisher of Highbury, mentioned as close friends in Period IV, sec. ii. Joseph Fisher (1795–1890) was an etcher-engraver who worked regularly for magazines and produced his own books of engravings.

My friends went south when I went west. Being detained by inundation on the borders of Austrian Italy, they were weary of their dull hotel. All other amusement being exhausted, Mr. F— sauntered round the open part of the house, reading whatever was hung against the walls. One document contained the names and description of persons who were not to be allowed to pass the frontier; and mine was among them. If I had been with my friends, our predicament would have been disagreeable. They could not have deserted me; and I must have deprived them of the best part of their journey.

In planning my next story, 'Berkeley the Banker,' I submitted myself to my reviewer's warning, and spared no pains in thoroughly incorporating the doctrine and the tale. I remember that, for two days, I sat over my materials from seven in the morning till two the next morning, with an interval of only twenty minutes for dinner. At the end of my plotting, I found that, after all, I had contrived little but relationships, and that I must trust to the uprising of new involutions in the course of my narrative. I had believed before, and I went on during my whole career of fiction-writing to be more and more thoroughly convinced, that the creating a plot is a task above human faculties. It is indeed evidently the same power as that of prophecy: that is, if all human action is (as we know it to be) the inevitable result of antecedents, all the antecedents must be thoroughly comprehended in order to discover the inevitable catastrophe. A mind which can do this must be, in the nature of things, a prophetic mind, in the strictest sense; and no human mind is that. The only thing to be done, therefore, is to derive the plot from actual life, where the work is achieved for us: and, accordingly, it seems that every perfect plot in fiction is taken bodily from real life. The best we know are so derived. Shakspere's are so: Scott's one perfect plot ('the Bride of Lammermoor') is so; and if we could know where Boccaccio and other old narrators got theirs, we should certainly find that they took them from their predecessors, or from the life before their eyes. I say this from no mortification at my own utter inability to make a plot. I should say the same, (after equal study of the subject) if I had never tried to write a tale. I see the inequality of this kind of power in contemporary writers; an inequality wholly independent of their merits in other respects; and I see that the writers (often inferior ones) who have the power of making the best plots do it by their greater facility in forming analogous narratives with those of actual experience. They may be, and often are, so inferior as writers of fiction to others who cannot make plots that one is tempted to wish that they and their superiors could be rolled into one, so as to make a perfect novelist or dramatist. For instance, Dickens cannot make a plot,—nor Bulwer,—nor Douglas Jerrold, nor perhaps Thackeray; while Fanny Kemble's forgotten 'Francis the First,' written in her teens, contains mines of plot, sufficient to furnish a groundwork for a score of fine fictions.[1] As for me, my incapacity in this direction is so absolute that I always worked under a sense of despair about it. In the 'Hour and the Man,' for instance, there are prominent personages who have no necessary connexion whatever with the story; and the personages fall out of sight, till at last, my hero is alone in his dungeon, and the story ends with his solitary death. I was not careless, nor unconscious of my inability. It was inability, 'pure and simple.' My only resource therefore was taking suggestion from facts, witnessed by myself, or gathered in any way I could. That tale of 'Berkeley the Banker' owed its remarkable success, not to my hard work of those two days; but to my taking some facts from the crisis of 1825–6 for the basis of my story. The toil of those two days was not thrown away, because the amalgamation of doctrine and narrative was more complete than it would otherwise have been: but no protraction of the effort would have brought out a really good plot, any more than the most prodigious amount of labour in practicing would bring out good music from a performer unendowed with musical faculty.

That story was, in a great degree, as I have already said, our own family history of four years before. The most amusing thing to me was that the relative (not one of my nearest relations) who was presented as Berkeley,[2]—(by no means exactly, but in the main characteristics and in some conspicuous speeches) was particularly delighted with that story. He seized it eagerly, as being about banking, and expressed his admiration, far and wide, of the character of the banker, as being so extremely natural! His unconscious pleasure was a great relief to me: for, while I could not resist the temptation his salient points offered me, I dreaded the consequences of my free use of them.

About the next number, 'Vanderput and Snoek,' I have a curious confession to make. It was necessary to advertise on the cover of each tale the title of the next. There had never been any difficulty thus far,—it

---

[1] Charles Dickens (1812–70), Edward Bulwer (later Bulwer-Lytton) (1803–73), and William Makepeace Thackeray (1811–63) were leading novelists in the 1840s and 50s. Douglas Jerrold (1803–57) wrote novels but was better known as a journalist and contributor to *Punch*. Frances' (Fanny) Kemble (1809–93) came from a distinguished theatrical family and became a famous actress.

[2] Possibly Martineau's uncle, Peter Martineau ((1755–1847), who, according to Valerie Sanders, was at one time a banker and partner in Martineau and Story of St. Albans.

being my practice, as I have said, to sit down to the study of a new number within a day or two, or a few hours, of finishing its predecessor. My banking story was, however, an arduous affair; and I had to write the first of my Poor-law series. I was thus driven so close that when urged by the printer for the title of my next number, I was wholly unprepared. All I knew was that my subject was to be Bills of Exchange. The choice of scene lay between Holland and South America, where Bills of Exchange are, or then were, either more numerous or more important than any where else. I thought Holland on the whole the more convenient of the two; so I dipped into some book about that country (Sir William Temple,[1] I believe it was), picked out the two ugliest Dutch names I could find, made them into a firm, and boldly advertised them. Next, I had to consider how to work up to my title: and in this I met with most welcome assistance from my friends, Mr. and Mrs. F—, of Highbury.[2] They were well acquainted with the late British Consul at Rotterdam, then residing in their neighbourhood. They had previously proposed to introduce me to this gentleman, for the sake of the information he could give me about Dutch affairs: and I now hastened to avail myself of the opportunity. The ex-consul was made fully aware of my object, and was delighted to be of use. We met at Mr. F.'s breakfast table; and in the course of the morning he gave me all imaginable information about the aspect and habits of the country and people. When I called on his lady, some time afterwards, I was struck by the pretty picture presented by his twin daughters, who were more exactly alike than any other twins I have ever seen. They sat beside a work-table, at precisely the same angle with it: each had a foot on a footstool, for the sake of her netting. They drew their silk through precisely at the same instant, and really conveyed a perplexing impression of a mirror where mirror there was none. The Dromios[3] could not be more puzzling. The temptation to put these girls into a story was too strong to be resisted: but, as I knew the family were interested in my Series at the moment, I waited a while. After a decent interval, they appeared in 'The Park and the Paddock;' and then only in regard to externals; for I knew nothing more of them whatever.

When I had to treat of Free Trade, I took advantage, of course, of the picturesque scenery and incidents connected with smuggling. The

---

[1] Sir William Temple, *Observations upon the United Provinces of the Netherlands* (London, 1793), frequently reprinted in the nineteenth century.
[2] Mr. and Mrs. Joseph Fisher; see p. 188, n. 1.
[3] The name comes from characters in Shakespeare's *Comedy of Errors*, about two pairs of twins involved in an elaborate series of mistaken identities.

only question was what part of the coast I should choose for my seventeenth and eighteenth numbers, 'The Loom and the Lugger.' I questioned all my relations and friends who had frequented Eastbourne and
that neighbourhood about the particulars of the locality and scenery. It
struck me as curious that, of all the many whom I asked, no one could
tell me whether there was a lighthouse at Beachy Head.[1] A cousin told
me that she was acquainted with a farmer's family living close by
Beachy Head, and in the very midst of the haunts of the smugglers. This
farmer was under some obligation to my uncle, and would be delighted
at the opportunity of rendering a service to any of the name. My
publisher was willing to set down the trip to the account of the
expenses of the Series; and I went down, with a letter of introduction
in my hand, to see and learn all I could in the course of a couple of
days. My time was limited, not only by the exigencies of my work, but
by an engagement to meet my Edinburgh reviewer for the first time,—
as I have mentioned above,—and to another very especial party for the
same evening. On a fine May evening, therefore, I presented myself at
the farm-house door, with my letter in my hand. I was received with
surpassing grace by two young girls,—their father and elder sister being
absent at market. Tea was ready presently; and then, one of the girls
proposed a walk to 'the Head' before dark. When we returned, every
thing was arranged; and the guest chamber looked most tempting to an
overworked Londoner. The farmer and one daughter devoted the
whole of the next day to me. We set forth, carrying a new loaf and a
bottle of beer, that we might not be hurried in our explorations. I then
and there learned all that appears in 'The Loom and the Lugger' about
localities and the doings of smugglers. Early the following morning I
went to see Pevensey Castle, and in the forenoon was in the coach on
my way back to town. I was so cruelly pressed for time that, finding
myself alone in the coach, I wrote on my knees all the way to London,
in spite of the jolting. At my lodging, I was in consternation at seeing
my large round table heaped with the letters and parcels which had
arrived during those two days. I dispatched fourteen notes, dressed, and
was at Lady S.'s by the time the clock struck six. The quiet, friendly
dinner was a pure refreshment; but the evening party was a singular trial.
I had been compelled to name the day for this party, as I had always

---

[1]   The Belle Tout Lighthouse was erected in 1831 on the chalk headland of Beachy Head,
near Eastbourne, on the south coast of England. Pevensey Castle, begun c. 1080, is seven
miles east.

been engaged when invited by my hostess. I thought it odd that my name was shouted by the servants, in preference to that of Lady C—, with whom I entered the room: and the way in which my hostess took possession of me, and began to parade me before her noble and learned guests showed me that I must at once take my part, if I desired to escape the doom of 'lionising.' The lady, having two drawing-rooms open, had provided a 'lion' for each. Rammohun Roy[1] was stationed in the very middle of one, meek and perspiring; and I was intended for the same place in the other. I saw it just in time. I took my stand with two or three acquaintances behind the folding-doors, and maintained my retirement till the carriage was announced. If this was bad manners, it was the only alternative to worse. I owe to that incident a friendship which has lasted my life. That friend, till that evening known to me only by name, had been behind the scenes, and had witnessed all the preparations; and very curious she was to see what I should do. If I had permitted the lionising, she would not have been introduced to me. When I got behind the door, she joined our trio; and we have been intimate friends to this day. Long years after, she gave me her account of that memorable evening. What a day it was! When Lady S. set me down at midnight, and I began to undress, and feel how weary I was, it seemed incredible that it was that very morning that I had seen Pevensey Castle, and heard the dash of the sea, and listened to the larks on the down. The concluding thought, I believe, before I fell into the deep sleep I needed, was that I would never visit a second time at any house where I was 'lionised.'

The Anti-corn law tale,[2] 'Sowers not Reapers,' cost me great labour,—clear as was the doctrine, and familiar to me for many a year past. I believe it is one of the most successful for the incorporation of the doctrine with the narrative: and the story of the Kays is true, except that, in real life, the personages were gentry. I had been touched by that story when told it, some years before; and now it seemed to fit in well

---

[1]   Rammohun Roy (1773–1833), an Indian educator and religious teacher, sought to preserve Hinduism, which he recognized as a strong unifying force in India, while removing from it the practice of idolatry, gender discrimination, and the caste system. His book, *The Precepts of Jesus* (1820), was an adaptation of Christian ethical and humanitarian teachings without its dogma or theology.

[2]   The Corn Law of 1815 protected the agricultural interests of Britain by prohibiting the importation of corn (i.e., grain) until the price on the domestic market had reached 80 shillings a quarter. The Anti-Corn Law League, officially formed in 1838 but unofficially active earlier, opposed this protective tariff, arguing that it helped the landed gentry and hurt both manufacturers who needed to export goods and workers who needed cheap bread.

with my other materials. Two years afterwards I met with a bit of strong
evidence of the monstrous vice and absurdity of our corn-laws in the
eyes of Americans. This story, 'Sowers not Reapers,' was republished in
America while I was there; and Judge Story,[1] who knew more about
English laws, manners and customs, condition, literature, and even
topography than any other man in the United States, told me that I
need not expect his countrymen in general to understand the book, as
even he, after all his preparedness, was obliged to read it twice,—first to
familiarise himself with the conception, and then to study the doctrine.
Thus incredible was it that so proud and eminent a nation as ours
should persist in so insane and suicidal a policy as that of protection, in
regard to the most indispensable article of food.

Among the multitude of letters of suggestion which had by this time
been sent me, was an anonymous one from Oxford, which gave me the
novel information that the East India Company constituted a great
monopoly. While thinking that, instead of being one, it was a nest of
monopolies (in 1833) I speculated on which of them I might best take
for an illustration of my anti-monopoly doctrine. I feared an opium
story might prove immoral, and I did not choose to be answerable for
the fate of any Opium-eaters. Salt was too thirsty a subject for a July
number. Cinnamon was fragrant, and pearls pretty and cool: and these,
of course, led me to Ceylon for my scenery. I gathered what I could
from books, but really feared being obliged to give up a singularly good
illustrative scene for want of the commonest facts concerning the social
life of the Cingalese. I found scarcely any thing even in Maria Graham
and Heber. At this precise time, a friend happened to bring to my lodging, for a call, the person who could be most useful to me, —Sir
Alexander Johnstone,[2] who had just returned from governing Ceylon,
where he had abolished Slavery, established Trial by Jury, and become
more thoroughly acquainted with the Cingalese than perhaps any other
man then in England. It was a remarkable chance; and we made the
most of it; for Sir Alexander Johnstone was as well pleased to have the
cause of the Cingalese pleaded as I was to become qualified to do it.
Before we had known one another half an hour, I confided to him my

---

[1] Joseph Story (1779–1845) was a constitutional scholar, justice of the American Supreme
    Court, and father of the sculptor, William Wetmore Story (1819–95).
[2] I.e., Maria Graham's *Journal of a Residence in India* (1812) and Bishop Reginald Heber's
    Narrative of a Journey through India (1828). Alexander Johnstone was appointed chief justice
    of Ceylon (now Sri Lanka) in 1805 and returned to England in 1809 to recommend a
    series of reforms.

difficulty. He started off, promising to return presently; and he was soon at the door again, with his carriage full of books, prints and other illustrations, affording information not to be found in any ordinarily accessible books. Among the volumes he left with me was a Colombo almanack,[1] which furnished me with names, notices of customs, and other valuable matters. The friend who had brought us together was highly delighted with the success of the introduction, and bestirred himself to see what else he could do. He invited me to dinner the next day (aware that there was no time to lose;) and at his table I met as many persons as he could pick up who had recently been in Ceylon. Besides Sir Alexander Johnstone, there was Holman, the blind traveller, and Captain Mangles, and two or three more;[2] and a curiously oriental day we had of it, in regard to conversation and train of thought. I remember learning a lesson that day on other than Cingalese matters. Poor Holman boasted of his achievements in climbing mountains, and of his always reaching the top quicker than his comrades; and he threw out some sarcasms against the folly of climbing mountains at all, as waste of time, because there were no people to be found there, and there was generally rain and cold. It evidently never occurred to him that people with eyes climb mountains for another purpose than a race against time; and that his comrades were pausing to look about them when he outstripped them. It was a hint to me never to be critical in like manner about the pleasures of the ear.—After I had become a traveller, Sydney Smith[3] amused himself about my acquaintance with Holman; and I believe it was reading what I said in the preface to my American book which put his harmless jokes into his head. In that preface I explained the extent to which my deafness was a disqualification for travel, and for reporting of it: and I did it because I knew that, if I did not, the slaveholders would make my deafness a pretext for setting aside any part

1   *The Ceylon Almanac and Compendium of Useful Information for the year 1833* (Colombo, Ceylon: P.M. Elders, 1833).

2   James Holman (1786–1857), known as the Blind Traveller, was a naval officer who lost his sight while in service and was appointed a royal knight of Windsor; he subsequently traveled through Europe, Asia, and Africa, and in 1833 wrote his memoirs, *A Voyage round the World, including Travels in Africa, Asia, Australasia, America, &c., from 1827 to 1832* (published, 1834–35). Captain Mangles is either C.E. Mangles, an M.P. connected with royal mail and the Union Steamship Company which transported it from England to India, or James Mangles (1786–1867), co-author of *Travels in Egypt and Nubia, Syria, and Asia Minor, during the years 1817 & 1818* (London, 1823).

3   Sydney Smith (1771–1845), a founder of the *Edinburgh Review*, was a clergyman-author who campaigned against slavery and transportation and in support of Catholic Emancipation.

of my testimony which they did not like. Soon after this preface appeared, and when he had heard from me of my previous meeting with Holman, Sydney Smith undertook to answer a question asked by somebody at a dinner party, what I was at that time about. 'She is writing a book,' said Sydney Smith, 'to prove that the only travellers who are fit to write books must be both blind and deaf.'

My number on the monopolies in cinnamon and pearls went off pleasantly after my auspicious beginning. Sir A. Johnstone watched over its progress, and seriously assured me afterwards, in a call made for the purpose, that there was, to the best of his belief, not a single error in the tale. There was much wrath about it in Ceylon, however; and one man published a book to show that every statement of mine, on every point, from the highest scientific to the lowest descriptive, was absolutely the opposite of the truth. This personage was an Englishman, interested in the monopoly: and the violence of his opposition was of service to the right side.

Soon after I went to my London lodgings, my mother came up, and spent two or three weeks with me. I saw at once that she would never settle comfortably at Norwich again; and I had great difficulty in dissuading her from at once taking a house which was very far beyond any means that I considered it right to reckon on. For the moment, and on occasion of her finding the particular house she had set her mind on quite out of the question, I prevailed on her to wait. I could not wonder at her desire to come up, and enjoy such society as she found me in the midst of; and I thought it, on the whole, a fortunate arrangement when, under the sanction of two of my brothers, she took the small house in Fludyer Street, Westminster,[1] where the rest of my London life was passed. That small house had, for a wonder, three sitting-rooms; and we three ladies needed this. The house had no nuisances, and was as airy as a house in Fludyer Street could well be: and its being on the verge of St James's Park was a prodigious advantage for us all,—the Park being to us, in fact, like our own garden. We were in the midst of the offices, people and books which it was most desirable for me to have at hand; and the house was exactly the right size for us; and of the right cost,—now that I was able to pay the same amount as my aunt towards the expenses of our household. My mother's little income, with these additions, just sufficed;— allowance being made for the generosity which she loved to exercise. I

---

[1]   Fludyer Street, now destroyed, was just south of Downing Street and ran directly into St. James's Park.

may as well finish at once what I have to say about this matter. For a time, as I anticipated, all went well. My mother's delight in her new social sphere was extreme. But, as I had also anticipated, troubles arose. For one of two great troubles, meddlers and mischief-makers were mainly answerable. The other could not be helped. It was, (to pass it over as lightly as possible) that my mother, who loved power and had always been in the habit of exercising it, was hurt at confidence being reposed in me, and distinctions shown, and visits paid to me; and I, with every desire to be passive, and being in fact wholly passive in the matter, was kept in a state of constant agitation at the influx of distinctions which I never sought, and which it was impossible to impart. What the meddlers and mischief-makers did was to render my old ladies, and especially my mother, discontented with the lowliness of our home. They were for ever suggesting that I ought to live in some sort of style,—to have a larger house in a better street, and lay out our mode of living for the society in which I was moving. Of course they were not my own earned friends who made such suggestions. Their officiousness proved their vulgarity; and my mother saw and said this. Yet every word told upon her heart; and thence every word helped to pull down my health and strength. No change could be made but by my providing the money; and I could not conscientiously engage to do it. It was my fixed resolution never to mortgage my brains. Scott's recent death impressed upon me an awful lesson about that.[1] Such an effort as that of producing my Series was one which could never be repeated. Such a strain was quite enough for one lifetime. I did not receive any thing like what I ought for the Series, owing to the hard terms under which it was published. I had found much to do with my first gains from it; and I was bound in conscience to lay by for a time of sickness or adversity, and for means of recreation, when my task should be done. I therefore steadily refused to countenance any scheme of ambition, or to alter a plan of life which had been settled with deliberation, and with the sanction of the family. To all remonstrances about my own dignity my reply was that if my acquaintance cared for me, they would come and see me in a small house and a narrow street: and all who objected to the smallness of either might stay away. I could not expose myself to the temptation to write in a money-getting spirit; nor yet to the terrible anxieties of assuming a position which could be maintained only by excessive toil. It was necessary to preserve my independence of thought and speech, and my power of resting, if necessary,—to have, in

---

[1]   Scott died prematurely in 1832 of overwork. See p. 156, n. 2.

short, the world under my feet instead of hanging round my neck: and therefore did I refuse all entreaty and remonstrance about our house and mode of living. I was supported, very cordially, by the good cousin who managed my affairs for me:[1] but an appeal to my brothers became necessary, at last. They simply elicited by questions the facts that the circumstances were unchanged;—that the house was exactly what we had expected; that our expenses had been accurately calculated; and that my mother's income was the same as when she had considered the house a proper one for our purposes: in short, that there was no one good reason for a change. The controversy was thus closed; but not before the train was laid for its being closed in another manner. The anxieties of my home were too much for me, and I was by that time wearing down fast. The illness which laid me low for nearly six years at length ensued; and when it did, there could be no doubt in any mind of its being most fortunate that I had contracted no responsibilities which I could not fulfil. It was a great fault in me, (and I always knew that it was) that I could not take these things more lightly. I did strive to be superior to them: but I began life, as I have said, with a most beggarly set of nerves; I had gone through such an amount of suffering and vicissitude as had weakened my *physique*, if it had strengthened my *morale*; and now, I was under a pressure of toil which left me no resource wherewith to meet any constant troubling of the affections. I held my purpose, because it was clearly right: but I could not hold my health and nerve. They gave way; and all questions about London residence were settled a few years after by our leaving London altogether. Soon after my illness laid me low, my dear old aunt died; and my mother removed to Liverpool, to be taken care of by three of her children who were settled there.

I was entering upon the first stage of this career of anxiety when I was writing my twenty-first number,—'A Tale of the Tyne.' The preparation of it was terribly laborious, for I had to superintend at that time the removal into the Fludyer Street house. The weather was hot, and the unsettlement extreme. I had to hire and initiate the servants, to receive and unpack the furniture; and to sit down at night, when all this was done, to write my number. At that time, of all seasons, arose a very serious trouble, which not only added to my fatigue of correspondence in the day, but kept me awake at night by very painful feelings of indignation, grief and disappointment. It was thought desirable, by myself as well as by others, that my plan of Illustration of Political Economy should be

---

[1]   Richard Martineau (1804–65); see Period III, sec. iv.

rendered complete by some numbers on modes of Taxation. The friends with whom I discussed the plan reminded me that I must make fresh terms with Charles Fox, the publisher. They were of opinion that I had already done more than enough for him by continuing the original terms through the whole series thus far, the agreement being dissoluble at the end of every five numbers, and he having never fulfilled, more or less, the original condition of obtaining subscribers. He had never obtained one. I accordingly wrote to Mr. Charles Fox, to inquire whether he was willing to publish five additional numbers on the usual terms of booksellers' commission. The reply was from his brother; and it was long before I got over the astonishment and pain that it caused. He claimed, for Charles, half the profits of the series, to whatever length it might extend. He supported the claim by a statement of eight reasons, so manifestly unsound that I was equally ashamed for myself and for him that he should have ventured to try them upon me. In my reply, I said that there was no foundation in law or equity for such a claim. As Mr. Charles Fox wrote boastfully of the legal advice he should proceed upon, I gladly placed this affair in the hands of a sound lawyer,—under the advice of my counsellors in the business. I put all the documents,—the original agreement and the whole correspondence, —into my lawyer's hands; and his decision was that my publisher, in making this claim, had 'not a leg to stand upon.' I was very sure of this; but the pain was not lessened thereby. I could not but feel that I had thrown away my consideration and my money upon a man who made this consideration the ground of an attempt to extort more. The whole invention and production of the work had been mine; and the entire sale was, by his own admission, owing to me. The publisher, holding himself free to back out of a losing bargain if I had not instantly succeeded, had complacently pocketed his commission of thirty per cent (on the whole) and half the profits, for simply selling the book to the public whom I sent to his shop: and now he was threatening to go to law with me for a prolongation of his unparalleled bargain. I sent him my lawyer's decision, and added that, as I disliked squabbles between acquaintances on money matters, I should obviate all pretence of a claim on his part by making the new numbers a supplement, with a new title,— calling them 'Illustrations of Taxation.' I did not take the work out of his hands, from considerations of convenience to all parties: but I made no secret of his having lost me for a client thenceforth. He owed to me such fortune as he had; and he had now precluded himself from all chance of further connexion. He published the Supplement, on the ordinary terms of commission: and there was an end. I remember nothing of that story,—

'A Tale of the Tyne;'[1] and I should be rather surprised if I did under the circumstances. The only incident that I read about it is that Mr. Malthus called on purpose to thank me for a passage, or a chapter, (which has left no trace in my memory) on the glory and beauty of love and the blessedness of domestic life; and that others, called stern Benthamites, sent round messages to me to the same effect. They said, as Mr. Malthus did, that they had met with a faithful expositor at last.

In 'Briery Creek' I indulged my life-long sentiment of admiration and love of Dr. Priestley, by making him, under a thin disguise, the hero of my tale.[2] I was staying at Lambton Castle[3] when that number appeared; and I was extremely surprised by being asked by Lady Durham who Dr. Priestley was, and all that I could tell her about him. She had seen in the newspapers that my hero was the Doctor; and I found that she, the daughter of the Prime Minister, had never heard of the Birmingham riots![4] I was struck by this evidence of what fearful things may take place in a country, unknown to the families of the chief men in it.

Of number twenty-three, 'The Three Ages,' I remember scarcely any thing. The impression remaining is that I mightily enjoyed the portraiture of Wolsey and More, and especially a soliloquy or speech of Sir Thomas More's.[5] What it is about I have no recollection whatever: and

---

[1]   A Tale of the Tyne describes press gangs, which legally captured and compelled British men to serve in the Navy. Martineau argues against impressment on the grounds that it violated "the free exercise of industry" (134) which the government had the responsibility to secure for all.

[2]   Briery Creek, set in America on a prairie settlement, illustrates the principles of productive versus unproductive consumption. Dr. Sneyd, the hero, is a philosopher-scientist who patiently continues his studies in astronomy while enduring the privations of settlement life, in contrast to his wealthy son-in-law, Mr. Temple, who complains about lack of luxuries without doing anything constructive to advance the state of the prairie settlement.

[3]   This nineteenth-century castle, complete with lion park, was the home of John George Lambton (1792–1840), Lord Durham as of 1828, and his wife, the daughter of the Prime Minister, Lord Charles Grey (1764–1845). Lord Durham, known as "Radical Jack," was a Whig who ardently supported the Reform Act of 1832, and was later governor general and high commissioner of British North America, issuing the Durham Report of 1838 for reform in the governance of Canada. Lambton Castle was not far from Newcastle upon Tyne, where Martineau's grandmother and oldest sister lived.

[4]   The Birmingham riots of July 14–18, 1791, also called the Priestley riots, broke out after a dinner held by Joseph Priestley (1733–1804) and others to commemorate the fall of the Bastille. The rioters, who considered this act of disloyalty to the established order, destroyed Dissenting chapels, houses of prominent Dissenters, and Priestley's chemical laboratory.

[5]   Thomas Wolsey (c. 1475–1530), Cardinal and Lord Chancellor under Henry VIII, and Sir Thomas More (c.1477–1535), executed for failing to swear an oath to Henry VIII above all other kings, including the Pope, appear in the first of The Three Ages. The second age is the Restoration; the third, the modern nineteenth century. The tale illustrates the uses and abuses of public expenditure for defense, public order, and social improvement.

I need not say that I have never looked at the story from the day of publication till now: but I have a strong impression that I should condemn it, if I were to read it now. I have become convinced that it is a mistake of serious importance to attempt to put one's mind of the nineteenth century into the thought of the sixteenth; and wrong, as a matter of taste, to fall into a sort of slang style, or mannerism, under the notion of talking old English. The temptation is strong to young people whose historical associations are vivid, while their intellectual sympathy is least discriminating; and young writers of a quarter of a century ago may claim special allowance from the fact that Scott's historical novels were then at the height of their popularity; but I believe that, all allowance being made, I should feel strong disgust at the affectations which not only made me very complacent at the time, but brought to me not a few urgent requests that I would write historical novels. Somewhere in that number there is a passage which Lord John Russell[1] declared to be treason, saying that it would undoubtedly bear a prosecution. The publisher smirked at this, and heartily wished somebody would prosecute. We could not make out what passage his Lordship meant; but we supposed it was probably that part which expresses pity for the Royal Family in regard to the mode in which their subsistence is provided;—such of them, I mean, as have not official duties. If it be that passage, I can only say that every man and every woman who is conscious of the blessing of living either by personal exertion or on hereditary property is thus declared guilty of treason in thought, whenever the contrast of a pensioned or eleemosynary condition and an independent one presents itself, in connexion with the Royal Family, as it was in the last generation. It might be in some other passage, however, that the liability lurked. I did not look very closely; for I cannot say that I should have at all relished the prosecution,—the idea of which was so exhilarating to my publisher.

Number twenty-four, 'The Farrers of Budge Row,' seems on the whole to be considered the best story of the Series. I have been repeatedly exhorted to reproduce the character of Jane in a novel.[2] This Jane was so far a personal acquaintance of mine that I had seen her, two or three times, on her stool behind the books, at the shop where we bought our cheese, in the neighbourhood of Fludyer Street. Her old

---

[1] Lord John Russell (1792–1878), Whig M.P. from 1813 to 1861.

[2] *The Farrers of Budge Row* discusses methods of taxation, arguing against taxes on commodities and in favor of a graduated property or income tax. In the 1830s Budge Row was a section of street between Watling and Cannon Streets in the city of London.

father's pride then was in his cheeses,—which deserved his devotion as much as cheeses can: but my mother and I were aware that his pride had once a very different object; and it was this knowledge which made me go to the shop, to get a sight of the father and daughter. There had been a younger brother of that quiet woman, who had been sent to college, and educated for one of the learned professions; but his father changed his mind, and insisted so cruelly and so long on the young man being his shopman, that the poor fellow died broken-hearted. This anecdote, and an observation that I heard on the closeness with which the daughter was confined to the desk, originated the whole story.

I wrote the chief part of the concluding number, 'The Moral of Many Fables,' during the journey to the north which I took to see my old grandmother before my departure for America, and to visit my eldest sister at Newcastle, and Lord and Lady Durham at Lambton Castle. The fatigue was excessive; and when at Lambton, I went down a coal-pit, in order to see some things which I wanted to know. The heats and draughts of the pit, combined with the fatigue of an unbroken journey by mail[1] from Newcastle to London, in December, caused me a severe attack of inflammation of the liver, and compelled the omission of a month in the appearance of my numbers. The toil and anxiety incurred to obtain the publication of the work had, as I have related, disordered my liver, two years before. I believe I had never been quite well, during those two years; and the toils and domestic anxieties of the autumn of 1833 had prepared me for overthrow by the first accident.—After struggling for days to rise from my bed, I was compelled to send word to printer and publisher that I must stop for a month. Mr. Fox (the elder) sent a cheering and consolatory note which enabled me to give myself up to the pleasure of being ill, and lying still, (as still as the pain would let me) without doubt or remorse. There was something to be done first, however; for the printer's note was not quite such a holiday matter as Mr. Fox's. It civilly explained that sixteen guineas' worth of paper had been wetted, which would be utterly spoiled, if not worked off immediately. It was absolutely necessary to correct two proofs, which, as it happened, required more attention than any which had ever passed under my eye, from their containing arithmetical statements. Several literary friends had offered to correct my proofs; but these were not of a kind to be so disposed of. So, I set to work, with dizzy eyes and a quivering brain; propped up with pillows, and my mother and the maid alter-

---

[1]   I.e., mail coach.

nately sitting by me with sal volatile, when I believed I could work a little. I was amused to hear, long afterwards, that it was reported to be my practice to work in this delightful style,—'when exhausted, to be supported in bed by her mother and her maid.' These absurd representations about myself and my ways taught me some caution in receiving such as were offered me about other authors.

It was no small matter, by this time, to have a month's respite from the fluctuations of mind which I underwent about every number of my work. These fluctuations were as regular as the tides; but I did not recognize this fact till my mother pointed it out in a laughing way which did me a world of good. When I told her, as she declared I did once a month, that the story I was writing would prove an utter failure, she was uneasy for the first few months, but afterwards amused: and her amusement was a great support to me. The process was indeed a pretty regular one. I was fired with the first conception, and believed that I had found a treasure. Then, while at work, I alternately admired and despised what I wrote. When finished, I was in absolute despair; and then, when I saw it in print, I was surprised to see how well it looked. After an interval of above twenty years, I have not courage to look at a single number,—convinced that I should be disgusted by bad taste and metaphysics in almost every page. Long before I had arrived at this closing number, my mother and aunt had got into the way of smiling at each other, and at me, whenever I bade them prepare for disgrace; and they asked me how often I had addressed the same exhortation to them before.—There was another misery of a few hours long which we had to bear once a month: and that was the sending the manuscript to the printing-office. This panic was the tax I have always paid for making no copy of any thing I write. I sent the parcel by a trusty messenger, who waited for a receipt. One day, the messenger did not return for several hours,—the official being absent whose duty it was to receive such packets. My mother said, 'I tell you what, Harriet; I can't bear this . . . .' 'Nor I either,' I replied. 'We must carry it ourselves next time.' So I would every time; but I doubt our being the safest messengers,' I was replying, when the note of acknowledgment was brought in. Now, at this new year 1834, I had a whole month of respite from all such cares, and could lie in bed without grudging the hours as they passed. It was indeed a significant yielding when, in 1831, I gave way to solicitations to produce a number a month. I did give way, (though with a trembling heart) because I knew that when I had once plunged into an enterprise, I always got through it, at whatever cost. I could not have asked any body to go into such an undertaking; and the cost was severe: but I got through; and,—if my twenty-fourth number was really the best, as people said,—without disgrace.

I was not through it yet, however. The 'Illustrations of Taxation' had still to be written. I had designed six; and I forget when and why I determined there should be only five: but I rather think it was when I found the first series must have an additional number. All I am sure of is that it was a prodigious relief, which sent my spirits up sky high, when I resolved to spare myself a month's work. Rest and leisure had now become far more important to me than fame and money. Nothing struck me so much, or left so deep and abiding an impression after the close of this arduous work, as my new sense of the value of time. A month had never before appeared to me what it now became; and I remember the real joy of finding in February, 1832, that it was leap year, and that I had a day more at my command than I had calculated. The abiding effect has perhaps not been altogether good. No doubt I have done more than I should without such an experience: but I think it has narrowed my mind. When I consider how some who knew me well have represented me as 'industrious in my pleasures;' and how some of my American friends had a scheme at Niagara to see whether I could pass a day without asking or telling what o'clock it was, I feel convinced that my respect for 'time and the hour' has been too much of a superstition and a bigotry. I say this now (1855) while finding that I *can* be idle; while, in fact, feeling myself free to do what I please,—that is, what illness admits of my doing, for above half of every day. I find, in the last stage of life, that I *can* play and be idle; and that I enjoy it. But I still think that the conflict between constitutional indolence and an overwrought sense of the value of time has done me some harm in the midst of some important good.

The Taxation numbers had, as I have said, still to be done; and, I think, the last of the Poor-law tales. I was aware that, of all the many weak points of the Grey administration, the weakest was Finance. Lord Althorp, then Chancellor of the Exchequer, complained of the hardship of being put into that office, when Nature had made him a grazier.[1] It

[1] Lord Charles Grey (1764–1845) became prime minister in 1831 as the Whigs moved ahead with the Reform Bill of 1832. John Charles Spencer (1782–1845), third Lord Althorp as of 1834, served as chancellor of the exchequer under Lord Grey and his successor, Lord Melbourne. Although he may have called himself a "grazier" (i.e., a person who grazes cattle), in fact Lord Althorp had studied political economy for many years and overseen various parliamentary committees dealing with economic reform. Thomas Drummond (1797–1840) then served on the Boundary Commission, set up to ensure fairly apportioned parliamentary districts as a result of the Reform Act of 1832; he later served as under-secretary of state for Ireland.

struck me that some good might be done, and no harm, if my Illustrations proceeded *pari passu* with the financial reforms expected from the Whig government; and I spoke on the subject to Lieutenant Drummond, who had just become private secretary to Lord Althorp. I was well acquainted with Mr. Drummond; and it occurred very naturally that I told him that if he knew of any meditated measure which would be aided by illustration, would help, in all silence and discretion,— provided always that I approved of the scheme. About this time the London shopkeepers were raising a selfish outcry against the House-tax, one of the very best on the list of imposts. It was understood on all hands that the clamour was not raised by the house-owners, but by their tenants, whose rents had been fixed in consideration of their payment of the tax. If they could get rid of the tax, the tenants would pocket the amount during the remaining term of their leases. Large and noisy deputations besieged the Treasury; and many feared that the good-natured Lord Althorp would yield. Just at this time, Mr. Drummond called on me, with a private message from Lords Grey and Althorp, to ask whether it would suit my purpose to treat of Tithes at once, instead of later,[1]— the reason for such inquiry being quite at my service. As the principles of Taxation involve no inexorable order, like those of Political Economy at large, I had no objection to take any topic first which might be most useful. When I had said so, Mr. Drummond explained that a tithe measure was prepared by the Cabinet which Ministers would like to have introduced to the people by my Number on that subject, before they themselves introduced it in parliament. Of course, this proceeded on the supposition that the measure would be approved by me. Mr. Drummond said he would bring the document, on my promising that no eye but my own should see it, and that I would not speak of the affair till it was settled; and, especially, not to any member of any of the Royal Commissions, then so fashionable. It was a thing unheard of, Mr. Drummond said, to commit any Cabinet measure to the knowledge of any body out of the Cabinet before it was offered to parliament. Finally, the Secretary intimated that Lord Althorp would be obliged by any suggestion in regard to principles and methods of Taxation.

Mr. Drummond had not been gone five minutes before the Chairman of the Excise Commission called, to ask, in the name of the

---

[1]   The tithe and church-rate bills were intended to reduce the obligations of non-Anglicans to pay mandatory taxes in support of the Anglican Church. Among Churchmen, these proposals were considered a preliminary move to disestablish the Church of England, and they set off the Tractarian (or Oxford) Movement.

Commissioners, whether it would suit my purpose to write immediately on the Excise, offering, on the part of Lord Congleton (then Sir Henry Parnell) and others, to supply me with the most extraordinary materials, by my exhibition of which the people might be enlightened and prepared on the subject before it should be brought forward in parliament.[1] The Chairman, Mr. Henry Wickham,[2] required a promise that no eye but my own should see the evidence; and that the secret should be kept with especial care from the Chancellor of the Exchequer and his secretary, as it was a thing unheard of that any party unconcerned should be made acquainted with this evidence before it reached the Chancellor of the Exchequer. I could hardly help laughing in his face; and wondered what would have happened if he and Mr. Drummond had met on the steps, as they very nearly did. Of course, I was glad of the information offered; but I took leave to make my own choice among the materials lent. A few days afterwards I met Mr. Wickham before the Horse Guards, and thought he would not know me,—so deep was he in reverie. Before I was quite past, however, he started, and stopped me with eagerness, saying intensely, 'O! Miss Martineau, Starch! Starch!' And he related the wonderful, the amazing evidence that had reached the Commissioners on the mischievousness of the duty on starch. I was obliged, however, to consider some other matters than the force of the evidence, and I declined expatiating on starch, finding the subject of green glass bottles, soap and sweets answer my purpose better. These two last, especially, yielded a very strong case.[3]

At the end of a note to Mr. Drummond on Tithes that evening, I expressed myself plainly about the House-tax and the shopkeepers, avowing my dread that Lord Althorp might yield to the clamour. Mr. Drummond called next day with the promised tithe document; and he told me that he had handed my note to Lord Althorp, who had said 'Tell her that I may be altogether of her mind; but that if she was here, in my place, with hundreds of shopkeepers yelling about the doors, she would yield, as I must do.' 'Never,' was my message back, 'so long as the House-tax is admitted to be the best on the list.' And I fairly told him

---

[1]   An "excise" taxes luxury goods; this 1833 reform reduced house and window taxes. Sir Henry Parnell (1776–1842), later Lord Congleton, was an Anglo-Irish parliamentarian, a treasury official, and the last paymaster of the forces (a cabinet-level position abolished in 1836); he was sympathetic to the plight of Irish Catholics, and well-known for his *A History of the Penal Laws Against the Irish Catholics, from the Treaty of Limerick to the Union* (1808).

[2]   Henry Lewis Wickham (1789–1864) was principal private secretary to Lord Althorp and chairman of the board of stamps and taxes from 1838 to 1848.

[3]   These taxable luxuries appear briefly in *The Farrers of Budge Row* and later in *The Jerseymen Meeting* and *The Jerseymen Parting* in the *Illustrations of Taxation*.

that the Whig government was perilling the public safety by yielding every thing to clamour, and nothing without it.

I liked the Tithe measure, and willingly propounded it in my tale 'The Tenth Haycock.' It was discussed that session, but deferred; and it passed, with some modifications, a session or two later.—Mr. Drummond next came to open to me, on the same confidential conditions, Lord Althorp's scheme for the Budget, then due in six weeks. His object was to learn what I thought of certain intended alterations of existing taxes. With some pomp and preface, he announced that a change was contemplated which Lord Althorp hoped would be agreeable to me as a dissenter,—a change which Lord Althorp anticipated would be received as a boon by the dissenters. He proposed to take off the tax upon saddle-horses, in the case of the clergy and dissenting ministers. 'What shall I tell Lord Althorp that you think of this?' inquired the Secretary. 'Tell him I think the dissenting Ministers would like it very much if they had any saddle-horses,' I replied.—'What! do you mean that they will not take it as a boon?'—'If you offer it as a boon, they will be apt to take it as an insult. How should dissenting Ministers have saddle-horses, unless they happen to have private fortunes?' He questioned me closely about the dissenting Ministers I knew; and we found that I could actually point out only two among the Unitarians who kept saddle-horses, and they were men of property.

'What, then, would you substitute?' was the next question. 'I would begin upon the Excise; set free the smallest articles first, which least repay the expense of collection, and go on to the greatest.'—'The Excise! Ah! Lord Althorp bade me tell you that the Commission on Excise have collected the most extraordinary evidence, which he will take care that you shall have, as soon as he gets it himself.' (It was at that moment in the closet, within two feet of my visitor.) I replied that the evils of the excise system were well known to be such as to afford employment to any Chancellor of the Exchequer for a course of years; and I should venture to send Lord Althorp my statement of them, hoping that he would glance at it before he brought out his Budget. I worked away at the two Excise stories ('The Jerseymen Meeting' and 'The Jerseymen Parting,') making out a strong case, among others, about Green Glass Bottles and Sweets, more as illustrative examples than as individual cases. I sent the first copy I could get to the Chancellor of the Exchequer, a day and a half before he brought out his Budget. When I opened the 'Times,' the morning after, I was highly amused at seeing that he had made a curious alteration in his intentions about the saddle-horse duty, applying the remission to those clergymen and

ministers only whose income was under two hundred pounds a year,—
having evidently no idea of the cost of keeping a horse. Not less amusing was it to see that he had taken off the duty from green glass bottles
and sweets. He was in fact open to suggestion and correction from any
quarter,—being consciously, as I have mentioned that he said, one of
Nature's graziers, and a merely man-made Chancellor of the Exchequer.

By this time, the summer of 1834 was far advanced, and I was much
exhausted with fatigue and hot weather, and the hurry of preparation
for my trip to America. I was drooping in idea over my last number,
'The Scholars of Arneside,' when a cordial friend of mine said, 'You will
go with great spirit through your last number, —the final task of such
an enterprise.' This prophecy wrought its own accomplishment. I did go
through it with spirit; and I found myself, after making my calls, with
one day left for packing and preparation. Many interruptions occurred
during the last few days which deferred my conclusion till I felt and saw
that my mother was so anxious that I must myself keep down worry of
nerves. On the Friday before I was to leave home for above two years,
my mother said, with anxious kindness, 'My dear, have you done?' 'No,
mother.' On Saturday night, she put her head in at my study door, with
'My dear, have you done?' 'Indeed I have not.' Sunday came,—my place
taken by mail for Tuesday, no packing done, and my number unfinished!
The case seemed desperate. My mother staid at home, and took every
precaution against my being disturbed: but some one came on indispensable business, and did not release me till our early Sunday dinner
hour. My mother looked anxiously in my face; and I could only shake
my head. After dinner, she in a manner mounted guard over my study
door. At five o'clock I flew down stairs with the last sheet, with the ink
still wet, in my hand. My sister Ellen was with us, and at the moment
writing to some Derbyshire friends. By a sudden impulse, I seized her
paper, and with the wet pen with which I had just written 'The End,' I
announced the conclusion of my work. My mother could say little but
'After all we have gone through about this work, to think how it has
ended!' I flew up stairs again to tie up parcels and manuscripts, and put
away all my apparatus; and I had just finished this when I was called to
tea. After tea I went into St. James's Park for the first thoroughly holiday walk I had taken for two years and a half. It felt very like flying. The
grass under foot, the sky overhead, the trees round about, were wholly
different from what they had ever appeared before. My business was not,
however, entirely closed. There were the proof-sheets of the last Number
to be looked over. They followed me to Birmingham, where Ellen and

I travelled together, in childish spirits, on the Tuesday.[1]

My mother had reason for her somewhat pathetic exultation on the conclusion of my Series. Its success was unprecedented, I believe. I am told that its circulation had reached ten thousand in England before my return from America. Mr. Babbage,[2] calling on me one day, when he was in high spirits about the popularity of his own work, 'Machinery and Manufactures,' said, 'Now there is nobody here to call us vain, we may tell each other that you and I are the only people in the market. I find no books are selling but yours and mine.' (It was a time of political agitation.) I replied, 'I find no books are selling but yours and mine.' 'Well!' said he, 'what I came to say is that we may as well advertise each other. Will you advertise mine if I advertise yours, &c. &c.?' And this was the work which had struggled into existence with such extreme difficulty! Under the hard circumstances of the case, it had not made me rich. I have at this time received only a little more than two thousand pounds for the whole work. But I got a hearing,—which was the thing I wanted. The barrier was down, and the course clear; and the money was a small matter in comparison. It was pleasant, too, to feel the ease of having money, after my straitened way of life for some years. My first indulgence was buying a good watch, —the same which is before my eyes as I write. I did not trouble myself with close economies while working to such advantage; and I now first learned the bliss of helping the needy effectually. I was able to justify my mother in removing to London, and to refresh myself by travel, at the end of my task. My American journey cost me four hundred pounds, in addition to one hundred which I made when there. I had left at home my usual payment to my mother; but she refused to take it, as she had a boarder in my place. Soon after my return, when my first American book was published, I found myself able to lay by one thousand pounds, in the purchase of a deferred annuity, of which I am now enjoying the benefit in the receipt of one hundred pounds a year. I may finish off the subject of money by saying that I lately calculated that I have earned altogether by my books somewhere about ten thousand pounds. I have had to live on it, of course, for five-and-twenty years; and

---

[1]   With her traveling companion, Louisa Jeffreys, Martineau left for America from Liverpool on the *United States* in August, 1834.

[2]   Charles Babbage (1791–1871), the inventor of standard railroad gauge, uniform postal rates, occulting lights for lighthouses, Greenwich time signals, and the difference engine to calculate polynomials, was at this time devising an analytical machine for mathematical computation, which is now considered the forerunner of modern computers. He had recently published *On the Economy of Machinery and Manufactures* (London: Charles Knight, 1832).

I have found plenty to do with it: but I have enough, and I am satisfied. I believe I might easily have doubled the amount, if it had been my object to get money; or even, if an international copyright law had secured to me the proceeds of the sale of my works in foreign countries. But such a law was non-existent in my busy time, and still is in regard to America. There is nothing in money that could pay me for the pain of the slightest deflexion from my own convictions, or the most trifling restraint on my freedom of thought and speech. I have therefore obtained the ease and freedom, and let slip the money. I do not speak as one who has resisted temptation, for there has really been none. I have never been at a loss for means, or really suffering from poverty, since the publication of my Series. I explain the case simply that there may be no mystery about my not being rich after such singular success as I so soon met with.

One more explanation will bring this long section to a close. I make it the more readily because it is possible that an absurd report which I encountered in America may be still in existence. It was said that I travelled, not on my own resources, but on means supplied by Lord Brougham and his relative Lord Henley,[1] to fulfil certain objects of theirs. Nobody acquainted with me would listen to such nonsense; but I may as well explain what Lord Henley had to do with my going to America. Lord Brougham had no concern with it whatever, beyond giving me two or three letters of introduction. The story is simply this. One evening, in a party, Lady Mary Shepherd[2] told me that she was commissioned to bring about an interview between myself and her nephew, Lord Henley, who had something of importance to say to me: and she fixed me to meet Lord Henley at her house at luncheon a day or two after. She told me meantime the thing he chiefly wanted, which was to know how, if I had three hundred pounds a year to spend in charity, I should employ it. When we met, I was struck by his excessive agitation, which his subsequent derangement might account for. His chief interest was in philanthropic subjects; and he told me, with extreme emotion, (what so many others have told me) that he believed he had been doing mischief for many years where he most meant to do good, by his methods of alms-giving. Since reading 'Cousin Marshall' and others of my Numbers, he had dropped his subscriptions to some hurtful charities, and had devoted his funds to Education, Benefit Societies and Emigration. Upon his afterwards asking whether I received visitors, and being surprised to find that I could afford

---

[1]   Robert Henley (1789–1841) was a Tory M.P. for Fowey from 1826 to 1830.
[2]   Lady Shepherd (1777–1847) was the second wife of Sir Samuel Shepherd, who had been a friend of many artists and authors.

the time, some remarks were made about the extent and pressure of my work; and then Lord Henley asked whether I did not mean to travel when my Series was done. Upon my replying that I did, he apologised for the liberty he took in asking where I thought of going. I said I had not thought much about it; but that I supposed it would be the usual route, to Switzerland and Italy. 'O! do not go over that beaten track,' he exclaimed. 'Why should you? Will you not go to America?' I replied, 'Give me a good reason, and perhaps I will.' His answer was, 'Whatever else may or may not be true about the Americans, it is certain that they have got at principles of justice and mercy in their treatment of the least happy classes of society which we should do well to understand. Will you not go, and tell us what they are?' This, after some meditation, determined me to cross the Atlantic. Before my return, Lord Henley had disappeared from society; and he soon after died. I never saw him, I believe, but that once.

After short visits, with my sister Ellen, at Birmingham, in Derbyshire and at Liverpool, I sailed (for there were no steamers on the Atlantic in those days) early in August, 1834.

SECTION II

ACCORDING to my promise, I reprint the bulk of an article on 'Literary Lionism,' written in 1837, which will show, better than anything which I can now relate, how I regarded the flatteries of a drawing-room while living in the midst of them. It makes me laugh as I read it to have recalled to my memory the absurd incidents which were occurring every day, and which drove me to write this article as a relief to feelings of disgust and annoyance. There is not a stroke that is not from the life. The works reviewed are 'The Lion of a Party,' from a publication of that time, 'Heads of the People;' and an Oration of Emerson's on the Life of the Scholar.[1]

---

[1]   *Heads of the People; or, Portraits of the English, drawn by Kenny Meadows with Original Essays by Distinguished Writers* (London: Robert Tyas, 1839); Douglas Jerrold wrote the chapter "The 'Lion' of the Party," which Martineau takes as the occasion for her remarks. She also discusses Ralph Waldo Emerson's *Critical and Miscellaneous Essays* (Boston, 1838–39), which includes "The American Scholar, an Address delivered to the Phi Beta Kappa Society at Harvard in 1837," and "Literary Ethics: An Oration delivered before the Literary Societies of Dartmouth College, July 24, 1838," both of which she quotes. Martineau's review appeared in the *London and Westminster Review* 32 (April 1839), 261–81.

Omitting only the review part and the extracts, I give the whole.

'This "Lion" is indeed one of the meanest of his tribe; but he is one of a tribe which has included, and does now include, some who are worthy of a higher classification. Byron was an "interesting creature," and received blushing thanks for his last "divine poem." Scott lost various little articles which would answer for laying up in lavender; and Madame de Stael was exhibited almost as ostensibly at the British Gallery as any of the pictures on the walls, on the evening when the old Marquis of A— obtained an introduction to her, and accosted her with "Come now, Madame de Stael, you must talk English to me."[1] As she scornfully turned from him, and continued her discourse in her own way, the discomfited Marquis seemed to think himself extremely ill used in being deprived of the entertainment he expected from the *prima donna* of the company. In as far as such personages as these last acquiesce in the modern practice of "Lionism," they may be considered to be implicated in whatever reproach attaches to it; but the truth seems to be that, however disgusting and injurious the system, and however guilty some few individuals may be in availing themselves of it for their small, selfish, immediate purposes, the practice, with its slang term, is the birth of events, and is a sign of the times,—like newspaper puffery,[2] which is an evidence of over-population, or like joint-stock companies and club-houses, which indicate that society has obtained a glimpse of that great principle of the economy of association, by which it will probably, in some future age, reconstitute itself.

'The practice of "Lionism" originates in some feelings which are very good,—in veneration for intellectual superiority, and gratitude for intellectual gifts; and its form and prevalence are determined by the fact, that literature has reached a larger class, and interested a different order of people from any who formerly shared its advantages. A wise man might, at the time of the invention of printing, have foreseen the age

---

[1]   George Gordon, Lord Byron (1788–1824) was lionized in London society after the publication of his semi-autobiographical *Childe Harold's Pilgrimage* in 1812. Sir Walter Scott (1771–1832) preceded Byron as the most famous poet of the early nineteenth century and continued to dominate the literary scene when his authorship of the Waverley novels became known. Anne-Louise-Germaine Necker, Madame de Staël (1766–1817), a French writer, became wildly popular in England, especially among women, with the publication of *Corinne, or Italy* (1807); she was praised for her critical writings on European societies and comparative literature, including *De la littérature considérée dans ses rapports avec les institutions sociales* (1800) and *De l'Allemagne* (1810), by a reviewer in *Blackwood's Edinburgh Magazine* (1818) as "the creator of the science of nations."

[2]   Excessively flattering reviews, called "puffs," were often written by friends or commissioned by publishers who wished to sell books.

of literary "Lionism," and would probably have smiled at it as a temporary extravagance. The whole course of literary achievement has prophesied its transient reign. The voluntary, self-complacent, literary "Lion" might, in fact, be better called the mouse issuing from the labouring mountain,[1] which has yet to give birth to the volcano.

'There was a time when literature was cultivated only in the seclusion of monasteries. There sat the author of old, alone in his cell,— alone through days, and months, and years. The echoes of the world have died away; the voice of praise could not reach him there, and his grave yawned within the very inclosure whence he should never depart. He might look abroad from the hill-side, or the pinnacle of rock where his monastery stood, on

> "the rich leas,
> The turfy mountains where live nibbling sheep,
> And flat meads thatch'd with stover them to keep:
> _____ the broom groves,
> Whose shadow the dismissed bachelor loves,
> Being lass-lorn: the pole-clipt vineyard,
> And the sea-marge, sterile and rocky hard."[2]

On these he might look abroad, but never on the assemblages of men. Literary achievement in such circumstances might be, to a certain degree, encouraged by visions of future usefulness and extended fame, but the strongest stimulus must have been the pleasure of intellectual exercise. The toil of composition must there have been its own reward, and we may even now witness with the mind's eye the delight of it painted upon the face under the cowl. One may see the student hastening from the refectory to the cell, drawn thither by the strong desire of solving a problem, of elucidating a fact, of indulging the imagination with heavenly delights, and contemplating the wealth stored in his memory. One may see him coming down with radiant countenance from the heights of speculation, to cast into the worship of the chapel

---

[1]   Proverbial, but perhaps recalling "Horace's Art of Poetry" by the Earl of Roscommon (1633–85):
> Begin not as th' old Poetaster did,
> (Troys famous War, and Priams Fate, I sing)
> In what will all this Ostentation end?
> The laboring mountain scarce brings forth a mouse;
> How far is this from the Meonian Stile?

[2]   Lines spoken by Iris, messenger of Ceres, in Shakespeare's *The Tempest*, IV, I, 68–75.

the devotion he had there gained. One may see the glow upon his cheek as he sits alone beside his lamp, noting his discoveries, or elaborating the expression of his ideas. There are many who think that no one ever wrote a line, even in the most private diary, without the belief, or the hope, that it would be read. It might be so with the monastic author; but in his case there could rarely be the appendage of praise to the fact of its being read; and the prospect of influence and applause was too remote to actuate a life of literary toil. It is probable that if an echo of fame came to him on any of the four winds, it was well, and he heartily enjoyed the music of the breeze; but that in some instances he would have passed his days in the same manner, cultivating literature for its own sake, if he had known that his parchments would be buried with him.

'The homage paid to such men when they did come forth into the world was, on the part of the many, on the ground of their superiority alone. A handful of students might feel thankfulness towards them for definite services, but the crowd gazed at them in vague admiration, as being holier or wiser than other people. As the blessings of literature spread, strong personal gratitude mingled with the homage,—gratitude not only for increase of fame and honour to the country and nation to which the author belonged, but for the good which each worshipper derived from the quickening of his sympathies, the enlargement of his views, the elevation of his intellectual being.[1] To each of the crowd the author had opened up a spring of fresh ideas, furnished a solution of some doubt, a gratification of the fancy or the reason. When, on a certain memorable Easter day in the fourteenth century, Petrarch mounted the stairs of the Capitol, crowned with laurel, and preceded by twelve noble youths, reciting passages of his poetry, the praise was of the noblest kind that it has been the lot of authorship to receive. It was composed of reverence and gratitude, pure from cold selfishness and from sentimental passion, which is cold selfishness in a flame-coloured disguise.[2] When, more than four centuries later, Voltaire was overpowered with acclamations in the theatre at Paris, and conveyed home in

---

[1]   In a two-part review for *Tait's Magazine* (1832), "Characteristics of the Genius of Scott" and "Achievement of the Genius of Scott," Martineau praised Walter Scott for effecting these important responses in his readers.

[2]   In 1341 Francesco Petrarca (1304–74), the great Italian poet and humanist, was crowned poet laureate in Rome. Madame de Staël rewrote this story in *Corinne* (1807), having a modern woman poet crowned at the Capitol in the Petrarchan mode. The episode recurs frequently in nineteenth-century literature as an example of the kind of social recognition that a writer's serious work ought to achieve.

triumph, crying feebly, "You suffocate me with roses," the homage, though inferior in character to that which greeted Petrarch, was honourable, and of better origin than popular selfishness.[1] The applauding crowd had been kept ignorant by the superstition which had in other ways so afflicted them, that they were unboundedly grateful to a man of power who promised to relieve them from the yoke. Voltaire had said, "I am tired of hearing it repeated that twelve men were sufficient to found Christianity: I will show the world that one is sufficient to destroy it;" and he was believed. He was mistaken in his boast, and his adorers in confiding in it; but this proves only that they were ignorant of Christianity, and not that their homage of one whom they believed to have exploded error and disarmed superstition, and whom they knew to have honoured and served them by his literary labours, was otherwise than natural and creditable to their hearts.

'The worship of popular authors at the present time is an expression of the same thoughts and feelings as were indicated by the crowning of Petrarch and the greeting of Voltaire in the theatre, but with alterations and additions according to the change in the times. Literary "lions" have become a class,—an inconceivable idea to the unreflecting in the time of Petrarch, and even of Voltaire. This testifies to the vast spread of literature among our people. How great a number of readers is required to support, by purchase and by praise, a standing class of original writers! It testifies to the deterioration of literature as a whole. If, at any one time, there is a class of persons to whom the public are grateful for intellectual excitement, how *médiocre* must be the quality of the intellectual production! It by no means follows that works of merit, equal to any which have yet blessed mankind, are not still in reserve; but it is clear that the great body of literature has entirely changed its character,—that books are no longer the scarce fruit of solemn and protracted thought, but rather, as they have been called, "letters to all whom they may concern."[2] That literary "lions" now constitute a class, testifies to the frequency of literary success,—to the extension of the number of minds from which a superficial and transient sympathy may be anticipated. But

---

[1] François-Marie Arouet (1694–1778), better known as Voltaire, was considered the great genius of the Enlightenment and applauded for his attacks on the *ancien régime*, including the Catholic Church. At a performance of his play, *Irène*, Voltaire was greeted at the theater with great festivity, including a band playing in his honor and an actor presenting him a laurel crown. Presumably this is the episode to which Martineau refers.

[2] Quotation untraced; a variation on the conventional address, "To Whom It May Concern."

the newest feature of all is the class of "lionisers,"—new, not because
sordid selfishness is new,—not because social vanity is new,—not because
an inhuman disregard of the feelings of the sensitive, the foibles of the
vain, the privileges of the endowed, is new: but because it is somewhat
new to see the place of cards, music, masks, my lord's fool, and my lady's
monkey,[1] supplied by authors in virtue of their authorship.

'It is, to be sure, quite to be expected that low-minded persons
should take advantage of any prevalent feeling, however respectable, to
answer their own purposes; but the effect, in this instance, would be odd
to a resuscitated gentleman of the fifteenth century. If he happened to
be present at one of the meetings of the British Association for the
Advancement of Science, he would there see the popular veneration
for intellectual achievement under a pretty fair aspect. There is no harm,
and some good, in seeing a group waiting for Sir John Herschel to
come out into the street, or a rush in the rooms to catch a sight of
Faraday,—or ladies sketching Babbage, and Buckland, and Back,—or a
train of gazers following at the heels of Whewell or Sedgwick, or any
popular artist or author who might be present among the men of
science.[2] In all this there is no reproach, and some honour, to both
parties, though of a slight and transient kind. The sordid characteristics
of the modern system appear when the eminent person becomes a
guest in a private house. If the resuscitated gentleman of the fifteenth
century were to walk into a country house in England in company with
a lady of literary distinction, he might see at once what is in the mind
of the host and hostess. All the books of the house are lying about,—
all the gentry in the neighbourhood are collected; the young men peep
and stare from the corners of the room; the young ladies crowd
together, even sitting five upon three chairs, to avoid the risk of being
addressed by the stranger. The lady of the house devotes herself to
"drawing out" the guest, asks for her opinion of this, that, and the other

---

[1] That is, the traditional entertainments of rich aristocrats have been replaced by the literary author.

[2] Martineau lists the famous English scientists of her day: John Herschel (1792–1871),
astronomer who specialized in stellar and nebular observation; Michael Faraday (1791–1867),
physicist and chemist who studied electromagnetism; Charles Babbage (1791–1871), mathematician and inventor of the first computer; William Buckland (1784–1856), geologist
known for his effort to reconcile sedimentary and fluvial processes with the biblical account
of creation; Sir George Back (1796–1878), naval officer who mapped the Arctic coastline
of North America; William Whewell (1794–1866), philosopher who formulated a scientific theory of induction; and Adam Sedgwick (1785–1873), geologist who studied the
Cambrian period.

book, and intercedes for her young friends, trembling on their three chairs, that each may be favoured with "just one line for her album."[1] The children are kept in the nursery, as being unworthy the notice of a literary person, or brought up severally into the presence, "that they may have it to say all their lives that they had been introduced," &c. &c. Some youth in a corner is meantime sketching the guest, and another is noting what she says, —probably something about black and green tea, or the state of the roads, or the age of the moon. Such a scene, very common now in English country houses, must present an unfavourable picture of our manners to strangers from another country or another age. The prominent features are the sufferings of one person, and the selfishness of all the rest. They are too much engrossed with the excitement of their own vanity and curiosity to heed the pain they are inflicting on one who, if she happens to have more feeling and less vanity than they, can hardly enjoy being told that children cannot be interesting to her, and that young people do not wish to speak to her.

'In a country town it is yet worse. There may be seen a coterie of "superior people" of the place, gathered together to make the most of a literary foreigner who may be passing through. Though he speaks perfect English, the ladies persist in uttering themselves, after hems and haws, in French that he can make nothing of,—French as it was taught in our boarding schools during the war. The children giggle in a corner at what the boys call "the jabber;" and the maid who hands the tea strives to keep the corners of her mouth in order. In vain the guest speaks to the children, and any old person who may be present, in English almost as good as their own; he is annoyed to the last by the "superior people," who intend that it should get abroad through the town that they had enjoyed a vast deal of conversation in French with the illustrious stranger.

'Bad as all this is, the case is worse in London,—more disgusting, if it is impossible to be more ridiculous. There, ladies of rank made their profit of the woes of the Italian and Polish refugees, the most eagerly in the days of the deepest unhappiness of the exiles, when the novelty was strongest.[2] These exiles were collected in the name of hospitality, but for

---

[1]   Then, as today, there was a vogue for collecting autographs of famous authors, though then the "favoured" might get a couplet of verse or a line or two of prose in addition to a signature.

[2]   Many Polish and Italian political refugees came to London in the 1830s after failed attempts at national independence. In Period IV, sec. i Martineau discusses meeting Julian Ursin Niemcewicz (1758–1841), who was driven into exile in 1831 after an unsuccessful resistance to Russia's annexation of Poland.

purposes of attraction, within the doors of fashionable saloons; there they were stared out of countenance amidst the sentimental sighs of the gazers; and if any one of them,—any interesting Count or melancholy-looking Prince, happened unfortunately to be the author of a "sweet poem," or a "charming tragedy," he was called out from among the rest to be flattered by the ladies, and secured for fresh services. It was not uncommon, during the days of the novelty of the Italian refugees, while they were yet unprovided with employments by which they might live, (and for aught we know, it may not be uncommon still,) for ladies to secure the appearance of one or two of these first-rate "lions" with them the next evening at the theatre or opera, and to forget to pay. Till these gentlemen had learned by experience to estimate the friendship of the ladies to whom they were so interesting, they often paid away at public places the money which was to furnish them with bread for the week. We have witnessed the grief and indignation with which some of them have announced their discovery that their woes and their accomplishments were hired with champagne, coffee, and fine words, to amuse a party of languid fine people.

'These gentlemen, however, are no worse treated than many natives. A new poet, if he innocently accepts a promising invitation, is liable to find out afterwards that his name has been inserted in the summonses to the rest of the company, or sent round from mouth to mouth to secure the rooms being full. If a woman who has written a successful play or novel attends the soirée of a "lionising" lady, she hears her name so announced on the stairs as to make it certain that the servants have had instructions; she finds herself seized upon at the door by the hostess, and carried about to lord, lady, philosopher, gossip, and dandy, each being assured that she cannot be spared to each for more than ten seconds. She sees a "lion" placed in the centre of each of the two first rooms she passes through,—a navigator from the North Pole in the one, a dusky Egyptian bey or Hindoo rajah in another; and it flashes upon her that she is to be the centre of attraction in a third apartment. If she is vain enough to like the position, the blame of ministering to a pitiable and destructive weakness remains with the hostess, and she is answerable for some of the failure of power which will be manifest in the next play or novel of her victim. If the guest be meek and modest, there is nothing for it but getting behind a door, or surrounding herself with her friends in a corner. If she be strong enough to assert herself, she will return at once to her carriage, and take care how she enters that house again. A few instances of what may be seen in London during any one season, if brought together, yield but a sorry exhibition of the manners of persons who give parties to gratify their own vanity, instead of enjoying the society and the pleasure of their friends. In one crowded room are three "lions,"—a new musical composer, an eminent divine who publishes, and a lady poet. These three stand in three corners of the room, faced by a gaping crowd. Weary at length of their position, they all happen to move towards the centre table at the same moment. They find it covered with the composer's music, the divine's sermons, and the lady's last new poem; they laugh in each other's faces, and go back to their corners. A gentleman from the top of Mont Blanc, or from the North Pole, is introduced to a lady who is dying to be able to say that she knows him, but who finds at the critical moment that she has nothing to say to him. In the midst of a triple circle of listeners, she asks him whether he is not surprised at his own preservation; whether it does not prove that Providence is everywhere, but more particularly in barren places? If a sigh or a syllable of remonstrance escapes from any victim, there is one phrase always at hand for use, a phrase which, if it ever contained any truth, or exerted any consolatory influence, has been long worn out, and become mere words,—"This is a tax you must pay for your eminence." There may, perhaps, be as much assumption with regard to the necessity of this tax as of some others. Every tax has been called absolutely necessary in its day; and the time may arrive when some shall dispute whether it be really needful that an accomplished actor should be pestered with the flattery of his art; that authors should be favoured with more general conversation only that any opinions they may drop may be gathered up to be reported; and that women, whom the hardest treatment awaits if their heads should be turned, should be compelled to hear what the prime minister, or the Russian ambassador, or the poet laureate, or the "lion" of the last season, has said of them. Those on whom the tax is levied would like to have the means of protest, if they should not see its necessity quite so clearly as others do. They would like to know why they are to be unresistingly pillaged of their time by importunity about albums, and despoiled of the privacy of correspondence with their friends by the rage for autographs, so that if they scribble a joke to an acquaintance in the next street, they may hear of its existence five years after in a far corner of Yorkshire, or in a book of curiosities at Hobart Town.[1] They would like to know why they must be civil when a stranger, introduced by an acquaintance at a

---

[1]   Capital of Tasmania, then known primarily as a convict colony.

morning call, makes her curtsey, raises her glass, borrows paper and pencil of the victim, draws a likeness, puts it into her reticule, and departs. They would like to know why they are expected to be gratified when eight or nine third-rate painters beg them to sit for their portraits, to be hung out as signs to entice visitors to the artist's rooms.'

*   *   *   *   *   *

'Authors would like to know why they must receive flattery as if it were welcome, and be made subject to fine speeches, which presuppose a disgusting degree of vanity in the listener. They would like to know whether it is absolutely necessary that they should be accused of pride and ingratitude if they decline honours of such spurious origin as most of these, and of absurd vanity if they do not repel them. They would like to know whether it is quite necessary, in generous and Christian England, that any class should submit to have its most besetting sin, its peculiar weakness, fostered and aggravated for the proposes of persons whose aim it is to have brilliant parties and a celebrated acquaintance. The being honoured through the broad land, while the soul is sinking under its sense of ignorance and weakness at home, is a tax which a popular author must pay; and so is the being censured for what may prove the best deeds of his life, and the highest thoughts of his mind. He may be obliged to submit to be gazed at in public, and to be annoyed with handfuls of anonymous letters in his study, where he would fain occupy himself with something far higher and better than himself and his doings. These things may be a tax which he must pay; but it may be questionable whether it is equally necessary for him to acquiesce in being the show and attraction of an assemblage to which he is invited as a guest, if not as a friend.

'This matter is not worth losing one's temper about,—just because nothing is worth it. There is another reason, too, why indignation would be absurd,—that no individuals or classes are answerable for the system. It is the birth of the times, as we said before, and those may laugh who can, and those who must suffer had better suffer good-humouredly; but not the less is the system a great mischief, and therefore to be exposed and resisted by those who have power. If its effects were merely to ensure and hasten the ruin of youthful poets, who are satisfied to bask in compliments and the lamp-light of saloons, to complete the resemblance to pet animals of beings who never were men, the world would lose little, and this species of coxcombry, like every other, might be left to have its day. But this is far from being all that is done. There is a grievous waste of time of a higher order of beings than the rhyming dandy—waste of the precious time of those who have only too few years in which to think and to live. There is an intrusion into the independence of their observation of life. If their modesty is not most painfully outraged, their idea of the literary life is depraved. The one or the other must be the case, and we generally witness both in the literary pets of saloons.

'Some plead that the evil is usually so temporary, that it cannot do much mischief to any one who really has an intellect, and is therefore of consequence to the world. But the mischief is not over with praise and publicity. The reverse which ensues may be salutary. As Carlyle says, "Truly, if Death did not intervene; or, still more happily, if Life and the Public were not a blockhead, and sudden unreasonable oblivion were not to follow that sudden unreasonable glory, and beneficently, though most painfully, damp it down, one sees not where many a poor glorious man, still more, many a poor glorious woman (for it falls harder on the distinguished female), could terminate, far short of Bedlam."[1] Such reverse may be the best thing to be hoped; but it does not leave things as they were before the season of flattery set in. The safe feeling of equality is gone; habits of industry are impaired; the delicacy of modesty is exhaled; and it is a great wonder if the temper is not spoiled. The sense of elevation is followed by a consciousness of depression: those who have been the idols of society feel, when deposed, like its slaves; and the natural consequence is contempt and repining. Hear Dryden at the end of a long course of mutual flatteries between himself and his patrons, and of authorship to please others, often to the severe mortification of his better nature:— "It will continue to be the ingratitude of mankind, that they who teach wisdom by the surest means shall generally live poor and unregarded, as if they were born only for the public, and had no interest in their own well-being, but were to be lighted up like tapers, and waste themselves for the benefit of others."[2]

★   ★   ★   ★   ★   ★

---

[1]   From the *Memoirs of Mirabeau* (1834–36), which Carlyle quotes in *The French Revolution* (1837).
[2]   Possibly taken from Samuel Johnson's essay on Dryden in *The Lives of the English Poets* (1779–81), a work quoted below (see p. 228, n. 1).

'The crowning evil which arises from the system of "lionism" is, that it cuts off the retreat of literary persons into the great body of human beings. They are marked out as a class, and can no longer take refuge from their toils and their publicity in ordinary life. This is a hardship shared by authors who are far above being directly injured by the prevalent practice. There are men who continue to enter society for the sake of the good it yields, enjoying intercourse, despising homage, smiling at the vanities of those who must needs be vain, and overlooking the selfishness of such as are capable of no higher ambition than of being noted for their brilliant parties,—there are men thus superior to being "lions" who yet find themselves injured by "lionism." The more they venerate their own vocation, and the more humbly they estimate the influence of their own labours on human affairs, the more distinctly do they perceive the mischief of their separation from others who live and think; of their being isolated as a class. The cabinet-maker is of a different class from the hosier, because one makes furniture and the other stockings. The lawyer is of a different class from the physician, because the science of law is quite a different thing from the science of medicine. But the author has to do with those two things precisely which are common to the whole race,—with living and thinking. He is devoted to no exclusive department of science; and the art which he practices,—the writing what he thinks,—is quite a subordinate part of his business. The very first necessity of his vocation is to live as others live, in order to see and feel, and to sympathize in human thought. In proportion as this sympathy is impaired, will his views be partial, his understanding, both of men and books, be imperfect, and his power be weakened accordingly. A man aware of all this will sigh, however good-naturedly he may smile, at such lamentations as may often be overheard in "brilliant parties." "How do you like Mrs.—, now you have got an introduction to her?" "O, I am so disappointed! I don't find that she has anything in her." "Nothing in her! Nothing, with all her science!" "O, I should never have found out who she was, if I had not been told; and she did not say a thing that one could carry away." Hence,—from people not finding out who she was without being told,—came Mrs.— 's great wisdom; and of this advantage was all the world trying to deprive her.'

★　★　★　★　★　★

'Amidst the "lower observances" of life, even the pedantry of literary coteries, the frivolities of the drawing-room, and the sentimentalities of "lion" worship, there is for the self-relying, "tuition in the serene and beautiful laws" of human existence.[1] But the tuition is for the self-relying alone,—for those who, in the deep interest of their vocation of thought, work from far other considerations than the desire of applause. None but a man who can do without praise can come out safe from the process of being "lionised:" and no one who cannot do without praise is likely to achieve anything better than he has already done. The newspapers may tell of his "expanding intellect," and his publisher may prophecy of the rich fruits of his coming years: but he has done his best. Having gained much applause by a particular quality of his writing, he will be always trying to get more applause by a stronger exhibition of the quality, till it grows into pure extravagance. If he has energy, it will grow into bombast in the hot-house of drawing-room favour. If he is suggestive, and excels in implication, he will probably end in a Lord Burleigh's shake of the head.[2] He deprives himself of the repose and independence of thought, amid which he might become aware of his own tendencies, and nourish his weaker powers into an equality with the stronger. Fashion, with all its lights, its music, its incense, is to him a sepulchre,—the cold deep grave in which his powers and his ambition must rot into nothingness. We have often wondered, while witnessing the ministering of the poison to the unwary, the weak and the vain, whether their course began with the same kind of aspiration, felt as early, as that which the greatest of the world's thinkers have confessed. It seems as if any who have risen so far into success as to attract the admiration (and therefore the sympathy) of numbers, must have had a long training in habits of thought, feeling, and expression; must have early felt admiration of intellectual achievement, and the consciousness of kindred with the masters of intellect; must have early known the stirring of literary ambition, the pleasure of thinking, the luxury of expressing thought, and the heroic longing to create or arouse somewhat in other minds. It is difficult to believe that any one who has succeeded has not gone through brave toils, virtuous struggles of modesty, and a noble glow of confidence: that he has not obtained glimpses of realities

---

[1]   Quoting Emerson's "Literary Ethics": "Out of love and hatred, out of earnings, and borrowings, and lendings, and losses; out of sickness and pain; out of wooing and worshipping; out of travelling, and voting, and watching, and caring; out of disgrace and contempt, comes our tuition in the serene and beautiful laws."

[2]   William Cecil, Lord Burleigh (1520–98), was lord treasurer under Queen Elizabeth I and her chief minister; Richard Sheridan made him a character in *The Critic*, where he comes onstage and shakes his head because he is too immersed in affairs of state to talk. The gesture was known as "Burleigh's nod."

unseen by the outward eye, and been animated by a sense of the glory of his vocation: that, up to the precincts of the empire of fashion, he has been, in all essential respects, on an equality with any of God's peerage. If so, what a sight of ruin is here: aspirations chained down by the fetter of complaisance! desires blown away by the breath of popularity, or the wind of ladies' fans! confidence pampered into conceit; modesty depraved into misgiving and dependence; and the music of the spheres exchanged for opera airs and the rhymes of an album! Instead of "the scholar beloved of earth and heaven,"[1] we have the mincing dandy courted by the foolish and the vain. Instead of the son of wisdom, standing serene before the world to justify the ways of his parent, we have the spoiled child of fortune, ready to complain, on the first neglect, that all the universe goes wrong because the darkness is settling down upon him after he has used up his little day. What a catastrophe of a mind which must have had promise in its dawn!

'Even where the case is not so mournful as this, the drawing-room is still the grave of literary promise. There are some who on the heath, or in the shadow of the wood, whispered to themselves, with beating hearts, while communing with some mastermind, "I am also a poet." In those days they could not hear the very name of Chaucer or Shakspere without a glow of personal interest, arising out of a sense of kindred. Now, lounging on sofas, and quaffing coffee and praise, they are satisfied with mediocrity, gratified enough that one fair creature has shut herself up with their works at noon-day, and that another has pored over them at midnight. They now speak of Chaucer and Shakspere with the same kind of admiration with which they themselves are addressed by others. The consciousness, the heart-felt emotion, the feeling of brotherhood,—all that is noble is gone, and is succeeded by a low and precarious self-complacency, a skeptical preference of mediocrity to excellence. They underrate their vocation, and are lost.'

*   *   *   *   *   *

---

[1]   Quoting Emerson's "Literary Ethics": "Thought is all light, and publishes itself to the universe. It will speak, though you were dumb, by its own miraculous organ. It will flow out of your actions, your manners, and your face. It will bring you friendships. It will impledge you to truth by the love and expectation of generous minds. By virtue of the laws of that Nature, which is one and perfect, it shall yield every sincere good that is in the soul, to the scholar beloved of earth and heaven."

'When we think how few writers in a century live for centuries, it is astonishing to perceive how many in every year dismiss all doubt of their own greatness, and strut about in the belief that men's minds are full of them, and will be full of them when a new age has arisen, and they and their flatterers have long been gone to learn elsewhere, perhaps, the littleness of all our knowledge. Any degree of delight, any excess of glee may be allowed for, and even respected, in one actually in the intense enjoyment of authorship, when all comparison with them is out of the question for the hour, and the charm of his own conceptions eclipses all other beauty, the fervor of his own persuasions excludes the influence of all other minds; but if a man not immediately subject to the inspiration of his art, deliberately believes that his thoughts are so far beyond his age, or his feelings so universal and so felicitously expressed as that he is even now addressing a remote posterity, no further proof of his ignorance and error is needed. The prophecy forbids its own accomplishment. There is probably no London season when some author is not told by some foolish person that he or she is equal to Shakspere; and it is but too probable that some have believed what they have been told, and in consequence stopped short of what, by patient and humble study and labour, they might have achieved; while it is almost certain, if such could but see it, that whenever Shakspere's equal shall arise, it will be in some unanticipated form, and in such a mode that the parity of glory shall be a secret to himself, and to the world, till he is gone from it.

'Another almost unavoidable effect of literary "lionism" is to make an author overrate his vocation; which is, perhaps, as fatal an error as underrating it. All people interested in their work are liable to overrate their vocation. There may be makers of dolls' eyes who wonder how society would go on without them. But almost all men, but popular authors, leave behind them their business and the ideas which belong to it when they go out to recreate themselves. The literary "lion," however, hears of little but books, and the kind of books he is interested in. He sees them lining the walls and strewing the tables wherever he goes: all the ideas he hears are from books; all the news is about books, till it is no wonder if he fancies that books govern the affairs of the world. If this fancy once gets fixed in his brain there is an end of his achievements. His sagacity about human interests, and his sympathy with human feelings, are gone. If he had not been enchanted, held captive within the magic circle of fashion, he might have stepped abroad to see how the world really goes on. He might have found there philosophers who foresee the imperishable nature of certain books; who would say to him, "Cast forth thy word into the everliving, ever-working universe; it is a seed grain that cannot die; unnoticed to-day, it will be found flourishing as a banyan-grove (perhaps, alas! as a hemlock forest) after a thousand years:"[1] all this, however, supposing vital perfection in the seed, and a fitting soil for it to sink into. He might have found some who will say with Fenelon, with all earnestness, "If the riches of both Indies, if the crowns of all the kingdoms of Europe were laid at my feet, in exchange for my love of reading, I would spurn them all."[2] But even among these, the reading and thinking class, he would be wise to observe how much more important are many things than books; how little literature can compete in influence with the winds of heaven, with impulses from within, with the possession of land and game, with professional occupations, with the news of the day, with the ideas and affections belonging to home and family. All these rank, as they ought to do, before books in their operation upon minds. If he could have gone out of the circle of the highly cultivated, he would have found the merchant on 'change, the shopkeeper at his ledger, mothers in their nurseries, boys and girls serving their apprenticeships or earning their bread, with little thought of books. It is true that in this class may be found those who are, perhaps, the most wrought upon by books,—those to whom literature is a luxury; but to such, two or three books are the mental food of a whole youth, while two or three more may sustain their mature years. These are they to whom the vocation of the author, in the abstract, is beyond comparison for nobleness, but to whom the vocation of this particular author is of less importance than that of the monkey that grimaces on Bruin's back, as he paces along Whitechapel or Cheapside.[3] If he could have gone further still, he would have heard little children talking to their haggard mothers of some happy possibility of bacon to their potatoes on some future day; he would have seen whole societies where no book is heard of but the

---

[1] Sartor Resartus, p. 38. [Martineau's note].

[2] François Fénelon (1651–1715), French theologian and educator, best known for his didactic romance, *Télémaque* (1699), which treats Telemachus's voyage as an educational experience, guided by the figure of "Mentor"; this is one of many didactic conclusions that Telemachus reaches in the course of his travels.

[3] A nineteenth-century entertainment in the poor areas of east London. Cheapside ("from *chepe* meaning "market") was the most important market in the city of London; Whitechapel (named for the Church of St. Mary Matfelon) was the principal entrance to the city from the east.

"Newgate Calendar."[1] How do books act upon the hundreds of thousands of domestic servants,—upon the millions of artisans who cannot sever the sentences they speak into the words which compose them,—upon the multitude who work on the soil, the bean-setters in spring, the mowers in summer, the reapers in autumn, who cover the broad land? How do books act upon the tribe who traverse the seas, obtaining guidance from the stars, and gathering knowledge from every strand? There is scarcely anything which does not act more powerfully upon them,—not a word spoken in their homes, not an act of their handicraft, not a rumour of the town, not a glimpse of the green fields. The time will doubtless come when books will influence the life of such; but then this influence will be only one among many, and the books which will give it forth will hardly be of the class in which the literary "lion" has an interest. Meantime, unless he goes abroad, in imagination at least, from the enchanted circle of which he is, for the time, the centre, he is in imminent peril, while relaxing in his intellectual toil, of overrating his vocation.

'This, however, is sometimes a preparation for being ashamed of the vocation. Some of the anxiety which popular authors have shown, towards the end of their career, to be considered as gentlemen rather than as authors, is no doubt owing to the desire, in aristocratic England, to be on a par with their admirers in the qualifications which most distinguish *them*: and much also to the universal tendency to depreciate what we possess in longing for something else,—the tendency which inclines so many men of rank to distinguish themselves as authors, statesmen, or even sportsmen, while authors and legislators are struggling for rank. But there can be no doubt that the subsidence of enthusiasm, which must sooner or later follow the excitement caused by popular authorship, the mortifications which succeed the transports of popularity, have a large share in producing the desire of aristocratic station, the shame of their vocation, by which some favourites of the drawing-room cast a shadow over their own fame. Johnson says of Congreve—"But he treated the muses with ingratitude; for, having long conversed familiarly with the great, he wished to be considered rather as a man of fashion than of wit; and when he received a visit from Voltaire, disgusted him by the despicable foppery of desiring to be considered, not as an author, but a gentleman: to which

---

[1]   *The Newgate Calendar* recorded the lives and notorious deeds of criminals. The first *Calendar* appeared in 1773, but Martineau may refer to the more modern versions published by the attorneys Andrew Knapp and William Baldwin in 1824–26.

the Frenchman replied, 'that if he had been only a gentleman, he should not have come to visit him."'[1]

'He must be a strong man who escapes all the pitfalls into this tomb of ambition and of powers. He must have not only great force of intellect to advance amidst such hindrances, but a fine moral vigour to hold the purpose of his life amidst the voices which are crying to him all the way up the mountain of his toil; syren voices, in which he must have an accurate ear to discover that there is little of the sympathy he needs, however much of the blandishment that he cannot but distrust.

'To any one strong enough to stand it, however, the experience of literary "lionism" yields much that is worth having. If authorship be the accomplishment of early and steady aspiration; if the author feels that it is the business of his life to think and say what he thinks, while he is far from supposing it the business of other people's lives to read what he says: if he holds to his aim, regarding the patronage of fashion, and the flattery of the crowd only as a piece of his life, like a journey abroad, or a fit of sickness, or a legacy, or anything which makes him feel for the time, without having any immediate connexion with the chief interest of his existence, he is likely to profit rather than suffer by his drawing-room reputation. Some essential conditions must be observed. It is essential that his mind should not be spent and dissipated amidst a crowd of pleasures; that his social engagements should not interfere with his labours of the study. He must keep his morning hours (and they must be many) not only free but bright. He must have ready for them a clear head and a light heart. His solitude must be true solitude while it lasts, unprofaned by the intrusions of vanities, (which are cares in masquerade) and undisturbed by the echoes of applause. It is essential that he should be active in some common business of life, not dividing the whole of his time between the study and the drawing-room, and so confining himself to the narrow world of books and readers.'

★   ★   ★   ★   ★   ★

'A man so seriously devoted to an object is not likely to find himself the guest of the coarsest perpetrators of "lionism." He is not likely to accept the hospitality on condition of being made a show; but he need not part with his good humour. Those who give feasts, and hire the

---

[1]   From Samuel Johnson, *The Lives of the English Poets* (1779–81), originally written as prefaces to reissues of their works.

talents of their neighbours to make those feasts agreeable, are fulfilling their little part,—are doing what they are fit for, and what might be expected of them, as the dispensers of intellectual feasts are doing *their* part in bringing together beauty and attraction from the starry skies, and the green earth, and the acts and thoughts of men. When once it is discerned that it is useless to look for the grapes and figs of these last among the thorns and thistles of the first, the whole matter is settled. Literary "lionism" is a sign of the times; and it is the function of certain small people to exhibit it and there is an end. Neither it nor they are to be quarrelled with for what cannot be helped.

'It will be hard upon the author faithful to his vocation, and it will be strange, if some valuable friendships do not arise out of the inter-courses of the drawing-room where his probation goes forward. This is one of the advantages which his popularity, however temporary, is likely to leave behind. He is likely, moreover, to shake off a few preju-dices, educational, or engendered in the study. He can hardly fail to learn something of the ways of thinking and feeling of new classes of persons, or orders of minds before unknown. He is pretty sure, also, to hear much that is said in his own dispraise that would never have reached him in retirement; and this kind of information has great weight, if not great virtue with every one; not only because there is almost invariably some truth involved in every censure, but because most people agree with Racine in his experience, that an adverse crit-icism gives more pain than the extremist applause can afford pleasure.[1] These things constitute altogether a great sum of advantages, in addi-tion to the enjoyments of relaxation and kindly intercourse which are supposed to be the attributes of all social assemblages. If many small wits and feeble thinkers have been extinguished by the system of literary "lionism," it may be hoped that some few have taken what is good and left what is bad in it, deriving from their exposure to it an improved self-reliance and fresh intellectual resources.

'Many are the thousands who have let the man die within them from cowardly care about meat and drink, and a warm corner in the great asylum of safety, whose gates have ever been thronged by the multitude who cannot appreciate the free air and open heaven. And many are the hundreds who have let the poet die within them that their complacency may be fed, their vanity intoxicated, and themselves securely harboured in the praise of their immediate neighbours. Few, very few are they who,

---

[1]   Jean Baptiste Racine (1639–99), French dramatist.

"noble in reason," and conscious of being "infinite in faculties," have faith to look before and after,—faith to go on to "reverence the dreams of their youth,"[1]—faith to appeal to the godlike human mind yet unborn,—the mind which the series of coming centuries is to reveal. Among the millions who are now thinking and feeling on our own soil, is it likely that there is not one who might take up the song of Homer,—not one who might talk the night away with Socrates,—not one who might be the Shakspere of an age when our volcanoes shall have become regions of green pasture and still waters, and new islands shall send forth human speech from the midst of the sea? What are such men about? If one is pining in want, rusting in ignorance, or turning from angel to devil under oppression, it is too probable that another may be undergoing extinction in the drawing-rooms,—surrendering his divine faculties to wither in lamplight, and be wafted away in perfume and praise. As surely as the human thought has power to fly abroad over the expanse of a thousand years, it has need to rest on that far shore, and meditate, "Where now are the flatteries, and vanities, and competitions, which seemed so important in their day? Where are the ephemeral reputations, the glow-worm ideas, the gossamer sentiments, which the impertinent voice of Fashion pronounced immortal and divine? The deluge of oblivion has swept over them all, while the minds which were really immortal and divine are still there, 'for ever singing as they shine'[2] in the firmament of thought, and mirrored in the deep of ages out of which they rose.'"[3]

Among the traits from the life is that paragraph of the foregoing extracts about the pedantry of the 'superior people' of a provincial town. Norwich, which has now no claims to social superiority at all, was in my childhood a rival of Lichfield itself, in the time of the Sewards, for literary pretension and the vulgarity of pedantry.[4] William Taylor was

---

[1]   A favorite phrase from Johann von Schiller ("Tell him to reverence the dreams of his youth"), which Martineau also uses in *Society in America* (1837): "The American people have not only much to learn, and a painful discipline to endure, but some disgraceful faults to repent of and amend. They must give a perpetual and earnest heed to one point: to cherish their high democratic hope, their faith in man. The older they grow, the more must they 'reverence the dreams of their youth.'"

[2]   The phrase comes from Joseph Addison's "The spacious firmament on high," in *Hymns based on Psalms*: "In reason's ear they all rejoice / And utter forth a glorious voice, / Forever singing as they shine, / 'The hand that made us is divine.'"

[3]   London and Westminster Review. No. LXIII., April, 1839. [Martineau's note]

[4]   The poet Anna Seward (1747–1809) was called the "Swan of Lichfield." Her father was canon at Lichfield cathedral, and her grandfather had taught Samuel Johnson, who was born there in 1709.

then at his best; when there was something like fulfillment of his early promise, when his exemplary filial duty was a fine spectacle to the whole city, and before the vice which destroyed him had coarsened his morale, and drowned his intellect.[1] During the war, it was a great distinction to know any thing of German literature; and in Mr. Taylor's case it proved a ruinous distinction. He was completely spoiled by the flatteries of shallow men, pedantic women, and conceited lads. We girls had the advantage. We could listen and amuse ourselves, without being called upon to take any part; and heartily amused we often were, after the example of our mother. When she went to Norwich, a bonny young bride, with plenty of sense and observation, and a satirical turn, and more knowledge, even of books, than the book people gave her credit for, she used to carry home her own intense amusement from the supper-tables of the time, and keep her good stories alive till we were old enough to enjoy them. We took our cue from her; and the blue-stocking ladies who crammed themselves from reviews and publishers' lists in the morning to cut a figure in the evening, as conversant with all the literature of the day, were little aware how we children were noting all their vanities and egotisms, to act them to-morrow in our play. The lady who cleared her throat to obtain a hearing for her question whether Mr. William Taylor had read the charming anecdote of the Chinese Emperor Chim-Cham-Chow, was a capital subject for us: and so was another who brought out her literary observations amidst an incessant complacent purring: and so was another who sported youthful vivacity, and political enthusiasm with her scanty skirts and uncovered head to past seventy. These and many more barely condescended to notice my mother, (who, in genuine ability, was worth them all,) except in her quality of hostess. The gentlemen took wine with her, and the ladies ate her fricassees and custards; but they talked vile French in her presence, knowing that she did not understand it, and that the foreigner they had caught could speak English very well. This sort of display, and the contrast which struck us whenever we chanced to meet with genuine superiority, was no doubt of service to us, as a preparation for the higher kind of life which we were afterwards to work out for ourselves. It enabled me, for one, to see, twenty years later, that there is no essential difference between the extreme case of a cathe-

---

[1]   William Taylor (1765–1836), born in Norwich, popularized German literature through his translations of Lessing, Goethe, and other poets, and his reviews in the *Monthly Magazine*. Martineau disapproved of the coterie of young men with which he surrounded himself and of his alcoholic excess.

dral city and that of literary London, or any other place, where dissipation takes the turn of book talk instead of dancing or masquerading. Among the mere pedants were some who were qualified for something better. Such women as Mrs. Opie and Mrs. John Taylor ought to have been superior to the nonsense and vanity in which they participated.[1] I do not remember Dr. Sayers;[2] and I believe he died before I could possibly remember him; but I always heard of him as a genuine scholar; and I have no doubt he was superior to his neighbours in modesty and manners. Dr. Enfield, a feeble and superficial man of letters, was gone also from these literary supper-tables before my time. There was Sir James Smith, the botanist,—made much of, and really not pedantic and vulgar, like the rest, but weak and irritable. There was Dr. Alderson, Mrs. Opie's father, solemn and sententious and eccentric in manner, but not an able man in any way.[3] William Taylor was managed by a regular process,—first, of feeding, then of wine-bibbing, and immediately after of poking to make him talk: and then came his sayings, devoured by the gentlemen, and making ladies and children aghast;—defences of suicide, avowals that snuff alone had rescued him from it: information given as certain, that 'God save the King' was sung by Jeremiah in the temple of Solomon,—that Christ was watched on the day of his supposed ascension, and observed to hide himself till dusk, and then to make his way down the other side of the mountain; and other such plagiarisms from the German Rationalists. When William Taylor began with 'I firmly believe,' we knew that something particularly incredible was coming. We escaped without injury from hearing such things half a dozen times in a year; and from a man who was often seen to have taken too much wine: and we knew, too, that he came to our house because he had been my father's schoolfellow, and because there had always been a friendship between his excellent mother and our clan.[4] His virtues as a son were before our eyes when we witnessed his endurance of his father's brutality of temper and manners, and his

[1] The poet and novelist Amelia Opie (1769–1853), daughter of the Norwich physician James Alderson, married the painter John Opie, a prominent member of the "Norwich School." When Martineau wrote her obituary for the London *Daily News*, she called her a member "of that curious class of English people—the provincial literary lion."

[2] Frank Sayers (1764–1817), poet and dramatist, friend of William Taylor, and author of *Dramatic Sketches of Northern Mythology* (1790).

[3] William Enfield (Unitarian minister), James Edward Smith (botanist), James Alderman (physician), and Mrs. John Taylor all actively promoted literature and the arts in Norwich and wrote for various local periodicals, including *The Cabinet* and *The Isis*.

[4] Thomas Martineau, William Taylor, and Frank Sayers attended the famous Palgrave School, a Dissenting academy, where they were taught by Anna Laetitia Aikins Barbauld.

watchfulness in ministering to the old man's comfort in his infirmities. When we saw, on a Sunday morning, William Taylor guiding his blind mother to chapel, and getting her there with her shoes as clean as if she had crossed no gutters in those flint-paved streets, we could forgive anything that had shocked or disgusted us at the dinner table. But matters grew worse in his old age, when his habits of intemperance kept him out of the sight of ladies, and he got round him a set of ignorant and conceited young men, who thought they could set the world right by their destructive propensities. One of his chief favourites was George Borrow, as George Borrow has himself given the world to understand.[1] When this polyglot gentleman appeared before the public as a devout agent of the Bible Society in foreign parts, there was one burst of laughter from all who remembered the old Norwich days. At intervals, Southey[2] came to see his old friend, William Taylor: and great was the surprise that one who became such a bigot on paper, in religion and politics, could continue the friend of so wild a rover in those fields as William Taylor, who talked more blasphemy, and did more mischief to young men (through his entire lack of conviction and earnestness and truth-speaking) than the Hones and Carliles and others whom Southey abhorred as emissaries of Satan.[3] After reading Southey's Life and Correspondence, the maintenance of that friendship appears to me more singular than when we young people used to catch a glimpse in the street of the author of 'Thalaba' and 'Kehama.' The great days of the Gurneys were not come yet. The remarkable family from which issued Mrs. Fry, and Priscilla and Joseph John Gurney,[4] were

---

[1]   George Borrow (1803–81), best known for his travel memoir *The Bible in Spain* (1843), also wrote two autobiographies, *Lavengro* (1851) and *The Romany Rye* (1857), which include his adventures with Norfolk gypsies.

[2]   The poet Robert Southey (1774–1843) was known for his "pantisocracy," a utopian scheme he devised with Samuel Coleridge in 1794–95 to set up an egalitarian commune in New England.

[3]   William Hone (1780–1842), bookseller and publisher of political satires, and Richard Carlile (1790–1843), freethinker and defender of a free press, incurred Southey's wrath when they circulated and reviewed *Wat Tyler* in 1817, a dramatic poem Southey had written in 1794 but left unpublished because of its radical views. Hone and Carlile used *Wat Tyler* to demonstrate Southey's political apostasy and acquiescence in the government's conservative politics when he was made poet laureate. In the *Reformists' Register*, on February 22, 1817, Hone wrote: "In consideration of a Court pension, he now regularly inflames his muse, in praise of official persons and business. . . . Poor Southey! a pensioned Laureate! compelled to sing like a blind linnet by a sly pinch, with every now and then a volume of his old verse flying into his face, and putting him out!"

[4]   The Gurneys, a prominent Quaker banking family, included the prison reformer Elizabeth Fry, as well as her siblings Priscilla and John Joseph, both known for their philanthropy and efforts to end slavery.

then a set of dashing young people,—dressing in gay riding habits and scarlet boots, as Mrs. Fry told us afterwards, and riding about the country to balls and gaieties of all sorts. Accomplished and charming young ladies they were; and we children used to overhear some whispered gossip about the effects of their charms on heart-stricken young men: but their final characteristics were not yet apparent.

There was one occasional apparition which kept alive in us a sense of what intellectual superiority ought to be and to produce. Mrs. Barbauld came to Norwich now and then; and she always made her appearance presently at our house.[1] In her early married life, before the happiness of the devoted wife was broken up by her gentle husband's insanity, she had helped him in his great school at Palgrave in Suffolk, by taking charge of the very little boys. William Taylor and my father had stood at her knee with their slates; and when they became men, and my father's children were older than he was when she first knew him, she retained her interest in him, and extended it to my mother and us. It was a remarkable day for us when the comely elderly lady in her black silk cloak and bonnet came and settled herself for a long morning chat. She used to insist on holding skeins of silk for my mother to wind, or on winding, while one of us children was the holder: and well I remember her gentle lively voice, and the stamp of superiority on all she said. We knew she was very learned, and we saw she was graceful, and playful, and kindly and womanly: and we heard with swelling hearts the anecdotes of her heroism when in personal danger from her husband's hallucinations, and when it was scarcely possible to separate her from him, when her life and his poor chance of restoration required it. I still think her one of the first of writers in our language, and the best example we have of the benefits of a sound classical education to a woman. When I was old enough to pass a few weeks with my aunt Lee, at Stoke Newington,[2] I went more than once with my aunt to Mrs. Barbauld's to tea, and was almost confounded at the honour of being allowed to make tea. It was owing to her that I had one literary acquaintance when I went to London in 1832. Miss Aikin,[3]

---

[1] Anna Laetitia Barbauld, née Aikin (1743–1825), poet, political essayist and educator. As Martineau explains, she was a key figure in her father's childhood; William Taylor called her "the mother of his mind."

[2] Margaret Lee (1756–1840), sister of Harriet's father, then lived in a village north of London; she later joined Martineau's household in Fludyer Street.

[3] Lucy Aikin (1781–1864), poet and historian, was at this time writing her *Memoirs of the Court of Queen Elizabeth* (1818), *Memoirs of the Court of James* (1822), and *Memoirs of the Court of Charles I* (1833).

niece of Mrs. Barbauld, came to Norwich now and then, and was well-known to my mother: and when I was in the City Road in that memorable spring of the success of the Prize Essays,[1] my mother gave me a letter of introduction to Miss Aikin, then living at Hampstead. She received me with kindness at once, and with distinction when the Prize Essays had come under her eye. When my Series was struggling for publication, I sent her my prospectus. She returned a bare message of acknowledgment. This rather surprised me; and it was not till some years afterwards that I learned how the matter was. The anecdote is so creditable to her candour, that it ought to be told. Naturally regarding me as a youngster, as my friendly elderly critics always did, even when I was long past thirty, she was so struck with the presumption of the enterprise that she thought it her duty to rebuke me for it. She accordingly wrote a letter which she showed to her literary friends, informing me that I could have no idea how far beyond any powers of mine was such a scheme; that large information, an extensive acquaintance with learned persons and with affairs, &c., &c., were indispensable; and that she counselled me to burn my prospectus and programme, and confine myself to humbler tasks, such as a young woman might be competent to. Those who saw the letter admired it much, and hoped I should have the grace to thank my stars that I had so faithful a friend, to interpose between me and exposure. She hesitated, however, about sending it; and she put off the act till my success was decided and notorious. She then burned the letter, and herself told the story with capital grace,—felicitating herself on her having burned the letter, instead of me on being the object of it. I heard unintelligible references to this letter, from time to time, and did not know what they meant, till the complete story, as told by herself, was repeated to me, after the lapse of years.—She rendered me a real service, about the time of the burning of the letter. Her friend, Mr. Hallam,[2] found fault at her house with two statements of mine about the operation of the law or custom of primogeniture; and she begged of him to make known his criticisms to me, and told me she had done so,—being assured that such an authority as Mr. Hallam would be fitly honoured by me. I was grateful, of course; and I presently received a long letter of pretty sharp criticism from Mr. Hallam. In my reply, I submitted myself to him about one point, but stood my ground in regard to

---

[1]   See Period III, sec. iii.
[2]   Henry Hallam (1777–1859), historian best known for his *Constitutional History of England* (1827).

the other,—successfully, as he admitted. He wrote then a very cordial letter,—partly of apology for the roughness of his method, by which he had desired to ascertain whether I could bear criticism, and partly to say that he hoped he might consider our correspondence a sufficient introduction, authorising Mrs. Hallam and himself to call on me. He was from that time forward, and is now, one of the most valued of my literary friends. One more transaction, however, was to take place before I could make him and Miss Aikin quite understand what my intentions and views were in indulging myself with the benefits and pleasures of literary society in London.

Mr. Hallam one day called, when, as it was the first of the month, my table was spread with new periodicals, sent me by publishers. I was not in the room when Mr. Hallam entered; and I found him with the 'Monthly Repository' in his hands, turning over the leaves. He pointed to the Editor's name (Mr. Fox) on the cover, and asked me some questions about him. After turning over, and remarking upon a few others, he sat down for a chat. A few days after, I received a note from Miss Aikin, kindly congratulating me on my 'success, thus far, in society,' and on my 'honours' generally; and then admonishing me that the continuance of such 'success' and such 'honours' would depend on my showing due deference to the opinions and standing of persons older and more distinguished than myself; so that she felt it was an act of friendship to warn me against appearing to know of periodicals so low as, for instance, the 'Monthly Repository,' and having any information to give about dissenting ministers, like Mr. Fox.

I replied without loss of time, that there might be no more mistake as to my views in going into society. I thanked her for her kindness and her frankness: told her that I objected to the word 'success,' as she had used it, because success implies endeavour; and I had nothing to strive for in any such direction. I went into society to learn and to enjoy, and not to obtain suffrages: and I hoped to be as frank and unrestrained with others as I wished them to be with me. I told her how I perceived that Mr. Hallam was her informant, and by what accident it was that he saw the periodical, and heard about its editor: but I said that I was a dissenter, and acquainted with dissenting ministers, and should certainly never deny it when asked, as I was by Mr. Hallam, or object to all the world knowing it. Once for all, I concluded, I had no social policy, and no personal aims; no concealments, nor reasons for compromise. Society was very pleasant; but it would cease to be so from the moment that it was any thing but a simple recreation from work, accepted without the restraint of politic conditions. She took my reply in good part; was somewhat aghast at my not being 'destroyed' by hostile reviews, when she trembled at the prospect of favourable ones of her own books; but was always gracious and kind when we met,—which seldom happened, however, when she grew old and I had left London.

Mr. Hallam's call opened to me a curious glimpse into some of the devices of this same London literary society. He told me that if I had not considered our correspondence a sufficient introduction, we should yet have become acquainted,—his friend, Dr.—, having promised him an introduction. I laughed, and said there must be some mistake, as Dr.— was an entire stranger to me. Mr. Hallam's surprise was extreme: Dr.— had told him we were relations, and had spoken as if we were quite intimate. I replied that there was a very distant connexion by marriage; but that we were utter strangers; and in fact, I had never seen Dr.— . I was less amazed than Mr. Hallam at the stroke of policy on the part of a courtier-like London physician, and was amused when Mr. Hallam said he must learn from him where the mistake lay.[1] My new friends had not been gone half an hour, when up drove Dr.—. In the presence of other visitors, he took my hand in both his, in true family style, and lavished much affection upon me,—though he had never recognised my existence during any former visits of mine to London. The excess of his humility in asking me to dinner was shocking. He, a physician in immense practice, entreated me to name my own day and hour, which I, of course, declined. When I went, on the first disengaged day, I met a pleasant, small party, and enjoyed the day,—except its close, when my host not only led me through all the servants in the hall, but leaned into my hackney-coach to thank me for the honour, &c., &c. This kind of behaviour was very disagreeable to me; and I never went to the house again but once. My mother and I were incessantly invited; and we really could not go because the invitations were short, and I was always engaged: but I was not very sorry, remembering the beginning of our acquaintance.—The one other time that I visited Dr.— was the occasion of an incident of which it may be worth while to give a true version, as a false one was industriously spread. I have said above, that there were three persons only to whom I have refused to be introduced; and two of these have been seen to be Mr. Lockhart and Mr. Sterling. The third was the poet Moore.[2] One day my mother was distressed at finding in the 'Times' a ribald song addressed to me. She folded it in the innermost part of the paper, and hoped, as I was in the

---

[1]   Unidentified.

[2]   Thomas Moore (1779–1852), poet known for his *Irish Melodies* (1808–34) and friendship with Byron.

country that morning, that I should not see it. The event showed her that it would not do to conceal any thing of the sort from me, as I could not conduct my own peculiar case without knowing as much of the circumstances of it as other people. The song was copied everywhere, and ascribed so positively to Moore that I was compelled to suppose it his, though there was not a trace of wit to redeem its coarseness. At Dr.—'s party, a few nights after, the host came to me to say that Mr. Rogers[1] and Mr. Moore had come for the purpose of making my acquaintance: and Mr. Moore was standing within earshot, waiting for his introduction. I was obliged to decide in a moment what to do; and I think what I did was best, under such a difficulty. I said I should be happy to be honoured by Mr. Rogers's acquaintance; but that, if Mr. Moore was, as was generally understood, the author of a recent insult to me in the 'Times' newspaper, I did not see how I could permit an introduction. I added that there might be a mistake about the authorship; in which case I should be happy to know Mr. Moore. Dr.— was, of course, very uncomfortable. Having seated Mr. Rogers beside me, he and Moore left the room together for a little while. When they returned, Moore went to the piano, and sang several songs. Then, he screened his little person behind a lady's harp; and all the time she was playing, he was studying me through his eye-glass. When she finished her piece he went away to another party, where a friend of mine happened to be; and there he apologised for being late, on the plea that he had been 'singing songs to Harriet Martineau.' The story told was that I had asked Dr.— to introduce us, and had then declined. The incident was, in one sense, a trifle not worth dwelling on: but in another view, it was important to me. At the outset of so very new a course of life, it seemed to me necessary to secure personal respect by the only means in a woman's power;—refusing the acquaintance of persons who have publicly outraged consideration and propriety. My mother thought me right; and so did the other friends who witnessed the transaction: and it was effectual. I never had any trouble of the sort again.

The first sight of Brougham,[2] then just seated on the wool-sack, and the object of all manner of expectation which he never fulfilled, was an incident to be remembered. I had not previously shared the general expec-

---

[1]   Samuel Rogers (1763–1855), poet, art critic, and famed host of literary "breakfasts," which he convened for over forty years.

[2]   Henry Peter, Baron Brougham and Vaux (1778–1868), Whig politician and eventually lord chancellor, was a founder of the *Edinburgh Review* and a moving force in the Society for the Diffusion of Useful Knowledge. See Period IV, sec. i for Martineau's dealings with him on *Poor Laws and Paupers Illustrated*.

tation of great national benefits from him. I believed that much of his effort for popular objects, even for education, was for party and personal purposes; and that he had no genuine popular sympathy, or real desire that the citizens at large should have any effectual political education. I distrusted his steadiness, and his disinterestedness, and his knowledge of the men and interests of his own time. I believed him too vain and self-ish, and too low in morals and unrestrained in temper, to turn out a really great man when his day of action came. Many a time has my mother said to me, 'Harriet, you will have much to answer for for speaking as you do if Brougham turns out what the rest of us expect:' to which my answer was 'Yes, Mother, indeed I shall.' She was at length very glad that I was not among the disappointed. Yet, there was a strong interest in meeting for the first time, and on the safe ground of substantial business, the man of whom I had heard so much from my childhood, and who now had more power over the popular welfare than perhaps any other man in the world. After two or three interviews, he was so manifestly wild, that the old interest was lost in pity and dislike; but at first I knew nothing of the manifesta-tions of eccentricity which he presently made public enough. Those were the days when he uttered from the platform his laments over his folly in accepting a peerage, and when he made no secret to strangers who called on him on business, of his being 'the most wretched man on earth.' But I first met him when nothing of the sort had taken place so publicly but that his adorers and toadies could conceal it.

A day or two after my arrival in London, I met him at dinner at the house of the correspondent of his through whom he engaged me to help in poor-law reform. By his desire, no one else was asked. The first thing that struck me was his being not only nervous, but thin-skinned to excess. Our hostess's lap-dog brought out the nervousness immediately, by jump-ing up at his knee. He pretended to play with Gyp, but was obviously annoyed that Gyp would not be called away. He was not accustomed to lap-dogs, it was clear. Before we went to dinner, I could not but see how thin-skinned he was. The 'Examiner' newspaper lay on the table; and it chanced to contain, that week, an impertinent article, warning me against being flattered out of my own aims by my host, who was Brougham's cat's-paw.[1] The situation was sufficiently awkward, it must be owned. Brougham did not read the article now, because he had seen it at home: but I saw by glances and pointings that the gentlemen were talking it

---

[1]   Probably Lady Shepherd (Brougham's aunt) and her husband, Sir Samuel Shepherd, who hosted many London gatherings of artists, authors, and politicians.

over, while my hostess and I were consulting about her embroidery: and
Brougham looked, not only very black upon it, but evidently annoyed
and stung. He looked black in another sense, I remember,—not a morsel
of his dress being anything but black, from the ridge of his stock to the
toes of his polished shoes. Not an inch of white was there to relieve the
combined gloom of his dress and complexion. He was curiously afraid
of my trumpet,[1] and managed generally to make me hear without. He
talked excessively fast, and ate fast and prodigiously, stretching out his long
arm for any dish he had a mind to, and getting hold of the largest spoons
which would dispatch the most work in the shortest time. He watched
me intently and incessantly when I was conversing with any body else.
For my part, I liked to watch him when he was conversing with gentlemen, and his mind and its manifestations really came out. This was never
the case, as far as my observation went, when he talked with ladies. I
believe I have never met with more than three men, in the whole course
of my experience, who talked with women in a perfectly natural manner;
that is, precisely as they talked with men: but the difference in Brougham's
case was so great as to be disagreeable. He knew many cultivated and
intellectual women; but this seemed to be of no effect. If not able to
assume with them his ordinary manner towards silly women, he was
awkward and at a loss. This was by no means agreeable, though the sin
of his bad manners must be laid at the door of the vain women who
discarded their ladyhood for his sake, went miles to see him, were early
on platforms where he was to be, and admitted him to very broad flirtations. He had pretty nearly settled his own business, in regard to conversation with ladies, before two more years were over. His swearing became
so incessant, and the occasional indecency of his talk so insufferable, that
I have seen even coquettes and adorers turn pale, and the lady of the
house tell her husband that she could not undergo another dinner party
with Lord Brougham for a guest. I, for my part, determined to decline
quietly henceforth any small party where he was expected; and this
simply because there was no pleasure in a visit where every body was on
thorns as to what any one guest might say and do next. My own impression that day was that he was either drunk or insane. Drunk he was not;
for he had been publicly engaged in business till the last moment. All
manner of protestations have been made by his friends, to this day, that
he is, with all his eccentricities, 'sane enough:' but my impression remains

---

[1]   I then used a caoutchouc tube, with a cup at one end for the speaker to speak into. It was
    a good exchange when I laid aside this in favour of a trumpet with which the speaker
    had no concern. [Martineau's note]

that no man who conducted himself as he did that summer day in 1834 could be sane and sober.[1]

I remember now, with no little emotion, a half hour of my visit at Lambton Castle, a few months before that uncomfortable dinner. One evening, when a guest, Lord H——,[2] had been talking with me about some matters of popular interest which led us to discuss the Society for the Diffusion of Useful Knowledge, Lord Durham invited me to the room where music was going on, and where we could not be overheard. He asked me whether Lord H—— had understood me right, that the surest way *not* to reach the people was to address them through the Society, and by the agency of the Whig managers. I replied that I had said so; and I told him why, giving him evidence of the popular distrust of Lord Brougham and his teaching and preaching clique. Lord Durham heard me with evident concern, and said at last, in his earnest, heart-felt way, 'Brougham has done, and will do, foolish things enough: but it would cut me to the heart to think that Brougham was false.' The words and the tone were impressed on my mind by the contrast which they formed with the way in which Brougham and his toadies were in the habit of speaking of Lord Durham. Brougham's envy and jealousy of the popular confidence enjoyed by Lord Durham at that time were notorious. If Lord Durham was unaware of it, he was the only person who was. I need not continue the story which is remembered by every body of my own generation, and which the next may read in the records of the time,— the Grey dinner at Edinburgh when Lord Durham involuntarily triumphed,—the attack on him at Salisbury and in a traitorous article in the Edinburgh Review, which revealed Cabinet secrets,—the challenge and anticipated encounter of the two noblemen on the floor of the House of Lords,—and the terror of the feeble King, who dissolved parliament to preclude the encounter, deprived Brougham of the Seals, and sent Lord Durham on a foreign mission.[3] I need not tell over again the

---

[1]   Lord Brougham's brother, Lord Henley (1789–1841), died insane, which may account for Martineau's speculation.

[2]   Perhaps Lord Henley.

[3]   Lords Durham and Brougham had a history of political disagreement—over Catholic emancipation, over Brougham's exclusion from the committee of four that drafted the Reform Act of 1832, and eventually over Durham's governance of Canada. When Durham was sent to Canada in 1838 to restore orderly government, he issued a proclamation of amnesty, excepting eight persons who had taken part in a rebellion and who were sent from Montreal to a Bermuda prison. Brougham vindictively attacked this Act of Amnesty and Durham's "interference" in another colonial territory, and urged Lord Melbourne, the prime minister, to disallow it. Martineau tells this story in *A History of the Peace*, Book V, ch. XII.

terrible story of the triumph of Brougham's evil passions, in perilling the safety, and overthrowing the government of Canada, and in destroying the career and breaking the heart of the generous, sensitive, honest and magnanimous statesman whom he chose to consider his enemy. It was as much as I could well bear to contrast the tones of the two men and their adherents before Lord Durham knew that there was anything wrong between them; and when the dismal story proceeded, my heart swelled, many a time, when I recalled the moment of Lord Durham's first reception of a doubt of Brougham's honesty, and the serious countenance and sweet voice of remonstrance in which he said 'It would cut me to the heart to think that Brougham was false.' In seven years from that time he was in his grave,—sent there by Brougham's falseness.

With Brougham, his ancient comrades were naturally associated in the mind of one who knew them only through books and newspapers. I saw much of Jeffrey, and the Murrays, and Sydney Smith.[1] My first sight of Jeffrey was odd enough in its circumstances. It makes me laugh to think of it now. My mother was with me in my second-floor lodgings in my first London winter. It happened to be my landlady's cleaning day; and the stair-carpets were up, and the housemaid on her knees, scouring, when Mrs. Marcet and Lord Jeffrey made their way as they could between the pail and the bannisters. While Mrs. Marcet panted for breath enough to introduce us, Jeffrey stood with his arms by his side and his head depressed,—the drollest spectacle of mock humility:—and then he made some solemn utterance about 'homage,' &c., to which I replied by asking him to sit down. Almost before we had well begun to talk, in burst Mrs. A.— , a literary woman whose ways were well known to my mother and me.[2] The moment she saw Lord Jeffrey, she forgot to speak to us, but so thrust herself between Lord Jeffrey and me as actually to push me backwards and sit on my knee. I extricated myself as soon as possible, and left my seat. As she turned her back on me, my mother cast a droll glance at me which I fancy Lord Jeffrey saw; for, though one of the most egregious flatterers of this lady,—as of vain

[1]   Francis, Lord Jeffrey (1773–1850) and Sydney Smith (1771–1845) were founders of the Whig *Edinburgh Review*. Sir John Archibald Murray (1779–1859), later Lord Murray, was lord advocate of Scotland in 1834–35 and a long-standing friend.

[2]   Jane Marcet (1769–1858) wrote *Conversations on Political Economy* (1816), which influenced Martineau's *Illustrations of Political Economy*. "Mrs.—" was most likely Sarah Austin, née Taylor, a Norwich-born author who married the jurist John Austin, and began to write to supplement her husband's income. She contributed to the *Edinburgh*, the *British and Foreign*, and the *Foreign Quarterly* reviews.

women in general,—he played her off in a way which she must have been very complacent not to understand. He showed that he wanted to talk to me, and said, when he saw she was determined to go away with him, that he considered this no visit, and would, if I pleased, come again on the first practicable day. I am convinced that he discovered in that short interview what my mother and I felt about the ways of literary people like Mrs. A——; and, though he could not easily drop, in any one case, his habit of flattery, he soon found that I did not like it, did not believe in it, and thought the worse of him for it. I never made any secret of my opinion of the levity, cruelty and unmanliness of literary men who aggravate the follies, and take advantage of the weakness of vain women; and this was Jeffrey's most conspicuous and very worst fault. As for my mother and me, we had a hearty laugh over this little scene, when our visitors were gone; it was so very like old Norwich, in the days of the suppers of the 'superior people!'

Whatever there might be of artificial in Jeffrey's manners,—of a set 'company state of mind' and mode of conversation,—there was a warm heart underneath, and an ingenuousness which added captivation to his intellectual graces. He could be absurd enough in his devotion to a clever woman; and he could be highly culpable in drawing out the vanity of a vain one, and then comically making game of it; but his better nature was always within call; and his generosity was unimpeachable in every other respect,—as far as I knew him. His bounties to needy men of letters,— bounties which did not stop to make ill-timed inquiries about desert,— were so munificent, that the world, which always knew him to be generous, would be amazed at the extent of the munificence: and it was done with so much of not only delicacy but respect,—in such a hearty love of literature, that I quite understand how easy it would be to accept money from him. If I had needed assistance of that kind, there is no one from whom I could more freely have asked it.—As for his conversation, it appeared to me that he cared more for moralizing than any other great converser I have known: but this might be adaptation to my likings; and I heard none of his conversation but what was addressed to myself. I must say that while I found (or perceived) myself regarded as romantic, high-flown, extravagant, and so forth by good Mr. Empson,[1] and the Jeffrey set generally (even including Sydney Smith), whenever I opened my mouth on matters of morals,—such as the aims of authorship, the rights and duties of opinion, the true spirit of citizenship, &c.,—I never failed to

---

[1]   William Empson (1791–1852), editor of the *Edinburgh Review* from 1847.

find cordial sympathy in Jeffrey. If at times he was more foolish and idle than most men of his power would choose to appear, he was always higher than them all when his moral sympathies and judgment were appealed to. I remember a small incident which impressed me, in connexion with this view of him; and, as it relates to him, it may be worth noting. At one of Mr. Rogers's breakfasts, I was seated between him and his friend Milman,[1] when the conversation turned on some special case (I forget what) of excessive vanity. I was pitying the person because, whatever flattery he obtained, there was always some censure; and the smallest censure, to the vain, outweighs the largest amount of praise. Milman did not think so, saying that the vain are very happy;—'no people more apt at making themselves happy than the vainest:'—'they feed upon their own praises, and dismiss the censure; and, having no heart, they are out of the way of trouble.' I made the obvious remark that if they have no heart they cannot be very happy. Jeffrey's serious assent to this, and remark that it settled the question, discomposed Milton extremely. He set to work to batter his egg and devour it without any reply, and did not speak for some time after. It was amusing that we two heretics should be administering instruction on morals to a Church dignitary of such eminence as a sacred poet as the Dean of St. Paul's.

I have however seen Milman so act, and so preserve a passive state, as to be a lesson to all present. One incident especially which happened at Mr. Hallam's dinner-table, gave me a hearty respect for his command of a naturally irritable temper. He behaved incomparably on that occasion. It was a pleasant party of eight or ten people, —every one, as it happened, of considerable celebrity, and therefore not to be despised in the matter of literary criticism, or verdict on character. I was placed near the top of the table, between Milman and Mr. Rogers; and the subject of animated conversation at the bottom presently took its turn among us. Mrs. Trollope's novel, 'Jonathan Jefferson Whitlaw,'[2] had just come out, and was pronounced on by everybody present but myself, —I not having read it. As I had lately returned from the United States, I was

---

[1]   Henry Hart Milman (1791–1868), clergyman, historian, poet, and author of the verse drama *Fazio* (1815), which was successful on stage.

[2]   Frances Trollope (1780–1863), popular novelist and mother of Anthony Trollope, had just published *Domestic Manners of the Americans* (1832), which she wrote after the failure of a commercial venture in Cincinnati. The book depicted what she saw as the vulgar and eccentric habits of North Americans. *The Life and Adventures of Jonathan Jefferson Whitlaw; or, Scenes on the Mississippi* (London, Richard Bentley, 1836) was Mrs. Trollope's venture into fiction, published as Martineau was reading proof for her own *Society in America* (London: Saunders and Otley, 1837).

asked what Mrs. Trollope's position was there. My reply was that I had
no scruple in saying that Mrs. Trollope had no opportunity of knowing what good society was in America, generally speaking. I added that
I intended to say this, as often as I was inquired of; for the simple reason
that Mrs. Trollope had thought proper to libel and slander a whole
nation. If she had been an ordinary discontented tourist, her adventures
in America would not be worth the trouble of discussing; but her slanderous book made such exposures necessary. Every body, except
Milman, asked questions, and I answered them. She certainly had no
admirers among the party when she was first mentioned; and the
account I gave of her unscrupulous method of reporting surprised
nobody. At last, Milman put in a word for her. He could not help thinking that she had been illused:——he knew facts indeed of her having been
taken in about her bazaar. 'No doubt,' said I. 'Any English traveller who
begins the game of diamond cut diamond with Yankee speculators is
likely to get the worst of it. No doubt she was abundantly cheated; and
hence this form of vengeance,——a vituperative book.' Milman continued that he was aware of what hard usage she had to complain of, by
his acquaintance with her. He was proceeding when Rogers broke in
with one of his odd tentative speeches,——one of those probings by
which he seemed to try how much people could bear. 'O yes,' said he;
'he *is* acquainted with Mrs. Trollope. He had the forming of her mind.'
There was a moment of dead pause, and then every body burst into a
hearty laugh; every body but Milman. He was beginning with a vehement 'No, no;' but he checked himself and said nothing. He had begun
to speak on behalf of Mrs. Trollope, and he would not give it up now
that Rogers had so spoken. His high colour and look of distress showed
what his magnanimous silence cost him; but not a word more did he
say. As I expected and hoped, he called on me the next morning. He
often did so, as we were neighbours; but that morning he came as soon
as the clock had struck two. His first care was to disclaim having
educated Mrs. Trollope, who was, in fact, about his own age. His mother
and hers, I think, were friends. At all events, he had known her nearly
all his life. He frankly told me now, in the proper place and time, why
he thought Mrs. Trollope ill-qualified to write travels and describe a
nation: 'but,' he continued, 'the thing is done, and can't be helped now;
so that, unless you feel bound in conscience to expose her,——which
might be to ruin her,——I would intercede for her.' Laying his finger on
a proof-sheet of my American book which lay at his elbow, he went
on, 'Can't you, now, say what you think of the same people, and let that

be her answer?' 'Why,' exclaimed I, 'you don't suppose I am going to occupy any of my book with Mrs. Trollope! I would not dirty my pages with her stories, even to refute them. What have I to do with Mrs. Trollope but to say what I know when inquired of?' 'O, well, that is all right,' said he. 'I took for granted you meant to do it in your book: and I don't say that you could be blamed if you did. But if you mean in conversation, you are certainly quite right, and Mrs. Trollope herself could have no title to complain.' I thought the candour, kindness and generosity shown in this incident quite remarkable; and I have always recalled it with pleasure.

With Jeffrey his old Edinburgh comrades were naturally associated, as far as the influences of time and chance yet permitted. Brougham had before this withdrawn himself almost entirely from those friends of his youth. Horner's Life and Correspondence had not then been published;[1] but I had gathered up enough about him to see him, in a spiritual sense, sitting in the midst of them. 'Did you know Horner?' inquired Sydney Smith. 'You should have known Horner; but I suppose he was gone before you were invented.' With Horner's name the most closely associated of all was that of John A. Murray, (Lord Murray who was Lord Advocate when I first knew him). Of all my acquaintance, no one was a greater puzzle to me than Horner's beloved John Murray, whose share of their published correspondence shows why there were once splendid expectations from him. His career as Lord Advocate and Judge was so little successful that the world could not but wonder how there could be such an issue from such promise. Jeffrey's failure in political office and as a parliamentary speaker, was easily accounted for by his uncertain health, his weak voice, his love of ease and literary trifling, and his eminence in a totally different function: and he ended by being an admirable Judge.[2] But in the other case, there was no success in any other direction to account or atone for the failure of Lord Murray, when opportunity opened before him in what should have been the vigour of his years. He was a kind neighbour, however, and a thoroughly good hearted man,—always happy to give pleasure, though reducing the amount he bestowed by a curious little pomposity of manner. His agreeable wife joined her efforts with his to make their guests happy, and enjoyed society as much as he did. When one could once put away the

---

[1]   Francis Horner (1778–1817), *Memoirs and Correspondence of Francis Horner, M.P.*, ed. by his brother Leonard Horner (London: J. Murray, 1843).

[2]   Lord Jeffrey stepped down as editor of the *Edinburgh Review* in 1829 when he became an M.P. and a Scottish judge.

association of Horner and those old Edinburgh days, the Murrays' parties were really delightful. I had a general invitation to their Thursday evenings at St. Stephen's;[1] and their carriage usually came for me and took me home. They lived at the Lord Advocate's Chambers, under the same roof with the Houses of Parliament; and there, on Thursday evenings during the session, was a long broad table spread, with a prodigious Scotch cake, iced and adorned, on a vast trencher in the midst. Members of both Houses dropped in and out, when the debates were tiresome; and there were always a few guests like myself, who went on their way to or from other visits, and gathered up the political news of the night, curiously alternating with political anecdotes or Edinburgh jokes of thirty or forty years before. It was pleasant to see the Jeffreys come in when Sydney Smith was there, and to look on these grey-headed friends as the very men who had made such a noise in the days of my childhood, and who were venerable for what they had done and borne in those days, though they had disappointed expectation when their opportunity came at last. It was at Lord Murray's table that Sydney Smith told me of the fun the Edinburgh reviewers used to make of their work. I taxed him honestly with the mischief they had done by their ferocity and cruel levity at the outset. It was no small mischief to have silenced Mrs. Barbauld;[2] and how much more utterance they may have prevented, there is no saying. It is all very well to talk sensibly now of the actual importance of reviews, and the real value of reviewers' judgments: but the fact remains that spirits were broken, hearts were sickened, and authorship was cruelly discouraged by the savage and reckless condemnations passed by the Edinburgh review in its early days. 'We *were* savage,' replied Sydney Smith. 'I remember' (and it was plain that he could not help enjoying the remembrance) 'how Brougham and I sat trying one night how we could exasperate our cruelty to the utmost. We had got hold of a poor nervous little vegetarian, who had put out a poor silly little book; and when we had done our review of it, we sat trying,—(and here he joined his finger and thumb as if dropping from a phial) 'to find one more chink, one more crevice, through which we might drop in one more drop of verjuice, to eat into his bones.' Very candid always, and sometimes very interesting, were the disclosures about

---

[1]   St. Stephen's Chapel, within the Royal Palace of Westminster, had been built by King Stephen c. 1141, and was later appropriated for the meeting place of the (old) House of Commons. Big Ben is officially "St. Stephen's tower."

[2]   The poet Anna Laetitia Barbauld (1743–1825) stopped publishing after the severe attacks on her anti-war poem, "Eighteen Hundred and Eleven."

the infant Edinburgh review. In the midst of his jocose talk, Sydney Smith occasionally became suddenly serious, when some ancient topic was brought up, or some life-enduring sensibility touched; and his voice, eye and manner at such times disposed one to tears almost as much as his ordinary discourse did to laughter. Among the subjects which were thus sacred to him was that of the Anti-slavery cause. One evening, at Lord Murray's, he inquired with earnest solicitude about the truth of some news from America, during the 'reign of terror,' as we used to call the early persecution of the abolitionists. As I had received letters and newspapers just before I left home, I could tell him what he wanted to know. He expressed, with manly concern, his sorrow for the sufferings of my friends in America,[1] and feared it must cause me terrible pain. 'Not unmixed pain,' I told him; and then I explained how well we knew that that mighty question could be carried only by the long perseverance of the highest order of abolitionists; and that an occasional purgation of the body was necessary, to ascertain how many of even the well-disposed had soundness of principle and knowledge, as well as strength of nerve, to go through with the enterprise: so that even this cruel persecution was not a pure evil. He listened earnestly, and sympathised in my faith in my personal friends among the abolitionists; and then a merry thought came into his head, as I saw by the change in his eye. 'Now, I am surprised at you, I own,' said he. 'I am surprised at your taste, for yourself and your friends. I can fancy you enjoying a feather (one feather) in your cap; but I cannot imagine you could like a bushel of them down your back with the tar.'

My first sight of Sydney Smith was when he called on me, under cover of a whimsical introduction, as he considered it. At a great music-party, where the drawing-rooms and staircases were one continuous crowd, the lady who had conveyed me fought her way to my seat,—which was, in consideration of my deafness, next to Malibran,[2] and near the piano. My friend brought a message which Sydney Smith had passed up the staircase;—that he understood we desired one another's acquaintance, and that he was awaiting it at the bottom of the stairs. He put it to my judgment whether I, being thin, could not more easily get down to him than he, being stout, could get up to me: and he would wait five minutes for

---

[1] Martineau traveled through the United States in 1834–35 (see Period IV, sec. iii) and maintained close friendships with Boston abolitionists, including Maria Weston Chapman, the editor of the "Memorials" added to her *Autobiography* as volume III.

[2] Maria Felicia Malibran (1808–36), a vocalist, was known for her dramatic songs, in which she often improvised to great effect.

my answer. I really could not go, under the circumstances; and it was a serious thing to give up my seat and the music; so Mr. Smith sent me a good-night, and promise to call on me, claiming this negotiation as a proper introduction. He came, and sat down, broad and comfortable, in the middle of my sofa, with his hands on his stick, as if to support himself in a vast development of voice; and then he began, like the great bell of St. Paul's, making me start at the first stroke. He looked with shy dislike at my trumpet, for which there was truly no occasion. I was more likely to fly to the furthest corner of the room. It was always his boast that I did not want my trumpet when he talked with me.

I do not believe that any body ever took amiss his quizzical descriptions of his friends. I was sure I never did: and when I now recal his fun of that sort, it seems to me too innocent to raise an uneasy feeling. There were none, I believe, whom he did not quiz; but I never heard of any hurt feelings. He did not like precipitate speech; and among the fastest talkers in England were certain of his friends and acquaintance;—Mr. Hallam, Mr. Empson, Dr. Whewell, Mr. Macaulay and myself.[1] None of us escaped his wit. His account of Mr. Empson's method of out-pouring stands, without the name, in Lady Holland's Life of her father.[2] His praise of Macaulay is well known;—'Macaulay is improved! Macaulay improves! I have observed in him of late,—flashes of silence!' His account of Whewell is something more than wit:—'Science is his forte: omniscience is his foible.' As for his friend Hallam, he knew he might make free with his characteristics, of oppugnancy and haste among others, without offence. In telling us what a blunder he himself made in going late to a dinner party, and describing how far the dinner had proceeded, and how every body was engaged, he said 'And there was Hallam, with his mouth full of cabbage and contradiction!' Nothing could be droller than his description of all his friends in influenza, in the winter of 1832–3; and of these, Hallam was the drollest of all that I remember. 'And poor Hallam was tossing and tumbling in his bed when the watchman came by and called "Twelve o'clock and a starlight night." Here was an opportunity for controversy when it seemed most out of the question! Up jumped Hallam, with "I question that,—I question that! Starlight! I see a star, I admit; but I doubt whether that constitutes starlight." Hours more of tossing and tumbling; and then comes

---

[1] Henry Hallam, historian; William Empson, contributor to the *Edinburgh Review*; William Whewell, philosopher and scientist; Thomas Babington Macaulay, Whig politician and historian.

[2] Lady [Saba] Holland, *A Memoir of the Reverend Sydney Smith. With a selection from his letters,* ed. by Mrs. Austin (London: Longman, Brown, Green, and Longmans, 1855).

the watchman again: "Past two o'clock, and a cloudy morning." "I question that,—I question that," says Hallam. And he rushes to the window, and throws up the sash,—influenza notwithstanding. "Watchman! do you mean to call this a cloudy morning? I see a star. And I question its being past two o'clock;—I question it, I question it!'" And so on. The story of Jeffrey and the North Pole, as told by Sydney Smith, appears to me strangely spoiled in the Life.[1] The incident happened while the Jeffreys were my near neighbours in London; and Mrs. Sydney Smith related the incident to me at the time. Captain (afterwards Sir John) Ross[2] had just returned from an unsuccessful polar expedition, and was bent upon going again. He used all his interest to get the government stirred up to fit out another expedition: and among others, the Lord Advocate was to be applied to, to bespeak his good offices. The mutual friend who undertook to do Captain Ross's errand to Jeffrey arrived at an unfortunate moment. Jeffrey was in delicate health, at that time, and made a great point of his daily ride; and when the applicant reached his door, he was putting his foot in the stirrup, and did not want to be detained. So he pished and pshawed, and cared nothing for the North Pole, and at length 'damned' it. The applicant spoke angrily about it to Sydney Smith, wishing that Jeffrey would take care what he was about, and use more civil language. 'What do you think he said to me?' cried the complainant. 'Why, he damned the North Pole!' 'Well, never mind! never mind!' said Sydney Smith, soothingly. 'Never mind his damning the North Pole. I have heard him speak disrespectfully of the equator.'

Much as I enjoyed the society of both in London, I cared more for the letters of Sydney Smith and Jeffrey during my long illness at Tynemouth than I ever did for their glorious conversation.[3] The air of the drawing-room had some effect on both; or I believed that it had: but our intercourse when Jeffrey was ill, and I was hopelessly so, and Sydney Smith old and in failing spirits (as he told me frequently) was thoroughly genuine. Sydney Smith wrote me that he hated the pen, now in his old age, when that love of ease was growing on him, common to aged dogs, asses and clergymen; and his letters were therefore a valuable gift, and, I am sure, duly prized. There was no drawback on intercourse with him except his being a clergyman. To a dissenter like myself, who had been brought up

1   I.e., Lady Holland's *Memoir of the Reverend Sydney Smith.*

2   John Ross (1777–1856), English explorer who led expeditions in search of the Northwest Passage.

3   See Period V, sec. i, where Martineau discusses her move from London to Newcastle upon Tyne for treatment of a debilitating illness (uterine tumors, which she does not name).

in strict nonconformist notions of the sacredness of the clerical office, and the absolute unworldliness which was its first requisite, there was something very painful in the tone always taken by Sydney Smith about Church matters. The broad avowals in his 'Letters to Singleton'[1] of the necessity of having 'prizes' in the Church, to attract gentlemen into it and keep them there;—his treatment of the vocation as a provision, a source of honour, influence, and money, are so offensive as to be really wonderful to earnest dissenters. His drawing-room position and manners were not very clerical; but that did not matter so much as the lowness of view which proved that he was not in his right place, to those who, like me, were unaware that the profession was not his choice. He discharged his duty admirably, as far as his conscience was concerned, and his nature would allow: but he had not the spiritual tendencies and endowments which alone can justify an entrance into the pastoral office.

He was not quite the only one of my new friends who did not use my trumpet in conversation. Of all people in the world, Malthus was the one whom I heard quite easily without it;—Malthus, whose speech was hopelessly imperfect, from defect in the palate.[2] I dreaded meeting him when invited by a friend of his who made my acquaintance on purpose. He had told this lady that he should be in town on such a day, and entreated her to get an introduction, and call and invite me; his reason being that whereas his friends had done him all manner of mischief by defending him injudiciously, my tales had represented his views precisely as he could have wished. I could not decline such an invitation as this; but when I considered my own deafness, and his inability to pronounce half the consonants in the alphabet, and his hare-lip which must prevent my offering him my tube, I feared we should make a terrible business of it. I was delightfully wrong. His first sentence,—slow and gentle, with the vowels sonorous, whatever might become of the consonants,—set me at ease completely. I soon found that the vowels are in fact all that I ever hear. His worst letter was *l*: and when I had no difficulty with his question, —'Would not you like to have a look at the Lakes of Killarney?' I had nothing more to fear. It really gratified him that I heard him better than anybody else; and whenever we met at dinner, I somehow found myself beside him, with my best ear next him; and then I heard all he said to every body at table.

---

[1]   Known as the "cathedral letters," Smith's *Letters to Archdeacon Singleton, on the Ecclesiastical Commission* appeared in 1837, 1838, and 1839.

[2]   Thomas Malthus (1766–1834), author of *An Essay on the Principle of Population* (1793), was a major influence on Martineau's Garveloch tales in the *Illustrations of Political Economy*.

Before we had been long acquainted, Mr. and Mrs. Malthus invited me to spend some of the hot weather with them at Haileybury,[1] promising that every facility should be afforded me for work. It was a delightful visit; and the well planted county of Herts was a welcome change from the pavement of London in August. Mr. Malthus was one of the professors of the now expiring College at Haileybury, and Mr. Empson was another: and the families of the other professors made up a very pleasant society,—to say nothing of the interest of seeing in the students the future administrators of India. On my arrival, I found that every facility was indeed afforded for my work. My room was a large and airy one, with a bay-window and a charming view; and the window side of the room was fitted up with all completeness, with desk, books, and every thing I could possibly want. Something else was provided which showed even more markedly the spirit of hospitality. A habit and whip lay on the bed. My friends had somehow discovered from my tales that I was fond of riding; and horse, habit and whip were prepared for me. Almost daily we went forth when work was done,—a pleasant riding party of five or six, and explored all the green lanes, and enjoyed all the fine views in the neighbourhood. We had no idea that it would be my only visit: but Mr. Malthus died while I was in America; and when I returned, his place was filled, both in College and home. I have been at Haileybury since, when Professor Jones was the very able successor of Mr. Malthus in the Chairs of Political Economy and History; and Mr. Empson lived in the pleasant house where I had spent such happy days. Now they are all gone; and the College itself, abolished by the new Charter of the East India Company, will soon be no more than a matter of remembrance to the present generation, and of tradition to the next. The subdued jests and external homage and occasional insurrections of the young men; the archery of the young ladies; the curious politeness of the Persian professor; the fine learning and eager scholarship of Principal Le Bas; and the somewhat old-fashioned courtesies of the summer evening parties, are all over now, except as pleasant pictures in the interior gallery of those who knew the place,—of whom I am thankful to have been one.

Mr. Hallam was one of the coterie of whom I have said so much: and Mr. Whishaw was another; and so were his then young friends,—his

---

[1]   Approximately 20 miles north of London, Haileybury was the site of the East India College, where Malthus taught political economy and history and William Empson, English law. Haileybury College, a boys' school founded in 1862, now occupies the buildings.

wards, the Romillys.[1] The elder Romillys found themselves in parliament, after the passage of the Reform Bill; and Sir John's career since that time speaks for itself. They had virtuous projects when they entered political life, and had every hope of achieving service worthy of their father's fame: but their aspirations were speedily tamed down,—as all high aspirations are lowered by Whig influences. They were warned by prudent counsellors to sit silent for a few years in the presence of their elders in the legislature: and, when months and years slid away over their silence, they found it more and more difficult, and at last impossible to speak. The lawyer brother got over this, of necessity; but Edward never did. With poor health and sensitive nerves, and brought up in the very hot-bed of Whiggism, they could perhaps be hardly expected to do more; but hope in them was strong, in the days of the Reform Bill, and still alive when I left London. Good old Mr. Whishaw was still fond and proud of his 'boys,' and still preaching caution while expecting great things from them, when I last saw him. I met that respected old man at every turn; and he did for me the same kind office as Mr. Rogers,[2]— coming for me, and carrying me home in his carriage. When the drive was a long one,—as to Hampstead, or even to Haileybury, there was time for a string of capital old stories, even at his slow rate of utterance: and he made me feel as if I had known the preceding generation of Whig statesmen and men of letters. Mr. Whishaw was not only lame, (from the loss of a leg in early life) but purblind and growing deaf, when I knew him: but every body was eager to amuse and comfort him. He sat in the dining-room before dinner, with host or hostess to converse with him till the rest came down; and every body took care that he carried away plenty of conversation. The attentions of the Romillys to their old guardian were really a beautiful spectacle.

His attached friend, Mr. Hallam, made abundant amends for the slowness of the Whishaw discourse. It would have been a wonderful spectacle, I have sometimes thought, if Hallam, Macaulay and Empson had been induced to talk for a wager;—in regard to quantity merely, with-

---

[1]   John Whishaw (1765–1840) was a lawyer, member of the exclusive London dining club, King of Clubs, and friend of Sir Samuel Romilly (1757–1818), a lawyer and legal reformer who committed suicide in grief over his wife's death. His son John Romilly (1802–74) entered parliament in 1832, became queen's counsel in 1843, was appointed solicitor-general in 1848, and achieved many legal reforms. Another son Edward (1804–70) was elected M.P. in 1832 and served from 1837–66 but with little action to his credit. There were four other sons: William, Henry, Charles, and Frederick (the last of whom served as an M.P. for Canterbury in 1850–52).

[2]   Samuel Rogers; see p. 238, n. 1.

out stopping to think of quality; while their friends Rogers, Whishaw and Malthus would have made good counterparts. Mr. Hallam was in the brightest hour of his life when I first knew him. His son Arthur was living and affording the splendid promise of which all have been made aware by Tennyson, in 'In Memoriam.'[1] In a little while, Arthur was gone,—found dead on the sofa by his father, one afternoon during a continental journey. Supposing him to be asleep, after a slight indisposition, Mr. Hallam sat reading for an hour after returning from a walk, before the extraordinary stillness alarmed him. Alone, and far from home, he was in a passion of grief. Few fathers have had such a son to lose; and the circumstances were singularly painful.—Then, there was the eldest daughter, on his arm at Carlyle's lectures, and the companion of her delightful mother; she died in just the same way,—on the sofa, after a slight illness, and while her mother was reading to her.[2] She exclaimed 'Stop!' and was dead within five minutes: and when Dr. Holland had come, and found that there was nothing to be done, he had to go in search of the father, who had gone for his walk, and tell him of the new desolation of his home. Not long after, Mrs. Hallam died with equal suddenness; and now, in his failing age, the affectionate family-man finds himself bereft of all his large household,—all his ten children gone, except one married daughter. His works show that, social as he has always been, he has enjoyed solitary study. I remember his once making a ludicrous complaint of London dinners, and of the sameness of the luxuries he and I saw every day; and he told me his greatest longing was for a few days of cold beef and leg of mutton. He was, like most of the set, a capital gossip. Nothing happened that we ladies did not hear from Whishaw, Empson, or Hallam: and Mr. Hallam poured it all out with a child-like glee and innocence which were very droll in a man who had done such things, and who spent so much of his time between passing judicial sentences in literature, and attending councils on politics and the arts with grave statesmen and with people of the highest rank, to whom he showed a most solemn reverence. He was apt to say rash and heedless things in his out-pourings, which were as amusing as they were awkward. I remember his blurting out, when seated on a sofa between Mr. Whishaw and the remarkably plain and literary Miss—, a joke on somebody's hobbling with a wooden leg; and then an observation on

---

[1] Arthur Henry Hallam (1811–33), college friend of both William Gladstone and Alfred Tennyson, whose untimely death in 1833 "In Memoriam" elegizes.

[2] Ellen Hallam, who died in 1837.

Mrs.— being the only handsome authoress. (As there were certainly two who would answer the description, I put no initials.) Of Mr. Hallam's works I say nothing, because they are fully discussed in the reviews of the time, by critics far more competent than myself. I enjoy them singularly; and especially his 'History of Literature.'[1] I had a profound respect for him as an author, long before I ever dreamed of having him for a friend: and nothing that I ever observed in him lessened that respect in any degree, while a cordial regard was, I believe, continually growing stronger between us, from the hour of our first meeting till now. It does not follow that we agreed on all matters of conduct, any more than of opinion. I could never sympathize fully with his reverence for people of rank: and he could not understand my principle and methods of self-defence against the dangers and disgusts of 'lionism.' For one instance; I never would go to Lansdowne House, because I knew that I was invited there as an authoress, to undergo, as people did at that house, the most delicate and refined process of being lionised,—but still, the process. The Marquis and Marchioness of Lansdowne, and a son and daughter, caused me to be introduced to them at Sir Augustus Callcott's;[2] and their not being introduced to my mother, who was with me, showed the footing on which I stood. I was then just departing for America. On my return, I was invited to every kind of party at Lansdowne House,—a concert, a state dinner, a friendly dinner party, a small evening party, and a ball; and I declined them all. I went nowhere but where my acquaintance was sought, as a lady, by ladies. Mr. Hallam told me,—what was true enough,—that Lady Lansdowne, being one of the Queen's ladies, and Lord Lansdowne, being a Cabinet Minister, could not make calls. If so, it made no difference in my disinclination to go, in a blue-stocking way, to a house where I was not really acquainted with any body. Mr. Hallam, I saw, thought me conceited and saucy: but I felt I must take my own

---

1   *Introduction to the Literature of Europe during the Fifteenth, Sixteenth, and Seventeenth Centuries* (London: John Murray, 1837–39).

2   Henry Petty-Fitzmaurice, Marquis of Lansdowne (1780–1863), was a champion of Catholic emancipation, popular education, and the abolition of the slave-trade. A leading Whig, he served in Canning's cabinet as secretary of state for home affairs in 1828 and was lord president of the council during the ministries of Grey, Melbourne, and Russell. He and his wife Louisa Emma, née Fox-Strangways, made their Wiltshire home, Bowood House, a center for social events at which local poets like Thomas Moore and William Bowles mingled with politicians, scientists and other "lions." Lansdowne House in London had a similar social function. The house was built like a country residence on a sizeable plot with extensive gardens. Sir Augustus Callcott (1779–1844) was a British landscape painter who with his wife, the writer Maria Graham, held a society salon for artistic London.

methods of preserving my social independence. Lord Lansdowne would not give the matter up. Finding that General Fox was coming one evening to a soirée of mine,[1] he invited himself to dine with him, in order to accompany him. I thought this somewhat impertinent, while Mr. Hallam regarded it as an honour. I did not see why a nobleman and Cabinet Minister was more entitled than any other gentleman to present himself uninvited, after his own invitations had been declined. The incident was a trifle; but it shows how I acted in regard to this 'lionising.'

Mr. Rogers was my neighbour from the time when I went to live in Fludyer Street; and many were the parties to which he took me in his carriage. Many also were the breakfasts to which he invited me;—those breakfasts, the fame of which has spread over the literary world. I could not often go;—indeed, scarcely ever,—so indispensable to my work were my morning hours and strength: and when Mr. Rogers perceived this, he asked me to dinner, or in the evening. But I did occasionally go to breakfast; and he made it easy by saving me the street passage. He desired his gardener to leave the garden gate unlocked; and I merely crossed the park and stepped in through the breakfast-room window. It was there that, besides my familiar friends, I met some whom I was glad to see after many years' acquaintance through books. It was there that I met Southey,[2] when he had almost left off coming to London. He was then indeed hardly fit for society. It was in the interval between the death of his first wife and his second marriage. He was gentle, kindly and agreeable; and well disposed to talk of old Norwich, and many things besides. But there was a mournful expression of countenance, occasionally verging upon the distress of perplexity: and he faltered for words at times; and once was painfully annoyed at being unable to recover a name or a date, rubbing his head and covering his eyes long before he would give it up. I told my mother, on coming home, that I feared that he was going the way of so many hard literary workers. We were greatly surprised to hear of his marriage, after what I had seen, and some worse indications of failure of which we had heard. The sequel of the story is known to every body.—I met Lord Mahon there (now Lord Stanhope) when his historical reputation was already established; and my agreeable friend Mr. Harness, whom I liked

---

[1]   Most likely Charles Richard Fox (1796–1873), son of Lord Holland and Elizabeth Vassall Webster, who was then a colonel, or possibly Henry Stephen Fox (1781–1846), the diplomat, who served as envoy to various Latin American countries.

[2]   The poet Robert Southey (1774–1843), who married fellow-poet Caroline Bowles (1786–1854) in 1839, when his mental health was deteriorating.

in all ways but as a dramatist.[1] The Milmans used to extol the 'finish' of his plays; and the author of 'Fazio'[2] ought to be a far better judge than I; but, as I told him, it seems to me that spirit is the first thing in a drama, and matter the next; and that 'finish' comes only third, if so soon; and I could never see or feel beauty and elevation enough in Mr. Harness's plays to make me think it worth his while to write them. But he was one of my very pleasantest acquaintances, for his goodness at home and abroad,—to his sister and niece, to his parishioners, and to his friends in society. With poor health, and literary tastes craving the gratification which was constantly within his reach, he was a devoted parish priest; and he made duty pleasure, and endurance an enjoyment, or at worst a matter of indifference,—by his cheerful and disinterested temper. He was a fine example of an accomplished gentleman and poet in the Church, who did his clerical duty to the utmost, and with simplicity, while as agreeable a man of the world as you could meet. I never could fully enter into his dramatic propensities and enthusiasms, any more than into Mr. Dickens's,—in both which cases the drama seems to have drawn to itself an unaccountable amount of thought and interest; but the fault is probably in me,—that I cannot extend my worship of Shakspere so as to take an interest in all forms of dramatic presentment, as these two of my friends do. To me Shakspere is so much of a poet as to be supreme and sole as a dramatist: and they probably appreciate him better than I do, and prove it by loving meaner labours and productions for his sake. Considering that Göthe[3] had the same preponderant taste, I can have no doubt that it is a case of deficiency in me, and not of eccentricity in them.

The Whig dinners of that day were at their highest point of agreeableness. The Queen on her accession found her ministers 'a set of pleasant fellows,' as was well understood at the time;—gentlemen of literary accomplishments, to a moderate extent, which seemed very great to her, accustomed as she had been to such society as her uncles had got about them. The Whigs were in the highest prosperity and briskness of spirits at the time when I first knew them,—in the freshness of power under

---

[1]   Philip Henry Stanhope (1805–75), then Lord Mahon, author of a *History of England from the Peace of Utrecht to the Peace of Versailles, 1713–1783* (London, 1839–54) and *History of the American Declaration of Independence* (London, 1855); William Harness (1790–1869), minor playwright and editor of Shakespeare's works.

[2]   The Henry Milmans, see p. 244, n. 1.

[3]   Johann Wolfgang von Goethe (1749–1832), who was called the German Shakespeare and wrote, besides his poetic drama *Faust*, an early exuberant play, *Götz von Berlichingen mit der eisernen Hand*, that Walter Scott translated into English in 1799.

the declining old King, who had not got out of humour with them, as he did after Brougham's pranks in the autumn of 1834.[1] And then again they were in high feather, after the Queen's accession, before they had arrived at presuming on their position, and while some vestiges of modesty remained among some of them. On returning to London a good many years later, I found a melancholy change which had occurred precisely through their desire that there should be no change at all. I found some who had formerly been 'pleasant fellows' and agreeable ladies, now saying the same things in much the same manner as of old, only with more conceit and contempt of every body but themselves. Their pride of station and office had swelled into vulgarity; and their blindness in regard to public opinion and the progress of all the world but themselves was more wonderful than ever. All that I have seen of late years has shown me that in those pleasant dinners I saw the then leading society in literary London to the utmost advantage;—a privilege which I certainly enjoyed exceedingly.

My place was generally between some one of the notabilities and some rising barrister. From the latter I could seldom gather much,—so bent were all the rising barristers I met on knowing my views on 'the progress of education and the increase of crime.' I was so weary of that eternal question that it was a drawback on the pleasure of many a dinner-party. In 1838, I went a journey of some weeks into the Lake district and Scotland, with a party of friends,—some of whom were over-worked like myself. We agreed to banish all topics connected with public affairs and our own labours, and to give ourselves up to refreshment, without any thought of improvement. We arrived at Fort William, where the inn was overcrowded with passengers for the Loch Ness steamer, in the evening, so tired that we (and I, especially) could scarcely keep awake till our room (where all the ladies of our party were to be lodged somehow,) was prepared. Mr. P—,[2] our leader, very properly brought in a gentleman who could not find a place to sit down in, to have tea with us. My companions, seeing me drooping with sleep, did their utmost to seat him at the opposite side of the table: but he

---

[1]   Martineau here refers to Brougham's public animosity at a banquet given in honor of Lord Grey (Lord Durham's father-in-law) at Edinburgh in September 1834, where he made a personal and political attack on Durham, repeated it afterwards at Salisbury, and published it anonymously in the *Edinburgh Review*. Brougham erred in this instance, and although Durham was no favorite with William IV, the king's disgust with Brougham, then lord chancellor, led to his dismissal of the Whig ministry in 1834.

[2]   Probably John Phillips Potter (1793–1861), Unitarian writer, whom Martineau mentions later as a friend (see p. 285).

seized a stool, forced himself in next me, and instantly began (rising barrister as he was) to ask my opinion on the progress of education and the increase of crime in Scotland. I had no clear idea what I replied: but my companions told me, with inextinguishable laughter, after our guest was gone, that I had informed him that I knew nothing of those matters, and had made no inquiry, because we had all agreed before we left home that we would not improve our minds. They said that his stare of astonishment was a sight to be remembered.—In my London days, Lord Campbell was 'Plain John Campbell:'[1] but Plain John was wonderfully like the present Lord;—facetious, in and out of place, politic, flattering to an insulting degree, and prone to moralising in so trite a way as to be almost as insulting. He was full of knowledge, and might have been inexhaustibly entertaining if he could have forgotten his prudence and been natural. When his wife, Lady Stratheden,[2] was present, there was some explanation of both the worldly prudence and the behaviour to ladies,—as if they were spoiled children,—which Plain John supposed would please them. Others were there, Judges then or since,—the Parkes, the present Lord Chancellor Cranworth, the then Lord Chancellor Brougham, Coltman, Crompton, Romilly, Alderson; (not Talfourd, who was then only a rising barrister, and not yet seen among the literary Whigs.)[3]

There were a few bishops;—Whately,[4] with his odd, overbearing manners, and his unequal conversation,—sometimes rude and tiresome, and at other times full of instruction, and an occasional drollery coming out amidst a world of effort. Perhaps no person of all my acquaintance has from the first appeared to me so singularly over-rated as he was then. I believe it is hardly so now. Those were the days when he said a candid thing which did him honour. He was quite a new bishop then; and he said one day, plucking at his sleeve, as if he had his lawn ones on, 'I don't know

---

[1]   John Campbell (1779–1861) was a moderate Whig who supported the first Reform Bill in 1831. In 1832 he was made solicitor-general, a knight, and M.P. for Dudley. For many years he was engaged in writing *The Lives of the Lord Chancellors and Keepers of the Great Seal of England, from the Earliest Times till the Reign of King George IV*, finally published in 1849. He was appointed lord chancellor in 1859 (after Martineau wrote her *Autobiography*).

[2]   John Campbell's wife, née Scarlett, was made Baroness Strathdene in 1836 to keep him in the Whig party after he was passed over for master of the rolls.

[3]   All Whig politicians: Joseph Parkes (1796–1865); Robert Monsey Rolfe, Lord Cranworth (1790–1868); Henry Peter, Lord Brougham (1778–1868); Sir Charles John Crompton (1797–1865); probably John Romilly (1802–74); and Thomas Talfourd (1795–1854).

[4]   Richard Whately (1787–1863), Archbishop of Dublin, and Edward John Stanley (1802–69), Bishop of Norwich and principal whip of the Whigs in the 1830s.

how it is: but when we have got these things on, we never do any thing more.' Then, there was the nervous, good-natured, indiscreet rattle,—the Bishop of Norwich (Stanley), who could never get under weigh without being presently aground. Timid as a hare, sensitive as a woman, heedless and flexible as a child, he was surely the oddest bishop that ever was seen: and, to make the impression the more strange, he was as like Dr. Channing as could well be, except that his hair was perfectly white, and Dr. Channing's dark.[1] That the solemn, curt, inaccessible, ever-spiritual Dr. Channing should so resemble the giddy, impressible Dr. Stanley, who carried his heart upon his sleeve (too often 'for daws to peck at') was strange enough: but so it was. Bishop Stanley was, however, admirable in his way. If he had been a rural parish priest all his life, out of the way of dissenters and of clerical *espionage*, he would have lived and died as beloved as he really was, and much more respected. In Norwich, his care and furtherance of the schools were admirable; and in the function of benevolence to the poor and afflicted, he was exemplary. But censure almost broke his heart and turned his brain. He had no courage or dignity at all under the bad manners of his Tory clergy; and he repeatedly talked in such a style to me about it as to compel me to tell him plainly that dissenters like myself are not only accustomed to ill-usage for differences of opinion, but are brought up to regard that trial as one belonging to all honest avowal of convictions, and to be borne with courage and patience like other trials. His innocent amazement and consternation at being ill-used on account of his liberal opinions were truly instructive to a member of a despised sect; but they were painful, too. I have often thought that if Bishop Stanley put himself in the power of other people as he did in mine he might expect at any hour the destruction of his peace, if not of his position,—so grievous were his complaints, and so desperate his criticisms of people who did not like his opinions, and teased him accordingly. His lady and daughters did much good in Norwich; and, on the whole, the city, which loved its old Bishop Bathurst, considered itself well off in his successor.—Then there was the somewhat shy but agreeable Bishop Lonsdale (Lichfield); and the gracious, kindly and liberal,—but not otherwise remarkable,—Bishop Otter (Chichester).[2]

[1]   William Ellery Channing (1780–1842), American Unitarian clergyman, forerunner of the Transcendentalists, whom Martineau visited during her American tour.
[2]   Henry Bathurst (1744–1837), Bishop of Norwich; John Lonsdale (1788–1867), Bishop of Lichfield; and William Otter (1768–1840), Bishop of Chichester—all known for their liberal views. Bishop Bathurst went to Parliament in his nineties to support the government of Lord Melbourne.

260

The common stream of Members of Parliament presented a curious uniformity, —even considering that they were almost all Whigs. They all had the same intense conviction that every thing but Whiggism was *bête*; that they could teach 'the people' every thing that it was good for them to know; and that the way to do it was by addressing them in a coaxing and admonitory way. They all had the same intense admiration of Whig measures before they were tried; and the same indifference and shamelessness in dropping those measures when it was found that they would not work. But among these there were a few who belonged to no party, and were too good to be confounded with the rest. There was Charles Buller,[1] the admired and beloved, and now and always the deeply mourned. He was more than a drawing-room acquaintance of mine. He was my friend; and we had real business to discuss occasionally, besides lighter matters. Many an hour he spent by my fireside, both before and after Lord Durham's government of Canada. By means of my American travel and subsequent correspondence, I was able,—or Charles Buller thought I was,—to supply some useful information, and afford some few suggestions; and I was quite as much impressed by his seriousness and fine sense in affairs of business as by his infinite cleverness and drollery in ordinary conversation.—The readers of my 'History of the Peace' must perceive that I had some peculiar opportunities of knowing the true story of that Canada governmental campaign.[2] I feared that it might be taken for granted that Lord Durham or his family gave me the information; whereas he and they were singularly careful to make no party, and to leave his case in silence till a time should arrive for explanation, without risk of turning out Lord Melbourne's government. They told me nothing of their personal grievances; and I have said so in a note in the History. But I could not then tell where I did get my information. It was mainly from Charles Buller's Journal of his residence in Canada,[3] which was confided to me on his return by a friend of his and mine. I felt myself bound not to say so while he was living, and with a political career before him which such a disclosure might have injured:

---

[1] Charles Buller (1806–48), Whig politician with a special interest in colonial policies; according to the *DNB*, "the celebrated report on Canada which bears Lord Durham's name was mainly written by Buller with the assistance of Gibbon Wakefield."

[2] *History of the Peace*, Book V, ch. XII. In this chapter Martineau includes a footnote: "It will be evident to the readers of this chapter that it is written from private knowledge, as well as from public documents. After the above notice of Lord Durham's generous silence, it is hardly necessary to say that no statement of the circumstances of his Canada mission was ever made to me by himself or any of his family."

[3] The journal was, at that time, unpublished.

but, now that he and his father and mother are gone, and that remarkable household has vanished, and is remembered as a dream, I see no
reason why I should not declare on what high authority I made the
statements relating to Lord Durham's residence in Canada. There was
another journal, by another of the party, put into my hands at the same
time, from which I have derived some incidents and suggestions: but
Charles Buller's narrative, written from day to day, was the one on which
I chiefly relied.—His capacity, and his probable future, could not be
adequately judged of by any thing he had said or done when his always
frail health finally gave way. The Canada Report is noted for its ability;
and the men of his generation remember how thorough were his
Colonization speeches, and how his fine temper and well-timed wit
soothed and brightened the atmosphere of the House in tempestuous
times. But the sound greatness that lay beneath was known only to his
intimates; and they mourned over an untimely arrest of a glorious career
of statesmanship, while the rest of the world regarded the loss simply as
of an effective and accomplished Member of Parliament.

Another, who stood out from the classification of Tory and Whig,
was my friend R. Monckton Milnes,[1] whom I know too well, and am
too sincerely attached to, to describe as if he were dead, or on less
friendly terms with me. When I first knew him, it was amidst the bustle
of the discovery of his being a poet; or, at least, I had seen him, as far as
I remember, only once before that. One evening, at Lady Mary
Shepherd's (where I never went again, for reasons which I will give
presently) my hostess told me that she was to introduce me, if I pleased,
to a young friend of hers who had just returned from travels in Greece.
I understood his name to be Mills, and did not think of connecting him
with the Yorkshire family whose name was so well known to me. When
the young friend arrived, he did look young,—with a round face and
a boyish manner, free from all shyness and gravity whatever. (Sydney
Smith had two names for him in those days: 'Dick Modest Milnes,' and
'the Cool of the Evening.') I was just departing, early, when he first had
some conversation with me in the drawing-room and then went down
to the cloak room, where he said something which impressed me

---

[1]   Richard Monckton Milnes (1809–85), later Baron Houghton, became an M.P. in 1837 and
worked for such reforms as the Copyright Act and the establishment of Mechanics'
Institutes. A friend of many literary men, he wrote poetry and edited the *Life, Letters, and
Literary Remains of Keats* (London: Edward Moxon, 1848). When Martineau met Milnes,
he had just published *Memorials of a Tour in Some Parts of Greece, Chiefly Poetical* (London:
Edward Moxon, 1834).

much, and made me distinctly remember the earnest youth, before I discovered that he was the same with 'the new poet,' Milnes. He asked me some question about my tales,—then about half done; and my answer conveyed to him an impression I did not at all intend,—that I made light of the work. 'No, now,—don't say that,' said he, bluntly. 'It is unworthy of you to affect that you do not take pains with your work. It is work which cannot be done without pains; and you should not pretend to the contrary.' I showed him, in a moment, that he had misapprehended me; and I carried away a clear impression of his sincerity, and of the gravity which lay under his *insouciant* manners. When his poems came out,—wonderfully beautiful in their way, as they have ever seemed to me,—they and their author were a capital topic for the literary gossips,—Empson and Whishaw, and their coterie; and I did not wonder at their going from house to house, to announce the news, and gather and compare opinions. My pleasure in those poems was greatest when I read them in my Tynemouth solitude. My copy is marked all over with hieroglyphics involving the emotions with which I read them. He came to see me there, and did me good by his kindness in various ways. He visited me there again on my recovery; and he has been here to see me, lately, in my present illness. From time to time, incidents which he supposes to be absolute secrets have come to my knowledge which prove him to be as nobly and substantially bountiful to needy merit and ability as he is kindly in intercourse, and sympathising in suffering. The most interesting feature of his character, as it stands before the world, is his catholicity of sentiment and manner,—his ability to sympathise with all manner of thinkers and speakers, and his superiority to all appearance of exclusiveness, while, on the one hand, rather enjoying the reputation of having access to all houses, and, on the other, being serious and earnest in the deepest recesses of his character.—This may look rather like doing what I said I could not;—describing a personal friend: but it is really not so: I have touched on none but the most patent aspects of an universally known man. If I were to describe him as a personal friend, I should have much more to say.

Another acquaintance who became a friend was Mr. Grote,[1] then one of the Members for London. That was not the period of his life

---

[1]   George Grote (1794–1871), classical scholar and author of *A History of Greece* (London: J. Murray 1846–57). As an M.P., Grote wrote several important political pamphlets, including *Essentials of Parliamentary Reform* (London: Baldwin and Craddock, 1831). His wife, née Harriet Lewin (1792–1878), was a biographer and after his death compiled the *Personal Life of George Grote* (London: J. Murray, 1873).

which he relished most. While doing his duty in parliament in regard to the Ballot, and Colonization, and other great questions of the time, and exercising hospitality as became his position, he looked back rather mournfully to the happy quiet years when, before his father suddenly made an eldest son of him, he was writing his History of Greece; and earnestly did he long for the time, (which arrived in due course) when he might retire to his study and renew his labours. I was always glad to meet him and his clever wife, who were full, at all times, of capital conversation;—she with all imaginable freedom; and he with a curious, formal, old-fashioned, deliberate courtesy, with which he strove to cover his constitutional timidity and shyness. The publication of his fine History now precludes all necessity of describing his powers and his tastes. He was best known in those days as the leading member of the Radical section in parliament; and few could suppose then that his claims on that ground would be swallowed up by his reputation as a scholar and author in one of the highest walks of literature. As a good man and a gentleman his reputation was always of the highest.—With him, the remembrance of his and my friend Roebuck is naturally associated.[1] Mr. Roebuck's state of health,—his being subject to a most painful malady,—accounted to those who knew him well for faults of temper which were singularly notorious. I always felt, in regard to both him and Lord Durham, that so much was said about faults of temper because there was nothing else to be fastened upon to their disadvantage. I can only say that, well as I knew them both, I never witnessed any ill temper in either. Mr. Roebuck was full of knowledge, full of energy, full of ability; with great vanity, certainly, but of so honest a kind that it did not much matter. When in pain, he was an example of wonderful fortitude; and there was a singular charm in the pathetic voice and countenance with which he discussed subjects that it was wonderful he could take an interest in under the circumstances. When he was well, his lively spirits were delightful; and a more agreeable guest or host could not be. Since I saw him last, he has undergone the severest trials of sickness; and it must be almost as great a surprise to himself as to me and others that he is now Chairman of the Sebastopol Committee,[2] and able to take a leading part in the politics of our present serious national crisis. His position

---

[1]   John Arthur Roebuck (1801–79), civil servant in the East India Company and Whig M.P. (almost without hiatus) from 1832 until his death.

[2]   A committee of inquiry formed to look into the inadequacies of the British military system in the Crimean War. Sebastopol, a port on the Black Sea which harbored the Russian fleet, was the site of a final key battle.

now seems to be a sort of retribution on Lord John Russell and other Whig politicians, who treated him with outrageous insolence, in public and private, while there was a Radical section for him to lead. Those who outlive me may yet see the balance struck between the popular and colonial tribune and the insolent official liberals, as they called themselves, who have one and all proved themselves incompetent to wield the power which they so greedily clutched, and held with so shameless a tenacity. I hope Mr. Roebuck may live to retrieve some mistakes, and to fulfill some of his long baffled aspirations. His chance seems at least better than that of his most insolent contemners.

Bulwer and Talfourd[1] were hardly thought of as Members of Parliament at that time, except in connexion with the international copyright treaty which authors were endeavouring to procure, and with the Copyright Act, which was obtained a few years after. Mr. Macaulay[2] was another Member of Parliament who associated his name very discreditably at first with the copyright bill, which was thrown out one session in consequence of a speech of his which has always remained a puzzle to me. What could have been the inducement to such a man to talk such nonsense as he did, and to set at naught every principle of justice in regard to authors' earnings, it is impossible, to me and others, to conceive. Nothing that he could propose,—nothing that he could do, could ever compensate to him for the forfeiture of good fame and public confidence which he seems to have actually volunteered in that speech. He changed his mind or his tactics afterwards; but he could not change people's feelings in regard to himself, or make any body believe that he was a man to be relied upon. He never appeared to me to be so. When I went to London he was a new Member of Parliament, and the object of unbounded hope and expectation to the Whig statesmen, who, according to their curious practice of considering all of the generation below their own as chicks, spoke rapturously of this promising young man. They went on doing so till his return from India, five years afterwards, by which time the world began to inquire when the promise was to begin to fructify,—this young fellow being by that time seven-and-thirty. To impartial observers, the true quality of Macaulay's mind was as

---

[1]   Edward Bulwer-Lytton (1803–73), elected M.P. for St. Ives in 1831, was better known as a writer of Newgate and historical fiction; Thomas Noon Talfourd (1795–1854), a judge and M.P., was a literary critic and author of blank verse tragedies.

[2]   Thomas Babington Macaulay (1800–59), Whig M.P., wrote regularly for the *Edinburgh Review* and published the first two volumes of his *History of England* in 1849; as Martineau notes, vols. 3–4 were scheduled for publication in 1855, as she wrote her autobiography.

clear then as now. In Parliament, he was no more than a most brilliant speaker; and in his speeches there was the same fundamental weakness which pervades his writings,—unsoundness in the presentment of his case. Some one element was sure to be left out, which falsified his statement, and vitiated his conclusions; and there never was perhaps a speaker or writer of eminence, so prone to presentments of cases, who so rarely offered one which was complete and true. My own impression is, and always was, that the cause of the defect is constitutional in Macaulay. The evidence seems to indicate that he wants heart. He appears to be wholly unaware of this deficiency; and the superficial fervour which suns over his disclosures probably deceives himself, as it deceives a good many other people; and he may really believe that he has a heart. To those who do not hold this key to the interpretation of his career, it must be a very mysterious thing that a man of such imposing and real ability, with every circumstance and influence in his favour, should never have achieved any complete success. As a politician, his failure has been signal, notwithstanding his irresistible power as a speaker, and his possession of every possible facility. As a practical legislator, his failure was unsurpassed, when he bought home his Code from India.[1] I was witness to the amazement and grief of some able lawyer, in studying that Code,—of which they could scarcely lay their finger on a provision through which you could not drive a coach and six. It has long been settled that literature alone remains open to him; and in that he has, with all his brilliancy and captivating accomplishment, destroyed the ground of confidence on which his adorers met him when, in his mature years, he published the first two volumes of his History. His review articles, and especially the one on Bacon, ought to have abolished all confidence in his honesty, as well as in his capacity for philosophy.[2] Not only did he show himself to be disqualified for any appreciation of Bacon's philosophy, but his plagiarisms from the very author (Basil Montagu) whom he was pretending to demolish, (one instance of plagiarism among many) might have shown any conscientious reader how little he was to be trusted in regard to mere integrity of statement. But, as he announced a History, the public received as a *bonâ fide* History the work on which he proposes to build his fame. If it had been announced as a historical romance, it might have been read with almost unmixed delight, though exception might

---

[1]   The code of criminal procedure, published in 1837.
[2]   The essay on Bacon appeared in the *Edinburgh Review* in July, 1837. Basil Montagu (1770–1851) was a prolific writer on legal issues.

have been taken to his presentment of several characters and facts. He has been abundantly punished, for instance, for his slanderous exhibition of William Penn.[1] But he has fatally manifested his loose and unscrupulous method of narrating, and, in his first edition, gave no clue whatever to his authorities, and no information in regard to dates which he could possibly suppress. Public opinion compelled, in future editions, some appearance of furnishing references to authorities, such as every conscientious historian finds it indispensable to his peace of mind to afford; but it is done by Macaulay in the most ineffectual and baffling way possible,—by clubbing together the mere names of his authorities at the bottom of the page, so that reference is all but impracticable. Where it is made, by painstaking readers, the inaccuracies and misrepresentations of the historian are found to multiply as the work of verification proceeds. In fact, the only way to accept his History is to take it as a brilliant fancypiece,—wanting not only the truth but the repose of history,—but stimulating, and even, to a degree, suggestive. While I write, announcement is made of two more volumes to appear in the course of the year. If the radical faults of the former ones are remedied, there may yet be before this gifted man something like the 'career,' so proudly anticipated for him a quarter of a century ago. If not, all is over; and his powers, once believed adequate to the construction of eternal monuments of statesmanship and noble edifices for intellectual worship, will be found capable of nothing better than rearing gay kiosks in the flower gardens of literature, to be soon swept away by the caprices of a new taste, as superficial as his own.—I have been led on to say all this by the vivid remembrance of the universal interest there was about Macaulay, when the London world first opened before me. I remember the days when he was met in the streets, looking only at the pavement as he walked, and with his lips moving,—causing those who met him to say that there would be a fine speech from Macaulay that night. Then came the sighs over his loss when he went to India for three years: then the joy at his return, and the congratulations to his venerable father: then the blank disappointment at the way in which he had done his work: and then his appearance in society,—with his strange eyes, which

---

[1]   William Penn (1644–1718), Quaker founder of Pennsylvania, about whom Macaulay wrote in his *History of England*: "The conduct of Penn was scarcely less scandalous. He was a zealous and busy Jacobite; and his new way of life was even more unfavourable than his late way of life had been to moral purity. It was hardly possible to be at once a consistent Quaker and a courtier; but it was utterly impossible to be at once a consistent Quaker and a conspirator."

appeared to look nowhere, and his full cheeks and stooping shoulders, which told of dreamy indolence; and then the torrent of words which poured out when he did speak! It did not do to invite him and Sydney Smith together. They interfered with one another. Sydney Smith's sense of this appears in his remarks on Macaulay's 'improvement,' as shown by 'flashes of silence;' and Macaulay showed his sense of the incompatibility of the two wits by his abstracted silence, or by signs of discomposure.

I had heard all my life of the vanity of women as a subject of pity to men: but when I went to London, lo! I saw vanity in high places which was never transcended by that of women in their lowlier rank. There was Brougham, wincing under a newspaper criticism, and playing the fool among silly women. There was Jeffrey flirting with clever women, in long succession. There was Bulwer, on a sofa, sparkling and languishing among a set of female votaries,—he and they dizened out, perfumed, and presenting the nearest picture to a seraglio to be seen on British ground,—only the indifference or hauteur of the lord of the harem being absent. There was poor Campbell the poet,[1] obtruding his sentimentalities, amidst a quivering apprehension of making himself ridiculous. He darted out of our house, and never came again, because, after warning, he sat down, in a room full of people (all authors, as it happened) on a low chair of my old aunt's which went very easily on castors, and which carried him back to the wall and rebounded, of course making every body laugh. Off went poor Campbell in a huff; and, well as I had long known him, I never saw him again: and I was not very sorry, for his sentimentality was too soft, and his craving for praise too morbid to let him be an agreeable companion. On occasion of the catastrophe, he came with about forty authors one morning, to sign a petition to parliament for an International copyright law. Then there was Babbage,—less utterly dependent on opinion than some people suppose; but still, harping so much on the subject as to warrant the severe judgment current in regard to his vanity.—There was Edwin Landseer,[2] a friendly and agreeable companion, but holding his cheerfulness at the mercy of great folks' graciousness to him. To see him enter a room, curled and cravatted, and glancing round in anxiety about his reception, could not but make a woman wonder where among her

---

[1] Thomas Campbell (1777–1824), Scottish poet remembered for war lyrics such as "Ye Mariners of England" and "The Battle of the Baltic" and the ballads "Lord Ullin's Daughter" and "The Maid of Neidpath," which Francis Palgrave included in *The Golden Treasury* (1859).

[2] Edwin Landseer (1802–73), English animal painter—as in his portrait of Sir Walter Scott surrounded by his dogs.

own sex she could find a more palpable vanity; but then, all that was forgotten when one was sitting on a divan with him, seeing him play with the dog.—Then there was Whewell,[1] grasping at praise for universal learning,—(omniscience being his foible, as Sydney Smith said,)—and liking female adoration, rough as was his nature with students, rivals and speculative opponents.—I might instance more: but this is enough. The display was always to me most melancholy; for the detriment was so much greater than in the case of female vanity. The circumstances of women render the vanity of literary women well nigh unavoidable, where the literary pursuit and production are of a light kind: and the mischief (serious enough) may end with the deterioration of the individual. Lady Morgan and Lady Davy and Mrs. Austin and Mrs. Jameson[2] may make women blush and men smile and be insolent; and their gross and palpable vanities may help to lower the position and discredit the pursuits of other women, while starving out their own natural powers: but these mischiefs are far less important than the blighting of promise and the forfeiture of a career, and the intercepting of national blessings, in the case of a Bulwer or a Brougham. A few really able women,—women sanctified by true genius and holy science,—a Joanna Baillie, a Somerville, a Browning,[3]—quickly repair the mischief, as regards the dignity of women; and the time has not yet arrived when national interests are involved in the moral dignity of individual women of genius. But, as a matter of fact, I conceive that no one can glance round society, as seen in London drawing-rooms, and pretend to consider vanity the appropriate sin of women. The instances I

---

1   William Whewell (1794–1866), Professor of Mineralogy, later of Moral Theology at Trinity College, where he became Master in 1841.

2   Sydney Morgan, née Owenson (1783–1859), made her fame with *The Wild Irish Girl* (1806); she wrote regularly for the *New Monthly Magazine*, and was a staple of Dublin and London literary society. Lady Davy, née Jane Kerr, then Mrs. Apreece (1780–1855), became the wife of the scientist, Sir Humphry Davy, and a celebrated hostess in the English community at Rome. Sarah Austin (1793–1867), from the Norwich Taylor family, was a reviewer and translator, particularly of German literature. Anna Jameson (1794–1860) rose to fame with *The Diary of an Ennuyée* (1826), a fictionalized version of her travels in France and Italy; she published *Winter Studies and Summer Rambles in Canada* (1838) after a brief residence in North America, and produced her more important art history, *Sacred and Legendary Art* (1848), after the period Martineau describes in this section.

3   Joanna Baillie (1762–1851) wrote poetry on Scottish subjects and produced a remarkably successful dramatic series, *Plays on the Passions*, between 1798 and 1812. Mary Somerville (1780–1872), mathematician and scientist, wrote popular treatises on the physical sciences. Elizabeth Barrett Browning (1806–61), an invalid like Martineau, had in this period translated *Prometheus Bound* (1833) and published *The Seraphim and Other Poems* (1838), including "The Dead Pan," which Martineau called a "very noble poem."

have given are of persons who, for the most part, were estimable and agree-able, apart from their characteristic foible. For Bulwer I always felt a cordial interest, amidst any amount of vexation and pity for his weakness. He seems to me to be a woman of genius enclosed by misadventure in a man's form. If the life of his affections had been a natural and fortunate one; and if (which would have been the consequence) he had not plunged over head and ears in the metaphysics of morals, I believe he would have made himself a name which might have lasted as long as our literature. He has insight, experience, sympathy, letters, power and grace of expression, and an irrepressible impulse to utterance and industry which should have produced works of the noblest quality; and these have been intercepted by mischiefs which may be called misfortune rather than fault. There is no need to relate his history or describe his faults. I can only lament the perversion of one of the most promising natures, and the intercepting of some of the most needful literary benefits offered, in the form of one man, in our time. His friendly temper, his generous heart, his excellent conver-sation (at his best) and his simple manners (when he forgot himself) have many a time 'left me mourning' that such a being should allow himself to sport with perdition. Perhaps my interest in him was deepened by the evident growth of his deafness, and by seeing that he was not, as yet, equal to cope with the misfortune of personal infirmity. He could not bring himself practically to acknowledge it; and his ignoring of it occasioned scenes which, painful to others, must have been exquisitely so to a vain man like himself. I longed to speak, or get spoken, to him a word of warn-ing and encouragement out of my own experience; but I never met with any one who dared mention the subject to him; and I had no fair oppor-tunity after the infirmity became conspicuous. From the time when, in contradicting in the newspapers a report of his having lost his hearing alto-gether, he professed to think conversation not worth hearing, I had no hope of his fortitude; for it is the last resource of weakness to give out that the grapes are sour.—Campbell was declining when I first knew him; and I disliked his visits because I was never quite sure whether he was sober,—his irritable brain being at the mercy of a single glass of sherry, or of a paroxysm of enthusiasm about the Poles: but I adored his poems in my youth; I was aware that domestic misfortune had worn out his affection-ate heart; and it was a pleasure to see that his sympathies were, to the last, warm on behalf of international morality and popular liberties.—As for Mr. Babbage, it seemed to me that few men were more misunderstood,—his sensitiveness about opinions perverting other people's impressions of him quite as much as his of them. For one instance: he was amused, as well as struck, by the very small reliance to be placed on opinion, public or private, for and against individuals: and he thought over some method of bringing his observation to a sort of demonstration. Thinking that he was likely to hear most of opinions about himself as a then popular author, he collected every thing he could gather in print about himself, and pasted the pieces into a large book, with the *pros* and *cons* in parallel columns, from which he obtained a sort of balance, besides some highly curious observations. Soon after he told me this, with fun and good humour, I was told repeatedly that he spent all his days in gloating and grumbling over what people said of him, having got it all down in a book, which he was perpetually poring over. People who so represented him had little idea what a domestic tenderness is in him,—though to me his singular face seemed to show it,—nor how much that was really interesting might be found in him by those who viewed him naturally and kindly. All were eager to go to his glorious soirées; and I always thought he appeared to great advantage as a host. His patience in explaining his machine in those days was really exemplary.[1] I felt it so, the first time I saw the miracle, as it appeared to me; but I thought so much more, a year or two after, when a lady, to whom he had sacrificed some very precious time, on the supposition that she understood as much as she assumed to do, finished by saying 'Now, Mr. Babbage, there is only one thing more that I want to know. If you put the question in wrong, will the answer come out right?' All time and attention devoted to lady examiners of his machine, from that time forward, I regarded as sacrifices of genuine good nature.

In what noble contrast were the eminent men who were not vain! There was the honest and kindly Captain (now Admiral Sir Francis) Beaufort,[2] who was daily at the Admiralty as the clock struck, conveying paper, pen and ink for any private letters he might have to write, for which he refused to use the official stores. There were the friends Lyell and Charles Darwin,[3]—after the return of the latter from his four years' voyage round the world;—Lyell with a Scotch prudence which gave way, more and more as years passed on, to his natural geniality, and to an

---

[1] Charles Babbage (1791–1871) invented an analytical machine for mathematical computation, considered the forerunner of modern computers.

[2] Sir Francis Beaufort (1774–1857), Hydrographer of the Admiralty, created the Beaufort scale for indicating wind force.

[3] Sir Charles Lyell (1797–1875) and Charles Darwin (1809–82), natural historians and geologists. Lyell was known for his *Principles of Geology; or Modern Changes of the Earth and Its Inhabitants* (1830). Darwin had published his *Journal of Researches into the Geology and Natural History of the various countries visited by H.M.S. Beagle* (1839) but not, of course, *On the Origin of Species* (1859).

expanding liberality of opinion and freedom of speech; and the simple, childlike, painstaking, effective Charles Darwin, who established himself presently at the head of living English naturalists. These well-employed, earnest-minded, accomplished and genial men bore their honours without vanity, jealousy, or any apparent self-regard whatever. They and their devoted wives were welcome in the highest degree. Lady Lyell was almost as remarkable in society as her husband, though she evidently considered herself only a part of him. Having no children, she could devote her life to helping him. She travelled over half the world with him, entered fully into his pursuits, and furthered them as no one else could have done; while there was not a trace of pedantry in her, but a simple, lively manner, proceeding from a mind at ease and nobly entertained. Mr. Rogers used to point out the beauty of her eye,—'The eye of the stag;' and truly she grew more charming-looking every year, and was handsomer and brighter than ever when I saw her not long ago in London. If she had no vanity for herself, neither had she for her husband, of whom her estimate was too lofty and just to admit the intrusion of so unworthy an emotion.

Many others there were in regard to whom the imputation of vanity was impossible. There were Dr. Dalton and Mrs. Somerville sitting with their heads close together,[1] on the sofa, talking their own glorious talk without a thought of what anybody in the world was saying about either of them. Dr. Dalton was simple in every way; Mrs. Somerville in all that was essential. Her mistakes in taking her daughters to court, and in a good many conventional matters, were themselves no worse than a misplaced humility which made her do as other people did, or as other people bade her do, instead of choosing her own course. I used to wish she had been wise in those matters, and more self-reliant altogether; but I am sure there was no ambition or vanity in her mind, all the time. It was delightful to find her with a letter from her publisher in her hand, considering it with anxiety; and to hear what her difficulty was. She was respectfully requested to make such alterations in the next edition of her 'Connexion of the Physical Sciences' as would render it more popular and intelligible. She could not at all see her way. The scientific mode of expression, with its pregnancy, its terseness and brevity, seemed to her perfectly simple. If she was to alter it, it could be only by amplifying; and she feared that would make her diffuse and comparatively unintelligible. It was delightful to see her always well-dressed and thoroughly womanly in her

---

[1]   Both were physical scientists, John Dalton (1766–1844) a meteorologist, physicist, and chemist, Mary Somerville, an astronomer (see also p. 269, n. 3).

conversation and manners, while unconscious of any peculiarity in her pursuits. It was delightful to go to tea at her house at Chelsea, and find every thing in order and beauty; —the walls hung with her fine drawings; her music in the corner, and her tea table spread with good things. In the midst of these household elegancies, Dr. Somerville one evening pulled open a series of drawers, to find something he wanted to show me.[1] As he shut one after another, I ventured to ask what those strange things were which filled every drawer. 'O! they are only Mrs. Somerville's diplomas,' said he, with a droll look of pride and amusement. Not long after this the family went abroad, partly for Dr. Somerville's health: and great has been the concern of her friends at so losing her, while it was well known that her longings were for England. Her husband and her daughters, (turned Catholics,) have kept her in Italy ever since, to the privation and sorrow of many who know that scientific London is the proper place for her, and that, unselfish as she is, she must long to be there. I own it went to my heart to hear of one thing that happened soon after she left England. The great comet of 1843 was no more seen by her than by any other woman in Italy. The only good observatory was in a Jesuits' College, where no woman was allowed to set foot. It is too bad that she should spend the last third of her life in a country so unworthy of her.

And there was Joanna Baillie, whose serene and cheerful life was never troubled by the pains and penalties of vanity;—what a charming spectacle was she! Mrs. Barbauld's published correspondence tells of her, in 1800, as 'a young lady of Hampstead whom I visited, and who came to Mr. Barbauld's meeting, all the while, with as innocent a face as if she had never written a line.' That was two years before I was born. When I met her, about thirty years afterwards, there she was 'with as innocent a face as if she had never written a line!' And this was after an experience which would have been a bitter trial to an author with a particle of vanity. She had enjoyed a fame almost without parallel, and had outlived it. She had been told every day for years, through every possible channel, that she was second only to Shakspere,—if second; and then she had seen her works drop out of notice so that, of the generation who grew up before her eyes, not one in a thousand had read a line of her plays:—yet was her serenity never disturbed, nor her merry humour in the least dimmed. I have never lost the impression of the trying circumstances of my first interview with her, nor of the grace, simplicity and sweetness with which

---

[1]   Dr. William Somerville, her cousin, was her second husband who, unlike her first, Samuel Greig, encouraged her intellectual pursuits.

she bore them. She was old; and she declined dinner-parties; but she wished to meet me,—having known, I believe, some of my connexions or friends of the past generation;—and therefore she came to Miss Berry's to tea,[1] one day when I was dining there. Miss Berry, her contemporary, put her feelings, it seemed to me, to a most unwarrantable trial, by describing to me, as we three sat together, the celebrity of the 'Plays on the Passions' in their day. She told me how she found on her table, on her return from a ball, a volume of plays; and how she kneeled on a chair to look at it, and how she read on till the servant opened the shutters, and let in the daylight of a winter morning. She told me how all the world raved about the plays; and she held on so long that I was in pain for the noble creature to whom it must have been irksome on the one hand to hear her own praises and fame so dwelt upon, and, on the other, to feel that we all knew how long that had been quite over. But, when I looked up at her sweet face, with its composed smile amidst the becoming mob cap, I saw that she was above pain of either kind. We met frequently afterwards, at her house or ours; and I retained my happy impression, till the last call I made on her. She was then over-affectionate, and uttered a good deal of flattery; and I was uneasy at symptoms so unlike her good taste and sincerity. It was a token of approaching departure. She was declining, and she sank and softened for some months more, and then died, revered and beloved as she deserved. Amidst all pedantry, vanity, coquetry, and manners ruined by celebrity which I have seen, for these twenty years past, I have solaced and strengthened myself with the image of Joanna Baillie, and with remembering the invulnerable justification which she set up for intellectual superiority in women, while we may hope that the injury done to that cause by blue-stockings and coquettes will be scarcely more enduring than their own trumpery notoriety.

I must own that I have known scarcely any political men who were not as vain as women are commonly supposed to be: and if any were not so themselves, their wives were sure to be so for them; and so conspicuously as to do the mischief effectually.[2] Lord Lansdowne was an exception, I believe; and so, I am sure, was his simple-minded, shy lady, with her rural tastes, and benevolent pursuits. The present Lord

---

[1] Mary Berry (1763–1852), minor dramatist and eighteenth-century woman of letters, was the subject of a *Daily News* obituary Martineau wrote in November 1852, and reprinted as an appendix to her *Autobiography*.

[2] Henry Petty-Fitzmaurice, Marquis of Lansdowne (1780–1863), Charles Grey, 2nd Earl Grey (1764–1845), and George Howard, Lord Morpeth (1802–64) were Whig politicians. Lord Grey was prime minister from November 1830 to July 1834.

Grey did not show in private life the sensitiveness which marred his temper and manners in his political function. Lord Morpeth (the present Lord Carlisle) has his weaknesses, which are evident enough; but I never saw a trace of vanity in him. His magnanimous, benevolent, affectionate temper, his pure integrity, and devout conscientiousness, are all incompatible with vanity. It seems a pity that his powers are so inadequate to his sensibilities; or that, his abilities being what they are, he has not chosen to remain in that private life which he conspicuously adorns: but it is a benefit, as far as it goes, that his fine spirit and manners should be present in official life, to rebuke the vulgar selfishness, levity, and insolence which have discredited his political comrades, from their accession to power, a quarter of a century since, till now, when their faults have brought on a crisis in the destinies of England. As an order of men, however, politicians are, as far as my experience goes, far inferior in dignity to scientific men, among whom there are, it is true, examples of egregious vanity, but not so striking as the simplicity and earnestness which characterize many whose lives are spent in lofty pursuits which carry them high above personal regards. And to nearly all, I believe, the pursuit of knowledge for its own sake yields more pleasure than any gain of fame or money. To one Lardner, there is many a Beaufort, Washington, Delabêche, Ehrenberg, Dalton, and Gregory.[1] Some, like Professor Nichol, may not be acquitted of vanity, while uniting with it, as he does, a simplicity, a kindliness, and a genial temper which make them delightful companions. Others, like Buckland, and Murchison, have a love of fun mingling with their genuine worship of science, which makes them highly agreeable, in spite of eccentricities of manner.[2] Sir Charles Bell was of too tender a nature for the conflicts which await a discoverer;[3] but his sensitiveness was of too refined and

---

[1]   Dionysius Lardner (1793–1859) was a popularizer of science and editor of *Lardner's Cabinet Cyclopaedia* (1830–44), a scientific library of 134 volumes. Francis Beaufort, hydrographer (see p. 271, n. 2); Washington (unidentified); Henry Thomas De La Beche (1796–1855), geologist; Christian Gottfried Ehrenberg (1795–1876), mineralogist and geologist; John Dalton, physicist and chemist (p. 272, n. 1); and William Gregory (1803–58), professor of chemistry at the University of Edinburgh or Olinthus Gregory (1774–1841), author of many practical books on mathematics, mechanics, and astronomy.

[2]   J.P. Nichols (1804–59) was an astronomer. William Buckland (1784–1856) and Sir Roderick Impey Murchison (1792–1871) were pioneering British geologists and leading members of the Geological Society of London.

[3]   Sir Charles Bell (1774–1842), Scottish anatomist, wrote his 1833 Bridgewater treatise on "The Hand: Its Mechanism and Vital Endowments as Evincing Design." With Lord Brougham, he annotated and illustrated an edition of William Paley's *Natural Theology*, published in 1836.

constitutional a kind to be insulted with the name of vanity; and he was beloved with a tenderness which no grossly vain person could ever win to himself. While he was grave, quiet and melancholy, men of stouter natures were making fun, if not of their science, of the uses to which they applied it, in that condescension to which their desire of reputation or of something lower led them. Sir Charles Bell wrote his Bridgewater Treatise, no doubt, with the grave sincerity with which he did every thing, and without any suspicion of the injury he was doing to theology, by attempting to bolster up the Design argument, which he ought to have seen tends directly, as is now widely admitted, to atheism. Among some of his comrades, the matter was viewed with more levity. When one of them was writing his successful treatise, he consigned his manuscript to a scientific friend for criticism. It had a good margin left for notes; and his critic, after gravely writing his observations on the scientific portion, scored in pencil the close of the sections, where the Bridgewater application was made, with the words 'Power, wisdom and goodness as per contract.' There was much covert laughter about this among the philosophers, while they presented a duly grave face to the theological world.

The artists are usually concluded to be the vainest of all orders of men. I have not found them so. A more dignified, simple-minded and delightful drawing-room companion I have hardly known than Sir Augustus Callcott, for one.[1] His tenderness of heart appeared in that devotion to his wife which cost him his health and his life. She (the Maria Graham of India and of South America, during Lord Dundonald's achievements there) was a clever woman in her way, with indomitable spirits, through years of slow consumption: but, when hearing her gossip and random talk, one could not, after all allowance for her invalid state and its seclusion contrasted with former activity, help regretting that her far superior husband should sink prematurely into melancholy and ill-health, from his too close attendance upon her, through years of hot rooms and night watching. A higher order of wife would not have permitted it; and a lower order of husband would not have done it.—Chantrey was abundantly aware of his own merits;[2] but there was an honesty in the avowal which distanced the imputation of vanity. As I sat next him one day at dinner, I was rather

[1]   Augustus Callcott (1779–1844), see p. 255, n. 2.
[2]   Francis Legatt Chantrey (1781–1841), sculptor; his son Peter Miller Chantry (b. 1789) became a surgeon in the navy.

disturbed at the freedom with which he criticised and directed the carving of a haunch of venison, fixing the attention of the whole table on the process, which the operator bore most gracefully. Chantrey turned apologetically to me with, 'You know I have a right. I am the first carver in London.' He always told every body who he was, and took for granted that every body knew all his works: but there was a good-humoured courage and naturalness about his self-estimate which made it amusing, instead of disgusting.

Allan Cunningham was, however, far more interesting than his employer and friend.[1] It was quite a sight to see stalwart Allan and his stalwart wife enter a drawing-room, and to see how his fine face and head towered above others in expression as much as in altitude. His simple sense and cheerful humour rendered his conversation as lively as that of a wit; and his literary knowledge and taste gave it refinement enough to suit any society. I always felt that Allan Cunningham was precisely the human example that I had long wished to see;—of that privileged condition which I think the very most advantageous that a man can be placed in; the original standing of a workman, with such means of intellectual cultivation as may open to him the life of books. Allan Cunningham was one of the hard-handed order, privileged to know the realities of practical life; while also a man of letters and a poet, exempt from the deficiencies and foibles of mere literary life. Thus, while a workman, a student and a poet, he was above all a man; and thorough manliness was his dominant characteristic. All this came back upon me when, in 1849, I met his son Peter, whose features recalled so much of his father, and whose industrious and effectual authorship reminds us all of his honourable descent.

Westmacott, again, was seriously full of his art; and that is the true charm in the manners of an artist.[2] Phillips was formal and self-complacent, but well read and communicative: and the friendship between himself and his accomplished family was a pretty spectacle. Macready's sensitiveness shrouded itself within an artificial manner; but a more delightful companion could not be,—not only on account of his learning and accomplishment, but of his uncompromising liberality of opinion, and his

---

[1]   Allan Cunningham (1784–1842) apprenticed as a stonemason but rose to fame in 1810 with *Remains of Nithsdale and Galloway Song,* many of which were his own but disguised as old Scottish songs to catch the current vogue. His publisher Robert Cromek (1720–1812) arranged for him to move to London and serve as secretary to Sir Francis Chantrey.

[2]   Richard Westmacott (1795–1856), sculptor; Giles Firman Phillips (1780–1867), landscape painter, especially of views on the Thames River; William Charles Macready (1793–1873), Shakespearean actor famous in the roles of Lear, Hamlet, and Macbeth.

noble strain of meditative thought. He enjoyed playing Jaques,[1]—thinking that character singularly like himself; and it was so, in one part of his character: but there was, besides the moralising tendency, a chivalrous spirit of rare vigilance, and an unsleeping domestic tenderness and social beneficence which accounted for and justified the idolatry with which he was regarded, through all trials occasioned by the irritable temper with which he manfully struggled.—The Kembles were of a different sort altogether; I mean Charles Kemble and his daughters.[2] They were full of knowledge and accomplishment, of course, and experienced in all manner of social intercourse: but there seemed to me to be an incurable vulgarity clinging to them, among all the charms of their genius, their cultivation, and their social privileges. I think it must have been from their passionate natures, and from their rather priding themselves on that characteristic of theirs. I liked Adelaide the best of the three, because she had herself more under control than the others, and because the womanly nature did itself more justice in her case than in her sister's. The admiration and interest which Fanny inspired were as often put to flight as aroused, —so provoking was her self-will, and so vexatious her caprice. And then, there was no relying on any thing she said, while the calmer and more devoted Adelaide was mistress of her own thought and speech, and composedly truthful in a way which ought to have been, and probably was, exemplary in Fanny's eyes. There was a green-room cast of mind about them all, from which Macready was marvelously free. He saw life by daylight, and they by stage lamps; and that was the difference. I am speaking of them as I met them in drawing-rooms: but I have other associations with them. I saw much of Fanny in America, during her early married life, and was present at the christening of her first child. She showed me the proof sheets of her clever 'Journal,'[3] and, as she chose to require my opinion of it, obtained a less flattering one than from most people. I might be, and probably was, narrow

---

[1] Jacques, discontented lord in Shakespeare's *As You Like It*, whose most famous line is "All the world's a stage."

[2] Charles Kemble (1775–1854), actor from an important theatrical family that included Sarah Siddons. His daughters were Frances Anne (Fanny), later Butler (1809–93), an actress and author, and Adelaide, later Sartoris (1816–79), a singer and fiction writer. By "best of the three," Martineau must include their brother, John Mitchell Kemble.

[3] Fanny Kemble published a *Journal of a Residence in America* (1835), which criticized American social and political institutions, including slavery. Martineau comments on Fanny's "self-inflicted" misfortunes because she married—and then divorced—a southern planter and slave owner. During the American Civil War, Kemble published *Journal of a Residence on a Georgia Plantation in 1838–39* (1863), which was frequently reprinted by supporters of emancipation.

and stiff in my judgment of it; but I was sufficiently shocked at certain passages to induce her to cancel some thirty pages. I really strove hard to like and approve her; and I imposed upon myself for a time, as on others in conversation, the belief that I did so: but I could not carry it on long. There was so radical an unreality about her and her sayings and doings, and so perverse a sporting with her possessions and privileges in life, and with other people's peace, that my interest in her died out completely, in a way which could not have happened if I could have believed her notorious misfortunes to have been other than self-inflicted. By her way of entering upon marriage, and her conduct in it afterwards, she deprived herself of all title to wonder at or complain of her domestic miseries, terrible as they were. She was a finely-gifted creature, wasted and tortured by want of discipline, principle and self-knowledge. Adelaide was morally of a far higher order; and when with her, I desired nothing more than that she had seen life through other than the stage medium, and that she had not been a Kemble. She was charming at their own soirées in London,—unobtrusively taking care of and amusing every body, with good nature and simplicity: and she was yet more charming when she sat beside my couch at Tynemouth, singing 'Auld Robin Gray' for my pleasure, and manifesting a true womanly sympathy with me, of whom she had personally known nothing except through drawing-room intercourse. It was she who sent me the chief luxury of my sick room,—the 'Christus Consolator' of Scheffer,[1] which truly affords study for as many years as I was ill. If, as I understand, she has found happiness in her domestic life, after such triumphs as hers on the stage, the genuine fine quality of her nature is sufficiently proved.

In those days, Eastlake was just home from Italy.[2] He had already left off landscape painting, with which he began. I have hanging up in the next room the engraving which he gave me of his last landscape,—'Byron's Dream.' He was now producing the early pictures of that short series which, full of charm at first, soon proved how *bornés* were his

---

[1] *Christus Consolator*, painted in 1837 by Ary Scheffer (1795–1856), portrays Christ surrounded by the afflicted and downtrodden. Scheffer's view of Christ as the Comforter of suffering humanity was inspired by Luke 4:18: "He hath sent me to heal the brokenhearted, to preach deliverance to the captives." The biblical text is carved in French on the frame.

[2] Sir Charles Eastlake (1793–1865) served in many public roles: as secretary of the Fine Arts Committee that oversaw the decoration of the House of Parliament; as keeper, then director of the National Gallery; and as president of the Royal Academy. His *Byron's Dream* was begun in 1824 and completed in 1828, just before his return to England after a fifteen-year residence in Italy; it depicts a dreaming figure amidst a Greek landscape with classical ruins and a party of "oriental" travelers.

resources. The mannerism of his colouring, and the sameness of his female faces, showing that he had but one idea of beauty, could be made evident only by time; and at first there was an exquisite charm in the grace, refinement and delicacy of both conception and execution. Since that time, his function has appeared to be the aiding and support of art by other means than himself painting. I always liked to meet him, —ignorant as I was on the subjects which were most important to him. He condescended to talk to me on them; and there was the wide field of literature in which we had a common interest. Kind and conversible as he was, I always felt that there was a certain amount of cynicism in his views, and skepticism in his temper, which must have interfered with his enjoyment of life. It was not very great, and was chiefly noticeable as being the only drawback on the pleasure of conversation with him. I have seen him only once for nearly twenty years; and that was at a distance in Thackeray's lecture room, in 1851.[1] I should hardly have known the careworn, aged face, if my attention had not been directed to him: and it gave me pain to see how the old tendency to anxiety and distrust seemed to have issued in care or ill-health, which could so alter a man not yet old. He has done so much for art, and given so much pleasure to society, that one wishes he could have enjoyed the strength and spirits which those who love art as he does should, and generally do, derive from its pursuit.—There was Uwins, in those days, with his sunny Italian groups; and, more recently, Rothwell, whose picture (when unfinished) of 'Rich and rare were the gems she wore,' seemed to me wonderfully beautiful: and, among portrait painters, the accomplished and earnest Richmond,— to whom I sat for the only good portrait taken of me.[2]

I seem to have got a long way from the dinner parties which led me into all these sketches; and I will not go back to them; but rather tell a little about the evening engagements which gave variety to my London life. There were blue-stocking evenings, now and then; and I never went twice to any house where I encountered that sort of reception, except the Miss

---

[1] Beginning in May 1851, Thackeray gave a lecture series on English humorists of the eighteenth century in Willis's Rooms, St. James's.

[2] Thomas Uwins (1782–1857), painter of literary subjects; Richard Rothwell (1800–68), Irish painter best known for his Regency portraits; and George Richmond (1809–1896), portrait painter for whom Martineau sat in 1849. The Richmond portrait is now in the National Gallery, London. The title of Rothwell's painting comes from a poem by Thomas Moore:
Rich and rare were the gems she wore,
And a bright gold ring on her wand she bore;
But oh! her beauty was far beyond
Her sparkling gems, or snow-white wand.

Berrys', where there was so much to relieve 'the blue,' and one was left so freely and pleasantly to be amused, that one's pride or one's modesty was safe from offence. By the way, an incident occurred at dinner at Miss Berry's which I recall with as much astonishment as paralysed me at the moment, and struck me dumb when it was of some importance that I should speak. I have told how a Prime Minister's daughter was for the first time informed of the Birmingham Church and King riots, when Dr. Priestley's chapel, house and library were destroyed.[1] A high-born lady betrayed to me, that evening at Miss Berry's, what her notion, and that of her associates, was of the politics of the liberal party after the passage of the Reform Bill. Lady G.S.W., whose husband, I think, had been in the United States, inquired of me about the prospects of Slavery there.[2] When she seemed surprised at the amount of persecution the abolitionists were undergoing, I attempted to show her how the vicious institution was implicated with the whole policy, and many of the modes, ideas and interests of society there; so that the abolitionists were charged with destructiveness, and regarded by timid persons, whether slaveholders or other, much as people would be among us who should be charged with desiring to overthrow every thing, from the throne to the workhouse. Her reply completely puzzled me for a moment, and then appeared so outrageously wide of the mark that I had not presence of mind to answer it; and the opportunity was presently gone. I wonder whether she really supposed she had given me a check and a set down! 'Come now,' said she; 'don't let us talk about that. I want to get this information from you, and we will talk only about what we agree in. You know we shall differ about pulling down, and all that.' Why she talked to me at all if she supposed that I wanted to pull down every thing, from the throne to the workhouse, I can't imagine. And, if she thought so of me, she must have regarded the then dominant liberals as unredeemed destructives. It is a curious state of mind in the Tory aristocracy that such incidents reveal. She seemed otherwise sensible enough; yet she had read my Series without finding out that I am for 'pulling down' nothing, and quietly superseding what can no longer be endured.

The ancient ladies themselves, the Miss Berrys and their inseparable friend, Lady Charlotte Lindsay,[3] (the youngest daughter of Lord North),

---

[1] Lady Durham, daughter of Lord Grey; see Period IV, sec. i.
[2] Martineau had toured the South extensively in 1834–35 to see slavery in action and, after witnessing its abuses, became closely allied with Northern abolitionists. Lady G.S.W. is unidentified.
[3] Lady Charlotte Lindsay (1770–1849), daughter of Lord North.

whose presence seemed to carry one back almost a century, were the main attraction of those parties. While up to all modern interests, the old-fashioned rouge and pearl-powder, and false hair, and the use of the feminine oaths of a hundred years ago were odd and striking. E.g: a footman tells his mistress that Lady So-and-so begs she will not wait dinner, as she is drying her shoes which got wet between the carriage and the door. The response is 'O! Christ! if she should catch cold! Tell her she is a dear soul, and we would not have her hurry herself for the world, &c., &c.' My mother heard an exclamation at our door, when the carriage door would not open, 'My God! I can't get out!' And so forth, continually. But they were all three so cheerful, so full of know-ledge and of sympathy for good ideas, and so evidently fit for higher pursuits than the social pleasures amidst which one met them, that, though their parties *were* 'rather blue,' they were exceedingly agreeable. I had a general invitation to go there, whenever, in passing their house in Mayfair from a dinner party, I saw light over the lower shutters; and they also invited me to spend summer days with them at their Petersham house.[1] I never did this, for want of time; and I went seldom to their evening parties, for the same reason that I seemed to neglect other invitations of the same general kind,—that I was always engaged three or four weeks in advance, by express invitation. When my aged friends perceived this, they gave me express invitations too, and made me fix my own day. The last of the trio, the elder Miss Berry, died in November, 1852. The announcement impelled me to record the asso-ciations it excited; and I did so in an obituary memoir of her in the 'Daily News.' My friend Milnes[2] offered his tribute in the form of some charming lines in the 'Times,' which show how strong was the natural feeling of concern, on such an occasion, at letting go our hold on the traditions of the last century.

How different were those parties from the express 'blue' assemblies of such pedants as Lady Mary Shepherd![3] She went about accompanied by the fame given her by Mr. Tierney,[4] when he said that there was not another head in England which could encounter hers on the subject of

---

[1]   Mary Berry and her sister Agnes inherited "Little Strawberry Hill" from Lord Orford at his death in 1797.

[2]   Richard Monckton Milnes (1809–85); see p. 262, n. 1.

[3]   Lady Shepherd (1777–1847) was an aunt of Lord Brougham and wife of Sir Samuel Shepherd, friend of many artists and authors. See Period IV, sec. i for other memories.

[4]   Possibly Mark A. Tierney (1795–1865), the Catholic historian. Lady Shepherd had writ-ten three philosophical treatises—hence, the reference to "Cause and Effect."

Cause and Effect, and some kindred topics: and it did indeed appear that she was, in relation to the subtlest metaphysical topics, what Mrs. Somerville was to mathematical astronomy. The difference was,—and a bottomless chasm separated the two,—that Mrs. Somerville was occupied with real science,—with the knowable; whereas, Lady Mary Shepherd never dreamed of looking out first for a sound point of view, and therefore wasted her fine analytical powers on things unknowable or purely imaginary. It was a story against her that when in a country house, one fine day, she took her seat in a window, saying in a business-like manner (to David Ricardo, if I remember rightly,)[1]—'Come, now; let us have a little discussion about Space.' I never went to her house but once. Though I there first made Mr. Milnes's acquaintance, I never would go again; and I then made my escape as soon as I could. First, I was set down beside Lady Charlotte Bury,[2] and made to undergo, for her satisfaction, a ludicrous examination by Lady Mary, about how I wrote my Series, and what I thought of it. Escaping from this, to an opposite sofa, I was boarded by Lady Stepney,[3] who was then, as she boasted, receiving seven hundred pounds apiece for her novels. She paraded a pair of diamond earrings, costing that sum, which she had so earned. She began talking to me on the ground of our mutual acquaintance with Mrs. Opie, who had once been an intimate friend and correspondent of hers. She complained of the inconvenience of Mrs. Opie's quakerism; and insisted on having my suffrage whether it was not very wrong in people to change their opinions, on account of the inconvenience to their friends.[4] The difficulty in conversing with this extraordinary personage was that she stopped at intervals, to demand an unqualified assent to what she said, while saying things impossible to assent to. She insisted on my believing that 'that dreadful Reform in Parliament took place entirely because the dear Duke' of Wellington had not my 'moral courage,' and would not carry a trumpet. She told me that the dear Duke assured her himself that if he had heard what had been said from the Treasury-benches, he should never have made that declaration against parliamentary reform which brought it on: and

---

[1] David Ricardo (1772–1823), economist and author of *On the Principles of Political Economy and Taxation* (1817).

[2] Lady Charlotte Bury (1775–1861), novelist of fashionable life whose anonymously published *Diary Illustrative of the Times of George IV* caused a stir in 1838.

[3] Catherine Pollock Manners Stepney (d. 1845), silver-fork novelist, author of *The New Road to Ruin* (1833), *The Heir Presumptive* (1835), *The Three Peers* (1840), and others.

[4] The Norwich-born writer Amelia Opie (1769–1853) converted to Quakerism in 1825 and ceased writing fiction.

thence it followed, Lady Stepney concluded, that if he had heard what was said behind him,—that is, if he *had* carried a trumpet, he would have suppressed his declaration; and the rest followed of course. I was so amused at this that I told Lady Durham of it; and she repeated it to her father,[1] then Prime Minister; and then ensued the most amusing part of all. Lord Grey did not apparently take it as a joke on my part, but sent me word, in all seriousness, that there would have been parliamentary reform, sooner or later, if the Duke of Wellington had carried a trumpet! Lady Stepney pointed to a large easy chair at my elbow, and said she supposed I knew for whom that was intended. She was surprised that I did not, and told me that it was for Captain Ross;[2] and that the company assembled were longing for him to come, that they might see the meeting between him and me, and hear what we should say to each other. This determined me to be off; and I kept my eye on the doors, in order to slip away on the entrance of the newest 'lion.' It was too early yet to go with any decency. Lady Stepney told me meantime that the Arctic voyagers had gone through hardships such as could never be told: but it only proved (and to this in particular she required my assent) 'that the Deity is every where, and more particularly in barren places.' She went on to say how very wrong she thought it to send men into such places, without any better reason than she had ever heard of. 'They say it is to discover the North Pole,' she proceeded; 'and, by the bye, it is curious that Newton should have come within thirty miles of the North Pole in his discoveries. They *say*, you know,' and here she looked exceedingly sagacious and amused; 'they *say* that they have found the magnetic pole. But you and I know what a magnet is, very well. *We* know that a little thing like that would be pulled out of its place in the middle of the sea.' When I reported this conversation to my mother, we determined to get one of this lady's novels immediately, and see what she could write that would sell for seven hundred pounds. If she was to be believed as to this, it really was a curious sign of the times. I never saw any of her books, after all. I can hardly expect to be believed about the anecdote of the magnet (which I imagine she took to be a little red horse-shoe;) and I had some difficulty in believing it myself, at the moment: but I have given her very words. And they were no joke. She shook her head-dress of marabout feathers and black bugles with her excitement as she talked. I got away before Captain

---

[1]   Charles, Lord Grey (1764–1845), prime minister from 1830–34.

[2]   Captain John Ross, who searched for a Northwest passage; see p. 250, n. 2.

Ross appeared, and never went to the house again, except to drop a card before I left London.

Some people may be disposed to turn round upon me with the charge of giving blue-stocking parties. I believe that to blue-stocking people my soirées might have that appearance, because they looked through blue spectacles: but I can confidently say that, not only were my parties as diverse in quality as I could make them,—always including many who were not literary; but I took particular care that no one was in any way shown off, but all treated with equal respect as guests. My rooms were too small for personages who required space for display: and such were not therefore invited. A gentleman who expected a sofa all to himself, while a crowd of adorers simpered in his face, was no guest for a simple evening party in a small house: nor a lady who needed a corner in which to confide her troubles with her husband; nor for another who hung her white hand over the arm of her chair, and lectured metaphysically and sentimentally about art, to the annoyance of true connoisseurs who felt that while she was exposing herself, she was misleading others who knew no more about the real thing than she did. Nor had I a place for rouged and made up old ladies who paraded literary flirtations in the style of half a century ago. Such were not therefore invited. I was too nervous about having parties at all to introduce any persons who might be disagreeable to people of better manners. All I ventured upon was to invite those who knew what to expect, and could stay away if they liked. What they had to expect was tea below stairs, and ices, cake and wine during the evening, with a very choice assembly of guests who did not mind a little crowding, for the sake of the conversation they afforded each other. I became more at ease when I found that all whom I invited always came: a test which satisfied me that they liked to come.

I have particularised only well-known persons: but it must be understood that these were not my intimates, or most valued acquaintances. If they had been intimate friends, I could not have characterised them. There were three or four houses where I went freely for rest and recreation; families too near and dear to me to be described in detail. There were country houses where I went every week or two, to meet pleasant little dinner parties, and to sleep, for the enjoyment of country air and quiet. Such as these were the H. Bellenden Kers', whose Swiss Cottage at Cheshunt was a sort of home to me: and the Porters', first at Norwood, and then on Putney Heath: and then the Huttons' at Putney Park; and the Fishers' at Highbury: and the Potters' at Notting Hill: and the Marshes' at Killburn: and the Hensleigh Wedgwoods'; in their Clapham home first, and then in Regent's Park: and my old friend, Mrs. Reid's, in Regent's Park: beside my own relations.[1] All these were home houses to me;—each a refuge from the wear and tear of my busy life, and from the incessant siege of lion-hunting strangers. One yearly holiday was especially refreshing to me. With the first fine weather in May, Mr. and Mrs. Fisher and I used to go, for a few days or a week, to Boxhill, or Godstone,[2] or some other pretty place not too far off, and carry a book or two, and lie on the grass, or ramble among hills, commons or lanes, as if we had nothing to do; and I never came home without fresh spirits for my work, and valuable suggestions about new efforts. With them I planned or thought of some of my tales: with them I discussed 'Deerbrook,' the week before I began it, though Mrs. Ker was my great confidante during its progress. I spent a month or more of every summer with her at her Swiss Cottage; and a month of luxury it always was,—well as my work proceeded in my own 'den' there.

I was spending a couple of days at Mrs. Marsh's, when she asked me whether I would let her read to me 'one or two little stories' which she had written. From her way of speaking of them, and from her devotion to her children, who were then for the most part very young, I concluded these to be children's tales. She ordered a fire in her room, and there we shut ourselves up for the reading. What she read was no child's story, but 'The Admiral's Daughter.' My amazement may be conceived. We were going to dine at the Wedgwoods': and a strange

---

[1]   Henry Bellenden Ker (1785–1871), legal reformer and unsuccessful Whig candidate for parliament from Norwich, and his wife Elizabeth Anne, née Clarke, lived in Cheshunt, Hertfordshire, ten miles north of London. The political economist George Richardson Porter (1792–1852) and his wife Sarah, née Ricardo (1791–1862), a writer on education, lived in Norwood Lane, Dulwich, south of London, in the 1840s. Robert Hutton, former M.P. for Dublin, and his wife were friends of Mrs. Anne Marsh, whom Martineau helped publish *Two Old Men's Tales* in 1834. Joseph Fisher (1795–1890) was an etcher-engraver who worked regularly for magazines and produced his own books, including *Sixty Reminiscences of the Models by Sir Francis Chantrey in the University Galleries, Oxford* (2nd ed., 1872). The Reverend John Phillips Potter (1793–1861) and his wife Ann, née Freeman (d. 1861), were Unitarians, he a writer on philosophy and education. Arthur Marsh and his wife Anne, née Caldwell (1791–1874), a novelist, were mutual friends of the Huttons and Wedgwoods. Hensleigh Wedgwood (1803–91) and his wife Fanny, née Mackintosh (1800–89), were not only London friends but corresponded regularly with Martineau during her illness in Tynemouth and residence in Ambleside. Elisabeth Jesser Reid, née Sturch, widow of Dr. John Reid, was a Unitarian philanthropist, an advocate of women's higher education, and one of Martineau's closest friends.

[2]   Boxhill, approximately 25 miles south of London, has fine walks through a woodland of box trees and superb views of the Sussex downs. Godstone, 21 miles south, has been consumed by the suburbs.

figure we must have cut there; for we had been crying so desperately that there was no concealing the marks of it. Mrs. Marsh asked me what I thought of getting her tales published. I offered to try if, on reading the manuscript at home, I thought as well of it as after her own most moving delivery of it. A second reading left no doubt on my mind; and I had the pleasure of introducing the 'Two Old Men's Tales' to the world through Messrs. Saunders and Otley, from whom, as from the rest of the world, the author's name was withheld as long as possible. Mr. Marsh made this the condition of our attempt: a condition which we thought perfectly reasonable in the father of many daughters, who did not wish their mother to be known as the author of what the world might consider second-rate novels. That the world did not consider them second-rate was immediately apparent; and the reason for secrecy existed no longer. But no one ever knew or guessed the authorship through my mother or me, who were for a considerable time the only possessors of the secret. From that time Mrs. Marsh managed her own affairs; and I never again saw her works till they were published. I mention this because, as I never concealed from her, I think her subsequent works very inferior to the first: and I think it a pity that she did not rest on the high and well-deserved fame which she immediately obtained. The singular magnificence of that tale was not likely to be surpassed: but I have always wished that she had either stopped entirely, or had given herself time to do justice to her genius. From the time of the publication of the 'Two Old Men's Tales' to the present hour, I have never once, as far as I remember, succeeded in getting another manuscript published for any body. This has been a matter of great concern to me: but such is the fact. I have never had to make any proposal of the kind for myself,—having always had a choice of publishers before my works were ready; but I have striven hard on behalf of others, and without the slightest success.

No kind of evening was more delightful to me than those which were spent with the Carlyles.[1] About once a fortnight, a mutual friend of theirs and mine drove me over to Chelsea, to the early tea table at number five, Cheyne Row,—the house which Carlyle was perpetually complaining of and threatening to leave, but where he is still to be found. I never believed that, considering the delicate health of both, they could ever flourish on that Chelsea clay, close to the river; and I

---

[1] Thomas Carlyle (1795–1881), essayist and historian, and his wife Jane Baillie, née Welsh (1801–66).

rejoiced when the term of lease had nearly expired, and my friends were looking out for another house. If they were living in a 'cauldron' and a 'Babel,' it seemed desirable that they should find an airy quiet home in the country,—near enough to London to enjoy its society at pleasure. Carlyle went forth, on the fine black horse which a friend had sent him with sanitary views, and looked about him. Forth he went, his wife told me, with three maps of Great Britain and two of the World in his pocket, to explore the area within twenty miles of London. All their friends were on the look out; and I, from my sick chamber at Tynemouth, sent them earnest entreaties to settle on a gravelly soil: but old habit prevailed, and the philosopher renewed the lease, and set to work to make for himself a noise-proof chamber, where his fretted nerves might possibly obtain rest amidst the London 'Babel.' I like the house for no other reason than that I spent many very pleasant evenings in it: but it has now become completely associated with the marvelous talk of both husband and wife. There we met Mazzini,[1] when he was exerting himself for the education of the Italians in London, and before he entered openly on the career of insurrection by which he has since become the most notorious man in Europe. I entirely believe in all that his adorers say of the noble qualities of his heart and temper. I can quite understand how it is that some of those who know him best believe him to be the best man in existence. There is no doubt whatever of his devotedness, his magnanimity, his absolute disinterestedness. But the more, and not the less, for all this does his career seem to me almost the saddest spectacle of our time. He is an ideologist who will preach for ever in a mood of exaltation and a style of fustian, without being listened to by any but those who do not need his incitements. Insurrection is too serious a matter to be stirred up by turgid appeals like his, vague and irreducible to the concrete. Accordingly, here are twenty years since I knew him gone by without success or the prospect of it. His beacon fire blazed longer at Rome than any where: but it went out; and it left in ashes many a glorious relic from ancient times, and the peace of many households. The slaughter of patriots from abortive insurrections has gone on through a long course of years, till, if Mazzini's heart is not broken, many others are; and the day of an Italian republic seems further off than ever. To Mazzini it seems always at hand, as the Millennium

---

[1]　Giuseppe Mazzini (1805–72), Italian nationalist and political refugee. Martineau refers to his abortive invasion of Italy from Switzerland in 1834, his participation in the revolutions of 1848, and his attempt in 1870 to lead a Sicilian revolt against the new unified Italian government of Victor Emmanuel II.

seems to Robert Owen;[1] but I cannot find that any one else who knows the Italians has the least belief that, as a people, they desire a republic, or that the small minority who do could ever agree to the terms of any republican constitution, or maintain it if established. His career will be, I fear, as it has hitherto been, one of failure; and of failure so disastrous as to set it above every other *vie manquée*. When I knew him, face to face, these purposes of his were growing in silence. His still, patient, grave countenance was that of a man who had suffered much, and could endure to any extremity: but I could not have supposed that experience and experiment could have been so lost on him as they appear to have been. His self-will was not the less strong for his disinterestedness, it appears; and it has taken possession of his intellect, causing him to believe, with a fatal confidence, what he wishes. When we consider how Sardinia has advanced, during the whole period of Mazzini's bloody and fruitless struggles, and how that State is now a striking spectacle of growing civil and religious liberty, while Mazzini, with his perfect plots, his occult armies, his buried arms and ammunition, his own sufferings and dangers, and his holocaust of victims, has aggravated the tyranny of Austria, and rendered desperate the cause of his countrymen, we can hardly help wishing that his own devotedness had met with acceptance, and that the early sacrifice of his life had spared that of hundreds of his followers who are wept by thousands more.

Another *vie manquée* was before my eyes at the Carlyles'. John Sterling[2] was then in the midst of his conflicts of all sorts,—with bad health, with the solemn pity and covert reprobation of orthodox friends and patrons, and with his own restless excitement about authorship. I cannot say that I knew him at all; for I never heard the sound of his voice. When we met at the tea table, he treated me like a chair; and so pointed was his rude ignoring of me that there was nothing to be done but for Carlyle to draw off apart with him after tea, while the rest of us talked on the other side of the room. When our meetings were over,— when I was on my couch at Tynemouth, and he was trying to breathe in Devonshire, he suddenly changed his mind, on meeting with 'Deerbrook,' and was as anxious to obtain my acquaintance as he had

---

[1] Robert Owen (1771–1858), Welsh-born socialist and founder of the New Harmony Community in America.

[2] John Sterling (1806–44), a member of the Cambridge Apostles, disciple of Coleridge, and friend of F.D. Maurice as well as Carlyle, wrote reviews and published poetry and a novel, *Arthur Coningsby* (1833), before his early death. Carlyle wrote a biography, *The Life of John Sterling* (1851).

been to avoid it. Supposing me to be at Teignmouth, and therefore within reach, he wrote to Mrs. Carlyle to ask whether it was too late, or whether she would sanction his going to Teignmouth to ask my friendship.[1] I should have been very happy to hear the voice belonging to the striking face and head I knew so well: but it *was* too late. The length of the kingdom lay between us; and before I emerged from my sick-room, he was in his grave. I am glad I saw him, whatever he might have been thinking of me; (and what it was I have not the remotest idea:) for I retain a strong impression of his noble head and vital countenance.

Another memorable head was there, now and then. Leigh Hunt[2] was there, with his cheery face, bright, acute, and full of sensibility; and his thick grizzled hair combed down smooth, and his homely figure;—black handkerchief, grey stockings and stout shoes, while he was full of gratitude to ladies who dress in winter in velvet, and in rich colours; and to old dames in the streets or the country who still wear scarlet cloaks. His conversation was lively, rapid, highly illustrative, and perfectly natural. I remember one evening when Horne[3] was there (the author of 'Orion,' &c.) wishing that the three heads, —Hunt's, Horne's and Carlyle's,— could be sketched in a group. Horne's perfectly white complexion, and somewhat coxcombical curling whiskers and determined picturesqueness contrasted curiously with the homely manliness of Hunt's fine countenance, and the rugged face, steeped in genius, of Carlyle. I have seen Carlyle's face under all aspects, from the deepest gloom to the most reckless or most genial mirth; and it seemed to me that each mood would make a totally different portrait. The sympathetic is by far the finest, in my eyes. His excess of sympathy has been, I believe, the master-pain of his life. He does not know what to do with it, and with its bitterness, seeing that human life is full of pain to those who look out for it: and the savageness which has come to be a main characteristic of this singular man is, in my opinion, a mere expression of his intolerable sympathy with the suffering. He cannot express his love and pity in natural acts, like other people; and it shows itself too often in unnatural speech. But to those who understand his eyes, his shy manner, his changing colour, his sigh, and the constitutional *pudeur* which renders him

---

[1]   Teignmouth is in Devonshire in the southwest of England; Tynemouth is in Northumberland in the northeast—a confusion of direction emblematic of the man.

[2]   James Henry Leigh Hunt (1784–1859), founder and editor of the *Examiner*, wrote poetry, essays, and an *Autobiography* (1850) much admired by Carlyle.

[3]   Richard Hengist Horne (1802–84) published *Orion* (1843), an allegorical epic "to mark the public contempt into which epic poetry had fallen."

silent about every thing that he feels the most deeply, his wild speech and abrupt manner are perfectly intelligible. I have felt to the depths of my heart what his sympathy was in my days of success and prosperity and apparent happiness without drawback; and again in sickness, pain, and hopelessness of being ever at ease again: I have observed the same strength of feeling towards all manner of sufferers; and I am confident that Carlyle's affections are too much for him, and the real cause of the 'ferocity' with which he charges himself, and astonishes others. It must be such a strong love and honour as his friends feel for him that can compensate for the pain of witnessing his suffering life. When I knew him familiarly, he rarely slept, was wofully dyspeptic, and as variable as possible in mood. When my friend and I entered the little parlour at Cheyne Row, our host was usually miserable. Till he got his coffee, he asked a list of questions, without waiting for answers, and looked as if he was on the rack. After tea, he brightened and softened, and sent us home full of admiration and friendship, and sometimes with a hope that he would some day be happy. It was our doing,—that friend's and mine,— that he gave lectures for three or four seasons.[1] He had matter to utter; and there were many who wished to hear him; and in those days, before his works had reached their remunerative point of sale, the earnings by his lectures could not be unacceptable. So we confidently proceeded, taking the management of the arrangements, and leaving Carlyle nothing to do but to meet his audience, and say what he had to say. Whenever I went, my pleasure was a good deal spoiled by his unconcealable nervousness. Yellow as a guinea, with downcast eyes, broken speech at the beginning, and fingers which nervously picked at the desk before him, he could not for a moment be supposed to enjoy his own effort; and the lecturer's own enjoyment is a prime element of success. The merits of Carlyle's discourses were however so great that he might probably have gone on year after year till this time, with improving success, and perhaps ease: but the struggle was too severe. From the time that his course was announced till it was finished, he scarcely slept, and he grew more dyspeptic and nervous every day; and we were at length entreated to say no more about his lecturing, as no fame and no money or other advantage could counterbalance the misery which the engagement caused him.—I remember being puzzled for a long while as to whether Carlyle

---

[1]   In 1837 Carlyle gave six lectures on German literature; in 1838 he gave twelve on the history of literature and culture. A third series on "The Revolution of Modern Europe" began in May, 1838. The fourth series, scheduled for May, 1840, became *On Heroes, Hero-Worship, and the Heroic in History* (1841).

did or did not care for fame. He was for ever scoffing at it; and he seemed to me just the man to write because he needed to utter himself, without ulterior considerations. One day I was dining there alone. I had brought over from America twenty-five copies of his 'Sartor Resartus,' as reprinted there; and, having sold them at the English price, I had some money to put into his hand. I did put it into his hand the first time: but it made him uncomfortable, and he spent it in a pair of signet rings, for his wife and me, (her motto being 'Point de faiblesse,' and mine 'Frisch zu!') This would never do; so, having imported and sold a second parcel, the difficulty was what to do with the money. My friend and I found that Carlyle was ordered weak brandy and water instead of wine; and we spent our few sovereigns in French brandy of the best quality, which we carried over one evening, when going to tea. Carlyle's amusement and delight at first, and all the evening after, whenever he turned his eyes towards the long-necked bottles, showed us that we had made a good choice. He declared that he had got a reward for his labours at last: and his wife asked me to dinner, all by myself, to taste the brandy. We three sat round the fire after dinner, and Carlyle mixed the toddy while Mrs. Carlyle and I discussed some literary matters, and speculated on fame and the love of it. Then Carlyle held out a glass of his mixture to me with, 'Here,—take this. It is worth all the fame in England.' Yet Allan Cunningham, who knew and loved him well, told me one evening, to my amazement, that Carlyle would be very well, and happy enough, if he got a little more fame. I asked him whether he was in earnest; and he said he was, and moreover sure that he was right; —I should see that he was. Carlyle's fame has grown from that day; and on the whole his health and spirits seem to be improved, so that his friend Allan was partly right. But I am certain that there are constitutional sources of pain (aggravated, no doubt, by excess in study in his youth) which have nothing to do with love of fame, or any other self-regards.

In 1837, he came to me to ask how he should manage, if he accepted a proposal from Fraser to publish his pieces as a collection of 'Miscellanies.'[1] After discussing the money part of the business, I begged him to let me undertake the proof-correcting, —supposing of course that the pieces were to be simply reprinted. He nearly agreed to let me do this, but afterwards changed his mind. The reason for my offer was that the sight of his proofs had more than once really alarmed me,—so

---

[1]   Hugh Fraser, founder and publisher of *Fraser's Magazine* (1830–82), in which Carlyle's *Sartor Resartus* appeared in 1833–34.

irresolute, as well as fastidious, did he seem to be as to the expression of his plainest thoughts. Almost every other word was altered; and revise followed upon revise. I saw at once that this way of proceeding must be very harassing to him; and also that profit must be cut off to a most serious degree by this absurdly expensive method of printing. I told him that it would turn out just so if he would not allow his 'Miscellanies' to be reprinted just as they stood, in the form in which people had admired, and now desired to possess them. As might be expected, the printing went on very slowly, and there seemed every probability that this simple reprint would stand over to another season. One day, while in my study, I heard a prodigious sound of laughter on the stairs; and in came Carlyle, laughing loud. He had been laughing in that manner all the way from the printing-office in Charing Cross. As soon as he could, he told me what it was about. He had been to the office to urge on the printer: and the man said 'Why, Sir, you really are so very hard upon us with your corrections! They take so much time, you see!' After some remonstrance, Carlyle observed that he had been accustomed to this sort of thing,—that he had got works printed in Scotland, and . . . 'Yes, indeed, Sir,' interrupted the printer. 'We are aware of that. We have a man here from Edinburgh; and when he took up a bit of your copy, he dropped it as if it had burnt his fingers, and cried out "Lord have mercy! have you got that man to print for? Lord knows when we shall get done,—with all his corrections!"' Carlyle could not reply for laughing, and he came to tell me that I was not singular in my opinion about his method of revising.

He has now been very long about his 'Frederick the Great,'[1] which I must, therefore, like a good many more, die without seeing. I could never grow tired of his biographies. From the time when I first knew him, I am not aware that he has advanced in any views, or grown riper in his conclusions; and his mind has always seemed to me as inaccessible as Wordsworth's, or any other constitutionally isolated like theirs: and there-fore it is that I prefer to an outpouring of his own notions, which we have heard as often as he has written didactically, and which were best conveyed in his 'Sartor Resartus,' a commentary on a character, as in biography, or on events, as in a history. For many reasons, I prefer his biog-raphies. I do not think that he can do any more effectual work in the field

---

[1] Carlyle's biography of Frederick the Great of Prussia, on which he spent fourteen years, came out in six volumes between 1858 and 1865—after the period in which Martineau wrote her autobiography but before her death. *Oliver Cromwell's Letters and Speeches* appeared in 1845, *Latter-Day Pamphlets*, in 1850.

of philosophy or morals: but I enjoy an occasional addition to the fine gallery of portraits which he has given us. I am now too much out of the world to know what is the real condition of his fame and influence: but, for my own part, I could not read his Latter Day Pamphlets, while heartily enjoying his Life of his friend Sterling, and, in the main, his 'Cromwell.' No one can read his 'Cromwell' without longing for his 'Frederick the Great:' and I hope he will achieve that portrait, and others after it. However much or little he may yet do, he certainly ought to be recognised as one of the chief influences of his time. Bad as is our political morality, and grievous as are our social short-comings, we are at least awakened to a sense of our sins: and I cannot but ascribe this awakening mainly to Carlyle. What Wordsworth did for poetry, in bringing us out of a conventional idea and method to a true and simple one, Carlyle has done for morality. He may be himself the most curious opposition to himself,—he may be the greatest mannerist of his age while denouncing conventionalism,—the greatest talker while eulogising silence,—the most woeful complainer while glorifying fortitude,—the most uncertain and stormy in mood, while holding forth serenity as the greatest good within the reach of Man: but he has nevertheless infused into the mind of the English nation a sincerity, earnestness, healthfulness and courage which can be appreciated only by those who are old enough to tell what was our morbid state when Byron was the representative of our temper, the Clapham Church of our religion,[1] and the rotten-borough system of our political morality. If I am warranted in believing that the society I am bidding farewell to is a vast improvement upon that which I was born into, I am confident that the blessed change is attributable to Carlyle more than to any single influence besides.

My mornings were, as I have said, reserved for work; and the occasions were very rare when I allowed any encroachment on the hours before two o'clock. Now and then, however, it was necessary; as when the Royal Academy Exhibition opened, and I really could not go, except at the early hour when scarcely any body else was there. The plain truth is that I was so stared at and followed in those days that I had not courage to go (indicated by my trumpet) to public places at their fullest time. Even at the Somerset House Exhibition, in the early morning, when the floors were still wet with watering, I was sure to be

---

[1]   The Clapham sect, as Sydney Smith dubbed them, were Evangelicals who worked on philanthropic projects, including the abolition of slavery. Martineau disliked their religion, not their abolitionism.

discovered and followed. There was a party, I remember, who so pushed upon me, and smiled at me under my bonnet (having recognised me by Evans's portrait on the wall)[1] that my mother exercised her sarcastic spirit with some effect. She said to me, after many vain attempts to get away from the grinning group,—'Harriet, these ladies seem to have some business with us. Shall we ask them how we can be of any service to them?' By Mr. Macready's kindness, we escaped this annoyance at the theatre, where we spent many a pleasant evening. He gave us the stage box, whenever we chose to ask for it; and there my mother, whose sight was failing, could see, and I, deaf as I was, could hear; and nobody saw us behind our curtain, so that we could go in our warm morning dress, and be as free and easy as if we were at home. This was one of my very greatest pleasures,—Macready's interpretation of Shakspere being as high an intellectual treat as I know of.

I have mentioned Evans's portrait of me,—of which Sir A. Callcott said to me, 'What are your friends about to allow that atrocity to hang there?' We could not help it. Mr. Evans was introduced to me by a mutual acquaintance, on the ground that he was painting portraits for a forthcoming work, and wanted mine. I could not have refused without downright surliness; but it appeared afterwards that the artist had other views. I sat to him as often as he wished, though I heartily disliked the attitude, which was one in which I certainly was never seen. The worst misfortune, however, was that he went on painting and painting at the portrait, long after I had ceased to sit,—the result of which was that the picture came out the 'atrocity' that Callcott called it. The artist hawked it about for sale, some years after; and I hope nobody bought it; for my family would be sorry that it should be taken for a representation of me. While on this subject, I must say that I have been not very well used in this matter of portraits. It signifies little now that Mr. Richmond's admirable portrait,[2] and the engraving from it exist to show what I really look like: but before that, my family were rather disturbed at the 'atrocities' issued, without warrant, as likenesses of me;

---

[1] The portrait by Richard Evans (1784–1871), painted 1832–34, is a three-quarter lengths depiction of a thin, unhealthy-looking Martineau in black silk with fur stole. One hand rests on the arm of a chair, the other on a side table. It is now owned by the National Portrait Gallery, London.

[2] George Richmond painted Martineau at the height of her fame in 1833, in one version with right hand to her ear, in a second without this symbol of her deafness. The first version is owned by the Armitt Trust, the second by the National Portrait Gallery. Richmond's portrait of 1849, owned by the National Gallery, shows Martineau in middle age in a simple mob cap.

and especially by Miss Gillies,[1] who covered the land for a course of
years with supposed likenesses of me, in which there was, (as introduced
strangers always exclaimed) 'not the remotest resemblance.' I sat to Miss
Gillies for (I think) a miniature, at her own request, in 1832 and from a
short time after that, she never saw me again. Yet she continued, almost
every year, to put out new portraits of me,—each bigger, more vulgar
and more monstrous than the last, till some of my relations, having seen
those of the 'People's Journal' and the 'New Spirit of the Age,' wrote to
me to ask whether the process could not be put a stop to, as certainly
no person had any business to issue so-called portraits without the sanction of myself or my family, and without even applying to see me after
the lapse of a dozen years. The drollest thing was to see the Editor of
the 'People's Journal,' when we first met.[2] He had been complacent and
gratified, as he told me, about presenting a likeness of me in the Journal;
on which I had made no observation, as it could answer no purpose to
object when the thing was done. When we did meet, his first words
were, as he sank back on the sofa,— 'Ma'am, the portrait! There is not
the remotest resemblance!'

I think there were fourteen or fifteen bad portraits before Mr.
Richmond's good one was obtained. I need not say that their fabrica-
tion was a disageeable process to me. That is of course: but I could not
prevent them. For some I did not sit: in other cases, I really could not
help myself. I refused to sit; but the artists came, with easel and imple-
ments, and established themselves in a corner of my study, requesting
me to go on with my work, and forget that they were there. The only
one besides Richmond's, and Miss Gillies's first, that has been liked by
any body, as far as I know, is Osgood's, taken in America.[3] I do not
myself think it good. It is too good-looking by far; and the attitude is
melodramatic. But it is like some of my relations, and therefore probably more or less like me. All the rest are, we think, good for less than
nothing.—Two casts have been taken of my head; one in 1833, and one
in 1853. They were taken purely for phrenological purposes. As I have

---

[1]   Margaret Gillies (1803–87), portrait painter.

[2]   Either John Saunders (1810–95) or William Howitt (1792–1879), both editors of the
        People's Journal, though more likely Saunders given her negative comments about Howitt
        (below). This periodical regularly featured portraits and short biographies of exemplary
        figures under the rubric "The People's Portrait Gallery." Margaret Gillies usually supplied
        the portraits, as she did with Martineau's in vol. 1 (March 14, 1846), p. 141.

[3]   Charles Osgood (1809–90), American painter. This portrait is now in the Essex Institute,
        Salem, Massachusetts.

bequeathed my skull and brain, for the same objects, I should not have thought it necessary to have a second cast taken (to verify the changes made by time) but for the danger of accident which might frustrate my arrangements. I might die by drowning at sea; or by a railway smash, which would destroy the head: so I made all sure by having a cast taken, not long before my last illness began.

It may be as well to explain here some transactions which might appear strange, if their reasons and their course were not understood. At the time of my removal to London, the special horror of the day was the Burke and Hare murders; and all wits were set to work to devise a remedy for the scarcity of bodies for dissection which bred such phenomena as the Burkes and Hares. The mischief was that the only authorised supply was from the gallows; and disgrace was added to the natural dislike of the idea of dissection. Good citizens set to work in various ways to dissolve the association of disgrace with *post mortem* dissection. Some sold the reversion of their bodies; and others followed Bentham's example of leaving his body for dissection, by an express provision of his will. I, being likely to outlive my only remaining parent, and to have no nearer connexion, did this, when my new earnings obliged me to make a new will in 1832. The passage of Mr. Warburton's bill, and its success, relieved the necessity of the case; and in my next will, the arrangement was omitted. This was one of the transactions I referred to. The next was much later in date. When I found that, easy as it is to procure brains and skulls, it is not easy to obtain those of persons whose minds are well known, so that it is rather a rare thing to be able to compare manifestations with structure, I determined to do what I could to remedy the difficulty by bequeathing my skull and brain to the ablest phrenologist I knew of; and this I did in the will rendered necessary by the acquisition of my Ambleside property. Soon after that will was made, I received a letter from Mr. Toynbee,[1] the well-known benevolent surgeon, enclosing a note of introduction from a mutual friend, and going straight to the point on which he wished to address me. He laid before me the same consideration in regard to cases of deafness that I have set down above in connexion with phrenology generally, saying that it is easy enough to obtain the skulls of deaf persons, in order to study the structure of the ear; and it is very easy to meet with deaf people in life; but it is very difficult to obtain the defunct ears of persons whose

---

[1] Dr. Joseph Toynbee (1815–66), aural surgeon, amassed a large collection of human ears with various diseases and defects, and later bequeathed it to the Royal College of Surgeons.

deafness has been a subject of observation during life. He therefore requested me to leave him a legacy of my ears. He added a few words, in explanation of his plain speaking, about the amount of mischief and misery caused by the ignorance of surgeons in regard to the ear; an ignorance which can be removed only by such means as he proposed. I was rather amused when I caught myself in a feeling of shame, as it were, at having only one pair of ears;—at having no duplicate for Mr. Toynbee after having disposed otherwise of my skull. I told him how the matter stood; and my legatee and he met, to ascertain whether one head could in any way be made to answer both their objects. It could not be, and Mr. Toynbee could not be gratified. I called on him in London afterwards, and showed him as much as he could see while I was alive: and he showed me his wonderful collection of preparations, by which malformation and impaired structure of the ear are already largely illustrated. This is the other transaction which I referred to, and which may as well be distinctly understood, as I do not at all pride myself on doing odd things which may jar upon people's natural feelings.

Two or three times during my residence in London, I was requested to allow my head to be pronounced upon by professional phrenologists, under precautions against their knowing who I was. I entirely disapprove, and always did, that summary way of deciding on the characters of utter strangers, whose very curiosity is a kind of evidence of their not being in a state to hear the sober truth;[1] while the imperfect knowledge of the structure of the brain at that time, and our present certainty of the complexity of its action, must obviate all probability of an accurate judgment being formed. At the time I speak of, every body was going to Deville,[2] to see his collection of bronzes, and to sit down under his hands, and hear their own characters,—for which they paid down their half-sovereigns, and came away, elated or amused. Among those who so

---

[1] Phrenologists believed that specific areas of the skull corresponded with moral and intellectual characteristics; for example, a prominent "bump" on the forehead would indicate that the individual had a well-developed "organ of benevolence" and thus would exhibit benevolent behavior.

[2] James De Ville (1777–1846), sometimes spelled Deville, apprenticed as a moulder in plaster and in 1803 opened his own plaster works in Soho. In 1817 he began to collect phrenological specimens, and by 1821 was taking moulds from living subjects. In 1824 De Ville published a standardized plaster bust demonstrating the layout of the phrenological organs with an explanatory booklet. He also began to "read" heads and give private lectures in his museum-shop. Despite his working-class dialect, which was often ridiculed by his middle-class and aristocratic clients, he became the most prominent practical phrenologist, supplier, and maker of phrenological casts in London from the 1820s to 1840s.

went was a remarkable trio,—of whom Lord Lansdowne and Sydney Smith were two; and I think, but am not sure, that Jeffrey was the third. They went on foot, and avoided naming each other, and passed for ordinary visitors. Lord Lansdowne, to whom was consigned at that time, on account of his aptitude for detail, all the small troublesome business of the Cabinet which every body else was glad to escape, was pronounced by Deville to be liable to practical failure at every turn by his tendency to lose himself in the abstract, and neglect particulars. What he said to Jeffrey (if Jeffrey it was) I forget; but it was something which amused his companions excessively. 'This gentleman's case,' said Deville of Sydney Smith, 'is clear enough. His faculties are those of a naturalist, and I see that he gratifies them. This gentleman is always happy, among his collections of birds and of fishes.' 'Sir,' said Sydney Smith, turning round upon him solemnly, with wide open eyes, 'I don't know a fish from a bird.' Of about the same accuracy was Deville's judgment of me. We were a large party,—seven or eight,—of whom my mother was one, and three others were acquaintances of Deville's. It was agreed that his friends should take the rest of us, as if to see the bronzes; that I should hide my trumpet in a bag, and that nobody should name me (or my mother) or speak to me as to a deaf person. We were certain to be invited by Deville, they said, to hear a little address on Phrenology; and he would then propose to pronounce on the character of any one of the company. I was instructed to take my seat at the end of the group, nearest Deville's right hand, and to take off my bonnet at a certain signal. All went exactly as foreseen. For some time, the party listened gravely enough to the oracle which I heard mumbling above my head; but at length all burst into a roar of laughter. Mr. Deville pronounced that my life must be one of great suffering, because it was a life of constant failure through timidity. I could never accomplish any thing, through my remarkable deficiency in both physical and moral courage. My mother then observed that it was so far true that I was the most timid child she had ever known. Satisfied with this, Deville proceeded. Amidst some truer things, he said I had wit. Some very properly denied this; but one exclaimed, 'Well, I say that any one who has read Miss Martineau's poor-law tale . . . . . .' And now the murder was out. Deville was much discomposed,—said it was not fair,—desired to do it all over again, —to come to our house and try, and so forth: but we told him that the whole proceeding was spontaneous on his own part, and that he had better leave the matter where it was. An amended judgment could not be worth any thing.—Another time, I went with my friends, Mr. and Mrs. F., to call on Mr. Holm the

Phrenologist.[1] They had some acquaintance with him, and had an appointment with him, to have him pronounce on Mrs. F.'s head. Mrs. F. thought this a good opportunity to obtain an opinion of my case; and I therefore accompanied her,—no trumpet visible, and no particular notice being taken of me. Mr. Holm pronounced my genius to be for millinery. He said that it was clear, by such and such tokens, that I was always on the look out for tasteful bonnets and caps: and that, my attention being fixed on one at a shop window, I should go home and attempt to make one like it; and should succeed. Such was the sum and substance of his judgment. I afterwards, at his request, attended a few private lectures of his, in a class of three members, the other two being the Duke of Somerset and Rammohun Roy.[2] I really used to pity the lecturer when, from the brain or cast which he held in his hand, he glanced at the heads of his pupils: for the Duke of Somerset had a brown wig, coming down low on his forehead: Rammohun Roy had his turban just above his eyebrows; and I, of course, had my bonnet. No one who knows me will suppose that in thus speaking of so-called phrenologists and their empirical practices, I am in the slightest degree reflecting on that department of physiological science. It is because such empirical practice is insulting and injurious to true science that I record my own experience of it. The proceedings of the fortune-telling oracles, which pronounce for fees, are no more like those of true and philosophical students of the brain than the shows of itinerant chemical lecturers, who burned blue lights, and made explosions, and electrified people half a century ago are like the achievements of a Davy or a Faraday.

One of my rare morning expeditions was to see Coleridge, at his Highgate residence.[3] I cannot remember on what introduction I went,

---

1   Probably the Joseph Fishers of Highbury, mentioned on pp. 285–86. The London phrenologist J.D. Holm was a friend of the famous Austrian phrenologist Johann Gaspar Spurzheim, who bequeathed his collection of skulls and casts to Holm in 1832.

2   Edward Adolphus Seymour (1804–85), 12th Duke of Somerset; Rammohun Roy (1773–1833), Indian educator and religious teacher, also mentioned in Period IV, sec. i.

3   In 1816 Samuel Taylor Coleridge (1772–1834) moved into Moreton House, the home of the surgeon Dr. James Gilman, who helped him in his struggle with opium addiction and suicidal depression. The *Reminiscences of Samuel Taylor Coleridge and Robert Southey* by Joseph Cottle (London: Houlston and Stoneman, 1847), the Unitarian publisher who encouraged Coleridge's early work and published the *Lyrical Ballads* in 1798, revealed Coleridge's extra-marital love for Sara Hutchinson and "sad habits" of addiction. Coleridge's periodical *The Friend*, which called itself "a literary, moral, and political weekly paper," ran for 28 issues in 1809–10.

nor whether I went alone: but I remember a kind reception by Mr. and Mrs. Gilman, and by Coleridge himself. I was a great admirer of him as a poet then, as I am, to a more limited extent, now. If I had thought of the man then as I have been compelled by Cottle's Life to think of him since, I should not have enacted the hypocrisy of going to see him, in the mode practiced by his worshippers. In these days, when it is a sort of fashion among wise men of all opinions to insist upon the disconnexion of religion and morals, one may have a strong sympathy with a man or a writer of eloquent religious sensibilities, even if his moral views or conduct may be unsatisfactory. But then, the religious eloquence must be of a sounder intellectual quality than Coleridge's appears to me to be. In truth, I do not know how to escape the persuasion that Coleridge was laughing in his sleeve while writing some of the characteristic pieces which his adorers go into raptures about. A great deal of cloud-beauty there is in the climate and atmosphere of his religious writings; and if his disciples would not attempt to make this charm, and his marvellous subtlety, go for more than they are worth, one could have no objection to any amount of admiration they could enjoy from such a source. But those who feel as strongly as I do the irreverence and vanity of making the most solemn and sacred subjects an opportunity for intellectual self-indulgence, for paradox, and word-play and cloud-painting, and cocoon-spinning out of one's own interior, will feel certain that the prophecied immortality of Coleridge will be not so much that of his writings as of himself, as an extreme specimen of the tendencies of our metaphysical period, which, being itself but a state of transition, can permit no immortality to its special products but as historical types of its characteristics and tendencies. If Coleridge should be remembered, it will be as a warning,—as much in his philosophical as his moral character.—Such is my view of him now. Twenty years ago I regarded him as poet,—in his 'Friend' as much as his verse. He was, to be sure, a most remarkable looking personage, as he entered the room, and slowly approached and greeted me. He looked very old, with his rounded shoulders and drooping head, and excessively thin limbs. His eyes were as wonderful as they were ever represented to be; —light grey, extremely prominent, and actually glittering: an appearance I am told common among opium eaters. His onset amused me not a little. He told me that he (the last person whom I should have suspected) read my tales as they came out on the first of the month; and, after paying some compliments, he avowed that there were points on which we differed: (I was full of wonder that there were any on which we agreed:) 'for instance,' said he, 'you appear to consider that society is an aggregate of individuals.' I replied that I certainly did: whereupon he went off on one of the several metaphysical interpretations which may be put upon the many-sided fact of an organised human society, subject to natural laws in virtue of its aggregate character and organisation together. After a long flight in survey of society from his own balloon in his own current, he came down again to some considerations of individuals, and at length to some special biographical topics, ending with criticisms on old biographers, whose venerable works he brought down from the shelf. No one else spoke, of course, except when I once or twice put a question; and when his monologue came to what seemed a natural stop, I rose to go. I am glad to have seen his weird face, and heard his dreamy voice; and my notion of possession, prophecy,—of involuntary speech from involuntary brain action, has been clearer since. Taking the facts of his life together with his utterance, I believe the philosophy and moralising of Coleridge to be much like the action of Babbage's machine;[1] and his utterance to be about equal in wonder to the numerical results given out by the mechanician's instrument. Some may think that the philosophical and theological expression has more beauty than the numerical, and some may not: but all will agree that the latter issues from sound premises, while few will venture to say that the other has any reliable basis at all. Coleridge appears to me to have been constitutionally defective in will, in conscientiousness and in apprehension of the real and true, while gifted or cursed with inordinate reflective and analogical faculties, as well as prodigious word power. Hence his success as an instigator of thought in others,[2] and as a talker and writer; while utterly failing in his apprehension of truth, and in the conduct of his life.

The mention of Coleridge reminds me, I hardly know why, of Godwin,[3] who was an occasional morning visitor of mine. I looked upon him as a curious monument of a bygone state of society; and there was still a good deal that was interesting about him. His fine head was striking, and his countenance remarkable. It must not be judged of by the

---

[1] I.e., a machine to make complex mathematical computations.

[2] Coleridge's *Aids to Reflection* (1825) were, as Martineau knew, deeply influential on John Sterling, Charles Kingsley, and other Christian Socialists.

[3] William Godwin (1756–1836), atheist and political radical, husband of Mary Wollstonecraft, and author of several novels, including *Caleb Williams* (1794), which defends Radicals accused of high treason (including his friends and fellow-writers Horne Tooke and Thomas Holcroft).

pretended likeness put forth in Fraser's Magazine about that time,[1] and attributed, with the whole set, to Maclise, then a young man, and, one would think, in great need of one sort or another, if he could lend himself to the base method of caricaturing shown in those sketches. The high Tory favourites of the Magazine were exhibited to the best advantage; while Liberals were represented as Godwin was. Because the finest thing about him was his noble head, they put on a hat: and they presented him in profile because he had lost his teeth, and his lips fell in. No notion of Godwin's face could be formed from that caricature: and I fear there was no other portrait, after the one corresponding to the well-known portrait of Mary Wollstonecraft.[2] It was not for her sake that I desired to know Godwin; for, with all the aid from the admiration with which her memory was regarded in my childhood, and from my own disposition to honour all promoters of the welfare and improvement of Woman, I never could reconcile my mind to Mary Wollstonecraft's writings, or to whatever I heard of her. It seemed to me, from the earliest time when I could think on the subject of Woman's Rights and condition, that the first requisite to advancement is the self-reliance which results from self-discipline. Women who would improve the condition and chances of their sex must, I am certain, be not only affectionate and devoted, but rational and dispassionate, with the devotedness of benevolence, and not merely of personal love. But Mary Wollstonecraft was, with all her powers, a poor victim of passion, with no control over her own peace, and no calmness or content except when the needs of her individual nature were satisfied. I felt, forty years ago, in regard to her, just what I feel now in regard to some of the most conspicuous denouncers of the wrongs of women at this day;—that their advocacy of Woman's cause becomes mere detriment, precisely in proportion to their personal reasons for unhappiness, unless they have fortitude enough (which loud complainants usually have not) to get their own troubles under their feet, and leave them wholly out of the account in stating the state of their sex. Nobody can be further than I am from being satisfied with the condition of my own sex, under

---

[1]   Godwin's portrait appeared in *Fraser's Magazine* in October 1836, as part of a series by Daniel Maclise (1806–70), the Irish portrait painter. Martineau's portrait appeared in November 1833; she, too, was depicted satirically because of her radical views.

[2]   Mary Wollstonecraft (1759–97), author of *Thoughts on the Education of Daughters* (1787), *A Vindication of the Rights of Man* (1790, a reply to Edmund Burke's *Reflections on the Revolution in France*), and *A Vindication of the Rights of Woman* (1792). She died giving birth to the future Mary Shelley. Martineau's judgment of Wollstonecraft as "a poor victim of passion" derives from learning, via Godwin's 1798 *Memoir* of his wife, of her love affair with Gilbert Imlay, her illegitimate daughter by him, and two suicide attempts after his desertion.

the law and custom of my own country; but I decline all fellowship and co-operation with women of genius or otherwise favourable position, who injure the cause by their personal tendencies. When I see an eloquent writer insinuating to every body who comes across her that she is the victim of her husband's carelessness and cruelty, while he never spoke in his own defence: when I see her violating all good taste by her obtrusiveness in society, and oppressing every body about her by her epicurean selfishness every day, while raising in print an eloquent cry on behalf of the oppressed; I feel, to the bottom of my heart, that she is the worst enemy of the cause she professes to plead.[1] The best friends of that cause are women who are morally as well as intellectually competent to the most serious business of life, and who must be clearly seen to speak from conviction of the truth, and not from personal unhappiness. The best friends of the cause are the happy wives and the busy, cheerful, satisfied single women, who have no injuries of their own to avenge, and no painful vacuity or mortification to relieve. The best advocates are yet to come,—in the persons of women who are obtaining access to real social business,—the female physicians and other professors in America, the women of business and the female artists of France; and the hospital administrators, the nurses, the educators and substantially successful authors of our own country. Often as I am appealed to to speak, or otherwise assist in the promotion of the cause of Woman, my answer is always the same:—that women, like men, can obtain whatever they show themselves fit for. Let them be educated,—let their powers be cultivated to the extent for which the means are already provided, and all that is wanted or ought to be desired will follow of course. Whatever a woman proves herself able to do, society will be thankful to see her do,—just as if she were a man. If she is scientific, science will welcome her, as it has welcomed every woman so qualified. I believe no scientific woman complains of wrongs. If capable of political thought and action, women will obtain even that. I judge by my own case. The time has not come which certainly will come, when women who are practically concerned

---

[1] These sentences have been read as an attack on Caroline Norton (1808–77), who was estranged from her husband (a man who accused her of adultery, and claimed a legal right to her income and to the custody of their children). In the 1830s and 40s Norton wrote poems addressing contemporary social conditions, *A Voice from the Factories* (1836) and *A Child of the Islands* (1845), as well as political pamphlets exposing the lack of legal rights for women. Her 1855 *Letter to the Queen on Lord Chancellor Cranworth's Marriage and Divorce Bill* influenced the passage of the Matrimonial Causes Act of 1857 and appeared as Martineau was writing the *Autobiography*.

in political life will have a voice in making the laws which they have to obey; but every woman who can think and speak wisely, and bring up her children soundly, in regard to the rights and duties of society, is advancing the time when the interests of women will be represented, as well as those of men. I have no vote at elections, though I am a tax-paying housekeeper and responsible citizen; and I regard the disability as an absurdity, seeing that I have for a long course of years influenced public affairs to an extent not professed or attempted by many men. But I do not see that I could do much good by personal complaints, which always have some suspicion or reality of passion in them. I think the better way is for us all to learn and to try to the utmost what we can do, and thus to win for ourselves the consideration which alone can secure us rational treatment. The Wollstonecraft order set to work at the other end, and, as I think, do infinite mischief; and, for my part, I do not wish to have any thing to do with them. Every allowance must be made for Mary Wollstonecraft herself, from the constitution and singular environment which determined her course: but I have never regarded her as a safe example, nor as a successful champion of Woman and her Rights.

Nothing struck me more in Godwin than an order of attributes which were about the last I should have expected to find in him. I found him cautious, and even timid. I believe this is often the case, towards the close of life, with reformers who have suffered in their prime for their opinions: but in Godwin's case, it was not about matters of opinion only that he was timid. My mother and I went, with a mutual friend, to tea at the Godwins' little dwelling under the roof of the Houses of Parliament, just before I went to America.[1] Godwin had a small office there, with a salary, a dwelling, and coals and candle; and very comfortable he seemed there, with his old wife to take care of him. He was so comfortable that he had evidently no mind to die. Three times in the course of that evening, he asked questions or made a remark on the intended length of my absence, ending with 'When you come back, I shall be dead:' or 'When you come back, you will visit my grave,'— evidently in the hope that I should say 'No, you will see me return.' I was much amused at the issue of a sudden impulse of complaisance towards me, under which he offered me letters of introduction to various friends and correspondents of his in America. I accepted the offer

---

[1] In 1833 Godwin was given a sinecure, officially "yeoman usher of the exchequer," and an office in New Palace Yard near the old House of Commons. His second wife was the former Mrs. Clairmont, whom he had married in 1801 after Mary Wollstonecraft's death.

exactly as I accepted every offer of the kind,—with thanks, and an explanation that my friends must not take it amiss if their letters should chance
not to be delivered, as I could not at all tell beforehand what would be
the extent or the circumstances of my American travel: and I observed
to my mother that this precaution might be particularly necessary in the
case of Mr. Godwin's introductions, if they should chance to be
addressed to persons whose views bore no relation to the politics of their
time and their republic. On the next Sunday, in came Godwin, in evident
uneasiness and awkwardness. He threw his gloves into his hat, as if
preparing for some great effort; and then he told me, with reluctance
and confusion, that he wished to recal his offer of letters to his American
correspondents; for this reason:—that I should be known there as a political economist; and, if he introduced me, it might be supposed that he
had changed his views in his old age, and become one of the order of
men against whom he had written in his earlier years. I told him I
thought he was quite right; and his spirits rose immediately when he
saw I was not offended.—I liked best getting him to speak of his novels;
and at times he was ready enough to gratify me. He told me, among
other things, that he wrote the first half of 'Caleb Williams' in three
months, and then stopped for six, —finishing it in three more. This pause
in the middle of a work so intense seems to me a remarkable incident.
I have often intended to read 'Caleb Williams' again, to try whether I
could find the stopping place: but it has never fallen in my way, and I
have not seen the book since my youth.

   That last evening at Godwin's was a memorable one to me. The place
is gone, and all who were there are dead except myself. Before it grew too
dusk (it was in July) Godwin took us through the passages of that old
Parliament House, and showed us the Star Chamber, and brought the old
tallies for us to examine, that we might finger the notches made by the
tax-collectors before accounts were kept as now. Within three months
those tallies burnt down that Star Chamber, and both Houses of
Parliament.[1] They burned old Godwin's dwelling too. His good wife saved
him from a fright and anxiety which might have destroyed him at once.
He was at the theatre; and she would not have him called, but packed and
removed his goods, and so managed as that he was met and told the story
like any body else. He was, however, dead before my return, as he had said

---

[1]   Martineau refers to the burning of the old Houses of Parliament on October 16, 1834.
      The fire, which destroyed almost everything except Westminster Hall, the Cloisters, and
      the Jewel Tower, was caused by burning a large quantity of elm sticks (used as tally sticks
      to keep the Exchequer's accounts) in a large furnace beneath the Lords' Chamber.

he should be. When I returned, he was in his grave; and faithful friends were taking kind care of the wife who had done so much for him.

Another old man, of a very different order, was a pretty frequent visitor of mine, and always a kind one,—Mr. Basil Montagu.[1] He, with his venerable head, and his majestic-looking lady were occasionally the ornaments of my evening parties: and I was well acquainted with the Procters, Mrs. Montagu's daughter and son-in-law.[2] I was always glad to see Mr. Procter in any drawing-room I entered. It was delightful to know the 'Barry Cornwall' who won his first fame when I was living on poetry, down at Norwich, and when his exquisite metres were on my tongue or in my head day and night: but all I found in him supported and deepened the interest with which I met him. He was always so kind and courteous, so simple and modest, so honest and agreeable that I valued his acquaintance highly, and have continued to do so, to this day.—As for Mr. Montagu, his benevolence was the first attraction; and the use of the gallows had not then been so long restricted as to permit the efforts of our Romillys and our Montagus to be forgotten. No one man perhaps did so much for the restriction of the punishment of death as Mr. Montagu; and none based the cause on so deep a ground. I was not aware of Mr. Montagu's philosophy till the latest period of my acquaintance with him. I wish I had been; but he was timid in the avowal of it to a wholly unnecessary, and, I think, faulty degree. Before his death, he distinctly declared in a message to me his approbation of the avowal which his friend Mr. Atkinson[3] and I had made of opinions like his own: and, if he could have lived to see how little harm, and how much good, the avowal has done us, he would have regretted his own caution,—though it was more justifiable in his time than it would have been in ours. I imagine that his curious strain of sentimentality was,—(as far as it was his at all, but I have always believed his lady to have intervened in that case)—to cover up to himself and others the differences between himself and others;—an attempt to find a ground of sympathy, when the broadest and firmest did not exist.

The rising up of his countenance before me as I write reminds me of an occasion when he drew me away from my morning work, to occupy

---

[1]   Basil Montagu (1770–1851) was a prolific writer on legal issues.

[2]   Brian Waller Procter (1787–1874), a.k.a. Barry Cornwall, achieved popular success with his songs and lyrics, though Keats and Shelley dismissed his work and the poet-critic George Darley (1795–1846) complained of his "eternal cud of rose-leaves."

[3]   Henry George Atkinson (1815?- 84), mesmerist, phrenologist, and amateur philosopher, with whom Martineau published *Letters on the Laws of Man's Nature and Development* (London: John Chapman, 1851).

an odd place, and witness a remarkable scene. I found a note from him on the breakfast table, one morning, to say that he would call at ten o'clock, and take me down to Westminster, to witness the trial of the Canadian prisoners, on whose behalf Mr. Roebuck was to plead that day. So early an hour was named, that I might be well placed for hearing. All London was in excitement about this trial, which followed the Canadian rebellion,[1] and the Court was daily crowded. My sister Rachel was with us at the time, and she was glad to accompany Mr. Montagu and me. Early as we were, the Court was full;—completely crowded to the back of the galleries. Mr. Montagu looked in at every door, and then committed us to the charge of one of the ushers while he disappeared for five minutes. He returned, threw his cloak over the arm of the usher, gave us each an arm, in perfect silence, and led us through a long succession of passages till we arrived at a door which he opened, lifting up a red curtain, and pushing us in. To our amazement and consternation, we found ourselves on the Bench, facing the sea of heads in the Court. It was dreadful; and at first, I crouched behind a bulwark: but we agreed that there was nothing to be done. There we were: Mr. Montagu had disappeared; and we could not help ourselves. The only vacant bench in the Court below was presently filled. In came the Canadian prisoners, and seated themselves there. We could hardly believe our eyes, but the men wore hand-cuffs, and we saw the gleam of the steel as they moved. Our consultation about this, and our observation of the prisoners while talking about it made us the subject of the hoax of the day.—We saw the prisoners lay their heads together, and make inquiries of their attendants; and then there was some bustle about handing paper, pen and ink to them. Presently a letter appeared, travelling over the heads of the crowd, and handed from counsel to counsel till it was presented to me by the one nearest the bench. It was a note of compliment and gratitude from the *chef* of the prisoners. Plenty of lawyers were in a minute pressing pen, ink and paper on me; and I again crouched down and wrote a civil line of reply, which was handed to my new correspondent. We found ourselves particularly stared at till we could bear it no longer, and slipped away,—meeting Mr. Montagu in time to save us from losing ourselves in the labyrinth of passages. We did not know till some time afterwards what pathos there was in the stare which followed the notes. A waggish acquaintance of ours was among the lawyers in the Court. He put on a grave look during

---

[1]   The Canadian rebellion of 1837, in response to which Lord John Russell condemned the protesters and, in January 1838, introduced a bill to suspend the Constitution of Lower Canada.

the transmission of the notes; and then, hearing speculation all round as to who we were, he whispered to one and another,— 'Don't you know? They are the wives of the Canadian prisoners.' As he intended, the news spread through the Court, and our countenances were watched with all due compassion. I am afraid we were pronounced to be very unfeeling wives, if we might be judged by our dress and demeanour.

When my morning work was done, there was usually a curious variety of visitors, such as it bewilders me more to think of now than it did to receive at the time. More than once, my study door was thrown open, and a Frenchman, Italian or German stood on the threshold, with one hand on his heart and the other almost touching the top of the door, clearing his throat to recite an ode, of which he wanted my opinion. Sometimes it was a lady from the country, who desired to pour her sorrows into my bosom, and swear eternal friendship. This kind of visitor could never be made to understand that it takes two to make a friendship; and that there was no particular reason why I should enter into it with a perfect stranger. By such as these I was favoured with the information that they had inquired my character before coming,—whether I was amiable and so forth; but they seemed to forget that I knew nothing of them. Sometimes some slight acquaintance or another would enter with a companion, and engage me in conversation while the companion took possession of a sheet of my writing paper, or even asked me for a pencil, sketched me, and put the sketch into her reticule; by which time the ostensible visitor was ready to go away. Sometimes my pen was filched from the inkstand, still wet, and taken away to be framed or laid up in lavender. Sometimes ambitious poets, or aspirants to poetic honours, obtained an introduction, on purpose to consult me as to how they should do their work. One young clergyman I remember, who felt that he was made for immortality in the line of Shaksperian tragedy; but he wanted my opinion as to whether he should begin in that way at once, or try something else; and especially, whether or not I should advise him to drink beer. Amidst such absurd people, whose names I have long forgotten, there were many agreeable visitors, beside the multitude whom I have sketched above, who made that time of the day exceedingly pleasant. It was then that I saw Dr. Chalmers[1] on his visits to town. His topics

---

[1]   Thomas Chalmers (1780–1847), professor of mathematics, then of moral philosophy at St. Andrews University, was an advocate of improving living conditions for the Scottish poor and a prolific writer on social welfare. His stance against the authority of the Established Church of Scotland in matters pertaining to local congregations led to disruption in the Church and the formation of the Free Church of Scotland, with Chalmers as its first Moderator.

were pauperism and (in those antediluvian days before the ark of the Free Church was dreamed of) the virtues of religious establishments: and fervid and striking was his talk on these and every other subject. Mr. Chadwick,[1] then engaged on the Poor-law, was a frequent visitor,—desiring to fix my attention on the virtues of centralisation,—the vices of which in continental countries were not then so apparent as they have since become. One always knew what was coming when he entered the room; and indeed, so busy a man could not make morning calls, but for the promotion of business. I regarded his visit, therefore, as a lesson; and I never failed to learn much from the master,—the first of our citizens, I believe, who fairly penetrated the foul region of our sanitary disorders, and set us to work to reform them. It might be that his mind was an isolated one; and his faculty narrow and engrossed with detail, so that it was necessary at length to remove him from the administrative position to which his services seemed to entitle him: but there is no question of his social usefulness in instituting the set of objects which he was found unequal to carry out. Twenty years ago, he was just discovered by the Whig Ministers, and he was himself discovering his own department of action. He was a substantial aid to me while I was writing about social evils and reforms; and he has gone on to supply me with valuable information, from that day to this,—from his first exposition of the way in which country justices aggravated pauperism under the old law, to the latest improvement in hollow bricks and diameter of drains.—Judging by the reforms then discussed in my study, that period of my life seems to be prodigiously long ago. Several of the beneficent family of the Hills came on their respective errands,—penny postage, prison administration, juvenile crime reformation, and industrial and national education.[2] Mr. Rowland Hill was then pondering his scheme, and ascertaining the facts which he was to present with so remarkable an accuracy. His manner in those days,—his slowness, and hesitating speech,—were not recommendatory of his doctrine to those who would not trouble themselves to discern its excellence and urgent

---

[1]   Edwin Chadwick (1800–90), social reformer responsible for the *Report … on an Enquiry into the Sanitary Condition of the Labouring Population of Great Britain* (1842) and the *Report on … the Practice of Interment in Towns* (the "Burials Report," 1843), which led to important reforms in urban sewage and drainage systems.

[2]   Rowland Hill (1795–1879) wrote *Post Office Reform: Its Importance and Practicability* (1837), which argued the need for pre-printed envelopes and adhesive postage. He is credited with the introduction of uniform penny postage (one penny per half-ounce a letter to anywhere in the British Isles), which took effect on January 10, 1840. Prior to this reform, the cost of postage depended on the number of sheets in the letter and the distance it traveled.

need. If he had been prepossessing in manner and fluent and lively in speech, it might have saved him half his difficulties, and the nation some delay: but he was so accurate, so earnest, so irrefragable in his facts, so wise and benevolent in his intentions, and so well timed with his scheme, that success was, in my opinion, certain from the beginning; and so I used to tell some conceited and shallow members and adherents of the Whig government, whose flippancy, haughtiness and ignorance about a matter of such transcendent importance tried my temper exceedingly. Rowland Hill might and did bear it; but I own I could not always. Even Sydney Smith was so unlike himself on this occasion as to talk and write of 'this nonsense of a penny postage:' as if the domestic influences fostered by it were not more promotive of moral good than all his preaching, or that of any number of his brethren of the cloth! Lord Monteagle got the nickname of 'the footman's friend,'[1] on that occasion, —the 'Examiner' being a firm and effective friend of Rowland Hill and his scheme. Lord Monteagle, who is agreeable enough in society to those who are not very particular in regard to sincerity, was, as Chancellor of the Exchequer or any thing else, as good a representative as could be found of the flippancy, conceit, and official helplessness and ignorance of the Whig administrations. He actually took up Rowland Hill's great scheme, to botch and alter and restrict it. With entire complacency he used to smile it down at evening parties, and lift his eyebrows at the credulity of the world, which could suppose that a scheme so wild could ever be tried: but he condescended to propose that it should supersede the London twopenny post. The 'Examiner' immediately showed that the operation would be to save flunkeys the fatigue of carrying ladies' notes; and Lord Monteagle was forthwith dubbed 'the footman's friend,'—a title which has perversely rushed into my memory, every time I have seen him since. The alteration in Rowland Hill himself, since he won his tardy victory, is an interesting spectacle to those who knew him twenty years ago. He always was full of domestic tenderness and social amiability; and these qualities now shine out, and his whole mind and manners are quickened by the removal of the cold obstruction he encountered at the beginning of his career. Grateful as I feel to him, as the most signal social benefactor of our time, it has been a great pleasure to me to see the happy influence of success on the man himself. I really should like to ask the surviving

---

[1]   Thomas Spring Rice (1790–1866), later Lord Monteagle, then chancellor of the exchequer, introduced the legislation to Parliament for the penny-postage scheme on July 5, 1839.

Whig leaders, all round, what they think now of 'the nonsense of the penny postage.'

Good Mr. Porter, of the Board of Trade,[1]—amiable and friendly, industrious and devoted to his business,—but sadly weak and inaccurate, prejudiced and *borné* in ability,—was a frequent and kindly visitor. His office was at hand, when we lived in Fludyer Street; and he found time to look in very often, and to bring me information, sometimes valuable, and sometimes not. His labours, industrious and sincere, were a complete illustration of Carlyle's doctrine about statistics.[2] Nothing could be apparently more square and determinate; while nothing could be in fact more untrustworthy and delusive. Some exposures of his mistakes have been made in parliament; and plenty more could be pointed out by parties qualified to criticise his statements; as, for instance, the Birmingham manufacturers, who find that the spirits of wine used in vast quantities for the burnishing of their goods are set down by Mr. Porter as alcoholic liquor drunk by the English people: and, again, the ship-owners, who find the tonnage of the kingdom estimated by him by the number of ships going to sea or returning in the course of the year,—no allowance being made for ships going more voyages than one. It is a serious injury to the nation that the Whig administrations have employed, to obtain and publish information, such unfortunate agents as Bowring, Macgregor and Porter, whose errors and incompetence any sensible man of business could have informed them of. Many thousands of pounds, much valuable time, and no little exertion, have been spent in actually misinforming the people, on the supposition of procuring valuable facts for them. Bowring and Macgregor were obviously unfitted for such work from the outset, by their vanity, incompetence and unscrupulousness. Mr. Porter was of a far higher order. His innocent vanity, which was far from immoderate, never interfered with his steady labour; and he was honourable, disinterested and generous: but his deficiency in sense and intellectual range, together with his confidence in himself and his want of confidence in all public men, was an insuperable disqualification for his sound discharge of an office

---

[1]   The political economist George Richardson Porter (1792–1852), mentioned earlier as a close friend (see pp. 285–86), was head of the statistical department of the board of trade from 1834, and joint secretary of the board of trade from 1847 to 1852. Edgar Alfred Bowring (1826–1911) served as librarian and registrar to the board of trade from 1848 to 1863. During the 1830s John Macgregor (1797–1857) assembled, with co-author James Hume, a vast work on the commercial statistics of European nations; in 1840 he succeeded Hume as one of the joint secretaries of the board of trade.

[2]   In *Chartism* (1839) Carlyle wrote: "A witty statesman said, you might prove anything by figures."

requiring a wholly different order of mind from his. His intimate friend, his guide and crammer, was David Urquhart,[1] whose accounts of royal, diplomatic and administrative personages he reverently accepted: and this accounts for a good deal of prejudice and perversion of judgment. It was at his table that I saw Mr. Urquhart for the only time that I ever met him. Once was enough; and that once was too like a pantomime to leave the impression of a rational dinner-party. Mr. Urquhart had arrived from Turkey with mighty expectations from what he called the friendship of William IV. But the King was dead, and Victoria reigned in his stead: and the oracle's abuse of the Queen,—a young girl entering upon the most difficult position in the world,—was something wonderful. He railed at her every where and perpetually,—with a vehemence which luckily prevented any harm, such as might have resulted from moderate censure. On the day that I met him, he engrossed the whole conversation, as he sat between our hostess and me. What he gave us, besides abuse of the Queen, was a series of oracular utterances on political doctrine, which he assured me from time to time I was incapable of comprehending; and an intense eulogium on Turkish life, which owed its excellence, political and moral, to the Turkish women being not allowed to learn to read and write. He addressed this to Mrs. Porter (the sister of David Ricardo, and the author of certain books),[2] on the one hand, and to me on the other. His odd ape-like gestures, his insane egotism, his frail figure and pale countenance, and the ferocious discontent which seemed to be consuming his life, left a strange and painful impression on my mind. His mother soon after died happy in the belief that he would be the saviour of his country: and now, after half a lifetime, he seems, by newspaper accounts, to be just the same man, talking in the same mood and style, with no other change than that he has been tried in parliament and has failed, and that he has been constantly moulting his tail, all these years. His adherents have fallen off and been replaced in constant succession. He has never retained any body's confidence long (he lost Mr. Porter's at last) and he has never failed to find impressible, half-informed and credulous people ready to shut their eyes and open their mouths, and swallow what doctrine he should please to give.

[1]   David Urquhart (1805–77), British diplomatist, was sent on several missions to Turkey during the 1830s, but his violently anti-Russia position brought him into conflict with many government officials, including Lord Palmerston, who was then head of the department of foreign affairs. Urquhart was recalled from his missions in 1833 and again in 1837.

[2]   Sarah Porter, née Ricardo (1791–1862), published several educational works, including *The Educator: Prize Essays on the Expediency and Means of Elevating the Profession of the Educator in Society* (London: Taylor & Walton, 1839) under the auspices of the Central Society of Education.

With Mr. Porter came Mr. Duppa,[1] the devoted and indefatigable friend of popular education, and the organiser and support of the Central Society of Education, which diffused some useful knowledge and good views in its day. Some foreigner or another, distinguished by eminence in some department within Mr. Porter's range, often gave me a call, and taught me something, or offered inducements to foreign travel, which I never was able to avail myself of, till the failure of my health made it too late. Mr. Senior[2] used to come and talk about the poor-law, or Ireland. The Combes came and talked about phrenology and educational improvement.[3] Mr. Robertson came to talk of the 'Westminster Review,' of which he was editor, under the direction of Mr. J.S. Mill.[4] He had prodigious expectations from his own genius, and an undoubting certainty of fulfilling a grand career: but he has long sunk out of sight. For fifteen years past, he seems to have been forgotten. I fear he has suffered much, and caused much suffering since the days when I knew him. I never understood him at all; and was duly surprised to find that he represented himself to be my most intimate friend,—philosopher, and guide! but the delusions of his vanity were so many and so gross that one may easily be let pass among the rest.—An even more unintelligible claim to my friendship has been advanced in print by the Howitts.[5] I can only say that I do not remember having seen Mrs. Howitt more

---

1   B[aldwin] F[rancis] Duppa (1828–73) published many practical works, including *The Causes of the Present Condition of the Labouring Classes in the South of England* (London: Saunders and Benning, 1831); *The Education of the Peasantry in England:What it Is, and What it Ought to Be* (London: Charles Knight, 1834); and *A Manual for Mechanics' Institutions* (London: Longman, Orme, Brown, Green, & Longmans, 1839).

2   William Nassau Senior (1790–1864), English economist and member of the Poor Law Inquiry Commission of 1832.

3   George Combe (1788–1858), an Edinburgh lawyer, was an early convert to phrenology and author of *The Constitution of Man in Relation to External Objects* (1828), not about phrenology *per se*, but a work of natural philosophy teaching that man is subject to the same natural laws (physical, organic, and moral) as the rest of nature. His brother Andrew Combe (1797–1847), a Scottish physiologist, investigated phrenology on anatomical principles and defended it before the Royal Medical Society of Edinburgh.

4   John Robertson (1811?- 75), protégé of J.S. Mill and nominal editor of the *Westminster Review* from 1837 to 1840.

5   William (1792–1879) and Mary (1799–1888) Howitt were poets, journalists, and popular educators. Martineau had contributed essays on the Lake District and on education to *The People's Journal* in 1846–47, when it was edited by John Saunders and William Howitt. When the two editors fell out over finances, Howitt bore the costs and created *Howitt's Journal*. Martineau sided with Saunders and ceased contributing, but she certainly knew William Howitt well enough for him to write the biographical sketch that appeared with her portrait in "The People's Portrait Gallery," *People's Journal* I (March 14, 1846), 141–43.

than twice in my life, and that I should not know her by sight: and that I have seen Mr. Howitt about four or five times:—three or four times in London, and once at Tynemouth, when he came with a cousin of mine to cool himself after a walk on the sands, and beg for a cup of tea. This he and Mrs. Howitt have represented in print as visiting me in my illness. Such service as they asked of me in London (to obtain a favourable review of a book of Mr. Howitt's in which he had grossly abused me) I endeavoured to render; but I really was barely acquainted with them; and I was glad the intercourse had gone no further when I witnessed their conduct to their partner in the 'People's Journal,' and in some other affairs. I so greatly admire some of their writings, in which their fine love of nature and their close knowledge of children are unmingled with passion and personal discontent, that I am thankful to enjoy the good their genius provides without disturbance from their unreasonable and turbulent tempers.

One of the most striking of my occasional visitors was Capel Lofft the younger, the author of that wonderful book, the merits of which were discovered by Charles Knight;—'Self-formation,' which should be read by every parent of boys.[1] Those who know the work do not need to be told that the author was a remarkable man: and if they happen to have met with his agrarian epic, 'Ernest,' a poem of prodigious power, but too seditious for publication, they will feel yet more desire to have seen him. When he called on me to ask my advice what to do with his poem, his card revived all I had heard about his eccentric father, the patron of the poet Bloomfield. He was neat and spruce in his dress and appearance,—with his glossy olive coat, and his glossy brown hair, parted down the middle, and his comely and thoughtful face. He was as nervous as his father; and by degrees I came to consider him as eccentric; especially when I found what was his opinion of the feminine intellect, and that his wife, to whom he appeared duly attached, did not know of the existence of his poem. (The Quarterly Review put an end to the secrecy, some time afterwards.) He died early; but not before he had left a name in the world, by his 'Self-formation,' and an impression of power and originality by his formidable epic.—

---

[1]   Capel Lofft (1806–73) published *Self-formation; or, The History of an Individual Mind* in 1837 and *Ernest*, a "Chartist epic poem," in 1839. He inherited the liberal views of his father Capel Lofft (1751–1824), a writer who advocated parliamentary and other reforms and who undertook the publication of *The Farmer's Boy: A Rural Poem* (1800) by the peasant-poet Robert Bloomfield (1766–1823).

Another poet whose face I was always glad to see was Browning.[1] It was in the days when he had not yet seen the Barretts. I did not know them, either. When I was ill at Tynemouth, a correspondence grew up between the then bedridden Elizabeth Barrett and myself; and a very intimate correspondence it became. In one of the later letters, in telling me how much better she was, and how grievously disappointed at being prevented going to Italy, she wrote of going out, of basking in the open sunshine, of doing this and that; 'in short,' said she, finally, 'there is no saying what foolish thing I may do.' The 'foolish thing' evidently in view in this passage was marrying Robert Browning: and a truly wise act did the 'foolish thing' turn out to be. I have never seen my correspondent, for she had gone to Italy before I left Tynemouth; but I knew her husband well, about twenty years ago. It was a wonderful event to me,—my first acquaintance with his poetry.—Mr. Macready put 'Paracelsus' into my hand, when I was staying at his house; and I read a canto before going to bed. For the first time in my life, I passed a whole night without sleeping a wink. The unbounded expectation I formed from that poem was sadly disappointed when 'Sordello' came out. I was so wholly unable to understand it that I supposed myself ill.[2] But in conversation no speaker could be more absolutely clear and purpose-like. He was full of good sense and fine feeling, amidst occasional irritability; full also of fun and harmless satire; with some little affectations which were as droll as any thing he said. A real genius was Robert Browning, assuredly; and how good a man, how wise and morally strong, is proved by the successful issue of the perilous experiment of the marriage of two poets. Her poems were to me, in my sick-room, marvellously beautiful: and, now that from the atmosphere of the sick-room, my life has been transferred to the free open air of real, practical existence, I still think her poetry wonderfully beautiful in its way, while

---

[1] Robert Browning (1812–89) met Elizabeth Barrett (1806–61) in 1845 and married her the next year. The letter from EBB to HM has not been published, but we know that EBB feared a visit from HM in late August or early September, 1846, just when she planned to elope with RB; see *The Letters of Robert Browning and Elizabeth Barrett Barrett, 1845–1846* (London: Smith, Elder, 1899), II, 462, where EBB refers to HM as a "formidable friend" whom unlike Anna Jameson, would not be "contented with a little confidence, ... and ask no questions."

[2] Martineau's response was typical: *Paracelsus* (1835), based on the life of the fifteenth-century physician and exploring the conflict of "love" and "knowledge," was a critical success; *Sordello* (1845), based on the life of a troubadour during the Guelf-Ghibelline wars of the late twelfth and early thirteenth centuries and exploring the political role of the poet, was a critical disaster.

wishing that she was more familiar with the external realities which are needed to balance her ideal conceptions. They are a remarkable pair, whom society may well honour and cherish.

Their friend Miss Mitford came up to town occasionally, and found her way to Fludyer Street.[1] I was early fond of her tales and descriptions, and have always regarded her as the originator of that new style of 'graphic description' to which literature owes a great deal, however weary we may sometimes have felt of the excess into which the practice of detail has run. In my childhood, there was no such thing known, in the works of the day, as 'graphic description:' and most people delighted as much as I did in Mrs. Ratcliffe's gorgeous or luscious generalities,—just as we admired in picture galleries landscapes all misty and glowing indefinitely with bright colours,—yellow sunrises and purple and crimson sunsets,—because we had no conception of detail like Miss Austen's in manners, and Miss Mitford's in scenery, or of Millais' and Wilkie's analogous life pictures, or Rosa Bonheur's adventurous Hayfield at noon-tide.[2] Miss Austen had claims to other and greater honours; but she and Miss Mitford deserve no small gratitude for rescuing us from the folly and bad taste of slovenly indefiniteness in delineation. School-girls are now taught to draw from objects: but in my time they merely copied their masters' vague and slovenly drawings: and the case was the same with writers and readers. Miss Mitford's tales appealed to a new sense, as it were, in a multitude of minds,—greatly to the amazement of the whole circle of publishers, who had rejected, in her works, as good a bargain as is often offered to publishers. Miss Mitford showed me at once that she undervalued her tales, and rested her claims on her plays. I suppose every body who writes a tragedy, and certainly every body who writes a successful tragedy, must inevitably do this. Miss Mitford must have possessed some dramatic requisites, or her success could have not been so decided as it was; but my own opinion always was that her mind wanted the breadth, and her character the depth, necessary for genuine achievement in the highest enterprise of literature. I must say

---

[1]   Mary Russell Mitford (1787–1855) wrote poetry, plays, and a series of popular sketches descriptive of rural life for the *Lady's Magazine*, which were collected in five volumes as *Our Village* (1824–32).

[2]   Martineau contrasts late eighteenth-century generality, as in the romances and travel writing of Ann Radcliffe (1764–1823, also spelled Ratcliffe or Rattcliffe), with the growing realism of the novelist Jane Austen (1775–1817), the essayist Mary Mitford, the Pre-Raphaelite painter John Everett Millais (1829–96), and the genre painters David Wilkie (1785–1841) and Rosa Bonheur (1822–99).

that personally I did not like her so well as I liked her works. The charming *bonhommie* of her writings appeared at first in her conversation and manners; but there were other things which presently sadly impaired its charm. It is no part of my business to pass judgment on her views and modes of life. What concerned me was her habit of flattery, and the twin habit of disparagement of others. I never knew her to respond to any act or course of conduct which was morally lofty. She could not believe in it, nor, of course, enjoy it: and she seldom failed to 'see through' it, and to delight in her superiority to admiration. She was a devoted daughter, where the duty was none of the easiest; and servants and neighbours were sincerely attached to her. The little intercourse I had with her was spoiled by her habit of flattery; but I always fell back on my old admiration of her as soon as she was out of sight, and her 'Village' rose up in my memory. The portrait of her which appeared in (I think) 1854 in the 'Illustrated London News' is one of the most remarkable likenesses I have ever seen:[1] and it recalls a truly pleasant trait of her conduct. Some years ago, Lady Morgan[2] published a furious comment on some unfavourable report of her beauty, at the very same time that Miss Mitford happened to be addressing a sonnet to an artist friend who had taken her portrait;—a morsel of such moral beauty that I was grateful to the friend (whoever it might be) who took the responsibility of publishing it. The absence of personal vanity, the *bonhommie*, and the thoughtful grace of that sonnet contrasted singularly, (and quite undesignedly) with the pettish wrath of the sister author.—When I knew Miss Mitford, she was very intimate with the Talfourds. Mr. Talfourd (as he was then) was one of my occasional visitors; and he was also exulting in his dramatic success as the author of 'Ion.'[3] To see Macready's representation of 'Ion' was a treat which so enraptured London as to swell Talfourd's reputation beyond all rational bounds. I shared the general enthusiasm; and I told Talfourd so; for which I was sorry when I knew better, and learned that the beauty of the play is actually in spite of its undramatic quality. During my absence in America, Talfourd's sudden rise in reputation and success, —professional, parliamentary and literary, was something extraordinary: but the inevitable collapse was not long in coming. His nature was a

---

[1]   *Illustrated London News*, 25 (1854). This portrait is most likely the one by John Lucas, engraved for the 1854 edition of Mitford's *Dramatic Works* and now in the National Portrait Gallery.

[2]   Lady Sydney Morgan (1783–1859), Irish novelist and author of *The Wild Irish Girl* (1806).

[3]   Thomas Noon Talfourd (1795–1854) had success with *Ion* (1836) largely because Charles Macready, the great tragic actor, played the lead role.

kindly, but not a lofty one; and his powers were prodigiously over-rated. He, of whom I had heard in my youth as a sentimental writer in the 'Monthly Repository,' died a judge; but he had outlived his once high reputation, which was a curious accident of the times, and might well mislead him when it misled society in general, for months, if not years. His most intimate friends loved him. By those who knew him less he was less liked,—his habits and manners being inferior to his social pretensions and position.

The most complete specimen of the literary adventurer of our time whom I knew was one who avowed his position and efforts with a most respectable frankness. Mr. Chorley,[1] who early went to town, to throw himself upon it, and see what he could make of it, was still about the same business as long as I knew him. He had a really kind heart, and helpful hands to needy brethren, and a small sort of generosity which was perfectly genuine, I am confident. But his best qualities were neutralised by those which belonged to his unfortunate position,— conceit and tuft-hunting, and morbid dread of unusual opinions, and an unscrupulous hostility to new knowledge. The faults of the 'Athenæum' are well known:—Mr. Chorley assumed to be the sub-editor of the 'Athenæum' at the time I knew him; and I suppose he is so still; and by a reference to it, his qualities, good and bad, may be best conveyed. For a considerable time, I over-rated him, trusting, from his real goodness of heart when his nature had fair play, that he would improve. But I fear,—by what I recently saw of his singular affectations in dress and manners in public places, and by the deteriorating quality of the 'Athenæum,' that the bad influences of his position have prevailed. From him alone,—unless it were also from Mr. Robertson,— I obtained a conception of the life of the literary adventurer as a voca-tion. Every author is in a manner an adventurer; and no one was ever more decidedly so than myself: but the difference between one kind of adventurer and another is, I believe, simply this:—that the one has something to say which presses for utterance, and is uttered at length without a view to future fortunes; while the other has a sort of general inclination toward literature, without any specific need of utterance, and a very definite desire for the honours and rewards of the literary career. Mr. Henry F. Chorley is, at least, an average specimen of the latter class; and perhaps something more. But the position is not a favourable

---

[1]   Henry Fothergill Chorley (1808–72), all-purpose journalist, unsuccessful writer of plays and novels, and music critic for the *Athenæum* (1833–68).

one, intellectually or morally, to the individual, while it is decidedly injurious to the sincerity and earnestness of literature.

I twice saw Miss Landon,—the well known 'L.E.L.' of twenty years ago.[1] Both times it was in our own house that I saw her;—once, when she was accompanying Mrs. A. T. Thomson in her round of calls,[2] and a second time when she came to me for information about her needful preparations for living at Cape Coast Castle,—a cousin of mine having recently undergone an experience of that kind as the wife of the Chief Justice of Sierra Leone. I was at first agreeably surprised by Miss Landon's countenance, voice and manners. I thought her very pretty, kind, simple and agreeable. The second time, it was all so sad that my mother and I communicated to each other our sense of dismay, as soon as the ladies were gone. Miss Landon was listless, absent, melancholy to a striking degree. She found she was all wrong in her provision of clothes and comforts, —was going to take out all muslins and no flannels, and divers pet presents which would go to ruin at once in the climate of Cape Coast. We promised, that day, to go to Dr. Thomson's, and hear her new play before she went: and I could not but observe the countenance of listless gloom with which she heard the arrangement made. Before the day of our visit came round, it was discovered that she had been secretly married, and I saw her no more. The shock of her mysterious death soon followed the uncomfortable impression of that visit.

Miss Edgeworth[3] happened never to be in London during my residence there; but she sought some correspondence with me, both before and after my American travel. Her kindly spirit shone out in her letters, as in all she did; but her vigour of mind and accuracy of judgment had clearly given way, under years and her secluded life. Her epistles,—three or four sheets to my one,—confirmed in me a resolution I had pondered before; to relax my habit of writing in good time; and to make to myself

---

[1]   Laetitia Elizabeth Landon (1802–38), who rose to fame writing love poetry under the initials "L.E.L.," married George Maclean, governor of Cape Coast Colony, and died mysterious shortly after she arrived in Africa—whether by an overdose of prussic acid (intended or inadvertent) or by poison administered by a native mistress in revenge for Maclean's abandonment.

[2]   Mrs. A.T. Thompson, author of a biography of Sir Walter Raleigh (1830). Her husband may have been Dr. Theophilus Thompson (1807–60), physician to the consumption hospital in Marlborough Street during this period.

[3]   Maria Edgeworth (1767–1849), novelist, children's author, and (with her father) writer on education, lived in Edgeworthtown, County Longford, Ireland, all her life; after her father's death in 1817 she was said to be distraught and depressed. Her novel *Helen* appeared in 1834 after a hiatus in her publishing.

such friends, among my nephews and nieces, as that I might rely on some of them for a check, whenever the quality of my writing should seem to deteriorate. A family connexion of Miss Edgeworth's had told me, long before, that there was a garret at Edgeworth's-town full of boxes of manuscript tales of Maria's which would certainly never see the light. This was before the appearance of 'Helen'; and the appearance of 'Helen,' notwithstanding the high ability shown in the first volume, confirmed my dread of going to press too often, and returning to it too late. An infamous hoax, in which Miss Edgeworth was betrayed to ridicule, in company with the whole multitude of eminent living authors, deepened the warning to me. That was a remarkable hoax. I was the only one of the whole order who escaped the toils. This happened through no sagacity of my own, but by my mother's acuteness in detecting a plot.

One day in 1833, when my mother and I were standing by the fire, waiting for the appearance of dinner, a note arrived for me, which I went up to my study to answer;—requesting that my mother and aunt would not wait dinner for me. The note was this:—

'82, Seymour Street, Somer's Town:
'October 4th, 1833.

'Madam,
'A Frenchman named Adolphe Berthier, who says he acted as Courier to you during one of your visits to France, has applied for a situation in my establishment. He says that you will give him a character. May I request the favour of an answer to this note, stating what you know of him.
'I have the honour to be, Madam,
'Your obedient Servant,
'GEORGE MILLAR.

'To Miss Martineau.'

My reply was easy and short. There must be some mistake, as I had never been in France. As I came down with the note, my mother beckoned me into her room, and told me she suspected some trick. There had been some frauds lately by means of signatures fraudulently obtained. She could not see what any body could do to me in that way; but she fancied somebody wanted my autograph. The messenger was a dirty little boy, who could hardly have come from a gentleman's house; and he would not say where he had come from.—I objected that I could not, in courtesy, refuse an answer; and my only idea was that I was mistaken for some other of the many Miss Martineaus of the clan. My mother said she would write the answer in the character of a secretary or deputy: and so she fortunately did. We never thought of the matter again till the great Fraser Hoax burst upon the town,[1]—to the ruin of the moral reputation of the Magazine, though to the intense amusement of all but the sufferers from the plot. Among these, I was not one. My mother's note was there, signed 'E.M.'; and the comment on it was fair enough. After a remark on their failure to get my autograph, the hoaxers observed that my story 'French Wines and Politics' might have saved me the trouble of assuring them that I had never travelled in France. Miss Edgeworth suffered most,—and it really was suffering to her modest and ingenuous nature. She sent a long letter about her lady's-maids,—sadly garrulous in her desire not to injure a servant whom she might have forgotten. The heartless traitors sent a reply which drew forth, as they intended, a mass of twaddle; and having obtained this from her very goodness, they made game of her.— Many of the other replies were characteristic enough. Scott's puzzles me most. I cannot see how there could be one from him, as he died in 1832, and was incapable of writing for long before: and the hoax could hardly have been whole years in preparation. Yet I distinctly remember the universal remark that Scott's was, of all, the most unlike the writer. He called the fictitious applicant a scoundrel, or a rascal, or something of that sort. Coleridge's was good,—'Should be happy to do any thing within my knowledge or power.' But I need say no more, as the whole may be seen by a reference to Fraser's Magazine. All who may look back to it will be of the same mind with every gentleman whom I heard speak of the trick,—that plotter and publisher deserved to be whipped from one end of London to the other.

Among the eminent women who sought my acquaintance by letter, and whom I have never seen, are Fredrika Bremer, and Miss Kelty, the author of the first successful 'religious novel,' 'the Favourite of Nature,' which I remember reading with much pleasure in my youth.[2] Miss Kelty wrote to me when I was ill at Tynemouth, under the notion that I had

---

[1]   See *Fraser's Magazine*, 8 (1833), 624–36. The hoax, as Martineau suggests, involved sending a phony request for a character reference and printing the responses of various famous persons, including Wordsworth, Coleridge, and Leigh Hunt.

[2]   Fredrika Bremer (1801–65), Swedish novelist whose works Mary Howitt translated into English; Bremer published *Homes of the New World: Impressions of America* in 1853. Mary Ann Kelty (1789–1873), a Cambridge writer who was influenced by the Evangelicalism of Charles Simeon, published *Favourite of Nature, A Tale* (1822), *Fireside Philosophy* (1842), and other religious meditations. Her memoir, *Reminiscences of Thought and Feeling*, appeared in 1852.

been her school-fellow some years before I was born. She then sent me her little volume, 'Fireside Philosophy;' and I have lately received from her her autobiography, published under the title of 'Reminiscences of Thought and Feeling.' It is a painfully impressive biography; but its tendency is to indispose me to intercourse with the writer,—sincere and frank and interesting as she appears to be. Systems of religion and philosophy are evidently something very different to her from what they are to me; and I cannot lay open, or submit to controversy, the most solemn and severe subjects of all, when they can be made a means of excitement, and a theme of mere spiritual curiosity. But I am glad to have read the Memoir; and glad that it exists,—painful as it is: for it is a striking emanation of the spirit of the time, and illustration of its experiences. Of the ability, courage and candour of the writer, there can be no question.

If Miss Kelty desired correspondence with me on the ground of the Atkinson Letters, Miss Bremer, I believe, dropped it for the same reason. Miss Bremer also accosted me when I was ill at Tynemouth, in a letter of pretty broken English. Her style is so well known now that I need not describe the mingled sentimentality, fun and flattery of her letters. The flattery, and the want of what we call common sense, rather annoyed me till I was made sure, by her American experiences, that those were her weak points, and quite irremediable. I was a good deal startled, before she went to America, at a little incident which filled me with wonder. A neighbour lent me her novel, 'Brothers and Sisters,' the first volume of which we thought admirable: but the latter part about Socialism, Mesmerism, and all manner of *isms* which she did not at all understand, made us blush as we read. Presently a letter arrived for me from her announcing the approach of a copy of this book, which she hoped I should more or less enjoy, as I had in fact, by my recovery and some other incidents and supposed views of mine, suggested and instigated the book. I mention this, because Miss Bremer may probably have explained the origin of her book in a similar manner elsewhere; and I am really bound to explain that, in that book, she does not represent any views and opinions that I ever had. I fear I did not answer that letter; for, if I remember right, I could not find any thing to say that she would like to hear; for she could not be satisfied with what I can truly say to others, that I enjoy and admire her books exceedingly, after throwing out the 'views' and the romance. The sketches of home life in Sweden are exquisitely done; and their coarseness of morals and manners is evidently merely Swedish, and not attributable to Miss Bremer,—unconscious as she evidently is of any unlikeness to the women around her. Her sentimental pietism is naturally offended by the accounts which have been given her of the Atkinson Letters, as I dare say it would be by the book itself; for philosophical research, with a view to truth, is quite out of her way. As she thinks every woman's influence springs from a hot-bed of sentiment, she naturally supposes that my influence must be destroyed by my having taken root on an opposite ground. But she is not aware how much further sound reason and appeals to science go with the best of our people than a floating religiosity which she proposes through the 'Times' newspaper as the means of reforming the world through the influence of women. Much more than she has lost in England through that singular obtrusion have I, as it proves, gained by a directly opposite method of proceeding. But I dare say it would be difficult to convince her of this, and painful to her, in her life of dreams, to be so convinced. I hoped to have enjoyed more of her exquisite pictures of Swedish homes; and I yet trust that others may. It would be a world-wide benefit if this gifted woman could be induced to leave social reforms and published criticism to other hands, and to discharge while she lives the special function by which she scatters a rare delight broadcast over whole nations.

A frequent topic of conversation between my morning guests and myself was the various methods of doing our work. Sooner or later, almost every author asked me about my procedure, and told me his or hers. The point on which I was at issue with almost every body was the time of beginning in the morning. I doubt whether I was acquainted with anybody who went to work during the fresh morning hours which have always been delightful to me,—before the post came in, and interruption was abroad. I found my friends differ much as to the necessity of revision, rewriting and delay,—on which I have already given my opinion and experience. The point on which perhaps they were most extensively agreed was that our occupation changes our relation to books very remarkably. I remember Miss Aikin[1] complaining of the difficulty of reading for amusement, after some years' experience of reading for purposes of historical or other authorship. I found this for a time when stopped in my career by illness: but, though I have never since read so fast or so efficiently as in my youth, I have experienced some return of the youthful pleasure and interest, though in regard to a different order of books. I could not now read 'Lalla Rookh' through before breakfast,

---

[1] Lucy Aikin (1781–1864), poet, historian, and writer on children's education; Aikin, the niece of Anna Barbauld, produced an edition of her aunt's works with a memoir.

as I did when it appeared. I cannot read new novels. It is an actual incapacity; while I can read with more pleasure than ever the old
favourites,—Miss Austen's and Scott's. My pleasure in Voyages and
Travels is almost an insanity; and History and philosophical disquisition
are more attractive than ever. Still, I can sympathise heartily with those
who declare that the privilege of being authors has deprived them of
that of being amateur readers. The state of mind in which books are
approached by those who are always, and those who have never been,
in print is no doubt essentially different.—I believe Miss Aikin's method
of writing is painstaking; and she has so high an opinion of revision by
friends, that I have no doubt she copies very conscientiously. Her enjoyment of her work is very great. I remember her saying, at a time when
her physician forbade her fatiguing herself with writing, that if ever she
saw a proof-sheet again, she thought she should dance.

Mrs. Opie wrote slowly, and amidst a strenuous excitement of her
sensibilities. She liked trying the effect of her tales on hearers before
they went to press. I remember my mother and sister coming home
with swollen eyes and tender spirits after spending an evening with Mrs.
Opie, to hear 'Temper,' which she read in a most overpowering way.[1]
When they saw it in print, they could hardly believe it was the same
story. Her handwriting was execrable, for smallness and irregularity. Miss
Aikin's is formal, but very legible. Miss Edgeworth's, an ordinary 'lady's
hand.' Mrs. Somerville's the same. Miss Brontë's was exceedingly small,
nervous and poor, but quite legible. Miss Edgeworth's method of
composition has been described already, on her own published authority. Mrs. Somerville, being extremely short-sighted, brings her paper
close to her eyes, supported on a square piece of pasteboard. Miss
Brontë did the same; but her first manuscript was a very small square
book, or folding of paper, from which she copied, with extreme care.
She was as much surprised to find that I never copy at all as I was at her
imposing on herself so much toil which seems to me unnecessary.—
Mr. Rogers used to give me friendly admonition, now and then, to do
every thing in my practice of composition in an exactly opposite
method to my own:—to write a very little, and seldom; to put it by,
and read it from time to time, and copy it pretty often, and show it to
good judges; all which was much like advising me to change my hair
and eyes to blonde and blue, and to add a cubit to my stature. It was a

---

[1] Amelia Opie (1769–1853) published *Temper, or, Domestic scenes* in 1812 when she lived in
Norwich.

curious commentary on his counsel to hear Sydney Smith's account of Mr. Rogers's method of composition. The story is in print, but imperfectly given, and evidently without any consciousness that 'the brooding dove' of Shakspere is concerned in it,—'the brooding dove, ere yet her golden couplets are disclosed.' The conversation took place soon after Rogers had given forth his epigram on Lord Dudley:

'Ward has no heart, they say: but *I* deny it.
Ward *has* a heart;—and gets his speeches by it.'

'Has Rogers written any thing lately?' asked somebody; to which another replied,—'No, I believe not. Nothing but a couplet.'

'Nothing but a couplet!' exclaimed Sydney Smith. 'Why, what would you have? When Rogers produces a couplet, he goes to bed:

And the caudle is made:

And the knocker is tied:

And straw is laid down:

And when his friends send to inquire,—"Mr. Rogers is as well as can be expected."'

Mr. Rogers's rate of advance would not suit a really earnest writer; and, granting that poetry is under wholly different conditions from prose, it will still occur to every body that the world may be thankful that Milton and Shakspere did not require so much time. Lope de Vega, with his eighteen hundred plays, may have been in excess of speed;[1] but literature would have no chance if the elaboration and expression of thought and feeling were so sophisticated as they must be by extreme timidity or excessive polish.

Mr. Hallam, taking up a proof-sheet from my table, one day, while I was at work on the second volume of the same book, expressed his surprise at my venturing to press before the whole was finished and tied up; and said that he should not have nerve to do this. I think he agreed with me that much depends on whether the work is or is not composed of complete sections,—of distinct parts,—each of which is absolutely finished in its own place. He was industrious when at work; but he did it for pleasure, and took as much time as he pleased about it. When I first knew him, his handwriting was one of the finest I ever saw; and there was a remarkable elegance about the whole aspect of his authorship.—Mr.

---

[1] Lope de Vega (1562–1635), Spanish dramatist, is said to have written over 2,000 plays, 500 of which have survived.

Rogers's hand was old-fashioned and formal, but so clear that you might teach a child to read from it.—I have mentioned the appearance of Carlyle's proof-sheets. His manuscript is beautifully neat, when finished; and a page holds a vast quantity of his small upright writing. But his own account of his toil in authorship is melancholy. He cannot sleep for the sense of the burden on his mind of what he has to say; rises weary, and is wretched till he has had his coffee. No mode of expression pleases him; and, by the time his work is out, his faculties are over-wearied. It is a great object in his case to have the evenings amused, that his work may not take possession of his mind before bedtime. His excessive slowness is a perfect mystery to me,—considering that the work is burdensome. If he dwelt lovingly on its details, and on his researches, I could understand it. But perhaps he does, more than he is aware of. If not, his noble vocation is indeed a hard one.

Almost every one of these is late in sitting down; and I believe few write every day. Mrs. Somerville's family did not breakfast early; and she ordered her household affairs before sitting down to work. She worked till two only: but then, it was such work! Dr. Somerville told me that he once laid a wager with a friend that he would abuse Mrs. Somerville in a loud voice to her face, and she would take no notice; and he did so. Sitting close to her, he confided to his friend the most injurious things,—that she rouged, that she wore a wig, and other such nonsense, uttered in a very loud voice; her daughters were in a roar of laughter, while the slandered wife sat placidly writing. At last, her husband made a dead pause after her name, on which she looked up with an innocent, 'Did you speak to me?'

Sir Charles Lyell sits down late, and says he is satisfied with a very few pages: but then, his work is of a kind which requires research as he proceeds; and pages are no measure of work in that case. In writing my 'History of the Peace,' I was satisfied with seven manuscript pages per day; whereas, in general, I do not like to fall short of ten or twelve.— Dr. Chalmers was another mystery to me. He told me that it was a heavy sin to write (for press) longer than two hours per day;—that two hours out of the twenty-four are as much of that severest labour as the human brain is fitted to endure. Yet he must have written faster than that, to produce his works. Dr. Channing entirely agreed with Dr. Chalmers, and was apt to tax people with rashness who wrote faster. His practice was, when in Rhode Island, to saunter round the garden once every hour, and then come back to the desk: and when in Boston, he went to the drawing-room instead, or walked about in his library.

No person can judge for another; but we used to compare notes. I wondered how he could ever get or keep his ideas in train, under such frequent interruption: and he was no less surprised at my experience;—that every hour is worth double the last for six hours; and that eight are not injurious when one's subject naturally occupies them: but then, it is an indispensable condition that there shall be no interruptions. The dissipation of mind caused by interruption is a worse fatigue than that of continuous attention.—Southey and Miss Edgeworth wrote in the common sitting-room, in the midst of the family. This I cannot understand, though I am writing this Memoir under circumstances which compel me to surrender my solitude. Under a heart-disease, I cannot expect or ask to be left alone: and I really find no *gêne* from the presence of one person, while writing this simple and plain account of my life. I can imagine that Miss Edgeworth's stories would not require very much concentration; but how a man can write epics in the midst of the family circle is inconceivable, even to some of Southey's warmest admirers. The comment is inevitable;—that his poems might have been a good deal better, if he had placed himself under the ordinary conditions of good authorship.—Wordsworth was accustomed to compose his verses in his solitary walks, carry them in his memory, and get wife or daughter to write them down on his return.—The varieties of method are indeed great. One acquaintance of mine takes a fit of writing,—a review or a pamphlet,—and sends his wife to an evening party without him. He scribbles, as fast as his pen will go, on half sheets of paper, which he lets fly to the floor when finished;—i.e., when a dozen or a score of lines run awry, so as to cover the greater part of the expanse. His wife, returning after midnight, finds him sitting amidst a litter of paper, some inches deep,—unless he has previously summoned the butler to sweep them up in his arms and put them somewhere. By five in the morning the pamphlet is done. How it is ever got into order for press, I cannot imagine.—But enough! I have met with almost every variety of method among living authors; and almost every variety of view as to the seriousness of their vocation. But I believe the whole fraternity are convinced that the act of authorship is the most laborious effort that men have to make: and in this they are probably right: for I have never met with a physician who did not confirm their conviction by his ready testimony.

SECTION III[1]

A LITTLE while before my departure for the United States, I met Mr.
James Mill[2] one evening, and had a good deal of conversation with
him. By the way, he made the frankest possible acknowledgment of his
mistake in saying what had so critically and mischievously alarmed Mr.
Fox;—that political economy could not be conveyed in fiction, and
that the public would not receive it in any but the didactic form.
Having settled this business, he asked me how long I meant to be
abroad; and then, whether I expected to understand the Americans in
that time;—that is, two years. He was glad to find I had no such idea,
and told me that five-and-twenty years before, he had believed that he
understood the Scotch; and that in another five-and-twenty, he should
no doubt understand the English; but that now he was quite certain
that he understood neither the one nor the other. As this looked rather
as if he supposed I went out on a book-making expedition, I told him
that it was not so. I would not say that I certainly should not write a
book on my return: but I had actually refused to listen to the urgent
recommendation of a gentleman who professed to have influence with
the booksellers, to allow him to obtain for me advances of money for
my travelling expenses from a publishing house which would be glad
to advance £500 or so, on my engaging to let them publish the book
on my return. I have since had strong reason to rejoice that I did not
permit such intervention. My reply was that I would not bind myself
by any pledge of the sort; and that my travelling money was in fact
ready. The friend who gave me credits to the American banks offered
to obtain from Lord Brougham the £100 he owed me, as part
payment: but that also I declined,—kindly as it was meant; because I
did not think it quite a proper way to obtain payment. I preferred
going out free from all misgiving and anxiety about pecuniary matters;
so I paid in my £400, and carried credits to that amount, without

---

[1]   In the original edition of 1877, volume II begins here.
[2]   James Mill (1773–1836), author of *Elements of Political Economy* (1821), associate of Jeremy
       Bentham and David Ricardo, and leading member of the Utilitarian philosophers, many
       of whose ideas Martineau popularized in her *Illustrations of Political Economy*. See Period
       III, sec. iv for Mill's objection to Martineau's original plan.

being under obligation to any body.—Mr. Bentley the publisher[1] met me one day at dinner at Miss Berry's, and he sounded me about a book on America. I rather think, from his subsequent conduct, that that was his real object in getting an introduction to me, though he put forward another:—his desire to issue my Series in a new form. I told him as I told others, that I knew nothing of any American book, and that I was going to the United States with other objects,—the first of which was to obtain rest and recreation. I went and returned entirely free from any kind of claim on me, on any hand, for a book. I can truly say that I travelled without any such idea in my mind. I am sure that no traveller seeing things through author spectacles, can see them as they are; and it was not till I looked over my journal on my return that I decided to write 'Society in America.'[2] (I never can bear to think of the title. My own title was 'Theory and Practice of Society in America;' but the publishers would not sanction it. They had better have done so.)

My first desire was for rest. My next was to break through any self-ish 'particularity' that might be growing on me with years, and any love of ease and indulgence that might have arisen out of success, flattery, or the devoted kindness of my friends. I believed that it would be good for me to 'rough it' for a while, before I grew too old and fixed in my habits for such an experiment. I must in truth add that two or three of my most faithful friends, intimate with my circumstances, counselled my leaving home for a considerable time, for the welfare of all who lived in that home. My position had become a difficult one there, even while my work afforded an incontestable reason for my being sought and made much of. If my social position remained the same after the work was done, my mother's happiness would not, they thought, be promoted by my presence. This was too obviously true already: and I took the advice of my friends to go without any misgiving, and to stay away as long as I found it desirable. I made provision for my mother's income not being lessened by my absence: but she declined, for generous reasons, all aid of that sort. She never touched the money I left for the purpose, but

---

[1]   Richard Bentley (1794–1871) first published with Henry Colburn (d. 1855) as Colburn and Bentley, then established the firm of Bentley & Son with his son George (1825–95). Bentley was known for "triple-decker" novels, but he published other popular genres, including biography and travel literature.

[2]   *Society in America*, 3 vols. (London: Saunders and Otley, 1837). After her American trip, Martineau also wrote *Retrospect of Western Travel*, 3 vols. (London: Saunders and Otley, 1838) and *How to Observe: Morals and Manners* (London: Charles Knight, 1838), the latter now considered a founding text of sociological method.

received in my place a lady who made an agreeable third in the little household. I have already said that Lord Henley's suggestions[1] first turned my project in the direction of the United States; and the reasons he urged were of course prominent in my mind during my travels.

I was singularly fortunate in my companion.[2] I had been rather at a loss at first what to do about this. There are great difficulties in joining a party for so very long a journey, extending over so long a time. To be with new friends is a fearful risk under such an ordeal: and the ordeal is too severe, in my opinion, to render it safe to subject an old friendship to it. There was a plan for a time that the same friends with whom I was to have gone to Italy (if the continent had been my playground) should go with me to America: but there were aged parents and other reasons against their going so far; and my friends and I went on our several ways.—It would never do, as I was aware, to take a servant, to suffer from the proud Yankees on the one hand and the debased slaves on the other: nor would a servant have met my needs in other ways. Happily for me a lady of very superior qualifications, who was eager to travel, but not rich enough to indulge her desire, offered to go with me, as companion and helper, if I would bear her expenses. She paid her own voyages, and I the rest: and most capitally she fulfilled her share of the compact. Not only well educated but remarkably clever, and, above all, supremely rational, and with a faultless temper, she was an extraordinary boon as a companion. She was as conscientious as able and amiable. She toiled incessantly, to spare my time, strength, and faculties. She managed the business of travel, and was for ever on the watch to supply my want of ears,—and, I may add, my defects of memory. Among the multitudes of strangers whom I saw, and the concourse of visitors who presented themselves every where, I should have made hourly mistakes but for her. She seemed to make none,—so observant, vigilant and retentive were her faculties. We fulfilled the term of our compact without a shadow of failure, but rather with large supererogation of good works on her part; and she returned under the care of the excellent captain,[3]—a friend of some of my family,—who brought me home four months later. I

---

[1]   See Period IV, sec. i for the role of Robert Henley Eden (1789–1841) in Martineau's decision to travel to North America rather than Italy and Switzerland.

[2]   Louisa Jeffrey, daughter of Francis Jeffrey (1773–1850), whom Martineau had met in London, offered to accompany her in return for expenses other than passage. Miss Jeffrey returned home early in 1836, while Martineau made a tour of the Great Lakes, from Niagara Falls to Detroit, Chicago, and Cleveland, and back to New York, finally sailing for England in August 1836.

[3]   Captain Bursley, also mentioned at the end of this section.

remained that much longer, for the purpose of accompanying a party of friends to the Northern Lakes, and some new territory which it was important that I should visit. I could not afford this additional trip to more than myself; and there was not room for more than one: so my comrade preceded me homewards, sorry not to have taken that northern trip, but well satisfied with the enterprise she had achieved. She has been married for many years; and it is pleasant still to talk over our American adventures in her house or in mine. Her husband and children must be almost as glad as she and I that she had the spirit to go.

After leaving home, I paid visits to my family and friends, (followed from place to place by my last proofs) and was joined by Miss J. at Liverpool, a day or two before we sailed. The first steam voyage to the United States took place in 1838: and I set forth in 1834:[1] so there was no thought of a quicker passage than a month. I did not wish for a shorter one; and when it stretched out to forty-two days, I was not at all discontented. I have enjoyed few things more in life than the certainty of being out of the way of the post, of news, and of passing strangers for a whole month: and this seems to show how over-wrought I must have been at the close of my long work. My felicity would have been complete if I could have looked forward to a month of absolute idleness: but my constitutional weakness,—my difficulty in saying 'No,' was in my way, and a good deal spoiled my holiday. A friend, whom indeed I was bound to oblige,[2] requested me to write for him a long chapter for a book he contemplated, to be called 'How to Observe.' The subject he gave me was Morals and Manners. Before my return, his proposed volume was given up; and Mr. Knight was arranging about a series of volumes, under that title. The Chapter I wrote on board ship served as the basis of my own volume for that series; and thus, the reluctant toil was not thrown away. But thoroughly reluctant it was. The task weighed upon me more than the writing of a quarto volume would have done at another time: and circumstances of time and place were indeed most unfavourable to work of the kind. My long confinement within stringent bounds of punctuality had produced bad effects,—narrowing my mind, and making my conscience tender about work. So, when that chapter was done at last, I wrote no more till I was settled at home again, in the autumn of 1836,—

---

[1]　On the sailing packet *United States*, with Nathan Holdrege as captain.

[2]　H. Bellenden Ker (1785–1871) proposed the series and wrote the preface to its first volume, *How to Observe: Geology* (1835) by Thomas de la Beche (1796–1855). Charles Knight (1791–1873) published Martineau's volume *How to Observe: Morals and Manners* (1838) as the second in the series.

with two small exceptions. It was necessary to accede to a request to bring out myself, while in America, two volumes of 'Miscellanies,' under penalty of seeing it done by some unauthorised person, with alterations, and probably the introduction of pieces which would be as new to me as to any body. In order to secure the copyright to the American proprietors, I wrote an essay for their edition: (on 'Moral Independence.')[1] Being asked to furnish a story for some Sunday school festival, I wrote the little tale 'The Children who lived by the Jordan.'[2] These two trifles were all I wrote for press, as far as I remember, for above two years. I need not say that I had a large correspondence to sustain,—a correspondence perpetually increasing as my travel and my intercourses extended: and I kept a very ample journal.

On the morning of the 4th of August, we were summoned on board our ship,—the United States. As I stood on the wharf in my sea-dress, watching the warping out of the vessel, I saw an old acquaintance observing the same process. Sir James Parke[3] was one of the Judges then at Liverpool on circuit; and he and some ladies were amusing themselves with seeing the American packet clear out. He would hardly believe me when I told him I was going to step on board presently; and for how long. He was the last of my London acquaintances whom I saw before that long absence.

I have said quite enough about that voyage, and very nearly enough about my American travel, in the two books I published after my return. One subject remains nearly untouched in those books; and on that alone I propose now to speak at any length. I refer to my own personal connexion with the great controversy on negro slavery which was then just beginning to stir the American community. While speaking largely of the controversy in my book, I said as little as possible of my own relation to it, because some undeserved suspicion of resentment on my own account might attach to my historical narrative; and because it was truly my object to present an impartial view, and by no means to create an interest in my personal adventures. In this place I feel it right to tell my story. Supported as it is by documents in the hands of my Executor,[4] and

---

1   *Miscellanies*, 2 vols. (Boston: Hilliard, Gray and Company, 1836).

2   *The Children Who Lived by the Jordan: A Story* (Salem [Mass.: Landmark Press], 1835).

3   James Parke (1782–1868), 1st Baron Wensleydale, Liverpool judge and member of the House of Lords.

4   Thomas and Robert Francis Martineau, her nephews, sons of Robert, were her executors. Thomas and his sister Maria were frequent visitors to the Knoll, the home Martineau built in Ambleside in 1845. Like his father, Thomas became mayor of Birmingham and served 1884–87.

by the testimony of Americans who know me best, it will stand as a record of what really took place, in answer to some false reports and absurd misrepresentations. For one instance of what Americans,— even American gentlemen,—will persuade themselves to do in the case of the Slavery question, which seems to pervert all its advocates;—I heard some time since that two American gentlemen,[1] who were college youths when I saw them, claim the credit of having beguiled me into publishing some nonsensical stories with which they mystified me when I was the guest of their parents. I not only clearly remember that I had no conversation with those boys (who were shy of my trumpet) but I possess the best possible evidence that it is their present statement which is the mystifying one. By some lucky inspiration of prudence, I kept a lock-up copy of my American books, in which the name of every authority for every statement is noted in the margin. I have referred to this copy since I heard of the claim of these two gentlemen; and I have called my biographer to witness that the names of the gentlemen in question do not once occur.—So many false things having been said about my American experiences, in regard to the anti-slavery agitation, during my life, it is probable that there may be more when I am no longer here to contradict them: and therefore it is that I now give a plain account of what really took place. I do not altogether trust my memory for an experience which is however deeply impressed upon it. My journal, and my entire American correspondence on that subject are my warrant: and I have before me also the narrative as written down many years ago, from the same materials, and when my remembrance of the events of 1835 and 1836 was so fresh as to obviate any objection that can be made to my statement on the score of lapse of time.

It will be remembered that I wrote, near the beginning of my Series, a number called 'Demerara,' which was as open a committal of myself, on every ground, to hostility to slavery as was possible. I therein declared myself satisfied that slavery was indefensible, economically, socially, and morally. Every body who knew any thing about me at all, at home or in America, knew that from the spring of 1832 I was completely committed against slavery. The American passengers on board our ship were certainly aware of it before they saw me; and so was a Prussian

---

[1]   One was possibly William Gilmore Simms, (1806–70), who published a pamphlet *Slavery in America: Being a Brief Review of Miss Martineau on that Subject by a South Carolinian* (Richmond [Va.]: T.W. White, 1838).

fellow-passenger, Dr. Julius,[1] who had been introduced to me in London as a philanthropist going to America with a direct commission from the late King of Prussia to inquire into the state of prison discipline there. Every one on board regarded Dr. Julius as so commissioned; but he told Miss J. and me one day, when in a communicative mood, that he had sought the sanction of the King to his object, and believed he had obtained it: but that when he was admitted to an audience, to take leave, he found that the King had forgotten all about it (if he had really known) and that nothing could make him understand that this was a leave-taking visit, or why Dr. Julius presented himself, though the King approved of inquiries into prison-discipline. Whether there was a prevalent doubt about the reality of his commission, or whether his habit of petty concealment induced suspicion, I do not know; but the impression on board ship, and in American society afterwards, certainly was that there was something mysterious and doubtful about him. I was disposed to conclude, on the whole, that there was nothing worse in the case than that he was a Jew, and was anxious to conceal the fact. The clearest thing in the matter was that, with all his big talk, he was in a continual state of panic. He was afraid of the elements and of man: convulsed with terror during a storm; and in great horror on the subject of Slavery, though the American 'reign of terror' was only then beginning, and it had not, I believe, been heard of in Europe. Mr. George Thompson[2] had half-engaged a cabin in our ship for himself and his family, but was by some accident prevented sailing so soon. It was very well: for, while we were crossing the sea, the first serious pro-slavery riots were taking place in New York;—those riots by which the Messrs. Tappan[3] were driven from the city, their houses destroyed, and their furniture burnt in the streets.

---

[1]   Before visiting the United States, Nicolaus Heinrich Julius (1783–1862) published *Amerika's Besserungs-System, und dessen Anwendung auf Europa* [*America's Reform System and its Application in Europe*] (Berlin, 1833), based on Alexis de Tocqueville's *Note sur le système pénitentiaire* [*On the Penitentiary System in the United States and its Application in France*] (Paris, 1831). Julius subsequently wrote *Amerikanischen Besserungs-Systeme* [*The American Reform System*] (Leipzig, 1837) and *Nordamerikas sittliche Zustände: Nach eigenen Anschauungen in den Jahren 1834, 1835 und 1836* [*North America's Moral State, from the particular perspective of the years 1834, 1835, and 1836*] (Leipzig, 1839).

[2]   George Thompson (1804–78), a well-known British abolitionist, was a friend of the American abolitionists William Lloyd Garrison and John Greenleaf Whittier. In 1835, he barely escaped from a Boston mob; later, during the American Civil War, he was given a warm reception in the House of Representatives.

[3]   Arthur (1786–1865) and Lewis (1788–1873) Tappan were wealthy merchants, philanthropists, and abolitionists who supported Garrison and his newspaper, *The Liberator*; they helped found the American Anti-Slavery Society in 1833, and arranged the defense of the crew of the *Amistad*, arguing that the mutineers were, in fact, kidnapped Africans. The New York riots

The last news I heard of Dr. Julius was some time after my return to England; and I acknowledge that I was considerably disturbed by it. After I had left Washington, he petitioned for certain State Papers, and government information, either in my name expressly, or on the ground of our being fellow-travellers. I need not say that this was without any authority whatever from me, or that I took pains to disavow in the right quarter all connexion with Dr. Julius's inquiries. I was distinctly informed that the papers and information would not have been granted, but on the supposition that they were asked for by me, for my own use.

When we took in a pilot at Sandy Hook,[1] we all observed how hastily he tossed down his bundle of newspapers for the amusement of the passengers, and then beckoned the captain to the stern; and we were not so absorbed in the newspapers as not to perceive that the conversation in the stern was earnest and long. Though there was a good deal about me and my reception in those newspapers, it never occurred to me that I was the subject of the conversation between the captain and pilot. When the pilot went to the wheel, the captain requested a private interview with an American lady who had talked with me a good deal during the voyage. Long after, I heard that he wanted to know from her what my opinions were upon Slavery; and, if anti-slavery, whether I had ever professed them publicly. It is odd that she did not tell him, (what she certainly knew) that I was completely committed to anti-slavery opinions by my writings. By her own account, her reply to the captain was that I was opposed to Slavery; but that I had been more than once heard to say on board, when questioned about my opinion of American institutions, that I went to learn, and not to teach. The captain seemed satisfied to let Slavery pass muster among 'American institutions;' and he declared that he should now know what to say. He avowed that if he had been less well satisfied, he should not have ventured to put me ashore: and he made it his particular request that I should hear nothing of what had passed. The pilot had warned him that if Mr. Thompson was on board, he had better hide him in his cabin; for, if his presence was known in New York, he would be a dead man before night.

Knowing nothing of all this, being carefully kept ignorant while in New York, (as many resident ladies were) of the fact of the riots, and

---

Martineau refers to broke out on 2 October 1833 when Lewis Tappan and other abolitionists organized a public meeting at which Garrison was to speak, and again on 7 July 1834 at Chatham Street Chapel, where a black preacher was to deliver a sermon. The mob ransacked not only the chapel, but the Tappan house.

[1]   The entry to the Narrows and New York harbor.

travelling for weeks among persons who either took no interest in the subject or anxiously ignored it, Miss J. and I long remained in a state of profound unconsciousness of the condition of society around us. It was not merely as travellers that we were thus kept in the dark. On the last occasion of my being at New York, I was assured by the ladies of Mrs. Jeffrey's family that I was entirely misinformed about there having been any disturbances there at all in the autumn of 1834. I told them the particulars,—some notorious, and others of unquestionable truth; but they believed me so little that they asked husband and brother about it, in the middle of dinner, in the presence of the servants. The gentlemen could not, of course, deny the facts; but they did their best to make light of them, on the one hand; and, on the other, accounted for their silence to the wondering ladies by declaring that they were ashamed of the whole business, and did not wish to alarm or annoy the ladies unnecessarily. Such was the bondage in which the inhabitants of the boasted republic were living so long ago as 1834. Such bondage was, to English women,[1] an inconceivable and incredible thing, till the fact was forced on our observation by further and more various travel.

We went among the Sedgwicks,[2] on our ascent of the Hudson: we went to Niagara, and by Western Pennsylvania to Philadelphia, where we staid six weeks, proceeding to Baltimore (a Slave State) in December. There was all this while scarcely any thing to remind us of the subject of Slavery but the virulent abuse of the Abolitionists in the newspapers. I afterwards learned that the whole country was divided into three parties: the Pro-slavery multitude, the Colonisationists (represented in Europe by the before-mentioned Elliot Cresson),[3] and the Abolitionists. The Colonisationists were simply a selection from the Pro-slavery multitude, who did the Slave States the service of ridding them of clever and dangerous slaves, and throwing a tub to the whale of adverse opinion, and easing lazy or weak consciences, by professing to deal, in a safe and beneficial manner, with the otherwise hopeless difficulty.[4] Care was taken, so early as my visit to Philadelphia, and yet more at Baltimore and Washington,

---

1   Martineau discusses the differences between the educations and practices of American and English women in her chapter "Women" in *Society in America*.

2   The Sedgwick family of Stockbridge, Massachusetts, included Theodore (1780–1839), Robert (1787–1841), Charles (1791–1856), and their sister, the novelist Catherine Maria (1789–1867), the last of whom spent considerable time with Martineau.

3   See Period IV, sec. i.

4   Martineau opposed the return of slaves to Liberia because she believed the plan was motivated primarily by the desire of slave owners to eliminate the voice and views of freed blacks in America.

that I should hear much in favour of the Colonisation scheme, and nothing but horrors of the Abolitionists. I acknowledge here, once for all, that it is very probable that expressions unfavourable to the Abolitionists may be fairly remembered and quoted against me throughout the Southern and Western States. I never wavered, of course, in my detestation of Slavery; and I never intended to take any part against the Abolitionists; but it is scarcely possible to hear from day to day, for ten months, that persons whom one has never seen are fanatical, bloodthirsty and so forth, without catching up some prejudice against them. We were constantly and gravely informed, as a matter of fact, that Garrison and his followers used incitements to the slaves to murder their masters, and sent agents and publications into the South to effect insurrections. Till we had the means of ascertaining that these charges were totally and absolutely false,—Garrison and most of his followers being non-resistants, and thoroughly consistent opponents of physical force,—it was really impossible to remain wholly unimpressed by them. I steadily declared my intention to hear, when opportunity offered, what the Abolitionists, as well as others, had to say for themselves: but it certainly never entered my imagination that I could possibly find them the blameless apostles of a holy cause which I afterwards saw that they were.

The first perplexing incident happened at Philadelphia, ten or twelve weeks after our landing. A lady of that city[1] whose manners were eminently disagreeable to us, beset us very vigorously,—obtruding her society upon us, and loading me with religious books for children,— some of her own writing, and some by others. When we made our farewell calls, we were not sorry to be told that this lady could see no visitors, as she had a cold. We were speeding away from the door, when a servant ran after us, with an unwelcome summons to the lady's chamber. She made me sit beside her on her sofa, while Miss J. sat opposite,— out of my hearing. The lady having somehow introduced the subject of the blacks, a conversation ensued between her and Miss J. of which I did not hear a syllable. I saw my companion look embarrassed, and could not conceive why, till the lady turned full upon me with, 'Can it be as your friend assures me? She says that if any young person known to you was attached to a negro, you would not interfere to prevent their marrying.' I replied that I had no notion of interfering between people who

---

[1]   Deborah Anna Logan, editor of Harriet Martineau's *Writings on Slavery and the American Civil War* (DeKalb: Northern Illinois UP, 2002), suggests that this may be Deborah Norris Logan (1761–1839), a prominent Philadelphia dowager whose diary includes accounts of Martineau's visits, conversations, and opinions.

were attached; that I had never contemplated the case she proposed; but that I did not believe I should ever interfere with lovers proposing to marry. The lady exclaimed against my thus edging off from the question,—which I had not the least intention of doing: and she drove her inquiries home. Mystery is worse than any other mischief in such matters; and I therefore replied that, if the union was suitable in other respects, I should think it no business of mine to interfere on account of complexion. The lady cried out in horror, 'Then you are an Amalgamationist!' 'What is that?' I asked: and then remonstrated against foreign travellers being classified according to the party terms of the country. I was not then aware of the extent to which all but virtuous relations are found possible between the whites and blacks, nor how unions to which the religious and civil sanctions of marriage are alone wanting, take place wherever there are masters and slaves, throughout the country. When I did become aware of this, I always knew how to stop the hypocritical talk against 'amalgamation.' I never failed to silence the cant by pointing to the rapidly increasing mulatto element of the population, and asking whether it was the priest's service which made the difference between holy marriage and abhorred 'amalgamation.' But I was not yet possessed of this defence when assailed by the Philadelphia saint.—When we rose to go, the woman insisted on kissing me, and poured out lamentations about my departure. The moment we were in the street, I said to my friend, 'You *must* be careful, and not get me or yourself into any more such scrapes till we know what people mean on this subject of the blacks.' Miss J. justified herself completely. She had been so questioned that she could not avoid saying as much as she did, unless by the more dangerous method of refusing to reply. This was the beginning of many troubles: but the troubles would have occurred from some other beginning, if we had escaped this.

The day before we left Philadelphia, Dr. Julius called at the house where we were staying. He had just arrived from New York. He burst into the room with an air of joy which did not look very genuine; and I presently saw that he was absent and uneasy. After staying an unconscionable time, while I was fidgety about my preparations, he explained a long series of unintelligible nods and winks by asking to speak with me alone for a few minutes. My host (a clergyman, and in character, though not in circumstances, the original of Hope in 'Deerbrook')[1] left

---

[1]   William Henry Furness (1802–96), pastor of the Unitarian church in Philadelphia established by Joseph Priestley, had been a visiting minister in New York when Martineau arrived in September 1834.

the room, taking his little boy with him: and then Dr. Julius, turning as white as the marble chimney-piece, said he came to warn me to proceed no further south than Philadelphia. He had not been two hours in the city before he heard that I had avowed myself an amalgamation-ist, and that my proceeding southwards would bring upon me certain insult and danger. It appeared to me that there was every reason why this conversation should *not* be private; and I summoned my host. While I repeated to him what Dr. Julius had been saying, he too turned as pale as ashes; and between his ghastly countenance, and the gesticulations of Dr. Julius, the scene was a strange one. Dr. Julius declared the whole city was ringing with the news.—After a moment's consideration, I declared that I should not alter my plans in any respect. I was a well-known anti-slavery writer before I thought of going to America; and my desire to see the operation of the system of Slavery could hardly be wrongly interpreted by any one who took an interest in my proceedings. I was disposed to trust to the openness of plans, and the simplicity of my purpose, and to the common sense of those among whom I was going. Dr. Julius shrugged his shoulders; and my host suggested a method by which the difficulty might be probably obviated. The Editors of the two leading Philadelphia newspapers were well acquainted with me, and would undoubtedly, according to custom, give their report of me on my departure. They could with perfect truth, and would on the slightest hint, declare that my opinions on slavery were candidly held, and that they afforded no obstacle to the most friendly intercourse with me. I positively forbade any such movement on the part of my personal friends, feeling that I should never succeed in seeing the Americans as they were, if my road was paved for me from one society to another. Knowing Dr. Julius's tendency to panic, I felt little apprehension from any thing he could say; and I particularly requested my host and host-ess not to alarm Miss J. with any account of what had passed. I took on myself the duty which belonged to me, of enlightening her sufficiently to put her own case into her own hands.

At Baltimore, further obscure intimations of danger were conveyed to me: and at Washington, so many, that I felt the time was come for laying the case before my companion. Reflecting that she and I had discussed the whole matter of my anti-slavery opinions before we left home; and that she was very prudent and extremely clever, and fully able to take care of herself, all I thought it necessary to do was this.

In our own room at Washington, I spread out our large map, showed the great extent of Southern States through which we should have to pass, probably for the most part without an escort; and always, where we were known at all, with my anti-slavery reputation uppermost in every body's mind.—'Now, Louisa,' said I, 'does it not look awful? If you have the slightest fear, say so now, and we will change our route.'—'Not the slightest,' said she. 'If you are not afraid, I am not.' This was all she ever heard from me of danger.

The intimations I refer to came to me in all manner of ways. I was specially informed of imprisonments for opinions the same as are found in 'Demerara;' which indeed might well be under the laws of South Carolina, as I found them in full operation. Hints were offered of strangers with my views not being allowed to come away alive. But the most ordinary cunning or sensitiveness of the slave-holders would account for attempts like these to frighten a woman from going where she might see slavery for herself. I was more impressed by less direct warning; by words dropped, and countenances of anxiety and pity.—Before I left Washington, I wrote to my Philadelphia host and hostess, who were not only my most intimate American friends, but witnesses of the first attempt to alarm me. I told them of the subsequent incidents of the same kind, and that I had communicated them to no other person whatever, supposing that they might be only empty threats. As they might however be real, I wrote to assure these friends, and other friends and my family through them, that I went into the danger warily: and I requested that my letter might be kept in evidence of this, in case of my never returning.

As for the terms on which I went, I took timely care that there should be no mistake about that. I carried letters to some of the leading states-men at Washington; and the first to acknowledge them were the senators from the Southern States. On the very first day, several of these gentlemen came straight from the senate, with their wives, not only to offer me their services at Washington, but to engage us to visit them at their homes, in our progress through the South. Before I pledged myself to make any visit whatever, I took care to make it understood that I was not to be considered as silenced on the subject of slavery by the hospitality of slave-owners. I made an express reservation of my freedom in this matter, declaring that I should not, of course, publish names or facts which could draw attention upon individuals in private life; but that it must not be forgotten that I had written upon Slavery, and that I should write on it again, if I saw reason. They all made in substance the same reply; that my having published 'Demerara' was the main reason why they wished me to visit them. They desired me to see their 'peculiar institu-tion' for myself: they would show me the best and the worst instances of its working; and their hope was—so they declared,—that I should publish exactly what I saw. The whole conduct and conversation of my southern entertainers showed an expectation of seeing in print all that was then passing. I often told them that they were much more sure than I was that I should write a book. I am not aware that there was ever any misunderstanding between them and me on this head; and if any charge of my having accepted hospitalities from slave-holders, and then denounced their mode of life has ever been brought, or should ever be brought against me, I repel it as wholly groundless. A fair lady of blue-stocking Boston said of me after my book appeared, 'She has ate of our bread and drunk of our cup; and she calls dear, delightful, intellectual Boston pedantic!' on which a countryman of the complainant remarked, 'If she thinks Boston pedantic, did you mean to bribe her, by a cup of tea, not to say so?' The southerners might be more easily excused for this sort of unreasonableness and cant: but I never heard that they were guilty of it. Angry as they were with my account of slavery, I am not aware that they imputed ingratitude and bad manners to me in consequence.

It was not in the south that I saw or heard any thing to remind me of personal danger: nor yet in the west, though the worst inflictions of Lynch law were beginning there about that time. My friend and I were in fact handed on by the families of senators, to the care and kindness of a long succession of them, from the day we reached Washington, till we emerged from the Slave States at Cincinnati. Governor Hayne and his friends, and Mr. Calhoun's family secured every attention to us at Charleston: and Colonel Preston was our host at Columbia.[1] Judge Porter, of the federal senate, and Chief Justice of the Supreme Court of Louisiana, was the familiar friend who took us in charge at New Orleans: and Mr. Clay conducted us on board the steamer there,—his son-in-law being our escort up the Mississippi, and our host afterwards in Kentucky, where Mr. Clay, whose estate adjoined, spent part of every day with us.[2] No one of these, nor any other of our intimate acquaintance can ever, I am sure, have complained of my act of publishing on the institution which they exhibited to me, however they may dislike my opinions on it.

---

[1]   Robert Young Hayne (1791–1839), governor of South Carolina from 1832 to 1834; John C. Calhoun (1782–1850), vice president of the United States from 1825 to 1832 and senator for South Carolina from 1833 until his death; William Campbell Preston (1794–1860), Whig senator for South Carolina and life-long friend of Washington Irving.

[2]   Alexander Porter (1796–1844), jurist and Whig senator for Louisiana; Henry Clay (1777–1852), Whig senator for Kentucky, who also served as president of the American Colonization Society.

Our host at Charleston was a clergyman from the north, with a northern wife, [1] who had rushed into that admiration of Slavery which the native ladies do not entertain. I never met with a lady of southern origin who did not speak of Slavery as a sin and a curse,—the burden which oppressed their lives; whereas Mrs. Gilman observed to me, in the slave-market at Charleston, in full view of a woman who, with her infant, was on the stand,—that her doctrine was that the one race must be subordinate to the other, and that if the blacks should ever have the upper hand, she should not object to standing on that table with her children, and being sold to the highest bidder. This lady's publications bear the same testimony. Her brother-in-law is Mr. Ellis Gray Loring of Boston, [2] well known as an avowed Abolitionist, and a most generous contributor to the cause. The Gilmans adored this brother-in-law,—speaking of his abolitionism as his only fault. I was gratified by receiving, in their house, a message from him, to say that his wife and he would call on me as soon as I went into their neighbourhood, and that they begged I would reserve some time for a visit to them. I was aware that this excellent pair, and also Dr. and Mrs. Follen,[3] were, though abolitionists, not 'blood-thirsty' nor 'fanatical.' One of my chief objects in meeting their advances was to learn what the abolitionists really thought, felt and intended. I had attended Colonisation meetings, whenever invited, and heard all that the advocates of slavery had to say; and I made no secret of my intention to give the same ample hearing to the abolitionists, if they should desire to instruct me in their views and objects.

My first intercourse with any abolitionist took place when I was staying in Kentucky, on my way northwards, and when Mr. Clay was daily endeavouring, at his daughter's house or his own, to impress me in favour of slavery. A long and large letter from Boston arrived one day. The hand

---

[1]   Samuel Gilman (1791–1858), Massachusetts-born minister of Archdale Street Unitarian Church in Charleston, South Carolina, married Caroline Howard (1794–1888), who wrote poetry, children's books, housekeeping manuals, and a memoir, *Recollections of a Southern Matron* (1838), which was later expanded into *Recollections of a New England Bride and of a Southern Matron* (1852).

[2]   Ellis Gray Loring (1803–58), Boston lawyer and abolitionist.

[3]   Charles Follen (1796–1840), professor of German language and literature at Harvard University, was a prominent Boston abolitionist whose appointment at Harvard was revoked in 1834 because of his strong anti-slavery views. His wife Eliza Lee, née Cabot (1787–1860), wrote children's books, including translations of German fairy tales, as well as treatises against slavery and an introduction to the American edition of Martineau's *Life in the Sick-Room* (Boston: L.C. Bowles and W. Crosby, 1844).

was strong and flowing; the wording wonderfully terse, the style wonderfully eloquent; but the whole appearing to me rather intrusive, and not
a little fanatical. It was from her who has been my dear, honoured and
beloved friend from that year to the present day. When I saw the signature 'Maria Weston Chapman,'[1] I inquired who she was, and learned that
she was one of the 'fanatics.' The occasion of her writing was that some
saying of mine had reached her which showed, she thought, that I was
blinded and beguiled by the slave-holders; and she bespoke for the abolitionists, in the name of their cause, a candid hearing. She then proceeded
to remonstrance. I cannot bear to think of my answer. I have no clear
remembrance of it; but I am sure it was repulsive, cold and hard. I knew
nothing of what was before her eyes,—the beginning of the reign of
terror in New England on the slave question;[2] and I knew myself to be
too thoroughly opposed to slavery to need caution from an abolitionist. I was not aware of the danger of the Colonisation snare. I was, in
short, though an English abolitionist, quite unaware of the conditions of
abolitionism in America. Mrs. Chapman received my reply, and then
myself, with a spirit of generosity, disinterestedness and thorough nobleness which laid a broad foundation for friendship between us, whenever
I should become worthy of it: but not one woman in a thousand (and
that one in a thousand only for the sake of the cause) would have ever
addressed me again after receiving my letter, if my general impression of
it is at all correct.

In August 1835, Miss J. and I were the guests of a clergyman at Medford,
near Boston: and there I saw Dr. and Mrs. Follen, and Mr. and Mrs. Ellis
Gray Loring, and enjoyed sufficient intercourse with them to find that
some abolitionists at least were worthy of all love and honour. We travelled in other parts of Massachusetts before paying our Boston visits; and
it was in passing through Boston, on my way from Salem to Providence,
that I saw, but without being aware of it, the first outbreak of Lynch law
that I ever witnessed. In that August, 1835, there had been a public meeting in Boston (soon and long repented of) to denounce, rebuke and silence

---

[1]   Maria Weston Chapman (1806–85), an early campaigner against slavery and a founder of
      the Boston Female Anti-Slavery Society, became a close friend. She edited the journal
      The Non-Resistant (1839–42) and, after Martineau's death, the "Memorials" volume of the
      Autobiography.

[2]   "Reign of terror" echoes the period of the French Revolution in which executions of
      aristocrats and their presumed sympathizers were daily occurrences; in an article for the
      Westminster Review 30 (December 1838), 1–59, Martineau called this period of American
      history "The Martyr Age of the United States."

the abolitionists; a proceeding which imposed on the abolitionists the onus of maintaining the liberty of speech and action in Massachusetts. How they did it, few or none can have forgotten; how, on the 21st of the following October, the women held their proper meeting, well knowing that it might cost them their lives; how Mr. Garrison was mobbed and dragged through the streets towards the tar-kettle which he knew to be heating near at hand, but was saved by the interference and clever management of a stout truckman, who got him into the gaol: and how Mrs. Chapman, the leader of the band of confessors, remained in possession of the moral victory of the day.[1] Miss J. and I asked the meaning of the crowded state of the streets in the midst of Boston that day; and our fellow-travellers in the coach condescended to explain it by the pressure near the post-office on foreign post day! At Providence, we heard what had really happened. President Wayland[2] agreed with me at the time about the iniquitous and fatal character of the outrage; but called on me, after a trip to Boston, to relieve my anxiety by the assurance that it was all right,—the mob having been entirely composed of gentlemen! Professor Henry Ware,[3] who did and said better things afterwards, told me that the plain truth was, the citizens did not choose to let such a man as Garrison live among them,—admitting that Garrison's opinions on slavery were the only charge against him. Lawyers on that occasion defended a breach of the laws; ladies were sure that the gentlemen of Boston would do nothing improper: merchants thought the abolitionists were served quite right,—they were so troublesome to established routine; the clergy thought the subject so 'low' that people of taste should not be compelled to hear any thing about it; and even Judge Story,[4] when I asked him whether there was not a public prosecutor who might prosecute for the assault on Garrison, if the abolitionists did not, replied that he had given his advice (which had been formally

---

1   A meeting of the Boston Female Anti-Slavery Society, held at the office of *The Liberator*, was mobbed because the abolitionist George Thompson was rumored to be speaking. Asked by the mayor to leave the building, Maria Chapman responded, "If this is the last bulwark of freedom, we may as well die here as anywhere." Chapman's sister, Deborah Weston, described it as "the day when 5,000 men mobbed 45 women." The mob included male members of Dr. Channing's Unitarian congregation.

2   Francis Wayland (1796–1865), Professor of Natural Philosophy, served as president of Brown University from 1827 to 1855.

3   Henry Ware, Jr. (1794–1843), Professor of Divinity at Harvard University and pastor of the Second Unitarian Church, Boston, was president of the Cambridge Anti-Slavery Society. His brother William (1797–1852) was pastor of the First Unitarian Church, New York, and a long-term correspondent with Martineau after her return to England.

4   Joseph Story (1779–1845), American Congressman and jurist, served on the Supreme Court from 1811 until his death.

asked) against any notice whatever being taken of the outrage,—the feeling being so strong against the discussion of slavery, and the rioters being
so respectable in the city. These things I myself heard and saw, or I would
not ask any body to believe what I could hardly credit myself. The rural
settlements were sounder in principle and conduct; and so were the working men of Boston, and many young men not yet trammelled and
corrupted by the interests of trade and the slavery of public opinion: but
the public opinion of Boston was what I have represented in the autumn
of 1835, when I was unexpectedly and very reluctantly, but necessarily,
implicated in the struggle.

It was in the interval between that dispersed meeting of the abolitionists and their next righteous attempt to assemble, that Miss J. and I
returned to the neighbourhood, —paying our first visit at Professor
Henry Ware's at Cambridge. Dr. and Mrs. Follen called on us there one
morning; and Dr. Follen said, with a mild and serious countenance, 'I
wish to know whether we understood you rightly,—that you would
attend an abolition meeting, if opportunity offered.' I repeated what I
had said before;—that, having attended Colonisation meetings, and all
others where I thought I could gain light on the subject of slavery, I
was not only willing but anxious to hear what the Abolitionists had to
say, on their public as well as their private occasions. Dr. Follen said that
the opportunity might presently occur, as there was to be a meeting on
the next Wednesday, (November 18th) adding that some were of opinion that personal danger was incurred by attending abolition meetings
at present. This was, of course, nothing to me in a case where a principle, political or moral, was involved; and I said so. Dr. Follen inquired
whether, if I should receive an invitation to attend a meeting in a day
or two, I would go. I replied that it must depend on the character of
the meeting. If it was one at which ladies would merely settle their
accounts and arrange their local affairs, I would rather defer it till a safer
time: but if it was one where I could gain the knowledge I wanted, I
would go, under any circumstances. Dr. Follen said the meeting would
be of the latter kind: and that, as it was impossible to hold it at the Anti-
slavery Office without creating a mob, the meeting was to be held at
the house of Mr. Francis Jackson. This house was only just finished, and
built according to the taste of this most faithful citizen, for himself and
his daughters: but he said he would willingly sacrifice it, rather than the
ladies of Boston should not have a place to meet in.

The Follens had not been gone many minutes before the invitation
arrived. It was signed by the President and the Secretary of the Ladies'

Society; and it included in its terms any friend whom I might like to take with me. The note was enclosed in one from Mr. Loring, proposing to call for Miss J. and me on the Wednesday, that we might dine early at his house, and go to the meeting with his family party. His house was near Mr. Jackson's,[1] and it was not considered safe to go otherwise than on foot. I had before satisfied myself as to the duty of not involving any of my hosts in any of my proceedings on the abolition question. But it was now necessary to give Miss J. time to consider the part she should take. Three ladies, all inadequate to the subject, were dining at Dr. Ware's that day; and it was impossible at the moment to have any private conversation with my companion. I therefore handed her the letters across the table, with a sign of silence; and she had five hours for reflection before the guests departed. 'Have you read those letters?' I then inquired of her.—'Yes.'—'Do you mean to go?'—'Certainly, if you do.'—'Shall I say so for you?'—'If you please.'—I therefore accepted both invitations for both of us, and returned to the drawing-room, where I soon found an opportunity of saying to my host and hostess, 'I do not ask or wish an opinion from you: but I tell you a fact. Miss J. and I are going to dine at Mr. Loring's on Wednesday, to attend an abolition meeting.' Dr. Ware turned round as he stood in the window, and said, 'You will be mobbed. You will certainly be mobbed.'—'Perhaps so,' I replied. I then explained that Mr. Loring was coming for us; so that none of our Cambridge friends would be seen in the streets, or involved in our proceeding. I was sorry to hear, the next morning, that my host had desired Mr. Loring not to trouble himself to fetch us, as Mrs. Ware had some shopping to do in Boston, and Dr. Ware would drive us there in his 'carry-all.'—From time to time during the intervening day, our host observed, 'You will certainly be mobbed:' and when I once more and finally explained that this would make no difference, he jokingly declared that he said it so often, partly to be proved right, if any accident should happen, and partly for a jest, if all went well.

At Mr. Loring's house we found Mrs. Chapman and one of her sisters,[2] and the Rev. Samuel J. May.[3] During dinner, the conversation was chiefly

---

[1]   Francis Jackson (1789–1861), a well-known Boston reformer who initiated many public improvements, also served as president of the Boston Anti-Slavery Society.

[2]   Three of Maria's sisters had co-founded the Boston Female Anti-Slavery Society with her: Caroline Weston (b. 1808), Anne Weston (b. 1812), and Deborah Weston (b. 1814). All were schoolteachers, as was Maria before her marriage to Henry Grafton Chapman.

[3]   Samuel J. May (1797–1871), Unitarian minister in Brooklyn, Connecticut (1836–42), was an abolitionist, pacifist, and early champion of equal rights for women.

on the Southern slave-holders, whose part was taken by Miss J. and myself, so far as to plead the involuntariness of their position, and the extreme perplexity of their case,—over and above the evil conditions of prejudice and ignorance in which they were brought up. Our line of argument was evidently worth little in the estimate of all present, who appeared to us, in our then half-informed state, hard and narrow. But we were now in the way to learn better. Mr. Loring was too ill to eat or speak: and it was plain that he ought to have been in bed: but he would not leave his wife's side on that day.—Immediately after dinner it was time to be gone. When I was putting on my shawl upstairs, Mrs. Chapman came to me, bonnet in hand, to say, 'You know we are threatened with a mob again to-day: but I do not myself much apprehend it. It must not surprise us; but my hopes are stronger than my fears.' I hear now, as I write, the clear silvery tones of her who was to be the friend of the rest of my life. I still see the exquisite beauty which took me by surprise that day;—the slender, graceful form,—the golden hair which might have covered her to her feet;—the brilliant complexion, noble profile, and deep blue eyes;—the aspect, meant by nature to be soft and winning only, but that day, (as ever since) so vivified by courage, and so strengthened by upright conviction, as to appear the very embodiment of heroism. 'My hopes,' said she, as she threw up her golden hair under her bonnet, 'are stronger than my fears.'

Mr. Loring and I walked first. Just before turning into the street where Mr. Jackson lived, he stopped, and looking me in the face, said, 'Once more,—have you physical courage? for you may need it now.' On turning the corner we were pleased to find only about a dozen boys yelling in front of Mr. Jackson's house, as often as the coloured women went up the steps. No one was detained there an instant. The door opened and shut as rapidly as possible. As it was a ladies' meeting, there were no gentlemen in the house but the owner, and the two who accompanied us. When all were admitted, the front door was bolted, and persons were stationed at the rear of the house, to keep a way clear for escape over the fence, if necessary. About a hundred and thirty ladies were assembled; all being members except Mrs. George Thompson, Miss J. and myself. The folding-doors between the two drawing-rooms were thrown back; and the ladies were seated on benches closely ranged in both rooms. The President's table was placed by the folding-door; and near her were seated the officers of the society. The three gentlemen overheard the proceedings from the hall. I may refer to my 'Retrospect of Western Travel,' (volume iii., page 153) for some account of the proceedings; and to an article of mine in the 'Westminster Review,' of December, 1838, entitled 'The Martyr Age of the United States,' for evidence of the perils dared by the women who summoned and held this meeting. To me, the commotion was a small matter,—provided we got away safely. I was going home in less than a year; and should leave peril and slander behind me. But these women were to pass their lives in the city whose wrath they were defying; and their persecutors were fellow-citizens, fellow-worshippers, and familiar acquaintances. I trust that any who may have the least doubt of the seriousness of the occasion will look back to that year of terror, 1835, in that sketch in the 'Westminster Review' or other records. The truth is, it was one of the crises which occur in the life of a youthful nation, and which try the quality of the people, bringing out the ten righteous from among the multitude who are doing evil.

In the midst of the proceedings which I have elsewhere detailed, a note was handed to me, written in pencil on the back of the hymn which the party were singing. It was from Mr. Loring; and these were his words. 'Knowing your opinions, I just ask you whether you would object to give a word of sympathy to those who are suffering here for what you have advocated elsewhere. It would afford great comfort.' The moment of reading this note was one of the most painful of my life. I felt that I could never be happy again if I refused what was asked of me: but, to comply was probably to shut against me every door in the United States but those of the Abolitionists. I should no more see persons and things as they ordinarily were: I should have no more comfort or pleasure in my travels; and my very life would be, like other people's, endangered by an avowal of the kind desired. George Thompson was then on the sea, having narrowly escaped with his life; and the fury against 'foreign incendiaries' ran high. Houses had been sacked; children had been carried through the snow from their beds at midnight: travellers had been lynched in the market-places, as well as in the woods; and there was no safety for any one, native or foreign, who did what I was now compelled to do.—Having made up my mind, I was considering how this word of sympathy should be given, when Mrs. Loring came up with an easy and smiling countenance, and said—'You have had my husband's note. He hopes you will do as he says; but you must please yourself, of course.' I said 'No: it is a case in which there is no choice.' 'O! pray do not do it unless you like it. You must do as you think right.' 'Yes,' said I: 'I must.'

At first, (out of pure shyness) I requested the President to say a few words for me: but, presently remembering the importance of the occasion, and the difficulty of setting right any mistake that the President might fall into, I agreed to that lady's request that I would speak for myself. Having risen therefore, with the note in my hand, and being introduced to the meeting, I said, as was precisely recorded at the time, what follows.

'I have been requested by a friend present to say something—if only a word—to express my sympathy in the objects of this meeting. I had supposed that my presence here would be understood as showing my sympathy with you. But as I am requested to speak, I will say what I have said through the whole South, in every family where I have been; that I consider Slavery as inconsistent with the law of God, and as incompatible with the course of his Providence. I should certainly say no less at the North than at the South concerning this utter abomination—and I now declare that in your *principles* I fully agree.'

I emphasized the word 'principles,' (involuntarily,) because my mind was as yet full of what I had heard at the South of the objectionable methods of the Abolitionists. I have already explained that I ascertained all reports of the kind to be entirely false.—As I concluded, Mrs. Chapman bowed down her glowing face on her folded arms, and there was a murmur of satisfaction through the room, while outside, the growing crowd (which did not however become large) was hooting and yelling, and throwing mud and dust against the windows.

Dr. Ware did the brave act of driving up to Mr. Jackson's door, to take us home. On our road home, he questioned me about the meeting. 'What have you been doing?' he asked. 'Why,' said I, 'I have been speaking.'—'No! you have not!' he exclaimed in alarm. I told him that I was as sorry for it as he could be; but that it was wholly unavoidable. He communicated the fact, first to his wife and then to his brother-in-law, at home, in a way which showed how serious an affair they considered it. They could only hope that no harm would come of it. As I heard nothing about it for nearly three weeks, I began to hope so too.— During those three weeks, however, the facts got into print. Dr. Follen went to the Anti-slavery office one day, and found the Secretary and Mr. May revising the report of the meeting,—Mr. May taking extreme care that my precise words should be given. Nothing could be more accurate than the report, as far as I was concerned.

About three weeks after the meeting, I was staying at the Rev. Dr. Walker's,[1] at Charlestown,—a suburb of Boston, the weather being extremely bad with snow-storms, so that visiting was almost out of the

---

[1] James Walker (1794–1864), a Unitarian minister in Charlestown, Massachusetts, edited the *Christian Examiner* during this period (1831–39) and was later president of Harvard University (1853–60).

question,—considering that a windy and immensely long bridge stretches between Charlestown and Boston. The weather prevented my being surprised that so few people came; but my host and hostess were in daily expectation of some remark about their seclusion from society. It was not till many months afterwards that I was told that there were two reasons why I was not visited there as elsewhere. One reason was that I had avowed, in reply to urgent questions, that I was disappointed in an oration of Mr. Everett's:[1] and the other was that I had publicly condemned the institution of Slavery. I hope the Boston people have outgrown the childishness of sulking at opinions, not in either case volunteered, but obtained by pressure. At the time, I could not have conceived of such pettishness; and it was now nearly twenty years ago; so we may hope that the weakness is more or less outgrown,—so little as the indulgence of it can matter to passing strangers, and so injurious as such tendencies are to permanent residents. At length, some light was thrown on the state of my affairs, which I found every body knew more of than Miss J. and myself.

Miss Peabody[2] of Boston was staying at Dr. Walker's at the same time with ourselves. The day before she returned home, she happened to be in the Doctor's library when his newspaper came in. It was the leading paper in Boston, conducted by Mr. Hale,[3] the brother-in-law of Mr. Everett. Mr. Hale knew me,—having travelled a whole day in company with me, during which the party conversed abundantly. His paper contained, on this day, an article on my attending an abolition meeting, very bad in itself, but made infinitely worse by giving, with its sanction, large extracts from a New York paper of bad repute (The Courier and Enquirer)—those extracts being, to speak plainly, filthy. Dr. Walker and Miss Peabody burned the paper, hoping that I might not hear of it. In the course of the morning, however, Miss Tuckerman called,[4] in

---

[1]   Edward Everett (1794–1865), pastor of the Brattle Street Unitarian Church in Boston, later served as American Minister to Great Britain (1841–45) and president of Harvard University (1846–49).

[2]   Elizabeth Palmer Peabody (1804–94), educator and owner of a Boston circulating library, was a sister-in-law of Horace Mann (1796–1859), the great advocate of universal popular education.

[3]   Nathan Hale, Sr. (1784–1863), who trained as a lawyer, purchased the *Daily Advertiser*, the first Boston daily, in 1814. His wife, Sarah Preston Everett (1796–1866), and their children were regular contributors.

[4]   Jane Tuckerman, daughter of Gustavus Tuckerman (1785–1860) of Boston and granddaughter of John Francis of Birmingham. Joseph Tuckerman (1778–1840), her uncle (mentioned below), devoted his life to a study of pauperism and effective methods of amelioration.

company with two other ladies, and was evidently full of something that she was eager to say. With a solemn countenance of condolence she presently told me that she had never seen Dr. Channing[1] so full of concern as on that day, on the appearance of a most painful article in the 'Daily Advertiser;' and she proceeded to magnify the misfortune in a way which astonished me. I begged her to tell Dr. Channing not to be troubled about it, as I was, in the first place, prepared for the consequences of what I might say or do; and, in the next, I acknowledged no foreign jurisdiction in the case. The next time I saw Dr. Channing, he quietly observed that it was all a mistake about his having been troubled on my account. His anxiety was for Mr. Hale, not for me. He did not offer an opinion, then or ever afterwards, as to whether I was right or wrong in regard to that act: and I never inquired. I found from others, some time afterwards, that he had written a strong remonstrance to Mr. Hale, declaring that he would not throw up the newspaper, as many other citizens did that day; because, having the independence of the newspaper press at heart, he thought it unjustifiable to desert an Editor for one slip, however great. Many others thought differently; and Mr. Hale lost so many subscribers before night as to be in a thorough ill-humour about the whole business. His excuse to the public for having delayed the 'exposure' of me so long was, like that of the New York editor, that he had not credited the fact of my attending an abolition meeting till he saw it confirmed in the Liberator, though daily assured of it by many anonymous letters.—In the course of that strange day, many other papers came out, full of fury against me, till Miss Peabody was almost frantic with grief. She had to return to Boston in the evening. Two hours after her return, late in the snowy night, a special messenger brought a letter from Miss Peabody, requiring an immediate answer. The letter told me that the Abolitionists were far from grateful for what I had done, while all the rest of society were alienated; and the justification of this assertion was that an abolition lady had made a saucy speech about it at the supper table of the boarding-house. (I was glad to find afterwards that this was a mistake,—the lady being no Abolitionist, and her meaning being also misapprehended by Miss Peabody.) The main business of the letter was to tell me that there was one newspaper not yet committed against me,—the 'Atlas'; and the Editor had just promised Miss Peabody to wait the return of her

---

[1]   William Ellery Channing (1780–1842), pastor of the Federal Street Church, Boston from 1803 to 1843 and a leading American Unitarian.

messenger for any explanation that I or my friends might send. My reply was, of course, that I had no explanation to give,—the report in the Liberator, on which all this censure was grounded, being perfectly accurate. I requested Miss Peabody to repeat to me no more conversations which were not intended for me to hear, and to burn no more newspapers, which I had a right to see. Next morning, the 'Atlas' came out against me, as strong as all the rest. I was truly concerned for Dr. and Mrs. Walker, who could obtain no guests to meet me but their own relatives, and those, I believe, only by special entreaty.

The day after the declaration of hostilities, while two ladies, yet ignorant of the hubbub, were calling on me, a coach drove up, and Mr. Loring entered, looking like a corpse from the grave. He had been confined to his bed ever since the day of the meeting, had risen from it that morning, to be wrapped in blankets, and put into the coach, and came over the long bridge, and through wind and snow to relieve his mind. He intimated that he must see me alone. I asked him if he could wait till the ladies were gone. 'I can wait all day,' he replied. When I could go to him, I took Miss J. with me as a witness, as I did on all occasions of importance, lest my deafness should cause mistake, or the imputation of it. With strong emotion, Mr. Loring said, 'I find I have injured you; and I have come to know if I can make reparation.' My good friend thought he could never be happy again! I bade him be comforted, telling him that the responsibility of the act of avowal was mine at bottom. The suggestion was his; the decision was mine. 'Thank God!' he exclaimed: 'then my mind is relieved. But the question is, what can I do?' 'Nothing,' I told him:—'that is, supposing the account is accurately given in the papers which have copied from the "Liberator."' I asked him whether he had the Advertiser with him. Yes, he had; but he never *could* show it me. I desired to see it, as I could not form a judgment without. He threw it into my lap, and walked to the window, and up and down the room, paler, if possible, than before. The facts were correctly stated, and I had therefore only to send my friend home, desiring him to get well, and trust me to bear the consequences of saying abroad what I had long ago printed at home. He left me much relieved, as he said; but he was long in getting over it. When Miss J. and I were staying at his house some weeks afterwards, we observed with pain the cloud that came over the faces of himself and his wife at every slight and insult, public and private, offered to me. I took occasion one day, when they and I were alone, to rebuke this, reminding them that when they devoted themselves to the cause, it was with a determination to bear, for themselves and each other, all its consequences; and that they ought to exert the same faith on behalf of their friends. To this they agreed, and never looked grave on the matter again.

As I anticipated, I saw nothing of Boston society, for some time, but what I had seen before; and at no time was I admitted as I should since have been, if I had accepted the invitations sent me in recent years, to go and see what reparation awaited me. I am told that many people who were panic-stricken during that reign of terror are heartily ashamed now of their treatment of me. I should be glad if they were more ashamed of the flatteries and worship with which the Americans received and entertained me, till I went to that meeting. The 'enthusiasm' of which they boasted, and which, I hereby declare, and my companion can testify, was always distasteful to me, collapsed instantly when I differed publicly from them on a sore point: and their homage was proved to be, like all such idolatries, a worship of the ideal, and no more related to myself, in fact, than to the heroine of a dream. There was something diverting, but more vexatious, in the freaks and whims of imaginative people, during the season of my being (in American phrase) 'Lafayetted'[1] in the United States; that is, during the first half of my stay; and the converse experience of the last few months was not devoid of amusement, though it was largely mingled with disgust. The 'lion-hunters' who embarrassed me with invitations which I had no inclination to accept, now backed out of their liability with a laughable activity. Mrs. Douglass Cruger,[2] of New York, who amused and bored Sir Walter Scott so wonderfully, and of whom most English celebrities have curious anecdotes to tell, was one of the most difficult to deal with, from her pertinacity in insisting that I should be her guest when I made my stay at New York: but, before I went there, I had made my abolition avowal; and never was there such a list of reasons why a hostess could not invite guests; as Mrs. Cruger poured out to me when we met in a crowd at a ball; nor any thing so sudden as her change of tone, with some hesitation lingering in it, when she saw that I was well received

---

[1] Celebrated, fêted, as Lafayette was when he visited American colonies in 1777 to aid their cause.

[2] The Crugers were a prominent New York family who had made their fortune in shipping. The grandfather, John Cruger (1710–92), served as colonial mayor of New York; in the next generation Henry Cruger (1739–1827) became a British M.P., and John (1738–1807) served as mayor of New York in 1764, returning to England after the Revolution as a Loyalist. In 1830 Harriet Douglas (1790–1872), a woman wealthy in her own right, had married Henry Cruger (of the third generation), with the agreement that she retain her own name and rights to her property. The couple's divorce in 1850 was a local scandal.

after all. A somewhat similar instance was that of General and Mrs. Sullivan,[1] of Boston, with whom Miss J. and I had travelled for many days together, and who had been urgent in their entreaties that we would spend a long time with them in Boston. On the appearance of the Advertiser article, they ceased their attentions, taking no further notice of me than once inviting me to a family party. Moreover, Dr. Channing inquired of some friends of mine whether I had been informed of the manner in which the Sullivans were speaking of me throughout Boston; for that I ought to be put on my guard against looking for, or accepting, attentions from persons who so treated my name. Again, I called one day on Mr. and Mrs. C.G.L.,[2] with whom we had had friendship on the Mississippi, and who had been then, and were always afterwards, kind to us in every possible way. I found Mr. L. ill, and almost unable to speak from a swelled face. Mrs. L. explained for him that he was wretched on my account, and had had two sleepless nights. Three gentlemen had called on him, entreating him to use his influence in persuading me not to expose myself to the censure and ridicule of the whole country. In answer to all that I said, Mrs. L. pleaded the wretchedness of her family in hearing 'such things' said of me; and she continued piteously beseeching me not to do 'such things.' She said all Boston was in an uproar about it. Alas! no power availed to put 'all Boston in an uproar' about the intolerable lot of millions of slaves, or about the national disgrace of their fate. My friends could lie awake at night from concern about what their neighbours were saying of a passing stranger, to whom Boston opinion would be nothing a year hence; and they could not spare a moment, or an emotion, for the negro mother weeping for her children, nor for the crushed manhood of hundreds of thousands of their countrymen whose welfare was their natural charge. In vain I told my friends how ashamed I was of my troubles being cared for, and how much better their grief and agitation might be bestowed on real sufferers whom they *could* aid, than on me who complained of nothing, and needed nothing. But really the subservience to opinion in Boston at that time seemed a sort of mania; and the sufferers under it were insane enough to expect that their slavery was to be shared by a foreigner accustomed to a totally different state of society.

---

[1] William Sullivan (1774–1839), brigadier-general of the state militia, was an able lawyer, an acclaimed orator, and a respected historian, on whom Harvard had conferred an LL.D. in 1826.

[2] Probably Charles Greeley Loring (1794–1868), a Boston lawyer and friend of Edward Everett.

For a considerable time, my intercourse was confined to the Abolitionists and their friends, and my own former friends; but before the end of my stay, it seemed to be discovered that I was not the monster that had been described; and sundry balls and parties were given for my entertainment. In other States, however, the prejudice remained as long as I was in the country, and some time after, giving place at length to an earnest desire (to judge by the warmth of invitations from various quarters) that I would return, and see their country in what my correspondents call its normal state. I am pleased to find, however, within the last few days, that in the South I am still reviled, as I was twenty years ago, and held up, in the good company of Mrs. Chapman and Mrs. Stowe,[1] to the abhorrence of the South. If I am proud of my company, in one sense, I am ashamed of it in another. Mrs. Chapman and Mrs. Stowe have really sacrificed and suffered, and thrown their whole future into the cause; whereas mine is so cheap a charity that I blush to have it associated with theirs. By their side, I am but as one who gives a half-penny to a beggar, in comparison with those who have sold all their goods to feed the poor.

From Boston I went to New York; and, though several months had passed, the impression against me was so strong that my host, on whose arm I entered a ball-room, was 'cut' by fourteen of his acquaintance on that account. When he told me this, as a sign of the time, he related that, seeing a group of gentlemen gathered round a pompous young man who was talking vehemently, he put his head in to see what it was all about, when he heard the following;—'My verdict is that Harriet Martineau is either an impertinent meddler in our affairs, or a woman of genius without common sense.' My host replied, with equal solemnity, 'If, sir, such be your sentence, Miss Martineau must bear it as she may!' thus exploding the serious business with a general laugh. These instances are mere samples of social rudenesses too numerous to be related.

To return to the 'Daily Advertiser';—in about ten days, an article appeared which the Editor declared to be his *amende*, and which the public seemed to consider such. The Editor professed to choose, from among an amazing number, a letter which was afterwards avowed to be by Mr. Minot,[2] a respected Boston merchant, and a connexion of the Sedgwicks. The insertion of this letter was considered by all who understood the principle involved in the case an aggravation of the original offense against that principle. It observed that American travellers were

---

[1]   Maria Chapman (see p. 344, n. 1) and Harriet Beecher Stowe (1811–96), author of *Uncle Tom's Cabin* (1851–52) and an early opponent of slavery.

[2]   Probably Charles Minot (1810–66), a Boston lawyer and railroad superintendent.

allowed in England, by courtesy, the liberty of expressing their opinions on all subjects; and it was to be hoped that Boston would not refuse a similar courtesy to a distinguished lady who was allowed in private relations to be, &c., &c., and to whom a debt of gratitude was owing for her writings. I have strong reason to believe that the discussions arising out of this treatment of me,—the attacks and the yet worse *amende*,—roused the minds of many young citizens to a consideration of the whole subject of freedom of opinion, and made many converts to that, and also to Abolitionism. One clear consequence of my conversation and experience together was that the next prosecution for Blasphemy in Massachusetts was the last. An old man, above seventy, was imprisoned in a grated dungeon for having printed that he believed the God of the Universalists to be 'a chimera of the imagination.' Some who had listened to my assertions of the rights of thought and speech drew up a Memorial to the Governor of the State for a pardon for old Abner Kneeland,[1]— stating their ground with great breadth and clearness, while disclaiming any kind of sympathy with the views and spirit of the victim. The prime mover being a well-known religious man, and Dr. Channing being willing to put his name at the head of the list of requisitionists, the principle of their remonstrance stood out brightly and unmistakably. The religious corporations opposed the petitioners with all their efforts; and the newspapers threw dirt at them with extraordinary vigour; so that the Governor did not grant their request: but when old Abner Kneeland came out of his prison every body knew that that ancient phase of society had passed away, and that there would never again be a prosecution for Blasphemy in Massachusetts. The civil rights of Atheists have not since been meddled with, though those of the coloured race and their champions are still precarious or worse.

The general indignation which I encountered at every step was, however disagreeable, far less painful to me than some experience among my personal friends. A letter from my Philadelphia host[2] (the same who turned pale at Dr. Julius's news) grieved me much. He told me that his first intimation of what I had done was from the abuse in the newspapers; that his great hope was that I had not acted without purpose; but that still, under any circumstances, he could not but greatly lament the

---

[1]   Abner Kneeland (1774–1844) began as a Baptist clergyman, then became a Universalist, and finally a Pantheist. In 1836 he was tried for blasphemy before the supreme court of Massachusetts. In the first British edition of the *Autobiography*, Martineau reprinted the "Memorial," signed by "Dr. Channing and 166 others."

[2]   William Furness; see p. 339, n. 1.

act, as he feared it would totally ruin the effect upon the American public of any book I might write. In my reply I reminded him of his own exhortation to me to forget all about writing a book, in order that my own impressions and ideas of what I witnessed might be true and free. He abandoned his objection to my attending the meeting, but still wished that I had not further committed myself. When I visited Philadelphia some months afterwards, I found the aspect of society much changed towards me; and my hostess and her coterie of friends surrendered none of their objections to what I had done. How changed is the whole scene now! That host of mine has become one of the most marked men in the cause. The scales fell from his eyes long years ago, and he perceived that there can be small virtue in preaching and teaching which covers up the master sin and sorrow of the time. He has seen from his pulpit a large proportion of his hearers rise and go away on his first mention of the subject on which they most needed to hear him. He has undergone social reproach and family solicitude for doing what I did—under the same objection, but at infinitely greater risk, and under temptations to silence which scarcely another in his profession has had grace to resist. In those days, however, I had to feel that I must stand alone; and, far worse, my friend's disapprobation (he being the most unworldly and upright of men) could not but cause some perplexity in my mind, even so simple an action as this, in the midst of a clamour which left me scarcely any quietness for reflexion. I found it best to accept this new trouble as retribution if I had indeed been wrong, and to defer too close a questioning of past acts to a calmer time. If any are surprised that I could be shaken even thus far, I can only say that they cannot conceive of the hubbub of censure in which I was living,—enough to confound the soberest senses.

On one occasion, my indignation was fairly roused. Among the passengers in my voyage out was the Rev. Charles Brooks,[1] who showed me great kindness during our whole acquaintance, and whose first wife was a special friend of mine. I was their guest at the time of the anniversary festival of Forefathers' Day,[2] at Plymouth, and I accompanied them to the celebration. The first incident of the day was a rather curious one. The orator of the occasion was Senator Sprague,[3]

---

[1] Charles Brooks (1795–1872), Congregational minister in Hingham, Massachusetts, advocated a version of the Prussian educational system and founded normal schools to train teachers.

[2] December 21st, the anniversary of the Pilgrims' landing at Plymouth Rock.

[3] Peleg Sprague (1793–1880) served as Whig senator from Maine from December, 1829, until January, 1835, when he resigned to practice law in Boston; from 1841 to 1865 he was a federal judge for the district of Massachusetts.

whom I had known well at Washington. He took particular pains to have me seated where I could hear him well; and then he fixed his eye on me, as if addressing to me particularly the absurd abuse of England which occupied much of his address, and some remarks which were unmistakably intended for my correction. On our returning to our quarters while the gentlemen went to dinner, an aged lady who could not brave the cold out of doors, asked me how I liked Mr. Sprague's address; on which her daughter burst out with an exclamation which I have never forgotten. The blood rose to her temples, and she threw her bonnet on the table as she cried 'O mother! I am sick of this boasting and exaltation of ourselves over others. When I think of what we might be and what we are, I want to say only "God be merciful to us sinners!"' While we were dressing for the ball, the gentlemen were dining. When Mr. Brooks came for us, he bent over my chair to inform me that my health had been proposed by the President to the Sons of the Pilgrims, and drunk with honour; and that it had fallen to him to return thanks for me, as my nearest friend present. I was struck by his perplexed and abashed countenance; but I might have gone to the ball believing his tale without deduction but for an accident which gave me some notion of what had really taken place. Mr. Brooks, who always went out of the room, or at least covered his face with a screen, when the subject of anti-slavery was mentioned, would willingly have kept from me, if it had been possible, all knowledge of the toast: but it was not possible; and he told me himself in order that I might know only what was convenient to him, at the risk of my making myself ridiculous at the ball. Happily, there was some one who served me better.—The method in which the President had introduced my health was this. After designating 'the Illustrious Stranger' who was to be toasted, he said that he was confident no son of the Pilgrims would refuse to drink, considering that the lady in question was their guest, and how they and their children were indebted to her for her writings. Considering these things, could they not forgive her, if, holding absurd and mischievous opinions, she had set them in operation in a sphere where she had no concern? Could they not forgive one such act in a guest to whom they were under such large obligations?—What Mr. Brooks took upon him to say for me, I was never able, with all my pains, to ascertain; for the newspapers gave merely an intimation that he acknowledged the toast. From his unwillingness that I should hear exactly what passed, I have always trembled to think what surrender of principle he may have made in my name.

From Boston, the abuse of me ran through almost every paper in the Union. Newspapers came to me from the South, daring me to enter the Slave States again, and offering mock invitations to me to come and see how they would treat foreign incendiaries. They would hang me: they would cut my tongue out, and cast it on a dunghill; and so forth. The calumnies were so outrageous, and the appeal to the fears of the Slave-holders so vehement that I could feel no surprise if certain interested persons were moved to plot against my life. My name was joined with George Thompson's, (who had already escaped with difficulty):[1] I was represented as a hired agent, and appeals were made to popular passions to stop my operations. I believe that almost all the extreme violences perpetrated against Abolitionists have been by the hands of slave-traders, and not by the ordinary kind of American citizens. The slave-traders on the great rivers are (or were then) generally foreigners,—outcasts from European countries,—England and Ireland among the number.[2] These desperate men, driving a profitable trade, which they believe to be endangered by the Abolitionists, were not likely to scruple any means of silencing their enemies. Such, and such only, have I ever believed to have designed any violence against me. Such as these were the instiga-tors of the outrages of the time,—the floggings in the market-places, as in Amos Dresser's case,[3]—the tarrings and featherings of travellers who were under suspicion of anti-slavery opinion, and the murder of Lovejoy[4] on his own threshold, in Illinois, on account of his gallant and heroic defence of the liberty of the press on the subject of Slavery.

These fellows haunted the Ohio at the time when I was about to descend the river with a party of friends, on a visit to the West which

[1] Thompson was pursued by a Boston mob, and escaped death by fleeing in a rowboat to an English vessel, going to St. Johns, New Brunswick, and sailing back to England in November, 1835.

[2] Martineau wrote in greater detail about the violent actions of these men in the "Compromise" chapter of *Retrospect of American Travel*, saying that the "Lynchers ... had triumphantly broken the laws, and trodden under foot their constitution of sixteen years" and concluding that the Missouri Compromise was ineffective.

[3] Amos Dresser (1812–1904), an Oberlin college student, was arrested and publicly whipped by a committee of citizens in Nashville, Tennessee, for being a member of an Ohio anti-slavery society and disseminating anti-slavery materials.

[4] Elijah Parish Lovejoy (1802–37), abolitionist and newspaper publisher, was murdered in Alton, Illinois, on November 7, 1837 (after Martineau's departure) for publishing anti-slav-ery opinions in his religious paper, *The Observer*; his brother Owen (1811–64), who witnessed the murder, devoted himself to abolitionism and held public anti-slavery meet-ings, despite their illegality in Illinois and the repeated threats of violence to which he was subjected.

was to occupy the last three months of my stay in America. The party consisted of Dr. and Mrs. Follen and their child, and Mr. and Mrs. Loring. We intended first to visit Birney at Cincinnati,[1] and afterwards to meet a brother of Dr. Follen's, who had a farm in Missouri. We knew that we could not enter Missouri with safety; but Mr. Follen was to cross the river, and join us in Illinois. Every thing was arranged for this in the winter, and we were rejoicing in the prospect, when the consequences of my abolition avowal interfered to spoil the plan. Miss J. and I were staying at Dr. Channing's towards spring, when, on our return about eleven o'clock one night from a visit, we were rather surprised to find Mr. Loring sitting in Dr. Channing's study. We were surprised, not only on account of the lateness of the hour, but because Mr. Loring was not then a visiting acquaintance of Dr. Channing's. Both of us were struck with the air of gloom in everybody's face and manner. We attempted conversation; but in vain: nobody supported it. Presently, Dr. Channing crossed the room to say to me 'I have requested Mr. Loring to remain, in order to tell you himself the news he has brought. I desire that you should hear it from his own lips.' It appeared that Mr. Loring had been waiting some hours. He told us that an eminent merchant of the city, with whom he was previously unacquainted, had that day called on him to say that he felt it his duty to give some intelligence to my friends of a matter which nearly concerned my safety. He took no interest whatever in the abolition question, on the one side or the other; but he could not allow the personal safety of a stranger to be imperilled without giving warning. He had been in the West on business, and had there learned that I was expected down the Ohio in the spring: that certain parties had sworn vengeance against me; and that they had set a watch upon the steamboats, where I should be recognised by my trumpet. At Cincinnati, the intention was to prosecute me, if possible; and, at any rate, to prevent my going further. Much worse things were contemplated at the slave-holding city of Louisville. My going upon the Ohio at all would not be permitted, the gentleman was sure, by any who cared for my security; and he explained that he was reporting what he positively knew, from the testimony of his own ears, as well as by trustworthy information; and that the people to be feared were not the regular inhabitants of the towns, but the hangers-on at the wharves; and especially the slave-traders. This gentleman's first business on his return was

---

[1]   James G. Birney (1792–1857), an advocate of the rights of Cherokees and former officer of the American Colonization Society, freed his slaves in 1834 and moved from Kentucky (a slave state) to Ohio (a free state).

to ascertain who were my most intimate friends, and to appeal to them to prevent my going near the Ohio. All this seemed so incredible to me that I made light of it at first: but the party looked more and more grave, and Mr. Loring said: 'Well, then, I must tell you what they mean to do. They mean to lynch you.' And he proceeded to detail the plan. The intention was to hang me on the wharf before the respectable inhabitants could rescue me.

Not wishing to detain Mr. Loring, as it was just midnight, I gave at once, as my decision, what seemed plain to my own mind. I told him that I had less means of judging what was likely to happen than natives of the country; and I would leave it to my own party to determine what should be done. I supposed that none of them would think of relinquishing such a scheme for mere threats; and if they were not afraid, neither was I. The decision must rest with them.—The gloom of the 'good-night' which the Channings gave me oppressed me even more than what I had just heard. While pondering the affair in the middle of the night, I recurred to what my brother James had suggested in a recent letter. He had abstained from giving any opinion of what I had done, as none from such a distance could be of any value: but he had proposed that I should transmit my papers piecemeal to England; for the obvious reason that destroying my papers would be the aim of the enemy, in order to prevent my publication of my journals at home. I had no immediate means of transmitting my papers: but I had obtained permission from a clergyman who was not an Abolitionist to deposit my papers in his unsuspected keeping. I had resolved now that this should be my first work in the morning.

After breakfast, while I was sealing up my parcel, Dr. Channing stood beside me, more moved than I had ever seen him. He went to his bookshelves, and came back again, and went again, as if to look at his books, but in truth to wipe away the tears that rolled down under his spectacles. What he said I remember, and the tone of his voice, as if it was five minutes ago. 'I am ashamed,' he said, 'that after what you have done for the people of this country, there should be any part of it in which you cannot set your foot. We are accustomed to say that we are under obligations to you; and yet you are not safe among us. I hope that, as soon as you return home, you will expose these facts with all the boldness of which you are capable.' I replied that I should not publish, in my accounts of America, any personal narrative of injury: for, besides the suspicion and odium that attach to a narrative of personal sufferings from insult, it was to me a much more striking fact that native citizens, like himself and Mr. Garrison and others, to whom the Constitution expressly guarantees the liberty of traversing all the States as freely as any one of them, should be excluded by intimidation from half the States of the Union. Dr. Channing said, 'As to this journey, you must indeed give it up. I think, if you consider that no immediate call of duty takes you to the Ohio, and that your destruction might involve that of the whole party, you will feel it to be your duty to change your plan.' My party unhesitatingly decided this for me. Mrs. Loring declared that she would not go; and the gentlemen were of opinion that the risk was too serious. I had myself no idea how I should suffer or act in circumstances so new. We therefore gave up the idea of visiting Messrs. Birney and Follen, and determined on another route.

During that spring, as during many preceding months, there were lynchings of Abolitionists in various parts of the country, and threatenings of more. Wherever we went, it was necessary to make up our minds distinctly, and with the full knowledge of each other, what we should say and do in regard to the subject which was filling all men's minds. We resolved, of course, to stand by our anti-slavery principles, and advocate them, wherever fair occasion offered: and we never did omit an opportunity of saying what we knew and thought. On every steamboat, and in every stage (when we entered public conveyances) the subject arose naturally; for no subject was so universally discussed throughout the country, though it was interdicted within the walls of the Capitol at Washington. Mr. Loring joined in the conversation when the legal aspects of the matter were discussed; and Dr. Follen when the religious and moral and political bearings of Slavery were the subject. Mrs. Follen and Mrs. Loring were full of facts and reasons about the working of Abolitionism in its head quarters. As for me, my topic was Texas, in regard to which I was qualified to speak by some recent inquiries and experience at New Orleans. This was three years before the annexation of Texas, and while the adventurers under Colonel Austin were straining every nerve to get Texas annexed.[1] They thought that if, among other devices, they could obtain any sort of sanction from the British government, or could induce English settlers, in any considerable number, to go to Texas, their chances of every sort would be improved. My visit to New Orleans was seized on, among other incidents,

---

[1]   After winning its independence from Mexico, Texas voted to seek annexation to the U.S. and sent Stephen F. Austin (1790–1836) to Washington in 1835 to negotiate the union. In part because of a debate over whether it would be admitted as a slave or free state, Texas remained separate until 1845.

for the prosecution of this chance. After duly preparing me by sending me 'information' in the shape of bragging accounts of the country, they sent a deputation to me at New Orleans, consisting of the notorious Mrs. Holley[1] (who did more than perhaps any other individual for the annexation of Texas) and two or three companions. Concealing from me the fact that Colonel Austin was at that very time in jail at Mexico,[2] my visitors offered me, in the name of the Texan authorities, an estate of several thousand acres in a choice part of the country, and every aid and kindness that could be rendered, if I would bind myself to live for five years in Texas, helping to frame their Constitution, and using my influence to bring over English settlers. The conversation was to me a most ludicrous one, from the boasts made by my guests of their happy state of society, though my questions compelled them to admit that they were living without a Constitution, or any safeguard of law; and in fact subject to the dictatorship of Colonel Austin, a mere adventurer, and then actually in the hands of the Mexicans, who were far too merciful in releasing him after a few months' imprisonment. One plea was urged on me which it was hoped I should find irresistible. There was to be no slave-trade or slavery in Texas. I knew there was none before the Americans intruded themselves; but I could not, and did not, believe in this piece of ostentatious virtue in a set of southern speculators who staked their all on the preservation of Slavery in the United States. I was not surprised to find that, in the absence of an avowed slave-trade, there were negroes conveyed from Louisiana, and landed at night on a spit of sand on the frontier, whence in the morning they immigrated into Texas, where they were not to be slaves:—O dear, no!—not slaves, but apprentices for ninety-nine years! I gave my visitors a bit of my mind, in return for their obliging offer. An English visitor, a scholar and a

---

[1]   Horace Holley (1781–1827), along with his wife Mary, née Austin (1784–1846), started as pastor of Hollis Street Unitarian Church in Boston, and served as president of Transylvania University in Lexington, Kentucky, from 1818 to 1827; he died while establishing a seminary in Louisiana. After five years of governessing, Mrs. Holley emigrated to Texas in 1831 with the help of her cousin, Stephen Austin. In 1833, she published *Texas: Observations Historical, Geographical and Descriptive in a Series of Letters Written during a Visit to Austin's Colony, with a View to a Permanent Settlement in That Country in the Autumn of 1831*.

[2]   In 1830 the Mexican government passed a law to prohibit further American immigration into Texas, hoping to limit American influence over the region. Austin nonetheless continued to expand the colony (as in the case of securing land for his cousin, Mrs. Holley), and helped to frame a constitution for the proposed state of Texas in 1833, which he took to Mexico City with a list of demands for redress of grievances. President Antonio López de Santa Anna repealed the law against further immigration, but refused the request for statehood and had Austin imprisoned for inciting an insurrection.

minister of religion, was deluded by similar offers and suggestions; and deeply concerned he was that I would not go into the enterprise. He wrote repeatedly to offer his assistance for any number of years, and implored me to consider well before I rejected so unequalled an opportunity of usefulness. He offered to come and see me wherever I might stop on the Mississippi; and he fully believed he should induce me to turn back. Poor gentleman! his was a mournful story. His wife died of consumption, on the bank of the Mississippi, just as I reached New Orleans; and he and his children were in their first desolation when he made up his mind to embrace the Texan enterprise. Soon after I answered his final appeal to me to go, I heard of his death by fever. The disease of the country laid him low at the outset of his first season. His children were most benignantly cared for by the American citizens. One died; but the two little daughters were adopted,—one by a planter's lady in the West, and the other by an English lady in the North.—My attention being thus turned towards Texas, I was qualified to bring the subject under Dr. Channing's notice as the interest of it deepened; and to converse upon it in our northern journey when we were perpetually encountering citizens who had been listening to the boasts of Austin's emissaries, at New York or elsewhere.—Dr. Channing's 'Letter' on the Annexation of Texas is perhaps the most honoured in England of all his writings.[1] The credit of originating it belongs in the first place, and chiefly, to Mr. David Lee Child,[2] who furnished an admirable history of the province, and of its sufferings from the Americans, in the Anti-slavery Quarterly Review. From that article I avowedly derived the facts which I gave as the basis of my own account of the Texas business, in my 'Society in America.' I besought Dr. Channing's especial attention to that chapter; and the whole subject so moved him that he sat down and wrote that noble 'Letter,' by the moral effect of which the annexation of Texas was unquestionably deferred for two years. It is not often that the writings of divines have even that much effect in bridling the lusts of ambition and cupidity.

---

[1]   William Ellery Channing's *Letter to the Hon. Henry Clay, On the Annexation of Texas to the United States, August 1, 1837* (Boston: J. Munroe and Company, 1837) viewed Austin's insurrection and the underlying scheme to take over Mexican territory as a step toward war and the extension of slavery.

[2]   David Lee Child (1794–1874), editor of the *Massachusetts Journal* and state congressman, denounced the annexation of Texas in the legislature and published a pamphlet against it, "Naboth's Vineyard."

Our route had for its chief objects (after Niagara) the Northern Lakes.[1] The further we went, the more we heard of lynchings which had lately taken place, or were designed for the next Abolitionists who should come that way. At Detroit, Mr. Loring entered the reading-room of the hotel, immediately on our arrival; and while he read the newspaper, he heard one citizen telling another how during the temporary absence of the latter, there had been a lynching of a fellow who pretended to be a preacher, but was suspected to be an Abolitionist. The speaker added that a party of Abolitionists was expected; and that every thing was in readiness to give them a similar reception. He finished off with saying that lynching did not look well in newspapers, or sound well at a distance; but that it was the only way. Our Abolitionism could be no secret, ready as we always were to say what we knew and thought: and that very evening, I had the pleasure of so far converting the Governor of the State (Michigan) as to possess him with a true idea of Garrison, and to obtain his promise,—which was indeed freely offered, as we took leave,—to protect to the utmost of his power, every Abolitionist within the boundary of the State.

The woods of Michigan were very beautiful; but danger was about us there, as everywhere during those three months of travel. It was out of such glades as those of Michigan that mobs had elsewhere issued to stop the coach, and demand the victim, and inflict the punishment earned by compassion for the negro, and assertion of true republican liberty. I believe there was scarcely a morning during those three months when it was not my first thought on waking whether I should be alive at night. I am not aware that the pleasure of that glorious journey was materially impaired by this; yet I learned by that experience to sympathise with the real griefs of martyrdom, and to feel something different from contemptuous compassion for those who quail under the terror of it.—At Pittsburg, sitting by our open window one hot night, we heard an uproar at a distance, the cause of which my companions truly divined to be a pro-slavery riot. 'What can it be?' I exclaimed, as it drew nearer. 'Only a little execration coming this way,' replied Dr. Follen, smiling, referring to our reputation as execrated persons. We were not the objects that night, however: but the houses of several free negro families were destroyed. What we met with was, usually, prodigious amazement, a little scorn, and a great many warnings.

---

[1]　The Great Lakes of Ontario, Erie, Huron, Michigan, and Superior, all of which she visited except the last.

After so many weeks, during which the idea of danger had become the rule, and safety the exception, we were struck with a kind of astonishment when we entered the great cities,—Philadelphia and New York,—where the comfortable citizens assumed an air of scepticism about the critical state of the country which was truly marvellous in republicans. I have mentioned before how the ladies of one of the first families in New York were kept in ignorance of riots so serious that one might almost as soon expect the ladies of Birmingham and Bristol to have been unaware of the High-church and Reform riots of 1791 and 1831.[1] We now found that selfish, or aristocratic, or timid citizens had kept themselves as ignorant of the dangers of their neighbours as the same kind of men of every country are, in times of great moral revolution. Quiet and complacent were the smiles with which some who ought to have known better declared their disbelief even that threats had been offered to a guest and a woman; and various were the excuses and special reasons given for the many instances of violence to their own citizens which could not be denied. Some were sorry that I believed such threats to myself, and such inflections upon others as were as certainly and notoriously true as the days of the month on which they happened. Some would not listen to the facts at the time: others, who could not doubt them at the time, have tried to get rid of the belief since, but are incessantly thrown back upon the old evidence by the new troubles which arise from day to day out of the cursed and doomed institution of Slavery. I happened to witness the opening of the martyr age of its reformers; and I am thankful that I did witness it. There were times when I was sorry that I was not the victim of the struggle, instead of Lovejoy, or some other murdered citizen. I was sorry, because my being a British subject would have caused wider and deeper consequences to arise from such a murder than followed the slaughter of native Abolitionists,—despised and disowned by their government for their very Abolitionism. The murder of an English traveller would have settled the business of American Slavery (in its federal sense) more speedily than perhaps any other incident. It is no wonder that some Americans, who shut their eyes to the whole subject, should disbelieve in any body being in any danger, and that others should try to make me forget my share of it. The latest and most general method of propitiating me has been by inviting me to go again,

---

[1] For the Birmingham riots of 1791 and the agitations before the Reform Act of 1832, see Period IV, sec. i; on ignorance in New England, see the opening of this section.

and see what Abolitionists my acquaintances have become, —every where north of Mason and Dixon's line.

When I returned home, the daily feeling of security, and of sympathy in my anti-slavery views gave me a pleasure as intense as if I had returned from a long exile, instead of a tour of recreation. I was not left without paltry disturbances, however. In the preface to 'Society in America,' I invited correction as to any errors in (not opinion, but) matters of fact. After this, I could not, of course, decline receiving letters from America. Several arrived, charged double, treble, even quadruple postage. These consisted mainly of envelopes, made heavy by all manner of devices, with a slip of newspaper in the middle, containing prose paragraphs, or copies of verses, full of insults, and particularly of taunts about my deafness. All but one of these bore the post-mark of Boston. I was ashamed to mention this back to America; and I hope that most of this expensive and paltry insult was the work of one hand.

My story seems a long one: but I do not think it could have been honestly omitted in a history of my life: and it seems to be worth telling for another reason,—that it may afford material for an instructive comparison between the state of the cause, (and of American society as determined by it,) in 1835 and 1855. When I was at Washington, the leading statesmen were, or declared themselves to be, confident that the abolition of Slavery would never be even named in Congress; to which I replied that when they could hedge in the wind and build out the stars from their continent, they might succeed in their proposed exclusion: and now, at the end of twenty years, what has come of the attempt? It was prosecuted with all diligence. A rigid censorship in the Southern States expunged from English and other classics every reference to Slavery, and every perilous aspiration after freedom. Abolitionists were kept out by the most vigilant cruelty, which inflicted torture on mere suspicion. Free negroes were lodged in prison, even when they were British sailors; as indeed they are still liable to be. The right of petition to Congress was temporarily abolished. Every liberty, personal and social, was sacrificed in the attempt to enforce silence on that one sore subject.[1] And now the whole world rings with it. Congress can, in fact, talk about nothing else: for, whatever subject a debate may ostensibly

---

[1] The "recapturing" of freed blacks of both American and British citizenship in the South was notorious, and detailed in Edward S. Abdy's *Journal of a Residence and Tour in the United States* (London, 1835) and in many anti-slavery periodicals. Before 1815, blacks had served in the British and American military, but in 1815 the American War Department issued a memorandum forbidding recruitment of black soldiers.

be upon, it always merges in a wrangle on Slavery. The entire policy of the Republic has been shaped by it; and the national mind also, in as far as the public mind depends on the national policy in a democratic republic. The moral deterioration has been more rapid than the most cautious of the early Presidents could have apprehended, or than the despots of the world could have hoped. Because it was necessary to obtain new territory for the support of the destructive institution, a process of aggression and annexation was entered upon; and that policy has dragged back the mind and morals of the people into that retrograde state in which territorial aggrandisement is the national aim. This, again, implicates foreign nations in the interest of the question. It was not enough that every political movement in the United States was modified by this great controversy;—that it ruined, and still ruins, every statesman who takes the immoral side;—that it destroyed the career and broke the hearts of the most eminent of them,—of Calhoun, of Clay, and of Webster;—that it shattered the reputation of more, and is now rendering absolutely certain the dissolution of the Union, in one way or another, and with more or less chance of its virtuous reconstitution:—it was not enough that all this has happened at home, amidst the most desperate efforts to cover up the difficulty under an enforced silence:—it has enlisted almost every people and ruler in the world on the one side or the other. The Czars are making friendships with the slave power, as the most hopeful ally on earth of Russian tyranny. Spain is immediately interested, because Cuba is the next morsel for which the ogre lusts. The friendship of Western Europe, otherwise so certain to be cordial and durable, is rendered in the last degree precarious by the lawless and barbaric proceedings of the pro-slavery Americans. The depressed nationalities of Europe, who might otherwise look up to America for protection and aid, can now only blush at the disgrace reflected by America on republicanism all over the world, and sigh at the hopelessness of any real assistance from a nation which cannot aid freedom abroad because it has to take care of its own slavery, and beware of its victims at home. That which was the protest of almost a solitary voice when I went to America has now expanded into a world-wide controversy.—It was in 1832 that Garrison, the apostle of the deepest and broadest cause of our century, said those immortal words. 'I am aware that many object to the severity of my language; but is there not cause for severity? I will be as harsh as truth, and as uncompromising as justice. I am in earnest—I will not equivocate—I will not excuse—I will not retreat a single inch—AND I WILL BE HEARD.' This

humble printer, so speaking after the first taste of persecution, a quarter of a century ago, has made himself 'heard' round the globe and from
pole to pole. There is no saying what fates and policies of nations were
involved in those first utterances of his. The negroes first heard him, by
some untraceable means; and the immediate consequence was the cessation of insurrection. There were frequent risings of the slaves before;
and there have been none since. But the lot of the negro race is by no
means the only or the chief fate involved in the controversy. Every
political and social right of the white citizens has been imperilled in
the attempt to enforce silence on the subject of slavery. Garrison will
be recognised hereafter, not only as at present,—as the Moses of the
enslaved race, leading them out of their captivity,—but as more truly
the founder of the republic than Washington himself. Under the first
Presidents, democratic republicanism made a false start. It has bolted
from the course, and the Abolitionists are bringing it back to the start-
ing-post. If it is found capable of winning the race against old despo-
tisms and temporary accommodations of constitutional monarchy, the
glory of the consummation will be awarded more plentifully to the
regenerators of the republic than to its originators, great as they were;
for they left in it a fatal compromise.—But I must not enlarge further
on this subject, on which I have written abundantly elsewhere. I could
say much; and it requires self-denial to abstain from a statement of what
Garrison's friends, Mr. and Mrs. Henry Grafton Chapman, and their
relatives on both sides of the house contributed to the cause by deeds
and sufferings. But my peculiar connexion with Mrs. Chapman in this
memoir[1] renders it impossible to speak as I would. Happily, the claims
of that privileged family are and will be understood without any appeal
from me to the veneration and gratitude of society.

The accident of my arriving in America in the dawning hour of the
great conflict accounts for the strange story I have had to tell about
myself. Any person from England, so arriving, pledged as I was to anti-
slavery views, and conspicuous enough to draw attention to those
views, was sure to meet with just such treatment;—a blinding incense
first; and then, if the incense failed to blind, a trial of the method of
intimidation. Other English persons were indeed so prepared for and
received. Some did not understand their position, and went unconsciously into the snare. Some took fright. Some thought prudence

---

[1]   I.e., the fact that Maria Chapman had been designated as editor of the *Autobiography* and
      its "Memorials."

necessary, for the sake of some other cause which they had more at heart. Some were even converted by the romancing of the slave-owners. Some did their duty. It is not, and it never will be, forgotten how Lord Carlisle did his, when, as Lord Morpeth,[1] he traversed the whole country, never failing in the kindliness and candour which adorn his temper, while never blinking the subject of slavery, or disguising his anti-slavery convictions. The reign of terror (for travellers at least) was over before he went; and he would have been safe under any circumstances: but he was subject to insults and slander, and was abundantly visited with a laborious contempt: and in bringing this upon himself and bearing it good-humouredly, he threw his mite into the treasury which is to redeem the slaves. He seems to have been pitied and excused in somewhat the same style as myself by persons who assumed to be our protectors. When I had conversed on board a steamboat with a young lady of colour, well educated and well mannered, and whom I had been acquainted with at Philadelphia, I was of course, the object of much wrath and denunciation on deck; and my spontaneous protectors thought themselves generous in pleading that I ought to be excused for such conduct, on the ground of the 'narrowness of my foreign education!' Such were the vindications with which Lord Carlisle also was insulted when he was vindicated at all.

It was impossible, during such a crisis, to avoid judging conspicuous persons more or less by their conduct in regard to the great conflict of their time. Ordinary persons might be living as common-place people do in such times,—in utter unconsciousness of their position. As in the days of Noah, such people buy and sell and build and plant, and are troubled by no forecast of what is to happen. But in a republic, it cannot be so with the conspicuous citizens. The Emersons, for instance, (for the adored Charles Emerson[2] was living then:)—they were not men to join an association for any object; and least of all, for any moral one: nor were they likely to quit their abstract meditations for a concrete employment on behalf of the negroes. Yet they did that which made me feel that I knew them, through the very cause in which they did not implicate themselves. At the time of the hubbub against me in Boston, Charles

---

[1] George William Frederick Howard (1802–64), Lord Morpeth from 1825 to 1848, visited America in 1841–42. In December, 1850 he delivered a lecture on the American situation to the Leeds Mechanics' Institute, published as *Travels in America* (London: Simpkin, Marshall, 1851). He also wrote a preface to the London edition of Stowe's *Uncle Tom's Cabin* (1852).

[2] Charles Chauncey Emerson (1808–36), fifth and youngest son of the Rev. William Emerson, minister of the First Church, Boston, and brother of Ralph Waldo.

Emerson stood alone in a large company in defence of the right of free thought and speech, and declared that he had rather see Boston in ashes than that I, or anybody, should be debarred in any way from perfectly free speech. His brother Waldo[1] invited me to be his guest, in the midst of my unpopularity, and, during my visit, told me his course about this matter of slavery. He did not see that there was any particular thing for him to do in it then: but when, in coaches or steamboats or any where else, he saw people of colour ill-used, or heard bad doctrine or senti- ment propounded, he did what he could and said what he thought. Since that date, he has spoken more abundantly and boldly the more critical the times became; and he is now, and has long been, completely identified with the Abolitionists in conviction and sentiment, though it is out of his way to join himself to their organisation.—The other eminent scholars and thinkers of the country revealed themselves no less clearly,—the literary men of Boston and Cambridge sneering at the controversy as 'low' and disagreeable, and troubling to their repose, and Edward Everett, the man of letters *par excellence*, burning incense to the south, and insulting the Abolitionists while they were few and weak, endeavoring to propitiate them as they grew strong, and finally break- ing down in irretrievable disgrace under a pressure to which he had exposed himself by ambition, but which he had neither courage nor conscience to abide.[2] I early saw in him the completest illustration I met with of the influences of republican life upon a man of powers without principle, and of knowledge without wisdom. He was still worshipped through vanity, when I knew him, though his true deserts were well

---

[1]   Ralph Waldo Emerson (1803–82), second son of William Emerson, became co-pastor of the Second Church, Boston in 1829 and had an active interest in public affairs, including philanthropic movements and anti-slavery efforts. In 1832, he resigned his pastorate after deciding that the communion elements were purely spiritual and refusing to compromise with his congregation (that he should retain the right to his own interpretation but leave them free to retain theirs). Martineau met Emerson in 1833 during his visit to England; by the time she toured America, he had begun his career as a lecturer, speaking on English literature in 1835, on the philosophy of history in 1836, and on human culture in 1837. It was a common view, not original with Martineau, that Emerson's mission was not to do practical work for reform, but to supply inspiration for others.

[2]   Edward Everett (1794–1865) served as American minister to Great Britain from 1841 to 1845. Martineau suspected his moral character (based on rumors that he was "licentious") and distrusted his late conversion to abolitionism; in a letter of 29 December 1841 to Catherine Macready, she wrote: "The present Amern Minister here, Everett, is an aboli- tionist:—a late convert,—for political reasons,—a man who nobody trusts in matters of high principles, tho' he has otherwise most valuable qualifications for his office,—talent, learn- ing, industry, accomplishment, friendliness of temper" (in Sanders, ed., *Selected Letters*, 63).

enough understood in private: he had plenty of opportunity to retrieve his political character afterwards: he obtained in England, when ambassador, abundance of the admiration which he sacrificed so much to win; and then at last, when the hour arrived which must test his quality, he sank, and must abide for the rest of his life in a slough of contempt from which there is no rescue. This is precisely what was anticipated twenty years ago by (not his enemies, for I believe he then had none, but) friends who mourned over his quitting a life of scholarship, for which he was eminently qualified, for one of political aspiration. They knew that he had not self-reliance or courage enough for effective ambition, nor virtue enough for a career of independence. It is all over now; and the vainest of men, who lives by the breath of praise, is placed for the sad remnant of his days between the scorn of the many and the pity of the few. Vindicators he has none; and I believe no followers. The Sedgwicks[1] were beginning to be interested in the great controversy; but they were not only constitutionally timid,—with that American timidity which we English can scarcely conceive of,—but they worshipped the parchment idol, —the Act of Union; and they did not yet perceive, as some of them have done since, that a human decree which contravenes the laws of Nature must give way when the two are brought into conflict. I remember Miss Sedgwick starting back in the path, one day when she and I were walking beside the sweet Housatonic,[2] and snatching her arm from mine when I said, in answer to her inquiry, what I thought the issue of the controversy must be. 'The dissolution of the Union!' she cried. 'The Union is sacred, and must be preserved at all cost.' My answer was that the will of God was sacred too, I supposed; and if the will of God which, as she believed, condemned slavery should come into collision with the federal constitution which sanctioned it, the only question was which should give way, —the Divine will or a human compact. It did not appear to me then, any more than now, that the dissolution of the Union need be of a hostile character. That the elimination of the two pro-slavery clauses from the constitution must take place sooner or later was always clear to me; but I do not see why the scheme should not be immediately and peaceably reconstituted, if the Americans will but foresee the necessity in time. The horror expressed by the Sedgwicks at what seemed so inevitable a consequence of the original compromise

---

[1]   On the Sedgwicks, see p. 337, n. 2.

[2]   The Housatonic River originates in northwestern Massachusetts, runs through Stockbridge, the Sedgwicks' home, and flows into Long Island Sound at Stratford, Connecticut.

surprised me a good deal: and I dare say it seems strange to themselves by this time: for Miss Sedgwick and others of her family have on occasion spoken out bravely on behalf of the liberties of the republic, when they were most compromised. I had a great admiration of much in Miss Sedgwick's character, though we were too opposite in our natures, in many of our views, and in some of our principles, to be very congenial companions. Her domestic attachments and offices were charming to witness; and no one could be further from all conceit and vanity on account of her high reputation in her own country. Her authorship did not constitute her life; and she led a complete life, according to her measure, apart from it: and this is a spectacle which I always enjoy, and especially in the case of a woman. The insuperable difficulty between us,—that which closed our correspondence, though not our good will, was her habit of flattery;—a national weakness, to which I could have wished that she had been superior. But her nature was a timid and sensitive one; and she was thus predisposed to the national failing;—that is, to one side of it; for she could never fall into the cognate error,—of railing and abuse when the flattery no longer answers. She praised or was silent. The mischief was that she praised people to their faces, to a degree which I have never considered it necessary to permit. I told her that I dreaded receiving her letters because, instead of what I wished to hear, I found praise of myself. She informed me that, on trial, she found it a *gêne* to suppress what she wanted to say; and thus it was natural for us to cease from corresponding. I thought she wanted courage, and shrank from using her great influence on behalf of her own convictions; and she thought me rash and rough. She thought 'safety' a legitimate object of pursuit in a gossiping state of society; and I did not care for it,— foreigner as I was, and witnessing, as I did, as critical a struggle as has ever agitated society. I said what I thought and what I knew of the Websters and the Everetts, and other northern men who are now universally recognised as the disgrace rather than the honour of the region they represented. Their conduct, even then, authorised my judgment of them: but she, a northern woman, shared the northern caution, if not the sectional vanity, which admired and upheld, as long as possible, the men of genius and accomplishment who sustained the intellectual reputation of New England. Through all our differences of view and temperament, I respected and admired Miss Sedgwick, and I was sorry to be absent from England in 1839 when she was in London, and when I should have enjoyed being of any possible use to her and her connexions, who showed me much hospitality and kindness in their own country. What

I think of Miss Sedgwick's writings I told in a review of her works in the Westminster Review of October, 1837.[1] Her novels, and her travels, published some years later, had better be passed over with the least possible notice; but I think her smaller tales wonderfully beautiful;—those which, as 'Home' and 'Live and Let Live,' present pictures of the household life of New England which she knows so well, and loves so heartily.

Of Webster, as of Clay, Calhoun, President Jackson and others, I gave my impressions in my books on America, nearly twenty years ago.[2] I will not repeat any thing I then and there said: but will merely point out how their fate corresponded with their ordeal. 'My dear woman,' said Mr. Webster to me at his own table, laying his finger on my arm to emphasize his words,—'don't you go and believe me to be ambitious. No man can despise that sort of thing more than I do. I would not sacrifice an hour of my ease for all the honours and powers in the world.' Mr. Clay made no protestations of the sort to me; nor Mr. Calhoun, whom, with all his absurdities, I respected by far the most of the three, in the long run. All were hugely ambitious: but Calhoun was honest in the main point. He lived and died for the cause of Slavery; and, however far such a career is from the sympathies of English people, the openness and directness of his conduct were at least respectable. He was infatuated by his sectional attachments: but he was outspoken and consistent. Mr. Clay never satisfied me of his sincerity on the great question of his time; but there was much, outside of that trying matter, that was interesting and even honourable;—a genuine warmth, a capacity for enthusiasm, and vast political ability. Our intercourse amounted to friendship at last; but his unworthy conduct during the closing years of his life overthrew my esteem, and destroyed my regard for him. While professing a desire to provide for the future abolition of slavery, he prevented in some parts its immediate abolition, and he extended in others the area of its prevalence. He was as well aware as any body of the true character of the Colonisation scheme of which he accepted the presidency; and he continued to laud it to foreigners as an agency of emancipation, when he knew that it was established and upheld by slaveholders like himself, for the protection and security of the institution of Slavery. His personal ambition

---

[1] "Miss Sedgwick's Works," *Westminster Review* 28 (October 1837), 42–65. The review treated all of Catharine Sedgwick's fiction and sketches, including *Tales and Sketches* (1835), which was dedicated to Martineau "as a humble expression of the respect and affection of the author."

[2] See the chapters "Life at Washington" and "The Capitol" in *Retrospect of American Travel*.

was as keen as Webster's; and the failure of both in their aspirations for the Presidentship destroyed them both.[1] In regard to genius, both were of so high an order, and their qualifications were so little alike that there is no need to set the one above the other. Webster's training was the higher; his position as a Massachusetts man the more advantageous, morally and politically; his folly and treachery in striving to win the supreme honours of the state by winning the south, through the sacrifice of the rights and liberties of the north were, of necessity, more extreme and more conspicuous than any double dealing of Mr. Clay's; his retribution was the more striking; and the disgrace which he drew down on his last days was the more damning of the two. But both these men, who might have rivalled the glory of Washington himself, by carrying the state through a stress as real and fearful as that of eighty years ago, will be remembered as warnings and not as examples. As far as appears, they were the last of the really great men who led the statesmanship of the republic; and to their failure, moral and political, may perhaps be mainly charged the fatal mischief which now hangs as a doom over the state, that the best men decline entering political life, and that there is every inducement for the least capable and the least worthy to be placed in the highest seats. The ablest men of their generation did not attempt to reverse, or even to retard the retrogression of their country; but, on the contrary, for their own ends they precipitated it. I feared this when I observed their proceedings on the spot; and they afterwards proved the fact to all the world; and sad has the spectacle been. There is not even the consolation that, being dishonest, they failed; for their failure was on account of their eminence and not their dishonesty. They were put aside to make way for knaves of an obscure cast, who might more readily beguile or evade the indignation of the world, which would not waste on a Fillmore or a Pierce[2] the reprobation which would have attended on a Webster or a Clay who had done

---

[1]   Daniel Webster (1782–1852) ran for president as a Whig in 1836. Henry Clay (1797–1852) was an unsuccessful presidential candidate of the Democratic-Republican Party in 1824, of the National Republican Party in 1832, and of the Whig Party in 1844.

[2]   Millard Fillmore (1800–74), unelected 13th president of the United States (1850–53), assumed office when Zachary Taylor died from food poisoning; Franklin Pierce (1804–69), Democratic 14th president, was elected on a platform that pledged support of the Compromise of 1850 and hostility to any anti-slavery efforts. Both were lackluster presidents. During the heated debates over the Compromise of 1850, Fillmore said nothing publicly, but privately told Taylor that, if there were a tie, he would vote in favor of Clay's compromise bill. Pierce was a dark horse nominated by the Democrats only after 48 ballots and after all the major candidates were eliminated.

their deeds and committed their *laches*.[1] Already, so long ago as twenty years, there was a striking contrast between the speech and manner of venerable elders, like Madison and Chief Justice Marshall,[2] and those of the aspiring statesmen, Webster, Clay, and, in a smaller way, Everett and other second-rate politicians. The integrity, simplicity and heart-breathing earnestness of the aged statesmen were singularly contrasted with the affectations, professions, cautious procedures, and premeditated speech of the leaders of the time. How rapid and how great the deterioration has been since, every new page of American history bears witness. Still, there is no reason for despair. A safe issue is always possible, and most probable, where there is any principled and active body of true patriots, like the Abolitionists of the United States. Their light shines the brighter for the gathering darkness about them; and they belong to a people who, however scared at new dangers for a time, cannot for ever love darkness rather than light. The choice is being offered to them more and more plainly; and my knowledge of them, personal and by study, gives me every hope that their choice will be the right one, if only they are compelled to make it before the lust of territorial aggrandisement has become overwhelming by indulgence.

In Margaret Fuller's Memoirs there is a letter which she declared she sent to me, after copying it into her common-place book.[3] It is a condemnatory criticism of my 'Society in America;' and her condemnation is grounded on its being what she called 'an abolition book.' I remember

---

[1]   Dastardly or cowardly deeds, e.g., the "Compromise of 1850." Fearing the dissolution of the Union, Clay emerged from retirement and was re-elected to the Senate, where he proposed an omnibus compromise bill, including the admission of California as a free state, the organization of the New Mexico and Utah territories without mention of slavery, the prohibition of the slave trade in the District of Columbia, the strengthened Fugitive Slave Act of 1850, and the settlement of Texas boundary claims by federal payment of $10 million to Mexico. Webster supported the Compromise of 1850, denouncing Southern threats of secession but urging Northern support for a stronger law for the recovery of fugitive slaves. In July, 1850 the new President Millard Fillmore appointed Webster secretary of state and, in that office, he supervised the strict enforcement of the Fugitive Slave Act. Webster's stand alienated anti-slavery forces in the North and divided the Whig party.

[2]   Martineau visited James Madison (1751–1836) and his wife Dolley (1768–1849) at their home in Montpelier, Virginia, and toured "Jefferson's University" in Charlottesville. In *Retrospect of Western Travel* she wrote that Madison and Jefferson were "men inspired by the true religion of statesmanship, faith in men, and in the principles on which they combine in an agreement to do as they would be done by." She met John Marshall (1755–1835), chief justice of the Supreme Court from 1801 until his death, through Justice Joseph Story (1779–1845) and observed the Court in action during her stay in Washington, D.C.

[3]   See the *Memoirs of Margaret Fuller Ossoli* (Boston: Phillips, Sampson, 1852), I, 151–53, for Fuller's comments on "Miss Martineau."

having a letter from her; and one which I considered unworthy of her and of the occasion, from her regarding the anti-slavery subject as simply a low and disagreeable one, which should be left to unrefined persons to manage, while others were occupied with higher things: but I do not think that the letter I received was the one which stands in her common-place book. I wish that she had mentioned it to me when my guest some years afterwards, or that my reply had appeared with her criticism. However, her letter, taken as it stands, shows exactly the difference between us. She who witnessed and aided the struggles of the oppressed in Italy must have become before her death better aware than when she wrote that letter that the struggle for the personal liberty of millions in her native republic ought to have had more of her sympathy, and none of the discouragement which she haughtily and complacently cast upon the cause. The difference between us was that while she was living and moving in an ideal world, talking in private and discoursing in public about the most fanciful and shallow conceits which the transcendentalists of Boston took for philosophy, she looked down upon persons who acted instead of talking finely, and devoted their fortunes, their peace, their repose, and their very lives to the preservation of the principles of the republic. While Margaret Fuller and her adult pupils sat 'gorgeously dressed,' talking about Mars and Venus, Plato and Göthe, and fancying themselves the elect of the earth in intellect and refinement, the liberties of the republic were running out as fast as they could go, at a breach which another sort of elect persons were devoting themselves to repair: and my complaint against the 'gorgeous' pedants was that they regarded their preservers as hewers of wood and drawers of water, and their work as a less vital one than the pedantic orations which were spoiling a set of well-meaning women in a pitiable way.[1] All that is settled now. It was over years before Margaret died.[2] I mention it now to show, by an example already made public by Margaret herself, what the difference was between me and her, and those who followed her lead. This difference grew up mainly after my return from America. We were there intimate friends; and I am disposed to consider

---

[1]   Martineau refers to the series of "Conversations," or seminars for women, that Fuller offered in Boston from 1839 to 1844.

[2]   Margaret Fuller (1810–50) went to Europe as a foreign correspondent for the New York *Tribune* and settled in Rome in 1847, where she took up the cause of Italian unification. She fell in love with one of Guiseppe Mazzini's lieutenants, the Marchese Giovanni Ossoli, with whom she played an active role in the Siege of Rome in 1849 and to whom she bore a son out of wedlock. Margaret and Ossoli married and sailed for America with their son in 1850. Just before arrival in New York, off Fire Island, the ship struck a sandbar, sank, and the family drowned.

that period the best of her life, except the short one which intervened between her finding her real self and her death. She told me what danger she had been in from the training her father had given her, and the encouragement to pedantry and rudeness which she derived from the circumstances of her youth. She told me that she was at nineteen the most intolerable girl that ever took a seat in a drawing-room. Her admirable candour, the philosophical way in which she took herself in hand, her genuine heart, her practical insight, and, no doubt, the natural influence of her attachment to myself, endeared her to me, while her powers, and her confidence in the use of them, led me to expect great things from her. We both hoped that she might go to Europe when I returned, with some friends of hers who would have been happy to take her: but her father's death, and the family circumstances rendered her going out of the question. I introduced her to the special care of R. Waldo Emerson and his wife: and I remember what Emerson said in wise and gentle rebuke of my lamentations for Margaret that she could not go to Europe, as she was chafing to do, for purposes of self-improvement. 'Does Margaret Fuller, —supposing her to be what you say,—believe her progress to be dependent on whether she is here or there?' I accepted the lesson, and hoped the best. How it might have been with her if she had come to Europe in 1836, I have often speculated. As it was, her life in Boston was little short of destructive. I need but refer to the memoir of her. In the most pedantic age of society in her own country, and in its most pedantic city, she who was just beginning to rise out of pedantic habits of thought and speech relapsed most grievously. She was not only completely spoiled in conversation and manners: she made false estimates of the objects and interests of human life. She was not content with pursuing, and inducing others to pursue, a metaphysical idealism destructive of all genuine feeling and sound activity: she mocked at objects and efforts of a higher order than her own, and despised those who, like myself, could not adopt her scale of valuation. All this might have been spared, a world of mischief saved, and a world of good effected, if she had found her heart a dozen years sooner, and in America instead of Italy. It is the most grievous loss I have almost ever known in private history,—the deferring of Margaret Fuller's married life so long. The noble last period of her life is, happily, on record as well as the earlier. My friendship with her was in the interval between her first and second stages of pedantry and forwardness: and I saw her again under all the disadvantages of the confirmed bad manners and self-delusions which she brought from home. The ensuing period redeemed all; and I regard her American life as a reflexion, more useful than agreeable, of the prevalent social spirit of her time and place; and the Italian life as the true revelation of the tender and high-souled woman, who had till then been as curiously concealed from herself as from others.

If eccentricities like Margaret Fuller's, essentially sound as she was in heart and mind, could arise in American society, and not impair her influence or be a spectacle to the community, it will be inferred that eccentricity is probably rife in the United States. I certainly thought it was, in spite (or perhaps in consequence) of the excessive caution which is prevalent there in regard to the opinion of neighbours and society.[1] It takes weeks or months for an English person to admit the conception of American caution, as a habit, and yet more as a spring of action: and the freedom which we English enjoy in our personal lives and intercourses must find an equivalent in Americans, somehow or other. Their eccentricities are, accordingly, monstrous and frequent and various to a degree incredible to sober English people like myself and my companion. The worst of it is, there seem to be always mad people, more or fewer, who are in waiting to pounce upon foreigners of any sort of distinction, as soon as they land, while others go mad, or show their madness, from point to point along the route. Something of the same sort happens elsewhere. A Queen, or a Prime Minister's secretary may be shot at in London, as we know; and probably there is no person eminent in literature or otherwise, who has not been the object of some infirm brain or another. But in America, the evil is sadly common. The first instance I encountered there was of a gentleman from the west who foretold my arrival in his country, and the time of it, before I had any notion of going, and who announced a new revelation which I was to aid in promulgating; and this incident startled and dismayed me considerably. I am not going into the history of the freaks of insanity, in that case or any other. Suffice it that, in any true history of a life, this liability must be set down as one condition of literary or other reputation. The case of the poor 'High Priest' at Philadelphia was not the only one with which I was troubled in America; and I have met with others at home, both in London and since I have lived at Ambleside.

I encountered one specimen of American oddity before I left home

---

[1] *Retrospect of Western Travel* includes a chapter on "American Originals," which treats eccentricity both negatively and positively; as positive examples, Martineau describes the public works of Noah Worcester (1758–1837), founder of American Peace Societies; "Father" Edward Taylor (1793–1871), founder of the Seaman's Bethel, Boston, and a temperance society; Joseph Tuckerman (1778–1840), scientific analyst and advocate of almsgiving; and William Lloyd Garrison, the abolitionist.

which should certainly have lessened my surprise at any that I met after-wards. While I was preparing for my travels, an acquaintance one day brought a buxom gentleman, whom he introduced to me under the name of Willis. There was something rather engaging in the round face, brisk air and *enjouement*[1] of the young man; but his conscious dandyism and unparalleled self-complacency spoiled the satisfaction, though they increased the inclination to laugh. Mr. N.P. Willis's[2] plea for coming to see me was his gratification that I was going to America: and his real reason was presently apparent;—a desire to increase his consequence in London society by giving apparent proof that he was on intimate terms with every eminent person in America. He placed himself in an attitude of infinite ease, and whipped his little bright boot with a little bright cane while he ran over the names of all his distinguished country-men and country-women, and declared he should send me letters to them all. This offer of intervention went so very far that I said (what I have ever since said in the case of introductions offered by strangers) while thanking him for his intended good offices, that I was sufficiently uncer-tain in my plans to beg for excuse beforehand, in case I should find myself unable to use the letters. It appeared afterwards that to supply them and not to have them used suited Mr. Willis's convenience exactly. It made him appear to have the friendships he boasted of without putting the boast to the proof. It was immediately before a late dinner that the gentlemen called; and I found on the breakfast-table, next morn-ing, a great parcel of Mr. Willis's letters, enclosed in a prodigious one to myself, in which he offered advice. Among other things, he desired me not to use his letter to Dr. Channing if I had others from persons more intimate with him; and he proceeded to warn me against two friends of Dr. and Mrs. Channing's, whose names I had never heard, and whom Mr. Willis represented as bad and dangerous people. This gratuitous defamation of strangers whom I was likely to meet confirmed the suspi-cions my mother and I had confided to each other about the quality of Mr. Willis's introductions. It seemed ungrateful to be so suspicious: but we could not see any good reason for such prodigious efforts on my behalf, nor for his naming any country-women of his to me in a way so spontaneously slanderous. So I resolved to use that packet of letters very

---

[1] Liveliness, playfulness.

[2] Nathaniel Parker Willis (1806–67), a Yale-educated author and editor, was famous for his smooth, sentimental style. He wrote, among others, *Pencillings by the Way* (1835), *Inklings of Adventure* (1836), *Romance of Travel* (1840), and *Life, Here and There: or, Sketches of Society and Adventure at Far-Apart Times and Places* (1850).

cautiously; and to begin with one which should be well accompanied.—
In New York harbour, newspapers were brought on board, in one of
which was an extract from an article transmitted by Mr. Willis to the
'New York Mirror,' containing a most audacious account of me as an
intimate friend of the writer. The friendship was not stated as a matter
of fact, but so conveyed that it cost me much trouble to make it understood and believed, even by Mr. Willis's own family, that I had never seen
him but once; and then without having previously heard so much as his
name. On my return, the acquaintance who brought him was anxious
to ask pardon if he had done mischief,—events having by that time
made Mr. Willis's ways pretty well known. His partner in the property
and editorship of the 'New York Mirror' called on me at West Point, and
offered and rendered such extraordinary courtesy that I was at first
almost as much perplexed as he and his wife were when they learned
that I had never seen Mr. Willis but once. They pondered, they
consulted, they cross-questioned me; they inquired whether *I* had any
notion what Mr. Willis could have meant by writing of me as in a state
of close intimacy with him. In like manner, when, some time after, I was
in a carriage with some members of a pic-nic party to Monument
Mountain,[1] a little girl seated at my feet clasped my knees fondly, looked
up in my face, and said 'O! Miss Martineau! you are *such* a friend of my
uncle Nathaniel's!' Her father was present; and I tried to get off without
explanation. But it was impossible,—they all knew how very intimate I
was with 'Nathaniel': and there was a renewal of the amazement at my
having seen him only once.—I tried three of his letters; and the reception was in each case much the same,—a throwing down of the letter
with an air not to be mistaken. In each case the reply was the same, when
I subsequently found myself at liberty to ask what this might mean. 'Mr.
Willis is not entitled to write to me: he is no acquaintance of mine.' As
for the two ladies of whom I was especially to beware, I became exceedingly well acquainted with them, to my own advantage and pleasure;
and, as a natural consequence, I discovered Mr. Willis's reasons for desiring to keep us apart. I hardly need add that I burned the rest of his letters.
He had better have spared himself the trouble of so much manoeuver-
ing, by which he lost a good deal, and could hardly have gained anything.
I have simply stated the facts because, in the first place, I do not wish to
be considered one of Mr. Willis's friends; and, in the next, it may be

---

[1]   A peak of 1,735 feet in Great Barrington, Massachusetts, overlooking the hills and valleys
of southern Berkshire County.

useful, and conducive to justice, to show, by a practical instance, what Mr. Willis's pretensions to intimacy are worth. His countrymen and countrywomen accept, in simplicity, his accounts of our aristocracy as from the pen of one of their own coterie; and they may as well have the opportunity of judging for themselves whether their notorious 'Penciller' is qualified to write of Scotch Dukes and English Marquises, and European celebrities of all kinds in the way he has done.

For some weeks, my American intercourses were chiefly with literary people, and with leading members of the Unitarian body,—far more considerable in America than among us. All manner of persons called on us; and every conceivable attention and honour was shown us, for the first year. Of this nothing appears in my journal, except in the facts of what we saw and did. Such idolatry as is signified by the American phrase, —that a person is Lafayetted,—is not conceivable in England: and its manifestations did not appear to me fit matter for a personal journal. Not a word is to be found in that journal therefore of either the flatteries of the first year or the insults of the second. A more difficult matter was how to receive them. I was charged with hardness and want of sympathy in casting back praise into people's faces: but what can one do but change the subject as fast as possible? To dwell on the subject of one's own merits is out of the question; but to disclaim praise is to dwell upon it. If one is silent, one is supposed to 'swallow everything.' I see nothing for it but to talk of something else, on the first practicable opening. While under the novelty of this infliction of flatterers, it was natural to turn to those most homelike of our acquaintance,—the chief members of the Unitarian body, clergymen and others. Among them we found a welcome refuge, many a time, from the hubbub which confounded our senses: and exemplary was the kindness which some few of the body showed me even throughout the year of my unpopularity. But before that, my destiny had led me much among the families of statesmen, and the interests of political society: and finally, as I have shown, the Abolitionists were my nearest friends, as they have ever since remained.

It was while my companion and I were going from house to house in the Unitarian connexion, between Philadelphia and our visits to our Congressional friends, that an incident occurred which is worth relating as curious in itself, and illustrative of more things than one. Our host in Philadelphia, (a Unitarian clergyman, as I have said)[1] had a little boy of six who was a favourite of mine,—as of a good many other people. Mr.

---

[1]   William Furness; see p. 339, n. 1.

Alcott,[1] the extraordinary self-styled philosopher, whose name is not unknown in England, was at Philadelphia at that time, trying his hand on that strange management of children of which I have given my opinion elsewhere.[2] Little Willie went to Mr. Alcott sometimes; and very curious were the ideas and accounts of lessons which he brought home. Very early in my visit, Willie's father asked me whether I could throw any light on the authorship of a parable which was supposed to be English, and which the children had learned from Mr. Alcott's lips. This parable, called 'The Wandering Child,' was creating such a sensation that it was copied and sent in all directions. It seemed to me, when Willie recited it, that I had somewhere seen it; but the impression was so faint as to be entirely uncertain, even to that extent. From Philadelphia, we went to the house of another clergyman at Baltimore; and there one of the first questions asked by my host was the origin of that parable. He had used the extraordinary license of taking the parable for the text of a recent sermon, instead of a passage of scripture; and his friends wanted to know where it came from. He was sadly disappointed that we could not tell him. More inquiries were made even at Washington, where we had no particular connexion with Unitarians. At Charleston, we found in our host a Unitarian clergyman who knew more of the 'Monthly Repository' than any English readers I was acquainted with. He possessed it; and he had a fancy to look there for the parable,—some notion of having seen it there remaining on his mind. I went with him to his study; and there we presently found the parable,—in a not very old volume of the Monthly Repository, and, to my unspeakable amazement, with my own signature, V., at the end of it.[3] By degrees my associations brightened and began to cohere; and at last I perfectly remembered when and where the conception occurred to me, and my writing the parable in my own room at Norwich, and carrying it down to my mother whom I saw in the garden, and her resting on her little spade as she listened.

The readers of Dr. Priestley's Life will not pronounce on me, (as I was

---

[1]   A. Bronson Alcott (1799–1888), Transcendentalist, abolitionist, vegetarian, friend of Thoreau and Emerson, and follower of Pestalozzi's child-centered educational innovations. Alcott served as superintendent of the Concord school system and founded the Concord School of Philosophy, a summer school for adults. His daughter, the novelist Louisa May Alcott, wrote of his methods: "My father taught in the wise way which unfolds what lies in the child's nature, as a flower blooms, rather than crammed it, like a Strasbourg goose, with more than it could digest."

[2]   Society in America, vol. iii, page 175. [Martineau's note]

[3]   "The Wandering Child" appeared in the *Monthly Repository*, N.S. 6 (January, 1832), 23–24. It is included in her *Miscellanies* (Boston: Hillard, Gray and Company, 1836), I, 301–2.

at first disposed to pronounce on myself) that I was losing my wits.[1] Dr. Priestley tells how he once found in a friend's library a pamphlet on some controverted topic which he brought to his friend with praise, as the best thing he had seen on the subject. He wanted to know, —the title-page being torn off,—who wrote it. His friend stared as my Charleston host did; and Dr. Priestley began to fear that he was losing his faculties: but he remembered (and this was my plea after him) that what we give out from our own minds, in speech or in writing, is not a subject of memory, like what we take in from other minds: and that there are few who can pretend to remember what they have said in letters, after a few years. There was the fact, in short, that we had completely forgotten compositions of our own; and that we were not losing our faculties.

Here is the parable which went through such curious adventures:—

THE WANDERING CHILD

'In a solitary place among the groves, a child wandered whithersoever he would. He believed himself alone, and wist not that one watched him from the thicket, and that the eye of his parent was on him continually; neither did he mark whose hand had opened a way for him thus far. All things that he saw were new to him; therefore he feared nothing. He cast himself down in the long grass, and as he lay he sang till his voice of joy rang through the woods. When he nestled among the flowers, a serpent arose from the midst of them; and when the child saw how its burnished coat glittered in the sun like a rainbow, he stretched forth his hand to take it to his bosom. Then the voice of his parent cried from the thicket "Beware!" And the child sprang up, and gazed above and around, to know whence the voice came; but when he saw it not, he presently remembered it no more.

He watched how a butterfly burst from its shell, and flitted faster than he could pursue, and soon rose far above his reach.

When he gazed and could trace its flight no more, his father put forth his hand, and pointed where the butterfly ascended, even into the clouds. But the child saw not the sign.

---

[1] In his *Memoirs and Correspondence*, Priestley tells of twice writing an account of the Jewish passover without remembering that he had already done so: "I have so completely forgotten what I have myself published, that in reading my own writings, what I find in them often appears perfectly new to me." See *The Theological and Miscellaneous Works of Joseph Priestley*, ed. John Towill Rutt (1817), vol. I, part I, 172.

A fountain gushed forth amidst the shadows of the trees, and its waters flowed into a deep and quiet pool.

The child kneeled on the brink, and looking in, he saw his own bright face, and it smiled upon him.

As he stooped yet nearer to meet it, the voice once more said "Beware!"

The child started back; but he saw that a gust had ruffled the waters, and he said within himself, "It was but the voice of the breeze."

And when the broken sunbeams glanced on the moving waves, he laughed, and dipped his foot that the waters might again be ruffled: and the coolness was pleasant to him. The voice was now louder, but he regarded it not, as the winds bore it away.

At length he saw somewhat glittering in the depths of the pool; and he plunged in to reach it.

As he sank, he cried aloud for help.

Ere the waters had closed over him, his father's hand was stretched out to save him.

And while he yet shivered with chillness and fear, his parent said unto him, "Mine eye was upon thee, and thou didst not heed; neither hast thou beheld my sign, nor hearkened to my voice. If thou hadst thought on me, I had not been hidden."

Then the child cast himself on his father's bosom and said,—"Be nigh unto me still; and mine eyes shall wait on thee, and my ears shall be open unto thy voice for ever more."'

I need say no more of my American travels. Besides that I have given out my freshest impressions in the two works on America which were published in the year after my return, it is as impossible to me here as in other parts of this Memoir to give any special account of my nearest and dearest friends. To those who have seen by the volumes I refer to how I lived and travelled with Dr. and Mrs. Follen no avowal or description of our intercourse can be necessary; and the relation in which Mrs. Chapman stands to me now, in the most deliberate and gravest hour of my life, renders it impossible to lay open our relation further to the world. I will simply state one fact which may show, without protestation, what my near and dear American friends were to me. They and I did not half believe, when I came away, that we had parted: and it was some years before I felt at all sure that I should not live and die in America, when my domestic duties should, in the course of nature, have closed. It was my Tynemouth illness, in fact, which decided the conflict. Something of a conflict it was. If I had gone to America, it would have been for the sole object of working in the cause which I believed then, and which I believe now, to be the greatest pending in the world. While my mother lived, my duty was clear—to remain with her if she and the family desired it. I did not think it the best arrangement; especially when I witnessed the painful effect on her of the resumption of my London life and acquaintances: but she and the others wished things to go on as they were; and I never thought of objecting. I did my utmost to make the two old ladies under my charge happy. It did not last very long,—only two years and a half, when I broke down under the anxiety of my position. During that time, the vision of a scheme of life, in which the anti-slavery cause (for the sake of the liberties of every kind involved in it) should be my vocation, was often before me,—not as a matter of imagination, but for decision by the judgment, when the time should arrive. The immediate objections of the judgment were two:—that, in the first place, it seldom or never answers to wander abroad for duty; every body doing best what lies nearest at hand: and, in the second place, that my relation to Mrs. Chapman required my utmost moral care.[1] The discovery of her moral power and insight was to me so extraordinary that, while I longed to work with and under her, I felt that it must be morally perilous to lean on any one mind as I could not but lean on hers. Thus far, whenever we had differed, (and that had not seldom happened) I had found her right: and so deeply and broadly right as to make me long to commit myself to her guidance. Such a committal can never be otherwise than wrong; and this it was which, more than any thing, made me doubt whether I ought to contemplate the scheme. As usual in such cases, events decided the matter. My mother was removed from under my care by my own illness; and, when I had recovered, and she died at an advanced age, I had a clear course of duty to pursue at home, in which perhaps there may be as decided an implication of human liberties of thought, action and speech as in the anti-slavery cause itself.

To a certain extent, my travels in America answered my purposes of self-discipline in undertaking them. Fearing that I was growing too much accustomed to luxury, and to an exclusive regularity in the modes of living, I desired to 'rough it' for a considerable time. The same

---

[1]   In the "Memorials" added to the *Autobiography*, Maria Chapman notes, "The idea of still further serving the anti-slavery cause in America never left her" (III, 220); Chapman quotes various letters and diary entries to support this commitment.

purpose would have been answered as well, perhaps, and certainly more according to my inclination, if I could have been quiet, instead of travelling, after my great task was done;—if I could have had repose of body and peace of mind, in freedom from all care. This was impossible; and the next best thing was such a voyage and journey as I took. America was the right country too, (apart from the peculiar agitation it happened to be in when I arrived); the national boast being a perfectly true one,— that a woman may travel alone from Maine to Georgia without dread of any kind of injury. For two ladies who feared nothing, there was certainly nothing to fear. We had to 'rough it' sometimes, as every body must in so new and thinly peopled a country; but we always felt ourselves safe from ill usage of any kind. One night, at New Orleans, we certainly did feel as much alarmed as could well be; but that was nobody's fault. From my childhood up, I believe I have never felt so desolating a sense of fear as for a few moments on that occasion,— which was simply this.

A cousin of mine[1] whom I saw at Mobile had a house at New Orleans, inhabited by himself or his partner, as they happened to be there or at Mobile. My cousin kindly offered us the use of this house during our stay, saying that we might thus obtain some hours of coolness and quiet in the morning which would be unattainable in a boarding-house, or in the capacity of guests. The 'people,' that is, the slaves, received orders to make us comfortable, and the partner saw that all orders were obeyed. We arrived at about ten in the forenoon,—exceedingly tired,—not only by long travel in the southern forests, but especially by the voyage of the preceding night,—in hot, thundery weather, a rough sea, and in a steamboat which so swarmed with cockroaches that we could not bring ourselves to lie down.—It was a day of considerable excitement. We found a great heap of letters from home; we saw many friends in the course of the day; and at night I wrote letters so late that my companion, for once, went to bed before me. We had four rooms forming a square, or nearly:—two sitting rooms, front and back; and two bedrooms opening out of them, and also reaching, like them, from the landing at the top of the stairs to the street front. On account of the heat, we decided to put all our luggage (which was of considerable bulk) into one room, and sleep in the other. The beds were very large, and as hard as the floor,—as they should be in such a climate. Mosquito nets hung from

---

[1]   Edward Martineau (1791–1862), son of her uncle Peter, was a merchant in Mobile, Alabama.

the top; and the room was plentifully provided with sponging baths and water.—Miss J. was in bed before I finished my writing: and I therefore did not call her when I found that the French window opening on the balcony could not be shut, as the spring was broken. Any one could reach the balcony from the street easily enough; and here was an entrance which could not be barred! I set the heaviest chair against it, with the heaviest things piled on it that I could lay my hands on. I need not explain that New Orleans is, of all cities in the civilised world, the most renowned for night robbery and murder. The reputation is deserved; or was at that time: and we had been in the way of hearing some very painful and alarming stories from some of our friends who spoke from their own experience. Miss J. was awake when I was about to step into bed, and thoughtlessly put out the candle. I observed on my folly in doing this, and on our having forgotten to inquire where the slave-quarter was. Here we were, alone in the middle of New Orleans, with no light, no bell, no servants within reach if we had had one, and no idea where the slaves were to be found! We could only hope that nothing would happen: but I took my trumpet with me within the mosquito curtain, and laid it within reach of Miss J.'s hand, in case of her having to tell me any news. I was asleep in a trice. Not so Miss J.

She gently awoke me after what seemed to her a very long time; and, putting the cup of my tube close to her mouth, whispered slowly, so that I could hear her, 'There is somebody or something walking about the room.' I whispered that we could do nothing: and that, in our helpless state, the safest way was to go to sleep. 'But I can't,' replied she. I cannot describe how sorry I was for her, sitting up listening to fearful sounds that I could not hear. I earnestly desired to help her: but there was nothing that I could do. To sit up, unable to hear anything, and thus losing nerve every minute, was the worst thing of all for us both. I told her to rouse me again if she had the slightest wish: but that I really advised her going to sleep, as I meant to do. She again said she could not. I did; and it must be remembered how remarkably tired I was. After another space, Miss J. woke me again, and in the same cautious manner said, 'It is a man without shoes; and he is just at your side of the bed.' We each said the same thing as before; and again I went to sleep. Once more she woke me; and this time she spoke with a little less caution. She said he had been walking about all that time,—for hours. He had pushed against the furniture, and especially the washstand, and seemed to be washing his hands: and now he had gone out at the door nearest the stairs. What did I think of her fastening that door? I feared she would let the mosquitoes in if she got up; and there were two other doors to the room; so I did not think we should gain much. She was better satisfied to try; and she drove a heavy trunk against the door, returned without letting in any mosquitoes, and at last obtained some sleep. In the morning we started up to see what we had lost. My watch was safe on the table. My rings were not there; but we soon spied them rolled off to the corners of the room. The water from the baths was spilled; and our clothes were on the floor; but we missed nothing.

We agreed to say and do nothing ungracious to the servants, and to make no complaint; but to keep on the watch for an explanation of the mystery; and, if evening came without any light being thrown on the matter, to consult our friends the Porters[1] about spending another night in that room.—At breakfast, the slave women, who had been to market, and got us some young green peas and other good things, hung over our chairs, and were ready to gossip, as usual. I could make nothing of their jabber; and Miss J. not much: but she persevered on this occasion; and, before breakfast was over, she gave me a nod which showed me that our case was explained. She had been playing with a little black dog the while: and she told me at length that this little black dog belonged to the personage at the back of my chair; but that the big dog, chained up in the yard, belonged to my cousin; and that the big dog was the one which was unchained the last thing at night, and allowed the range of the premises, to deal with the rats, which abounded in that house as in every other in New Orleans. The city being built in a swamp, innumerable rats are a necessary consequence. The intruder was regarded very differently the next night; and we had no more alarms. I own that the moments when my companion told me that a man without shoes was walking about the room, and when, again, she heard him close by my bedside, were those of very painful fear. I have felt nothing like it on any other occasion, since I grew up.

Safe as we were from ill usage, our friends in America rather wondered at our fearlessness about the perils of the mere travel. We were supposed, before we were known, to be fine ladies; and fine ladies are full of terrors in America, as elsewhere. When it was seen that we could help ourselves, and had no groundless fears, some of our friends reminded us that their forests and great rivers were not like our own mailroads; and that untoward accidents and detentions might take place,

---

[1]   Probably Alexander Porter (1796–1844), justice of the Supreme Court of Louisiana from 1821 to 1833, and Whig senator from 1834 to 1837.

when we should be glad of such aid as could be had from its being known who we were. Chief Justice Marshall, the survivor of the great men of the best days of the republic, and the most venerated man in the country, put into my hands 'a general letter,' as he called it, commending us to the good offices of all citizens, in case of need. The letter lies before me; and I will give it as a curiosity. No occasion of peril called it forth for use; but it was a show, in many a wild place,—gratifying the eyes of revering fellow citizens of the majestic old Judge. Here it is.

'I have had the honour of being introduced to, and of forming some acquaintance with, Miss Martineau and Miss J—, two English ladies of distinction who are making the tour of the United States. As casualties to which all travellers, especially those of the female sex, are liable may expose these ladies to some difficulties in situations remote from those populous towns in which they may find persons to whom they will be known, it gives me pleasure to state that these ladies have the fairest claims to the aid, protection and services which their possible situation may require: that they are of high worth and character, and that I shall, individually, feel myself under obligations to any gentleman who, in the event described, shall be in any manner useful to them.

J. MARSHALL.'

A parting act of gallantry has puzzled me many a time; and the more I have thought of it, the less have I known what to make of it. For many months it had been settled, as I have mentioned, that I was to return in Captain Bursley's ship,—he being a friend, in virtue of mutual friendships on both sides the water. Some days before I sailed, my last American host undertook the business of paying my passage, and changing my American money for English. We were not aware of any extraordinary precipitation in settling this business. When I was out at sea, however, a fellow-passenger, one of our party of six, put into my hands a packet of money. It was the amount of my fare; and my fellow-passenger either could not or would not tell me who sent it. She said she was as helpless in the matter as I was. All that she could tell me was that somebody had gone, in supposed good time, to pay my passage, was disconcerted to find I had paid it, and could think of no other way than returning the money through a fellow-passenger.—I know no more of the motive than of the person or persons. Whether it was shame at the treatment I had received on the anti-slavery question, or a primitive method of hospitality, or any thing else, I have never been able to satisfy myself, or to get any light from any body. I could do nothing, and say nothing. The only certain thing about the case is that the act was meant in kindness: and I need not say that I was grateful accordingly.

The New York host whom I have referred to was an intimate friend of our captain: and he knew enough of one or two of the passengers to be pretty well aware that there would be moral tempests on board, however fair the weather might be overhead. He and his wife kindly forbore to give me any hint of coming discomfort which could not be avoided; but they begged me to keep a very full journal of the voyage, and send it to them, for their private reading. I did so: and they next requested that I would agree to a proposal to print it,—the names being altered; and the most disgraceful of the incidents (e.g., a plot for the seduction of an orphan girl) being omitted. The narrative accordingly appeared in the 'Penny Magazine' of October and November, 1837, under the title of 'A Month at Sea.' As it may amuse somebody to see, in such detail, what such a voyage was like, the narrative will be found in the Appendix.[1] It is enough to say here that I had the advantage of the companionship of Professor and Mrs. Farrer, of Harvard University; of Lieutenant Wilkes, who was on his way to England to prepare for the American Exploring Expedition, of which he was Commander; and of two or three younger members of the party, who were good-humoured and agreeable comrades, in the midst of a set of passengers who were as far as possible from being either.[2]

We arrived at Liverpool on the 26th of August, 1836; and there I found several members of my family awaiting me.

---

[1]   This appendix has been omitted from this edition. "A Month at Sea: Narrative of a Voyage from New York to Liverpool" originally appeared in installments in the *Penny Magazine*, 6 (1837), 398–400, 405–08, 414–16, 429–31.

[2]   John Farrar (1779–1853) served as Greek tutor, then as Hollis professor of mathematics and natural philosophy at Harvard University from 1807 to 1836; his wife, Eliza Ware (1791–1870), born in Flanders and educated in England, wrote juvenile literature. Lt. Wilkes is probably Charles Wilkes (1798–1877), a naval officer appointed to the department of charts and instruments in 1830 to improve astronomical instruments and navigation techniques; from 1838 to 1842 he led an exploratory expedition in the southern oceans.

SECTION IV

My mother and I spent two months among my brothers and sisters before returning home to settle for the winter. I was aware that I must presently make up my mind about a book or no book on America: but I had no idea how soon my decision would be called for. As I have mentioned, I declined the offer made before I left home to obtain an advance of £500 from a publisher, who would be glad thus to secure the book. Mr. Murray[1] also sent me a message through a mutual friend, intimating his wish to publish my travels on my return. In America such applications were frequent: and on all occasions my reply was the same; that I did not know, nor should till I got home, whether I should write on the subject at all. One personal application made to me in New York at once amused and shocked me. I had not then, and I have not to this day, got over the wonder and disgust caused by the tone in which so serious and unworldly a vocation as that of authorship is spoken of; and, of all the broad instances of such coarseness that I have met with, this New York application affords the very grossest. Mr. Harper,[2] the head of the redoubtable piratical publishing house in New York, said to me in his own shop, 'Come, now! tell me what you will take for your book.'—'What book?'—'O! you know you will write a book about this country. Let me advise you.'—'But I don't know that I shall write one.'—'O! but I can tell you how easily you may do it. So far as you have gone, you must have picked up a few incidents. Well! then you might Trollopize a bit, and so make a readable book. I would give you something handsome for it. Come! what will you take?'

Even people who know nothing of books in a mercantile view seem to have as little conception of the true aim and temper of authorship as the book-merchants themselves, who talk of a book as an 'article,'—as the mercer talks of a shawl or a dress. A good, unselfish, affectionate

---

[1]   John Murray (1778–1843), the "son" of the publishing firm Murray and Son.

[2]   Probably Fletcher Harper (1806–77), editor-in-chief of Harper & Brothers. In the 1830s the firm included James, John, Fletcher, and Wesley Harper. In an age without international copyright, the Harpers were known for pirating English novels and issuing American editions of novelists who had sold their rights to other American publishers.

woman, whom I really love, showed me one day how she loves me still as in the old times when I was not yet an author, by evidencing her total lack of sympathy in my thoughts and feelings about my work. I am to her the Harriet of our youth,—the authorship being nothing more between us than something which has made her happy for me, because it has made me happy. I like this,—the being loved as the old Harriet: but, still, I was startled one day by her congratulating me on my success in obtaining fame. I had worked hard for it, and she was so glad I had got it! I do not like disclaiming, or in any way dwelling on this sort of subject; but it was impossible to let this pass. I told her I had never worked for fame. 'Well then,—for money.' She was so glad I was so successful, and could get such sums for my books. This, again, could not be let pass. I assured her I had never written, or omitted to write, any thing whatever from pecuniary considerations. 'Well, then,' said she, 'for usefulness. I am determined to be right. You write to do good to your fellow-creatures. You must allow that I am right now.' I was silent; and when she found that I could allow no such thing, she was puzzled. Her alternatives were exhausted. I told her that I wrote because I could not help it. There was something that I wanted to say, and I said it: that was all. The fame and the money and the usefulness might or might not follow. It was not by my endeavour if they did.[1]

On landing at Liverpool, I found various letters from publishers awaiting me. One was from Mr. Bentley,[2] reminding me of his having met me at Miss Berry's, and expressing his hope of having my manuscript immediately in his hands. My reply was that I had no manuscript. Another letter was from Messrs. Saunders and Otley to my mother, saying that they desired the pleasure of publishing my travels. I was disposed to treat with them, because the negotiation for the 'Two Old Men's Tales'[3] had been an agreeable one. I therefore explained to these gentlemen the precise state of the case, and at length agreed to an interview when I should return to town. My mother and I reached home before London began to fill; and I took some pains to remain unseen

[1] While true enough, this account does not entirely square with Martineau's private resolution of 1829, included in the "Memorials" volume, that she would pursue a writing career "on subjects of universal concern as to inform some minds and stir up others." See Appendix B.

[2] Richard Bentley (1794–1871), publisher of *Bentley's Miscellany* and popular literature. Despite being on bad terms with Colburn, the two continued to publish their Standard Novelists series until 1841 under the Colburn and Bentley imprint.

[3] On Martineau's recommendation, the firm Saunders and Otley published Anne Marsh's *Two Old Men's Tales* (1834); see Period III, sec. iii.

for two or three weeks, while arranging my books, and my dress and my other affairs. One November morning, however, my return was announced in the 'Morning Chronicle;' and such a day as that I never passed, and hoped at the time never to pass again.

First, Mr. Bentley bustled down, and obtained entrance to my study before any body else. Mr. Colburn[1] came next, and had to wait. He bided his time in the drawing-room. In a few minutes arrived Mr. Saunders,[2] and was shown into my mother's parlour. These gentlemen were all notoriously on the worst terms with each other; and the fear was that they should meet and quarrel on the stairs. Some friends who happened to call at the time were beyond measure amused.

Mr. Bentley began business. Looking hard into the fire, he 'made no doubt' I remembered the promise I had made him at Miss Berry's house. I had no recollection of having promised any thing to Mr. Bentley. He told me it was impossible I should forget having assured him that if any body published for me, except Fox, it should be himself. I laughed at the idea of such an engagement. Mr. Bentley declared it might be his silliness; but he should go to his grave persuaded that I had made him such a promise. It might be his silliness, he repeated. I replied that indeed it was; as I had a perfect recollection that no book of mine was in question at all, but the Series, which he had talked of putting among his Standard Novels. He now offered the most extravagant terms for a book on America, and threw in, as a bribe, an offer of a thousand pounds for the first novel I should write. Though my refusals were as positive as I could make them, I had great difficulty in getting rid of him: and I doubt whether I was so rude to Mr. Harper himself as the London speculator.—Mr. Colburn, meantime, sent in his letter of introduction, which was from the poet Campbell,[3] with a message that he would shortly return. So Mr. Saunders entered next. I liked him, as before; and our conversation about the book became quite confidential. I explained to him fully my doubt as to the reception of the work, on the ground of its broad republican character. I told him plainly that I believed it would ruin me, because it would be the principle of the book to regard every thing American from the American point of view: and this method, though the only fair one, was so unlike the usual practice, and must lead to a judgment so unlike what English people were

[1]   Henry Colburn (d. 1855), founder of the *New Monthly Magazine* in 1814 and *Literary Gazette* in 1817.

[2]   John Saunders (1810–95), co-publisher of the firm Saunders and Otley.

[3]   Thomas Campbell (1777–1844), Scottish poet.

prepared for, that I should not be surprised by a total condemnation of my book and myself. I told him that, after this warning, he could retreat or negotiate, as he pleased: but that, being thus warned, he and not I must propose terms: and moreover, it must be understood that, our negotiation once concluded, I could listen to no remonstrance or objection, in regard to the contents of my book. Mr. Saunders replied that he had no difficulty in agreeing to these conditions, and that we might now proceed to business. When he had ascertained that the work would consist of three volumes, and what their probable size would be, the amusing part of the affair began. 'Well, Ma'am,' said he, 'What do you propose that, we should give you for the copyright of the first edition?' 'Why, you know,' said I, 'I have written to you, from the beginning, that I would propose no terms. I am quite resolved against it.'— 'Well, Ma'am; supposing the edition to consist of three thousand copies, will you just give me an idea what you would expect for it?'—'No, Mr. Saunders: that is your business. I wait to hear your terms.'

So I sat strenuously looking into the fire,—Mr. Saunders no less strenuously looking at me, till it was all I could do to keep my countenance. He waited for me to speak; but I would not and I wondered where the matter would end, when he at last opened his lips. 'What would you think, Ma'am, of £900 for the first edition?'— 'Including the twenty-five copies I stipulated for?'—'Including twenty-five copies of the work, and all proceeds of the sale in America, over and above expenses.' I thought these liberal terms; and I said so; but suggested that each party should take a day or two for consideration, to leave no room for repentance hereafter. I inquired whether Messrs. Saunders and Otley had any objection to my naming their house as the one I was negotiating with, as I disliked the appearance of entertaining the proffers of various houses, which yet I could not get rid of without a distinct answer to give. Apparently amused at the question, Mr. Saunders replied that it would be gratifying to them to be so named.

On the stairs, Mr. Saunders met Mr. Colburn, who chose to be confident that Campbell's introduction would secure to him all he wished. The interview was remarkably disagreeable, from his refusing to be refused, and pretending to believe that what I wanted was more and more money. At last, on my giving him a broad hint to go away, he said that, having no intention of giving up his object, he should spend the day at a coffee-house in the neighbourhood, whence he should shortly send in terms for my consideration. He now only implored a promise that I would not finally pass my word that day. The moment he was gone, I slipped out into the Park to refresh my mind and body; for I was heated and wearied with the conferences of the morning. On my return, I found that Mr. Colburn had called again: and while we were at dinner, he sent in a letter, containing his fresh terms. They were so absurdly high that if I had had any confidence in the soundness of the negotiation before, it would now be overthrown. Mr. Colburn offered £2,000 for the present work, on the supposition of the sale of I forget what number, and £1,000 for the first novel I should write. The worst of it was, he left word that he should call again at ten o'clock in the evening. When we were at tea, Mr. Bentley sent in a set of amended proposals; and at ten, Mr. Colburn arrived. He set forth his whole array of 'advantages,' and declared himself positive that no house in London could have offered higher terms than his. I reminded him that I had been telling him all day that my objections did not relate to the amount of money; and that I was going to accept much less: that it was impossible that my work should yield what he had offered, and leave anything over for himself; and that I therefore felt that these proposals were intended to bind me to his house,—an obligation which I did not choose to incur. He pathetically complained of having raised up rivals to himself in the assistants whom he had trained, and concluded with an affected air of resignation which was highly amusing. Hanging his head on one side, and sighing, he enunciated the sentiment: 'When, in pursuing any praiseworthy object, we have done all we can, and find it in vain, we can but be resigned.' With great satisfaction I saw him lighted down stairs, and heard the house-door locked, at near midnight, on the last of the booksellers for that day. From that time forward, Mr. Colburn was seen, on the appearance of any of my works, to declare himself 'singularly unfortunate' in having been always too late. He professed to have the best reason to know that if he had been a day or so earlier in his application, he would have been my publisher. This was in each case a delusion. I never, for a moment, encouraged any such expectation; and when, in course of time, Mr. Colburn's piracies of Sparks's Washington[1] and other works were brought before the law

---

[1] Jared Sparks's *The Life of George Washington* (Boston: F. Andrews, 1837) was issued in England as *The Life of George Washington, Commander-in-chief of the American Armies, and First President of the United States: to which are added his diaries and speeches; and various miscellaneous papers relating to his habits & opinions* (London: H. Colburn, 1839). Sparks's authorized 12–volume edition of Washington's letters became the focus of an important American copyright case over the ownership of letters, Folsom v. Marsh, when Charles Upham used the letters without permission for his auto/biography, *The Life of General Washington, First President of the United States, Written by Himself, Comprising his Memoirs and Correspondence, as Prepared by Him for Publication* (1856).

courts, I was glad to have avoided all connection with the house.—The only reasons for dwelling on the matter at all are that, in the first place, it is desirable to put on record exactly what did happen on an occasion which was a good deal talked about; and next, because it may be well to show how the degradation of literature comes about, in times when speculating publishers try to make grasping authors, and to convert the serious function of authorship into a gambling match. The way in which authors allowed themselves to be put up to auction, and publishers squabbled at the sale was a real and perpetual grief to me to witness. It reminded me but too often of the stand and the gesticulating man with the hammer, and the crowding competitors whom I had seen jostling each other in the slave-markets of the United States. I went to bed that night with a disgusted and offended feeling of having been offered bribes, all day long, with a confidence which was not a little insulting.

My transactions with Messrs. Saunders and Otley were always very satisfactory. I did not receive a penny from the sale of my American books in the United States, though my American friends exerted themselves to protect the work from being pirated:[1] but the disappointment was the fault of my publishers' agent; and they were as sorry for it as I was. Soon after the appearance of 'Society in America,' Mr. Saunders called on me to propose a second work, which should have more the character of travel, and be of a lighter quality to both writer and reader. I had plenty of material; and, though I should have liked some rest, this was no sufficient reason for refusing. The publishers offered me £600 for this, in addition to the attendant advantages allowed with the former work.—Even through these liberal and honourable publishers, however, I became acquainted with one of the tricks of the trade which surprised me a good deal. After telling me the day of publication, and announcing that my twenty-five copies would be ready, Mr. Saunders inquired when I should like to come to their back parlour, 'and write the notes.'—'What notes?'—'The notes for the Reviews, you know, Ma'am.' He was surprised at being obliged to explain that authors write notes to friends and acquaintances connected with periodicals, 'to request favourable notices of the work.' I did not know how to credit this; and Mr. Saunders was amazed that I had never heard of it. 'I assure you, Ma'am,— —does it; and all our authors do it.' On my emphatically declining, he replied 'As you please, Ma'am: but it is the universal

---

[1]   The title page of the American edition of *Retrospect of Western Travel* lists Saunders and
       Otley as the English publisher, Harper & Brothers as the American.

practice, I believe.' I have always been related to the Reviews exactly like the ordinary public. I have never inquired who had reviewed me, or known who was going to do so, except by public rumour. I do not very highly respect reviews, nor like to write them; for the simple reason that in ninety-nine cases out of a hundred, the author understands his subject better than the reviewer. It can hardly be otherwise while the author treats one subject, to his study of which his book itself is a strong testimony; whereas the reviewer is expected to pass from topic to topic, to any extent, pronouncing, out of his brief survey, on the results of deep and protracted study. Of all the many reviews of my books on America and Egypt, there was not, as far as I know, one which did not betray ignorance of the respective countries. And, on the other hand, there is no book, except the very few which have appeared on my own particular subjects, that I could venture to pronounce on; as, in every other case, I feel myself compelled to approach a book as a learner, and not as a judge. This is the same thing as saying that reviewing, in the wholesale way in which it is done in our time, is a radically vicious practice; and such is indeed my opinion. I am glad to see scientific men, and men of erudition, and true connoisseurs in art, examining what has been done in their respective departments: and everybody is glad of good essays, whether they appear in books called Reviews or elsewhere. But of the reviews of our day, properly so called, the vast majority must be worthless, because the reviewer knows less than the author of the matter in hand.

In choosing the ground of my work, 'Society in America,'—(which should have been called, but for the objection of my publishers, 'Theory and Practice of Society in America,') I desired fairness in the first place: and I believed it was most fair to take my stand on the American point of view,—judging American society, in its spirit and methods, by the American tests,—the Declaration of Independence, and the constitutions based upon its principles. It had become a practice so completely established to treat of America in a mode of comparison with Europe, that I had little hope of being at first understood by more than a few. The Americans themselves had been so accustomed to be held up in contrast with Europeans by travellers that they could not get rid of the prepossession, even while reading my book. What praise there was excited vanity, as if such a thing had never been heard of before: and any censure was supposed to be sufficiently answered by evidence that the same evils existed in England. I anticipated this; and that consternation would be excited by some of my republican and other principles. Some of this consternation, and much of the censure followed, with a good deal that I had not conceived of. All this was of little consequence, in comparison with the comfort of having done some good, however little, in both countries. The fundamental fault of the book did not become apparent to me for some time after;—its metaphysical framework,[1] and the abstract treatment of what must necessarily be a concrete subject. The fault is not exclusively mine. It rests with the American theory which I had taken for my standpoint: but it was the weakness of an immature mind to choose that method of treatment; just as it was the act of immature politicians to make after the same method the first American constitution,—the one which would not work, and which gave place to the present arrangement. Again, I was infected to a certain degree with the American method of dissertation or preaching; and I was also full of Carlylism, like the friends I had left in the Western world. So that my book, while most carefully true in its facts, had a strong leaning towards the American fashion of theorising; and it was far more useful on the other side of the Atlantic than on this. The order of people here who answer to the existing state of the Americans took the book to heart very earnestly, if I may judge by the letters from strangers which flowed in upon me, even for years after its publication. The applications made to me for guidance and counsel,—applications which even put into my hand the disposal of a whole life, in various instances,—arose, not from agreement in political opinion, nor from discontent with things at home; but from my hearty conviction that social affairs are the personal duty of every individual, and from my freedom in saying what I thought. The stories that I could tell, from letters which exist among my papers, or from those which I thought it right to burn at once, would move the coldest, and rouse the laziest. Those which touched me most related to the oppressions which women in England suffer from the law and custom of the country. Some offered evidence of intolerable oppression, if I could point out how it might be used. Others offered money, effort, courage in enduring obloquy, every thing, if I could show them how to obtain, and lead them in obtaining, arrangements by which they could be free in spirit, and in outward liberty to make what they could of life. I feel strongly tempted to give here two or three narratives: but it would not be right. The applicants and their friends may be living; and I might be betraying confidence, though nearly twenty years

---

[1] In making this judgment, Martineau adopts the three stages of human development from Auguste Comte's *Positive Philosophy*—religious, metaphysical, positive—as she does throughout her *Autobiography* in treating her personal development; on her translation of Comte, see Period VI, sec. vii.

have elapsed. Suffice it that though I now disapprove the American form and style of the book, not the less standing by my choice of the American point of view, I have never regretted its boldness of speech. I felt a relief in having opened my mind which I would at no time have exchanged for any gain of reputation or fortune. The time had come when, having experienced what might be called the extremes of obscurity and difficulty first, and influence and success afterwards, I could pronounce that there was nothing for which it was worth sacrificing freedom of thought and speech. I enjoyed in addition the consolidation of invaluable friendships in America, and the acquisition of new ones at home. Altogether, I am well pleased that I wrote the book, though I now see how much better it might have been done if I had not been at the metaphysical period of my life when I had to treat of the most metaphysical constitution and people in the world.

Some of the wisest of my friends at home,—and especially, I remember Sydney Smith and Carlyle,—gently offered their criticism on my more abstract American book in the pleasant form of praise of the more concrete one. The 'Retrospect of Western Travel' was very successful,—as indeed the other was, though not, I believe, to the extent of the publishers' expectations. Sydney Smith showed but too surely, not long after, in his dealings with American Repudiation,[1] that he did not trouble himself with any study of the Constitution of the United States; for he crowded almost as many mistakes as possible into his procedure,—supposing Congress to be answerable for the doings of Pennsylvania, and Pennsylvania to have repudiated her debts; which she never did. Readers who thus read for amusement, and skip the politics, liked my second book best: and so did those who, like Carlyle, wisely desire us to see what we can, and tell what we see, without spinning out of ourselves systems and final causes, and all manner of notions which, as self-derived, are no part of our business or proper material in giving an account of an existing nation. Carlyle wrote me that he had rather read of Webster's cavernous eyes and arm under his coat-tail, than all the political speculation that a cut-and-dried system could suggest. I find before me a memorandum that Lord Holland sent me by General Fox a motto for the chapter on Washington. How it came about, I do not exactly remember; but I am

---

[1]   In May 1843, Smith petitioned Congress to ask the repayment of £1000 in bonds issued by the state of Pennsylvania. Like other states, Pennsylvania was seriously in debt and had defaulted on its loans. Martineau here alludes to Smith's letters to the *Morning Chronicle* in November 1843, which were brilliantly satirical about Pennsylvania's "repudiation" of its debts, but bitter in tone and ill-informed on matters of American government.

sure my readers, as well as I, were obliged to Lord Holland for as exquisite an appropriation of an exquisite eulogy as was ever proposed. The
lines are the Duke of Buckingham's on Lord Fairfax.

> 'He might have been a king
> But that he understood
> How much it was a meaner thing
> To be unjustly great than honourably good.'[1]

It was in September of that year (1837) that I began to keep a Diary. My
reason was that I saw so many wise people, and heard so much valuable
conversation, that my memory would not serve me to retain what I was
sorry to lose. I continued the practice for about five years, when I found
it becoming, not only burdensome, but, (as I was ill and living in solitude,)
pernicious. I find, by the first portion of my Diary, that I finished the
'Retrospect of Western Travel' on the first of December, 1837, having written a good many other things during the autumn, of which I now remember nothing. It was in August of that year that the Editor of the
Westminster Review (then the property of Mr. J.S. Mill) called on me, and
asked me to write a review of Miss Sedgwick's works. I did so for the
October number,[2] and I believe I supplied about half-a-dozen articles in
the course of the next two years,—the best known of which is 'The
Martyr Age of the United States,'[3]—a sketch of the history of
Abolitionism in the United States, up to that time. I find mentioned in
my Diary of articles for the 'Penny Magazine,' before and after the one
already referred to—the 'Month at Sea:'[4] and I remember that I earned
Knight's 'Gallery of Portraits,'[5] and some other valuable books in that
pleasant way. The most puzzling thing to me is to find repeated references
to a set of Essays called 'The Christian Seer,'[6] with some speculation on

---

[1]   From stanza iv of "A Pindaric Poem on the Death of the Lord Fairfax," by George Villiers
      (1628–87), Duke of Buckingham and husband of Lord Fairfax's daughter Mary.
[2]   "Miss Sedgwick's Works," *London and Westminster Review*, 28 (October 1837), 42–65.
[3]   "The Martyr Age of the United States," *London and Westminster Review*, 30 (December
      1838), 1–59.
[4]   *Penny Magazine* 6 (1837), 398–400, 405–08, 414–16, 429–31.
[5]   *Gallery of Portraits: Distinguished Men of Modern Times*, 4 vols. (London, C. Knight, 1838).
[6]   "The Christian Seer," *The Christian Teacher and Chronicle of Benevolence* 3 (1837), 532–44,
      576–82, 661–70, 704–12. This short-lived Unitarian periodical was edited by John H.
      Thom and published by Charles Fox; the same volume included her essay on "Moral
      Independence," written for the American edition of her *Miscellanies* (pp. 330–38) and a
      review of *Society in America* (pp. 340–53).

their quality, while I can recal nothing whatever about them,—their object, their subject, their mode of publication, or any thing else. I can only hope that others have forgotten them as completely as I have; for they would not have been worth much, if I have never heard thought of them since. They seem to have cost me some pains and care; and they were probably not the better for that.—The entry in my Diary on the comple- tion of the 'Retrospect' brings back some very deep feelings. 'I care little about this book of mine. I have not done it carelessly. I believe it is true: but it will fill no place in my mind and life; and I am glad it is done. Shall I despise myself hereafter for my expectations from my novel?'

Great were my expectations from my novel, for this reason chiefly;— that for many years now my writing had been almost entirely about fact: facts of society and of individuals: and the constraint of the effort to be always correct, and to bear without solicitude the questioning of my correctness, had become burdensome. I felt myself in danger of losing nerve, and dreading criticism on the one hand, and of growing rigid and narrow about accuracy on the other. I longed inexpressibly for the liberty of fiction, while occasionally doubting whether I had the power to use that freedom as I could have done ten years before. The intimate friend, on whose literary counsel, as I have said, I reposed so thankfully, and at whose country-house I found such sweet refreshment every autumn, was the confidante of my aspirations about a novel;[1] and many a talk she and I had that autumn about the novel I was to write in the course of the next year. She never flattered me; and her own relish of fiction made her all the more careful not to mislead me as to my chances of success in a new walk of literature. But her deliberate expectation was that I should succeed; and her expectation was grounded, like my own, on the fact that my heart and mind were deeply stirred on one or two moral subjects on which I wanted the relief of speech, or which could be well expressed in fiction as in any other way,—and perhaps with more freedom and earnestness than under any other form. After finishing my American subjects, I was to take a holiday,—to spend whole days with- out putting pen to paper; and then I was to do my best with my novel.

Such was the scheme: and so it went on up to the finishing of the year's engagements, and the first day of holiday, when I found reason to suspect that I had been under too long a strain of work and of anxiety. During that summer, I failed somewhat in strength, and, to my own surprise, in

---

[1]   Elizabeth Ann Ker, whose Swiss Cottage in Hertfordshire Martineau calls "a sort of home to me" in Period IV, sec. ii.

spirits. I told no person of this, except the friend and hostess just referred to. Within two years we found that I had already begun to sink under domestic anxieties, and the toil which was my only practicable refuge from them. The illness which prostrated me in 1839 was making itself felt,—though not recognised,—in 1837. I was dimly aware of overstrained strength, on the first experiment of holiday, when something happened which threw me into great perturbation. Nothing disturbs me so much as to have to make a choice between nearly equal alternatives; and it was a very serious choice that I had to make now.—A member of an eminent publishing firm called on me on the eleventh of December, to propose that his house should set up a periodical which was certainly much wanted,—an Economical Magazine,—of which I was to have the sole charge.[1] The salary offered was one which would have made me entirely easy about income: the subject was one which I need not fear to undertake: the work was wanted: and considerations like these were not strongly balanced by the facts that I felt tired and longed for rest, or by the prospect of the confinement which the editorship would impose. The vacillation of my mind was for some days very painful. I find, two days later, this entry. 'In the morning, I am *pro*, and at night, and in the night, *con* the scheme. I wonder how it will end. I see such an opening in it for things that I want to say! and I seem to be the person to undertake such a thing. I can toil—I am persevering, and in the habit of keeping my troubles to myself. If suffering be the worst on the *con* side, let it come. It will be a fine discipline of taste, temper, thought and spirits. But I don't expect — — and — — will accede to my last stipulations. If not, there's an end. If they do, I think I shall make the plunge.' Two days later:—'After tea, sat down before the fire with pencil and paper, to make out a list of subjects, contributors and books, for my periodical. Presently came a letter from — — and —, which I knew must nearly decide my fate in regard to the project. I distinctly felt that it could not hurt me, either way, as the *pros* and *cons* seem so nearly balanced that I should be rather thankful to have the matter decided for me. — — and — — grant all that I have asked; and it looks much as if we were to proceed. So I went on with my pondering till past ten, by which time I had got a sheetful of subjects.' I certainly dreaded the enterprise more than I desired it. 'It is an awful choice before me!'[2] Such facilities for usefulness and activity of knowledge; such certain toil and

---

[1]   The proposal came from Saunders and Otley.

[2]   Chapman quotes the entire journal entry in the *Memorials* (III, 204), with slight variation at the start: "It is an awful subject; such facilities for usefulness and activity of knowledge," etc.

bondage; such risk of failure and descent from my position! The realities of life press upon me now. If I do this, I must brace myself up to do and suffer like a man. No more waywardness, precipitation, and reliance on allowance from others! Undertaking a man's duty, I must brave a man's fate. I must be prudent, independent, serene, good-humoured; earnest with cheerfulness. The possibility is open before me of showing what a periodical with a perfect temper may be:—also, of setting women forward at once into the rank of men of business. But the hazards are great. I wonder how it will end.' I had consulted two or three intimate friends, when I wrote these entries; and had written to my brother James for his opinion. The friends at hand were all in favour of my undertaking the enterprise. If the one remaining opinion had been in agreement with theirs, I should have followed the unanimous advice: but on the nineteenth, I find, 'James is altogether against the periodical plan.'[1] I wrote my final refusal on that day; and again I was at liberty to ponder my novel.

My doctrine about plots in fiction has been given at sufficient length. It follows of course that I looked into real life for mine. I attached myself strongly to one which it cost me much to surrender. It is a story from real life which Miss Sedgwick has offered in her piece called 'Old Maids,' in her volume of 'Tales and Sketches,'[2] not likely to be known in England:—a story of two sisters, ten years apart in age, the younger of whom loves and finally marries the betrothed of the elder. Miss Sedgwick told me the real story, with some circumstances of the deepest interest which she, for good reasons, suppressed, but which I might have used. If I had wrought out this story, I should of course have acknowledged its source. But I deferred it,— and it is well I did. Mrs. S. Carter Hall relates it as the story of two Irish sisters, and impresses the anecdote by a striking woodcut, in her 'Ireland:' and Mrs. Browning has it again, in her beautiful 'Bertha in the Lane.'[3]

I was completely carried away by the article on St. Domingo in the Quarterly Review, (vol. xxi.)[4] which I lighted upon, one day at this

---

[1]   In a letter to Fanny Wedgwood of 19 December 1837, Martineau wrote, "I have just written to decline the enterprize, on James's strongly expressed opinion, which is right, I am confident." As Elisabeth Arbuckle notes (in *Letters*, p. 4), this version is milder than the "fuller and less complacent account [in the *Autobiography*] written after HM's break with her brother."

[2]   *Tales and Sketches* (Philadelphia: Carey, Lea, and Blanchard). Sedgwick dedicated this collection to Martineau.

[3]   Mr. and Mrs. S.C. Hall, *Ireland: Its Scenery, Character, &c.* (London: Hall, Virtue, 1841); Elizabeth Barrett, "Bertha in the Lane," first published in *Poems* (1844).

[4]   "Past and Present State of Hayti," *Quarterly Review* 21 (1819), 430–60. The article is a review essay of four books about Haiti, including *History of the Island of St. Domingo, from its First Discovery by Columbus to the Present Period.*

time, while looking for the noted article on the Grecian Philosophy in the same volume. I pursued the study of Toussaint L'Ouverture's character in the Biographie Universelle;[1] and, though it is badly done, and made a mere patch-work of irreconcilable views of him, the real man shone out into my mind, through all mists and shadows. I went to my confidante, with a sheetful of notes, and a heartful of longings to draw that glorious character,—with its singular mixture of negro temperament, heathen morality, and as much of Christianity as agreed with the two. But my friend could not see the subject as I did.[2] She honestly stood by her objections, and I felt that I could not proceed against the counsel of my only adviser. I gave it up: but a few years after, when ill at Tynemouth, I reverted to my scheme and fulfilled it:[3] and my kind adviser, while never liking the subject in an artistic sense, graciously told me that the book had kept her up, over her dressing-room fire, till three in the morning. There was a police report, during that winter,—very brief,—only one short paragraph,—which moved me profoundly, and which I was sure I could work out into a novel of the deepest interest. My fear was that that one paragraph would affect other readers as it did me, and be remembered, so that the catastrophe of my tale would be known from the beginning: so we deferred that plot, meaning that I should really work upon it one day. The reason why I never did is that, as I have grown older, I have seen more and more the importance of dwelling on things honest, lovely, hopeful and bright, rather than on the darker and fouler passions and most mournful weaknesses of human nature. Therefore it was that I reverted to Toussaint, rather than to the moral victim who was the hero of the police-court story.

What then was to be done? We came back, after every divergence, to the single fact (as I then believed it) that a friend of our family, whom I had not seen very often, but whom I had revered from my youth up, had been cruelly driven, by a match-making lady, to propose to the sister of the woman he loved,—on private information that the elder had lost her heart to him, and that he had shown her attention enough to warrant it. The marriage was not a very happy one, good as were the

---

[1]   Toussaint L'Ouverture (1743–1803), a black revolutionary, assumed leadership of the French colony of San Domingo (Haiti) when a decree of 1791 freeing the slaves was revoked; he was removed by a military force sent by Napoleon and transported to France. The *Biographie Universelle, ou Dictionnaire Historique* is a 52-vol. French biographical dictionary, published between 1811 and 1828.

[2]   Elizabeth Ker; see Period IV, sec. ii.

[3]   In *The Hour and the Man: A Historical Romance,* 3 vols. (London: Edward Moxon, 1841).

persons concerned, in their various ways. I altered the circumstances as much as I could, and drew the character, not of our English but of an American friend, whose domestic position is altogether different: and lo! it came to my knowledge, years afterwards, that the story of our friend's mischance was not at all true. I was rejoiced to hear it. Not only was I relieved from the fear of hurting a good man's feelings, if he should ever read 'Deerbrook:' but 'Deerbrook' was a fiction, after all, in its groundwork.[1]

The process was an anxious one. I could not at all tell whether I was equal to my enterprise. I found in it a relief to many pent-up sufferings, feelings, and convictions: and I can truly say that it was uttered from the heart. But my friend seemed nearly as doubtful of success as I was. She feared to mislead me; and she honestly and kindly said less than she felt in its favour. From the time when one day I saw a bright little tear fall on her embroidery, I was nearly at ease; but that was in the last volume. I have often doubted whether I could have worked through that fearful period of domestic trouble, with heart and hope enough to finish a book of a new kind, but for a singular source of refreshment, —a picture. Mr. Vincent Thompson[2] and his lady took me to the private view of the pictures at the British Institution; and I persisted in admiring a landscape in North Wales by Baker, to which I returned again and again, to feast on the gush of sunlight between two mountains, and the settling of the shadows upon the woods at their base.[3] Mr. Thompson at length returned too, and finally told me that it *was* a good picture. Several weeks afterwards, I heard an unusual lumbering mode of coming upstairs; and Mr. Thompson was shown in, bearing the picture, and saying that as I should certainly be getting pictures together some time or other, Mrs. Thompson had sent me this to begin with. I sat opposite that landscape while writing 'Deerbrook;' and many a dark passage did its sunshine light me through. Now that I live among mountains, that landscape is as beautiful as ever in my eyes: but nowhere could it be such a benefaction as in my little study in Fludyer Street, where dingy red walls rose up almost within reach, and idle clerks of the Foreign Office lolled out of dusty windows, to stare down upon their opposite neighbours.

---

[1]   *Deerbrook*, 3 vols. (London: Edward Moxon, 1839).

[2]   Possibly a gentleman from Fairfax, Virginia (1785–1845), whom she had met in America.

[3]   Probably Samuel Baker (1824–1909), a Birmingham landscape painter known for his watercolors of the Welsh countryside, but possibly Thomas Baker (1809–69), a Midlands landscape painter more famous during this period.

I was not uneasy about getting my novel published. On May-day, 1838, six weeks before I put pen to paper, I received a note from a friend who announced what appeared to me a remarkable fact;—that Mr. Murray, though he had never listened to an application to publish a novel since Scott's, was willing to enter into a negotiation for mine.[1] I was not aware then how strong was the hold on the public mind which 'the silver-fork school'[2] had gained; and I discovered it by Mr. Murray's refusal at last to publish 'Deerbrook.' He was more than civil;—he was kind, and, I believe, sincere in his regrets. The execution was not the ground of refusal. It was, as I had afterwards reason to know, the scene being laid in middle life. I do not know whether it is true that Mr. Lockhart advised Mr. Murray to decline it; but Mr. Lockhart's clique gave out on the eve of publication that the hero was an apothecary. People liked high life in novels, and low life, and ancient life; and life of any rank presented by Dickens, in his peculiar artistic light, which is very unlike the broad daylight of actual existence, English or other: but it was not supposed that they would bear a presentment of the familiar life of every day. It was a mistake to suppose so; and Mr. Murray finally regretted his decision. Mr. Moxon, to whom, by Mr. Rogers's advice, I offered it, had reason to rejoice in it. 'Deerbrook' had a larger circulation than novels usually obtain; two large editions having been long exhausted, and the work being still in constant demand.—I was rather amused at the turn that criticism took among people of the same class as my personages,—the class which I chose because it was my own, and the one that I understood best. It was droll to hear the daughters of dissenting ministers and manufacturers expressing disgust that the heroine came from Birmingham, and that the hero was a surgeon. Youths and maidens in those days looked for lords and ladies in every page of a new novel.—My own judgment of 'Deerbrook' was for some years more favourable than it is now. The work was faithful in principle and sentiment to the then state of my mind; and that satisfied me for a time. I should now require more of myself, if I were to attempt a novel,— (which I should not do, if I were sure of living another quarter of a century.) I should require more simplicity, and a far more objective character,—not of delineation but of scheme. The laborious portions of meditation, obtruded at intervals, are wholly objectionable in my

[1] John Murray; see p. 393, n. 1.
[2] Novels about aristocrats and fashionable life written by Benjamin Disraeli, Susan Ferrier, Catherine Gore, and others.

eyes. Neither morally nor artistically can they be justified. I know the book to have been true to the state of thought and feeling I was then in, which I now regard as imperfect and very far from lofty:—I believe it to have been useful, not only in overcoming a prejudice against the use of middle-class life in fiction, but in a more special application to the discipline of temper; and therefore I am glad I wrote it: but I do not think it would be fair to judge me from it, any later than the time in which it was written.

When Mr. Murray perceived that the book had a decided though gradual success, he sent a mutual friend to me with a remarkable message, absolutely secret at the time, but no longer needing to be so. He said that he could help me to a boundless fortune, and a mighty future fame, if I would adopt his advice. He advised me to write a novel in profound secrecy, and under appearances which would prevent suspicion of the authorship from being directed towards me. He desired to publish this novel in monthly numbers; and was willing to pledge his reputation for experience on our obtaining a circulation as large as had ever been known. It would give him high satisfaction, he declared, to see my writings on thousands of tables from which my name would exclude every thing I published under it: and he should enjoy being the means of my obtaining such fortune, and such an ultimate fame as I might confidently reckon on, if I would accept his offer. I refused it at once. I could not undertake to introduce a protracted mystery into my life which would destroy its openness and freedom. This was one reason: but there was a far more serious one;—more important because it was not personal. I could not conscientiously adopt any method so unprincipled in an artistic sense as piecemeal publication. Whatever other merits it may have, a work of fiction cannot possibly be good in an artistic sense which can be cut up into portions of an arbitrary length. The success of the portions requires that each should have some sort of effective close; and to provide a certain number of these at regular intervals, is like breaking up the broad lights and shadows of a great picture, and spoiling it as a composition. I might never do any thing to advance or sustain literary art; but I would do nothing to corrupt it, by adopting a false principle of composition. The more license was afforded by the popular taste of the time, the more careful should authors be to adhere to sound principle in their art. Mr. Murray and our friend evidently thought me very foolish; but I am as sure now as I was then that, my aim not being money or fame, I was right.

While pondering my novel, I wrote (as I see by my diary) various small pieces, stories, and didactic articles, for special purposes,—religious or benevolent, American and English: and in April and May I cleared my mind and hands of a long-standing engagement. The chapter which I mentioned having written at sea, on 'How to observe Morals and Manners,' was, by the desire of the proposer and of Mr. Knight, to be expanded into a volume; and this piece of tough work, which required a good deal of reading and thinking, I accomplished this spring. The earlier numbers of the 'Guide to Service,' beginning with 'The Maid of All Work,'[1] were written in the same spring. In the first days of June, I wrote an article on 'Domestic Service in England' for the Westminster Review:[2] and then, after a few days with my friends the Fs.[3] on one of our Box Hill expeditions, I was ready and eager to sit down to the first chapter of my first novel on my birthday,—June 12th, 1838. By the end of August, I had finished the first volume, and written 'The Lady's Maid,' for the 'Service' series. As I then travelled, it was November before I could return to 'Deerbrook.' I finished it on the first of the next February; and it was published before Easter.

The political interests of this period were strong. The old King[4] was manifestly infirm and feeble when I last saw him, in the spring of 1837. I was taking a drive with Lady S—,[5] when her carriage drew up to the roadside and stopped, because the King and Queen were coming. He touched his hat as he leaned back, looking small and aged. I could not but feel something more than the ordinary interest in the young girl who was so near the throne. At a concert at the Hanover Square Rooms, some time before (I forget what year it was) the Duchess of Kent sent Sir John Conroy[6] to me with a message of acknowledgment of the usefulness of my books to the Princess: and I afterwards heard more particulars of the eagerness with which the little lady read the stories on the first day of the month. A friend of mine who was at Kensington Palace one evening when my Political Economy series was

---

[1] *The Guide to Service*, published by Charles Knight, included *The Maid of All-work* (1838), *The Lady's Maid* (1838), and *The Housemaid* (1839).

[2] "Domestic Service," *London and Westminster Review* 29 (1838), 405–32. Ostensibly a review of Charles Knight's *The Guide to Service* (1838) and Catharine Sedgwick's *Live and Let Live* (1838), Martineau was in fact announcing the need for Knight's series and reviewing her own contribution to it, *The Maid of All Work*.

[3] Mr. and Mrs. Joseph Fisher of Highbury; see Period IV, sec. ii.

[4] King William IV (1765–1837).

[5] Probably Lady Shepherd (1777–1847); see Period IV, sec. i.

[6] The Duchess of Kent, the future Queen Victoria (1819–1901), ascended the throne in 1837 at age eighteen. Sir John Conroy was then comptroller of the Duchess of Kent's household and, as a great friend of Victoria's mother, saw himself as the future power behind the throne. Victoria disliked him, and in 1839 dismissed him from her Court.

coming to an end, told me how the Princess came, running and skipping, to show her mother the advertisement of the 'Illustrations of Taxation,' and to get leave to order them. Her 'favourite' of my stories is 'Ella of Garveloch.'—It was at breakfast that we heard of the King's death. In the course of the morning, while I was out, a friend came to invite my old ladies to go with him to a place near, where they could at their ease see the Queen presented to the people. They went into the park, and stood in front of the window at St. James's Palace, where, (among other places) the sovereigns are proclaimed and presented. Scarcely half-a-dozen people were there; for very few were aware of the custom. There stood the young creature, in the simplest mourning, with her sleek bands of brown hair as plain as her dress. The tears ran fast down her cheeks, as Lord Melbourne[1] stood by her side, and she was presented to my mother and aunt and the other half-dozen as their sovereign.—I have never gone out of my way to see great people; but the Queen went abroad abundantly, and I saw her very often. I saw her go to dissolve Parliament;[2] and on the 9th of November, to the Guildhall banquet; and several times from Mr. Macready's box at the theatre. It so happened that I never saw her when she was not laughing and talking, and moving about. At a tragedy, and going to a banquet and to dissolve her predecessor's parliament, it was just the same. It was not pleasant to see her, when Macready's 'Lear' was fixing all other hearts and eyes, chattering to the Lord Chamberlain, and laughing, with her shoulder turned to the stage. I was indignant, like a good many other people: but, in the fourth act, I saw her attention fixed; and then she laughed no more. She was interested like the rest of the audience; and, in one way, more than others. Probably she was the only person present to whom the play was entirely new. I heard from one who knew her and the incidents of that evening too well to be mistaken, that the story was absolutely new to her, inasmuch as she was not previously aware that King Lear had any daughters. In remarkable contrast with her was one of the gentlemen in attendance upon her,—the Lord Albemarle of that day.[3] He forgot every thing but the play,—by degrees

[1]   William Lamb (1779–1848), 2nd Viscount Melbourne, prime minister when Victoria came to the throne, served as her mentor and advisor on matters of state and politics.

[2]   In June 1837, the newly-crowned Victoria decreed (as reported in the Manchester *Guardian*) "that, so soon as the money bills and the most pressing business before the house of commons have been disposed of, a dissolution will take place." In November 1837 she paid a ceremonial visit to the City of London, where the lord mayor presided over a 700-guest dinner at the Guildhall and presented her with the City Sword.

[3]   Augustus Frederick Keppel (1794–1851), 5th Earl of Albemarle.

leaned forward between the Queen and the stage, and wept till his limp handkerchief would hold no more tears.

Those were the days when there was least pleasure to the loyal in seeing their Queen. At her accession, I was agreeably surprised at her appearance. The upper part of her face was really pretty, and there was an ingenuous and serene air which seemed full of promise. At the end of a year, the change was melancholy. The expression of her face was wholly altered. It had become bold and discontented. That was, it is now supposed, the least happy part of her life. Released from the salutary restraints of youth, flattered and pampered by the elated Whigs who kept her to themselves, misled by Lord Melbourne, and not yet having found her home, she was not like the same girl that she was before, nor the same woman that she has been since. Her mother had gone off the scene, and her husband had not come on; and in the lonely and homeless interval there was much cause for sorrow to herself and others. The Whigs about her made a great boast of the obligations she was under to Lord Melbourne: but the rest of the world perceives that all her serious mistakes were made while she was in Lord Melbourne's hands, and that all went well after she was once fairly under the guidance of Sir Robert Peel,[1] and happy in a virtuous home of her own.

I was at her Coronation: and great is the wonder with which I have looked back to the enterprise ever since. I had not the slightest desire to go, but every inclination to stay at home: but it was the only coronation likely to happen in my lifetime, and it was a clear duty to witness it. I was quite aware that it was an occasion (I believe the only one) on which a lady could be alone in public, without impropriety or inconvenience: and I knew of several daughters of peeresses who were going singly to different parts of the Abbey, their tickets being for different places in the building. Tickets were offered me for the two brothers who were then in London;[2] but they were for the nave; and I had the luck of one for the transept-gallery. The streets had hedges of police from our little street to the gates of the Abbey; and none were allowed to pass but the bearers of tickets; so nothing could be safer. I was aware

---

[1]   Robert Peel (1788–1850) served as Tory prime minister in 1834–1835, and assumed that office again from 1841 to 1846. Martineau approved of his repeal of the Corn Laws and of the duties on raw materials and manufactured goods in his free trade budgets of 1842 and 1845.

[2]   Henry, who had remained in Norwich overseeing the family's wine importing business but had recently moved to London to take a position as a clerk at Somerset House, and either Robert of Birmingham or James of Liverpool.

of all this, and had breakfasted, and was at our hall-door in time, when
one of my brothers, who would not believe it, would not let me go
for another half-hour, while he breakfasted. As I anticipated, the police
turned him back, and I missed the front row where I might have heard
and seen every thing. Ten minutes sooner, I might have succeeded in
witnessing what would never happen again in my time. It was a bitter
disappointment; but I bent all my strength to see what I could from
the back row. Hearing was out of the question, except the loudest of
the music.—The maids called me at half-past two that June morning,—mistaking the clock. I slept no more, and rose at half-past three.
As I began to dress, the twenty-one guns were fired which must have
awakened all the sleepers in London. When the maid came to dress
me, she said numbers of ladies were already hurrying to the Abbey. I
saw the grey old Abbey from my window as I dressed, and thought
what would have gone forward within it before the sun set upon it.
My mother had laid out her pearl ornaments for me. The feeling was
very strange of dressing in crape, blonde and pearls at four in the morning. Owing to the delay I have referred to, the Poets' Corner entrance
was half full when I took my place there. I was glad to see the
Somervilles[1] just before me, though we presently parted at the foot of
the staircase. On reaching the gallery, I found that a back seat was so
far better than a middle one that I should have a pillar to lean against,
and a nice corner for my shawl and bag of sandwiches. Two lady-like
girls, prettily dressed, sat beside me, and were glad of the use of my
copy of the service and programme. The sight of the rapid filling of
the Abbey was enough to go for. The stone architecture contrasted
finely with the gay colours of the multitude. From my high seat I
commanded the whole north transept, the area with the throne, and
many portions of galleries, and the balconies which were called the
vaultings. Except a mere sprinkling of oddities, every body was in full
dress. In the whole assemblage, I counted six bonnets.[2] The scarlet of
the military officers mixed in well; and the groups of the clergy were
dignified; but to an unaccustomed eye the prevalence of court-dresses
had a curious effect. I was perpetually taking whole groups of gentlemen for quakers till I recollected myself.[3] The Earl Marshal's assistants,

---

[1] The scientist Mary Somerville and her husband, Dr. William Somerville; see Period IV,
     sec. ii.

[2] Because the custom was court dress, bonnets for day dress would be atypical.

[3] Quaker men retained their hats and, in a belief in the equality of all, did not doff them in
     respect to a person of higher social status.

called Gold Sticks,[1] looked well from above, lightly flitting about in white breeches, silk stockings, blue laced frocks, and white sashes. The throne, an armchair with a round back, covered, as was its footstool, with cloth of gold, stood on an elevation of four steps, in the centre of the area. The first peeress took her seat in the north transept opposite at a quarter before seven: and three of the bishops came next. From that time, the peers and their ladies arrived faster and faster. Each peeress was conducted by two Gold Sticks, one of whom handed her to her seat, and the other bore and arranged her train on her lap, and saw that her coronet, footstool and book were comfortably placed. I never saw any where so remarkable a contrast between youth and age as in those noble ladies. None of the decent differences of dress which, according to middle-class custom, pertain to contrasting periods of life seem to be admissible on these grand court occasions. Old hags, with their dyed or false hair drawn to the top of the head, to allow the putting on of the coronet, had their necks and arms bare and glittering with diamonds: and those necks and arms were so brown and wrinkled as to make one sick; or dusted over with white powder which was worse than what it disguised. I saw something of this from my seat in the transept gallery, but much more when the ceremonial was over, and the peeresses were passing to their carriages, or waiting for them. The younger were as lovely as the aged were haggard. One beautiful creature, with a transcendent complexion and form, and coils upon coils of light hair, was terribly embarrassed about her coronet. She had apparently forgotten that her hair must be disposed with a view to it: and the large braids at the back would in no way permit the coronet to keep on. She and her neighbour tugged vehemently at her braids; and at last the thing was done after a manner, but so as to spoil the wonderful effect of the simultaneous self-coroneting of all the peeresses.—About nine, the first gleams of the sun slanted into the Abbey, and presently travelled down to the peeresses. I had never before seen the full effect of diamonds. As the light travelled, each peeress shone like a rainbow. The brightness, vastness, and dreamy magnificence of the scene produced a strange effect of exhaustion and sleepiness. About nine o'clock, I felt this so disagreeably that I determined to withdraw my senses from the scene, in order to reserve my strength (which was not

---

[1]   So named because they carry a golden rod. Even in Parliament today, four people (the Earl Marshal, the Lord Great Chamberlain, and the carriers of the Sword of State and the Cap of Maintenance) walk in front of Queen Elizabeth at the opening of Parliament as "Gold Sticks."

great at that time) for the ceremonial to come. I had carried a book; and I read and ate a sandwich, leaning against my friendly pillar, till I felt refreshed.

The guns told when the Queen had set forth; and there was renewed animation. The Gold Sticks flitted about; there was tuning in the orchestra; and the foreign ambassadors and their suites arrived in quick succession. Prince Esterhazy,[1] crossing a bar of sunshine, was the most prodigious rainbow of all. He was covered with diamonds and pearls; and as he dangled his hat, it cast a dancing radiance all round. While he was thus glittering and gleaming, people were saying, I know not how truly, that he had to redeem those jewels from pawn, as usual, for the occasion.—At half-past eleven, the guns told that the Queen had arrived: but, as there was much to be done in the robing-room, there was a long pause before she appeared. A burst from the orchestra marked her appearance at the doors, and the anthem 'I was glad'[2] rang through the abbey. Every body rose: and the holders of the first and second rows of our gallery stood up so high that I saw nothing of the entrance, nor of the Recognition, except the Archbishop of Canterbury reading at one of the angles of the platform. The 'God save the Queen' of the organ swelled gloriously forth after the recognition. The services which followed were seen by a very small proportion of those present. The acclamation when the crown was put on her head was very animating: and in the midst of it, in an instant of time, the peeresses were all coroneted:—all but the fair creature already described. In order to see the enthroning, I stood on the rail behind our seats, holding by another rail. I was in nobody's way; and I could not resist the temptation, though every moment expecting that the rail would break. Her small dark crown looked pretty, and her mantle of cloth of gold very regal. She herself looked so small as to appear puny. The homage was as pretty a sight as any;—trains of peers touching her crown, and then kissing her hand. It was in the midst of that process that poor Lord Rolle's[3] disaster sent a shock through the whole assemblage. It turned me very sick. The large, infirm old man was held up by two peers, and

---

1   Prince Paul Anthony (1786–1866), of the Magyar family Esterhazy of Galantha, was a career diplomat who served the Austrian government in embassies at London, Paris, and Rome, and from 1830 to 1836 was the premier Austrian commissioner in London.

2   Probably Henry Purcell's version based on Psalm 122, "I was glad when they said unto me," originally composed for the coronation of James II; more recent coronations have used music by Sir Hubert Parry (1848–1918), composed in 1902.

3   John Rolle (1750–1842), Baron Rolle of Stevenstone, was a Tory M.P. from 1779 onward.

had nearly reached the royal footstool when he slipped through the hands of his supporters, and rolled over and over down the steps, lying at the bottom, coiled up in his robes. He was instantly lifted up; and he tried again and again, amidst shouts of admiration of his valour. The Queen at length spoke to Lord Melbourne, who stood at her shoulder, and he bowed approval; on which she rose, leaned forward, and held out her hand to the old man, dispensing with his touching the crown. He was not hurt, and his self-quizzing on his misadventure was as brave as his behaviour at the time. A foreigner in London gravely reported to his own countrymen, what he entirely believed on the word of a wag, that the Lords Rolle held their title on the condition of performing the feat at every coronation.

The departure of a large proportion of the assemblage when the Communion-service began afforded me a good opportunity for joining some friends who, like myself, preferred staying to see more of the Queen in the Abbey, to running away for the procession. I then obtained a good study of the peers, and of the Queen and her train-bearers when she returned to the throne. The enormous purple and crimson trains, borne by her ladies, dressed all alike, made the Queen look smaller than ever. I watched her out at the doors, and then became aware how fearfully fatigued I was. I never remember any thing like it. While waiting in the passages and between the barriers, several ladies sat or lay down on the ground. I did not like to sink down in dust half a foot deep, to the spoiling of my dress and the loss of my self-respect; but it was really a terrible waiting till my brothers appeared at the end of the barrier. The crowd had rendered our return impossible till then; and even then, we had to make a circuit. I satisfied my thirst, and went to sleep; and woke up to tea, and to keep house with my mother, while every body else went out to see the illuminations. I did not; but was glad to go to bed at midnight, and sleep eight hours at a stretch, for once.

It was a wonderful day; and one which I am glad to have witnessed; but it had not the effect on me which I was surprised to observe in others. It strengthened, instead of relaxing my sense of the unreal character of monarchy in England. The contrast between the traditional ascription of power to the sovereign and the actual fact was too strong to be overpowered by pageantry, music, and the blasphemous religious services of the day. After all was said and sung, the sovereign remained a nominal ruler, who could not govern by her own mind and will; who had influence, but no political power; a throne and crown, but with the knowledge of every body that the virtue had gone out of them. The festival was a highly barbaric one, to my eyes. The theological part especially was worthy only of the old Pharaonic times in Egypt, and those of the Kings in Palestine. Really, it was only by old musical and devotional association that the services could go down with people of any reverence at mixing up of the Queen and the God, such homage to both, and adulation so like in kind and degree that, when one came to think of it, it made one's blood run cold to consider that this was commended to all that assemblage as religion. God was represented as merely the King of kings and Lord of lords;—the lowest of the low views in which the Unknown is regarded or described. There is, I believe, no public religious service which is not offensive to thoughtful and reverent persons, from its ascription of human faculties, affections, qualities and actions to the assumed First Cause of the universe: but the Jewish or heathen ascription to him of military and aristocratic rank, and regal prerogative, side by side with the same ascription to the Queen, was the most coarse and irreverent celebration that I was ever a witness to. The performance of the Messiah, so beautiful and touching as a work of art, or as the sincere homage of superstition, is saddening and full of shame when regarded as worship. The promises—all broken; the exultation—all falsified by the event; the prophecies—all discredited by the experience of eighteen centuries, and the boasts of prevalence, rung out gloriously when Christianity is dying out among the foremost peoples of the earth;—all these, so beautiful as art or history, are very painful when regarded as religion. As an apotheosis of Osiris,[1] under his ancient name, or his more modern image of Christ, the Messiah of Handel is the finest treat in the whole range of art: but it is too low for religion. Yet more striking was the Coronation service to me, in the same light. Splendid and moving as addressed to a Jehovah, on the coronation of a Solomon,[2] it was offensive as offered to the God of the nineteenth century in the western world.—I have refreshed my memory about the incidents of that twenty-eighth of June, 1838, from my Diary. The part which least needs refreshing is this last. I remember remarking to my mother on the impiety of the service, when a copy of it was kindly sent to me the evening before; and I told her when the celebration was over, that this part of it had turned out even worse than I expected; and that I could not imagine how so many people could hear it as a matter of course.

---

[1]   Osiris, the Egyptian god of the dead, but also the source of renewed life.

[2]   Solomon (970–928 BCE), Jewish king whose reign was marked by its faithfulness to Judaic religious precepts against foreign influences, and the splendor and ostentation of its court.

One of the strongest interests of the year 1838 was Lord Durham's going out as Governor-General of the North American colonies.[1] I have given my account of that matter in my History of the Peace, and I will not enlarge on it now. I was concerned when I heard of his acceptance of the post, because the difficulties appeared all but insuperable at best; and I knew too much of Lord Brougham's jealousy and Lord Melbourne's laxity to hope that he would be duly supported from home, or even left unmolested. He said himself that he felt 'inexpressible reluctance' to undertake the charge: but his confiding temper misled him into trusting his political comrades,—Lord Melbourne and his Ministry—for 'cordial and energetic support,' and his political opponents,—Lord Brougham and those who pulled his wires,—for 'generous forbearance.' In talking over the matter one day with our mutual friend, Lady Charlotte Lindsay,[2] I did not conceal my regret and apprehension. She called one day, soon after, to tell me honestly that she had told Lord Durham, the night before, that I was not sanguine about his success. He questioned her anxiously as to my exact meaning; and she referred him to me. I had no wish to disturb him, now that it was too late, with my bad opinion of those in whose hands he was placing his fate: and I did not do so. I answered all his questions about Canada and the United States as well as I could. Charles and Arthur Buller[3] obtained introductions and information from me; and Charles spent many hours by my fireside, diligently discussing business, and giving me the strongest impression of his heart being deep in his work. His poor mother, who worshipped him, came one day, just before they sailed, nervous and flushed, and half laughing, telling me what a fright she had had: —that she had been assured that the Hastings man-of-war, in which her sons were to attend Lord Durham, would certainly sink from the weight of the Governor-General's plate. This was a specimen of the vulgar jokes of the Brougham clique: and it produced an effect on others than poor Mrs. Buller. Lord Chandos[4] founded a motion on it, —objecting to the

---

[1]   John George Lambton (1792–1840), 1st Earl Durham, was a friend and fellow radical; see Period IV, sec. i for another account of his career, as well as *A History of England during the Thirty Years' Peace, 1816–1848* (1849), vol. 3, ch. 12.

[2]   Lady Charlotte Lindsay (1770–1849), daughter of Lord North; see Period IV, sec. ii.

[3]   Charles Buller (1806–48), Radical M.P., went as secretary to Lord Durham on his Canadian mission and contributed to the "Report on the Affairs of British North America" of 1839; after Durham's death, Buller became the spokesman for the colonial reformers, speaking frequently in the House of Commons on colonial issues and urging various reforms, including fair wages and education for Canadian workers. Arthur Buller was his younger brother. See Period IV, sec. ii for another version of this story.

[4]   Samuel Egerton Brydges (1762–1837), Baron Chandos of Sudeley, who died soon thereafter.

expense to the country!—the Governor-General going out unsalaried, to save a group of colonies to the empire, in an hour of extreme danger! The intolerable treatment he met with shocked me as much as if I had anticipated any thing better: and his own magnanimous conduct on his return moved me as deeply as if I had not known him to be capable of it. He was calm, cheerful, winning in his manners as ever, and quite willing to trust his friends for their friendship while himself desiring no demonstration of it which should overthrow the tottering Government, and embarrass the Queen for his sake. Lady Durham necessarily resigned her office about the Queen's person:[1] but no word or sign of reproach ever reached her royal mistress for her fatal fickleness in first writing an autograph letter of the warmest thankfulness for his ordinances, and then disallowing those same ordinances, and permitting every kind of insult to be offered to the devoted statesman who had sacrificed his comfort and ease in her service, and was about to yield his life under the torture which she allowed to be inflicted on him.[2] To the last moment, her old friends, who might have expected something very different from her sense of early obligation, maintained that she meant well, but was misguided. When I last saw Lord Durham it was in his own house in Cleveland Row, when a note was brought in from the Colonial Office, the contents of which he communicated to me:— that he could not have any copies of his own Report without paying four shillings and threepence apiece for them. He had gone unsalaried, had spent 10,000£ out of his private property, and had produced a Report of unequalled value, at an unparalleled sacrifice; and he was now insulted in this petty way. He smilingly promised me a four-and-threepenny Report notwithstanding.—His successor, Lord Sydenham[3] (who had not yet got his patent) was diligently studying Canadian affairs every day, with Lord Durham and the Bullers, in order to carry out their scheme. We had a world of talk about the Western Continent that night: but I never much liked Poulett Thomson. He had great qualities,—a very remarkable industry, and personal fortitude, long and thoroughly tested: but he was luxurious, affectedly indolent in manner, and with a curious stamp of meanness on both person and manners. I never

---

[1]   Lady Durham, the former Lady Louisa Elizabeth Grey (d. 1841), was appointed a lady of the bedchamber to Queen Victoria in 1837 but resigned on her husband's return from Canada.

[2]   Lord Durham died in 1840, after many years of bad health and weakened by his Canadian experience.

[3]   Charles Poulett-Thomson (1799–1841), Lord Sydenham, governor general of Canada from 1839 to 1841, executed the Union Act of 1840 that united Upper and Lower Canada.

saw him again, either. He was on the eve of departure for his government, whence he never returned. If I remember right, that was the day of Lord Normanby's[1] appointment to the Colonial Office. He complained, half in earnest, of the hardship of never getting a foreign tour, like other people,—passing as he had done from Jamaica to Ireland, and now having all the colonies on his hands. I entirely agreed with him as to the weight of the charge: whereupon he asked me what I should have done first, if I had been in his place that day. My answer was that I should have gone immediately to the globe, to see where the forty-three colonies were that I was to govern. He laughed; but I thought it a serious matter enough that any Minister should be burdened with a work which it was so impossible that he should do properly. Well!—that night I bade Lord and Lady Durham farewell, little imagining that I should never more see either of them. I knew he was more delicate in health even than usual; and that he was exerting himself much to keep up till the Ministry or the session should close. 'Till Easter' politicians said the Ministry might last; and this was a pretty good hit, as the Bedchamber Question came on just after Easter.[2] Before that time I was abroad; and I was brought home on a couch, and carried through London at once to Newcastle-on Tyne, where I staid some months at my brother-in-law's.[3] Repeated invitations to Lambton Castle came to me there; but I was too ill to leave the house. In the course of the next spring, Lord Durham was ordered to the south of Europe; but he got no further than Cowes,[4] where he died in July,—the vitality of his heart and animation of his mind flattering the hopes of his family to the last. Lady Durham took her young family to Italy, but died before they had reached their destination.[5] For his death I was

---

[1]   In February, 1839, Constantine Henry Phipps (1797–1863), 1st Marquis of Normanby, succeeded Charles Grant (1778–1866), Baron Glenelg, as colonial secretary.

[2]   In the "Bedchamber Crisis" of 1839, the Whig prime minister Lord Melbourne tried to resign, and Queen Victoria rejected the request of Robert Peel, the prospective Tory prime minister, that she dismiss some of the wives and daughters of Whig M.P. s who made up her household. Victoria insisted that "the ladies of the bedchamber" were not political appointees but members of her family circle, and that she would not countenance the traditional system, in which new prime ministers chose the ladies of the new court from among their own parliamentary supporters. The "Bedchamber Question" saved Lord Melbourne's government for another term (until 1841).

[3]   In May, 1839, Martineau returned from a European tour, stricken by the uterine tumors that were to plague her for the rest of her life. Dr. Thomas Greenhow, her brother-in-law, treated her until she turned to mesmerism for a cure.

[4]   On the Isle of Wight, off the southern coast of England.

[5]   Lady Durham died on 26 November 1841 in Genoa, Italy.

prepared: but the news of hers was a great shock. I was very ill then; and when the orphaned girls came to see me at Tynemouth, I behaved (it seemed to me) unpardonably. I could not stop my tears, in the presence of those who had so much more reason and so much more right to be inconsolable. But I always have felt, and I feel still, that that story is one of the most tragic I have ever known. In my early youth I had been accustomed to hear my revered eldest brother say that the best man in the House of Commons—the one who would turn out a hero and a statesman in the worst or the best of times,—was John George Lambton. I had watched his career through the worst of times till he came into power, and made the Reform Bill. I then became acquainted with him, and found in him a solid justification of the highest hopes; and now he was dead, in middle life, broken-hearted by injury, treachery and insult; and his devoted wife presently followed him.

Their eldest daughter was profoundly impressed by the serious responsibilities which rested on her as the head of the family during her brother's boyhood; and she took me along with her in her efforts and her cares. It was she and I who originated the 'Weekly Volume,'[1]— our scheme being taken up and carried out by Mr. Charles Knight, in the way which is so well known. The singular satisfaction has been hers of seeing the redemption of Canada carried out by her husband from her father's beginning.[2] She has the best possible consolation for such a fate as that of her parents that their work has been gloriously achieved by one whom she has made their son.

On looking at my Diary, I am not at all surprised that it was considered desirable for me to take another journey in the autumn of 1838. I was sorry to leave 'Deerbrook' at the end of the first volume: but there was every other reason why I should take the refreshment of a journey after two years of close work, and no other reason why I should not. Either the growing domestic anxiety or the ever-increasing calls of work and of society would have been enough for the strongest and gayest-hearted: and I had both kinds of burdens on me. I find in my Diary more and more self-exhortations and self-censures about the

---

[1]   The "Weekly Volume," a cheap, popular library launched by Charles Knight in June 1844, was intended for working men and women who might either "club together" to purchase volumes or read volumes in libraries; in a letter to Edward Bulwer-Lytton of 21 April 1844, Martineau describes the audience and distribution: "for Prisons, Ships, Barracks, Police & Coast Guards stations, workhouses, rail-road stations, palace and mansion libraries, pit & factory villages &c." (in Sanders, ed. *Letters*, 91).

[2]   Mary Louisa Lambton (d. 1898) married James Bruce (1811–63), 8th Earl of Elgin, in 1846; he served as governor general of Canada from 1847 to 1854.

sufferings of that year 1838. I had by that time resolved on the wisdom which I try to this day to practise:—longing for quiet, and yet finding it impossible in the nature of things that my life should be any thing but a busy, public, and diversified one,—*to keep a quiet mind*. I did strive; and to a considerable extent I succeeded; but my nerves were, and had long been, overstrained; and my wisest friends continued to advise me to leave home more frequently than my inclination would have disposed me to do. My mother was well pleased to let me go on this occasion, as my rooms would be at her disposal for her hospitalities; and I therefore agreed to join a party of friends, to attend the meeting of the British Association at Newcastle first,[1] and then proceed to the Lake District, which I had never seen, and into Scotland, visiting both Western and Northern Highlands. It is always pleasant, I find, to have some object in view, even in the direction of a journey of pleasure: and this was supplied to me by Mr. Knight's request that I would explore the topography of Shakspere's Scotch play now; and of the Italian plays when I went to the continent the next year. 'Do this for me,' said Mr. Knight, 'and I will give you ten copies of my Shakspere.' Two copies of the Shakspere satisfied me; for indeed the work was purely pleasurable. A few months after that time, my companions were walking Padua through and through with me, for the shrewish Katherine's and delectable Portia's sake; and looking for Juliet at Verona, and exploring the Jew quarter at Venice, and fixing on the very house whence Jessica eloped; and seeing at the arsenal what Othello meant by his business at the Sagittary. In like manner we now traced out the haunts of Macbeth, living and dead. When we were at Lord Murray's, at Strachur, his brother gave us a letter of introduction which opened to us all the known recesses of Glammis Castle.[2] We sat down and lingered on the Witches' Heath, between Nairn and Forres, and examined Cawdor Castle. Best of all, we went to Iona,[3] and saw Macbeth's grave in the line of those of the Scottish kings. I have seen many wonders and beauties in many lands; but no one scene remains so deeply impressed on my very heart as that sacred Iona, as we saw it, with

---

1   British Association for the Advancement of Science, founded in 1831.

2   Sir John Archibald Murray (1779–1859), later Lord Murray, was lord advocate of Scotland in 1834–35; his elder brother was William, Lord Henderland. Glamis Castle is the home of the Earls of Strathmore and Kinghorne, and the legendary setting for Shakespeare's *Macbeth*. A more detailed account of Lord Murray appears in Martineau's *Biographical Sketches* (1869), 309–15.

3   Small island off the Isle of Mull, site of a ruined abbey founded by St. Columba in 563 A.D., and burial place of 48 Scottish kings, including Macbeth and Duncan I.

its Cathedral standing up against a bar of yellow western sky, while the myrtle-green tumbling sea seemed to show it to be unattainable. We had reached it however; and had examined its relics with speechless interest. I do not know whether any of the air of the localities hangs about those notes of mine in Mr. Knight's Shakspere; but to me, the gathering up of knowledge and associations for them was almost as pleasant work as any I ever had to do.

We were tempted to go to Newcastle by sea, by a steamer having been engaged to convey a freight of *savans*. A curious company of passengers we were on board the Ocean:—sound scientific men; a literary humbug or two; a statistical pretender or two; and a few gentlemen, clerical or other. When we entered Shields Harbour,[1] the whole company were on deck, to see Tynemouth Priory,[2] and the other beauties of that coast; and the Shields people gathered on the quays to stare at the strange vessel. When they hailed, and asked who we were, the great men on the deck shouted in reply '*savans*,' 'philosophers,' 'nondescripts.'

That was the Meeting of the British Association at which (Dr. Lardner[3] being present) the report was industriously spread that the Great Western,—the first steamer to America on her first voyage,—'had been seen in the middle of the Atlantic, broken-backed, and in great distress.'[4] The words sank heavily upon my heart; for I was acquainted with several persons on board; and it shed more or less gloom over the whole week. Many observed at the time that it was just the thing likely to be said by Dr. Lardner and his friends, considering his pledges of his scientific reputation on the impossibility of crossing the Atlantic by steam; and in this every body agreed: but the suspense was painful; and it outlasted the week; as it was intended to do. Dr. Lardner's final disgraces had not yet taken place;[5] but I saw how coldly he was noticed, when he was not entirely ignored: and when I curtseyed to him at the

---

[1]   Shields Harbour, at the mouth of the Tyne River, nine miles from the city of Newcastle.

[2]   This eighth-century priory, rebuilt in the eleventh century, expanded in the fourteenth and fifteenth, but in ruins by the nineteenth, stood on a high cliff at the mouth of the Tyne.

[3]   Dionysius Lardner (1793–1859), a scientific writer, urged the establishing of a steamship service to India via the Red Sea in an 1837 public "Letter" to Lord Melbourne. As Martineau suggests, he made disparaging remarks about the trans-Atlantic steamship *Great Western*, rebutted by Samuel Hall in his *Address to the British Association, Explanatory of the Injustice done to his Improvements on Steam Engines by Dr. Lardner* (Liverpool, 1837).

[4]   The *Great Western* steamship was launched on 19 July 1837. It left Bristol on 8 April 1838 and arrived in New York, without difficulty, on 23 April 1838.

[5]   Lardner eloped with the wife of a cavalry officer, Captain Henry Heaviside, and was sued for an "act of seduction," with £8000 damages.

ball, I was warned by a friend not to notice him if I could avoid it. I was glad then that I had not entertained his proposal when, as editor of the Encyclopedia which goes under his name, he wrote to me, and called, and endeavoured to obtain my promise to write a volume for him. A cousin of mine, who is so little fond of the pen as to find letter-writing a grievance, was highly amused at receiving (I think while I was abroad) a flattering letter from Dr. Lardner, requesting a volume from her for his series. Not very long after that Newcastle meeting, he made his notorious flight to America; and I have heard nothing of him since.

What I saw of that meeting certainly convinced me of the justice, in the main, of Carlyle's sarcasms on that kind of celebration.[1] I have no doubt of the opportunity afforded for the promotion of science in various ways: but the occasion is really so sadly spoiled (or was in those days) by the obtrusions of coxcombs, the conceit of third-rate men with their specialities, the tiresome talk of one-idead men, who scruple no means of swelling out what they call the evidence of their doctrines, and the disagreeable footing of the ladies, that I internally vowed that I would never again go in the way of one of those anniversaries. I heard two or three valuable addresses; but, on the whole, the humbugs and small men carried all before them: and, I am sorry to say, Sir John Herschel[2] himself so far succumbed to the spirit of the occasion as to congratulate his scientific brethren on the 'crowning honour' among many, of the presence of the fair sex at their sections! That same fair sex, meantime, was there to sketch the *savans*, under cover of mantle, shawl or little parasol, or to pass the time by watching and quizzing the members. Scarcely any of the ladies sat still for half an hour. They wandered in and out, with their half-hidden sketch-books, seeking amusement as their grandmothers did at auctions. I was in truth much ashamed of the ladies; and I wished they had staid at home, preparing hospitalities for the tired *savans*, and showing themselves only at the evening promenade in the Green Market,[3] and at the ball. The promenade was really a pretty sight,—not only from the beauty of the place and its decorations, but on account of the presence of the Quaker body,

---

[1] Possibly an allusion to Carlyle's critique of the modern "Mechanical Age" in "Signs of the Times" (1829).

[2] Sir John Herschel (1792–1871), an astronomer who participated regularly in the British Association and, at the meeting in Newcastle in 1838, was appointed a member of a committee to study Lacaille's stars.

[3] Originally named for an open-air market outside St. Andrew's church in the center of Newcastle.

who, excluded from the other forms of social amusement, eagerly grasp at this one lawful exception. They made the very most of it; and I, for one, can testify to their capacity for staring at an anti-slavery confessor. My sister,[1] who bore a family likeness to me, proposed to dress her hair like mine, borrow a trumpet from a deaf friend who was present, and walk up and down the opposite side, to draw off my 'tail,' which was declared to be 'three times as long as O'Connell's.'

It was the accident of Professor Daubeney[2] putting some American newspapers into my hand one day that week which occasioned the appearance of one of my most heart-felt writings. The Editor of the Westminster Review was impressed by what I showed and told him of the life and murder of Lovejoy, the first American witness unto death in the cause of liberty of speech; and he requested from me a vivid historical sketch of the cause, from the beginning to Lovejoy's murder. This was the origin of 'The Martyr Age of the United States' which has been elsewhere sufficiently referred to.[3] It appeared in the Christmas number of the Westminster Review.

With joy we left the crowded scene which was such a mixture of sound-ness and pretence, wisdom and vanity, and matter for pride and shame, and betook ourselves to the Lake District. I had never seen it before, and had no distinct anticipation of seeing it again. What should I have felt, if I had been told that, after one more painful stage of my life, I should make my home in that divine region till death! It was on the 2nd of September that we drove through Ambleside, from Bowness to Grasmere,[4] passing the field in which I am now abiding,—on which I am at this moment looking forth. I wonder whether my eye rested for a moment on the knoll whereon my house now stands. We returned through Ambleside to go to Patterdale; and a pencil entry in my diary calls up the remembrance of the soft sadness with which we caught 'our last view of Windermere;'—that Windermere which was to become to me the most familiar of all waters.

While at Strachur, Lord Murray's seat in Argyleshire, we found ourselves treated with singular hospitality. Lord Murray placed the little Loch Fyne steamer at our disposal. He and Lady Murray insisted on receiving our entire party; and every facility was afforded for all of us seeing

---

1   Most likely Elizabeth Greenhow, the sister who lived in Newcastle.
2   Charles Giles Daubeney (1795–1867), M.D., chemist, and botanist, became professor of botany at Oxford.
3   See p. 344, n. 2, as well as Martineau's account in Period IV, sec. iii.
4   Bowness, Grasmere, Ambleside, and Patterdale are villages in the Lake District in Cumbria in northwestern England. Windermere is one of the larger lakes.

every thing. Every Highland production, in the form of fish, flesh and fowl, was carefully collected; salmon and Loch herrings, grouse pies, and red-deer soup, and so forth. What I best remember, however, is a conversation with Lord Murray by the loch side. He invited me there for a walk; and he had two things to say. He wanted me to write some papers on prison management, for Chambers's Journal,[1] or some other popular periodical, for the purpose of familiarising the Scotch with the principle of punishment, and the attendant facts of American imprisonment. He lost his Prisons Bill in the preceding session,[2] and wanted the support of Scotch public opinion before the next. This being settled, he wrote to Messrs. Chambers at Edinburgh; and I there saw one of the brothers for the first time.[3] The papers were agreed upon, written and published. Mr. Robert Chambers I did not see till some few years later, when he called on me at Tynemouth, during my recovery by mesmerism, for the purpose of investigating the subject. Our acquaintance, then begun, has since ripened into friendship, both on his own account, and for the sake of his brother-in-law and sister, Mr. and Mrs. Wills,[4] who, becoming known to me through my being a contributor to 'Household Words,' have largely increased the pleasures of my latest years by their friendly offices of every kind, and their hearty affection. Edinburgh was quite a different place to me when I went for my third Scotch journey in 1852, by Robert Chambers's charming home being open to me; and London has a new familiar interest to me now that I have another home there at Mr. Wills's.

To return to that walk with the Lord Advocate. He wished to know my opinion on a subject which was then more talked of than almost any other,—our probable relations with Russia.[5] I hardly know now

[1]   These articles appeared under the title "Prison Life" in *Chambers's Edinburgh Journal*, 7 (1838), 353–54, 362–63, 370–71. Martineau described American innovations with the "separate system," which isolated prisoners from fellow criminals and attempted reformation through reading, vocational education, and association with positive influences.

[2]   The basic proposals of prison reform appeared in an anonymous article, "Proposed Re-Arrangement in the Prison System," in *Chambers's Edinburgh Journal*, 7 (1838), 154, which appeared before Martineau's signed articles. In *A History of the Peace*, book V, ch. xv, Martineau discusses reforms proposed by the criminal law commission, including elimination of the death penalty in 21 cases, a reform enacted in 1839.

[3]   William Chambers (1800–83) and his brother Robert (1802–71) were Edinburgh publishers.

[4]   William Henry Wills (1810–80), journalist and sub-editor of Dickens's periodical *Household Words*, married Janet, the younger sister of the Chambers brothers (above).

[5]   A dominant concern in nineteenth-century British foreign policy was the "Eastern Question," which included a fear of Russian encroachment, especially in India, and a related shoring up of the Ottoman Empire to prevent it. Rumors of Russian encroachment were frequent during the build-up to the Crimean War (1853–56).

how the notion came to spread as it did that the Czar had a mind to annex us: but it was talked over in all drawing-rooms, and, as I now found, in the Cabinet. I had nothing to say,—so astonished was I to hear it thus gravely and expressly brought forward. I could only say that the idea of our ever submitting to Russia seemed too monstrous to be entertained. Lord Murray had no formed opinion to produce; but he offered,—'as a speculation,—just as a ground for speculation,'—the fact that for centuries no quarter of a century had passed without the incorporation of some country with Russia; some country which no doubt once regarded its absorption by Russia as the same unimaginable thing that our own appeared to us now. He said that if we commit two stone bottles to the stream, and one breaks the other, it is nearly an even chance whether it will break or be broken next time: but, when the same has broken a score, the chances are almost anything to nothing that it will break the twenty-first. Therefore he thought we might as well not be so entirely complacent and secure as we were, but think over such a liability with some little sobriety and sense. So there was a new and very horrible speculation for me to carry away with me: and highly curious it is to recur to now (August, 1855) when we find that Russia, after nearly twenty years' more leisure for preparation, cannot meet us at sea, or win a battle on land. At least, after a year and a half of warfare, she has as yet done neither.[1]

From Strachur, we pursued our way to the Western Islands:[2] and, after being weather-bound in Mull, we accomplished the visit to Iona which I have referred to. We saw Staffa,[3] and had the captain's spontaneous promise to take us round by Garveloch, that I might see the homes of the personages about whom I had written so familiarly: but the weather was too rough; and I did not see the Garveloch Isles till a glorious sunny day in July, 1852.

It was October before we reached Edinburgh; and there my kind companions and I parted. Miss Rogers[4] and a young friend were staying at Lord Jeffrey's, where I met them; and Miss Rogers urged me to

---

[1]   In September 1855, the month after Martineau wrote this paragraph, the British and French defeated the Russians at Sebastopol, effectively ending the Crimean War.

[2]   The islands off the western coast of Scotland: Mull, Skye, Harris, Tweed, and others known as the Hebrides. The Garveloch (or Garvellach) Isles are small islands settled by the Christian mission of St. Columba in the sixth century, now visited for their stone beehive huts and other monastic remains.

[3]   Famous for the columnar basalt of Fingal's Cave.

[4]   Sarah Rogers (d. 1854), sister and confidant of the poet Samuel Rogers.

take a seat in her carriage as far as Newcastle, where I was to stop for a week or two. We saw Abbotsford and Dryburgh[1] under great advantages of weather; but my surprise at the smallness and toy-character of Abbotsford was extreme. It was impossible but that both Scott and Lockhart must know what a good Scotch house is; and their glorification of this place shakes one's faith in their other descriptions.

That journey of 1838 was beneficial to me to a certain extent; and it would have been more so, but for its close. I was called home from Newcastle under circumstances which made my long solitary mail journey a very heavy one, full of apprehension and pain. I was, though without being fully conscious of it, becoming too ill to bear the shocks of that unhappy year as I had borne all manner of shocks, all my life. The internal disease which was soon to prostrate me entirely had made considerable progress, though I had no more than a vague notion that there was something wrong. The refreshment from the journey was not lasting; but its pleasures were. One of the noticeable things about it was that it introduced me to Mrs. Crowe,[2] whose acquaintance has since yielded me very great pleasure. And she, again, has been the main cause or occasion of my friendship with Dr. Samuel Brown[3] and his wife, who have been intimates of my latest years,—too much so to permit more than such a notice as this. Another marked thing about that autumn trip was that it introduced me to that pleasant experience of middle age,—the consideration of the young. I had always been among the youngest at home in my childhood; and of late years had ministered, in the capacity of youngster, to my old ladies. Now, for the first time, I experienced the luxury of being tended as an elderly person. Though some years younger than the two heads of our travelling party, I was of their generation; and the four young people were most attentive in saving us elders fatigue, making tea, giving us the sofas and warm corners, and so on. From that time I have taken rank among the elders, and enjoyed the comfort of it.

The readers of my 'Retrospect of Western Travel' may remember the story[4] of the slave child Ailsie, whose mistress died at New Orleans, leav-

---

[1] Abbotsford, a pseudo-baronial home built by Walter Scott on the Tweed River; Dryburgh, an abbey on the Tweed founded in 1150, and destroyed by the English in 1322, 1385, and finally in 1544.

[2] Catherine Ann Crowe, née Stevens (1790–1872), author of novels, plays, and juvenile literature.

[3] Dr. Samuel Brown (1817–56), Scottish chemist and historian of science.

[4] Retrospect of Western Travel, vol. ii., page 146 [Martineau's note].

ing that beautiful little creature to be a most embarrassing charge to the widower.[1] My description of this child, and of the interest felt in her fate by me and mine, reached the eye of the widower; and he wrote to entreat me to take charge of the girl (by that time twelve years old). He avowed his inability to protect her, and offered to send over a yearly allowance for her maintenance, if I would receive and adopt her. I declined the annual allowance, because my friend's money was derived from slave-labour, and I would not touch it; but otherwise, I accepted his proposal, and did not see why he should not lodge in a bank, for her ultimate bene-fit, such money as he believed her to have earned. I intended first to train her as my little maid, and have her attend a school near, so that I might ascertain what she was most fit for. All this winter, we were in daily expectation of her arrival. Her little bed awaited her in my room; and we had arranged about having her vaccinated at once, and clothed like English children, instead of having her brilliant eyes and beautiful mulatto face surmounted by the yellow turban which became her so well. But Ailsie, for whose reception all arrangements were complete when I went to Scotland, did not appear all the winter; and I wrote again, very urgently, to her master. I had to make arrangements again when I went to the continent in April; but his final letter came at last. It was the letter of an almost broken-hearted man; and it almost broke our hearts to read it. He, Irish by birth, had never been more or less reconciled to 'the peculiar institutions.' Involved in it before he was of age, he had no power to extri-cate himself from it,—at least till he had paid off all the liabilities under which young planters enter life. His beloved young wife had received this child as a gift from her mother in Tennessee,—the child's life being in danger on her native plantation, through the fierce jealousies which attend upon a system of concubinage. It never occurred to the widower that he could not freely dispose of his wife's little slave: but his mother-in-law demanded the girl back again. In her ripening beauty she was too valuable to be given to me. For what purposes she was detained as of course, there is no need to describe. She was already lost and gone; and I have never heard of her since. Her voice often comes back upon my memory, and her vivid affectionate countenance, as she pulled at her mistress's gown, and clasped her knees with the anxious question,—'Ain't you well?' This one illustration of the villainy of the system roused more

---

[1]   The story appears in the chapter "New-Orleans," where Martineau explains that Ailsie was sent from a Tennessee plantation to New Orleans because the husband of her black mother hated Ailsie, the mulatto offspring of his black wife and a local white man.

indignation and sympathy in many hearts than a whole row of books of
argument or description of Slave institutions in the abstract. I could not
have done for Ailsie what I purposed, as my affairs turned out; but there
were many of my friends who could, and who were anxious to assume
the charge. But she was never to be heard of more.

The continental journey that I have referred to was undertaken
chiefly for the sake of escorting an invalid cousin to Switzerland.[1] As
soon as 'Deerbrook' was published, and my 'Guides to Service' finished,
the weather was fine enough to permit our departure. Two mutual
friends joined us; and our party thus consisted of four ladies, a maid-
servant and a courier. We crossed to Rotterdam on the 17th of April,
went up the Rhine, and by the usual route to Lausanne, except that one
of my companions slipped across the frontier with me, for the sake of
seeing Toussaint L'Ouverture's prison and grave.[2] I was furnished with
a copious and comprehensive passport for myself and maid, obtained
by the Lord Advocate's kindness from the Secretary of State, as the
Austrian interdict against my entrance into the empire might otherwise
be still an impediment. My friend offered to personate my maid just for
the day which would take us from the frontier to the castle of Joux. We
excited great wonder at the *douane*, of course, with our destitution of
baggage, and our avowed intention of leaving France in the afternoon;
but we accomplished our purpose, and it was virtually decided that 'The
Hour and the Man' should be written.

While I was walking up a hill in Germany, one of my companions
had observed to another that I was, in her opinion, on the verge of some
terrible illness. It was at Venice that the extent of my illness became
unquestionable. My cousin had been deposited at her place of abode;
and the rest of us had gone on to Venice, intending to take a look at her
at Lausanne on our return. My illness, however, broke up all our plans.
My kind nurses contrived a couch for me in the carriage; and on that
I was brought home by the straightest road,—by the Via Emilia, and the
St. Gothard, down the Rhine, where we were joined by one of my
brothers and a brother-in-law.[3] We took passage to London, from

---

[1] In April 1839, Martineau crossed to Rotterdam with Elisabeth Reid, her cousin Isabella
Rankin, a maid, and a courier, intending to sail down the Rhine to Switzerland, leave her
cousin there, and travel on in Italy.

[2] The castle of Joux dominates a narrow passage between two mountains in the Alps on
the Besançon (France)-Lausanne (Switzerland) road. Toussaint L'Ouverture was imprisoned and died there.

[3] Her brother James and future brother-in-law Alfred Higginson, who married Ellen in
1841, escorted her home.

Antwerp: and I was soon on my mother's couch in Fludyer Street. Not to remain, however. I was conveyed without delay to Newcastle-upon-Tyne, to be under the care of my brother-in-law; and from that neighbourhood I did not remove for nearly six years.

Here closed the anxious period during which my reputation, and my industry, and my social intercourses were at their height of prosperity; but which was so charged with troubles that when I lay down on my couch of pain in my Tynemouth lodging, for a confinement of nearly six years, I felt myself comparatively happy in my release from responsibility, anxiety and suspense. The worst sufferings of my life were over now; and its best enjoyments and privileges were to come,— though I little knew it, and they were as yet a good way off.

FIFTH PERIOD

TO THE AGE OF FORTY-THREE

————

SECTION I

————

THE LITTLE volume which I wrote during my illness,—'Life in the Sick-room,'[1]—tells nearly as much as it can be interesting or profitable for any body to hear about this period of my life. The shorter I can make my narrative of it, the better on all accounts. Five years seem a long time to look forward; and five years of suffering, of mind or body, seem sadly like an eternity in passing through them: but they collapse almost into nothingness, as soon as they are left behind, and another condition is fairly entered on. From the monotony of sick-room life, little beyond the general impression remains to be imparted, or even recalled; and if it were otherwise, I should probably say little of that dreary term, because it is not good to dwell much on morbid conditions, for any other purpose than scientific study, for the sake of the prevention or cure of the suffering in other cases. I am aware that the religious world, proud of its Christian faith as the 'Worship of Sorrow,'[2] thinks it a duty and a privilege to dwell on the morbid conditions of human life; but my experience of wide extremes of health and sickness, of happiness and misery, leads me to a very different conclusion. For pathological purposes, there must be a study of morbid conditions; but

---

1   *Life in the Sick-Room: Essays by an Invalid* (London: Edward Moxon, 1844) was published anonymously near the end of Martineau's five-year illness at Tynemouth, and just before her successful experiment with mesmerism. The American edition (Boston: Leonard C. Bowles and William Crosby, 1844) included a preface, written by her friend E[liza] L[ee] Follen, which revealed the author's identity.

2   Martineau refers to the religious belief, especially common among nineteenth-century Evangelicals, that suffering is a spiritual trial intended to strengthen a Christian's faith and reliance on God. She may also allude to the chapter "The Everlasting Yea," in Thomas Carlyle's *Sartor Resartus* (1833–34), in which the editor declares: "Knowest thou that 'Worship of Sorrow'? The Temple thereof, founded some eighteen centuries ago, now lies in ruins, overgrown with jungle, the habitation of doleful creatures: nevertheless, venture forward; in a low crypt, arched out of falling fragments, thou findest the Altar still there, and its sacred Lamp perennially burning."

that the study should be general,—that it should be enforced as a duty, and held up as a pleasure—seems to me one of those mistakes in morals which are aggravated and protracted by the mischievous influence of superstition. Tracts and religious books swarm among us, and are thrust into the hands of every body by every body else, which describe the sufferings of illness, and generate vanity and egotism about bodily pain and early death,—rendering these disgraces of our ignorance and barbarism attractive to the foolish and the vain, and actually shaming the wholesome, natural desire for 'a sound mind in a sound body.' The Christian superstition, now at last giving way before science, of the contemptible nature of the body, and its antagonism to the soul, has shockingly perverted our morals, as well as injured the health of Christendom: and every book, tract, and narrative which sets forth a sick-room as a condition of honour, blessing and moral safety, helps to sustain a delusion and corruption which have already cost the world too dear. I know too much of all this from my own experience to choose to do any thing towards encouragement of the morbid appetite for pathological contemplation,—physical or moral. My youthful vanity took the direction which might be expected in the case of a pious child. I was patient in illness and pain because I was proud of the distinction, and of being taken into such special pupilage by God; and I hoped for, and expected early death till it was too late to die early. It is grievous to me now to think what an amount of time and thought I have wasted in thinking about dying,—really believing as I did for many years that life was a mere preparation for dying: and now, after a pretty long life, when I find myself really about to die, the event seems to me so simple, natural, and, as I may say, negative in comparison with life and its inter-ests, that I cannot but marvel at the quantity of attention and solicitude I lavished upon it while it was yet so far off as to require no attention at all. To think no more of death than is necessary for the winding up of the business of life, and to dwell no more upon sickness than is neces-sary for its treatment, or to learn to prevent it, seems to me the simple wisdom of the case,—totally opposite as this is to the sentiment and method of the religious world.

On the other hand, I do not propose to nourish a foolish pride by disguising, through shame, the facts of sickness and suffering. Pain and untimely death are, no doubt, the tokens of our ignorance, and of our sins against the laws of nature. I conceive our business to be to accept these consequences of our ignorance and weakness, with as little personal shame on the one hand as vanity or pride on the other. As far as any

sickness of mine can afford warning, I am willing to disclose it; and I
have every desire to acknowledge my own fault or folly in regard to it,
while wholly averse to treat it as a matter of sentiment,—even to the
degree in which I did it, sincerely enough, in 'Life in the Sick-room,' a
dozen years ago.[1] I propose, therefore, to be now as brief as I can, and at
the same time, as frank, in speaking of the years between 1839 and
1845.—I have mentioned before, in regard to my deafness, that I have
no doubt of its having been seriously aggravated by nervous excitement,
at the age when I lived in reverie and vanities of the imagination; and
that it was suddenly and severely increased by a sort of accident. That
sort of accident was the result of ignorance in a person whom I need
not point out: and thus it seems that my deafness is largely ascribable to
disobedience to the laws of nature. And thus in regard to the disease
which at this time was laying me low for so many years. It was unquestionably the result of excessive anxiety of mind,—of the extreme tension
of nerves under which I had been living for some years, while the three
anxious members of my family were, I may say, on my hands,—not in
regard to money, but to care of a more important kind.[2] My dear aunt,
the sweetest of old ladies, was now extremely old, and required shield-
ing from the anxiety caused by the other two. My mother was old, and
fast becoming blind; and the irritability caused in her first by my position in society, and next by the wearing trial of her own increasing infirmity, told fearfully upon my already reduced health. My mother's
dignified patience in the direct endurance of her blindness was a really
beautiful spectacle: but the natural irritability found vent in other directions; and especially was it visited upon me. Heaven knows, I never
sought fame; and I would thankfully have given it all away in exchange
for domestic peace and ease: but there it was! and I had to bear the
consequences. I was overworked, fearfully, in addition to the pain of
mind I had to bear. I was not allowed to have a maid, at my own expense,
or even to employ a workwoman; and thus, many were the hours after

---

[1]   Although *Life in the Sick-Room* dismisses the idea of pain "inflicted by the malignity of a
       superior being," it retains a sense of a "divinely-appointed instrumentality" that made
       Martineau treat suffering as "wholly brought out and directed by Him [God] who framed
       and actuated us." By 1855, when she wrote the *Autobiography*, she viewed this stage of thought
       as "metaphysical" rather than "scientific" in its understanding of human development.

[2]   Martineau emphasizes the psychological aspects of her illness, but it had a physical source
       in the uterine tumors ("enlarged and retroverted uterus") that her brother-in-law diag-
       nosed, treated, and eventually wrote about in "Medical Report of the Case of Miss H—
       M— " by T.M. Greenhow (London: Samuel Highley, 1845); rpt. in Maria Frawley, ed.,
       Life in the Sick-Room, pp. 187–95.

midnight when I ought to have been asleep, when I was sitting up to mend my clothes. Far worse than this, my mother would not be taken care of. She was daily getting out into the crowded streets by herself, when she could not see a yard before her. What the distress from this was to me may be judged of by the fact that for many months after my retreat to Tynemouth, I rarely slept without starting from a dream that my mother had fallen from a precipice, or over the bannisters, or from a cathedral spire; and that it was my fault. These cares, to say nothing of the toils, had long been wearing me down, so that I became subject to attacks of faintness, on occasion of any domestic uneasiness; and two or three intimate friends, as well as some members of the family, urged my leaving home as frequently as possible, for my mother's sake as well as my own, as my return was always a joyful occasion to her. My habits and likings made this moving about a very irksome thing to me; and especially when arrangements had to be made about my work,—from which I had never any holiday. I loved, as I still love, the most monotonous life possible: but I took refuge in change, as the only relief from a pressure of trouble which was breaking me down,—I was not aware how rapidly. An internal disease was gaining ground for months or years before I was aware of it. A tumour was forming of a kind which usually originates in mental suffering; and when at last I broke down completely, and settled myself in a lodging at Tynemouth, I long felt that the lying down, in solitude and silence, free from responsibility and domestic care, was a blessed change from the life I had led since my return from America. My dear old aunt soon died: my mother was established at Liverpool, in the neighbourhood of three of her children; and the other claimant of my anxious care emigrated.[1] It is impossible to deny that the illness under which I lay suffering for five years was induced by flagrant violations of the laws of nature: and I then failed to appropriate the comforts with which Christians deprave their moral sense in such a case, as I also felt unable to blame myself individually for my incapacity. No doubt, if I had felt less respect and less affection for my mother, I might have taken the management of matters more into my own hands, and should have felt her discontent with me less than I did; and again, if I had already found the supports of philosophy on relinquishing the selfish complacencies of religion, I should have borne my troubles with strength and

---

[1] James was pastor of a Unitarian congregation in Paradise Street, Liverpool; Rachel, head-mistress of a Liverpool girls' school; and Ellen, married to Alfred Higginson, a Liverpool surgeon. Their brother Henry emigrated to New Zealand in 1839 or 1840 after his wine-importing business failed.

ease. But, as it was, I was neither proud or vain of my discipline on the one hand, nor ashamed of it on the other, while fully aware that it was the result of fault and imperfection, moral and intellectual.

On my return from Italy, ill, my sister and her husband[1] hospitably urged my taking up my abode with them, at least till the nature and prospects of my case were ascertained. After spending a month at a lodging in their neighbourhood in Newcastle-upon-Tyne, I removed to their hospitable house, where I was taken all possible care of for six months. They most generously desired me to remain: but there were various reasons which determined me to decline their kindness. It would have been clearly wrong to occupy their guest chamber permanently, and to impose restraints upon a healthy household: and, for my own part, I had an unspeakable longing for stillness and solitude. I therefore decided for myself that I would go to a lodging at Tynemouth, where my medical brother-in-law could reach me by railway in twenty minutes, while I was removed from the bustle and smoke of Newcastle by an interval of nine miles. With an affectionate reluctance and grudging, my family let me try this as an experiment,—all of them being fully convinced that I could not long bear the solitude and monotony, after the life of excitement and constant variety to which I had been accustomed for above seven years. I was right, however, and they were wrong. On the sofa where I stretched myself after my drive to Tynemouth, on the sixteenth of March, 1840, I lay for nearly five years, till obedience to a newly-discovered law of nature raised me up, and sent me forth into the world again, for another ten years of strenuous work, and almost undisturbed peace and enjoyment of mind and heart.

I had two rooms on the first floor in this house of my honest hostess, Mrs. Halliday,[2] who little imagined, that March day, that the luck was happening to her of a lodger who would stay, summer and winter, for nearly five years. I had no servant with me at first; for I was not only suddenly cut off from my literary engagements, and almost from the power of work, but I had invested £1,000 of my earnings in a deferred annuity, two years before;—a step which seemed prudent at the time, and which I still consider to have been so; but which deprived me of immediate resources. It was not long before two generous ladies, (sisters) old friends of mine,[3] sent me, to my amazement, a bank-note for £100, saying that

---

[1]   Her eldest sister Elizabeth and Thomas Greenhow, a surgeon in Newcastle-upon-Tyne.

[2]   Mrs. Halliday's house was No. 12 Front Street, Tynemouth.

[3]   Possibly Emily Taylor and her sister Sarah Austin, but see p. 443, n. 1 for evidence of Martineau's frustration with their interference.

my illness had probably interfered with certain plans which they knew I entertained. The generosity was of a kind which it was impossible to refuse, because it extended through me to others. I took the money, and applied it as intended. I need hardly say that when my working days and my prosperity returned, I repaid the sum, which was, as I knew it would be, lodged in the hands of sufferers as needy as I was when it came to me.

I was waited upon in my lodging by a sickly-looking, untidy little orphan girl of fourteen,—untidy, because the state of her eyes was such that she could not sew, or have any fair chance for cleanliness. She was the niece and dependent of my hostess,[1] by whom she was scolded without mercy, and, it seemed to me, incessantly. Her quiet and cheerful submission impressed me at once; and I heard such a report of her from the lady who had preceded me in the lodgings, and who had known the child from early infancy, that I took an interest in her, and studied her character from the outset. Her character was easily known; for a more simple, upright, truthful, ingenuous child could not be. She was, in fact, as intellectually incapable as morally indisposed to deception of any kind. This was 'the girl Jane' who recovered her health by mesmerism in companionship with me, and whom I was required by the doctors, and by the Athenæum, to 'give up' as 'an impostor,' after five years' household intercourse with her, in addition to my indirect knowledge of her, through my neighbour, from the age of three. I may mention here that my unvarying good opinion of her was confirmed after the recovery of both by the experience of her household qualities for seven years, during which period she lived with me as my cook, till she emigrated to Australia, where she has lived in high credit from the beginning of 1853 till now. This Jane, destined to so curious an experience, and to so discreditable a persecution (which she bore in the finest spirit), was at the door of my Tynemouth lodging when I arrived: and many were the heartaches I had for her, during the years that her muscles looked like dough, and her eyes like .... I will not say what. I suffered from the untidiness of my rooms, I own; and I soon found that my Norfolk notions of cleanliness met with no response at Tynemouth. Before long, I was shifted from purgatory to paradise in this essential matter. An uncle and some cousins,[2] who had always been

---

[1] Jane Arrowsmith (b. 1824 or 1825), who later played an important role in Martineau's experiments with mesmerism, and received mesmeristic treatments for headaches and inflamed eyes.

[2] Probably David Martineau and his children, who had supported her work on the *Illustrations of Political Economy*; see Period III, sec. iv.

kind to me, were shocked to find that I was waited upon by only the people of the house; and they provided me with a maid, who happened to be the cleanliest of her sex. She remained with me during the whole of my illness: and never, in all that time, did I see a needless grain of dust on the furniture, nor a speck on the window panes that was not removed next morning.

For the view from my window, and the details of my mode of life as an invalid I must refer all who wish to know my Tynemouth self to 'Life in the Sick-room.' They will find there what the sea and shore were to me, and how kind friends came to see me, and my family were at my call; and for what reasons, and how peremptorily, I chose to live alone. One half year was rendered miserably burdensome by the cheating intrusion of an unwelcome and uncongenial person who came (as I believed because I was told) for a month, and stayed seven, in a lodging next door. More serious mischiefs than the immediate annoyance were caused by this unwarrantable liberty taken with my comfort and convenience; and the suffering occasioned by them set me back in health not a little: but with the exception of that period, I obtained the quiet I so needed and desired.

During the first half of the time, I was able to work,—though with no great willingness, and with such extreme exhaustion that it became at length necessary to give up every exertion of the kind. 'Deerbrook' had come out in the spring of 1839, just before my illness declared itself. That conception being wrought out and done with, I reverted to the one which I had held in abeyance, through the objections made to it by my friend Mrs. — —,[1] whom alone I consulted in such matters, and on whose knowledge of books and taste in literature I reposed my judgment. Now that she was far away, my affections sprang back to the character and fortunes of Toussaint L'Ouverture.[2] I speedily made up my mind to present that genuine hero with his actual sayings and doings (as far as they were extant) to the world. When I had been some time at Tynemouth, finding my strength and spirits declining, I gave up the practice of keeping a diary, for two reasons which I now think good and sufficient;—first, that I found it becoming a burden; and next, that a diary, kept under such circumstances, must be mainly a record of frames and feelings, —many of them morbid, and few fit for any but pathological

---

[1] Mrs. Bellenden Ker; see Period IV, sec. iii.

[2] Toussaint L'Ouverture (1743–1803), black revolutionary, symbol of freedom in French colonial Haiti, and the hero of Martineau's historical romance, *The Hour and the Man*; see Period IV, sec. iii.

uses: but I cannot be sorry that I continued my journal for some months, as it preserves the traces of my progress in a work which I regard with some affection, though, to say the truth, without any admiration whatever. I find, in the sickly handwriting of that spring of 1840, notices of how my subject opened before me, and of how, as I lay gazing upon the moon-lit sea, in the evenings of April and May, new traits in the man, new links between the personages, and a clearer perception of the guiding principle of the work disclosed themselves to me. I find, by this record, that I wrote the concluding portion of 'The Hour and the Man' first, for the same reason that I am now writing the fifth period of this Memoir before the fourth,—lest I should not live to do the whole. It was on Saturday, the 2nd of May, 1840, that I began the book, with Toussaint's arrival at the Jura.[1] My notice is that I was sadly tired with the effort, but more struck than ever with the springing up of ideas by the way, in the act of writing, so much more than in that of reading,—though in reading, the profit is more from the ideas suggested than from those received. This work was a resource, and some anxiety to me, all summer: on the 17th of November, I corrected the last proof-sheet, and before the end of the month, the opinions of my friends were, for the most part, known to me. I find in my diary of this period, under the date of November 26th, an entry which it may be worth while to give here, both as an authentication of some things I have said elsewhere, and as saving explanations which might appear like afterthoughts, in regard to a point in my character which has been important to my happiness, if not to matters of higher consequence. 'A letter from Moxon about the publication of my book holds out a very poor prospect. Under 500 copies are subscribed for. He offers me twenty-five copies more, both of it and of "Deerbrook," if I like to have them,—showing that he does not expect to sell them. If the book succeeds after this, it will be by its own merits purely. This seems the only good derivable from the news. Yet, as I sat at work, my spirits rose, the more I thought it over. It always is the way with me, and has been since I grew up, that personal mortifications (except such as arise from my own faults, and sometimes even then) put me in a happy state of mind. This is the news of all others (about my own affairs) which I had rather not have had: yet I don't know when I have been more cheery than now, in consequence of it. It is always so with hostile reviewers; — the more brutal, the more animating, in a very little while. In that case it

---

[1]   L'Ouverture was imprisoned by Napoleon in the citadel of Joux in the Jura Mountains (Swiss Alps).

is that one's feelings are engrossed in concern for the perpetrators, and in an anxious desire to do them good,—and looking forward to the day when their feelings will be healthier.' The lighting upon this entry reminds me of some marked days of my literary life, made happy by this tendency in me; and especially the two days which might seem to have been the most mortifying;—that of the publication of the brutal review of my Political Economy series in the Quarterly, and that on which I received the news from the publisher of the total failure (as far as money was concerned) of my 'Forest and Game Law tales,'—of which no more than 2,000 copies have been sold to this day. In the first case, there was every sort of personal insult which could make a woman recoil; and in the other there was that sense of wasted labour which to me, with my strong economic faculty, was always excessively disagreeable: yet did both carry with them so direct an appeal to one's inner force, and especially to one's disinterestedness, that the reaction was immediate, and the rebound from mortification to joyful acquiescence was one of the most delightful experiences I have ever had. Those several occasions are white days in the calendar of my life.—As for the success of 'The Hour and the Man' and 'Deerbrook,' it is enough to say that both passed through two editions, and have been purchased of me for a third.[1]

Before my book was well out, I had planned the light and easy work, (for which alone I was now fit) of a series of children's tales, for which a friend then nursing me suggested the capital title of 'The Playfellow.'[2] While in spirits about the reception of my novel, I conceived the plot of the first of those tales,—'Settlers at Home,' concerning which I find this entry in my diary. 'How curious it would be to refer back to the sources of as many ideas as possible, in any thing one writes! Tait's Magazine of last year had an article of De Quincy's which made me think of snow-storms for a story:[3]—then it occurred to me that floods were less hack-neyed, and would do as well for purposes of adventure and peril. But De Quincy's tale (a true one) is fairly the origin of mine. —Floods suggested Lincolnshire for the scene and Lauder's book (Sir Thomas Dick Lauder's

---

[1] I find that 'The Hour and the Man' is re-issued. [Martineau's note]

[2] *The Playfellow* (London: Charles Knight, 1841) included four tales, originally issued separately: "The Settlers at Home," "The Peasant and the Prince," "Feats on the Fiord," and "The Crofton Boys."

[3] Thomas De Quincey (1785–1859), writing as "The English Opium-Eater," published his reminiscences of the Lake Poets in seven installments in *Tait's Edinburgh Magazine* 6 (1839), 1–12, 90–103, 246–54, 453–64, 513–17, 569–81, 804–08; he describes a severe snowstorm (and a method for finding wanderers lost in it) in the sixth number.

"Floods in Morayshire,"[1] read many years before) for the material. For Lincolnshire I looked into the Penny Cyclopedia, and there found references to other articles,—particularly "Axholme."[2] Hence,—finding *gypsum* in that region,—came the precise scene and occupations. A paragraph in a Poor Law Report on a gypsy "born in a long meadow," suggested (together with fishers and fowlers in the marshes) the Roger of my tale.' I finished this first of my four volumes of 'The Playfellow' by the end of the year,—of my first year of solitary residence at Tynemouth. The close was, on the whole, satisfactory. I found the wintry aspects of the sea wonderfully impressive, and sometimes very beautiful. I had been visited by affectionate members of my own family, and by friends,—one of whom devoted herself to me with a singular power of sympathy, and consummate nursing ability.[3] I had reason to hope that my book had done good to the Anti-slavery cause by bringing into full notice the intellectual and moral genius of as black a negro as was ever seen; and I had begun a new kind of work,—not too heavy for my condition of health, and sure of a prosperous circulation in Mr. Knight's hands. All this was more or less spoiled in actual experience by the state of incessant uneasiness of body and unstringing of nerves in which I was: but it was one year of the five over, and I can regard it now, as I did even then, (blank as was the future before me,) with some complacency. The remnant of life was not wholly lost, in regard to usefulness: and, as to the enjoyment, that was of small consequence.

The second volume of 'The Playfellow' was wrought upon the suggestion of a friend, for whose ability in instigation I had the highest respect. By this time I hardly needed further evidence that one mind cannot (in literature) work well upon the materials suggested by another: but if I had needed such evidence, I found it here. The story of 'the Prince' was by far the least successful of the set, except among poor

---

[1] Thomas Dick Lauder, *An Account of the Great Floods of August 1829, in the Province of Moray, and Adjoining Districts*, 2nd edition (London: Longman, Rees, Orme, Brown & Green, 1830).

[2] *Penny Cyclopædia of the Society for the Diffusion of Useful Knowledge* (London: Charles Knight, 1835), III, 181, s.v. "Axholme": "a river-island in the county of Lincoln," separated from the rest of the county by the rivers Trent, Don, and Idle.

[3] Julia Smith (1799–1883), daughter of the Liberal M.P. for Norwich and aunt of Florence Nightingale, nursed her through most of the first winter. Another friend and frequent visitor was Elisabeth Reid (1789–1866), Unitarian philanthropist, widow of Dr. John Reid, and a companion on the European tour of 1839 during which Martineau fell ill. Reid brought a telescope for viewing the sea and scenery. A distant cousin and childhood friend, Emily Taylor (1795–1872), also came for long visits, one of seven months, but this long stay came to annoy Martineau more than aid her.

people, who read it with wonderful eagerness. Some of them called it 'the French revelation,' and the copy in Lending Libraries was more thumbed than the others; but among children and the general reading public, there was less interest about it than any of the rest. I suppose other authors who have found, as I have, that plenty of friends have advice to give them how to write their books, (no two friends agreeing in their advice) have also found themselves called self-willed and obstinate, as I have, for not writing their books in some other way than their own. In this case, I liked the suggestion, and felt obliged by it, and did my best with it; and yet the result was a failure, in comparison with those which were purely self-derived. Throughout my whole literary career, I have found the same thing happen; and I can assure any young author who may ever read this that he need feel no remorse, no misgiving about conceit or obstinacy, if he finds it impossible to work so well upon the suggestions of another mind as upon those of his own. He will be charged with obstinacy and conceit, as I have been. He is sure of that, at all events; for among a dozen advisers, he *can* obey only one; and the other eleven will be offended. He had better make it known, as I had occasion to do, that advice is of value in any work of art when it is asked, and not otherwise; and that in a view more serious than the artistic,— when convictions have to be uttered,—advice cannot, by the very nature of things, be taken, because no conscience can prescribe or act for another. This seems to be the place for relating what my own practice has been in this important matter. In regard to literature, and all other affairs, my method has been to ask advice very rarely,—always to follow it when asked, —and rarely to follow unasked advice. In other words, I have consulted those only whom I believed to be the very best judges of the case in hand; and, believing them the very best judges, I have of course been thankful for their guidance: whereas, the officious givers of unsought advice are pretty sure not to be good judges of the case in hand; and their counsel is therefore worth nothing. The case of criticism as to what is already wrought is different. I have accepted or neglected that, according as it seemed to me sound or unsound; and I believe I have accepted it much oftener than not. I have adopted subjects suggested by others, invariably with ill-success. I have always declined assistance as to the mode of treating my own subjects from persons who could not possibly be competent to advise, for want of knowing my point of view, my principle, and my materials. I was rather amused, a few weeks ago, by the proffer of a piece of counsel, by an able man who, on the mere hearing that I was too ill to defer any longer the writing of this

Memoir, wrote me his advice how to do it,—to make it amusing, and 'not too abstract' &c., &c., while in total ignorance of the purposes with which I was undertaking the labour,—whether to make an 'amusing,' book, or for a more serious object. It reminded me of an incident which I may relate here, though it occurred three years before the time under notice. It is so immediately connected with the topic I am now treating, that there could not be a better place for it.

When I was writing 'Society in America,' a lady of my acquaintance[1] sat down in a determined manner, face to face with me, to ask me some questions. A more kind-hearted woman could not be; but her one requirement was that all her friends,—or at least all her protégés,—should let her manage their affairs for them,—either with her own head and hands, or by sending round her intelligence or her notions, so as to get somebody else to do the managing before the curtain while she prompted from behind. This lady brought her sister up to me, one day, in her own house, and they asked me, point blank, whether I was going to say any thing about this, that, and the other, in my book on America. Among the rest, they asked whether I was going to say something about the position of women in the United States. I replied 'Of course. My subject is Society in America; and women constitute one half of it.' They entreated me 'to omit that.' I told them that the thing was done; and that when the book appeared, they would see that it was necessary. Finding me impracticable (conceited and obstinate, of course) they next called on my mother, for the purpose of alarming her into using her influence with me. They reckoned without their host, however; for my mother was thoroughly sound in doctrine, and just and generous in practice, on that great matter. She told them that she never interfered with my work,—both because she considered herself incompetent to judge till she knew the whole bearing of it, and because she feared it would be turned into patch-work if more minds than one were employed upon it without concert. Foiled in this direction, the anxious meddler betook herself to a mutual friend,—a literary man,—the Edinburgh reviewer of my Political Economy tales,[2]—and most unwarrantably engaged his interference. He did not come to me, or write, but actually sent a message through a third friend, (who was most reluctant

---

[1]   Possibly the writer Sarah Austin (1793–1867), née Taylor, or her sister Emily Taylor (1795–1872), who was one of Martineau's friends. In Period IV, sec. ii, Martineau describes another of Mrs. Austin's attempt to influence—and alter—her work. But the reference to "Mrs. W—" in the letter below suggests another woman friend.

[2]   William Empson; see Period III, sec. iii.

to convey it) requesting me to say nothing about the position of women in America, for fear of the consequences from the unacceptableness of the topic, &c, &c. When matters had come to this pass, it was clear that I must plainly assert the principle of authorship and the rights of authors, or be subject to the interference of meddlers, and in constant danger of quarrels, from that time forward. I therefore wrote to my reviewer the letter which I will here cite. It was not sent at once, because our intermediary feared it would hurt him so deeply as to break off our intercourse: but he questioned her so closely as to learn that there *was* a letter; and then he read it, declared we could never quarrel, and sent the reply which, in fairness to him, I append to my letter. The reply shows that he no more discerned the principle of the case after reading my letter than before; and in fact, if he had been restricted in his habit of advising every body on all occasions, he would have felt his occupation gone: but his kindly and generous temper abundantly compensated for that serious mistake in judgment, and our good understanding remained unimpaired to the day of his death.

'March 5th, 1837.

My dear friend,

'I have received through Mrs. W— a message from you, advising me not to put into my book any opinions concerning what are vulgarly called the "Rights of Woman."

'My replying to you is rendered unnecessary by the fact that what I have to say on that subject at present has been printed these two months: but I think it desirable to write, to settle at once and for ever this matter of interference with opinions, or the expression of them. You and I differ so hopelessly on the very principle of the matter, that I have no expectation of converting you: but my declaration of my own principle may at least guide you in future as to how to treat me on such matters.

'I say nothing to you of the clear impertinence (in some through whom I conclude you had your information) of questioning an author as to what is to be in his book, in order to remonstrate, and get others to remonstrate, against it. You will agree with me in this. It was in answer to questions only that I mentioned the subject at all, to some friends of ours.

'Nor need I tell you how earnestly I have been besought by various persons to say nothing about Democracy, nothing about Slavery, Commerce, Religion, &c.; and again, to write about nothing else but each of these. In giving me advice how to write my book, you are only following a score of other friends, who have for the most part far less weight with me.

'But you ought to know better than they what it is to write a book. You surely must know that it is one of the most sacred acts of conscience to settle with one's own intellect what is really and solemnly believed, and is therefore to be simply and courageously spoken. You ought to be aware that no second mind can come into the council at all;—can judge as to what are the actual decisions of the intellect, or felt obligations of the conscience.—If you regard a book in the other aspect, of a work of Art, are you not aware that only one mind can work out the conceptions of one mind? If you would not have the sculptor instructed how to bring out his Apollo; or Handel helped to make an oratorio,—on the same principle you should not interfere with the very humblest efforts of the humblest writer who really has any thing to say. In the present case, the appearance of my book will show you the impossibility of any one who does not know the scheme of it being able to offer applicable advice. I analyse society in America,—of which women constitute the half. I test all by their own avowed democratic principles. The result, you see, is inevitable.

'Either you think the opinions objectionable, or you kindly fear the consequences to myself, or act from a more general regard to my influence. Probably you are under all the three fears. If the opinions are objectionable, controvert them. The press is as open to you as to me. But do not seek to suppress the persuasions of a mind which, for aught you know, has been as patient, and careful, and industrious in ascertaining its convictions as your own.

'Perhaps you fear for my influence. I fully agree with an American friend of mine who says, in answer to the same plea addressed to him as an abolitionist, "I do not know what influence is good for if it is not to be used." For my own part, I have never sought influence: and by God's blessing, I never will seek it, nor study how to use it, as influence. This is a care which God has never appointed to creatures so incapable of foresight as we are. Happily, all we have to do is to be true in thought and speech. What comes of our truth is a care which we may cast with our other cares, upon Him.

'This is answer enough to your kind concern for myself. I know well enough what are likely to be the consequences of a perfectly free expression of opinion on any moral subject whatever. I will not say how I can bear them: but I must try. You and I differ as to what I can do; and what, if I am to render any service to society, is the kind of service which I am likely to render. You estimate what would be commonly called my talent far higher than I do. We will not dispute about what can be proved only by the event. But I will tell you what I *know*,—that any human being, however humble or liable to error, may render an essential service to society by making, through a whole lifetime, a steady, uncompromising, dispassionate declaration of his convictions as they are matured. This is the duty to which I some time ago addressed myself. What my talents, my influence, my prosperity may turn out to be, I care little. What my fidelity may be eventually proved to have been, I do care,—more than for life, and all that makes life so sweet as it is. My best friends will not seek to divert me from my aim.

'You may think I am making too serious a matter of this. I can only say that I think it a very serious one. The encroachment of mind upon mind should be checked in its smallest beginning, for the sake of the young and timid who shrink from asserting their own liberty.

'May I ask you not to destroy this letter: but to keep it as a check upon any future solicitudes which may arise out of your friendship for me? When shall we see you?

'Believe me &c., &c.,
'H. MARTINEAU.'

[ANSWER]

'My dear friend,

'Many thanks for the unreservedness of your letter, which I only got yesterday, when I called on Mrs. W——. It sets me quite at ease, in this instance, on the serious question of self-reproach at the reluctance and almost cowardice with which I usually set about to offer my advice to my friends. It would be personally an infinite relief to me if all those in whom I am interested would release me from what I feel to be one of the most painful obligations of friendship, by telling me with equal frankness, that advice tendered under any of the points of view which you enumerate was an undue encroachment of mind on mind.

'Do not imagine that my personal interest in your happiness and usefulness will be one jot less sincere when the expression of it is limited within the conditions which you require.

'If I can call to-day, &c., &c.

'W. EMPSON.'

I will add only one more incident in connexion with this subject. The friend who suggested the taking the life of Louis XVII. for my tale was one of my rebukers for not taking counsel;—that is, for not adopting all his suggestions when he would suggest a dozen volumes in the course of a single evening. I adopted more of his than of any body's, because I often admired them.[1] (I wrote 'How to Observe' at his request, and a good many things besides.) He one day desired to be allowed to see and criticize the first chapter of my 'Retrospect of Western Travel.' I gave him the MS. at night; and in the morning he produced it, covered with pencil marks. I found on examination, and I convinced him, that he had altered about half the words;—on an average, every other word in the chapter: and I put it to him what would become of my book if I submitted the MS. to other friendly critics, equally anxious to deal with it. He could not answer the question, of course; so he called me conceited and obstinate, and I rubbed out his pencil marks,—without any detriment on either side to our friendship. My chapter would have cut a curious figure, dressed in his legal phraseology; as I should expect his legal opinions to do, if I were to express them in my own unprofessional style. Painters complain of interference: musicians, I believe, do not. Amateurs let *them* alone. It is to be hoped that, some time or other, literary works of art,—to say nothing of literary utterance being a work of conscience,—will be left to the artist to work out, according to his own conception and conviction. At present, it seems as if few but authors had any comprehension whatever of the seriousness of writing a book.

There is something to be told about the origin of the third volume of 'The Playfellow.' I had nearly fixed on a subject of a totally different kind when Mr. Laing's book on Norway fell in my way,[2] and set my imagination floating on the fiords, and climbing the slopes of the Dovre Fjeld. I procured Inglis's travels,[3] and every thing that I could get hold of about the state of Norway while connected with Denmark; and hence arose 'Feats on the Fiord.' Two or three years afterwards, a note from Mr. Laing to a relative of his in Scotland travelled round to me, in which he inquired whether his relative could tell him, or could learn, when and for how long I had resided in Norway, as he

---

[1]   Henry Bellenden Ker, who initiated the "How to Observe" series; see Period IV, sec. ii.

[2]   Samuel Laing, *Journal of a Residence in Norway, during the Years 1834, 1835, and 1836* (London, 1836). Dovre Fjeld (or, more commonly, Dovre Fjell) is a mountainous region in Norway now part of Hardangervidda National Park.

[3]   Henry D. Inglis, *A Personal Narrative of a Journey through Norway, Part of Sweden, and the Islands and State of Denmark* (London: Hurst, Chance, 1829).

concluded I had, on the evidence of that story. I had the pleasure of transmitting to him the fact that I knew scarcely any thing about Norway, and had chosen another scene and subject, when his book caught my fancy, and became the originator of my tale. I hope he enjoyed the incident as much as I did.

The fourth and last volume,—'The Crofton Boys'—was written under the belief that it was my last word through the press. There are some things in it which I could not have written except under that persuasion. By that time, I was very ill, and so sunk in strength that it was obvious that I must lay aside the pen. I longed to do so; and yet I certainly had much enjoyment in the free outpouring of that book. When it was sealed up and sent, I stretched myself on my sofa, and said to myself, with entire sincerity, that my career as an author was closed. I find an entry in my Diary of the extreme need in which I was,—not of idleness, but of my mind being free of all *engagement* to work. I was under the constant sense of obligation to do what I am doing now,— to write my life; but otherwise I was at liberty and leisure. The strictest economy in my way of living was necessary from the time of my ceas- ing to earn; but my relations now, as I explained before, enabled me to have a servant. My lodgings were really the only considerable expense I had besides; for I had left off dining from total failure of appetite, and my consumption of food had become so small that the wonder was how life could be supported upon it.

To finish the subject of my authorship during this period, I will now tell how my anonymous volume, 'Life in the Sick-room,' came into existence, and how I, who never had a secret before or since, (as far as I can now remember) came to have one then.—In the book itself it is seen what I have to say on the subject of sympathy with the sick. When I had been living for above three years alone (for the most part) and with merely the change from one room to another,—from bed to sofa,—in constant uneasiness, and under the depression caused both by the nature of my disease and by heavy domestic cares, I had accumu- lated a weight of ideas and experiences which I longed to utter, and which indeed I needed to cast off. I need not repeat (what is amply explained in the book) that it was wholly my own doing that I lived alone, and why such was my choice; and the letters which I afterwards received from invalids satisfied me, and all who saw those letters, that my method was rational and prudent. It was not because I was desti- tute of kind nurses and visitors that I needed to pour out what was in my mind, but because the most perfect sympathy one can meet with in any trial common to humanity is reached by an appeal to the whole mind of society. It was on the fifteenth of September 1843 that this mode of relief occurred to me, while I lay on my sofa at work on my inexhaustible resource, fancy-work. I kept no diary at that time; but I find inserted under that date in a note-book, 'A new and imperative idea occurred to me,'—"Essays from a Sick-room." This conception was certainly the greatest refreshment I had during all those heavy years. During the next few days, while some of my family were with me, I brooded over the idea; and on the nineteenth, I wrote the first of the Essays. I never wrote any thing so fast as that book.[1] It went off like sleep. I was hardly conscious of the act, while writing or afterwards,— so strong was the need to speak. I wrote the Essays as the subject pressed, and not in the order in which they stand. As I could not speak of them to any body, I suspended the indulgence of writing them while receiving the visits which I usually had in October,—preparatory to the long winter solitude; and it was therefore November when I finished my volume. I wrote the last Essay on the fourth. It was now necessary to tell one person;—viz, a publisher. I wrote confidentially to Mr. Moxon who, curiously enough, wrote to me on the same day, (so that our letters crossed,) to ask whether I was not able, after so long an interval of rest, to promise him some work to publish. My letter had a favourable reception; he carefully considered my wishes, and kept my secret, and I corrected my last proof on the twenty-sixth of November. On the seventh of December, the first news of the volume being out arrived in the shape of other letters than Mr. Moxon's. I was instantly and universally detected, as I had indeed supposed must be the case. On that day, my mother and eldest sister came over from Newcastle to see me. It was due to them not to let them hear such a fact in my history from the newspapers or from strangers; so, assuring them that it was the first time I had opened my lips on the subject, and that Mr. Moxon was the only person who had known it at all, I told them what I had done, and lent them my copy to take home. They were somewhat hurt, as were one or two more distant friends, who had no manner of right to be so. It proved to me how little reticence I can boast of, or have the credit for, that several friends confidently denied that the book was mine, on the ground that I had not told them a word about it,—a conviction in which I think them perfectly justified. There could not be a stronger proof of how I *felt* that book than my inability to speak

---

[1]   She wrote it between September 19 and November 4, 1843.

of it except to my unknown comrades in suffering. My mother and sister had a special trial, I knew, to bear in discovering how great my suffering really was; and I could not but see that it was too much for them, and that from that time forward they were never again to me what they had been.

What the 'success' of the book was, the fact of a speedy sale of the whole edition presently showed. What my own opinion of it is, at the distance of a dozen years, it may be worth while to record. My note-book of that November says that I wrote the Essays from the heart, and that there never was a truer book as to conviction. Such being the fact, I can only now say that I am ashamed, considering my years and experience of suffering, that my state of mind was so crude, if not morbid, as I now see it to have been. I say this, not from any saucy elevation of health and prosperity, but in an hour of pain and feebleness, under a more serious and certainly fatal illness than that of 1843, and after ten intervening years of health and strength, ease and prosperity. All the facts in the book, and some of the practical doctrine of the sick-room, I could still swear to: but the magnifying of my own experience, the desperate concern as to my own ease and happiness, the moaning undertone running through what many people have called the stoicism, and the total inability to distinguish between the metaphysically apparent and the positively true, make me, to say the truth, heartily despise a considerable part of the book. Great allowance is to be made, no doubt, for the effect of a depressing malady, and of the anxieties which caused it, and for an exile of years from fresh air, exercise, and change of scene. Let such allowance be made; but the very demand shows that the book is morbid,—or that part of it which needs such allowance. Stoical! Why, if I had been stoical I should not have written the book at all:—not *that* book; but, if any, one wholly clear of the dismal self-consciousness which I then thought it my business to detail. The fact is, as I now see, that I was lingering in the metaphysical stage of mind, because I was not perfectly emancipated from the *débris* of the theological.[1] The day of final release from both was drawing nigh, as I shall have occasion to show: but I had not yet ascertained my own position. I had quitted the old untenable point of view, and had not yet found the one on which I was soon to take my stand. And, while attesting the truth of the book on the whole,—its truth as a reflexion of my mind

---

[1] In evaluating her intellectual state, Martineau uses the three Comtean stages of development: theological, metaphysical, and positive (or scientific); see Period VI, sec. vii.

450

of that date,—I still can hardly reconcile with sincerity the religious remains that are found in it. To be sure, they are meagre and incoherent enough; but, such as they are, they are compatible, I fear, with only a metaphysical, and not a positive order of sincerity. I had not yet learned, with decision and accuracy, what *conviction* is. I had yet no firm grasp of it; and I gave forth the contemporary persuasions of the imagination, or narratives of old traditions, as if they had been durable convictions, ascertained by personal exertion of my faculties. I suffered the retribution of this unsound dealing,—the results of this crude state of mind,—in the latent fear and blazoned pain through which I passed during that period; and if any one now demurs to my present judgment, on the score of lapse of time and change of circumstances, I would just remind him that I am again ill, as hopelessly, and more certainly fatally than I was then. I cannot be mistaken in what I am now feeling so sensibly from day to day,—that my condition is bliss itself in comparison with that of twelve years ago; and that I am now above the reach (while my brain remains unaffected by disease) of the solicitudes, regrets, apprehensions, self-regards, and in-bred miseries of various kinds, which breathe through these Sick-room Essays, even where the language appears the least selfish and cowardly. I should not now write a Sick-room book at all, except for express pathological purposes: but, if I did, I should have a very different tale to tell. If not, the ten best years of my life,—the ten which intervened between the two illnesses,— would have been lost upon me.

Before I dismiss this book, I must mention that its publisher did his duty amply by it and me. I told him at first to say nothing to me about money, as I could not bear to think of selling such an experience while in the midst of it. Long after, when I was in health and strength, he wrote that circumstances had now completely changed, and that life was again open before me; and he sent me a cheque for £75. On occasion of another edition, he sent me £50 more.

The subject of money reminds me that by this time a matter was finally settled which appears of less consequence to me than many have supposed,—probably because my mind was clear on the point when the moment of action came. On my first going to reside in London, at the end of 1832, a friend of Lord Brougham's told me that there was an intention on the part of government to give me a pension which should make me independent for life. The story then told me I believed, of course, though it was not long before I found that it was almost entirely one of Lord Brougham's imaginations or fictions. He said that Lord Grey, then

Premier, wished to make me independent, that I might not be tempted, or compelled, to spend my powers (such as they were) on writing for periodicals: that he (Lord Brougham) had spoken to the King about it, and that the King had said divers gracious things on the occasion; but that the two Ministers had judged it best for me to wait till my Political Economy series was finished, lest the Radicals should charge me with having been bought by the Whigs. Fully believing this story, I consulted, confidentially, three friends,—a Tory friend, my Whig Edinburgh reviewer, and my brother James.[1] The two first counselled my accepting the pension, —seeing no reason why I should not. My brother advised my declining it. If it had then been offered, I believe I should have accepted it, with some doubt and misgiving, and simply because I did not then feel able to assign sufficient reasons for doing an ungracious act.— The next I heard of the matter was a year afterwards, when I was two-thirds through my long work. Lord Durham then told me, after inquiring of Lord Grey, that the subject had never been mentioned to the King at all; but that Lord Grey intended that it should be, and that I should have my pension. Some months afterwards, when I was about to go to America, Lord Grey sent to Lord Durham for my address, for the avowed purpose of informing me of the intended gift. I left England immediately after, and fully understood that, on my return, I should be made easy for life by a pension of £300 a year. Presently, the Whigs went out, and Sir R. Peel was Premier for five months, to be succeeded by the Whigs, who were in power on my return. But, meantime, my mind had become clear about refusing the pension. When at a distance from the scene of my labours, and able to think quietly, and to ascertain my own feelings at leisure, the latent repugnance to that mode of provision came up again, and I was persuaded that I should lose more independence in one way than I should gain in another. I wrote to Lord Durham from America, requesting him to beg of Lord Grey that the idea might be laid aside, and that no application might be made to me which would compel me to appear ungrateful and ungracious. Lord Grey saw that letter of mine; and I supposed and hoped that the whole subject was at an end.

After my return, however, and repeatedly during the next two years (1837 and 1838) some friends of the government, who were kind friends of my own, remonstrated with me about my refusal. I could never make them understand the ground of my dislike of a pension. One could see

---

[1]   Probably Richard Monckton Milnes (1809–85), then a Tory M.P., and William Empson, who reviewed her *Illustrations* for the *Edinburgh Review*; see Period III, sec. iii.

in it nothing but pride, and held up to me the name of Southey, and others whom I cordially honoured, and told me that I might well accept what they had not demurred to. Another chid me for practically censuring all acceptors of pensions; whereas, it was so earnestly my desire to avoid all appearance of such insolence and narrowness, that I entreated that the express offer might not be made. As for Lord Brougham, he said testily, before many hearers, when my name was mentioned, — 'Harriet Martineau! I hate her!' Being asked why, he replied 'I hate a woman who has opinions. She has refused a pension,—making herself out to be better than other people.' Having done all I could to be quiet about the matter, and to avoid having to appear to imply a censure of other people by an open refusal, I took these misconceptions as patiently as I could; and I can sincerely declare that I never did, in my inmost mind, judge any receiver of a pension by my own action in a matter which was more one of feeling than of judgment or principle. When my part was taken beyond recal, a friend of mine showed me cause for belief that it would have been convenient for me to have accepted a pension at that time, on account of an exposure of some jobbery, and a consequent stir about the bestowal of pensions. Certainly, the few most popular pensioners' names were paraded in parliament and the newspapers in a way which I should not relish; and though no suspicion of my name being desired for justificatory reasons had any thing to do with my refusal, I was more than ever satisfied with what I had done when I saw the course that matters were taking.

The subject was revived at the close of 1840, through an old friend of mine; and again in August 1841, just before Lord Melbourne went out of office.[1] Mr. Charles Buller wrote to me to say that Lord Melbourne understood how my earnings were invested (in a deferred annuity) and was anxious to give me present ease in regard to money: that he was sorry to have no more to offer at the moment than £150 a year, (which however I was given to understand might be increased when opportunity offered); and that my answer must be immediate, as Lord Melbourne was going out so soon as to require the necessary information by return of post. I was very ill, the evening that this letter arrived,—too ill to write myself: but my brother Robert and his wife happened to be with me; and my brother transmitted my reply. I did

---

[1]   Richard Holt Hutton (1826–97), Unitarian minister and essayist, and Charles Buller (1806–48), first-secretary to Lord Durham during his Canadian mission and later member of the India Board, wrote to her about a government pension. An appendix to the 1877 *Autobiography* included letters from them.

not feel a moment's hesitation about it. While fully sensible of Lord Melbourne's kindness, I felt that I could not, with satisfaction to myself, accept such a boon at his hands, or as a matter of favouritism from any minister. I should have proudly and thankfully accepted ease and independence in the form of a pension bestowed by parliament, or by some better judge than Minister or Sovereign can easily be: but, distinct and generous as were the assurances given that the pension was offered for past services, and ought not to interfere with my political independence, I felt that practically the sense of obligation would weigh heavily upon me, and that I could never again feel perfectly free to speak my mind on politics. At that time, too, the popular adversity was very great; and I preferred sharing the poverty of the multitude to being helped out of the public purse. From time to time since, I have been made sensible of the prudence of my decision; and especially in regard to that large undertaking of a subsequent period,—my 'History of the Thirty Years' Peace.' No person in receipt of a pension from government, bestowed by Lord Melbourne, could have written that History;[1] and I have had more satisfaction and pleasure from that work than any amount of pension could have given me. My family,—the whole clan,—behaved admirably about the business, except the adviser in the former case, who had changed his mind, and blamed me for my decision. All the rest, whether agreeing with me or not as to my reasons or feelings, said very cordially, that, as such were my reasons and feelings, I had done rightly; and very cheering to me, in those sickly days of anxious conscience, was their generous approval. Some of the newspapers insulted me: but I did not care for that. All the mockery of strangers all over the world could be nothing in comparison with the gratification afforded by one incident, with which the honoured name of Lady Byron is connected. Lady Byron,[2] with whom I had occasionally corresponded, wrote to a visitor of mine at that time that henceforth no one could pity me for narrow circumstances which were my own free choice: but that she thought it hard that I should not have the pleasure of helping people poorer than myself. She had actually placed in the bank, and at my disposal, £100 for beneficent purposes: and, lest there

---

[1]   In her discussion of the Melbourne administration in Book V, ch. II of *The History of the Thirty Years' Peace*, Martineau is critical of Melbourne's personal manner as well as his government—as in her judgment, "He was out of his place as the head of a reforming administration, from his inability to originate, and his indisposition to guide."

[2]   Lady Noel Byron, née Millbank (1792–1860), became a close friend; after her death, Martineau published an obituary, included in *Biographical Sketches* (1869).

should be any possible injury to me from the circumstances becoming known, she made the money payable to another person. How rich and how happy I felt with that £100! It lasted nearly the whole time of my illness; and I trust it was not ill-spent.

During the whole time of my illness, comforts and pleasures were lavishly supplied to me. Sydney Smith said that every body who sent me game, fruit and flowers was sure of Heaven, provided always that they punctually paid the dues of the Church of England. If so, many of my friends are safe. Among other memorials of that time which are still preserved and prized in my home are drawings sent me by the Miss Nightingales, and an envelope-case, (in daily use) from the hands of the immortal Florence. I was one of the sick to whom she first ministered; and it happened through my friendship with some of her family.[1]

Some time after the final settlement of this pension business, some friends of mine set about the generous task of raising a Testimonial Fund for my benefit.[2] It is necessary for me to offer the statement, as expressly and distinctly as possible, that I had nothing whatever to do with this proceeding, and that I did every thing in my power to avoid knowing any particulars while the scheme was in progress. This declaration, indispensable to my honour, is rendered necessary by the behaviour of one person whose indiscretion and double-dealing involved me in trouble about the testimonial business. It is enough to say here that so determined was I to hear nothing of the particulars of the affair that, when I found it impossible to prevent that officious person telling me all she knew, and representing me as compelling her to tell it, in excuse for her own indiscretion, I engaged my aunts, who were then lodging close by, to come in whenever that visitor entered,—to stop her when she spoke on the forbidden subject, and to bear witness that it was my resolute purpose to hear nothing about it. One of my dear aunts was always instantly on the spot, accordingly, to the discomfiture of the gossip, who complained that she never saw me alone: and at last, (but not till I was liable to serious injury in the minds of many people) I

---

[1] Florence Nightingale (1820–1910) was introduced by her aunt, Julia Smith; they exchanged letters about illness and information on nursing, and Martineau favorably reviewed her *Notes on Nursing: What it is, What it is not* (1860) in an attempt to further the cause.

[2] In 1843 Erasmus Darwin, Hensleigh Wedgwood, and other friends gave her a testimonial fund of £1358. 8s. 10d., which gave her an additional £200 yearly income. The "one person" she mentions as double-dealing is most likely Emily Taylor, who infuriated Martineau by writing to potential contributors without consulting her and who intruded herself (in Martineau's view) on the Wedgwood family.

succeeded in being so completely outside of the affair as to be ignorant of all but the first steps taken. To this day I have never seen the list of subscribers, nor heard, probably, more than ten or twelve of them. The money raised was mainly invested, with the entire approbation of the managers of the business, in the Long Annuities,—the object being to obtain the latest income procurable from £1,400 for the period during which it was then supposed that I might live. I have since enjoyed ten years of health, (after many months more of that sickness) and it seemed probable that I should outlive that investment. Now again the scene is changed; and it appears that I shall leave the remnant of the kindly gift behind me. I do not know that I could better express the relief and satisfaction that I derived from that movement of my friends than by citing here the circular in which I made my acknowledgments.

'TO THE CONTRIBUTORS TO A TESTIMONIAL TO H. MARTINEAU

'My dear friends,

'To reach you individually from my retirement is not very easy; and to convey to you the feelings with which I accept your kindness is impossible: yet I cannot but attempt to present to each of you my acknowledgments, and the assurance of the comfort I feel, from day to day, in the honour and independence which you have conferred upon me. By your generous testimony to my past services you have set me free from all personal considerations, in case of my becoming capable of future exertion. The assurance which I possess of your esteem and sympathy will be a stimulus to labour, if I find I have still work to do: and if I remain in my present useless condition, it will be a solace to me under suffering, and a cordial under the depressions of illness and confinement.

'I am, with affectionate gratitude,
'Your Friend and Servant,
'HARRIET MARTINEAU.'

'Tynemouth,
October 22nd, 1843.'

AFTER what I have said of my Sick-room Essays, which were written only the year before my recovery, it may seem strange to say that my mind made a progress worth noting during the five heavy years from 1839 to 1844: but, small as my achievements now appear to me, there *was* achievement. A large portion of the transition from religious inconsistency and irrationality to free-thinking strength and liberty was gone over during that period. Not only had I abundant leisure for thought, and undiminished faculty of thought, but there was abundance of material for that kind of meditation which usually serves as an introduction to a higher. I was not yet intellectually capable of a wide philosophical survey, nor morally bold enough for a deep investigation in regard to certain matters which I had always taken for granted: but the old and desultory questions—such as that of 'a divine government,' 'a future life,' and so on—were pressed upon me by the events and experiences of those years. At the outset of the period, my revered and beloved friend, Dr. Follen, was lost by the burning of the Lexington steam-packet, under circumstances which caused anguish to all who heard the story.[1] Just about the same time, my old instructor, who had for years of my youth been my idol, Dr. Carpenter, perished in a singularly impressive manner,—by being thrown overboard, no doubt by a lurch of the steamer in which he was traversing the Mediterranean.[2] The accident happened in the evening, so that he was not missed till the morning. The hour was shown by the stopping of his watch,—his body being afterwards cast upon the Italian coast. A strange and forlorn mode of death for a minister, the idol of a host of disciples, and for a family-man whose children would thankfully, any one of them, have given their lives to prolong his!—During that period, my grandmother, the head of one side of our house, died; and, on the other, the beloved old aunt who had lived with us, and the old uncle whose effectual sympathy in

---

[1]   Charles Follen died in the explosion of the steamboat *Lexington* on January 13, 1840, as it traveled through Long Island Sound en route to Boston.

[2]   Lant Carpenter was drowned on April 5, 1840, having been washed overboard from a steamer traveling from Leghorn to Marseilles; see Period II, sec. iii for his influence.

my great enterprise of the Political Economy series I described in its place; and three cousins of my own generation; and a nephew of the generation below.[1] Several friends of my father and mother, to whom I had looked up during my childhood and youth, slipped away during the period when I was lying waiting for death as my release from dreary pain: and also a whole group of my political friends, acquired since I entered the world of literature. Lord and Lady Durham died, after having sympathised with me in my illness; and Lord Sydenham, who had made me known to them in my writings: and Lord Congleton: and Thomas Drummond, who had been the medium of some of my communications with Lord Grey's government: and Lord Henley, who had suggested and determined my going to America: and old Lord Leicester, who had been, under the name of Mr. Coke, my early ideal of the patriot gentleman of England;[2] and others of less note, or a remoter interest to myself. Most various and impressive had been the modes of their death. Some few by mere old age and ordinary disease; but others by heart-break, by over-anxious toil in the public service, by suicide, and by insanity! Then, among my American friends, there were several whom I had left not long before, in the full exercise of important functions, and in the bright enjoyment of life;—Judge Porter of Louisiana, one of the leading Senators of the United States, and perhaps the most genial and merry of my American friends; Dr. Henry Ware, the model of a good clergyman; and Dr. Channing, who had just cheered me by his fervent blessing on my portraiture of Toussaint L'Ouverture.[3] And then again, there were literary men who were much connected with the last preceding phase of my life;—Southey, after his

[1] The relatives who died during this period include her grandmother, Mrs. Robert Rankin, Sr. (d. 1840); her aunt Margaret Lee (d. 1840); her uncle David Martineau (d. 1841); her cousins Eleanor Rogers Martineau (d. 1841), John Scott Martineau (d. 1845), and Margaret Hester Martineau (d. 1845); and her nephew Herbert Martineau (d. 1846). Interestingly, she does not mention the death of her brother Henry (d. 1844), who had come to live in her London household after his wine importing business failed and who emigrated to New Zealand, in large part because his alcoholism had become a serious problem.

[2] Lord Durham died in 1840, weakened by the failure of his Canadian mission; Lady Durham died soon after in 1841; see Period IV, sec. iv. Lord Henley died insane in 1843. Some deaths were unexpected—e.g., Lord Sydenham's in 1841 at the age of 42, during his second year as governor general of Canada, and Thomas Drummond's in 1840 at the age of 43, by some accounts from overwork as under-secretary of Ireland. Some died of old age—e.g., Lord Congleton in 1842 at the age of 88, and Lord Leicester in 1842 at the age of 76.

[3] Although perhaps unexpected, these deaths were not untimely—Henry Ware's in 1845 at age 81 and William Ellery Channing's in 1842 at age 62. Alexander Porter died young in 1844 at age 48.

dreary decline, and Campbell; and Dr. Dalton, who remains a venerable picture in my memory; and John Murray who had refused (with hesitation) to publish 'Deerbrook,' and had found the refusal a mistake.[1] And there were others who were living influences to me, as they were to multitudes more, who had never seen them,—as Grace Darling, of whom every storm of that same sea reminded me.[2] The departure of these and many more kept the subject of death vividly before me, and compelled me to reduce my vague and fanciful speculations on 'the divine government' and human destiny to a greater precision and accuracy. The old perplexity about the apparent cruelty and injustice of the scheme of 'divine government' began at last to suggest the right issue. I had long perceived the worse than uselessness of enforcing principles of justice and mercy by an appeal to the example of God. I had long seen that the orthodox fruitlessly attempt to get rid of the difficulty by presenting the two-fold aspect of God,—the Father being the model of justice, and the Son of love and mercy,—the inevitable result being that he who is especially called God is regarded as an unmitigated tyrant and spontaneous torturer, while the sweeter and nobler attributes are engrossed by the man Jesus,—whose fate only deepens the opprobrium of the Divine cruelty: while the heretics whose souls recoil from such a doctrine, and who strive to explain away the recorded dogmas of tyranny and torture, in fact give up the Christian revelation by rejecting its essential postulates. All this I had long seen: and I now began to obtain glimpses of the conclusion which at present seems to me so simple that it is a marvel why I waited for it so long;—that it is possible that we human beings, with our mere human faculty, may not understand the scheme, or nature, or fact of the universe! I began to see that we, with our mere human faculty, are not in the least likely to understand it, any more than the minnow in the creek, as Carlyle has it,[3] can comprehend the perturbations caused in his world of existence by the tides. I saw that no revelation can by possibility set men right on these matters, for want of faculty in man to understand anything beyond human ken; as all instruction whatever offered to the minnow must fail

---

[1]   Robert Southey died insane in 1843; the poet Thomas Campbell died in 1844; the scientist John Dalton in 1844; and the publisher John Murray in 1843.

[2]   Grace Darling and her father, a lighthouse keeper, rescued nine survivors of the S.S. Forsfarshire on September 7, 1838, by rowing in a storm to the rock to which they were clinging. Grace died three years later of tuberculosis, and her heroism was memorialized in the churchyard of her native village, Bamburgh, Northumberland.

[3]   In *Sartor Resartus*.

to make it comprehend the action of the moon on the oceans of the earth, or receive the barest conception of any such action. Thus far I began to see now. It was not for long after that I perceived further that the conception itself of moral government, of moral qualities, of the necessity of a preponderance of happiness over misery, must be essentially false beyond the sphere of human action, because it relates merely to human faculties. But this matter,—of a truer stand-point, —will be better treated hereafter, in connexion with the period in which I perceived it within my horizon. As to death and the question of a future life,—I was some time in learning to be faithful to my best light,—faint as it yet was. I remember asserting to a friend who was willing to leave that future life a matter of doubt, that we were justified in expecting whatever the human race had agreed in desiring. I had long seen that the 'future life' of the New Testament was the Millennium looked for by the apostles, according to Christ's bidding,—the glorious reign of 1,000 years in Judea, when the Messiah should be the Prince, and his apostles his councillors and functionaries, and which was to begin within the then existing generation.[1] I had long given up, in moral disgust, the conception of life after death as a matter of compensation for the ills of humanity, or a police and penal resource of 'the divine government.' I had perceived that the doctrines of the immortality of the soul and the resurrection of the body were incompatible; and that, while the latter was clearly impossible, we were wholly without evidence of the former. But I still resorted, in indolence and prejudice, to the plea of instinct,—the instinctive and universal love of life, and inability to conceive of its extinction. My Sick-room book shows that such was my view when I wrote those essays: but I now feel pretty certain that I was not, even then, dealing truly with my own mind, — that I was unconsciously trying to gain strength of conviction by vigour of assertion. It seems to me now that I might then have seen how delusive, in regard to fact, are various genuine and universal instincts; and, again, that this direction of the instinct in question is by no means so universal and so uniform as I declared it to be. I might then have seen,

---

[1]   Many nineteenth-century Evangelicals were "millenarians," i.e., they believed that Christ would return to earth to reign for 1000 years, as prophesied in Isaiah 32:1 ("Behold, a king shall reign in righteousness"), Revelation 11:15 ("The kingdom of this world is become the kingdom of our Lord, and of his Christ, and he shall reign forever and ever"), and other biblical passages. In *Traditions of Palestine* (1829) Martineau's stories, especially "The Hope of the Hebrews" and "Songs of Praise," incorporate the Jewish belief in a Messiah to explain the reception of Christ and his preaching.

if I had been open-minded, that the instinct to fetishism, for instance, is more general,—is indeed absolutely universal, while it is false in regard to fact; and that it is, in natural course, overpowered and annihilated by higher instincts, leading to true knowledge.

In such progress as I did make, I derived great assistance from the visits of a remarkable variety of friends, and from the confidence reposed in me during tête-à-tête conversations, such as could hardly have occurred under any other circumstances. Some dear old friends came, one at a time, and established themselves at the inn or in lodgings near, for weeks together, and spent with me such hours of the day as I could render (by opiates) fit for converse with them. Others stopped at Tynemouth, in the midst of a journey, and gave me a day or two; and with many I had a single interview which was afterwards remembered with pleasure. During many a summer evening, while I lay on my window-couch, and my guest of the day sat beside me, overlooking the purple sea, or watching for the moon to rise up from it, like a planet growing into a sun, things were said, high and deep, which are fixed into my memory now, like stars in a dark firmament. Now a philosopher, now a poet, now a moralist, opened to me speculation, vision, or conviction; and numerous as all the speculations, visions and convictions together, were the doubts confided to my meditation and my discretion. I am not going to violate any confidence here, of course, which I have considered sacred in life. I refer to these conversations with the thoughtful and the wise merely to acknowledge my obligations to them, and to explain certain consequences to myself which may perhaps be best conveyed by an anecdote.—During the latter part of my Tynemouth sojourn, a friend, who could minister to me in all manner of ways except philosophy, was speaking of the indispensableness of religion, and of her mode of religion especially, to a good state of mind. Not at all agreeing with her, I told her I had had a good deal of opportunity of knowing states of mind since I lay down on that sofa; and that what I had seen had much deepened the impression which I had begun to have long before,—that the best state of mind was to be found, however it might be accounted for, in those who were called philosophical atheists. Her exclamation of amazement showed me that I had said something very desperate: but the conversation had gone too far to stop abruptly. She asked me what on earth I could mean: and I was obliged to explain. I told her that I knew several of that class,—some avowed and some not; and that I had for several years felt that they were among my most honoured acquaintances and friends; and that now that I knew them more deeply and thoroughly, I must say that, for conscientiousness, sincerity, integrity,

seriousness, effective intellect, and the true religious spirit, I knew nothing like them. She burst out a laughing, and said she could conceive how,
amidst fortunate circumstances, they might have been trained to morality; but how they could have the religious spirit, she could in no way
conceive. It seemed to her absolute nonsense. I explained what I meant,
being very careful, according to my state of mind at that time, to assure
her that I was not of their way of thinking: nevertheless, it did seem to
me, I said, that the philosophical atheists were the most humble-minded
in the presence of the mysteries of the universe, the most equable in spirit
and temper amidst the affairs of life, the most devout in their contemplation of the unknown, and the most disinterested in their management
of themselves, and their expectations from the human lot;—showing, in
short, the moral advantages of knowledge (however limited) and of freedom (however isolated and mournful) over superstition as shared by the
multitude. I have reason to believe that, amazed as my visitor was, she was
not so struck as to derive benefit from the statement of an unusual experience like mine, in my sudden translation from the vividness of literary
and political life in London to the quietness of the sick-room and its
converse. She had not forgotten the conversation many years afterwards;
but it had not borne fruit to her. On the contrary, she was so shocked at
my opinions, as avowed in the 'Letters on Man's Nature and Development'
as to be one of the very few who retreated from intercourse with me on
account of them. There was a pretext or two for ceasing to correspond;
but I believe there is no doubt that my heresies were the cause. What I
said to her I said to several other people; and I doubt whether any one
of them was unprepared for what was pretty certain to be the result when
I had once attained to the estimate of the free-thinkers of my acquaintance which I have just recorded.

SECTION III

———

ABOUT the middle of the period of this illness, Sir E.L. Bulwer Lytton[1]
wrote to me an earnest suggestion that I should go to Paris to consult
a somnambule about the precise nature and treatment of my disease.

---

[1]   The novelist Edward Bulwer-Lytton (1803–73).

He said I should probably think him insane for making such a proposition, but offered to supply me with his reasons, if I would listen to him. My reply was that I needed no convincing of the goodness of his advice, if only the measure was practicable. I had long been entirely convinced of the truth of the insight of somnambules, and should have been thankful to be able to make use of it: but there were two obstacles which appeared insurmountable. I could not move, in the first place. My medical adviser, my brother-in-law, had much wished to take me to London, for other opinions on my case; but my travelling was altogether out of the question. Sir Charles Clarke had come into Northumberland afterwards, and he had visited me, and, after a careful inquiry into the case, had decided that the disease was incurable.[1] After this, it was agreed on all hands that I could not travel. In the next place, I had to explain that the penalty on my consulting a somnambule, even if one could be brought to me, was, not only the loss of my medical comforts at Tynemouth, but of family peace,—so strong was the prejudice of a part of my family against mesmerism. There the matter rested till May 1844, when, in the course of a fortnight, there were no less than three letters of advice to me to try mesmerism. My youngest sister wrote to me about a curious case which had accidentally come under the notice first, and then the management, of her husband,—a surgeon:—a case which showed that insensibility to pain under an operation could be produced, and that epilepsy of the severest kind had given way under mesmerism, when all other treatment had long been useless. Mr. and Mrs. Basil Montagu[2] wrote to entreat me to try mesmerism, and related the story of their own conversion to it by seeing the case of Ann Vials treated by their 'dear young friend, Henry Atkinson,'[3]—of whom I had never heard. The third was from a wholly different quarter, but contained the same counsel, on very similar grounds. Presently after, I was astonished at what my brother-in-law said in one of his visits. He told me that Mr. Spencer Hall,[4] of whom I had never heard, was lecturing in Newcastle on mesmerism; that he (my brother) had gone to the lecture out of curiosity, and had

1   Sir Charles Mansfield Clarke (1782–1857), a leading London obstetrician and gynecologist, was author of a 2-vol. treatise, *Observations on those Diseases of Females which are attended by Discharges* (London: Longman, 1821). Clarke examined Martineau in September, 1841, and confirmed her brother-in-law's diagnosis of "an enlargement of the BODY of the Uterus."

2   Basil Montagu (1770–1851) and his wife were old London friends.

3   Henry George Atkinson (1815?- 84), a phreno-mesmerist with whom Martineau later wrote *Letters on the Laws of Man's Nature and Development* (London: John Chapman, 1851).

4   Spencer Timothy Hall (1812–85), a popular lecturer and practitioner of mesmerism.

been put into the chair, on the clear understanding that he accepted the post only to see fair play, and not at all as countenancing mesmerism, of which he fairly owned that he knew nothing whatever: that he had been deeply impressed by what he saw, and was entirely perplexed,— the only clear conviction that he had brought away being of the honesty and fairness of the lecturer, who was the first to announce such failures as occurred; and that he (my brother) was anxious to see more of the lecturer, and disposed to advise my trying the experiment of being mesmerised, as possibly affording me some release from the opiates to which I was obliged to have constant recourse. I was as much pleased as surprised at all this, and I eagerly accepted the proposal that Mr. Spencer Hall should be brought to see me, if he would come. Some of my family were sadly annoyed by this proceeding; but, as the move was not mine, I felt no scruple about accepting its benefits. For between five and six years, every thing that medical skill and family care could do for me had been tried, without any avail; and it was now long since the best opinions had declared that the case was hopeless,—that, though I might live on, even for years, if my state of exhaustion should permit, the disease was incurable. I had tried all the methods, and taken all the medicines prescribed, 'without' as my brother-in-law declared in writing, 'any effect whatever having been produced on the disease'; and, now that a new experiment was proposed to me by my medical attendant himself, I had nothing to do but try it. This appears plain and rational enough to me now, as it did then; and I am as much surprised now as I was then that any evil influence should have availed to persuade my mother and eldest sister that my trial of mesmerism was a slight to the medical adviser who proposed it, and my recovery by means of it a fit occasion for a family quarrel. For my part,—if any friend of mine had been lying in a suffering and hopeless state for nearly six years, and if she had fancied she might get well by standing on her head instead of her heels, or reciting charms or bestriding a broomstick, I should have helped her to try: and thus was I aided by some of my family, and by a further sympathy in others: but two or three of them were induced by an evil influence to regard my experiment and recovery as an unpardonable offence; and by them I never was pardoned. It is a common story. Many or most of those who have been restored by mesmerism have something of the same sort to tell; and the commonness of this experience releases me from the necessity of going into detail upon the subject.

I may also omit the narrative of my recovery, because it is given in

'Letters on Mesmerism' which I was presently compelled to publish.[1] There is among my papers my diary of the case,—a record carefully kept from day to day of the symptoms, the treatment, and the results. The medical men, and the few private friends who have seen that journal (which I showed to my medical adviser) have agreed in saying that it is as *cool* as if written by a professional observer, while it is so conclusive as to the fact of my restoration by the means tried in 1844, that 'we must cease to say that any thing is the cause of any other thing, if the recovery was not wrought by mesmerism.' These are the words which are before me in the hand-writing of a wholly impartial reader of that journal.

I had every desire to bear patiently any troubles sure to arise in such a case from professional bigotry, and popular prejudice; but I must think that I had more than my share of persecution for the offence of recovery from a hopeless illness by a new method.—Occasion of offence was certainly given by some advocates of mesmerism, strangers to me, by their putting letters into the newspapers, praising me for my experiment, and ridiculing the doctors for their repugnance to it; and one at least of these officious persons made several mistakes in his statement. I knew nothing of this for some time; and then only by the consequences. I must repeat here, what I have said elsewhere, that Mr. Spencer Hall had nothing to do with all this. Though he might naturally have been pleased with his own share in the business, and though many men would have considered themselves released from all obligation to silence by the publicity the matter soon obtained, he remained honourably silent, till he had my express permission to tell the story when and where he pleased. When he did tell it, it was with absolute accuracy. The first letters to the newspapers, meanwhile, drew out from the grossest and more ignorant of the medical profession, and also from some who ought to have been above exposing themselves to be so classified, speculations, comments, and narratives, not only foolish and utterly false in regard to facts, but so offensive that it was absolutely necessary to take some step, as no one intervened for my protection from a persecution most odious to a woman.[2] After much consideration, it seemed to me best to send to (not a newspaper, but) a scientific journal, a simple narrative of the facts,—making no allusion to any thing already published, but so offering the story as to

---

[1]   The letters appeared in the *Athenæum* from November 23 to December 21, 1844, and were then published as *Letters on Mesmerism* (London: Edward Moxon, 1845).

[2]   In addition to her mother and sister Elizabeth, Dr. Thomas Greenhow's nephew, Headlam Greenhow (1814–88), also a surgeon, opposed mesmerism and published a derogatory statement in the *Athenæum* after the appearance of Martineau's letters.

lift it out of the professional mire into which it had been dragged, and to place it on its right ground as a matter of scientific observation. This was the act which was called 'rushing into print.'

The conduct of the editor[1] who accepted and profited by my 'Letters on Mesmerism' is so capital an illustration of the mode in which I and my coadjutors were treated on this occasion, and of that in which persons concerned in any new natural discovery are usually treated, that it may be profitable to give a brief statement of the facts as a compendium of the whole subject.—I wrote to one of the staff of the *Athenæum*, saying that I found it necessary to write my experience; and that I preferred a periodical like the Athenæum to a newspaper, because I wanted to lift up the subject out of the dirt into which it had been plunged, and to place it on a scientific ground, if possible. I said that I was aware that the editor of the Athenæum was an unbeliever in mesmerism; but that this was no sufficient reason for my concluding that his periodical would be closed against a plain story on a controverted subject. I begged, at the outset, to say that I could take no money for my articles, under the circumstances; and that, if it was the rule of the Athenæum, as of some publications, to take no contributions that were not paid for, perhaps the editor might think fit to give the money to some charity. What I did require, I said, was, that my articles should appear unaltered, and that they and I should be treated with the respect due to the utterance and intentions of a conscientious and thoughtful observer. I hold the reply, in the hand-writing of the editor, who eagerly accepted the proposed articles; and agreed without reserve to my conditions. The six 'Letters' that I sent carried six numbers of the Athenæum through three editions. Appended to the last was a string of comments by the editor, insulting and slanderous to the last degree. For a course of weeks and months from that time, that periodical assailed the characters of my mesmeriser and of my fellow-patient, the excellent girl whom I before described.[2] It held out inducements to two medical men to terrify some of the witnesses, and traduce others, till the controversy expired in the sheer inability of the honest party to compete with rogues who stuck at no falsehoods: and finally, the Athenæum gave public notice that it would receive communications from our adversaries, and not from us. Meantime, Mr. Moxon wrote to ask me to allow him to reprint the

---

[1] Charles Wentworth Dilke (1789–1864), editor of the *Athenæum*, ridiculed Martineau's cure by mesmerism in the issue of December 28, 1844, just after the last of Martineau's letters had appeared.

[2] Jane Arrowsmith, her maid and mesmeristic assistant, was ridiculed primarily for her prediction of the outcome of a shipwreck while in a mesmeric state.

'Letters' as a pamphlet; and I gave permission, declining to receive any profit from the sale. While the 'Letters' were reprinting, the editor of the Athenæum actually wrote, and then sent his lawyer, to forbid Mr. Moxon to proceed, declaring that he claimed the property of the 'Letters' by which he had already pocketed so large a profit. Of course the claim was absurd,—nothing having been paid for the articles,—which I had also told the editor it was my intention to allow to be reprinted. The editor finally stooped to say that I did not know that he had not given money on account of the 'Letters' to some charity: but, when we asked whether he had, there was no reply forthcoming. Mr. Moxon of course proceeded in his re-publication, and the editor gained nothing by his move but the reputation, wherever the facts were known, of having achieved the most ill-conditioned transaction, in regard to principle, temper and taste, known to any of those who read his letters, public and private, or heard the story.—As for me, what I did was this. When I found that a conscientious witness has no chance against unscrupulous informers, I ceased to bandy statements in regard to the characters of my coadjutors: (nobody attacked mine)[1] but I took measures which would avail to rectify the whole business, if it should ever become necessary to any of the injured parties to do so. I sent my solicitor to one of the unscrupulous doctors, to require from him a retractation of his original statement. This retractation, obtained in

[1]   Martineau appended this footnote: "The only doubtful point, as far as I know, about my own accuracy is one which is easily explained. I explained it in private letters at the time, but had no opportunity of doing more. My medical attendant charged me with first desiring that he should publish my case, and then being wroth with him for doing so. The facts are these. He spoke to me about sending an account of the case to a Medical Journal: I could not conceive why he consulted me about it; and I told him so; saying that I believed the custom was for doctors to do what they thought proper about such a proceeding; and that, as the patients are not likely ever to hear of such a use of their case, it does not, in fact, concern them at all. Some time after, he told me he was going to do it; and the very letter in which he said so enclosed one of the many very disagreeable applications at that time sent both to him and me from medical men, —requesting to know the facts of the case. My reply was that I was glad he was going to relieve me of such correspondence by putting his statement where medical men could learn what they wanted better than from me.— He then or afterwards changed his mind, forgetting to tell me so; and published the case,— not in a Medical Journal, where nobody but the profession would ever have seen it, and where I should never have heard of it,—but in a shilling pamphlet,—not even written in Latin,—but open to all the world! When, in addition to such an act as this, he declared that it was done under my sanction, I had much ado to keep any calmness at all. But the sympathy of all the world,—even of the medical profession,—was by this act secured to me: and the whole affair presently passed from my mind. The only consequence was that I could never again hold intercourse with one from whom I had so suffered." The pamphlet that her brother-in-law, T.M. Greenhow, published was "Medical Report of the Case of Miss H— M—" (Newcastle: E. Charney, 1845; London: Samuel Highley, 1845).

the presence, and under the sanction, of the doctor's witness (his pastor) I now hold, in the slanderer's own hand-writing: and it effectually served to keep him quiet henceforward.[1] I hold also an additional legal declaration which establishes the main fact on which the somnambule's story of the shipwreck was attempted to be overthrown. The whole set of documents has been shown to a great variety of people,—lawyers and clergymen, among others; and all but medical men have declared, under one form of expression or another, that the evidence is as strong as evidence can be on any transaction whatever. One eminent lawyer told me that the twelve Judges would be unanimous in regard to the truth of the parties concerned, and the certainty of the facts, from the documents which were offered to the public, and the two or three which I have held in readiness to fill up any gaps of which we were not in the first instance aware.—Such a persecution could hardly be repeated now, in regard to the particular subject,—after the great amount of evidence of the facts of mesmerism which the intervening years have yielded; but it will be repeated in regard to every new discovery of a power or leading fact in nature. Human pride and prejudice cannot brook discoveries which innovate upon old associations, and expose human ignorance; and, as long as any thing in the laws of the universe remains to be revealed, there is a tolerable certainty that somebody will yet be persecuted, whatever is the age of the world. We may hope, however, that long before that, men will have become ashamed of allowing rapacity and bad faith to make use of such occasions, as the Athenæum did in the year 1844.—I may just mention that the editor was an entire stranger to me. I had never had any acquaintance with him then; and I need not say that I have desired none since.

I was as familiar as most people with the old story of the unkindly reception of new truth in natural or moral science. I had talked and moralized, like every body else, on the early Christians, on Galileo, on Harvey and his discovery, and so forth:[2] but it all came upon me like novelty when I saw it so near, and in a certain degree, though slightly, felt it myself. It is a very great privilege to have such an experience; and especially to one who, like me, is too anxious for sympathy, and for the good opinion of personal friends. That season of recovery was one of most profitable discipline to me. At times my heart would swell that people could be so cruel to sufferers, like poor Jane and myself, recovering from years of hopeless pain; and again my spirit rose against the

---

[1] Headlam Greenhow is the "slanderer" referred to here.

[2] I.e., on the reception of Christianity, Galileo's discovery of the sun as the center of our solar system, and Harvey's theory of the circulation of blood.

rank injustice of attempting to destroy reputations in a matter of scientific inquiry. But, on the whole, my strength kept up very well. I kept to myself my quiverings at the sight of the postman, and of newspapers and letters. After the first stab of every new insult, my spirit rose, and shed forth the *vis medicatrix*[1] of which we all carry an inexhaustible fountain within us. I knew, steadily, and from first to last, that we were right,—my coadjutors and I. I knew that we were secure as to our facts and innocent in our intentions: and it was my earnest desire and endeavour to be no less right in temper. How I succeeded, others can tell better than I. I only know that my recovery, and the sweet sensations of restored health disposed me to good-humour, and continually reminded me how much I had gained in comparison with what I had to bear. I owed much to the fine example of poor Jane. That good girl, whose health was much less firmly established, at that time, than mine, was an orphan, and wholly dependent on her own industry,—that industry being dependent on her precarious health, and on the character which two or three physicians first, and two or three journalists after them, strove by the most profligate plotting,[2] to deprive her of. They tried to confound her with a woman of loose character; they bullied

---

[1] Usually, *vis medicatrix naturae*, "the healing power of nature."

[2] Martineau inserted this footnote: "I think I ought to relate the anecdote alluded to, to show what treatment medical men inflict on women of any rank who have recourse to mesmerism.—A girl called on my mesmeriser (the widow of a clergyman) to say that a physician of Shields, who had enjoined her not to tell his name, had desired her to ask my friend to mesmerise her for epilepsy. We took time to consider, and found on inquiry that the patient belonged to a respectable family, her brother, with whom she lived, being a banker's clerk, and living in a good house in Tynemouth, with his name on a brass plate on the door. We allowed her to come, attended by her sister; and she was mesmerised with obvious benefit. On the second occasion, two gentlemen from Newcastle were at tea with us. She had been introduced by the name of Ann; and Ann we called her. One of the gentlemen said, in an odd rough way, 'Jane: her name is Jane:' and she said her name was Jane Ann. The next morning, he called, and very properly told us that the girl had been seduced at the age of fifteen, and had been afterwards too well known among the officers of the garrison. On inquiry, we found that she had long been repentant and reformed, so that she was now an esteemed member of the Methodist body; so we did not dismiss her to disease and death, but, with the sanction of my landlady, let her come while we remained at Tynemouth,—taking care so to admit her as that our own Jane should not see her again.—Some weeks after I had left Tynemouth, I was written to by a clergyman at Derby, who thought I ought to know what was doing by the 'first physician in Derby.' He was driving about, telling his patients, as by authority, about our Tynemouth proceedings. Among other things, he related that he was informed *by a physician at Shields*, that those proceedings of ours were most disreputable, as 'Jane of Tynemouth was a girl of loose character, too well known among the officers there.' The plot was now clear: and surely the story needs no comment. What were my wrongs, in comparison with my good Jane's?" The mesmeriser referred to in the second sentence was Mrs. Montague Wynyard.

and threatened her; they tried to set her relations against her. But she said cheerfully that people ought not to grumble at having some penalty to pay for such blessings as rescue from blindness and restoration to health by a new method; and, moreover, that they should be glad to tell the truth about it, under any abuse, and to spread the blessing if they could. So she bore her share very quietly, and with wonderful courage resisted the bullies who waited for my separation from her to frighten her into concessions: and, from that day to this, her healing hand, her time and her efforts have ever been at the service of the sick, to not a few of whom she has been a benefactress in their time of need. She has long been valued as she deserved; and she has probably forgotten that season of trial of her temper: but I felt at the time that I should never forget it; and I never have.

I was much aided and comforted during the five months that my recovery was proceeding by the visits of friends who knew more about mesmerism than I did, and who entirely approved my recourse to it. Among others came a gentleman and his wife whose name and connexions were well known to me,[1] but whom I had not chanced ever to meet. The gentleman was one of the very earliest inquirers into mesmerism in England in our time; and he was a practiced operator. He came out of pure benevolence, at the suggestion of a mutual friend who saw, and who told him, that this was a case of life and death, which might terminate according to the preponderance of discouragement from my own neighbouring family, or encouragement from those who understood the subject better. He came, bringing his wife; and their visit was not the less pleasant for the urgent need of it being almost past. They found me going on well under the hands of the kind lady who was restoring me. But it is clear that even then we were so moderate in our hopes as not to expect any thing like complete restoration. When they bade us farewell, we talked of meeting again at Tynemouth,—having no idea of my ever leaving the place; and in truth a journey did then appear about the most impossible of all achievements. A few weeks later, however, we had agreed that I should confirm my recovery by change of scene, and that the scene should be Windermere, on the shores of which my new friends were then living. They kindly urged their invitation on the ground that I must not give up being mesmerised suddenly or too soon, and that in their house there

---

[1]   William R. Greg (1809–81), essayist and mesmerist, and his wife lived in the Lake District at Wansfell, east of the village of Ambleside where Martineau eventually settled and built her home, The Knoll.

would be every facility for its daily use. So, early in January, 1845, my mesmeriser[1] and I left Tynemouth, little thinking that I should never return to it. I had no sooner left my late home, however, than the evil spirit broke out so strongly, in the medical profession and in the discontented part of the family, that the consideration was forced upon me—why I should go back. There was indeed no attraction whatever but the sea; and if there had been every thing that there was not,—society, books, fine scenery, &c.,—they could have been no compensation for non-intercourse with the relations who were disconcerted at my mode of recovery.

My first anxiety was to ascertain whether, in the opinion of the family, my mother should be left undisturbed in her present arrangements at Liverpool, or whether I had further services to render to her. To allow time for the fullest understanding on this head, I resolved to spend six months or more in visiting those of my family who had approved my proceedings, and in lodgings near Windermere; [2] after which, I would determine on my course of life.

One wintry morning, while walking to Waterhead with my host, we said 'what wonderful things do come to pass!' We looked back to that day twelve-months, when I was lying, sick and suffering for life, as every body supposed, on my couch at Tynemouth; and we wondered what I should have said if any prophet had told me that that day twelve months I should be walking in a snow storm, with a host whom I had then never seen, looking for lodgings in which to undergo my transformation into a Laker![3]

---

[1] Elizabeth Montague Wynyard, described in a letter of September 16, 1844, to Elizabeth Barrett as "a first-rate mesmerist," "a benevolent lady," and "widow of a clergyman" (see Sanders, ed., *Letters*, p. 106).

[2] Some of this time was spent with her brother Robert and his family in Birmingham; some was spent in lodgings at Waterhead, where she could be near the Gregs and within walking distance of the Arnolds and Wordsworths.

[3] The term "Laker" was used for poets like Wordsworth and Coleridge, who lived in the Lake District, and more generally for any resident of the region. Waterhead, at the north end of Lake Windermere, was the starting place for steamers across the lake.

SIXTH PERIOD

SECTION I

My life, it has been seen, began with winter. Then followed a season of storm and sunshine, merging in a long gloom. If I had died of that six years' illness, I should have considered my life a fair average one, as to happiness,—even while thinking more about happiness, and caring more for it, than I do now. I did not know, ten years ago,[1] what life might be, in regard to freedom, vigour, and peace of mind; and, not knowing this, I should have died in the persuasion that I had been, on the whole, as happy as the conditions of human existence allow. But the spring, summer, and autumn of life were yet to come. I have had them now,— all rapidly succeeding each other, and crowded into a small space, like the Swedish summer, which bursts out of a long winter with the briefest interval of spring. At past forty years of age, I began to relish life, without drawback; and for ten years I have been vividly conscious of its delights, as undisturbed by cares as my anxious nature, and my long training to trouble could permit me ever to be. I believe there never was before any time in my life when I should not have been rather glad than sorry to lay it down. During this last sunny period, I have not acquired any dread or dislike of death; but I have felt, for the first time, a keen and unvarying relish of life. It seems to be generally supposed that a relish of life implies a fear or dislike of death, except in the minds of those shallow and self-willed persons who expect to step over the threshold of death into just the same life that they quitted,—with the same associates, employments, recreations,—the same every thing, except natural scenery. But this does not at all agree with my experience. I have no expectation of that kind,—nor personal expectation of any kind after death; and I have a particularly keen relish of life,—all the keener for being late: yet now, while in daily expectation of death, I certainly feel

---

[1]   Martineau wrote Period VI in 1855, ten years after recovering from her Tynemouth illness. Early that year, she consulted two heart specialists, Dr. Peter Mere Latham (1789–1875) and Sir Thomas Watson (1792–1882), who concluded that she had a "mortal disease" (*Autobiography*, p. 35). Latham was physician extraordinary to Queen Victoria and author of *Lectures on Subjects Connected with Clinical Medicine, Comprising Diseases of the Heart* (London, 1845).

no dislike or dread of it; nor do I find my pleasant daily life at all over-shadowed by the certainty that it is near its end. If this seems strange to people who hold other views than mine, their baseless conclusions,—that I must dread death because I enjoy life, —appear no less strange to me. They surely do not refuse to enjoy any other pleasure because it must come to an end; and why this? And if they feel sad as the end of other pleasures draws near, it is because they anticipate feeling the absence and the blank. Thus, we grieve, and cannot but grieve, at the death of a friend, whose absence will leave a blank in our life: but the laying down our own life, to yield our place to our successors, and simply ceasing to be, seems to me to admit of no fear or regret; except through the corruption introduced by false and superstitious associations. I suppose we must judge, each for ourselves, in such matters: but I cannot but remember that I have gone through the Christian experience in regard to the expectation of death, and feel that I understand it, while Christians have not experienced, and I perceive do not understand, my present view and feeling in the expectation of death. But if they care to have my own statement, they are welcome to it. It is what I have said:—that for ten years I have had as keen a relish of life as I believe my nature to be capable of; and that I feel no reluctance whatever to pass into noth-ingness, leaving my place in the universe to be filled by another. The very conception of *self* and *other* is, in truth, merely human, and when the self ceases to be, the distinction expires.

I remember that when the prospect of health and prolonged life opened before me, there was a positive drawback, and a serious one, in the dread of having the whole thing to go over again, some time or other. I had recourse to desperate comforts under this apprehension. I hoped I might die by a railway crash, or some other sudden accident; or that I might sink away in mere old age; or I trusted that time might somehow make some change. I little thought how short a time would make so vast a change! I little thought that in ten years I should find myself far more fatally ill, without the slightest reluctance, and with the gayest feeling that really it does not matter whether I feel ill or well,—(short of acute and protracted pain, of which I have still a great dread) if only other people are not made unhappy. All the solemn, doleful feeling about my suffer-ings, which seemed right and appropriate, if not religious, a dozen years ago, now appears selfish, and low, and a most needless infliction on myself and others. Once become aware of how little consequence it is, and how the universe will go on just the same, whether one dies at fifty or seventy, one looks gaily on the last stage of one's subjection to the great laws of nature,—notes what one can of one's state for the benefit of others, and enjoys the amusement of watching the course of human affairs from one's fresh and airy point of view, above the changes of the elements with which one has no further personal concern. The objective and disinterested contemplation of eternity is, in my apprehension, the sublimest pleasure that human faculties are capable of; and the pleasure is most vivid and real when one's disinterestedness is most necessary and complete,—that is, when our form of its life is about to dissolve, to make way for another.

After spending a month on the shores of Windermere, I went for a long visit to my dear elder brother's, some of whose children had grown up from infancy to youth during my illness.[1] He and his wife had attached me to them more than ever by their recent conduct. Thinking me right in my effort to recover health, and wronged in much of the treatment I had received, they upheld me steadily and effectually, while, at the same time, they saw how the wrong was mainly owing to prejudice and want of the knowledge pertinent to the case; and they therefore did not find it necessary to quarrel with any body. I thought then, and I think now, that they were just and kind all round; and I am sure they were no small assistance to me in keeping my temper. They took a great interest in the subject of mesmerism, and enjoyed seeing its operation in cases similar to my own, and in many others, in which sufferers, pronounced incurable by the doctors, were restored as I had been. One amusement to us all at that time was the pity with which the doctors regarded me. I could quote several medical men who reasoned that, *as* my disease was an incurable one, I could not possibly be radically better; that I was then in a state of exhilaration, infatuation, and so forth; and that in six months (or three months or a year, as might be) I should be as ill as ever, and mourning over my having been duped by the mesmerists. Now and then we heard, or saw in the newspapers, that I *was* as ill as ever, and mourning my infatuation,—though I was walking five or seven miles at a time, and giving every evidence of perfect health. The end of it was that I went off to the East,— into the depths of Nubia, and traversing Arabia on a camel; and then the doctors said I had never been ill![2] It is very curious,—this difficulty of

---

[1]   Robert Martineau (1798–1870) and his wife Jane, née Smith (d. 1874), had six children: Susan (b. 1826), Maria (b. 1827), Thomas (b. 1828), Robert Francis (b. 1831), Jane (b. 1832), and Edward (b. 1834). As Martineau testifies, they remained good friends and avoided family disputes—as her siblings Elizabeth and James did not.

[2]   In 1846–47 Martineau traveled in northern Africa and the Middle East with Richard V. Yates (1785–1856) of Liverpool, his wife, and Joseph C. Ewart (1799–1868), later M.P. for Liverpool. On her return she wrote *Eastern Life, Present and Past* (London: Edward Moxon, 1848), which treats Judaism and Christianity from a historical perspective, not as divine revelation.

admitting evidence about any new, or newly revived, fact in nature. I remember Mr. Hallam (the last man open to the charge of credulity) telling me at Tynemouth a story which struck me very much. He told me how he and his friend Mr. Rogers had had the privilege of witnessing that very rare spectacle, 'the reception by a great metropolis, of the discovery of a pregnant natural fact.'[1] He told me,—and he has so manfully told plenty of other people, that I am betraying no confidence in repeating the story once more,—that Mr. Rogers and he had, many years before, seen some mesmeric facts in Paris which convinced and impressed them for life. When they returned, they told what they had seen, and were met by such insulting ridicule that they were compelled to be silent, or to quarrel with some of their pleasantest friends. One physician in particular he named, who treated them at his own table in a way which prevented their ever again communicating their knowledge to him, if they wished to remain on civil terms with him. By degrees, in course of years, facts became known; higher scientific authorities on the continent declared themselves convinced, or in favour of that genuine inquiry which has always ended in conviction; and the tone of London society began to change. The physician referred to ceased to gibe and jeer, and sat silent and embarrassed while the subject was discussed; and at length began to ask questions, and show a desire to learn: 'and now,' continued Mr. Hallam, 'we can say that we are acquainted with nobody who has attended to the subject with any earnestness who does not consider certain facts of mesmerism to be as completely established as any facts whatever in the whole range of science.' He added, 'this reception of a great truth is a great thing to have seen.'—In a note I had from Mr. Hallam before I left Tynemouth, he declared his view to be this. 'I have no doubt that mesmerism, and some other things which are not mesmerism properly so-called, are fragmentary parts of some great law of the human frame which we are on the verge of discovering.' It appears to be the method of the London doctors now to admit the facts (being unable longer to suppress them) and to account for them, each according to his own favourite physiological view; and thus the truth is near its full admission. When the facts are admitted in London, the medical men in the provinces will not long continue to scoff and perpetrate slander: and when a score of commentators on a single class of facts offer a score of explanations, the true solution is so much needed that it must soon be obtained.

---

[1]   Henry Hallam (1777–1859), the historian, and Samuel Rogers (1763–1855), the poet. See Period IV, sec. ii for Martineau's reminiscences of these two London friends.

Amidst the happiness of my visit at my brother's, I felt a really painful longing to see verdure and foliage. On leaving Newcastle, I had been carried swiftly past a railway embankment covered with broom; and the dark green of that bank made my heart throb at the time, and bred in me a desperate longing to see more. I did not think I could have wished so much for any thing as I did to see foliage. I had not seen a tree for above five years, except a scrubby little affair which stood above the haven at Tynemouth, exposed to every wind that blew, and which looked nearly the same at midsummer and Christmas. It was this kind of destitution which occasioned some of the graceful acts of kindness which cheered my Tynemouth sojourn. An old friend sent me charming coloured sketches of old trees in Sherwood Forest: and an artist who was an entire stranger to me, Mr. McIan, stayed away from a day's excursion at a friend's house in the country, to paint me a breezy tree.[1] For months the breezy tree was pinned up on the wall before me, sending many a breeze through my mind. But now I wanted to see a real tree in leaf; and I had to wait sadly long for it. The spring of 1846 was the latest I remember, I think,—unless it be the present one (1855). My impatience must have been very apparent, for my sister-in-law 'fooled' me, when I came down to breakfast on the 1st of April, with lamentations about 'the snow under the acacia.' There was no snow there; but the hedges seemed dead for ever; and there was scarcely a tinge of green on them when I left Edgbaston[2] for Nottingham, on the second of May.

There,—at Lenton, near Nottingham,—new pleasures awaited me. Spring is always charming on the Trent meadows at Nottingham, where the clear shoaly river runs between wide expanses of meadow, where crocuses almost hide the grass for a few weeks of the year. It was an unspeakable pleasure to me to move freely about blossoming gardens; but no one but a restored invalid can conceive what it was to ramble for miles, to Clifton woods, or to Woollaton, drinking in the sunshine in the fields, and the cool shade under the green avenues.[3] Now, at the end of ten years, I do not find my thirst for foliage fully quenched, after the long absence at Tynemouth. There were excursions from Nottingham to Newstead

[1]   Robert Ronald McIan (d. 1856), Scottish painter best known for his *Clans of the Scottish Highlands* (London: Ackerman, 1845–47).

[2]   The Robert Martineau family lived in Edgbaston, near (now in) Birmingham, where he owned a brass foundry and nail factory. In 1846, when Martineau visited, Robert was Lord Mayor of Birmingham.

[3]   Catherine Turner, née Rankin (1797–1852), Harriet's cousin on her mother's side, lived in Lenten, near (now in) Nottingham. Clifton and Wollaton are nearby villages.

and elsewhere,—all delightful; but I don't know that I had not more pleasure from the common lawn, with the shadows of the trees flickering upon it, than from any change of objects. The surprise to my friends, and also to myself, was that I was so little nervous,—so capable of doing like other people, as if I had not led a sick and hermit life for so many years. This exemption from the penalties of long illness I believe I owe to mesmerism being the means of cure. I had left off all drugs for ten months, except the opiates, which had been speedily reduced from the outset of the experiment, and now discontinued for half a year. I had not therefore to recover from the induced illness and constitutional poisoning caused by drugs; and my nerves had been well strung by the mesmerism which I had now discontinued. I certainly felt at first, when at the Lakes and at Edgbaston, by no means sure that I knew how to behave in society; but old associations soon revived, and I fell into the old habit of social intercourse. It was not very long indeed before we proposed,—my friends and I,—to ignore altogether the five years at Tynemouth,—to call me 38 instead of 43, and proceed as if that awful chasm had never opened in my path which now seemed closed up, or invisible as it lay behind. There were things belonging to it, however, which I should have been sorry to forget, or to lose the vivid sense of; and chief among these was the kindness of a host of friends. I have observed, however, at intervals since, that though the sense of that kindness is as vivid as ever, the other incidents and interests of that term of purgatory have so collapsed as to make the period which seemed in experience to be an eternity, like a momentary blank,—a night of uneasy dreams, soon forgotten between the genuine waking interests of two active days.

With this new day of activity arose a strong fresh interest. It was at Lenton, near Nottingham, that I first saw Mr. Atkinson, whose friendship has been the great privilege of the concluding period of my life. I have told above that Mr. and Mrs. Basil Montagu mentioned him to me in the letter in which they besought me to try mesmerism. I had never heard of him before, as far as I know. I have often said, as I am ready to say again, that I owe my recovery mainly to him,—that my ten last happy years have been his gift to me: but it is not true, as many people have supposed and led others to believe, that I was mesmerised by him at Tynemouth. I am careful in explaining this, because many persons who think it necessary to assign some marvellous reason for my present philosophical views, and who are unwilling to admit that I could have arrived at them by my own means and in my own way, have asserted that Mr. Atkinson was my mesmeriser, and that he infused into me his own views by the power he thus gained over my brain. I might explain that I never was unconscious,—never in the mesmeric sleep,—during the whole process of recovery; but the simplest and most incontestible reply is by dates. I was first mesmerised on the 22nd of June, 1844; I was well in the following November: I went forth on my travels in January, 1845, and first saw Mr. Atkinson on the 24th of May of that year. The case was this. Mr. and Mrs. Montagu, earnest that I should try mesmerism, brought about a meeting at their house, in June, 1844, between Mr. Atkinson and an intimate friend of mine who had visited me, and was about to go to me again. They discussed the case: and from that time Mr. Atkinson's instructions were our guidance. He, too, obtained for me the generous services of the widow lady mentioned above, when my maid's operations were no longer sufficient; and we followed his counsel till I was well. As for the share he had in the ultimate form assumed by my speculations, on their becoming opinions,—he himself expressed it in a saying so curiously resembling one uttered by a former guide and instructor that it is worth quoting both. The more ancient guide said, when I was expressing gratitude to him, 'O! I only helped you to do in a fortnight what you would have done for yourself in six weeks.' Mr. Atkinson said 'I found you out of the old ways, and I showed you the shortest way round the corner—that's all.' I certainly knew nothing of his philosophical opinions when we met at Lenton; and it was not till the close of 1847, when, on my setting about my book on Egypt, I wrote him an account of my opinions, and how I came by them, and he replied by a somewhat similar confidence, that I had any clear knowledge what his views were. I shall probably have more to say about this hereafter. Meantime, this is the place for explaining away a prevalent mistake as to my recovery having been wrought by the mesmerising of a friend whom I had, in fact, never seen.

I vividly remember the first sight of him, when one of my hostesses and I having gone out to meet him, and show him the way, saw him turn the corner into the lane, talking with the gardener who was conveying his carpet-bag. He also carried a bag over his shoulder. He looked older than I expected, and than I knew he was. His perfect gentlemanliness is his most immediately striking and uncontested attribute. We were struck with this; and also with a certain dryness in his mode of conversation which showed us at once that he was no sentimentalist; a conviction which was confirmed in proportion as we became acquainted with his habit of thought. We could not exactly call him reserved; for he was willing to converse, and ready to communicate his thoughts; yet we felt it difficult to know him. It was years before I, in particular, learned to know him, certainly and soundly, though we were in constant correspondence, and frequently met: but I consider myself no rule for others in the matter. All my faults, and all my peculiarities, were such as might and did conspire to defer the time when I might understand my friend as he was perfectly willing to be understood. One of the bad consequences of my deafness has been the making me far too much of a talker: and, though friends whom I can trust aver that I am also a good listener, I certainly have never allowed a fair share of time and opportunity to slower and more modest and considerate speakers. I believe that, amidst the stream of talk I poured out upon him, it was impossible for him to suppose or believe how truly and earnestly I really did desire to hear his views and opinions; and as, in spite of this, he did tell me much which I thought over, and talked over when he was gone, it is plain that he was not reserved with me. A yet greater impediment to our mutual understanding was that I, hitherto alone in my pursuit of philosophy, had no sufficient notion of other roads to it than that which I had found open before me; and Mr. Atkinson's method was so wholly different that it took me, prepossessed as I was, a very long time to ascertain his route and ultimate point of view. I had, for half my life, been astray among the metaphysicians, whose schemes I had at my tongue's end, and whose methods I supposed to be the only philosophical ones. I at first took Mr. Atkinson's disregard of them and their methods for ignorance of what they had done, as others who think themselves philosophers have done since. Let it not be supposed that I set this down without due shame. I have much to blush for in this matter, and in worse. I now and then proffered him in those days information from my metaphysical authors, for which he politely thanked me, leaving me to find out in time how he knew through and through the very matters which the metaphysicians had barely sketched the outside of. In truth, he at his Baconian point of view, and I at my metaphysical, were in our attempts to understand each other something like beings whose reliance is on a different sense,—those who hear well and those who see well,—meeting to communicate. When the blind with their quick ears, and the deaf and dumb with their alert eyes meet, the consequences usually are desperate quarrels. In our case, I was sometimes irritated; and when irritated, always conceited and wrong; but my friend had patience with me, seeing what was the matter, and knowing that there were grand points of agreement between us which would secure a thorough understanding, sooner or later. If, amidst my metaphysical wanderings I had reached those points of agreement, there was every reason to suppose that when

I had found the hopelessness of the metaphysical point of view, with its uncertain method and infinite diversity of conclusions,—corresponding with the variety of speculators,—I should find the true exterior point of view, the positive method, and its uniform and reliable conclusions. In this faith, and in wonderful patience, my friend bore with my waywardness and occasional sauciness, till at length we arrived at a complete understanding. When our book,—our 'Letters on Man's Nature and Development,'[1]—came out, and was abused in almost every periodical in the kingdom, it amused me to see how very like my old self the metaphysical reviewers were;—how exclusively they fastened on the collateral parts of the book, leaving its method, and all its essential part, wholly untouched. It is a curious fact that, of all the multitude of adverse reviewers of our book that we read, there was not one that took the least notice of its essential part,—its philosophical Method. Scarcely any part of it indeed was touched at all, except the anti-theological portion, which was merely collateral.

Such was my method of criticism of Mr. Atkinson, on the first occasion of our meeting. As we walked up and down a green alley in the garden, he astonished and somewhat confounded me by saying how great he thought the mistake of thinking so much and so artificially as people are for ever striving to do about death and about living again. Not having yet by any means got out of the atmosphere of selfishness which is the very life of Christian doctrine, and of every theological scheme, I was amazed at his question,—what it could signify whether we, with our individual consciousness, lived again? I asked what could possibly signify so much,—being in a fluctuating state then as to the natural grounds of expectation of a future life, (I had long given up the scriptural) but being still totally blind to the selfish instincts involved in such anxiety as I felt about the matter. I was, however, in a certain degree struck by the nobleness of his larger view, and by the good sense of the doctrine that our present health of mind is all the personal concern that we have with our state and destiny: that our duties lie before our eyes and close to our hands; and that our business is with what we know, and have it in our charge to do, and not at all with a future which is, of its own nature, impenetrable. With grave interest and

---

[1]   *Letters on the Laws of Man's Nature and Development* (1851). The book was criticized for, among other things, its attack on dogmatic Christianity, its rejection of immortality and an afterlife, its reliance on science and Baconian method, and its insistence that humans can know nothing but phenomena and the laws that govern them. "There is no God," Douglas Jerrold quipped, "and Harriet is his prophet."

an uneasy concern, I talked this over afterwards with my hostess.[1] At first she would not credit my account of Mr. Atkinson's view; and then she was exceedingly shocked, and put away the subject. I, for my part, soon became able to separate the uneasiness of contravened associations from that of intellectual opposition. I soon perceived that this outspoken doctrine was in full agreement with the action of my mind for some years past, on the particular subject of a future life; and that, when once Christianity ceases to be entertained as a scheme of salvation, the question of a future life becomes indeed one of which every large-minded and unselfish person may and should say, —'What does it signify?' Amidst many alternations of feeling, I soon began to enjoy breathings of the blessed air of freedom from superstition,—which is the same thing as freedom from personal anxiety and selfishness;—that freedom, under a vivid sense of which my friend and I, contrasting our superstitious youth with our emancipated maturity, agreed that not for the universe would we again have the care of our souls upon our hands.

At length, the last day of May arrived, and my longings for my Lake lodgings were to be gratified. The mossy walls with their fringes of ferns; the black pines reflected in the waters: the amethyst mountains at sunset, and the groves and white beaches beside the lake had haunted me almost painfully, all spring; and my hosts and hostesses must have thought my unconcealable anticipations somewhat unmannerly. They could make allowance for me, however: and they sent much sympathy with me. It was truly a gay life that was before me now. My intention was not to work at all; an intention which I have never been able to fulfil when in health, and which soon gave way now, before a call of duty which I very grudgingly obeyed. On the day of my arrival at Waterhead, however, I had no idea of working; and the prospect before me was of basking in the summer sunshine, and roving over hill and dale in fine weather, and reading and working beside the window overlooking the lake (Windermere) in rainy hours, when lakes have a beauty of their own. My lodging, taken for six months, was the house which stands precisely at the head of the lake, and whose grass-plat is washed by its waters.[2] The view from the windows of my house was wonderfully beautiful,— one feature being a prominent rock, crowned with firs, which so projected into the lake as to be precisely reflected in the crimson, orange

---

[1]   Catherine Turner was the widow of Henry Turner, formerly Unitarian pastor of Hanover Square Chapel, Newcastle.

[2]   The house, owned by Mrs. Jackson Thompson, had six bedrooms as well as dining and sitting rooms.

and purple waters when the pine-crest rose black into the crimson, orange, and purple sky, at sunset. When the young moon hung over those black pines, the beauty was so great that I could hardly believe my eyes. On the day of my arrival, when I had met my new maid from Dublin (my Tynemouth nurse being unable to leave her mother's neighbourhood),[1] and when I had been welcomed by a dear old friend or two, I found an intoxicating promise of bliss whichever way I turned. I was speedily instructed in the morality of lakers,—the first principle of which is (at least, so they told me) never to work except in bad weather. The woods were still full of wild anemones and sorrel, and the blue bells were just coming out. The meadows were emerald green, and the oaks were just exchanging their May-golden hue for light green, when the sycamores, so characteristic of the region, were growing sombre in their massy foliage. The friends whom I had met during my winter visit were kind in their welcome; and many relations and friends came that summer, to enjoy excursions with me. It was all very gay and charming; and if I found the bustle of society a little too much,—if I felt myself somewhat disappointed in regard to the repose which I had reckoned on, that blessing was, as I knew, only deferred.

As to this matter,—of society. There is a perpetual change going on in such neighbourhoods in the Lake District as that of Ambleside. Retired merchants and professional men fall in love with the region, buy or build a house, are in a transport with what they have done, and, after a time, go away. In five or six years, six houses of friends or acquaintance of mine became inhabited by strangers. Sorry as I was, on each occasion, to lose good friends or pleasant acquaintances, I did not call on their successors,—nor on any other new-comers: nor did I choose, from the beginning, to visit generally in Ambleside. When I made up my mind to live there, I declined the dinner and evening engagements offered to me, and visited at only three or four houses; and very sparingly at those. It did not suit me to give parties, otherwise than in the plainest and most familiar way; and I had some idea of the mischiefs and dangers of such society as is found promiscuously cast into a small neighbourhood like this. I had not time to waste in meeting the same people,—not chosen as in London, but such as chanced to be thrown together in a very small country town,—night after night: I was aware how nearly impossible it is to keep out of the gossip and

---

[1]   Martineau had two maids: Jane Arrowsmith from Tynemouth and Martha Fulcher Andrews, originally from Norfolk.

the quarrels which prevail in such places; and there was no adequate reason for encountering them. I foresaw that among a High-church squirearchy, and Low-church evangelicals, and the moderate-church few, who were timid in proportion to their small numbers, I might be tolerated, and even courted at first, on account of my reputation, but must sooner or later give deadly offence by some outbreak of heresy or reforming tendency, stronger than they could bear. I therefore confined my visiting to three or four houses, merely exchanging calls with others: and it is well I did. Of those three or four, scarcely one could endure my avowal of my opinions in 1851. Even with them, I had before ceased, or did then cease, to exchange hospitalities.[1] As they had sought me, and even urgently pressed themselves upon me (one family in particular, whose mere name I had never heard when I arrived), they were especially in need of my compassion at the plight they found themselves in,—with goodness of heart enough to remember that our acquaintance was all of their seeking, but with too much narrowness and timidity to keep up intercourse through such opprobrium as my opinions brought on me among their High-church neighhours. They had the shame (which I believe them to be capable of feeling) of being aware, and knowing that *I* was aware, that they sought me, as they are wont to seek and flatter all celebrities, for my fame, and to gratify their own love of excitement; and that their weakness stood confessed before the trial of my plain avowal of honest opinions. It made no difference that, after a time, when the gossip had blown over, and my neighbours saw that I did not want them, and did not depend on their opinions in any way, they came round, and began to be attentive and kind;—their conduct at a moment of crisis proved to me that I had judged rightly in declining Ambleside visiting from the beginning; and their mutual quarrelling, fierce and wide and deep, certainly confirmed my satisfaction with my independent plan of life. My interests lay among old friends at a distance; and I had as much social intercourse as I at all desired when they came into the district. I was amused and instructed by the words of an ingenuous young friend, who, taking leave of me

---

[1]   These neighbors included Mrs. Eliza Fletcher and her daughter, Mrs. John Davy, wife of Dr. John Davy. In a letter of 25 October 1852 to Mary Carpenter, Elizabeth Gaskell wrote that both women "have thought it right to decline intercourse with Miss Martineau, (except for causes of humanity,) since the publication of her book"; see letter 138, *The Letters of Mrs Gaskell*, ed. J.A.V. Chapple and Arthur Pollard (Manchester: Manchester UP, 1966). Some members of the Arnold family disapproved of the book co-authored with Atkinson, but did not break relations. In the "Memorials," Maria Chapman states, "Her friends outside of Unitarianism were not wrathful or distressed" (III, 320).

one winter afternoon at her own gate, said: 'Ah! now,—you are going home to a comfortable quiet evening by your own fire! Really, I think it is quite hypocritical in us!—We dress and go out, and seem to be so pleased, when we are longing all the time to be at home! We meet the same people, who have only the same talk; and we get *so* tired!' It was not long before that family withdrew from the Ambleside visiting which I had always declined. A very few faithful friends, whose regard did not depend on the popular nature of my opinions, remained true and dear to me; and thus I found that book—the 'Atkinson Letters,'— do me the same good and welcome service in my own valley that it did in the wide world;—it dissolved all false relations, and confirmed all true ones. Finally, now that that business has long been settled, and that all my other affairs are drawing near their close, I may make my decla- ration that I have always had as much society as I wished for, and some- times a great deal more. And this leads me to explain why I came to live where I am;—a prodigious puzzle, I am told, to the great majority of my London acquaintance.

When I had been thoroughly and avowedly well for half a year, I found my family had made up their minds, as I had scarcely a doubt that they would, that my mother's settlement at Liverpool had better not be disturbed. She was among three of her children settled there, and she was suited with a companion better adapted to aid her in her nearly blind condition than any deaf person could be. It would have been a most serious and injurious sacrifice to me to live in a provincial town. The choice for me, in regard to my vocation, was between London and a purely country residence. I was partly amused and partly shocked at the amazement of some of my really intimate friends, to whom I supposed my character fully known, at my choosing the latter. One of these friends wrote to me that she could not at all fancy me 'a real coun- try lady'; and another told Mr. Atkinson that she did not believe I had any genuine love of natural scenery. Mr. Hallam told me, some years afterwards, that he and others of my friends had considered my retreat from London, after having known the delights of its society, 'a most doubtful and serious experiment,—a *most* doubtful experiment'; but that they found, by the testimony of mutual friends who had visited me, that it had 'answered completely.'—My reasons are easily told. I was now, when at liberty to form my own plan of life, past the middle of its course. I had seen the dangers and moral penalties of literary life in London for women who had become accustomed to its excitements; and I knew that I could not be happy if I degenerated into 'a hackney-coach

and company life.' No true woman, married or single, *can* be happy without some sort of domestic life;—without having somebody's happiness
dependent on her; and my own ideal of an innocent and happy life was
a house of my own among poor improvable neighbours, with young
servants whom I might train and attach to myself; with pure air, a
garden, leisure, solitude at command, and freedom to work in peace and
quietness. When to all this could be added fine natural scenery, the
temptations were such as London could not rival. If I had country, I
would have the best; and my mind was made up at once,—to live at the
Lakes, —as soon as I was sure of my liberty to choose. I began to look
about in the neighbourhood at cottages to let or on sale. The most
promising was one at Clappersgate, at the head of Windermere, which
was offered me for £20 a year. It had more rooms than I wanted, and
an exceedingly pretty porch; and a little garden, in which was a tempting copper-beech. But the ceilings were too low for my bookcases, and
the house was old; and it commanded no great beauty, except from the
attic windows. A friend who went with me to view it said that £20
was the interest of £500; and that for £500 I could build myself a
cottage after my own heart.[1] This was strikingly true: and thus the idea
of having at once a house of my own was suggested. By the necessity
of the case, the matter was soon settled. A dissenting minister, an opulent
man who had built a chapel and school, and bought a field for cottage-
building, found life too hard for a dissenter among the orthodox at
Ambleside, and especially after he had proposed to supply the want of
cottages which is there the screw which the rich put upon the labouring classes; and, after his health had sunk under the treatment he
encountered, he was obliged to leave the place to save his life. My
house-viewing friend brought me, on the 27th of June, the plan of this
minister's field, which was to be sold in lots the next day but one. The
time was short; but land was becoming rare in the neighbourhood; and
I went to see the field. One of the lots was a rocky knoll, commanding
a charming view. I knew no one whom I could ask to go and bid; and
I could not feel sure of a due supply of water; not knowing then that
wherever there is rock, there is a tolerable certainty of water. The other
lots appeared to me to lie too low for building; and I, in my simplicity,
concluded that the pretty knoll would be the first and surest to sell.
Next day, I found that that lot, and the one at the foot of the rise,

---

[1] Probably William Rathbone Greg (1809–81), with whom Martineau stayed in June, 1845
at Wansfell Holme on Lake Windermere, after recovering from her illness.

remained unsold. I went to the minister for a consultation. His wife satisfied me about the water-supply; and she moreover said that as the other unsold slip, valued at £70, would not sell by itself, if I would buy the Knoll, I should have the other for £20. I agreed on the spot. There was one other three-cornered piece, lying between these and the meadows which were entailed land, certain never to be built on: and this bit had been bought at the sale by an exciseman, to graze his pony when he came his rounds. My friends all agreed in lamenting over that sale, and said the exciseman would soon be running up some hideous structure, to make me pay 'through the nose' for his nook. I replied that I must stop somewhere; and that the matter seemed settled by the land having been sold. It makes me grateful now to think what pains my friends took on my behalf. Mrs. Arnold consulted the Wordsworths;[1] and they all came to exhort me to try to get the nook, for the sake of myself and my heirs; and my original adviser found up the exciseman, and came back with the news that no conveyance had yet been made out, and that the man would let me have the land for a bonus of £5. I whipped out my five sovereigns; and the whole was mine. It may seem that I have gone into much detail about a trifle: but I am giving an account of myself; and there have been few things in my life which have had a more genial effect on my mind than the possession of a piece of land. Those who consider what some scenes of my life had been,—my being left with a single shilling at the time of our losses, my plodding through London mud when I could not get my series published, and my five years' confinement at Tynemouth, may conceive what it was to me to go, in the lustrous days of that summer, to meditate in my field at eventide, and anticipate the healthful and genial life before me. The kind cousin whom I have mentioned as always at my elbow in all time of need, or when a graceful service could be rendered, came with his family to the Lakes at that precise time.[2] Knowing my affairs,—of which he generously took the management,—he approved my scheme; and he did more. I asked him plainly whether he thought me justified in building a house of the kind I explained, and of which I showed him the builder's estimate. He called on me alone one morning,—on business, as he said; and his 'business' was this. He told me that he considered me abundantly justified; he added that there could be no difficulty in obtaining, on such securities as I could offer, whatever additional

---

[1]   Mary Arnold, née Penrose (1791?-1873), widow of Thomas Arnold of Rugby; William and Mary Wordsworth lived at Rydal Mount, about two miles away.
[2]   Richard Martineau, who managed her financial affairs.

money would be requisite for finishing the house (the land was already paid for,) but that, to save trouble and speculation, I had better send in the bills to him; and he would, to save me from all sense of obligation, charge me with interest till I had paid off the whole. The transaction, of which this was the graceful beginning, was no less gracefully carried on and ended. The amount was (as always happens in such cases) more than we expected; and I was longer, owing to the failure of one of my plans, in repaying the loan; but my cousin cheered me by his approbation and sympathy; and at last presented me with the final batch of interest, to purchase something for the house to remember him by.

Then came the amusement of planning my house, which I did all myself. It was the newest of enterprises to me; and seriously did I ponder all the requisites,—how to plan the bedrooms, so that the beds should not be in a draught, nor face the window nor the fireplace, &c. I did not then know the importance of placing beds north and south, in case of illness,[1] when that position may be of the last consequence to the patient; but it so happens that all my beds stand or may stand so. The whole scheme was fortunate and charming. There is not a single blunder or nuisance in my pretty house; and now that it is nearly covered with ivy, roses, passion flowers, and other climbers, and the porch a bower of honeysuckles, I find that several of my neighbours, and not a few strangers, consider my knoll,—position and house together,—the prettiest dwelling in the valley;—airy, gay, and 'sunny within and without,' as one family are pleased to say. 'It is,' said Wordsworth, 'the wisest step in her life; for' ... ... and we supposed he was going on to speak of the respectability, comfort, and charm of such a retreat for an elderly woman; but not so. 'It is the wisest step in her life; for the value of the property will be doubled in ten years.'

One of those London friends whom I have mentioned as doubting my discretion in settling here,[2] was paying me a morning visit at my lodgings when I was planning my house; and while taking a kind interest in looking over the plan and elevation, she thought it right to make a remonstrance which she has since recalled with a generous amusement. 'Now, my dear friend,' said she, 'I take a real interest in all this: but,—do be persuaded,—sell your field, and stay where you are, in this nice lodging. Do, now! Why should you not stay here?'

'First,' said I, 'because it costs me more to live here in three rooms

---

[1]   A popular belief (still current today) that sleeping in one direction (n-s) is more health-ful than others.

[2]   Untraced.

than it would in a whole house of my own.

'Second: there is no room here for my book-cases; and I want my library.

'Third: I am paying for house-room for my furniture at Tynemouth.

'Fourth: this house stands low, and is apt to be flooded and damp in winter.

'Fifth: this house was a barn; and the dust lies a quarter of an inch thick, in some weathers, on every thing in the sitting-room.

'Sixth: the chimney smokes so that I could not have a fire without keeping a window open.

'Seventh: Being close on the margin of the lake, the house is swarming with rats.

'Eighth: ... ... '

'O! stop—stop!' cried my friend, now quite ready to leave my own affairs in my own hands. She long after spent some days with me at the Knoll, and pronounced my house and my scheme of life perfect for me.

SECTION II

———

THE whole business of the house-building went off without a difficulty, or a shadow of misunderstanding throughout. The Contractor proposed his own terms; and they were so reasonable that I had great pleasure in giving him all his own way. It is the pernicious custom of the district to give very long credit, even in the case of workmen's wages. One of my intentions in becoming a housekeeper was to discountenance this, and to break through the custom in my own person. I told all the tradesmen that I would not deal with them on any other terms than ready money payments, alleging the inconvenience to persons of small income of having all their bills pouring in at Candlemas. At first I was grumbled at for the 'inconvenience'; but, before I had lived here two years, I was supplicated for my custom, my reputation being that of being 'the best paymaster in the neighbourhood.' I began with the house itself, offering to pay down £100 every alternate month, on condition that the work-people were paid weekly. At the end, when the contractor received his last £100, I asked him whether he and all his people were fully satisfied, saying that if there was any discontent, however slight, I wished to hear of it, there and then. His answer was 'Ma'am, there has not been a rough

word spoken from beginning to end.''Are *you* satisfied?' I asked.'Entirely,'
he replied.'I underrated the cost of the terrace; but you paid me what I
asked; a bargain is a bargain: and I gained by other parts, so as to make
up for it, and more; and so I am satisfied,—entirely.' When I afterwards
designed to build a cottage and cow-stable, he came to beg the servants
to help to get the job for him,—complimenting my mode of payment.
I mention this because the poor man, whom I greatly esteemed, got his
head turned with subsequent building speculations, fell into drinking
habits, and died of a fever thus brought on,—leaving debts to the amount
of £1,000: and I wish it to be clearly understood that I was in no degree
connected with his misfortunes.

The first sod was turned on the 1st of October, by Mr. Seymour
Tremenheere, in the presence of my elder brother and myself.[1] There
was only one tree on the summit of the knoll; and that was a fine thorn,
which the builder kindly managed to leave, to cover a corner; and I
seldom look at it, powdered with blossom in May and June, without
thinking of the consideration of the poor fellow who lies in the churchyard, so miserably cut off in the vigour of his years. The winter of 1845–6
was (as the potato-rot makes us all remember) the rainiest in the experience of our generation: but the new house was not injured by it; and
it was ready for occupation when April arrived. If I am to give an
account of my most deep-felt pleasures, I may well mention that of my
sunset walks, on the few fine days, when I saw from the opposite side of
the valley the progress of my house. One evening I saw the red sunset
glittering on the windows, which I did not know were in. Another day,
I saw the first smoke from the chimney;—the thin blue smoke from a
fire the workmen had lighted, which gave a home-like aspect to the
dwelling.—When the garden was to take form, new pleasures arose. The
grass was entirely destroyed round the base of the knoll by the carts
which brought the stone and wood; and I much wished for some sods.
But the summer had been as dry as the winter and spring were wet; and
no sods were to be had for love or money,—every gardener assured me.
In riding over Loughrigg terrace,[2] I saw where large patches of turf had
been cut; and I asked Mr. Wordsworth whether one might get sods from
the mountain. He told me that the fells were the property of the dales-
men, and that it takes 100 years to replace turf so cut. So I made up my

---

1   Hugh Seymour Tremenheere (1804–93) was a commissioner appointed to enact Lord
     Ashley's 1842 bill for the protection of women and children working in mines. Robert
     Martineau was, in 1845, her eldest surviving brother.
2   Loughrigg Terrace is a mountainous area at the end of Lake Grasmere.

mind to wait till grass-seed would grow, and wondered how I was to secure the seed being good. One morning, the servants told me that there was a great heap of the finest sods lying under the boundary wall; and that they must have been put over during the night. It was even so: and, though we did our best to watch and listen, the same thing happened four times,—the last load being a very large one, abundantly supplying all our need. A dirty note, wafered, lay under the pile. It pretended to come from two poachers, who professed to be grateful to me for my Game Law Tales,[1] and to have rendered me this service in return for my opinion about wild creatures being fair game. The writing and spelling were like those of an ignorant person; and I supposed that the inditing was really so, at the bidding of some neighbour of higher quality. The Archbishop of Dublin, who was at Fox How at the time,[2] offered me the benefit of his large experience in the sight of anonymous letters: (not the reading of them, for he always burns unread, before the eyes of his servants, all that come to him) and he instantly pronounced that the note was written by an educated person. He judged by the evenness of the lines, saying that persons who scrawl and misspell from ignorance never write straight. Every body I knew declared to me, sooner or later, in a way too sincere to be doubted, that he or she did not know any thing whatever about my sods: and the mystery remains unsolved to this day. It was a very pretty and *piquant* mystery. Several friends planted a young tree each on my ground. Some of the saplings died and some lived: but the most flourishing is one of the two which Wordsworth planted. We had provided two young oaks: but he objected to them as not remarkable enough for a commemorative occasion. We found that the stone pine suited his idea: and a neighbour kindly sent me two. Wordsworth chose to plant them on the slope under my terrace wall, where, in my humble opinion, they were in the extremest danger from dogs and cats,— which are our local nuisance. I lay awake thinking how to protect them. The barriers I put up were broken down immediately; but I saved one by making a parterre round it: and there it flourishes,—so finely that my successor will have to remove my best pear-tree ere long, to leave room for the forest tree.

The planting-scene was characteristic. Wordsworth had taken a

---

[1]   *Forest and Game-Law Tales* (London: Edward Moxon, 1845–46).

[2]   Richard Whately (1787–1863) served as Archbishop of Dublin from 1831 until his death. His close friend, Dr. Thomas Arnold (1795–1842) of Rugby, build Fox How as a family retreat, where Arnold's widow and children lived year-round after his death.

kindly interest in the whole affair; and where my study now is, he had thrown himself down, among the hazel bushes, and talked of the meadows, and of the right aspect and disposition of a house, one summer day when he and his wife and daughter had come to view the site,[1] and give me the benefit of their experience; and long after, when I had begun to farm my two acres, he came to see my first calf. On occasion of the planting of his pine, he dug and planted in a most experienced manner,—then washed his hands in the watering-pot, took my hand in both his, and wished me many happy years in my new abode,—and then, proceeded to give me a piece of friendly advice. He told me I should find visitors a great expense, and that I must promise him,—(and he laid his hand on my arm to enforce what he said) I must promise him to do as he and his sister had done, when, in their early days, they had lived at Grasmere.

'When you have a visitor,' said he, 'you must do as we did;—you must say "if you like to have a cup of tea with us, you are very welcome: but if you want any meat,—you must pay for your board." Now, promise me that you will do this.' Of course, I could promise nothing of the sort. I told him I had rather not invite my friends unless I could make them comfortable. He insisted: I declined promising; and changed the subject. The mixture of odd economies and neighbourly generosity was one of the most striking things in the old poet. At tea there, one could hardly get a drop of cream with any ease of mind, while he was giving away all the milk that the household did not want to neighbouring cottagers, who were perfectly well able to buy it, and would have been all the better for being allowed to do so.—It was one of the pleasures of my walks, for the first few years of my residence here, to meet with Wordsworth, when he happened to be walking, and taking his time on the road. In winter, he was to be seen in his cloak, his Scotch bonnet, and green goggles, attended perhaps by half-a-score of cottagers' children,—the youngest pulling at his cloak, or holding by his trowsers, while he cut ash switches out of the hedge for them. After his daughter's death, I seldom saw him except in his phaeton, or when I called. He gave way sadly (and inconsiderately as regarded Mrs. Wordsworth) to his grief for his daughter's loss; and I heard that the evenings were very sad. Neither of them could see to read by candle-light; and he was not a man of cheerful temperament, nor of much practical sympathy.

[1]   William Wordsworth and his wife, née Mary Hutchinson (d. 1859), lived with their daughter Dora at Rydal Mount, about two miles from the Knoll. Dora died in 1847, a few years after her marriage to the minor poet Edward Quillinan.

Mrs. Wordsworth often asked me to 'drop in' in the winter evenings: but I really could not do this. We lived about a mile and a half apart; I had only young girls for servants, and no carriage; and I really could not have done my work but by the aid of my evening reading. I never went but twice; and both times were in the summer. My deafness was a great difficulty too, and especially when his teeth were out, as they were in the evenings, when the family were alone. He began a sentence to me, and then turned his head away to finish it to somebody on the other side: so that I had no chance with him unless we were *tête-à-tête*, when we got on very well.—Our acquaintance had begun during the visit I paid to the Lakes in January 1845, when he and Mrs. Wordsworth had requested a conversation with me about mesmerism, which they thought might avail in the case of a daughter-in-law, who was then abroad, mortally ill.[1] After a long consultation, they left much disposed for the experiment: but I supposed at the time that they would not be allowed to try; and I dare say they were not. They invited me to Rydal Mount, to see the terrace where he had meditated his poems; and I went accordingly, one winter noon. On that occasion, I remember, he said many characteristic things, beginning with complaints of Jeffrey and other reviewers,[2] who had prevented his poems bringing him more than £100, for a long course of years,—up to a time so recent indeed that I will not set it down, lest there should be some mistake. Knowing that he had no objection to be talked to about his works, I told him that I thought it might interest him to hear which of his poems was Dr. Channing's favourite. I told him that I had not been a day in Dr. Channing's house when he brought me 'the Happy Warrior,'—(a choice which I thought very characteristic also.) 'Ay,' said Wordsworth: 'that was not on account of the *poetic conditions* being best fulfilled in that poem: but because it is' (solemnly) 'a chain of extremely *valooable* thoughts.—You see,—it does not best fulfil the conditions of poetry; but it is' (solemnly) 'a chain of extremely valooable thoughts.' I thought this eminently true; and by no means the worse for the description being given by himself.—He was kind enough to be very anxious lest I should overwalk myself. Both he and Mrs. Wordsworth repeatedly bade me take warning by his sister, who had lost first her strength, and then her sanity by extreme imprudence in that way, and its conse-

---

[1]   Isabella, née Curwen, wife of John Wordsworth, who had just lost her youngest son. William Wordsworth referred to her "weakness of body and distressed state of mind" in a letter of June 2, 1846 to a cousin.

[2]   Lord Francis Jeffrey (1773–1850), reviewer from 1802, editor from 1829, of the *Edinburgh Review*.

quences.[1] Mrs. Wordsworth told me what I could not have believed on any less trustworthy authority,—that Miss Wordsworth had—not once, but frequently,—walked forty miles in a day. In vain I assured them that I did not meditate or perpetrate any such imprudence, and that I valued my recovered health too much to hazard it for any self-indulgence whatever. It was a fixed idea with them that I walked all day long. One afternoon Mr. Atkinson and I met them on the Rydal road. They asked where we had been; and we told them. I think it was over Loughrigg terrace to Grasmere; which was no immoderate walk. 'There, there!' said Wordsworth, laying his hand on my companion's arm. 'Take care! take care! Don't let *her* carry you about. She is killing off half the gentlemen in the county!' I could not then, nor can I now, remember any Westmoreland gentleman, except my host on Windermere, having taken a walk with me at all.

There had been a period of a few years, in my youth, when I worshipped Wordsworth. I pinned up his likeness in my room; and I could repeat his poetry by the hour. He had been of great service to me at a very important time of my life. By degrees, and especially for ten or twelve years before I saw him, I found more disappointment than pleasure when I turned again to his works,—feeling at once the absence of sound, accurate, weighty thought, and of genuine poetic inspiration. It is still an increasing wonder with me that he should ever have been considered a *philosophical* poet,—so remarkably as the very basis of philosophy is absent in him, and so thoroughly self-derived, self-conscious and subjective is what he himself mistook for philosophy. As to his poetic genius, it needs but to open Shelley, Tennyson, or even poor Keats, and any of our best classic English poets, to feel at once that, with all their truth and all their charm, few of Wordsworth's pieces are poems. As eloquence, some of them are very beautiful; and others are didactic or metaphysical meditations or speculations poetically rendered; but, to my mind, this is not enough to constitute a man a poet. A benefactor, to poetry and to society, Wordsworth undoubtedly was. He brought us back out of a wrong track into a right one;—out of a fashion of pedantry, antithesis and bombast, in which thought was sacrificed to sound, and common sense was degraded, where it existed, by being made to pass for something else. He taught us to say what we had to say in a way,—not only the more rational but the more beautiful;

---

[1]   After a serious illness in 1829, Dorothy Wordsworth (1771–1855) suffered from severe arteriosclerosis from which she never recovered; for the remaining years of her life, she lived at Rydal Mount, with bouts of lucidity punctuated by long periods of insanity.

and, as we have grown more simple in expression, we have become more unsophisticated and clear-seeing and far-seeing in our observation of the scene of life, if not of life itself. These are vast services to have rendered, if no more can be claimed for the poet. In proportion to our need was the early unpopularity of the reform proposed; and in proportion to our gratitude, when we recognized our benefactor, was the temporary exaggeration of his merits as a poet. His fame seems to have now settled in its proper level. Those who understand mankind are aware that he did not understand them; and those who dwell near his abode especially wonder at his representation of his neighbours. He saw through an imagination, less poetic than metaphysical; and the heart element was in him not strong. He had scarcely any intercourse with other minds, in books or in conversation; and he probably never knew what it was to have anything to do. His old age suffered from these causes; and it was probably the least happy portion of a life too self-enclosed to be very happy as a whole. In regard to politics, however, and even to religion, he grew more and more liberal in his latter years. It is in that view, and as a neighbour among the cottagers, that he is most genially remembered: and considering the course of flattery he was subjected to by his blue-stocking and clerical neighbours, who coaxed him into monologue, and then wrote down all he said for future publication, it is wonderful that there is any thing so genial to record. His admirable wife, who, I believe, never suspected how much *she* was respected and beloved by all who knew them both, sustained what was genial in him, and ameliorated whatever was not so. Her excellent sense and her womanly devotedness,—(especially when she grew pale and shrunk and dim-eyed under her mute sorrow for the daughter whom *he* mourned aloud, and without apparent consideration for the heart-sufferer by his side) made her by far the more interesting of the two to me. But, while writing these recollections, the spring sunshine and air which are streaming in through my open window remind me of the advent of the 'tourist season,' and of the large allowance to be made for a 'lake poet,' subject to the perpetual incursions of flatterers of the coarsest order. The modest and well-bred pass by the gates of celebrated people who live in the country for quiet, while the coarse and selfish intrude,—as hundreds of strangers intruded every year on Wordsworth. When I came into the district, I was told that the average of utter strangers who visited Rydal Mount in the season was five hundred! Their visits were not the only penalty inflicted. Some of these gentry occasionally sent letters to the newspapers, containing their opinions of the old man's state of health or of intellect: and then, if a particularly intrusive lion-hunter got a surly reception, and wrote to a newspaper that Wordsworth's intellects were failing, there came letters of inquiry from all the family friends and acquaintances, whose affectionate solicitudes had to be satisfied.

For my part, I refused, from the first, to introduce any of my visitors at Rydal Mount, because there were far too many already. Mrs. Wordsworth repeatedly acknowledged my scrupulosity about this: but in time I found that she rather wished that I would bear my share in what had become a kind of resource to her husband. I never liked seeing him go the round of his garden and terraces, relating to persons whose very names he had not attended to, particulars about his writing and other affairs which each stranger flattered himself was a confidential communication to himself. One anecdote will show how the process went forward, and how persons fared who deserved something better than this invariable treatment. In the first autumn of my residence,—while I was in lodging,—Mr. Seymour Tremenheere and his comrade in his Educational Commissionership, Mr. Tufnell,[1] asked me to obtain lodgings for them, as they wished to repose from their labours beside Windermere. When they came, I told them that I could not take them to Rydal Mount. They acquiesced, though much wishing to obtain some testimony from the old poet on behalf of popular education. In a week or two, however, I had to call on Mrs. Wordsworth, and I invited the gentlemen to take their chance by going with me. We met Mr. and Mrs. Wordsworth just coming out of their door into the garden. I twice distinctly named both gentlemen; but I saw that he did not attend, and that he received them precisely after his usual manner with strangers. He marched them off to his terraces; and Mrs. Wordsworth and I sat down on a garden seat. I told her the state of the case; and she said she would take care that, when they returned, Mr. Wordsworth should understand who his guests were. This was more easily promised than done, however. When they appeared, Mr. Wordsworth uncovered his grey head as usual, wished the gentlemen improved health and much enjoyment of the lake scenery, and bowed us out. My friends

---

[1]   Edward Carleton Tufnell, an education reformer, founded with James Kay-Shuttleworth the first training college for school teachers (1839–40) at Battersea, London. Later, he and Tremenheere headed the Royal Commission on the Employment of Children, Young Persons and Women in Agriculture (1867), whose charge was to inquire into the situation of agricultural workers, "for the purpose of ascertaining to what extent, and with what modifications, the principles of the Factory Acts can be adopted for the regulation of such employment, and especially with a view to the better education of such children."

told me (what I could have told them) that Mr. Wordsworth had related many interesting things about his poems, but that they doubted whether he had any idea who they were; and they had no opportunity of introducing the subject of popular education. That evening, when a party of friends and I were at tea, an urgent message came, through three families, from Rydal Mount, to the effect that Mr. Wordsworth understood that Mr. Seymour Tremenheere was in the neighbourhood; and that he was anxious to obtain an interview with Mr. Tremenheere for conversation about popular education!—Mr. Tremenheere arrived at the Mount the next day. He told me on his return that he had, he hoped, gained his point. He hoped for a sonnet at least. He observed, 'Mr Wordsworth discoursed to me about Education, trying to impress upon me whatever I have most insisted on in my Reports for seven years past: but I do not expect him to read Reports, and I was very happy to hear what he had to say.' The next time I fell in with Mr. Wordsworth, he said 'I have to thank you for procuring for me a call from that intelligent gentleman, Mr. Tremenheere. I was glad to have some conversation with him. To be sure, he was bent on enlightening me on principles of popular education which have been published in my poems these forty years: but that is of little consequence. I am very happy to have seen him.'

In no aspect did Wordsworth appear to more advantage than in his conduct to Hartley Coleridge, who lived in his neighbourhood.[1] The weakness,—the special vice,—of that poor, gentle, hopeless being is universally known by the publication of his life; and I am therefore free to say that, as long as there was any chance of good from remonstrance and rebuke, Wordsworth administered both, sternly and faithfully: but, when nothing more than pity and help was possible, Wordsworth treated him as gently as if he had been—(what indeed he was in our eyes)—a sick child. I have nothing to tell of poor Hartley, of my own knowledge. Except meeting him on the road, I knew nothing of him. I recoiled from acquaintanceship,—seeing how burdensome it was in the case of persons less busy than myself, and not having, to say the truth, courage to accept the conditions on which his wonderfully beautiful conversation might be enjoyed. The simple fact is that I was in company with him five times; and all those five times he was drunk. I should think there are few solitary ladies, whose time is valuable, who

---

[1] Hartley Coleridge (1796–1849), eldest son of Samuel Coleridge, had many of his father's gifts but few successes; he lost his Oxford fellowship for repeated drunkenness and then failed as a schoolmaster. His brother Derwent published his *Essays and Marginalia* posthumously (London: Edward Moxon, 1851), with a brief memoir.

would encourage intercourse with him after that. Yet I quite understood the tenderness and earnestness with which he was tended in his last illness, and the sorrow with which he was missed by his personal friends. I witnessed his funeral; and as I saw his grey-headed old friend Wordsworth bending over his grave, that winter morning, I felt that the aged mourner might well enjoy such support as could arise from a sense of duty faithfully performed to the being who was too weak for the conflicts of life. On his tombstone, which stands near Wordsworth's own, is the cross wreathed with the thorny crown, and the inscription, so touching in this case, 'By thy Cross and Passion, Good Lord, deliver me!'

One of my objects during this summer was to become acquainted with the Lake District, in a complete and orderly manner. It has been a leading pleasure and satisfaction of mine, since I grew up, to compass some one department of knowledge at a time, so as to feel a real command of it, succeeding to a misty ignorance. The first approach to this was perhaps my acquaintance with the French and Latin languages; and the next my study of the Metaphysical schools of Mental Philosophy. But these pursuits were partly ordained for me in my educational course; and they belonged to the immature period of my mind. Perhaps my first thorough *possession* was of the doctrine of Necessity, as I have explained in its place.[1] Then, there was the orderly comprehension of what I then took to be the science of Political Economy, as elaborated by the Economists of our time: but I believe I should not have been greatly surprised or displeased to have perceived, even then, that the pretended science is no science at all, strictly speaking; and that so many of its parts must undergo essential change, that it may be a question whether future generations will owe much more to it than the benefit (inestimable, to be sure) of establishing the grand truth that social affairs proceed according to great general laws, no less than natural phenomena of every kind. Such as Political Economy was, however, I knew what it meant and what it comprehended.—Next came my study of the United States republic: and this study yielded me the satisfaction I am now referring to in full measure. Before I went, I actually sat down, on the only spare evening I had, to learn how many States there were in the American Union.—I am not sure that I knew that there were more than thirteen: and in three years after, one of the first constitutional lawyers in America wrote me

---

[1]   See Period III, sec. i.

the spontaneous assurance that there was not a single mistake in my 'Society in America,' in regard to the political constitution of the republic. I really had learned something thoroughly:—not the people, of course, whom it would take a lifetime to understand: but the social system under which they were living, with the geography and the sectional facts of their country.—The next act of mastery was a somewhat dreary one, but useful in its way. I understood sickness and the prospect of death, with some completeness, at the end of my five years at Tynemouth.—Now, on my recovery, I set myself to learn the Lake District, which was still a *terra incognita*, veiled in bright mists before my mind's eye: and by the close of a year from the purchase of my field, I knew every lake (I think) but two, and almost every mountain pass. I have since been complimented with the task of writing a Complete Guide to the Lakes,[1] which was the most satisfactory testimony on the part of my neighbours that they believed I understood their beloved District.—After that, there was the working out for myself of the genealogy of the faiths of the East, as represented in my 'Eastern Life.'[2] Lastly, there was the history of the last half century of the English nation, as shown in my 'History of the Peace,' and in my articles for the 'Daily News,' at the beginning of the present war.[3] I need not say that I feel now, as I have ever felt, hedged in by ignorance on every side: but I know that we must all feel this, if we could live and learn for a thousand years: but it is a privilege, as far as it goes, to make clearings, one at a time, in the wilderness of the unknown, as the settler in the Far West opens out his crofts from the primeval forest. Of these joyous labours, none has been sweeter than that of my first recovered health, when Lake-land became gradually disclosed before my explorations, till it lay before me, map-like, as if seen from a mountain top.

I had not been settled many days in my lodging at Waterhead before I was appealed to by my landlady and others on behalf of sick neighbours, to know whether mesmerism would serve them, and whether I would administer it. After what I owed to mesmerism, I could not refuse to try; and, though my power has always been very moderate, I found I could do some good. Sometimes I had seven patients asleep at one time in my sitting-room; and all on whom I tried my hand were either cured

---

[1] *A Complete Guide to the English Lakes* (Windermere: John Garnett, 1855).

[2] *Eastern Life, Present and Past,* 3 vols. (London: Edward Moxon, 1848).

[3] *A History of England during the Thirty Years' Peace, 1816–1846,* 2 vols. (London: Charles Knight, 1849–50). Martineau wrote "leaders" for the *Daily News* not only during the Crimean War, but also about the American Civil War and beyond, from 1852 to 1869.

or sensibly benefited.[1] One poor youth who was doomed to lose both arms, from scrofulous disease in the elbows, was brought to me, and settled beside me, to see what could be done till it could be ascertained whether his lungs were or were not hopelessly diseased. I mesmerised him twice a day for ten weeks, giving up all engagements which could interfere with the work. He obtained sleep, to the extent of thirteen hours in twenty-four. He recovered appetite, strength, and (the decisive circumstance) flesh. In six weeks, his parents hardly knew him, when they came over to see him. He lost his cough, and all his consumptive symptoms; we made him our postman and errand-boy; and he walked many miles in a day. But alas! my house was not built: he could not remain in the lodging when the weather broke up: his return to his father's cottage for the winter was inevitable; and there he fell back: and the damps of February carried him off in rapid decline. None who knew him doubt that his life was lengthened for several months, and that those were months of ease and enjoyment through the mesmeric treatment. The completest case under my hands was one which I always think of with pleasure. My landlady came up one day to ask my good offices on behalf of a young nursemaid in the service of some ladies who were lodging on the ground floor of the house. This girl was always suffering under sick headache, so that her life was a burden to her, and she was quite unfit for her place. I agreed to see her; but her mistress declared that she could not spare her, as she was wanted, ill or well, to carry the baby out. One day, however, she was too ill to raise her head at all; and, as she was compelled to lie down, her mistress allowed her to be brought to my sofa. In seven minutes, she was in the mesmeric trance. She awoke well, and never had a headache again. The ladies were so struck that they begged I would mesmerise her daily. They came, the second day, to see her asleep, and said she looked so different that they should not have known her; and they called her the 'little Nell,' of Dickens.[2] In a few days she went into the trance in seven seconds: and I could do what I pleased with her, without her being conscious that I sent her all over the house, and made her open windows, make up the fire, &c., &c. She began to grow fast, became completely altered, and was in full health, and presently very pretty. Her parents came many miles to thank me; and their reluctant and hesitating request was that I would not mesmerise

---

[1]   In a letter to Fanny Wedgwood of 29 September 1845, Martineau described "one poor youth" who had been condemned to lose both arms "from diseased elbows" whose pain abated whenever Martineau mesmerized him (*Letters*, ed. Arbuckle, pp. 83–84).

[2]   The young heroine of Charles Dickens's novel, *The Old Curiosity Shop* (1841).

her in the presence of any body who would tell the clergy, on account of the practice of unbelievers of traducing the characters of all who were cured by mesmerism. I was sorry, because Professor Gregory and his lady,[1] and some other friends, were coming for the purpose of pursuing the subject; and this girl would have been valuable to us in the inquiry: but, of course, I could not resist the wish of the parents, which I thought perfectly reasonable. —This reminds me of an incident too curious not to be related. There is at Ambleside a retired surgeon, confined to the sofa by disease. A former patient of his, an elderly woman, went to him that summer, and told him that the doctors so completely despaired of her case that they would give her no more medicine. Mr. C— was very sorry, of course; but what could be said? The woman lingered and hesitated, wanting his opinion. There *was* a lady,—she was lodging at Waterhead,—and she did wonderful cures. What did Mr. C— think of an application to that lady? 'Why not?' asked Mr. C—, if the doctors would do nothing more for the patient? He advised the attempt. After more hesitation, the scruple came out. 'Why, Sir, they *do* say that the lady does it through the Old 'Un.' The sick woman feared what the clergy would say; and, in spite of Mr. C—'s encouragement, she never came.

My own experience that year was an instructive one. I have mentioned that, during my recovery, I was never in the mesmeric sleep,—never unconscious. From the time that I was quite well, however, I fell into the sleep,—sometimes partially and sometimes wholly: though it took a long while to convince me that I was ever unconscious. It was only by finding that I had lost an hour that I could be convinced that I had slept at all. One day, when mesmerised by two persons, I had begun to speak; and from that time, whenever I was thus double mesmerised, I discoursed in a way which those who heard it call very remarkable. I could remember some of the wonderful things I had seen and thought, if questioned immediately on my waking; but the impressions were presently gone. A short-hand writer took down much of what I said; and certainly those fragments are wholly unlike any thing I have ever said under any other circumstances. I still believe that some faculties are thus reached which are not, as far as can be known, exercised at any other time; and also that the conceptive and imaginative faculties, as well as those of insight and of memory, are liable to be excited to very vigorous action. When consciousness is incomplete,—or, rather, when unconsciousness is all but complete,—so that actual experience is interfused with the dreams of the

---

[1]   William Gregory (1803–1858), Professor of Chemistry, University of Edinburgh.

mesmeric condition, there is danger of that state of mind which is not uncommon under mesmeric treatment, and which renders the superintendence of an experienced and philosophical mesmeriser so desirable as we see it to be, —a state of exaltation almost amounting to delusion, when imaginative patients are concerned. Nobody would consider me, I think, a particularly imaginative patient: and nothing could be more common-place and safe than the practice while I was either wide awake or so completely asleep as to remember nothing of my dreams afterwards; but, in the intermediate case, I was subject to a set of impressions so strong that,—having seen instances of the *clairvoyant* and prophetic faculty in others,—it was scarcely possible to avoid the belief that my constant and highly detailed impressions were of the same character. It is impossible to be absolutely certain, at this moment, that they were not: but the strongest probability is that they were of the same nature with the preachments and oracular statements of a host of mesmeric patients who give forth their notions about 'the spiritual world' and its inhabitants.[1] It is observed, in all accounts of spirit-rappings and mesmeric speculation, that, on the subject of religion, each speaker gives out his own order of opinions in the form of testimony from what he sees. We have all the sects of Christendom represented in their mesmeriser members,—constituting, to the perplexity of inexperienced observers, as remarkable a Babel in the spiritual world as on our European and American soil; and, when there is no hope of reconciling these incompatible oracles, the timid resort to the supposition of demoniacal agency. There is no marvel in this to persons who, like myself, are aware, from their own experience, of the irresistible strength of the impressions of mesmeric dreaming, when more or less interfused with waking knowledge; nor to philosophical observers who, like my guardian in this stage of my experience, have witnessed the whole range of the phenomena with cool judgment, and under a trained method of investigation. Under different management, and without his discouragements and cool exposure of the discrepancies of dreaming, I

---

[1]   Martineau added this footnote: "An eminent literary man said lately that he never was afraid of dying before; but that he now could not endure the idea of being summoned by students of spirit-rapping to talk such nonsense as their ghosts are made to do. This suggests to me the expediency of declaring my conviction that if any such students should think fit to summon me, when I am gone hence, they will get a visit from,—not me,— but the ghosts of their own thoughts: and I beg beforehand not to be considered answerable for any thing that may be revealed under such circumstances.—I do not attempt to offer any explanation of that curious class of phenomena, but I do confidently deny that we can be justified in believing that Bacon, Washington, and other wise men are the speakers of the trash that the 'spiritual circles' report as their revelations."

might have been one of the victims of the curiosity and half-knowledge of the time; and my own trust in my waking faculties, and, much more, other people's trust in them, might have been lost; and my career of literary action might have prematurely come to an end. Even before I was quite safe, an incident occurred which deeply impressed me.—Margaret Fuller, who had been, in spite of certain mutual repulsions, an intimate acquaintance of mine in America, came to Ambleside while Professor and Mrs. Gregory and other friends were pursuing the investigations I have referred to.[1] I gave her and the excellent friends with whom she was travelling the best welcome I could. My house was full: but I got lodgings for them, made them welcome as guests, and planned excursions for them. Her companions evidently enjoyed themselves; and Margaret Fuller as evidently did not, except when she could harangue the drawing-room party, without the interruption of any other voice within its precincts. There were other persons present, at least as eminent as herself, to whom we wished to listen; but we were willing that all should have their turn: and I am sure I met her with every desire for friendly intercourse. She presently left off conversing with me, however; while I, as hostess, had to see that my other guests were entertained, according to their various tastes. During our excursion in Langdale, she scarcely spoke to any body; and not at all to me; and when we afterwards met in London, when I was setting off for the East, she treated me with the contemptuous benevolence which it was her wont to bestow on common-place people. I was therefore not surprised when I became acquainted, presently after, with her own account of the matter. She told her friends that she had been bitterly disappointed in me. It had been a great object with her to see me, after my recovery by mesmerism, to enjoy the exaltation and spiritual development which she concluded I must have derived from my excursions in the spiritual world: but she had found me in no way altered by it: no one could have discovered that I had been mesmerised at all; and I was so thoroughly common-place that

---

1   Margaret Fuller (1810–50) visited Ambleside before traveling to Italy as a journalist. There she married the Marchese Giovanni Ossoli, one of Mazzini's followers, in 1849 and devoted herself to him, their child, and the cause of Italian unification. Martineau refers to comments published posthumously in the *Memoirs of Margaret Fuller Ossoli* (Boston: Phillips, Sampson, 1852). After reading the *Memoirs*, Martineau wrote to Ralph Waldo Emerson: "The whole thing is more painful than I cd have anticipated, ... I had no idea that she was another instance of the old fate,—of a woman of strong nature, debarred from a home of her own, & seeking a refuge in mysticism. How plain this becomes when we see her marry as she did, & become so thoroughly the mother;—so rational & humble too!" (in Sanders, ed., *Selected Letters*, p. 122).

she had no pleasure in intercourse with me.—This was a very welcome confirmation of my hope that I had, under Mr. Atkinson's wise care,[1] come back nearly unharmed from the land of dreams; and this more than compensated for the unpleasantness of disappointing the hopes of one whom I cordially respected for many fine qualities, intellectual and moral, while I could not pretend to find her mind unspoiled and her manners agreeable. She was then unconsciously approaching the hour of that remarkable regeneration which transformed her from the dreaming and haughty pedant into the true woman. In a few months more, she had loved and married; and how interesting and beautiful was the closing period of her life, when husband and child concentrated the powers and affections which had so long run to waste in intellectual and moral eccentricity, the concluding period of her memoirs has shown to us all. Meantime, the most acceptable verdict that she could pronounce upon me in my own function of housekeeper and hostess, while the medical world was hoping to hear of my insanity, was that I was 'common-place.'

Some members of the medical world were, in that summer at Waterhead (1845), demonstrating to me what my duty was in regard to poor Jane, at Tynemouth,[2]—usually called my maid, but not yet so, nor to be so till the spring of 1846. The sudden cessation of mesmerism was disastrous to the poor girl.—Her eyes became as bad as ever; and the persecution of the two doctors employed by Dr. Forbes fell upon her alone,[3]—her ignorant and selfish aunt refusing to let her be mesmerised, and permitting her rather to go blind. When she was blind, these two men came to her with a paper which they required her to sign, declaring that she had been guilty of imposture throughout; and they told her that she should be taken to prison if she did not, then and there, sign their paper. She steadily refused, not only to sign, but to answer any of their questions, saying that they had set down false replies for both her aunts; and in this her aunts took courage to support her, in the face of

---

[1]   In contrast, Fuller was impressed by Henry Atkinson, whom she described as "tall and finely formed, with a head for Leonardo to paint; mild and composed, but thoughtful and sagacious" (quoted in "Memorials," III, 297).

[2]   Jane Arrowsmith; see Period V, sec. i and iii. Her aunts Mrs. Halliday and Mrs. Arrowsmith ran boarding houses in Tynemouth, where Jane worked as a housemaid.

[3]   Probably Dr. John Forbes, founder and editor of the *British and Foreign Medical Review* and author of *Illustrations of Modern Mesmerism from Personal Investigation* (London: John Churchill, 1845). In *Mesmerized* (Chicago: U of Chicago P, 1998), Alison Winter classifies him as an "ambivalent supporter" who "urged doctors to evaluate mesmerism—not ignore it" (p. 172).

threats from the doctors that they would prevent these poor widows having any more lodgers. An Ambleside friend of mine, calling on Jane at Tynemouth, found her in this plight, and most kindly brought over from South Shields a benevolent druggist, accustomed to mesmerise. The aunt refused him admission to her house; and he therefore went to the bottom of the garden, where Jane was supported to a seat. At the end of the *séance*, she could see some bright thing on her lap; and she had an appetite, for the first time in some weeks. The aunt could not resist this appeal to her heart and her self-interest at once; and she made the druggist welcome. As soon as I heard all this, I begged my kind aunts to go over from Newcastle, and tell Jane's aunt that if she could restore Jane so far as to undertake the journey to Ambleside, I would thenceforth take charge of her. It was a fearful undertaking, under the circumstances; but I felt that my protection and support were due to the poor girl. The aunt had her mesmerised and well cared for; and in two or three weeks she said she could come. I had, as yet, no house; and there was no room for her in my lodging; so I engaged a cottager near Ambleside to receive the girl, and board her for her services in taking care of the children till my house should be habitable. She was so eager to reach me, that, when she found the Keswick coach full, she walked sixteen miles, rather than wait, and presented herself to me tearful, nervous, in sordid clothes (for her aunt had let the poor girl's wardrobe go to rags while she was too blind to sew) and her eyes like those of a blind person, looking as if the iris was covered with tissue paper. My heart sank at the sight. I told her that I had not mentioned mesmerism to her hostess, because, after all she had gone through, I thought the choice should be hers whether to speak of it or not. I had simply told the woman that I wished Jane to take a walk to my lodgings, three or four times a week. Jane's instant reply was that she did not wish for any secret about the matter; and that she thought she ought not to mind any ill-treatment while God permitted sick people to get well by a new means, whether the doctors liked it or not. I soon found that she was mesmerising a diseased baby in the cottage, and teaching the mother to do it; — whereby the child lived for months after the medical man declined visiting it any more, because it was dying. I mesmerised Jane three times a week; and in ten days her eyes were as clear as my own. When, henceforth, I saw any doubtful appearance in them, I mesmerised her once or twice; and that set all right. She never had any more trouble with them, except during my long absence in the East. They looked ill when I returned; when again, and finally, a few *séances* cured them. She lived with me seven years, and then went, with my entire approbation, to Australia. She immediately became cook in the family of the High Sheriff of Melbourne, where she is still.[1] The zeal with which she assisted in furnishing and preparing my new house may be imagined; and how happy she was in those opening spring days when we met at the house early in the mornings, and staid till nine at night, making all ready in the new house which we longed to occupy. The first night (April 7th, 1846) when we made our beds, stirred up the fires, and locked the doors, and had some serious talk, as members of a new household, will never be forgotten, for its sweetness and solemnity, by my maids or myself.

Many persons, before doubtful or adverse, began to take a true view of this girl and her case when I was in the East. When they saw that, instead of accepting large sums of money to go about as a *clairvoyante*, with lecturers on mesmerism, she remained at her post in my house, during the long fourteen months of my absence, they were convinced that she was no notoriety seeker, or trickster, or speculator for money. She practiced the closest economy, and invested her savings carefully, because she doubted her eyes, and wished to provide against accidents; and, when she emigrated, she had money enough for a good outfit, and to spare. But she might have had ten times as much if she had been tempted to itinerate as a *clairvoyante*. With these facts I close her history. I have given it fully, because it happened repeatedly during the seven years that she lived with me, that reports appeared in the newspapers, or by applications to myself through the post, that I had dismissed her in disgrace. My reply always was that if I had seen reason to doubt her honesty in the matter of the mesmerism, or in any other way, I should have felt myself bound to avow the fact in print, after all that had happened. My final declaration is that I have never known a more truthful person than my Jane; and I am confident that, among all the neighbours to whom she was known for seven years, and among her Tynemouth neighbours, who knew her for the nineteen preceding years of her life, there are none who would dissent from my judgment of her.

My notion of doing no work during the gladsome year 1845 soon gave way,—not before inclination, (for I was sorely reluctant) but duty. When the potato famine was impending, and there was alarm for the farming interest, Mr. Bright's Committee on the Game-laws published

---

[1]   Jane emigrated to Australia in April, 1853. Alister (or Alexander) McKenzie, became high sheriff of Melbourne in 1847.

the evidence laid before them; and it appeared that there could not be a better time for drawing public attention to a system more detrimental to the farming class, and more injurious to the production of food than any of the grievances put forth by the complaining 'agricultural interest.'[1] I was told that I ought to treat the subject as I had treated the topics of Political Economy in my Series; and I agreed that I ought. Mr. Bright supplied me with the evidence; I collected historical material; and I wrote the three volumes of 'Forest and Game-Law Tales' in the autumn of 1845.[2] Above 2,000 copies of these have sold; but, at the time, the publication appeared to be a total failure;—my first failure. The book came out, as it happened, precisely at the time when Sir R. Peel was known to be about to repeal the Corn-laws.[3] It was said at the time that for three weeks no publisher in London sold any thing, with the one exception of Wordsworth's new and last edition of his works, wherein he took his farewell of the public.[4] Nearly 1,000 copies of my book were sold at once; but, reckoning on a very large sale, we had stereotyped it;[5] and this turned out a mistake,—the stereotyping more than cutting off the profits of the sale. From that work I have never received a shilling. On my own account, I have never regretted doing the work,—reluctant as I was to work that happy autumn. I know that many young men, and some of them sure to become members of the legislature, have been impressed by those essentially true stories to a degree which cannot but affect the destination and duration of the Game-laws; and this is enough. That the toil was an encroachment on my fresh pleasures at the time, and

1 John Bright (1811–89) headed a parliamentary committee to investigate the operation and effects of the game laws—a tactic of the Anti-Corn Law League to set farmers against landlords and increase resentment against squires whose hunting practices destroyed farmers' crops.

2 *Forest and Game-Law Tales* (London: Edward Moxon, 1845–46).

3 Robert Peel (1788–1850), Tory prime minister from 1841 to 1846, tried for repeal in December, 1845 but failed, and he then resigned. Lord John Russell (1792–1878) could not, however, form a Whig government, and Peel continued in office, proposing a lowered duty on corn immediately and complete abolition in three years. The repeal of the Corn Laws passed the House of Lords on June 26, 1846.

4 This would be the single-volume edition of Wordsworth's *Poems* (London: E. Moxon, 1845); Moxon also issued a six-volume edition, *The Poetical Works of William Wordsworth* (London: E. Moxon, 1849–50).

5 Stereotyping is a "process of printing in which a solid plate of type-metal, cast from a papier-mâché or plaster mould taken from the surface of a forme of type, is used for printing from, instead of the forme itself" (OED). According to John Carter in *ABC for Book Collectors*, 4th ed. (London: Rupert Hart-Davis, 1966), p. 187, "In England, unless a large or continuing sale is expected, a book is seldom 'plated,' as the printers call it."

has proved gratuitous, is of no consequence now, while it is certain that a few young lords and gentry have had their eyes opened to the cost of their sport, and to their duty in regard to it. If I could but learn that some of the 2,000 copies sold had gone into the hands of the farmers, and had put any strength into their hearts to assert their rights, and resist the wrongs they have too tamely submitted to, I should feel that the result deserved a much greater sacrifice. As it was, I set down the gratuitous labour as my contribution to, or fine upon, the repeal of the Corn-laws.

That repeal was now drawing nigh. It was in the November and December of that year that Lord John Russell condescended to that struggle for power with Sir R. Peel which will damage his fame in the eyes of posterity, and which reflected disgrace at the time on the whole Whig party, as it waned towards dissolution. During the struggle, and the alternate 'fall' of the two statesmen, much wonder was felt by people generally, and, it is believed, especially by Sir R. Peel, that the great middle-class body, including the Anti-corn-law League, showed so little earnestness in supporting Peel; so that when the matter was placed in Peel's hands by his restoration to power, it did not seem to *get on*. I had occasion to know where the hitch was; and, as it appeared to me, to act upon that knowledge, in a way quite new to me,—indisposed as I have always been to meddle in matters which did not concern me.—While I was ill at Tynemouth, Colonel Thompson and Mr. Cobden[1] called on me; and we had a long talk on League affairs, and the prospect of a repeal of the Corn-Laws. Mr. Cobden told me that he and his comrades were so incessantly occupied in lecturing, and in showing up to multitudes the facts of a past and present time, that they had no leisure or opportunity to study the probable future; and that the opinions or suggestions of a person like myself, lying still, and reading and thinking, might be of use to the leaders of the agitation; and he asked me to write to him if at any time I had any thing to criticise or suggest in regard to League affairs. I had not much idea that I could be of any service; but I made the desired promise.

In the autumn of 1845, when Sir R. Peel retired from the government to make way for Lord J. Russell, Mr. Cobden made a speech to his Stockport constituents, in which he spoke in terms of insult of

---

[1] Thomas Peronnet Thompson (1783–1869), political writer, M.P. for Hull, and author of *Catechism of the Corn Laws* (1827), considered the most effective pamphlet published on the subject. Richard Cobden (1804–65), founder, with John Bright, of the Anti-Corn Law League in 1839.

Peel.[1] I saw this with much regret; and, recalling my promise, I wrote to Mr. Cobden, telling him that it was as a member of the League, and not as a censor that I wrote to him. It was no business of mine to criticise his temper or taste in addressing his constituents; but I reminded him that his Stockport speech was read all over the kingdom; and I asked him whether he thought the object of the League would be furthered by his having insulted a fallen Minister;—whether, indeed, any thing had ever been gained, since society began, by any man having insulted any other man. Before my letter reached Mr. Cobden, he had spoken in yet more outrageous terms of Peel, at a crowded meeting in Covent Garden theatre, leaving himself without the excuse that, in addressing his constituents, he had lost sight of the consideration of the general publicity of his speech. Mr. Cobden's reply was all good-humour and candour as regarded myself; but it disclosed the depth of the sore in his mind in regard to his relations with Sir R. Peel. There is no occasion to tell at length the sad story of what had passed between them in February 1843, when Peel charged Cobden with being answerable for assassination, and Cobden, losing his presence of mind, let the occasion turn against him.[2] It was the worst act of Peel's public life, no doubt; and the moment was one of such anguish to Cobden that he could never recall it without agitation. He referred to it, in his reply to me, in extenuation of his recent outbreak,—while declining to justify himself. I wrote again, allowing that Peel's conduct admitted of no justification; but showing that there were extenuating circumstances in his case too. Of these circumstances I happened to know more than the public did; and I now laid them before my correspondent,—again saying that I did not see why the cause should suffer for such individual griefs. In the course of two or three weeks, plenty of evidence reached me that the great manufacturing classes were holding back on account of this unsettled reckoning between Peel and their leader; and also that Cobden had suffered much and magnanimously, for a course of years, from the remonstrances and instigations of liberal members, who urged his seeking personal satisfaction from his enemy.

---

[1]   Cobden was M.P. for Stockport, Cheshire. Martineau first asked Richard Monckton Milnes (1809–85), 1st Baron Houghton, to intervene; when he would not, she wrote in February, 1846 to both Peel and Cobden.

[2]   During a debate on social distress in the House of Commons on February 17, 1843, Cobden declared that Peel should be held personally responsible for the state of the country, and Peel retorted that Cobden's words were an incitement to assassination. Since Peel's private secretary, Edward Drummond (1792–1843), had been shot in mistake for Peel a month earlier, on January 21, 1843, this charge was extremely serious, and Cobden felt it to be an accusation of murder.

Mr. Cobden had steadily refused, because he was in parliament as the representative of the bread-eaters, and had no right, as he thought, to consume the time and attention of parliament with his private griev-ances. It struck me that it was highly important that Sir R. Peel should know all this, as he was otherwise not master of his own position. I there-fore wrote to a neutral friend of his and mine, laying the case before him.[1] He was a Conservative M.P., wholly opposed to the repeal of the Corn-laws; but I did not see that that was necessarily an obstacle. I told him that he must see that the Corn-laws must be repealed, and that there would be no peace and quiet till the thing was done; and I had little doubt that he would be glad of the opportunity of bringing two earnest men to a better understanding with each other. My friend did not answer my letter for three weeks; and when he did, he could send me nothing but fierce vituperation of his abjured leader. Time was now pressing; and I had not felt it right to wait. The whole move would have failed but for the accident that Mr. Cobden had sat in a draught, and suffered from an abscess in the ear which kept him from the House for three weeks or so. What I did was this.

As I sat at breakfast on New Year's day, (1846) thinking over this matter, it struck me that no harm could be done by my writing myself to Sir R. Peel. He would probably think me meddlesome, and be vexed at the womanish folly of supposing that, while the laws of honour which are so sacred in men's eyes remain, he could make any move towards a man who had insulted him as Mr. Cobden had recently done. But it was nothing to me what Sir R. Peel thought of the act. He was a stranger to me; and his opinion could not weigh for an instant against the remotest chance of abridging the suspense about the Corn-laws. I frankly told him this, in the letter which I wrote him after breakfast.[2] I laid the case before him; and, when I came to the duelling consider-ations, I told him what a woman's belief is in such a case,—that a devoted man can rise above arbitrary social rules; and that I believed him to be the man who could do it. I believed him to be capable of doing the impossible in social morals, as he was proving himself to be in politics. I told him that my sole object was to put him in possession of a case which I suspected he did not understand; and that I therefore

---

[1]   Richard Monckton Milnes (1809–85), M.P. for Pontefract, West Yorkshire; after the Corn Law debates, he switched from Peel's Tory party and aligned himself with Palmerston's Liberal politics.

[2]   Martineau's letters to Peel of February 22 and 24, 1846, are reprinted in Sanders, ed., *Selected Letters*, pp. 112–15.

desired no answer, nor any notice whatever of my letter, which was written without any body's knowledge, and would be posted by my own hand. By return of post came a long letter from Sir R. Peel which moved me deeply. Nothing could be more frank, more cordial, or more satisfactory. It was as I suspected. He had not had the remotest idea that what he had said in the House by way of *amende*, the next (Monday) evening after the insult,[1] had not been considered satisfactory. He wrote strongly about the hardship of being thus kept in the dark for years,—neither Mr. Cobden nor any other member on either side of the House having hinted to him that the matter was not entirely settled.—Now that it was clear that Sir R. Peel would act on his new knowledge in one way or another, the question occurred to me,—what was to be done with Mr. Cobden, whose want of presence of mind had aggravated the original mischief. The same deficiencies might spoil the whole business now.—I had told Sir R. Peel, whilst praising Mr. Cobden, that of course he knew nothing of what I was doing. I now wrote to Mr. Cobden the most artful letter I ever penned. It really was difficult to manage this, my first intrigue, all alone. I told Mr. Cobden that the more I pondered the existing state of the Corn-law affair, the more sure I felt that Sir R. Peel must become aware of the cause of the backwardness of the Manchester interest; and also, that my view of certain unconspicuous features of the Minister's character led me to expect some magnanimous offer of an *amende*: and I ventured to observe what a pity it would be if Mr. Cobden should be so taken by surprise as to let such an occasion of reconciliation be lost. I also wrote to Sir R. Peel, telling him that, however it might appear to him, Mr. Cobden was of a relenting nature, likely to go more than half way to meet an adversary; and that, though he knew nothing of my interference, I had a confident hope that he would not be found wanting, if an occasion should present itself for him finally to merge his private grief in the great public cause of the day.

The next morning but one, the post brought me a newspaper directed by Sir R. Peel, and autographed by him; and, as usual, the 'Times.' There was also a note from Mr. Cobden which prepared me for something interesting in the report of the Debates. His note was scrawled in evident feebleness, and expressive of the deepest emotion. He dated at 3 A.M., and said he had just returned from the House, and that he could not lay his head on his pillow till he had sent me the bless-

---

[1] I.e., after the bitter retort to Cobden in the House of Commons on February 17, 1843.

ing on the peace-maker. He declared that his mind was eased of a load which had burdened it for long and miserable years; and now he should be a new man. The 'Times' told me how immediately Sir R. Peel had acted on his new information, and that that union of effort was now obtained under which the immediate repeal of the Corn-laws was certain. How well the hostile statesmen acted together thenceforth, every body knows. But scarcely any body knows (unless Sir R. Peel thought proper to tell) how they came to an understanding. Mr. Cobden has told his friends that it was somehow my doing; but he never heard a word of it from or through me.—He wrote, after some time, to beg me to burn any letters of his which contained his former opinion of Sir R. Peel. I had already done so. I wished to preserve only what all the parties implicated would enjoy seeing twenty years later: and I should not have related the story here if I had not considered it honourable to every body concerned.

I little dreamed during that winter how I should pass the next. The months slipped away rapidly, amidst the visits of family and friends, writing, study, house-building, and intercourse with the few neighbours whom I knew. A young nephew and niece came late in the autumn, and others in the spring;[1] and we went little journeys on foot among the mountains, carrying knapsack or basket, and making acquaintance among the small country inns. In the spring, there was the pleasure of bringing home basketsful of the beautiful ferns and mosses of the district, and now and then a cartful of heather, to cover my rocks; and primroses and foxgloves and daffodils and periwinkle for the garden; and wood-sorrel for the copses, where the blue-bells presently eclipsed the grass. A friend in London, who knew my desire for a sundial, and heard that I could not obtain the old one which had told me so important a story in my childhood, presented me with one, to stand on the grass under my terrace wall, and above the quarry which was already beginning to fill with shrubs and wild-flowers.[2] The design of the dial is beautiful, —being a copy of an ancient font; and in grey granite, to accord with the grey-stone house above it. The motto was an important affair. A neighbour had one so perfect in its way as to eclipse a whole

---

[1] Among the visitors were her aunt Mrs. Philip Meadows Martineau, née Ann Clarke (1772–1851), and daughter, Harriet's cousin Fanny; her brother Robert, his wife Jane, and their children; and Henry Atkinson. The niece and nephew were Robert's children Susan (1826–94) and Frank (1831–1909), frequent visitors to The Knoll.

[2] The sundial was a gift of her friend Mary Sturch, sister of Elisabeth Reid ("Memorials," III, 264).

class;—the class of bible sayings about the shortness of life and the flight of time. 'The night cometh.'[1] In asking my friends for suggestions, I told them of this; and they agreed that we could not approach this motto, in the same direction. Some good Latin ones, to which I inclined, were put aside because I was besought, for what I considered good reasons, to have nothing but English. It has always been my way to ask advice very rarely, and then to follow it. But on this occasion, I preferred a motto of my own to all that were offered in English; and Wordsworth gave it his emphatic approbation. 'Come, Light! visit me!' stands emblazoned on my dial: and it has been, I believe, as frequent and impressive a monitor to me as ever was any dial which bore warning of the fugacious nature of life and time.

Summer brought a succession of visitors,—very agreeable, but rather too many for my strength and repose. I began to find what are the liabilities of Lake residents in regard to tourists. There is quite wear and tear enough in receiving those whom one wishes to see; one's invited guests, or those introduced by one's invited friends. But these are fewer than the unscrupulous strangers who intrude themselves with compliments, requests for autographs, or without any pretence whatever. Every summer they come and stare in at the windows while we are at dinner, hide behind shrubs or the corner of the house, plant themselves in the yards behind or the field before; are staring up at one's window when one gets up in the morning, gather handfuls of flowers in the garden, stop or follow us in the road, and report us to the newspapers. I soon found that I must pay a serious tax for living in my paradise: I must, like many of my neighbours, go away in 'the tourist season.' My practice has since been to let my house for the months of July, August and September,—or for the two latter at least, and go to the sea, or some country place where I could be quiet.

I do not know that a better idea of the place could be given than by the following paragraphs from a palpable description of our little town (under the name of Haukside,—a compound of Hawkshead and Ambleside) which appeared some time since in 'Chambers's Journal.'[2]

'The constitution of our town suffers six months of the year from fever, and the other six from collapse. In the summertime, our inns are filled to bursting; our private houses broken into by parties desperate after lodgings; the prices of every thing are quadrupled; our best meat,

---

[1] John 9:4: "I must work the works of him that sent me, while it is day; the night cometh, when no man can work."

[2] Untraced; perhaps Martineau recalls the article "Sauntering Among the English Lakes," *Chamber's Edinburgh Journal*, N.S. 2 (1844), 162–65, or a parody published subsequently.

our thickest cream, our freshest fish, are reserved for strangers; our letters, delivered three hours after time, have been opened and read by banditti assuming our own title; ladies of quality, loaded with tracts, fusillade us; savage and bearded foreigners harass us with brazen wind instruments; coaches run frantically towards us from every point of the compass; a great steam-monster ploughs our lake, and disgorges multitudes upon the pier; the excursion-trains bring thousands of curious vulgar, who mistake us for the authoress next door, and compel us to forge her autograph; the donkeys in our streets increase and multiply a hundredfold, tottering under the weight of enormous females visiting our waterfalls from morn to eve; our hills are darkened by swarms of tourists; we are ruthlessly eyed by painters, and brought into foregrounds and backgrounds, as "warm tints" or "bits of repose;" our lawns are picnicked upon by twenty at a time, and our trees branded with initial letters; creatures with introductions come to us, and can't be got away; we have to lionise poor, stupid, and ill-looking people for weeks, without past, present, or future recompense; Sunday is a day of rest least of all, and strange clergymen preach charity-sermons every week with a perfect kaleidoscope of religious views.

'The fever lasts from May until October.

'When it is over, horses are turned out to grass, and inn-servants are disbanded; houses seem all too big for us; the hissing fiend is "laid" upon the lake; the coaches and cars are on their backs in outhouses, with their wheels upward; the trees get bare, the rain begins to fall, grass grows in the streets, and Haukside collapses.

'Our collapse generally lasts from November to May. During this interval, we residents venture to call upon each other. Barouches and chariots we have none, but chiefly shandrydans[1] and buggies; we are stately and solemn in our hospitalities, and retain fashions amongst us that are far from new; we have evening-parties very often, and at every party—whist! Not that it is our sole profession: not that it is our only amusement; it is simply an eternal and unalterable custom—whist! We have no clubs to force it into vigour: the production is indigenous and natural to the place. It is the attainment of all who have reached years of maturity; the dignity of the aged, and the ambition of the young; a little whirling in the dance, a little leaning over the piano, a little attachment to the supper-table, a little flirting on both sides—all this is at

---

[1]   Old-fashioned chaises with hoods—a term used, by mid-nineteenth century, for any rickety, unfashionable vehicle.

Haukside as elsewhere; but the end, the bourne to which male and female alike tend at last after experiencing the vanity of all things else, and from which none ever returns, is—the whist-table.'

The autumn of 1846 had been fixed on for a series of visits to some of my family, and to London; and I let my house to a young couple of my acquaintance for their honeymoon,[1] and went to Liverpool, to my younger sister's, on the last day of August, little dreaming how long it would be before I came back again. I should have gone away even more sad than I was, if I had known.[2]

SECTION III

WHILE at Liverpool, I was the guest of my old friends, the Misses Yates, for a few days; on one of which days, Miss E. Yates and I went out to dinner, while Miss Yates paid a family visit.[3] On our return, she looked very bright and happy; but it did not strike me that it was from any hidden secret. Mr. Richard V. Yates came to breakfast the next morning; and he was placed next to me,—and next to my best ear. The conversation soon turned on his projected Eastern journey, about which I had before had some talk,—remarkably free in regard to the dangers and disagreeables,—with Mrs. R. V. Yates, as we afterwards remembered with much amusement. Mr. Yates now renewed that conversation, consulting me about turning back at the first cataract of the Nile, or going on to the second. From 'Would you go on to the second?' Mr. Yates changed his question to 'Will you go on to the second?' and, after a few moments of perplexity to me, he said 'Now, seriously,—will you go with us? Mrs. Yates will do every thing in her

---

[1] James Dawson and his wife, later of Wray Castle, Ambleside.

[2] Martineau intended to visit her sister Ellen Higginson and other Liverpool friends for three weeks from September 1–21, 1846, and then proceed to London; instead, she accepted the invitation of Mr. and Mrs. Richard Yates to travel in northern Africa and the Middle East; she left London in October, 1846, returning to Ambleside in June, 1847.

[3] The Yates family were prominent Unitarians. According to Elisabeth Sanders Arbuckle (*Letters*, 93–94), their father, John Yates, served as "minister of Kaye Street and Paradise Street churches in Liverpool, the ancestors of James Martineau's church at Hope Street"; Richard Yates was a prominent Unitarian philanthropist; and his brother James, who retired from the Unitarian ministry in 1835, became a distinguished antiquary.

power to render the journey agreeable to you; and I will find the pias-
tres.'[1] At first, I felt and said, while deeply gratified, that I could not
go; and for hours and days it seemed impracticable. I was engaged to
write a new series of 'The Playfellow' for Mr. Knight, and had sent
him the MS. of the first ('The Billow and the Rock.') I had just begun
housekeeping, and had left home without any other idea than returning for the winter: and the truth was, I had the strongest possible inclination to return, and indisposition to wander away from the repose
and beauty of my home. But the way soon cleared so as to leave me
no doubt what I ought to do. My family urged my accepting an
opportunity too fine ever to recur: Mr. Knight generously proposed
to put my story into his 'Weekly Volume,' and wait for more
'Playfellows,'—sending the money at once, to make my outfit easy; and
my neighbours at Ambleside promised to look after my house and
servant, and let the house if possible. Tenants were in it for a part of
the time, and Jane was well taken care of for the rest; so that nothing
could turn out better than the whole scheme. We were joined *en route*
by Mr. J.C. Ewart, the present representative of Liverpool; and he
remained with us till we reached Malta on our return. He thence
wrote to his sister about our parting,—he to go to Constantinople, and
we homewards; saying that our experience was, he feared, a very rare
one;—that of a travelling party who had been in the constant and close
companionship imposed by Nile and Desert travelling, for eight
months, and who, instead of quarrelling and parting, like most such
groups, had travelled in harmony, were separating with regret, and
should be more glad to meet in future than we were before we set out.
It is worth mentioning this, because I heard, a year or so afterwards,
that a report was abroad that our party had quarrelled immediately,—
in France,—and that I had prosecuted my Eastern journey alone. My
book, however, must have demolished that fiction, one would think:
but such fictions are tenacious of life. In my preface to that book, I
related the kindness of my companions in listening to my journal, and
in authorising me to say that they bore testimony to the correctness
of my facts, to the best of their judgment, while disclaiming all connexion with the resulting opinions.[2] I have a letter from Mr. Yates, in

---

[1]   The currency of the Arab world—viz., Richard Yates funded the entire trip.
[2]   In the preface to *Eastern Life*, Martineau states: "About these facts there is entire agree-
      ment between them and me.—For the opinions expressed in this book no one is answer-
      able but myself."

acknowledgment of his copy of the book, in which he bears the same testimony, with the same reservation, and adds an expression of gratification, on Mrs. Yates's part and his own, at the manner in which they are spoken of throughout the work. Some idle reports about this matter, injurious to those excellent friends of mine, are probably extinct already: and if not, this statement will extinguish them.

My travelling companions and I met in London in October, after I had secured my outfit there, and run down into Norfolk to see old Norwich again. We had had hopes that Mr. Atkinson could go with us; and the plan had been nearly arranged; but he was prevented at the last, and could accompany us no further than Boulogne. We traversed France to Marseilles, resting for two days at Paris, where, strange to say, I had never been before. We were quite late enough at best; but the evil chance which sent us on board the mail-packet Volcano caused a most vexatious delay. We were detained, at the outset, for the mails. The captain started with a short supply of coal, because it was dear at Marseilles, and soon found that he had been 'penny wise and pound foolish.' The engines of the vessel were too weak for her work; and the wind was dead against us. The captain forsook the usual route, and took the northerly one, for I forget what reason; and thus we were out of the way of succour. The vessel swarmed with cockroaches; two ill-mannered women shared the cabin with Mrs. Yates and me; the captain was so happy flirting with one of them as to seem provokingly complacent under our delays. It was really vexatious to see him and the widow sitting hand-in-hand, and giggling on the sofa, while our stomachs turned at the sea-pie to which we were reduced, and our precious autumn days were slipping away, during which we ought to have been at Cairo, preparing for our ascent of the Nile. It was worse with others on board,—gentlemen on their way to India, whose clothes and money were now sure to have left Malta before they could arrive there. One of these gentlemen was to meet at Malta a sister from Naples, whom he had not seen for twenty years, and who must either be in agony about his fate, or have given up the rendezvous as a failure. This gentleman, whose good manners and cheerfulness in company never failed, told me on deck, when no one was within hearing, that the trial was as much as he could bear. Some passengers were ill,—some angry, —some alarmed; and the occasion was a touch-stone of temper and manners. All our coal was consumed, except enough for six hours,—that quantity being reserved to carry us into port. Every morning, the captain let us sail about a little, to make believe that we were on our way; but every evening we found ourselves again off Pantellaria,[1] which seemed as much an enchanted island to us as if we had seen Calypso on its cliffs. Now and then, Sicily came provokingly into view, and the captain told us he was bound not to touch there or any where till we were in extremity; and we should not be in extremity till he had burned the cabin wainscot and furniture, and the stairs and berths, and there was nothing whatever left to eat. We now had cheese and the materials for plum-pudding. Every thing else on table began to be too disgusting for even sea-appetites. A young lieutenant offered us a receipt for a dish which he said we should find palatable enough when we could get nothing better,—broiled boot leather, well seasoned.—As for me, I was an old sailor; and, when the sickness was once over, I kept on deck and did very well. The weather was dreary,—the ship sticky and dirty in every part,—and our prospects singularly obscure; but there was clearly nothing to be done but to wait as good-humouredly as we could.

One afternoon, just before dinner, the fellow-passenger who pined for his sister, hastily called the captain, who, looking towards the southern horizon, was in earnest for once. A thread of smoke was visible where all had been blank for so many days; and it was astonishing to me that the wise as well as the foolish on board jumped to the conclusion that it was a steamer sent from Malta in search of us. They were right; and in another hour we were in tow of our deliverer. There had been time for only two or three questions before we were on our course. I left the dinner-table as soon as I could, and went to the bows, to see how her Majesty's mail-steamer looked in tow. The officers of the two vessels wanted to converse; but the wind was too high. 'Try your trumpet,' was written on a black board in the other vessel. 'Have not got one,' was our Lieutenant's reply; to which the black board soon rejoined, 'Why, that lady has got it.' They actually took my special trumpet for that of the ship. When in sight of Malta, we burned our remnant of coal; and at midnight a gun in Valetta harbour[2] told the inhabitants that the Volcano was safe in port. Our party remained on board till the morning; but the brother and sister met that night; and we saw them on the ramparts next day, arm-in-arm, looking as happy as could be. I was made uneasy about my own family by hearing that Valetta newspapers had gone to England the day before, notifying the non-arrival of the Volcano, and the general belief that she was gone to the bottom, with the addition that I was on board. My first business was to close and

---

[1]   A volcanic island in the southern Mediterranean between Sicily and Tunisia, usually spelled *Pantelleria*.

[2]   The harbor of Malta's capital city, considerably east of Pantelleria.

dispatch the journal-letter which I had amused myself with writing on board. Before it arrived, some of my relatives had been rendered as uneasy as I feared by the inconsiderate paragraph in the Valetta paper.

At Malta I began to feel (rather than see) the first evidences of the rivalry then existing between the English and French at the Egyptian Court. I could not conceive why Captain Glasscock,[1] whose ship was then in the port, made so much of me; but his homage was so exaggerated that I suspected some reason of policy. He came daily, bringing his lady, and all his officers in parties; he loaded me with compliments, and seized every occasion of enforcing certain views of his own, which I was glad to hear in the way of guidance in a new scene; and his most emphatic enforcement of all was in regard to the merits of a certain Englishman who was waiting, he intimated, to worship us on our landing at Alexandria. Captain Glasscock insisted on sending my party in his man-of-war's boat to the Ariel, in which we were to proceed to Egypt. We saw his friend at Alexandria,[2] and received the promised homage, and, really, some agreeable hospitality, but not the impressions of the gentleman's abilities of which we had been assured. By degrees it became apparent to me that what was wanted was that I should write a book on Egypt, like Mrs. Romer,[3] who had preceded me by a year or two; and that, like Mrs. Romer, I should be flattered into advocating the Egyptian Railway scheme by which the English in Egypt hoped to gain an advantage over the French, and for which the Alexandrian gentleman had already imported the rails. There they lay, absorbing his capital in a very inconvenient manner; and he seized every chance of getting his scheme advocated. With Mrs. Romer he succeeded, but not with me. At Cairo I had the means of knowing that much more was involved in the scheme,—much difficulty with the Bedoueens and others besides the French,—than I had been told at Alexandria. I knew what would be the consequences of my treatment of the matter in my book; and I learned them in an amusing way. An acquaintance of mine in London told me, a day or two after publication, that the brother of the Alexandrian gentleman, and part-owner of the rails, had got a copy of the book already. 'And he does not like it,' said I: 'he tells

---

[1]   William Glasscock (1787?-1847); according to the *DNB*, "From April 1843 to January 1847 he commanded the Tyne frigate on the Mediterranean station."

[2]   Most likely, R.H. Galloway who with his brother wished to build a railroad from Cairo to Suez.

[3]   Isabella Frances Romer, *A Pilgrimage to the Temples and Tombs of Egypt, Nubia and Palestine, in 1845–6*, 2 vols. (London: Richard Bentley, 1846). Mrs. Romer does, indeed, endorse the railway scheme and recommends a pamphlet, "Observations on the Overland Communication with India" by J.G. Galloway, Esq. for the rationale (I, 99–100).

you it is damned humbug.' My friend burst into a fit of laughter, shouting out, 'Why, that is exactly what he did say.'

The greater was my reluctance to go this journey under my new and happy domestic circumstances, the stronger is the evidence of my estimate of its advantages. I should not have gone but for the entire conviction that it would prove an inestimable privilege. Yet, I had little idea what the privilege would turn out to be, nor how the convictions and the action of the remnant of my life would be shaped and determined by what I saw and thought during those all-important months that I spent in the East. I need say nothing here of the charms of the scenery, and the atmosphere, and the novelty, and the associations with hallowed regions of the earth. The book I wrote on my return gives a fresher impression of all that enjoyment than any thing I could write now: but there were effects produced on my own character of mind which it would have been impertinent to offer there, even if the lapse of years had not been necessary to make them clear to myself. I never before had better opportunity for quiet meditation. My travelling companions, and especially the one with whom I was the most inseparably associated, Mrs. Yates, had that invaluable travelling qualification,—the tact to leave me perfectly free. We were silent when we chose, without fear of being supposed unmannerly; and I could not have believed beforehand that so incessant and prolonged a companionship could have entailed so little restraint. My deafness which would, in the opposite case, have imposed a most disabling fatigue, was thus rather an advantage. While we had abundance of cheerful conversation at meals and in the evenings, and whenever we were disposed for it, there were many hours of every day when I was virtually as much alone as I could have been in my own house; and, of the many benefits and kindnesses that I received from my companions, none excited my lasting gratitude more than this. During the ten weeks that we were on the Nile, I could sit on deck and think for hours of every morning; and while we were in the desert, or traversing the varied scenery of Palestine, or winding about in the passes of the Lebanon, I rode alone,—in advance or in the rear of the caravan, or of our own group, without a word spoken, when it was once understood that it was troublesome and difficult to me to listen from the ridge of my camel, or even from my horse. I cannot attempt to give an idea what I learned during those quiet seasons. All the historical hints I had gained from my school days onward now rose up amidst a wholly new light. It is impossible for even erudite home-stayers to conceive what is gained by seeing for one's self the scenes of history, after any considerable preparation of philosophical thought. When, after my return, the Chevalier Bunsen[1] told me that he would not go to Egypt, if he had the leisure, because he already knew every thing that could be learned about it, I could not but feel that this was a matter which could be judged of nowhere but on the spot; and that no use of the eyes and mind of Lepsius[2] could avail him so well as the employment of his own. Step by step as we proceeded, evidence arose of the true character of the faiths which ruled the world; and my observations issued in a view of their genealogy and its results which I certainly did not carry out with me, or invent by the way side. It was not till we had long left the Nile, and were leaving the desert, that the plan of my book occurred to me. The book itself had been determined on from the time when I found the influx of impressions growing painful, for want of expression; and various were the forms which I imagined for what I had to say; but none of them satisfied me till that in which it afterwards appeared struck me, and instantly approved itself to me. It happened amidst the dreariest part of the desert, between Petra and Hebron,—not far from the boundary of Judea.[3] I was ill, and in pain that day, from the face-ache which troubled me in the dryest weather, amidst the hottest part of the desert; and one of our party rode beside me, to amuse me with conversation. I told him that I had just been inspired with the main idea of my book about the East. 'That is,' said he, 'you think it the best scheme till you prefer another.' 'No,' I replied; 'there can be but one perfect one; and this completely answers to my view. My book will illustrate the genealogy, as it appears to me, of the old faiths,—the Egyptian, the Hebrew, the Christian and the Mohammedan.'[4] After my life-long study of the Hebrew and Christian, our travels in Palestine brought a rich accession of material for thought; and the Syrian part of the journey was the more profitable for what had gone before. The result of the whole, when

---

1   Christian Charles Josias Bunsen (1791–1860), Prussian diplomat, scholar of early Christianity, and author of *Egypt's Place in Universal History: An Historical Investigation in Five Books*, trans. Charles H. Cottrell (London: Longman, Brown, Green, and Longmans, 1846–47), a work that reconstructs Egyptian chronology and attempts to determine the development of the Egyptian language and religion in relation to those of other ancient peoples.

2   Karl Richard Lepsius (1810–84), Prussian Egyptologist who surveyed important Egyptian monuments, including the pyramids. Before touring northern Africa, Martineau might have seen his *A Tour from Thebes to the Peninsula of Sinai*, trans. Charles Herbert Cottrell (London: J. Petheram, 1846).

3   Hebron is in modern-day Israel; the Petra ruins are in modern-day Jordan; and the border is about half-way between, south of the Dead Sea.

4   *Eastern Life* follows this plan with sections on "Egypt and Its Faith," "Sinai and Its Faith," "Palestine and Its Faith," and "Syria and Its Faith."

reconsidered in the quiet of my study, was that I obtained clearness as to the historical nature and moral value of all theology whatever, and attained that view of it which has been set forth in some of my subsequent works. It was evident to me, in a way which it could never have been if I had not wandered amidst the old monuments and scenes of the various faiths, that a passage through these latter faiths is as natural to men, and was as necessary in those former periods of human progress, as fetishism is to the infant nations and individuals, without the notion being more true in the one case than in the other. Every child, and every childish tribe of people, transfers its own consciousness, by a supposition so necessary as to be an instinct, to all external objects, so as to conclude them all to be alive like itself; and passes through this stage of belief to a more reasonable view: and, in like manner, more advanced nations and individuals suppose a whole pantheon of Gods first,—and then a trinity,—and then a single deity;—all the divine beings being exaggerated men, regarding the universe from the human point of view, and under the influences of human notions and affections. In proportion as this stage is passed through, the conceptions of deity and divine government become abstract and indefinite, till the indistinguishable line is reached which is supposed, and not seen, to separate the highest order of Christian philosopher from the philosophical atheist. A future point of my narrative will be the proper one for disclosing how I reached the other point of view for which I was now exchanging the theological and metaphysical. What I have said will indicate the view under which I set about relating what I had seen and thought in the birthplaces of the old family of faiths.

I have said thus much, partly to show how I came by the views which I have been absurdly supposed to derive, in some necromantic way, from Mr. Atkinson.[1] The fact is, our intercourse on these subjects had as yet hardly amounted to any thing. It may be dated, I think, from a letter which I wrote him in November 1847, and his reply. I had returned from the East in June 1847, after an absence of eight months. I had then paid the visits which had been intercepted by my eastern travel, and had returned home early in October. After settling myself, and considering the plan and materials of my book, I consulted Mr. Atkinson as to whether honesty required that I should avow the total extent of my dissent from the world's theologies. I thought *not*, as my

---

[1]   Some of Martineau's friends and critics assumed that she had been unduly influenced by Atkinson in her rejection of theology, either because he mesmerized her or because she was lonely and needed the intellectual companionship that he offered.

subject was the mutual relation of those theologies, and not their relation to science and philosophy. I had no desire to conceal, as my subsequent writings have shown, my total relinquishment of theology; but it
did not seem to me that this book was the natural or proper ground for
that kind of discussion. The birthplaces of the four faiths had been my
study; and the four faiths were my specific subject; and it seemed to me
that it would spoil the book to intrude any other. Thus it was settled;
and the consideration of the point led to my writing the following letter
to Mr. Atkinson. I give it here that it may be seen how my passage from
theology to a more effectual philosophy was, in its early stages, entirely
independent of Mr. Atkinson's influence. It is true, these letters exhibit
a very early stage of conviction,—before I had attained firmness and
clearness, and while a large leaven of the old anxiety and obscurity
remained. I was, as Mr. Atkinson said, out of the old ways; and he was
about to show me the shortest way round the corner.

'Sunday evening, Nov. 7th, 1847.

'My dear friend,

'I seem to have much to say; but I waited to hear from you, because,
when people's letters once cross, as ours did last time, they generally
continue to do so. How I pity you for your yellow fog! Here it is grey
mist, hanging or driving about the mountain ridges. In the early morning I love to see it rising from the lake. I always go out before it is quite
light; and in the fine mornings I go up the hill behind the church—the
Kirkstone road—where I reach a great height, and see from half way
along Windermere to Rydal. When the little shred of moon that is left,
and the morning star, hang over Wansfell, among the amber clouds of
the approaching sunrise, it is delicious. On the positively rainy mornings, my walk is to Pelter Bridge and back. Sometimes it is round the
south end of the valley. These early walks (I sit down to breakfast at
half-past seven) are good, among other things, in preparing me in mind
for my work. It is *very serious* work. I feel it so, more and more. The
more I read (and I am reading a good deal) and the more I am struck
with the diversity of men's views, and the weakness, in some point or
other, of all, in the midst of great learning, the more presumptuous it
appears in me to speak at all. And yet, how are we to learn, if those who
have travelled to the birthplaces of the old world do not tell what they
think, in consequence of what they have seen? I have felt a good deal
depressed,—or rather, say oppressed,—today about this. Tomorrow

morning I begin upon my (necessary) sketch of the history of Egypt; and in preparation, I have been today reading again Heeren and Warburton.[1] While I value and admire their accumulation of facts, I cannot but dissent from their inferences; that is, some of the most important of them. For instance, Warburton declares that rulers have ever strenuously taught the people the doctrines of a future life, and reward and punishment, without believing them; admits that some of the Egyptian priests believed in the Unity of God, and that Moses knew their opinions; and then argues that it is a proof that Moses' legation was divine that he did not teach a future life, but a protracted temporal reward and punishment, extending to future generations. The existence, on the temple walls, of representations of judgment scenes, from the earliest times, and the presumption that the Egyptian priests believed in One (national) god,—Moses being in their confidence,—are inestimable facts to me; but my inference from the silence of Moses about a future life is that he was too honest to teach what he did not know to be true. But no more of this.

'The depressing feeling is from the conflict of opinions among people far wiser than myself about points which I do not believe at all; points which they believe, but in different ways. I am pretty confident that I am right in seeing the progression of ideas through thousands of years,—a progression advanced by every new form of faith (of the four great forms)—every one of these faiths being beset by the same corruptions. But I do not know of any one who has regarded the matter thus: and it is an awful thing to stand alone in;—for a half-learned person at least. But I cannot decline speaking about it. We cannot understand the old Egyptians and Arabians through any other channel of study. I must speak as diffidently as I truly feel, and as simply as possible. One thing (which I am to work out tomorrow) I cannot be wrong in;—in claiming for the old heathens the same rule we claim to be judged by. If we refuse to have our faith judged by our state of society, we must not conclude on theirs by *their* state of society. If we estimate our moral ideas by the minds of our best thinkers, we must estimate theirs by their philosophers, and not by the commonalty. Insisting on this, I think I

---

[1]   Arnold Hermann Ludwig Heeren (1760–1842), *Historical Researches into the Politics, Intercourse, and Trade of the Carthaginians, Ethiopians, and Egyptians,* trans. from the German (Oxford: D.A. Talboys, 1832). William Warburton (1698–1779), *The Divine Legation of Moses Demonstrated: on the principles of a religious deist, from the omission of the doctrine of a future state of reward and punishment in the Jewish dispensation* (London: F. Gyles, 1738–41). There are several nineteenth-century editions of both works which Martineau could have consulted.

can show that we have no right to despise either their faith or their best men. I must try, in short, to show that Men's faculties exist complete, and pretty much alike, in all ages; and that the diversity of the objects on which they are exercised is of far less consequence than the exercise itself.—Do you not feel strangely alone in your views of the highest subjects? I do. I really know of no one but you to whom I can speak freely about mine. To a great degree, I always did feel this. I used to long to be a Catholic, though I deeply suspected that no reliance on authority would give me peace of mind. Now, all such longings are out of the question; for I feel that I never *could* believe on any ground of reasoning what I once took for granted in prejudice. But I do feel sadly lonely, for this reason,—that I could not, if I tried, communicate to any one the *feeling* that I have that the theological belief of almost every body in the civilized world is baseless. The very statement between you and me looks startling in its presumption. And if I could, I dare not, till I have more assurance than I have now that my faith is enough for my own self-government and support. I know, as well as I ever knew any thing, that for support I really need nothing else than a steady desire to learn the truth and abide by it; and, for self-government, that it is enough to revere my own best nature and capabilities: but it will require a long process of proof before I can be sure that these convictions will avail me, under daily pressure, instead of those by which I have lived all my life. At my age, when the season of moral resolution, and of permanent fervour from the reception of new ideas is pretty well over, one's goodness must be, I fear, more the result of habit than of new inspiration.—And yet there is hope that some youthfulness is left in me, too. I trust so from my interest in the subjects I am now writing about: and I have lately fairly broken the only two bad habits that ever had much power over me. ... ...

'I quite enjoy your letter. I am always pleased to have your thoughts on your present subjects of study,—as I show by sending you mine. I agree emphatically with you about philosophers inventing methods instead of learning from nature how to teach.

'My house is so pretty, now it is finished! I hope Emerson is coming. Would you like to come and meet him or not? I don't know whether he interests you. ... ...'

Mr. Atkinson's reply was delightful to me at the time; and it is so now, in remembrance of that time,—the beginning of my free communication to him of my views and studies. It is no fair specimen of his letters when I rose to a more equal reciprocity of intercourse, and when the comfort and satisfaction which I derived from standing firm on a higher standpoint than I had at this time reached rendered unnecessary the kind of encouragement which I derived from the following letter:

'November 13, 1847,

'18, Upper Gloucester Place.

'My dear friend,

'Your letter has interested me *extremely*.—Most certainly we must judge the tree by its fruit, and the doctrine by its influence; calculating, of course, the whole circumstances and material in which that doctrine has to operate: and it would appear that all opinions with regard to a God and a future life had much the same fruits and sustaining influence, though producing results in proportion to the grossness and immorality of the times. But we must consider each view as a stage in the progress of knowledge and reason, and so, perhaps, essential to the circumstances of the times in which it existed. I would strongly urge a full consideration of this view; that Man cannot interfere with truth or nature; but that himself and his opinions are evolved in due course,— not in a perceptible direct line, but necessarily so, as regards the whole; so that in a wide view of the question, whatever is, is right, in its general and ultimate bearing, and ever must be so. That legislators have ever given forth certain views from motives of policy, and not from conviction of their truth, seems to me a most unwarrantable assertion, and certainly not agreeing with facts of the present times which we are able to recognise; though doubtless it was and is often so. You will do a great and good thing if you can trace the origin and progress of opinion in Egypt. I had designed to do this in a general and philosophical sense in the Introduction to my contemplated work, and to wage war, tooth and nail, as they say, against the assumptions of natural theology. Philosophers, with hardly an exception, cling to the idea of a God creator: Bacon at the head of them, saying that he would rather believe in all things most gross and absurd, than that creation was without a mind. How unphilosophical—I had almost said contemptible![1] I recognised a godhead long after I rejected a revelation; but I can now perceive no tittle of evidence, in the mind or out of the mind, so to speak,—for such a belief, but that

---

[1]   See in explanation of this, 'Letters on the Law of Man's Nature and Development,' pp. 180, 182, 183. [Martineau's note]

all evidence, reason and analogy are against it; and that the origin of the idea is traceable to the errors (and necessary errors) of the mind striving in ignorance.

'I delight in the tone of mind in which you enter on the inquiry with regard to Egypt's Faith. That noble feeling—faith, how sadly is it cramped and misapplied,—though never to be considered sad in its position in the chain of progress, any more than pain or death is sad, as essential to the progress of life, and the fulfilment of the law. It is well that men feel loneliness in advancing in truth, for it holds them back to instruct and bring others forward, and gives them a mission to perform, to save their fellows from that to which they cannot return. For knowledge, to the truthful and earnest, is a mistress to whom you are wedded for life: and in confidence and constancy must you seek your self-respect and happiness, whatever may be the peril and disaffection of the world. 'I place a sword in the world,' said Christ, 'and set brother against brother.'—'But blessed are those who are persecuted for righteousness' sake.' I see no pleasure in martyrdom: but I feel it necessary to die if it must be, in maintaining what I believe—earnestly, and in reason and faith believe,—to be true: to sacrifice friendship and every other thing to maintain this predominating impulse and want. You feel, nevertheless, a sense of loneliness now; and so do I; and have done more than I do now. But this is passing away, and one friend in truth is a host against the world assembled. The time may come when you, and perhaps I, may be pointed at and despised by thousands. Pshaw! what matter? I have more fear of an east wind or a November fog, than of all the hubbub they can make. But we may reasonably hope that it will not be so. There are too many believing as we believe on vital questions, and many more who are indifferent; and others may be convinced. Yet, still, the sense of loneliness will accompany you more or less through much of your social intercourse; and friends may grow cold, and you may be misrepresented and misunderstood. But out of this sense of loneliness shall grow your strength, as the oak, standing alone, grows and strengthens with the storm; whilst the ivy, clinging for protection to the old temple wall, has no power of self-support. Be sure that you will find sufficient, if you hold to the truth, and are true to yourself. How well does the great philosopher speak of the pleasure of standing fortified in truth watching the wandering up and down of other minds, and in pity and charity bending over their weakness! Strong in the faith and knowledge of good intentions, we must endeavour to fix the good, true, and noble impulses, and obliterate the evil ones. Thus we shall be strong in resignation and gratitude, enjoying all things that we may; indifferent as to the end, seeing that it is of no more consequence that we should live again, than that the pebble-stones should rise and become living beings. The difficulty is not in the condition of self-reliance, but in the want of sympathy under the pressure of adverse opinion, and the mass of our prejudices which still encumber the brain's action, and the soil where better thoughts and habits should have been early sown. Lesser minds will hereafter float easily and merrily down the stream where you find impediments; but the necessity of self-support will give you strength, and pleasures which they shall not feel; and so the balance and opportunity are more even than would at first appear. A noble path lies before you, and stern necessity bids you accept unmoved what was "designed"—for you from all time,—that link of being in which you exist and act. Not alone are we, but bound in the eternal laws of the whole. Let us unindividualize ourselves; —merge our personality in the infinite;—raise the ideal in our mind;—see each as but a part of that ideal;—and we lose the sense of imperfection—the sense of individual opinions and character, and rise into a new life of god-like conceptions—active, practical, and earnest; but above the accidents of life: not altogether separate from, but superior to them; enjoying all the harmonious action of mind and body; loving with all our heart and in spirit, all that is good and noble and most beautiful;—casting out and destroying every wrong ·action of the mind, as we would the pains and ills of the body:—warming with affection and interest for every human being; untouched except by pity for their ill thoughts of us:—such are aspirations which may live in the breast which has rejected its Man-God, and lost all faith in consciousness revived in the same shape and being from the grave. At least we lose the fear (if we have not the hope), and the curse of a cruel uncertainty, and are left free to enjoy the present in seeking our best and highest happiness and exaltation. The highest minds will still impress the world with the sense of what is right; and the religion of morals and philosophy will advance, until theology is in the grave, and man will be free to think, and, morally expanded, will be more free to act than perhaps has yet entered into many brains to conceive; because men, in their fears and ignorance, look into the darkness and not into the light, and cannot measure beyond their knowledge. But this is too much of a preachment,—so I say stop!

'I should like, indeed, very much to see Emerson if it could be, you may be sure. I think you have a very high opinion of him. I fear I have filled up my letter with nothing, when I have so much in my thoughts to say that has engaged my attention.

'Well, well,—all in time. I am glad to hear Mr. — — is talking over such important questions with you. I hope you will find him free and wise. Pray remember me to them, will you? and to that cheerful, dear woman, Mrs. —. You have not told me what is to be the motto of your dial. Never mind but you should differ from the world; and, with that wise doubt of self which you express, you need not fear; for that will lead you to dwell on evidence, and on the cause of your opponent's errors, and how you should be satisfied if your convictions be indeed the truth.

> 'Adieu, &c., &c.,
> 'H.G. ATKINSON.

'P.S.—A friend just writes to me that he cannot understand the consciousness of doing wrong, if we have no free will, and are not accountable. This is at the root of the errors of philosophers, who take a particular state of feeling for the simple and essential condition of an innate sense. They argue a God from a similar error. Conscience arises from a sense of right, with the desire that the right should be done. But what is felt to be right depends much on the state of opinion and society. The sense of sinning is a mere condition and habit of thinking, arising from a belief in free will—a deifying of the mind.

'Much of the manner that has been thought pride in me, has arisen from a sense of loneliness and non-sympathy with the opinions of others, and that they would dislike my opinions if they fully knew them. But I am passing over this barrier, in losing the care and thought of sympathy, in a livelier interest and care for the happiness of all, and in the thought of the ultimate glory and triumph of all truth—when the wrong shall prove right, and the right shall become wrong.'

My reply will close, for the present, the subject of my anti-theological views, at the beginning of my intimate correspondence with Mr. Atkinson.

> 'Ambleside, November 21, 1847.

'My dear friend,

'It was very kind of you to write that last letter to me. I agree in, and like, almost every word of it: but I was especially pleased to see your distinct recognition of the good of the old superstitions in their day. As a necessarian, you are of course bound to recognize this: but the way in which you point it out pleases me, because it is the great idea I have before me in my book. I have found the good of those old superstitions in my day. How it might have been with me (how much better) if I had had parents of your way of thinking, there is no saying. As it was, I was *very* religious (far beyond the knowledge and intentions of my parents) till I was quite grown up. I don't know what I should have done without my faith; for I was an unhealthy and most unhappy child, and had no other resource. Yet it used to strike me often, and most painfully, that whatever relief and comfort my religion gave to my feelings, it did not help me much against my faults. Certainly, my belief in a future life never was either check or stimulus to me in the matter of self-government. Five-and-twenty years ago I became a thoroughly grounded necessarian. I have never wavered for an hour on that point since; and nothing ever gave me so much comfort. Of course this paved the way for the cessation of prayer. I left off praying however, less from seeing the absurdity (though I did see it) of petitioning about things already ordained, than from a keen sense of the impiety of prayer. First, I could not pray for daily bread, or for any outward good, because I really did not wish to ask for them,—not knowing whether they would be good for me or not. So, for some years, I prayed only for good states of mind for myself and others. Of course, the feeling grew on me that true piety required resignation about spiritual matters as much as others. So I left off express prayer: and without remorse. As for Christ's example and need of prayer,—I felt that he did not mean what we mean by prayer: and I think so still. I think he would condemn our prayers as much as he did those of the Pharisees of his time: and that with him prayer was contemplation and aspiration chiefly.—Next, I saw very painfully (I mean with the pain of disgust) how much lower a thing it is to lead even the loftiest life from a regard to the will or mind of any other being, than from a natural working out of our own powers. I felt this first as to resignation under suffering, and soon after as to moral action. Now, I do know something of this matter of resignation. I know it to the very bottom. I have been a very great sufferer,—subject to keen miseries almost all my life till quite lately; and never, I am pretty confident, did any one acquiesce in God's will with a more permanent enthusiasm than I did;—because this suited the bent of my nature. But I became ashamed of this;—ashamed of that kind of support when I felt I had a much higher ground of patience in myself. (Only think how shocked the orthodox would be at this, and how they would talk of the depravity of our nature, and of my awful presumption! I saw a sort of scared smile on Mrs. —'s face the other day, when, in talking about education, I said we had yet to see what could be done by a direct appeal to our noble human nature. She, liberal as she is, thinks we have such active bad tendencies, such interior corruption, that we can do nothing without—not effort, or toil, but—Help. Yet she, and Mrs. — too, devours my Household Education papers, as if she had never met with any thing true before on that subject.[1] She says I most certainly have been a mother in a pre-existent state: and yet, if she knew that these papers were founded on 'infidel' and phrenological principles, she would mourn over me with deep grief.)—Well but, —you see now, how long a preparation I have had; and how gradual, for my present freedom.—As to what my present views are, when clearly brought to the point of expression, they are just these. I feel a most reverential sense of something wholly beyond our apprehension. Here we are, in the universe! this is all we know: and while we feel ourselves in this isolated position, with obscurity before and behind, we must feel that there is something above and beyond us. If that something were God (as people mean by that word, and I am confident it is not), he would consider those of us the noblest who must have evidence in order to belief;— who can wait to learn, rather than rush into supposition. As for the whole series of Faiths, my present studies would have been enough, if I had not been prepared before, to convince me that all the forms of the higher religions contain (in their best aspect) the same great and noble ideas, which arise naturally out of our own minds, and grow with the growth of the general mind; but that there is really *no* evidence whatever of any sort of revelation, at any point in the history. The idea of a future life, too, I take to be a necessary one (I mean necessary for support) in its proper place, but likely to die out when men better understand their nature and the *summum bonum* which it incloses. At the same time, so ignorant as I am of what is possible in nature, I do not deny the possibility of a life after death: and if I believed the desire for it to be as universal as I once thought it, I should look upon so universal a tendency as some presumption in favour of a continuous life. But

---

[1]   Most likely, Elisabeth Jesser Reid, widow of Dr. John Reid (who had died before Martineau moved to Tynemouth), and Eliza Fletcher (1770–1858), mother of her friend and neighbor Mrs. Margaret Davy (b. 1798), or possibly Mary Arnold, widow of Thomas Arnold (d. 1842), Despite their different views, Elisabeth Reid maintained her friendship with Martineau; Mrs. Fletcher "cut" her after the publication of the Atkinson letters.

I doubt the desire and belief being so general as they are said to be: and then, the evidence in favour of it is nothing;—except some unaccountable mesmeric stories.—As for your correspondent's very young question, about why we should do right,—how such remarks show that we neglect our own nature while running after the supposed pleasure of another! I am sure I never felt more desirous of the right than I do now, or more discomposed when it flashes across me that I have done wrong. But I need not write about this to you, of all people. —What a long confession of faith I have written you! Yes, it *is* faith, is it not?—and not infidelity, as ninety-nine hundredths of the world would call it.—As for the loneliness I spoke of, I don't generally mind it: and there is abundant ground of sympathy between me and my best friends, as long as occasion does not require that I should give names to my opinions. I have not yet had any struggle with my natural openness or indiscretion. I never could conceal any opinion I hold, and I am sure I never would: and I know therefore that I am at the mercy (in regard to reputation and some of my friendships) of accident, which may at any hour render an avowal necessary. But I do not fear this. I have run so many inferior risks, and suffered so little in peace by divers avowals and heresies, that I am not likely to tremble now. What does give me a qualm sometimes, is thinking what such friends as — and as — will suffer, whenever they come to know that I think their 'Christian hope' baseless. They are widows, and they live by their expectation of a future life.[1] I seriously believe that — would go mad or die, if this hope was shaken in her: and my opinions are more to her than any others since her husband's death. But I say to myself as you would say, —that these matters must take care of themselves. If the truth comes to me, I must believe it.—Yes, I should not wonder if there is a prodigious clamour against me, some day, as you say;—perhaps after this book comes out. But I don't think I should care for that, about a matter of opinion. I should (or might) about a matter of conduct; for I am sadly weak in my love of approbation: but about a matter of opinion, I can't and don't believe what I once did; and there's an end. It is a thing which settles itself;—for there is no going back to discarded beliefs. It is a great comfort to me to have you to speak to, and to look to for sympathy. It is a delightful indulgence and refreshment: but if you were to die, or to be engrossed by other interests and occupations, so as to diverge from

---

[1]   Martineau added this footnote: "I need not have feared. The one was offended and the other grieved; but neither understood me. The one behaved ill and the other well; and both presently settled down into their habitual conceptions."

me, I think I could do without sympathy, in a matter so certain as my inability to believe as I once did.—But enough and too much. There will surely never be occasion to write you such a letter again. But I have written, not so much about *my* mind, as about *a* mind, which you, as a philosopher, may like to see into, as well as to sympathise with as a friend …

I walk every morning, never stopping for weather. I shall have the young moon now for ten days. Emerson is engaged (lecturing) deep at present, but hopes to come by and by. He is free, if any man is. So I hope you can come when he does.—The motto of the dial is, 'Come, light! Visit me!' Old Wordsworth likes this much.

'O! your letter was very pleasant to me. We rarely agree as completely as I do in that.

'Good night!—it is late. Ever yours truly,

'H. MARTINEAU.'

Mr. Emerson did come. He spent a few days in February with me; and, unfavourable as the season was for seeing the district,—the fells and meadows being in their dunnest hay-colour instead of green,—he saw in rides with a neighbour and myself some of the most striking features in the nearer scenery. I remember bringing him, one early morning, the first green spray of the wild currant, from a warm nook. We met soon after in London, where Mr. Atkinson made acquaintance with him. It was a great pleasure to me to have for my guest one of the most honoured of my American hosts, and to find him as full as ever of the sincerity and serenity which had inspired me with so cordial a reverence twelve years before.

The mention of 'Household Education' in the letter just quoted reminds me of some work that I was busy about when invited to go to the East. 'The People's Journal' was then in the hands of Mr. Saunders,[1] who has since shown more of his quality than he had scope for in that periodical, but who engaged my respect by the spirit in which he carried on his enterprise. He was a perfect stranger to me before; but we soon became friends on the ground of that enterprise of his; and I wrote a good deal for him;—a set of papers called 'Surveys from the Mountain,'

---

[1]   John Saunders (1810–95) edited the short-lived *People's Journal*, to which Martineau contributed three articles titled "Lake and Mountain Holidays" (*People's Journal* 2 [1846], 1–2, 72–74, 149–50), as well as a monthly column, "Survey from the Mountain," which allowed her to comment on topics of current interest.

and many on desultory subjects: I forget when it was that he suggested the subject of 'Household Education' to me, as one which required different treatment from any that it had hitherto met with: but it was certainly after my return from the East, and after his discontinuance of the 'People's Journal,' that I planned the volume,—the first chapters of which had been written at his request.[1] When I was entirely independent of him, and had nothing to consider but the best use to make of my opportunity, I resolved to write the book for the Secularist order of parents. It had been conveyed to me, before this time, that there was a great want of juvenile literature for the Secularists, who could obtain few story-books for their children which were not stuffed with what was in their eyes pernicious superstition. People of all beliefs can see the hardship of this; and I was forcibly struck by it. If the age of fiction-writing had not been over with me, so that I felt that I *could not* write good stories, I should have responded to the appeal by writing more children's tales. The next best thing that I could do was to write for the Secularists a familiar book on 'Household Education.' Two surprises awaited me, on the appearance of that volume: —the bulk of the Secularist body, and the cordial reception of the book by Christian parents. After the publication of the 'Atkinson Letters,' I had reason to know how very different was the state of opinion in England from any thing that I had supposed when I had felt lonely in my views. I then found that I was, as far as I can discover, actually on the side of the majority of sensible and thoughtful persons; and that the Christians, who are apt to look on a seceder as, in some sort, a fallen person, are in fact in a minority, under that mode of reckoning. The reception of my book, when its qualities came to be understood, prepared me for the welcome discovery of the actual condition of the Secularists, and their daily extending prospects; while it proved that there are a good many Christian parents who can accept suggestion and aid from one who will not pronounce their Shibboleth; and that they can enter into moral sympathy with one who finds aspiration to be wholly unconnected with notions of inherent human corruption, free will, and the immortality of the soul. The book was published in 1848; and it must be published again; for it has been for some time out of print.[2]

The winter of 1847–8 passed delightfully in the preparation of my book. I doubt whether there is any higher pleasure, in which intellectual

---

[1]   Three articles became the core of *Household Education* (1848): "The Natural Possessions of Man," "How to Expect," and "The Golden Mean"; see *People's Journal* 2 (1846), 128–30, 205–07, 274–76.

[2]   *Household Education* (London: Edward Moxon, 1849; Philadelphia: Lea & Blanchard, 1849).

and moral enjoyment are commingled, than in writing a book from the heart;—a book of one's own conception and wrought out all alone: and I doubt whether any author could feel more satisfaction, (in proportion to individual capacity for pleasure, of course) in the production of a book than I did in regard to 'Eastern Life.' I wrote on in entire security about its publication; for I had made an agreement with Mr. Murray in the autumn. His father had wished to publish for me,[1] and had made more than one overture; and I wished to try whether there was advantage, in point of circulation, in being published by Murray. After the failure of the 'Game Law Tales,' I considered myself fully authorised to do the best I could for my next work; and especially for one so considerable as 'Eastern Life.' I had every desire that Mr. Murray should know precisely what he was undertaking; and I explained to him, in the presence of a witness, as distinctly as possible, and even with reiteration, what the plan and agreement of the book were designed to be. He seemed so entirely satisfied, and offered his terms afterwards with so much good will, that I never dreamed of difficulty, and sent him the MS. of the two first volumes when finished. After a note of acknowledgment and compliment, the MS. was immediately returned, with a curt note which afforded no explanation. Mr. Murray could not publish the book; and that was all. The story goes that Mr. Murray was alarmed by being told,—what he then gave forth as his plea for breach of contract,—that the book was a 'conspiracy against Moses.' Without crediting this joke in full, we may suppose that his clerical clients interfered to compel him to resign the publication; and I understood, on good authority, long after, when the success of the book was secure, that he heartily regretted the mischance. I wrote by the same day's post to Mr. Moxon, to tell him the facts of the case, and to offer him the publication, which he accepted by return of post,—on the usual terms; viz., that Mr. Moxon should take the risk, and give me two-thirds of the profits. The first year's proceeds made my house and its contents my own.[2] I declined all interest in the second edition, desiring that my share of the proceeds should go to the cheapening of the book. I had got all I wanted from it, in the way of money, and I had an earnest desire that it should circulate widely among the less opulent class who were most

---

[1]   The "father" is John Murray II (1778–1843), son of the founder of the publishing house, John Murray I (1745–1793). The "son" referred to here is John Murray III (1808–92).

[2]   According to Martineau's financial records, she made £620 on the sale of *Eastern Life*—considerably more than from any prior publications except the *Illustrations of Political Economy* and *Society in America*.

likely to sympathise with its contents. I do not know why I should not relate an incident, in connexion with this matter, which it gratifies me to recall. One day in the desert, when some hostile Arabs waylaid our party, my camel-leader trotted me away, against my will, from the spectacle of the fight which was to ensue. The same thing happened to Mr. and Mrs. Yates; and we three found ourselves near a clump of acacias where we were to await the event of the feud, and the rest of our caravan. We alighted, and sat down in the scanty shade. Mr. Yates observed that this encounter would be a picturesque incident for my book: and this led us to talk of whether there should be a book or not. I told Mr. Yates that this was a good opportunity for mentioning my chief scruple about writing the book at all. I knew he and Mrs. Yates would not sympathise in it; but yet it was best to utter it frankly. I scrupled about making money by a journey which was his gift. The surprise expressed in his countenance was really amusing. 'O, dear!' said he: 'I am sure Mrs. Yates and I shall be very happy indeed if you should be able so soon to make your house completely your own. It will be, indeed, *another* pleasant consequence of this journey, that we had not thought of.' It gave me hearty satisfaction, after this, to write to them that, through this book, their kind wish was fulfilled.

SECTION IV

The same mail which brought back my MS. from Mr. Murray brought the news of the flight of Louis Philippe.[1] My petty interests seemed unworthy of mention, even to myself, in the same day with that event. Mine were rearranged in three days, while the affairs of the Continent became more exciting from hour to hour. Towards the end of March, when my book was finished, and nearly ready for publication, letters came in, in increasing numbers, appealing to me for help, in one form or another, for or against popular interests, so far as they were supposed

---

[1]   Louis Philippe (1773–1850), the "Orleanist" King of France from 1830 to 1848, was initially admired as the "Citizen King," but his popularity suffered as his government became increasingly conservative and monarchical. When an economic crisis hit in 1847, the French working classes revolted, and Louis Philippe abdicated, fleeing Paris in an ordinary cab under the name of "Mr. Smith" and escaping to England.

to be represented by Chartism.[1] Of these letters, one was from the wife of a Cabinet Minister, an old acquaintance,[2] who was in a terrible panic about Feargus O'Connor and the threatened Chartist outbreak of the tenth of April, then approaching. She told me that she wrote under her husband's sanction, to ask me, now that they saw my book was advertised for publication, to use my power over the working-classes, to bring them to reason, &c., &c. The letter was all one tremor in regard to the Chartists, and flattery to myself. I replied that I had no influence, as far as I knew, with the Chartists; and that, as a matter of fact, I agreed with them in some points of doctrine while thinking them sadly mistaken in others, and in their proposed course of action. I told her that I had seen something in the newspapers which had made me think of going to London: and that if I did go, I would endeavour to see as many political leaders (in and out of parliament) as possible, and would, if she pleased, write her an account of what should seem to me the state of things, and the best to be done, by myself and others. It was an advertisement in the newspapers which had made me think of going;—the advertisement of a new periodical to be issued by Mr. Knight, called 'The Voice of the People.'[3] It was pointed out to me by several of my friends, as full of promise in such hands at such a time. The day after my letter to Lady —— —— was sent, I heard from Mr. Knight. He desired to see me so earnestly that he said, if I could not go to town, he would come to me,—ill as he could just then spare the time: or, he would come and fetch me, if I wished it. Of course, I went immediately; and I helped to the extent Mr. Knight wished, in his new periodical. But I saw immediately, as he did, that the thing would never do. The Whig touch perished it at once. The Whig officials set it up, and wished to dictate and control its management in a way which no literary man could have endured, if their ideas and feelings had been as good as possible. But the poverty and perverseness of their ideas and the insolence of their feelings were precisely what might be expected by all who really knew that remarkably vulgar class of men. They proposed to lecture the working-classes, who were by far the wiser party of the two,

---

[1]   A working-class movement for political equality. Its "charter"—expressed in a bill for parliamentary approval—included six points: universal manhood suffrage, equal electoral districts, annual parliamentary elections, voting by closed ballot, abolition of property qualifications for M.P.s, and payment for M.P.s.

[2]   Unidentified; possibly Lady Lansdowne, wife of Henry Petty-Fitzmaurice (1780–1863), 3rd Marquess of Lansdowne, or Lady Molesworth, wife of Sir William Molesworth (1810–55), 8th Baronet, and Radical politician.

[3]   Knight's *Voice of the People* lasted for three weeks only.

in a jejune, coaxing, dull, religious-tract sort of tone, and criticised and deprecated everything like vigour, and a manly and genial tone of address in the new publication, while trying to push in, as contributors, effete and exhausted writers, and friends of their own who knew about as much of the working-classes of England as of those of Turkey. Of course the scheme was a complete and immediate failure. On the insertion of an article by a Conservative Whig (which was certainly enough to account for the catastrophe), the sale fell to almost nothing at all; and Mr. Knight, who had before stood his ground manfully against the patrons of the scheme, threw up the business.

Meantime, the tenth of April arrived (while I was near London) and passed in the way which we all remember.[1] Lady — — wrote to me in a strain of exultation, as vulgar, to say the least, as Feargus O'Connor's behaviour,[2] about the escape of the government. She told of O'Connor's whimpering because his toes were trodden on; and was as insolent in her triumph about a result which was purely a citizen work as she had been abject when in fear that the Chartists would hold the metropolis. I felt the more obliged to write the promised letter, when I had seen several leading politicians of the Liberal party; and I did it when I came home. I did it carefully; and I submitted my letter to two ladies who were judges of manners, as well as of politics; and they gave it their sanction—one of them copying it, with entire approbation. Lady —'s reply was one of such insolence as precluded my writing to her again. She spoke of the 'lower classes' (she herself being a commoner by birth) as comprising all below the peerage; so that she classed together the merchants and manufacturers with 'cottagers' and even paupers: and, knowing me to be a manufacturer's daughter, she wrote of that class as low, and spoke of having been once obliged to pass a week in the house of a manufacturer, where the governess was maltreated with the tyranny which marks low people. My two consultees reddened with indignation at the personal insolence to myself; which I had overlooked in my disgust at the wrong to my 'order,' and to the 'cottagers' with whom she classed us. By their advice, I wrote a short note to this lady's husband, to explain that my letter was not a

---

[1]   On April 10, 1848, the Chartists planned a massive demonstration in London, including a march from Kennington Common to Parliament to present a petition with 5,706,000 signatures. Fearing insurrection, the Duke of Wellington put the military on guard, but the event fizzled out. It rained heavily, the petition was delivered by cab, and the crowds dispersed.

[2]   Feargus O'Connor (1794–1855), Chartist leader and founder of the influential *Northern Star* weekly, was elected M.P. for Nottingham in 1847 and presented the Chartist petition in Commons in 1848. He was considered to be a good public orator, but a poor organizer.

spontaneous address, as his lady now assumed, but written in answer to her request. This little transaction confirmed the impression which I had derived from all my recent intercourse with official Whigs;—that there was nothing to be expected from them now that they were spoiled by the possession of place and power. I had seen that they had learned nothing by their opportunities: that they were hardened in their conceit and their prejudices, and as blind as bats to the new lights which time was introducing into society. I expected what became apparent in the first year of the war,[1] when their incapacity and aristocratic self-complacency disgraced our administration, and lowered our national character in the eyes of the world, and cost their country many thousands of lives and many millions of treasure. I have seen a good deal of life and many varieties of manners; and it now appears to me that the broadest vulgarity I have encountered is in the families of official Whigs, who conceive themselves the cream of society, and the lights and rulers of the world of our empire. The time is not far off, though I shall not live to see it, when that coterie will be found to have brought about a social revolution more disastrous to themselves than anything that could have been rationally anticipated from poor Feargus O'Connor and his Chartist host of April 10th, 1848.

What Mr. Knight wanted of me at that time was not mainly my assistance in his new periodical, but to carry on an old enterprise which had been dropped. The 'History of the Thirty Years' Peace' had been begun long before; but difficulties had occurred which had brought it to a stand for two years past.[2] That his subscribers should have been thus apparently deserted, and left with the early numbers useless on their hands, was a heavy care to my good friend; and he proposed to me to release him from his uncomfortable position by undertaking to finish the work. I felt tempted; but I did not at all know whether I could write History. Under his encouragement I promised to try, if he could

---

1   I.e., the Crimean War, 1853–56. Martineau alludes to the disastrous loss at Balaclava, memorialized in Tennyson's "Charge of the Light Brigade," and the more widespread organizational failure that eventually brought down the ministry of George Gordon (1784–1860), Lord Aberdeen.

2   The first sixteen chapters of *The History of the Peace* were written by Knight, George Lillie Craik (1798–1866), and Charles McFarlane (d. 1858). Martineau finished the *History* and, at Knight's request, added a volume on the first fifteen years of the century, *Introduction to the History of the Peace: From 1800–1815* (1851). In a letter of May 23, 1850 to Fanny Wedgwood, Martineau explained: "After writing up to 1815, I am to rewrite the *dull* chapters of Craik and McFarlane; and in the winter, if I live, finish off with the next Xmas,— the close of the Half Century" (see Arbuckle, ed. *Letters*, pp. 108–9).

wait three months. I was writing 'Household Education,' and I had promised him an account of the Lake District, for the work he was publishing, called 'The Land we Live in.' It was on or about the 1st of August that I opened, for study, the books which Mr. Knight had been collecting and forwarding to me for the sources of my material.

This year was the beginning of a new work which has afforded me more vivid and unmixed pleasure than any, except authorship, that I ever undertook;—that of delivering a yearly course of lectures to the mechanics of Ambleside and their families. Nothing could have been further from my thoughts, at the outset, than such an extension of the first effort. On my return from the East, I was talking with a neighbour about the way in which children, and many other untravelled persons, regard the Holy Land. When Dr. Carpenter taught me in my youth, among his other catechumens, the geography of Palestine, with notices from Maundrell's travels there,[1] it was like finding out that a sort of fairy land was a real and substantial part of our everyday earth; and my eagerness to learn all about it was extreme, and highly improving in a religious sense. I remarked now to my neighbour that it was a pity that the school-children should not learn from me something of what I had learned in my youth from Maundrell. She seized upon the idea, and proposed that I should give familiar lectures to the monitors and best scholars of the national school,—sometimes, when convenient, to escape visitation, called the Squire's school.[2] I was willing, and we went to the school-mistress, whose reception of the scheme amused us much. She said she knew, and had taught the children, 'all about the sources of the Nile;' but that she should be glad to hear anything more that I had to tell. We could hardly refrain from asking her to teach us 'all about the sources of the Nile:' but we satisfied ourselves with fixing the plan for my addressing the children in the schoolhouse. I was more nervous the first time than ever after,—serious as was the extension of the plan. After the first lecture, which was to two or three rows of children and their school-mistress, a difficulty arose. The incumbent's lady[3] made a speech in School Committee, against our scheme, saying that the incumbent had found so much discontent in the parish

---

1   Henry Maundrell, *Journey from Aleppo to Jerusalem, at Easter, A.D. 1697.* In the most common nineteenth-century edition (London: J. White, 1810), an *Account of the Author's Journey to the Banks of Euphrates at Beer, and to the Country of Mesopotamia* was added.

2   I.e., to escape a visit from Her Majesty's school inspectors by attaching a private name to the school.

3   Possibly Mrs. Samuel Irton Fell, wife of the Anglican vicar, who remained on good terms with Martineau and whom Martineau called "kind Mrs. Irton Fell" in a letter to Effie Wedgwood (see Arbuckle, ed., *Letters*, p. 300).

from a dissenter having been allowed to set foot in the school-house, that its doors must be closed against me. She added some compliments to me and the lectures, which she expressed a great wish to hear, and so on. My neighbour immediately took all the blame on herself, saying that I had not even known where the school-house was till she introduced me to it; and that what I had done was at her request. She went straight to the authorities of the chapel which stands at the foot of my rock, and in an hour obtained from them in writing an assurance that it would give them 'the greatest pleasure' that I should lecture in their school-rooms. Armed with this, and blushing all over, my neighbour came, and was relieved to find that I was not offended but amused at the transaction. I proposed to have the children in my kitchen, which would hold them very well; and that we should invite the incumbent's lady to be present. My neighbour said 'No, no: she does not deserve that,' and produced the Methodists' gracious letter. I may add here that last year the incumbent's lady said, in a railway carriage, in the hearing of a friend of mine, that there was great alarm among the clergy when I first came to live at Ambleside; but that it had died away gradually and completely (even after the publication of the Atkinson Letters) from their finding that, while I thought it right to issue through the press whatever I thought, I never meddled with anybody's opinions in private. I may add, too, that I have been treated with courtesy and kindness, whenever occasion brought us together.

It occurs to me also to add an anecdote which diverted me and my friends at the time, and which seems more odd than ever, after the lapse of a few years. There is a book-club at Ambleside, the members of which are always complaining to outsiders of the dullness of the books, and the burdensomeness of the connection. I had had hints about the duty of neighbours to subscribe to the book-club; and when one or two books that I wished to see were circulating, I told a member that I was not anxious to join, at an expense which could hardly be compensated,—judging by what I heard about the choice of books: but that, if I ever joined, it should be then. She mentioned this to another member; and it was agreed that I should be proposed and seconded. But the gentleman she spoke to—always a friendly neighbour to me—called on her to communicate, with much concern, his apprehension that I might possibly be black-balled. He was entirely uncertain; but he had some notion that it might be so. The lady came, very nervous, to ask whether I would proceed or not. I had half a mind to try the experiment,—it would have been such a rich joke,—so voluminous a writer, and one so familiar in literary society in London, being black-balled in a country book-club! But I thought it more considerate not to thrust myself into any sort of connection with anybody who might be afraid of me. I profited by an invitation to join a few families in a subscription to a London library, by which, for less money, I got a sight of all the books I wished to see,—and no others; for my friends and I are of the same mind in our choice of reading.

At the second lecture, some of the parents and elder brothers and sisters of the children stole in to listen; and before I had done, there was a petition that I would deliver the lectures to grown people. I saw at once what an opportunity this was, and nerved myself to use it. I expanded the lectures, and made them of a higher cast; and before another year, the Mechanics of Ambleside and their families were eager for other subjects. I have since lectured every winter but two; and with singular satisfaction. The winter was the time chosen, because the apprentices and shop-keepers could not leave their business in time, when the days lengthened. No gentry were admitted, except two or three friends who took tea with me, and went as my staff,—in order to help me, if any difficulty arose, and to let me know if I spoke either too loud or too low; a matter of which, from my deafness, I could not judge. It is rather remarkable that, being so deaf, and having never before spoken in any but a conversational tone, I never got wrong as to loudness. I placed one of my servants at the far end of the room; and relied on her to take out her handkerchief if she failed to hear me; but it always went well. I made notes on half-a-sheet of paper, of dates or other numbers, or of facts which might slip my memory; but I trusted entirely to my power at the time for my matter and words. I never wrote a sentence; and I never once stopped for a word.—The reasons why no gentry were admitted were, first, because there was no room for more than the 'workies'; and next, that I wished to keep the thing natural and quiet. If once the affair got into the newspapers, there would be an end of the simplicity of the proceeding. Again, I had, as I told the gentry, nothing new to tell to persons who had books at home, and leisure to read them.—My object was to give rational amusement to men whom all circumstances seemed to conspire to drive to the public-house, and to interest them in matters which might lead them to books, or at least give them something to think about. My lectures were maliciously misrepresented by a quizzer here and there, and especially by a lawyer or two, who came this way on circuit, and professed to have been present; but they were welcome to their amusement, as long as it was an indisputable matter that they had *not* been present.

The second course was on Sanitary matters; and it was an effectual preparation for my scheme of instituting a Building Society. In a place like Ambleside, where wages are high, the screw is applied to the working men in regard to their dwellings. The great land-owners, who can always find room to build mansions, have never a corner for a cottage: and not only are rents excessively high, but it is a serious matter for a working man to offend his landlord, by going to chapel instead of church, for instance, when he may be met by the threat—'If you enter that chapel again, I will turn your family out of your cottage; and you know you can't get another.' When the people are compelled to sleep, ten, twelve, or fourteen in two rooms, there can be little hope for their morals or manners; and one of the causes of the excessive intemperance of the population is well known to be the discomfort of the crowded dwellings. When the young men come home to bad smells and no room to turn, they go off to the public-house. The kindhearted among the gentry tend the sick, and pray with the disheartened, and reprove the sinner; but I have found it singularly difficult to persuade them that, however good may be wine and broth, and prayers and admonition, it is better to cut off the sources of disease, sin and misery by a purer method of living. My recourse was to the 'workies' themselves, in that set of lectures; in which I endeavoured to show them that all the means of healthy and virtuous living were around them,—in a wide space of country, slopes for drainage, floods of gushing water, and the wholesomest air imaginable. I showed them how they were paying away in rent, money enough to provide every head of a household with a cottage of his own in a few years; and I explained to them the principle of such a Building Society as we might have,—free from the dangers which beset such societies in large towns, where the members are unknown to each other, and sharp lawyers may get in to occasion trouble. They saw at once that if twenty men lay by together, instead of separately, a shilling a week each, they need not wait twenty weeks for any one to have the use of a pound; but the twentieth man may have his pound, just the same, while the other nineteen will have had earlier use of theirs and be paying interest for it. Hence arose our Building Society; the meeting to form it being held in my kitchen. A generous friend of mine advanced the money to buy a field, which I got surveyed, parcelled out, drained, fenced, and prepared for use.[1] The lots were immediately purchased, and paid for without default. Impediments and diffi-

---

[1]   Elisabeth Reid advanced funds in January, 1849 for two cottages; Mary Arnold and her daughter Mary Twining (1825–88) also purchased plots for cottages; and others were built from collective funds of the Building Society.

culties arose, as might be expected. Jealousy and ridicule were at work against the scheme. Some who might have helped it were selfish, and others timid. Death (among a population where almost every man drinks) and emigration, and other causes impeded an increase of members; and the property was less held by working men, and more by opulent persons, than I had desired and intended; but the result is, on the whole, satisfactory, inasmuch as thirteen cottages have arisen already; and more are in prospect: and this number is no small relief in a little country town like Ambleside. The eye of visitors is now caught by an upland hamlet, just above the parsonage, where there are two good houses, and some ranges of cottages which will stand, as the builders say, 'a thousand years,'—so substantial is the mode of building the grey stone dwellings of the district. I scarcely need add that I made no reference, in the lectures or otherwise, to the form of tyranny exercised by the owners of land and houses. My business was to preclude the tyranny, by showing the people that their own interests were in their own hands, and by no means to excite angry feelings about grievances which I hoped to mitigate, or even extinguish.

The generous friend who enabled me to buy the land declined to receive the money back. She is the proprietress of two of the cottages and their gardens; and she placed the rest of the money at my disposal, for the benefit of the place, as long as it was wanted. Since my illness began, three months ago, I have transferred the trust to other hands; and there is reason to hope that the place will be provided with a good Mechanics' Institute, and Baths,—which are now the next great want.

In the two last lectures of the Sanitary course, there was an opportunity for dealing with the great curse of the place,—its intemperance. Those two lectures were on the Stomach and Brain. I drew the outline of the stomach on a large expanse of paper, which was fixed in front of the desk; and I sent round the coloured prints, used in Temperance Societies, of the appearances of progressive disease in the drunkard's stomach,—from the first faint blush of inflammation to the schirrous condition. It was a subject which had long and deeply engaged my attention; and my audience, so closely packed as that the movement of one person swayed the whole, were as much interested as myself; so that my lecture spread out to an hour and twenty minutes, without my being at all aware of the time. The only stir, except when the prints were handed round, was made by a young man who staggered out, and fainted at the door. He was a recent comer to the place, and had lately begun to tipple, like his neighbours. After that night, he joined my Building Society, that he might have no money for the public-house.

Many told me afterwards that they were sick with pain of mind during that lecture; and I found, on inquiry, that there was probably hardly a listener there, except the children, who had not family reasons for strong emotion during an exposure of the results of intemperate habits.

The longest course I have given was one of twenty lectures on the History of England, from the earliest days of tradition to the beginning of the present century. Another was on the History of America, from its discovery by Columbus to the death of Washington. This was to have been followed by a course which I shall not live to offer;—the modern History of the United States—with a special view to recommend the Anti-slavery cause. Last November and December, I addressed my neighbours for the last time,—On Russia and the War. At the close, I told them that if I were alive and well next winter, we would carry on the subject to the close of the campaign of 1855. I should be happy to know that some one would take up my work, and not allow my neighbours to suffer by my departure. I found myself fatigued and faint during the two last lectures; and I spoke seriously when making my conditional promise for another season; but I had no clear notion how ill I was, even then, and that I should never meet that array of honest, earnest faces again.

There was some fear that the strong political interests of the spring of 1848 would interfere with the literary prosperity of the season. Whether they did or not, I do not know. For my own part I cared more for newspapers than books in that exciting year; but my own book had an excellent sale.[1] The remembrance of the newspaper reading of those revolutionary times recalls a group of circumstances in my own experience which may be worth recording,—to show how important a work it is to give an account of the constitution and politics of a foreign nation.— Ten years before this,—(I think it was the year before my long illness began) a gentleman was brought to a *soirée* at my mother's house, and introduced to me by a friend, who intimated that the stranger had a message to deliver to me. The gentleman had been for some time resident in Sweden, where he was intimately acquainted with the late Prime Minister. The Crown Prince Oscar of that day (the present King)[2] was earnestly desirous of introducing constitutional reforms on a large scale, many of which, as we all know, he has since achieved. The retired Prime

---

[1]   The large print run of *Eastern Life*, published in 1848, had nearly sold out by January, 1849.
[2]   Oskar I, King of Sweden from 1844 to 1859.

Minister desired my guest of that evening to procure an introduction to me, and to be the bearer of an invitation to me to spend a Swedish summer at the Minister's country-house, where his lady and family would make me welcome. His object was, he said, to discuss some political topics of deep interest to Sweden; and he conceived that my books on America showed me to be the person whom he wanted;—to be capable, in fact, of understanding the working of the constitutions of foreign nations. He wanted to talk over the condition and prospects of Sweden in the light of the experiments of other countries. I could not think of going; and I forgot the invitation till it was recalled to memory by an incident which happened in April 1839. I was then going to Switzerland with three friends, and our passage to Rotterdam was taken, when a friend of my family, the English representative of an Irish county, called on me with an earnest request that I would suspend my scheme, for reasons which he would assign in a few days.[1] I explained that I really could not do so, as I was pledged to accompany a sick cousin. In a day or two, my friend called, to insist on my dining at his house the next Wednesday, to meet Mr. O'Connell on business of importance. Mr. O'Connell could not be in town earlier, because the freedom of some place (I forget what) was to be presented to him on Tuesday; and travelling all night would bring him to London only on Wednesday afternoon. I could not meet him, as we were to go on board the packet on Wednesday evening.—My friend, hoping still to dissuade me, told me what Mr. O'Connell wanted. He had private reasons for believing that 'Peel and the Tories' would soon come into power: (in fact, the Bedchamber Question occurred within a month after)[2] and he feared more than ever for the liberties of Ireland, and felt that not a day must be lost in providing every assistance to the cause that could be obtained. He had long been convinced that one of the chief misfortunes of Ireland was that her cause was pleaded in print by authors who repre-sented only the violent, and vulgar, and factious elements of Irish discon-tent; by Irish people, in fact, who could not speak in a way which the English were willing to listen to. He considered that my American books established my capacity to understand and represent the political and social

---

[1] This was the ill-fated trip during which Martineau collapsed in Venice and returned to nearly six years of illness in Tynemouth. The Irish representative for Dublin City was Robert Hutton, of Putney Park, Surrey (according to Hansard's *Members of Parliament: Return … of the names of every member returned to serve in each parliament … up to the present time*). The Martineaus knew the Huttons through James's work with Joseph Hutton, Unitarian minis-ter at Eustace Street Chapel in Dublin, under whom James served in the 1830s.

[2] See Period IV, sec. iv, p. 420, n. 2.

condition of another country; and what he had to request was that I would study Irish affairs on the spot, and report of them. He offered introductions to the best-informed Catholic families in any or every part of Ireland, and besought me to devote to the object all the time I thought needful,— either employing twelve months or so in going over the whole of Ireland, or a shorter time in a deeper study of any particular part,—publishing the results of my observations without interference from anybody, or the expression of any desire from any quarter that my opinions should be of one colour rather than another.

It was impossible for me to say anything to this scheme at the time: but my family and friends were deeply impressed by it. It was frequently discussed by my comrades and myself during our continental journey; and one of them,—the same generous friend to whom I have had occasion to refer in connexion with my Ambleside schemes,[1]—offered to accompany me, with a servant, to help and countenance me, and *hear* for me, and further the object in every possible way; and she was not the only one who so volunteered. It stood before my mind as the next great work to be undertaken: but, in another month, not only were 'Peel and the Tories' sent to the right-about for the time, but I was prostrate in the illness which was to lay me aside for nearly six years. On our return from Italy, we fell in with the family of Lord Plunket,[2] to whom, in the course of conversation about Ireland, we related the incident. Miss Plunket seemed as much struck with the rationality of the scheme as we were; and, after some consultation apart, Miss Plunket came to me with an express offer of introductions from Lord Plunket to intelligent Protestants, in any or every part of Ireland where this business might carry me. My illness, however, broke up the scheme.

This incident, again, was recalled to my memory by what happened the next time I was abroad. It occurred in the spring of 1847. Our desert party agreed, at Jerusalem, to make an excursion of three days to the Jordan and the Dead Sea. On the eve of the trip, three European gentlemen sent a petition to Lady Harriet K— —,[3] that they might be allowed to ride with our party, on account of the dangerous state of the road to Jericho. They joined our troop in the Valley of Jehosaphat, and rode among us all day. It did not occur to me to ask who they were. In

---

[1]   Elisabeth Reid; see p. 542, n. 1.

[2]   William Conyngham Plunket (1764–1854), 1st Baron Plunket, Irish lawyer and lord chancellor of Ireland from 1830 to 1841.

[3]   In Part III, ch. iv, of *Eastern Life*, Martineau records that "four strangers—European gentlemen ... asked permission to ride with us," without revealing their names as she does below.

the course of the next morning, when the ladies of the party were going through the wood on the bank of the Jordan, to bathe northwards, while the gentlemen went southwards, we met one of these strangers; and I told him where he might find his companions. I never doubted his being English,—he looked so like a country squire, with his close-cropped, rather light hair, and sunburned complexion. He appeared to be somewhere about five-and-thirty. On leaving the Jordan, we had to traverse an open tract, in excessive heat, to the margin of the Dead Sea. The hard sand looked trustworthy; and I put my horse to a gallop, for the sake of the wind thus obtained. I soon heard other horses coming up; and this gentleman, with two others, appeared: and he rode close by my side till an accident to one of the party obliged him to dismount and give help. I was among those who rode on when we found that no harm was done; and presently after I was asked by Lady Harriet K— — whether I would allow Count Porro to be introduced to me,—he being desirous of some conversation with me.[1] For Silvio Pellico's sake, as well as Count Porro's father's and his own, I was happy to make his acquaintance; and I supposed we should meet at our halting place,—at Santa Saba. But Count Porro and his companions were to strike off northwards by the Damascus road; and they were gone before I was aware.—A few weeks afterwards, when we four, of the Nile party, rode up to our hotel at Damascus, Count Porro was awaiting us; and he helped us ladies down from our horses. He had remained some days, in order to see me. He desired some conversation with me at a convenient time; and that convenient time proved to be the next morning, when he joined me on the divan, in the alcove in the quadrangle. He was so agitated that he could scarcely speak. His English, however, was excellent. He told me that in what he was going to say he was the mouth-piece of many of his countrymen, as well as of his own wishes; and especially of several fellow-citizens of Milan. What he said was as nearly as could be a repetition of O'Connell's plea and request. He said it was the misfortune of his country to be represented abroad by injured and exasperated patriots, who demanded more than the bulk of the people desired, and gave forth views which the citizens in general disclaimed. It was believed by the leading men in Lombardy that the changes which were really most essential might

---

[1] Silvio Pellico (1788–1854) was an Italian dramatist imprisoned by the Austrians for his revolutionary writings, including articles in *Il Conciliatore*; his autobiography, *The Imprisonments of Silvio Pellico* (Edinburgh, 1839), details his suffering during his ten years in a Milanese prison. He was tutor to the two sons of Count Porro Lambertenghi; both Counts Porro, father and son, were anti-Austrian patriots and active supporters of Italian unification.

be obtained from Austria, if sought in a temperate and rational manner;[1] and that the best way of obtaining these changes would be by means of a report on the condition of affairs by some traveller of reputation, who had shown, as they considered that I had done by my work on the United States, a capacity to understand and report of a foreign state of society. He was therefore authorised to request that I would reside in Milan for six months or a year, and to say that every facility should be afforded for my obtaining information, and all possible respect shown to my liberty of judgment and representation. All they wanted was that I should study their condition, and report it fully, on my return to England. He told me (in consideration of my deafness, which disabled me for conversation, though not, of course, for reading, in a foreign language) that every educated Milanese speaks English; and that every thing should be done to render my abode as pleasant as possible; and so forth.—I positively declined, being, in truth, heartily home-sick,—longing for my green, quiet valley, and the repose of my own abode. My duties there seemed more congenial and natural than investigating the politics of Lombardy; and I did not therefore think it selfish to refuse. With increasing agitation, Count Porro declared that he would take no refusal. He asked how much time these home duties would occupy; said, in spite of all my discouragements, that he should go to England the next spring; and declared, when taking his leave next day, that, on landing at Southampton, his first step would be to put himself into the train for Ambleside, whence he would not depart without my promise to go to Milan.

When that 'next spring' arrived,—the anniversary of those conversations of ours at Damascus,—Count Porro was a member of the Provisional Government at Milan, telling Austria by his acts and decrees what it was that Lombardy required. The mention, in my narrative, of the revolutions of 1848 brought up these three stories at once to my recollection; and their strong resemblance to each other seems to show that there must be something in them which makes them worth the telling.

I began my great task of the History under much anxiety of mind. My mother was known to be dying from the spring onwards; and she died in August.[2] She was removed, while yet able, to the house of her eldest surviving son, at Edgbaston; and there, amidst the best possible tendance, she declined and died. Her life hung upon perfect quiet; and

---

[1]   1848 was a year of uprisings to support Italian independence and unification ("Risorgimento"); as this passage suggests, some Italian patriots advocated negotiation rather than military action.

[2]   1848.

therefore, as all her children had seen her not long before, it was considered best to leave her in the good hands of one of the families. I saw her
at Liverpool, on my return home from the East. By evil offices, working on her prejudice against mesmerism, she had been prevented from
meeting me after my recovery:[1] but such a cause of separation was too
absurd to be perpetual. I knew that the sound of my voice, and my mere
presence for five minutes, would put to flight all objections to my mode
of recovery: and we did meet and part in comfort and satisfaction. I did
hope to have had the pleasure of a visit from her that summer, though
I proposed it with much doubt. She was now blind; and she could not
but be perpetually hearing of the charms of the scenery. She could walk
only on smooth and level ground; and walking was essential to her
health: and it is not easy to find smooth level ground in our valley. Yet,
as one main inducement to my building and settling here was that there
might be a paradise for any tired or delicate members of my family to
rest in, I did wish that my mother should have tried it, this first practicable summer: but she was too ill to do more than go to Edgbaston, and
find her grave there. She was in her seventy-sixth year,—I have never
felt otherwise than soundly and substantially happy, during this last term
of my life: but certainly those months of July and August 1848 were the
most anxious of the whole ten years since I left Tynemouth. The same
faithful old friend to whom I have often referred, must come into my
history again here.[2] She came to me when I was becoming most
anxious, and remained above two months,—saving me from being overwhelmed with visits from strangers, and taking me quiet drives when
my work was done;—a recreation which I have always found the most
refreshing of all. Some of my own family came before the event, and
some after; and a few old and dear friends looked in upon me in the
course of the season.

When I had laid out my plan for the History and begun upon the
first portion, I sank into a state of dismay. I should hardly say 'sank;' for
I never thought of giving up or stopping; but I doubt whether, at any
point of my career, I ever felt so oppressed by what I had undertaken
as during the first two or three weeks after I had begun the History.
The idea of publishing a number of my Political Economy series every
month was fearful at first: but that was only the quantity of work. The

---

[1]   Although the passive construction allows Martineau to avoid naming names, her letters
    suggest that her brother James and sister Elizabeth caused the family to take sides on the
    mesmeristic "cure."
[2]   Elisabeth Reid.

Discontented Pendulum[1] comforted me then,—not only because every month's work would have its own month to be done in, but because there was a clear, separate topic for each number, which would enable the work to take care of itself, in regard to subject as well as time. In America, I was overwhelmed with the mass of material to be dealt with; but then, I was not engaged to write a book; and by the time I had made up my mind to do so, the mass had become classified. Now, the quantity and variety of details fairly overpowered my spirits, in that hot month of August. I feel my weakness,—more in body than (consciously) in mind—in having to deal with many details. The most fatiguing work I ever have to do is arranging my library; and even packing my trunks for a journey, distributing the contents when I come home, fatigues me more than it seems to do other people. In this case, I fear I afflicted my friend by my discouragement,—the like of which she had never seen in me. At times, she comforted me with assurances that the chaos would become orderly; but, on the whole, she desired that I should throw up the work,—a thing which I could not even meditate for a moment, under the circumstances in which Mr. Knight found himself. No doubt, the nervous watching of the post at that time had much to do with my anxiety. My habit was to rise at six, and to take a walk,—returning to my solitary breakfast at half-past seven. For several years, while I was strong enough, I found this an excellent preparation for work. My household orders were given for the day, and all affairs settled, out of doors and in, by a quarter or half-past eight, when I went to work, which I continued without interruption, except from the post, till three o'clock, or later, when alone. While my friend was with me, we dined at two; and that was, of course, the limit of my day's work. The post came in at half-past ten; and my object was to keep close to my work till the letters appeared. When my mother became so ill that this effort was beyond my power, I sent to meet the coach, and got my letters earlier; but the wear and tear of nerve was very great. One strong evidence of the reality of my recovery was that my health stood the struggle very well. In a few weeks, I was in full career, and had got my work well in hand. My first clear relief came when I had written a certain passage about Canning's eloquence, and found in the course of it that I really was interested in my business. Mr. Knight, happily, was satisfied; and I was indebted to him for every kind of

---

[1]   "The Discontented Pendulum," a children's tale by Jane Taylor (1783–1824), tells of an old clock that suddenly stops ticking when the pendulum announces, "I am tired of ticking."

encouragement. By the 1st of February, the last MS. of the first volume was in the hands of the printer. I mention this because a contemporary review spoke of 'two years' as the time it had occupied me,—calling it very rapid work; whereas, from the first opening of the books to study for the History to the depositing of the MS. of the first volume at press was exactly six months. The second volume took six months to do, with an interval of some weeks of holiday, and other work. I delivered the last sheets into Mr. Knight's hands in November 1849.

During the year 1849,—the dismal cholera year,[1]—I found that I had been overworking; and in the autumn I accepted Mrs. Knight's invitation to join their family at St. Leonards for a month, and then to stay with them for the remaining weeks which were necessary to finish the History.[2] The Sunday when I put the last batch of MS. into Mr. Knight's hands was a memorable day to me. I had grown nervous towards the end; and especially doubtful, without any assignable reason, whether Mr. Knight would like the concluding portion. To put it out of my mind, I went a long walk after breakfast with Mr. Atkinson to Primrose Hill (where I had never been before) and Regent's park.[3] My heart fluttered all the way; and when I came home, to meet a farewell family party at lunch, I could not eat. Mr. Knight looked at me, with an expression of countenance which I could not interpret; and when he beckoned me into the drawing-room, I was ready to drop. I might have spared myself the alarm. His acknowledgments were such as sent me to my room perfectly happy; and I returned to my Knoll with a light heart. I was soon followed by an invitation from Mr. Knight to write the introductory period, from the opening of the century to the Peace, to be followed by the four years to 1850, if we should live to see the close of that year, so as to make a complete 'History of the Half Century.' The work would be comparatively light, from the quantity of material supplied by the Memoirs of the statesmen now long dead. I was somewhat disappointed in regard to the pleasure of it from Mr. Knight's frequent changes of mind as to the form in which it was to be done. I imagine he had become somewhat tired of the scheme; for, not only was I kept waiting weeks, and once three months, for a promised letter which should guide me as to space and other particulars; but he three times

---

[1]   By 1848 another cholera epidemic reached Britain from the Continent, killing over 100,000 by 1849; see Period IV, sec. i, for the impact of the first cholera epidemic.

[2]   Martineau went to visit the Knights in October, 1849. St. Leonards is a sea-side town near Hastings on the English Channel; the Knights' London home was then in St. John's Wood.

[3]   Primrose Hill is north of London, above Regent's Park.

changed his mind as to the form in which he should present the whole. He approved, as cordially as ever, what I wrote; but finally decided to print the portion from 1800 to the Peace as an Introductory volume,[1] relinquishing the project of completing the Half Century by a History of the last four years. I state these facts because it was afterwards believed by many people, who quoted his authority, that he broke off the scheme, to his own injury, from terror at the publication of the Atkinson Letters,—as if he had been taken by surprise by that publication. I can only say that it was as far as possible from being my intention to conceal our plan of publishing those Letters. I not only told him of it while at his house in the autumn of 1849, and received certain sarcasms from him on our 'infidel' philosophy; but I read to Mrs. Knight two of the boldest of Mr. Atkinson's letters: and it was after this that Mr. Knight invited me to write the Introductory volume. Moreover, it was after some of his changes of plan that he stayed at my house (May 1850) with Mr. Atkinson and Mr. Jerrold,[2] and considerately took Mr. Jerrold for a walk, on the last day of their visit, to leave Mr. Atkinson and me at liberty to read our manuscript. He was certainly panic-stricken when the volume appeared, in January 1851; but, if he was surprised, it was through no fault of mine, as the dates show. In July 1851, half-a-year after the 'Letters' appeared, when he paid me for my work at his own house, he expressed himself more than satisfied with the Introductory History, and told me that, though the Exhibition had interfered with the publishing season, he had sold two-thirds of the edition, and had no doubt of its entire success in the next. Before the next season opened, however, he sold off the whole work. With his reasons for doing so I have no concern, as the preceding facts show. In regard to him, I need only say,—which I do with great pleasure,—that he has continued to show me kindness and affection, worthy of our long friendship. In regard to the History,—it has passed into the hands of Messrs. Chambers of Edinburgh, who invited me, last summer, to bring the History of the Peace down to the War. I agreed to do so; and the scheme was only broken off by my present illness, which, of course, renders the execution of it impossible.[3]

---

[1]   *Introduction to the History of the Peace: From 1800–1815* (London: Charles Knight, 1851).

[2]   Douglas Jerrold (1803–57), dramatist, journalist, and contributor to *Punch* from its founding in 1841.

[3]   Despite this statement, the work was later issued in its entirety as *A History of England from the Commencement of the XIXth Century to the Crimean War* by two American publishers (Philadelphia, Porter & Coates, 1864; Boston, Walker, Wise, 1865–66). The Chambers brothers issued yet another version, *The Pictorial History of England; Being a History of the People as well as a History of the Kingdom* (London: W. and R. Chambers, 1855–58).

SECTION V

On the last evening of my stay at Mr. Knight's a parcel arrived for me, enclosing a book, and a note which was examined as few notes ever are. The book was 'Shirley;' and the note was from 'Currer Bell.' Here it is:

'Currer Bell offers a copy of "Shirley" to Miss Martineau's acceptance, in acknowledgment of the pleasure and profit ~~she~~ (sic) he has derived from her works. When C.B. first read "Deerbrook" he tasted a new and keen pleasure, and experienced a genuine benefit. In his mind, "Deerbrook" ranks with the writings that have really done him good, added to his stock of ideas, and rectified his views of life.'
'November 7th, 1849.'

We examined this note to make out whether it was written by a man or a woman. The hand was a cramped and nervous one, which might belong to any body who had written too much, or was in bad health, or who had been badly taught. The erased 'she' seemed at first to settle the matter; but somebody suggested that the 'she' might refer to me under a form of sentence which might easily have been changed in the penning. I had made up my mind, as I had repeatedly said, that a certain passage in 'Jane Eyre,' about sewing on brass rings, could have been written only by a woman or an upholsterer. I now addressed my reply externally to 'Currer Bell, Esq.,' and began it 'Madam.'—I had more reason for interest than even the deeply-interested public in knowing who wrote 'Jane Eyre;' for, when it appeared,[1] I was taxed with the authorship by more than one personal friend, and charged by others, and even by relatives, with knowing the author, and having supplied some of the facts of the first volume from my own childhood. When I read it, I was convinced that it was by some friend of my own, who had portions of my childish experience in his or her mind. 'Currer Bell' told me long after, that she had read with astonishment those parts of 'Household Education' which relate my own experience. It was like

---

[1]   *Jane Eyre* was published by Smith, Elder in October, 1847.

meeting her own fetch,—so precisely were the fears and miseries there described the same as her own, told or not told in 'Jane Eyre.'

A month after my receipt of 'Shirley,' I removed, on a certain Saturday, from the house of a friend in Hyde Park Street to that of a cousin in Westbourne Street,[1] in time for a dinner party. Meanwhile, a messenger was running about to find me, and reached my cousin's when we were at dessert, bringing the following note:

'December 8th, 1849.

My dear Madam,

'I happen to be staying in London for a few days; and having just heard that you are likewise in town, I could not help feeling a very strong wish to see you. If you will permit me to call upon you, have the goodness to tell me when to come. Should you prefer calling on me, my address is ... ... [2]

'Do not think this request springs from mere curiosity. I hope it has its origin in a better feeling. It would grieve me to lose this chance of seeing one whose works have so often made her the subject of my thoughts.

'I am, my dear Madam,

'Yours sincerely,

'CURRER BELL.'

My host and hostess desired me to ask the favour of C.B.'s company the next day, or any subsequent one. According to the old dissenting custom of early hours on Sundays, we should have tea at six the next evening:—on any other day, dinner at a somewhat later hour. The servant was sent with this invitation on Sunday morning, and brought back the following reply:

'My dear Madam,

'I hope to have the pleasure of seeing you at six o'clock to-day:— and I shall try now to be patient till six o'clock comes.

'I am, &c., &c.'

---

[1] Her cousin Richard Martineau, managing director of Whitbread Brewery, lived at 17 Westbourne St., Hyde Park.

[2] Charlotte Brontë left Haworth on November 29, 1849, to visit her publisher, George Smith (1824–1901) of Smith, Elder, and stayed with his family at their home in Westbourne Place, Paddington, very near Richard Martineau's home.

'That is a woman's note,' we agreed. We were in a certain state of excitement all day, and especially towards evening. The footman would certainly announce this mysterious personage by his or her right name; and, as I could not hear the announcement, I charged my cousins to take care that I was duly informed of it. A little before six, there was a thundering rap:—the drawing-room door was thrown open, and in stalked a gentleman six feet high. It was not 'Currer,' but a philanthropist, who had an errand about a model lodging-house. Minute by minute I, for one, wished him away; and he did go before anybody else came. Precisely as the time-piece struck six, a carriage stopped at the door; and after a minute of suspense, the footman announced 'Miss Brogden;' whereupon, my cousin informed me that it was Miss Brontë; for we had heard the name before, among others, in the way of conjecture.—I thought her the smallest creature I had ever seen (except at a fair) and her eyes blazed, as it seemed to me. She glanced quickly round; and my trumpet pointing me out, she held out her hand frankly and pleasantly. I introduced her, of course, to the family; and then came a moment which I had not anticipated. When she was seated by me on the sofa, she cast up at me such a look,—so loving, so appealing,—that, in connexion with her deep mourning dress, and the knowledge that she was the sole survivor of her family, I could with the utmost difficulty return her smile, or keep my composure. I should have been heartily glad to cry. We soon got on very well; and she appeared more at her ease that evening than I ever saw her afterwards, except when we were alone. My hostess was so considerate as to leave us together after tea, in case of C.B. desiring to have private conversation with me. She was glad of the opportunity to consult me about certain strictures of the reviewers which she did not understand, and had every desire to profit by. I did not approve the spirit of those strictures; but I thought them not entirely groundless. She besought me then, and repeatedly afterwards, to tell her, at whatever cost of pain to herself, if I saw her afford any justification of them. I believed her, (and I now believe her to have been) perfectly sincere: but when the time came (on the publication of 'Villette,' in regard to which she had expressly claimed my promise a week before the book arrived) she could not bear it. There was never any quarrel, or even misunderstanding, between us.[1] She thanked me for

---

[1] Brontë was deeply wounded by Martineau's review of *Villette* in the *Daily News* on February 3, 1853, which criticized the novel's obsession with love: "the book is almost intolerably painful. ... All the female characters, in all their thoughts and lives, are full of one thing, or are regarded by the reader in the light of that one thought—love. It begins with the child of six years old, at the opening—a charming picture—and it closes with it at the

my sincere fulfilment of my engagement; but she could not, she said, come 'at present' to see me, as she had promised: and the present was alas! all that she had to dispose of. She is dead, before another book of hers could (as I hoped it would) enable her to see what I meant, and me to re-establish a fuller sympathy between us.—Between the appearance of 'Shirley' and that of 'Villette,' she came to me;—in December, 1850. Our intercourse then confirmed my deep impression of her integrity, her noble conscientiousness about her vocation, and her consequent self-reliance in the moral conduct of her life. I saw at the same time tokens of a morbid condition of mind, in one or two directions;—much less than might have been expected, or than would have been seen in almost any one else under circumstances so unfavourable to health of body and mind as those in which she lived; and the one fault which I pointed out to her in 'Villette' was so clearly traceable to these unwholesome influences that I would fain have been spared a task of criticism which could hardly be of much use while the circumstances remained unchanged. But she had exacted first the promise, and then the performance in this particular instance; and I had no choice. 'I know,' she wrote (January 21st, 1853) 'that you will give me your thoughts upon my book,—as frankly as if you spoke to some near relative whose good you preferred to her gratification. I wince under the pain of condemnation-like any other weak structure of flesh and blood; but I love, I honour, I kneel to Truth. Let her smite me on one cheek—good! the tears may spring to the eyes; but courage! There is the other side—hit again—right sharply!' This was the genuine spirit of the woman. She might be weak for once; but her permanent temper was one of humility, candour, integrity and conscientiousness. She was not only unspoiled by her sudden and prodigious fame, but obviously unspoilable. She was somewhat amused by her fame, but oftener annoyed;—at least, when obliged to come out into the world to meet it, instead of its reaching her in her secluded home in the wilds of Yorkshire. There was little

---

last page, and, so dominant is this idea—so incessant is the writer's tendency to describe the need of being loved, that the heroine, who tells her own story, leaves the reader at last under the uncomfortable impression of her having either entertained a double love, or allowed one to supercede another without notification of the transition. It is not thus in real life. There are substantial, heartfelt interests for women of all ages, and under ordinary circumstances, quite apart from love." Although Martineau here insists that there was no "quarrel" or "misunderstanding," and later insisted that Elizabeth Gaskell remove the statement from *The Life of Charlotte Brontë* (1857) that Charlotte was "wounded to the quick by expressions of censure which she believed to be unjust and unfounded," in fact Brontë wrote to George Smith on March 26, 1853, that "she has hurt me a good deal." Brontë also wrote to Martineau to say that she no longer wished to continue any communication.

hope that she, the frail survivor of a whole family cut off in childhood or youth, could live to old age; but, now that she is gone, under the age of forty, the feeling is that society has sustained an unexpected, as well as irreparable loss.

I have often observed that, from the time I wrote the Prize Essays, I have never come to a stand for work;—have never had any anxiety as to whether there would be work for me;—have, in short, only had to choose my work. Holiday I have never had, since before that time, except in as far as my foreign travels and a few months of illness could be called such: and it had now been a weight on my mind for some years that I had not got on with my autobiography,—which I felt to be a real duty. I find that I wrote this to Mr. Atkinson, when under uneasiness about whether Murray would hold to his engagement to publish 'Eastern Life' (February 1848.) 'It is a very great and pressing object with me to go on with my own Life; lest it should end before I have recorded what I could trust no one to record of it. I always feel this a weight upon my mind, as a duty yet undone; and my doing it within a moderate time depends on my getting this book out now.' It was got out; but then came the History, which could not be delayed, and which I should have done wrong to refuse. Now that those three great volumes were nearly done, Mr. Dickens sent me an invitation to write for 'Household Words.' That kind of work does not, in my own opinion, suit me well; and I have refused to write for Magazines by the score; but the wide circulation of 'Household Words' made it a peculiar case;[1] and I agreed to try my hand,—while I was yet a good way from the end of my History. I did this with the more ease because a scheme was now rising to the light which would relieve me of much of the anxiety I felt about recording the later experiences of my life. The Atkinson Letters were by this time in preparation.

The publication of those letters was my doing. Having found, after some years of correspondence with Mr. Atkinson, that my views were becoming broader and clearer, my practice of duty easier and gayer, and my peace of mind something wholly unlike what I had ever had experience of before; and, being able to recognize and point out what fundamental truths they were that I had thus been brought to grasp, I thought that much good might be done by our making known, as master and pupil, what truths lay at the root of our philosophy. If I had known—what

---

[1]   *Household Words* had an initial circulation of 100,000 in 1850 when Martineau agreed to write; its average circulation was 40,000. See Richard D. Altick, *The English Common Reader* (Chicago: U of Chicago P, 1957), p. 394.

I could not know till the reception of our volume revealed it to me,—how small is the proportion of believers to the disbelievers in theology to what I imagined,—I might have proposed a different method; or we might have done our work in a different way. In regard to disbelief in theology, much more had already taken place than I, at least, was aware of. But there is an essential point,—the most essential of all,—in regard to which the secular and the theological worlds seem to need conviction almost equally: viz., the real value of science, and of philosophy as its legitimate offspring. It seems to us, even now, the most impossible, or, speaking cautiously, the rarest thing in the world to find any body who has the remotest conception of the indispensableness of science as the only source of, not only enlightenment, but wisdom, goodness and happiness. It is, of course, useless to speak to theologians or their disciples about this, while they remain addicted to theology, because they avowedly give their preference to theology over the science with which it is incompatible. They, in the face of clear proof that science and theology are incompatible, embrace theology as the foundation of wisdom, goodness and happiness. They incline, all the while, to what they call philosophy;—that is, to theologico-metaphysics, from which they derive, as they say, (and truly) improvement in intellectual power, and confirmation of their religious faith in one direction, nearly equivalent to the damage inflicted on it in another. The result must be, when the study is real and earnest, either that the metaphysics must dwindle away into a mere fanciful adornment of the theology, or the theology must be in time stripped of its dogmatic character, exhausted thereby of its vitality, and reduced to a mere name and semblance. Examples of the first alternative are conspicuous in the argumentative preachers and writers of the Church of England, and other Christian sects; and, we may add, in the same functionaries of the Romish Church, who thus unconsciously yield to the tendencies of their age so far as to undermine the foundations of their own 'everlasting' Church. Examples of the second alternative are conspicuous, in our own country and in America, in the class of metaphysical Deists, —who may be, by courtesy, called a class because they agree in being metaphysical, and, in one way or another, Deists; but who cannot be called a sect, or a body, because it is scarcely possible to find any two of them who agree in anything with any approach to precision. One makes the Necessarian doctrine his chief reliance, while another denounces it as Atheistic.[1] One insists on the immortality of the soul, while

[1]   This statement may reflect Martineau's disagreement with her brother James, who had introduced her to Necessarianism but later renounced it as incompatible with his approach to Unitarian theology.

another considers a future life doubtful, and a matter of no great consequence. Others belong, amid an unbounded variety of minor views, to
one or another of the five sorts of Pantheism. All these claim to be philosophers, and scientific in the matter of mental philosophy; while observers
discover that all are wandering wide of the central point of knowledge
and conviction,—each in his own balloon, wafted in complacency by
whatever current he may be caught by, and all crossing each other, up and
down, right or left, all manner of ways, hopeless of finding a common
centre till they begin to conceive of, and seek for, a firm standpoint.

The so-called scientific men, who consider themselves philosophers,
are, for the most part, in a scarcely more promising condition. Between
their endless subdivision as labourers in the field of research, before they
have discovered any incorporating principle; and the absorbing and
blinding influence of exclusive attention to detail; and some remaining
fear of casting themselves loose from theology, together with their share
of the universal tendency to cling to the old notions even in their own
department,—the men of science are almost as hopelessly astray, as to
the discovery of true wisdom, as the theologians. Well read men, who
call themselves impartial and disinterested, as they stand aloof and
observe all these others, are no nearer to the blessed discovery or
conviction. They extol philosophy, perhaps; but it is merely on the
ground that (conceiving metaphysics to be philosophy) it is a fine exercise of the subtle powers of the intellect. As to science, they regard it
either as a grave and graceful pastime, or they see no use in it, or they
consider it valuable for its utilitarian results. As for the grand conception,—the inestimable recognition,—that science (or the knowledge
of fact inducing the discovery of laws) is the sole and the eternal basis
of wisdom,—and therefore of human morality and peace,—none of all
these seem to have obtained any view of it at all. For my part, I must in
truth say that Mr. Atkinson is the only person, of the multitude I have
known, who has clearly apprehended this central truth. He found me
searching after it; and he put me in clear possession of it. He showed
me how all moral evil, and much, and possibly all, physical evil arises
from intellectual imperfection, —from ignorance and consequent error.
He led me to sympathise in Bacon's philosophy, in a truer way than the
multitude of Bacon's theological and metaphysical professed adorers;
and to see how a man may be happier than his fellows who obey
Bacon's incitements to the pursuit of truth, as the greatest good of man.
There is plenty of talk of the honour and blessedness of the unflinching pursuit of truth, wherever it may lead; but I never met anyone else

who lived for that object, or who seemed to understand the nature of the apostleship. I have already told where I was in (or in pursuit of) this path when Mr. Atkinson found me. Learning what I could from him, and meditating for myself, I soon found myself quite outside of my old world of thought and speculation,—under a new heaven and on a new earth; disembarrassed of a load of selfish cares and troubles; with some of my difficulties fairly solved, and others chased away, like bad dreams; and others, again, deprived of all power to trouble me, because the line was clearly drawn between the feasible and the unknowable. I had got out of the prison of my own self,[1] wherein I had formerly sat trying to interpret life and the world,—much as a captive might undertake to paint the aspect of Nature from the gleams and shadows and faint colours reflected on his dungeon walls.[2] I had learned that, to form any true notion whatever of any of the affairs of the universe, we must take our stand in the external world,—regarding man as one of the products and subjects of the everlasting laws of the universe, and not as the favourite of its Maker; a favourite to whom it is rendered subservient by divine partiality. I had learned that the death-blow was given to theology when Copernicus made his discovery that our world was not the centre and shrine of the universe, where God had placed man 'in his own image,' to be worshipped and served by all the rest of creation. I had learned that men judge from an inverted image of external things within themselves when they insist upon the Design argument, as it is called, —applying the solution from out of their own peculiar faculties to external things which, in fact, suggest that very conception of design to the human faculty. I had learned that whatever conception is transferred by 'instinct' or supposition from the human mind to the universe cannot possibly be the true solution, as the action of any product of the general laws of the universe cannot possibly be the original principle of those laws. Hence it followed that the conceptions of a God with any human attributes whatever, of a principle or practice of Design, of

---

[1] 'Fear only has its seat,' says Schiller, 'where heavy and shapeless masses prevail, and the gloomy outlines waver between uncertain boundaries. Man rises superior to every terror of Nature as soon as he is able to give it a form, and can make it a definite object. When he begins to assert his independence against Nature as an appearance, he also asserts his dignity against Nature as a power, and in all freedom stands up boldly before his gods. He tears away the masks from the spectres which terrified his childhood; and they surprise him with his own image; for they are merely his own imaginations.' [Martineau's note]

[2] A reformulation of Plato's allegory in the *Republic*, where men are viewed as imprisoned in a cave, able to see only their own shadows or the shadows of one another, which a fire throws on the cave walls.

an administration of life according to human wishes, or of the affairs of the world by the principles of human morals, must be mere visions, — necessary and useful in their day, but not philosophically and permanently true. I had learned, above all, that only by a study of the external and internal world in conjunction can we gather such wisdom as we are qualified to attain; and that this study must be *bonâ fide*,—personal and diligent, and at any sacrifice, if we would become such as we hint to ourselves in our highest and truest aspirations. The hollowness of the popular views of philosophy and science,—as good intellectual exercise, as harmless, as valuable in a utilitarian sense, and even as elevating in their mere influence,—was, by this time, to me the clearest thing I ever saw: and the opposite reality,—that philosophy founded upon science is the one thing needful,—the source and the vital principle of all intellectuality, all morality, and all peace to individuals, and goodwill among men,—had become the crown of my experience, and the joy of my life.

One of the earliest consequent observations was, of course, that the science of Human Nature, in all its departments, is yet in its infancy. The mere principle of Mental Philosophy is, as yet, very partially recognised; and the very conception of it is new. It is so absolutely incompatible with theology that the remaining prevalence of theology, circumscribed as it is, sufficiently testifies to the infant state of the philosophy of Man. I have found Mr. Atkinson's knowledge of Man, general and particular, physical, intellectual and moral, theoretical and practical, greater than I ever met with elsewhere, in books or conversation; and I immediately discovered that his superior knowledge was due to his higher and truer point of view, whereby he could cast light from every part of the universe upon the organisation and action of Man, and use and test the analogies from without in their application to the world within. I had long desired that the years should not pass over his head without the world being the better, as I felt myself, for his fresh method of thought, and conscientious exercise of it.[1] I wished that some others besides myself should be led by him to the true point of view which they were wandering in search of; and I therefore went as far as I dared in urging him to give the world a piece of his mind. At length he consented to my scheme of publishing a set of 'Letters on Man's Nature and Development.' Certainly I have reason to congratulate myself on my pertinacity in petitioning for this.

---

[1]   Although Martineau does not say it directly, Atkinson pursued many projects but produced few books or articles as a result. The *Letters on the Laws of Man's Nature and Development* (London: John Chapman, 1851) was, practically speaking, Martineau's doing and his only book; his chief publications were articles for the *Zoist*, a journal devoted to mesmerism.

I do not often trouble my friends with requests or advice as to their doings: and in this case, I was careful not to intrude on my friend's independence. But I succeeded; and I have rejoiced in my success ever since,—seeing and hearing what that book has done for others, and feeling very sensibly what a blessing it has been to myself.[1]

Once embarked in the scheme, my friend was naturally anxious to get on; but he was wonderfully patient with the slowness to which the pressure of my other work condemned us. I have mentioned that I read two of his letters to my hostess in the autumn of 1849. The book did not appear till January 1851. My literary practice indicated that I ought to copy out the whole of Mr. Atkinson's portion in proper order for press; and this was the more necessary because Mr. Atkinson's handwriting is only not so bad as Dr. Parr's and Sydney Smith's.[2] When I began, I supposed I must alter and amend a little, to fit the expression to the habit and taste of the reading world; but, after the first letter, I did not alter a single sentence. The style seems to me,—as it does to many better judges than myself,—as beautiful as it is remarkable. Eminent writers and readers have said that they could not lay the book down till they had run it through,—led on through the night by the beauty of the style, no less than by the interest of the matter. Such opinions justify my decision not to touch a sentence. (I speak of the volume without scruple, because, as far as its merits are concerned, it is Mr. Atkinson's. The responsibility was mine, and a fourth or fifth part of its contents; but my letters were a mere instigation to his utterance.)

It appears, by the dates above, that nearly the whole of 1850 elapsed during my copying. I was writing the Introductory volume of the History, and was in the midst of a series of papers, (the title of which I cannot recal) for an American periodical, whereby I wanted to earn some money for the Abolition cause there.[3] I sent off the last of them in April. By that time, my season guests began to arrive; and my evenings were not at my own disposal. I had engaged myself to 'Household Words' for a

---

[1]   This account of the response to the *Letters* omits the shocked and offended responses of many readers, including her friends Elisabeth Reid, Mary Arnold, Julia Smith, Crabb Robinson, William Macready, and family members. Sec. vi gives a more accurate account of the critical reaction.

[2]   Samuel Parr (1747–1825), Latin scholar known as "the Whig Johnson" for his witty conversation; Sydney Smith (1771–1845), founder of the *Edinburgh Review*; see Period IV, sec. ii.

[3]   These monthly articles, "A Year at Ambleside," appeared in *Sartain's Union Magazine* of Philadelphia throughout 1850; the proceeds went to William Lloyd Garrison's *Liberator*. They have been collected in a modern edition, *Harriet Martineau at Ambleside*, ed. Barbara Todd (Carlisle: Bookcase, 2002).

series of tales on Sanitary subjects; and I wrote this spring the two first,—
'Woodruffe the Gardener' and 'The People of Bleaburn.'[1]

I spent a fortnight at Armathwaite, a beautiful place between Penrith
and Carlisle; (departing, I remember, on the day of Wordsworth's funeral)[2]
and, though I carried my work, and my kind friends allowed me the
disposal of my mornings, I could not do any work which would bear postponement. I looked forward hopefully to a ten weeks' sojourn at a farm-
house near Bolton Abbey, where I went to escape the tourist-season;[3] and
there I did get on. My house had been full of guests, from April till the
end of July, with little intermission: and the greater the pleasure of receiving one's friends, the worse goes one's work. Among the guests of that
spring were three who came together, and who together made an illustrious week,—Mr. Charles Knight, Mr. Douglas Jerrold, and Mr. Atkinson.
Four days were spent in making that circuit of the district which forms
the ground-plan of my 'Complete Guide:'[4] and memorable days they
were. We were amused at the way in which some bystander at Strands[5]
recorded his sense of this in a Kendal paper. He told how the tourists were
beginning to appear for the season, and how I had been seen touring with
a party of the *élite* of the literary world, &c., &c. He declared that I, with
these *élite*, had crossed the mountains 'in a gig' to Strands, and that wit and
repartee had genially flowed throughout the evening;—an evening, as it
happened, when our conversation was rather grave. I was so amused at this
that I cut out the paragraph, and sent it to Mr. Jerrold, who wrote back
that, while the people were about it, they might as well have put us into
a howdah on an elephant. It would have been as true as the gig, and far
grander.—I owed the pleasure of Mr. Jerrold's acquaintance to Mr. Knight;
and I wish I had known him more. My first impression was one of

---

1   "The Sickness and Health of the People of Bleaburn," *Household Words* 1 (May-June, 1850),
    193–99, 230–38, 256–61, 283–88; rpt. in America as *The Sickness and Health of the People of
    Bleaburn* (Boston: Crosby, Nichols, 1853; New York: Charles S. Francis, 1853). "The Home
    of Woodruffe the Gardener" appeared in *Household Words* 1 (August-September, 1850),
    518–24, 540–47, 569–74. Between 1850 and 1855, Martineau wrote almost fifty articles for
    Dickens's journal, earning £200.
2   Wordsworth died on April 23, 1850. Armathwaite, on the Eden river, is north of the Lake
    District.
3   A twelfth-century Augustinian priory at the southern edge of the Yorkshire dales. On
    May 23, 1850, Martineau wrote to Fanny Wedgwood that she had taken "rooms at the
    Steward's house at Bolton Abbey, for 8 or 10 weeks from the end of July" (*Letters*, ed.
    Arbuckle, p. 109).
4   *Complete Guide to the English Lakes* (Windermere: John Garnett, 1855).
5   Strands was a starting point for walks in the Lake District to Wast Water and Wastdale
    Head; see "Third Tour" in Martineau's *Complete Guide to the English Lakes*.

surprise,—not at his remarkable appearance, of which I was aware;—the eyes and the mobile countenance, the stoop and the small figure, reminding one of Coleridge, without being like him,—but at the gentle and thoughtful kindness which set its mark on all he said and did. Somehow, all his good things were so dropped as to fall into my trumpet, without any trouble or ostentation. This was the dreaded and unpopular man who must have been hated (for he *was* hated) as 'Punch' and not as Jerrold,[1]— through fear, and not through reason or feeling. His wit always appeared to me as gentle as it was honest,—as innocent as it was sound. I could say of him as of Sydney Smith, that I never heard him say, in the way of raillery, any thing of others that I should mind his saying of me. I never feared him in the least, nor saw reason why any but knaves or fools should fear him.— The other witty journalist of my time, Mr. Fonblanque, I knew but little, having met him only at Mr. Macready's, I think.[2] I once had the luck to have him all to myself, during a long dinner; and I found his conversation as agreeable for other qualities as for its wit. The pale face, the lank hair, the thin hands, and dimmed dark eye, speaking of ill health, made the humour of his conversation the more impressive, as recommended by patience and amiability.

But to return to my summer of 1850. At Bolton I was not by any means lonely; for tourists came there too; and relations and friends gave me many a pleasant day and evening. But, on the whole, the History got on very well in the mornings, and the transcribing of the Letters in the evening; and, but for the relaxing air of the place, which injured my health, that Bolton sojourn would have been a season of singular enjoyment. With the same dear, faithful old friend whom I have so often referred to, I saw Ilkley and Benrhydding, and some of the finest parts of the West of Yorkshire.[3] I found time to write another long story for 'Household Words,' ('The Marsh Fog and the Sea Breeze') and engaged to make my subscription to the new weekly journal, the 'Leader' (which has lagged terribly, instead of leading) in the form of twelve 'Sketches from Life,' which I began before the Atkinson Letters were well off my hands.[4]

---

[1] Jerrold wrote political articles for *Punch* (signed "Q") and the highly popular "Mrs. Caudle's Curtain Lectures."

[2] Albany Fonblanque (1793–1872), journalist and editor of the *Examiner*; William Charles Macready (1793–1873), tragic actor and long-time friend.

[3] Ilkley is the site of a Roman fort and other Iron and Bronze Age ruins; Ben Rhydding, a high point in the surrounding moors. Her companion was probably Elisabeth Reid.

[4] "The Marsh Fog and the Sea Breeze," *Household Words* 3 (April 1851), 53–38, 88–94. The "Sketches from Life" in *The Leader*, a periodical for working-class readers, appeared from November 9, 1850 to July 12, 1851.

Another small piece of authorship which interposed itself was really no fault of mine. In 1848 (I think it was) I had begun an experiment of very small farming, which I never intended to become an affair of public interest. My field, let to a neighbour, was always in such bad condition as to be an eyesore from my windows. I found myself badly and expensively served with cream and butter, and vegetables, and eggs. In summer there was no depending on the one butcher of the place for meat, even though joints had been timely ordered and promised,—so great and increasing was the pressure of the tourist multitude. In winter, when I was alone, and did not care what came to table, I could have what I liked: but in summer, when my house was full, it was frequently an anxiety how to get up a dinner when the butcher was so set fast as to have to divide the promised joint between three houses. All the while, I had to pay an occasional gardener very high, to keep the place in any order at all,—over and above what my maids and I could do. A more serious consideration was the bad method of farming in the Lake District, which seemed to need an example of better management, on however humble a scale. My neighbours insisted on it that cows require three acres of land apiece; whereas I believed that, without emulating Cobbett, I could do better than that.[1] I procured an active, trustworthy married labourer from Norfolk, and enlisted his ambition and sympathy in the experiment.[2] We have since kept about a cow and a half on my land, with the addition of half an acre which I rent from the adjoining field; and the purchase of a fourth part of the food is worth while, because I am thus kept constantly supplied with milk, while able to sell the surplus; besides that the stable may as well hold a second cow; and that two cows are little more trouble than one. My whole place is kept in the highest order: I have the comfort of a strong man on the premises (his cottage being at the foot of the knoll) for the protection of my household and property; and I have always had the satisfaction of feeling that, come who may, there are at all times hams, bacon and eggs in the house. The regular supply of fresh vegetables, eggs, cream and butter is a substantial comfort to a housekeeper. A much greater blessing than all these together is that a plentiful subsistence for two worthy people has been actually created out of my field; and that the spectacle has certainly not been lost

---

[1]   In addition to writing his *Political Register*, which included his famous *Rural Rides* commenting on the state of English agriculture, Cobbett conducted experimental farming in Surrey and Hampshire, publishing *Cottage Economy, containing information relative to the brewing of beer, making of bread, keeping of cows, pigs, bees, ewes, goats, poultry and rabbits and relative to other matters deemed useful in the conducting of the affairs of a labourer's family* (London: C. Clement, 1822).

[2]   Robert Fulcher, who lived with his wife in the cottage below Martineau's terrace wall.

on my neighbours. At first, we were abundantly ridiculed, and severely condemned for our methods; and my good servant's spirits were sometimes sorely tried: but I told him that if we persevered good-humouredly, people would come round to our views. And so they did. First, I was declared deluded and extravagant: next, I was cruel to my live stock; then, I petted them so that they would die of luxury; and finally, one after another of our neighbours admitted the fine plight of my cows; and a few adopted our methods. At the end of a year's experience, I wrote a letter, by request, to an Assistant Poor-law Commissioner, who was earnest in his endeavours to get workhouses supplied with milk and vegetables, by the labour of the inmates on the land. To my amazement, I found my letter in the 'Times,' one day while I was at Bolton. How it got there, I know not. Other papers quoted portions of it which, separated from the rest, gave rise to wrong impressions; so that I found it necessary to write a second letter, giving the result of the second year's tillage; and to issue the two as a small pamphlet.[1] I need say nothing here about our method of farming, as the whole story is told in that pamphlet. I may simply add that we go on with it very comfortably, and that my good farm-servant is a prosperous man. Strangers come every summer to see the place as a curiosity; and I am assured that the invariable remark is that not a foot of ground is lost, and not a sign of neglect appears in any corner. I have added a little boiling-house, a root-house, and a capital manure-pit, since those letters were written; and I have put up a higher order of fences,—to the improvement at once of the appearance and the economy of my little estate. All this, with the growth of the shrubs and little copses, and the spread of roses and evergreen climbers over the house, makes my Knoll dwelling, to say the truth, a charming spectacle to visitors;—though not half so much as to me. Some have called it 'a perfect poem:' and it is truly that to me: and so, speaking frankly, is the life that I have passed within it.

---

[1] *Two Letters on Cow-Keeping* (Edinburgh, 1850). She later contributed "Our Farm of Two Acres," in three installments, to Dickens's *Once a Week* on July 9, 16, and 30, 1859.

SECTION VI

———

WITH all the writing that I have particularised on my hands, it is not to be wondered at that November arrived before Mr. Atkinson was wanted, to finish off our work for press: and by that time, my winter course of lectures was due. So much for the 'leisure,' and the 'dulness' which distant friends have attributed to my life at the Lakes. This winter's course was the arduous one of twenty lectures on the History of England,[1] —the first of which was delivered on the fifth of November, and the last on the first of April, 1851. Amidst the undeniable overwork of that winter, I had a feeling, which I remember expressing to one friend at least, that this might probably be the last season of work for me. It seemed to me probable that, after the plain-speaking of the Atkinson Letters, I might never be asked, or allowed, to utter myself again. I had, on four previous occasions of my life, supposed the same thing, and found myself mistaken; but the 'audacity,' (as a scientific reader called my practice of plain avowal) was so much greater in appearance (though not in reality) in the present case than ever before, that I anticipated excommunication from the world of literature, if not from society. This seems amusing enough, now, when I have enjoyed more prosperity since the publication of that volume, realised more money, earned more fame of a substantial kind, seen more of my books go out of print, and made more friendships and acquaintance with really congenial people than in any preceding four years of my life. But the anticipation was very sincere at the time; and I took care that my comrade in the work knew what my anticipation was. —There was to me, I must observe, no choice about making known, in this form or some other, my views at this period. From the time when, in my youth, I uttered my notions and was listened to, I had no further choice. For a quarter of a century past I had been answerable to an unknown number of persons for a declaration of my opinions as my experience advanced; and I could not stop now. If I had desired it, any concealment would have been most imprudent. A life of hypocrisy was wholly impracticable to me, if it had been endurable in idea; and disclosure by bits, in

———

[1] For the origin of the lectures, see Part VI, sec. iv.

mere conversation, could never have answered any other purpose than misleading my friends, and subjecting me to misconception. So much for the necessity and the prudence of a full avowal. A far more serious matter was the duty of it, in regard to integrity and humanity. My comrade and I were both pursuers of truth, and were bound to render our homage openly and devoutly. We both care for our kind; and we could not see them suffering as we had suffered without imparting to them our consolation and our joy. Having found, as my friend said, a spring in the desert, should we see the multitude wandering in desolation, and not show them our refreshment? We never had a moment's doubt or misgiving; though we anticipated (or I did, for I ought only to speak for myself) all manner of consequences which never ensued.

Just as I am writing on this subject, an old letter of mine to Mr. Atkinson is put before my eyes. It was written before the publication of 'Eastern Life;' and I will insert a part of it, both because it indicates the kind of difficulty I had to deal with, on these occasions, and because it is an honest comfort to see what I had gained in courage, strength and cheerfulness in the three years which intervened between the publication of the two books.

'I am not afraid of censure,' I wrote in February 1848, 'from individuals or from the world. I don't feel, at present, any fear of the most thorough pulling to pieces that I suppose can ever befall me. The book once out, I am in for it, and must and will bear every thing. ... ... The fact is, however,—this book is, I believe, the greatest effort of courage I ever made. I only hope I may not fail in the proof. Some people would think the Population number of my Political Economy, and the Women and Marriage and Property chapters in my American books, and the Mesmerism affair, bolder feats: but I know that they were not. I was younger and more ardent then; and now the forecast and love of ease belonging to age are coming upon me. Then, I believed in a Protector who ordered me to do that work, and would sustain me under it: and, however I may now despise that sort of support, I had it then, and have none of that sort now. I have all that I want, I believe, in the absolute necessity of saying what I really believe, if I speak at all, on those Egyptian and Mosaic subjects; and I would not exchange my present views, imperfect and doubtful as they are,— I had better say, I would not exchange my freedom from old superstition, if I were to be burned at the stake next month, for all the peace and quiet of orthodoxy, if I must take the orthodoxy with the peace and quiet. Nor would I, for any exemption, give up the blessing of the power of appeal to thoughtful minds. There was —— ——, the other day, at the reading of the Sinai part of my book.[1] I should have expected her to be purely shocked at so much of it as to carry away a bad impression of the whole: but she was beyond all measure interested,—beyond anything ever seen in her. So I would not have anything otherwise than as it is, as to my fate in consequence of my opinions, or absence of belief. What I dread is being silenced, and the mortification and loss of the manner of it: (from a refusal to publish the book). Yet, if it happens, I dare say it will become clear to me what I ought to do; and that is the only really important thing... ... ... Well: I have had plenty of painful enterprises to go through, and found support from the two considerations that I could not help being so circumstanced, and that I believed myself right. ... ... I will tell you of a terrible pain I have had about this matter of religious opinion. When I was at —— in September, I was told about a Town Missionary, Mr. ——,[2] who desired particularly to see me. He came to the house, when it appeared (—no, we knew it before; but, however,) he had formed himself upon my books,—the more serious ones particularly,—and we found, had taken up that notion of me which we know to be idealism,—all but idolatry. In every thing else he seemed a rational, as he certainly was a very interesting young man. Such a face! so full of life and happiness,—all made up of benevolence. He was delicate; and so was his young wife. He was then thinking of undertaking the —— City Mission. He did so: and soon sank;—had influenza, and fell into rapid consumption. A friend of his at Birmingham wrote me that he declared himself dying, in his letter to her received that day: and she immediately wrote to suggest to me that a letter from me would gratify him. There was scarcely any thing I would not rather have done: but it was impossible to refuse. I wrote at once; and every word was as true to my own state of mind as what I write to you now: but I feared it would be taken for a Christian letter. There was not a word about the future, or of God, or even Christ. It was a letter of sympathy in his benevolent and happy life, and also, of course, in his present weakness. It reached him on the

---

[1]   Part II of *Eastern Life* was "Sinai and Its Faith." In the chapter "Moses at Mount Sinai," Martineau treats the Jewish faith and Moses' promulgation of the ten commandments as a political necessity, given the historical moment: "Sin was not corrupt thought, but failure of allegiance to the Divine King. The Commandments, therefore,—even the first ten, which are moral and not merely ritual like the second,—relate only to political or social virtue, leaving it to Christianity to work out the nobler object of personal holiness" (II, v, 301).

[2]   Town missionaries worked among the urban poor, just as foreign missionaries took the Christian gospel to the heathen poor around the globe. The man is unidentified.

last day of his life. It was read to him. When a little revived, he asked for it, and read it himself; and then desired his wife to tell all who loved him of 'this last flush on his darkness.' This is dreadful pain to me. I feel as if I had told him a lie for my last words to him. I cannot now see how I could have acted otherwise. It would have been hard and unkind not to write: and it was impossible to disturb his life at the last. Yet I feel that that letter did not carry my real mind to him, and does not to the many who are reading it. His poor delicate young widow is strong in heart; but she has two young infants to maintain, and not a shilling in the world. But missionaries' widows are, I believe, always cared for,— as I am sure they ought to be.'

It is cheering to read this letter now, and feel how much clearer and stronger my mind had become before the time arrived for the far greater enterprise which caused me so much less apprehension, and which was to release me for ever from all danger of misleading missionaries, or any body else, by letters of sympathy under solemn circumstances, which they would interpret by their preconceptions. I can write such letters now to all kinds of sufferers, in full assurance that, whether they satisfy or not, they are not misapprehended.

On the nineteenth of November, my friend and I revised his last letter, I wrote my preface, and we tied up our MS. for press; and on the twentieth, he went away. As we were going to the coach he said, 'I am glad we have done this work. We shall never repent it.' We next met in London, in the summer, when our book had run the gauntlet of all the reviews, and we found ourselves no worse for the venture we had made, and well satisfied that we had borne our testimony to the truth,—not in vain,—for many who had sorely needed the support and blessing which our philosophy had long afforded to ourselves.

When Mr. Atkinson was gone, the printing began; and I highly enjoyed the proof-correcting. That is always the time when I begin to relish any book that I have part in. The conception I enjoy, of course, or I should not write the book; but during the work, I am doubtful, and the manuscript disgusts me. Then come the proofs, when one sees exactly, and in order, what one has really said; and the work appears to that time is shown by a sad piece of weakness of mine, which I have sorely repented since;—trusting to the printing-office the proof-correcting of the Appendix. Almost three-fourths of the Appendix being sent in print to the office, and the rest in the remarkably good handwriting of a helpful neighbour, I did hope that errors might be avoided; and I inquired about it, and was assured that I might trust the printer. But never did I see such a shameful mess as those sheets; and never could I have conceived of such an ignorant sort of blunders being allowed to pass. I have never forgiven myself for my laziness in letting any part of the business out of my own hands.

The neighbour who helped me kindly in getting up the Appendix was a sickly retired clerk living close by my gate,—a man of good tastes and fond of reading.[1] I, as I thought, hired him for a succession of evenings to write for me; and, by working together, we soon finished the business. He would not have supper, nor any refreshment whatever; and, to my consternation, (and admiration too) he declined all remuneration in such a way that I could only accept his gift of his time and labour. Since that time he has had the loan, daily, of my newspaper:—his wife buys milk of my dairy; and he sends me many a dish of trout; and I lend books to his good son. Thus we go on; and very pleasant it is.

It was while our evenings were thus filled up, that Mr. Quillinan,[2] Wordsworth's son-in-law, called one day, full of kindly pleasure, to tell me that I must dine with him next Thursday; and sadly blank he looked when I told him I was engaged every evening that week. Could I not put off my engagement?—No: Miss Brontë was coming on Monday; and I had business which must be finished first.[3] His disappointment was great; for he had a benevolent scheme of bringing me into the favourable acquaintance of certain clergy of the neighbourhood, and of a physician whose further acquaintance I by no means desired. I have before mentioned that, from the first, I avoided visiting among all my neighbours, except a very few intimates; and, of course, I had no intention of beginning now, when a book was in the press which would make them gnash their teeth at me in a month or two. Mr. Quillinan had ascertained from the whole party that they should be happy to meet me; and he enjoyed, as he told me, 'bringing neighbours together, to like each other.' It had never occurred to him that I might not like to meet them; and sadly disconcerted he was. However, I promised to take Miss Brontë with me, one day, if he would dine early enough to enable my delicate guest to return before nightfall. That was a truly pleasant

---

[1] Possibly John Carter, a clerk who helped Wordsworth compile the manuscripts for editions of his poems.
[2] Edward Quillinan, who lived at Loughrigg Holme.
[3] Charlotte Brontë visited for a week, December 16–22, 1850. She and Martineau dined at Quillinan's house, where Matthew Arnold was the other guest. Brontë found Arnold "striking and prepossessing—his manner displeases from its seeming foppery"; see Juliet Barker, *The Brontës* (New York: St. Martin's Press, 1994), pp. 663–65.

day,—no one being there, in addition to the family, but Mr. Arnold, from Fox How, and ourselves. And when 'Currer' and I came home, there were proof-sheets lying; and I read her Mr. Atkinson's three letters about the distribution of the brain. She was exceedingly impressed by what she called 'the tone of calm power in all he wrote;' moreover, she insisted on having the whole book, when it came out; and no one, so little qualified by training to enter into its substance and method, did it more generous justice. She was very far indeed from sympathising in our doctrine; and she emphatically said so; but this did not prevent her doing justice to us, under our different view.[1] In a preceding letter, she had said, 'I quite expect that the publication of this book will bring you troublous times. Many who are beginning to draw near to you will start away again affrighted. Your present position is high. Consequently there are many persons, very likely, precisely in the mood to be glad to see it lower. I anticipate a popular outcry which you will stand much as the Duke of Wellington would;—and in due time, it will die round you; but I think not soon.' A month afterwards she wrote, 'Having read your book, I cannot now think it will create any outcry. You are tender of others:—you are serious, reverent and gentle. Who can be angry?' This appreciation, from one who declared (as she did to me) that our doctrine was to her 'vinegar mingled with gall,' was honourable to her justice and candour. And so was the readiness with which she admitted and accepted my explanation that I was an atheist in the vulgar sense,—that of rejecting the popular theology,—but not in the philosophical sense, of denying a First Cause. She had no sympathy whatever with the shallow and foolish complaint that we were 'taking away people's faith.' She thought that nobody's faith was worth much which was held, more or less, because I held it too; and of course she saw that truth and Man would never advance if they must wait for the weak, who have themselves no means of progression but by the explorations of the strong, or of those more disposed for speculation than themselves. As I have had occasion to say to some people who seem to have forgotten all they knew of the history of Opinion, and as Luther and many others greater than I have had to say, 'If your faith is worth anything, it

---

[1] Brontë's private view, expressed to James Taylor, was one of horror: the "unequivocal declaration of disbelief in the existence of God or a Future Life" was not to be borne. "The strangest thing is that we are called upon to rejoice over this hopeless blank—to receive this bitter bereavement as a great gain—to welcome this unutterable desolation as a state of pleasant freedom. Who *could* do this if he would? Who *would* do it if he could?" (quoted in Barker, p. 664).

does not depend on me: and if it depends on me, it is not worth anything.' This reminds me of an incident perhaps worth relating, in connexion with this absurd plea for standing still, which, under the laws of the mind, means retrogression.

When I was publishing 'Eastern Life,' I rather dreaded its effects on two intimate friends of mine, widows, both far removed from orthodoxy, and zealous all their lives long for free thought, and an open declaration of it.[1] If I might judge by their profession of principle, I should become more dear to them in proportion to my efforts or sacrifices in the discovery and avowal of truth: but I knew that they could not be so judged, because neither of them had encountered any serious trial of their principle. They bore 'Eastern Life' better than I expected,—not fully perceiving, perhaps, the extent of the speculation about belief in a future life. In the 'Atkinson Letters,' the full truth burst upon them; and it was too much for them. They had been accustomed to detail to me their visions of that future life, which were curiously particular,— their 'heaven' being filled with the atmosphere of their respective homes, and framed to meet the sufferings and desires of their own individual minds. I never pretended to sympathise in all this, of course; but neither had I meddled with it, because I never meddle, except by invitation, with individual minds. After 'Eastern Life,' they must have been thoroughly aware that they had not my sympathy; but, while they insisted (against my wish) in reading the 'Atkinson Letters,' which was altogether out of their way, they blamed me excessively,—wholly forgetting their professions in favour of free-thought and speech. One partially recovered herself: the other had not power to do so. She went about every where, eloquently bemoaning my act, as a sort of fall, and doing me more mischief (as far as such talk can do damage) than any enemy could have done; and, by the time she began to see how she stood, she had done too much for entire reparation,—earnestly as I believe she desires it. As for the other, an anecdote will show how considerable her self-recovery was. The very woman who had taken on herself to inform me that God would forgive me was not long in reaching the point I will show.—She came to stay with me a year afterwards; and when she departed, I went down to the gate, to put her into the coach, when an old acquaintance greeted me,—an aged lady living some miles off. The two fellow-passengers talked me over, and the aged one related how fierce an opinionated old lady of the neighbourhood

---

[1]   One was Elisabeth Reid; see Period VI, sec. iii, p. 530, n. 1.

was against me,—without having read the book;—the narrator confessing that she herself thought I was 'exceedingly wrong to take away people's faith.' Did not my friend think so? She replied that if I was wrong on that ground,—in seeking truth, and avowing it in opposition to the popular belief, so was every religious reformer, in all times, mounting up through Luther to St. Paul. 'Why, that's true!' cried the old lady. 'I will remember that and tell it again.' 'And as to the moral obligation of the case,' continued my friend, 'we must each judge by our own conscience: and perhaps Harriet is as able to judge as Mrs. —.' 'Yes, indeed, and a great deal better,' was the reply.

I certainly had no idea how little faith Christians have in their own faith till I saw how ill their courage and temper can stand any attack upon it. And the metaphysical deists who call themselves free-thinkers are, if possible, more alarmed and angry still. There were some of all orders of believers who treated us perfectly well: and perhaps the settled orthodox had more sympathy with us than any other class of Christians. They were not alarmed,—safely anchored as they are on the rock of authority; and they were therefore at leisure to do justice to our intentions, and even to our reasoning. Having once declared our whole basis to be wrong,—their own being divine,—they could appreciate our view and conduct in a way impossible to persons who had left the anchorage of authority, and not reached that of genuine philosophy. Certainly the heretical,—from reforming churchmen to metaphysical deists,—behaved the worst. The reviews of the time were a great instruction to us. They all, without one exception, as far as we know, shirked the subject-matter of the book, and fastened on the collateral, anti-theological portions. In regard to these portions, the reviewers contradicted each other endlessly. We had half a mind to collect their articles, and put them in such juxtaposition as to make them destroy one another, so as to leave us where they found us. It is never worth while, however, to notice reviews in their bearing upon the books they discuss. When we revert to reviews, so-called, it is for their value as essays; for it is, I believe, a thing almost unknown for a review to give a reliable account of the book which forms its text, if the work be of any substance at all. This is not the place for an essay on reviewing. I will merely observe that the causes of this phenomenon are so clear to me, and I think them so nearly unavoidable, that I have declined reviewing, except in a very few instances, since the age of thirty; and in those few instances, my articles have been avowedly essays, and not, in any strict sense, reviews.

As for the 'outcry' which 'Currer Bell' and many others anticipated, I really do not know what it amounted to,—outside of the reviewing world. If I knew, I would tell: but I know very little. To the best of my recollection, we were downright insulted only by two people;—by the opinionated old lady (above eighty) above referred to, and by one of my nearest relations;—the former in a letter to me (avowing that she had not seen the book) and the latter in print.[1] Another old lady and her family, with whom I was barely acquainted, passed me in the road thenceforth without speaking,—a marriage into a bishop's family taking place soon after. Others spoke coldly, for a time; and one family, from whom more wisdom might have been expected, ceased to visit me, while continuing on friendly terms. I think this is all, as regards my own neighbourhood. My genuine friends did not change; and the others, failing under so clear a test, were nothing to me. When, in the evening of that spring, I went out (as I always do, when in health) to meet the midnight on my terrace, or, in bad weather, in the porch, and saw and felt what I always do see and feel there at that hour, what did it matter whether people who were nothing to me had smiled or frowned as I passed them in the village in the morning? When I experienced the still new joy of feeling myself to be a portion of the universe, resting on the security of its everlasting laws, certain that its Cause was wholly out of the sphere of human attributes, and that the special destination of my race is infinitely nobler than the highest proposed under a scheme of 'divine moral government,' how could it matter to me that the adherents of a decaying mythology,—(the Christian following the heathen, as the heathen followed the barbaric-fetish) were fiercely clinging to their Man-God, their scheme of salvation, their reward and punishment, their arrogance, their selfishness, their essential pay-system, as ordered by their mythology? As the astronomer rejoices in new knowledge which compels him to give up the dignity of our globe as the centre, the pride, and even the final cause of the universe, so do those who have escaped from the Christian mythology enjoy their release from the superstition which fails to make happy, fails to make good, fails to make wise, and has become as great an obstacle in the way of progress as the prior mythologies which it took the place of nearly two thousand years ago. For three centuries it has been undermined, and its overthrow

---

[1]   The old lady was most likely Eliza Fletcher (1770–1858), mother of her friend Mrs. Margaret Davy; see Period VI, sec. iii, p. 530, n. 1. The "nearest relation" was her brother James, who wrote a negative review attacking the book and Atkinson's intellectual credentials, "Mesmeric Atheism," *Prospective Review* 7 (June, 1851), 224–62.

completely decided,[1] as all true interpreters of the Reformation very well know. To the emancipated, it is a small matter that those who remain imprisoned are shocked at the daring which goes forth into the sunshine and under the stars, to study and enjoy, without leave asked, or fear of penalty. As to my neighbours, they came round by degrees to their former methods of greeting. They could do no more, because I was wholly independent of all of them but the few intimates on whom I could rely. As one of these last observed to me,—people leave off gossip and impertinence when they see that one is independent of them. If one has one's own business and pleasure and near connexions, so that the gossips are visibly of no consequence to one, they soon stop talking. Whether it was so in my case, I never inquired. I am very civilly treated, as far as I see; and that is enough.

As to more distant connexions, I can only say the same thing. I had many scolding letters; but they were chiefly from friends who were sure to think better of it, and who have done so. For a time there was a diminution of letters from mere acquaintances, and persons who wanted autographs, or patronage, or the like: but these have increased again since. I went to London the summer after the publication of the book, and have done so more than once since; and my friends are very kind. I think I may sum up my experience of this sort by saying that this book has been an inestimable blessing to me by dissolving all false relations, and confirming all true ones. No one who would leave me on account of it is qualified to be my friend; and all who, agreeing or disagreeing with my opinions, are faithful to me through a trial too severe for the weak, are truly friends for life. I early felt this; and certainly no ardent friendships of my youthful days have been half so precious to me as those which have borne unchanged the full revelation of my heresies. As to my fortunes,—I have already said that my latest years have been the most prosperous since the publication of my Political Economy Series.[2]

When my friends in Egypt and I came down from, and out of, the Great Pyramid, we agreed that no pleasure in the recollection of the adventure, and no forgetfulness of the fatigue and awfulness of it, should ever make us represent the feat as easy and altogether agreeable. For the

---

[1]   As Comte pithily puts it, the three reformers who were all living at the same time, provided among them for the total demolition of Christianity,—Luther having overthrown the discipline, Calvin the hierarchy, and Socinus the dogma. [Martineau's note]

[2]   The financial prosperity was due largely to the sale of her *History of the Peace*, for which she recorded profits of £1000, but she also made £200 on *Household Words* (1849) and £220 on her translation of Comte's *Positive Philosophy* (1853).

sake of those who might come after us, we were bound to remember the pains and penalties, as well as the gains. In the same way, I am endeavouring now to revive the faded impressions of any painful social consequences which followed the publication of the 'Atkinson Letters,' that I may not appear to convey that there is no fine to pay for the privilege of free utterance. I do not remember much about a sort of pain which was over so long ago, and which there has been nothing to revive; but I am aware, in a general way, that the nightly mood which yields me such lofty pleasure, under the stars, and within the circuit of the solemn mountains, was not always preserved: and that if I had not been on my guard in advance, and afterwards supported by Mr. Atkinson's fine temper, I might have declined into a state of suspicion, and practice of searching into people's opinion of me. To renew the impressions of the time, I have now been glancing over Mr. Atkinson's letters of that spring, which I preserved for some such purpose: and I am tempted to insert one or two, as faithful reflexions of his mood at the time, which was the guide and aid of mine. This reminds me that one of our amusements at the time was at the various attempts,—in print, in letters, and in conversation,—to set us at variance. One of our literary magnates, who admires the book,[1] said that this was the first instance in history of an able man joining a woman in authorship; and the novelty was not likely to be acquiesced in without resistance. In print, Mr. Atkinson was reproached,—in the face of my own preface,— with drawing me into the business, and making me his 'victim,' and so forth, by persons who knew perfectly well that, so far from wanting any aid in coming forward, he had lectured, and published his lecture, containing the same views, both physiological and anti-theological, before we had any acquaintance whatever:[2] and, on the other hand, I was scolded for dragging forth a good man into persecution which I had shown I did not myself care for. On this sort of charge, which admitted of no public reply, (if he had replied to any thing) Mr. Atkinson wrote these few words,—after reading the one only review which stooped to insult,—insult being, in that instance, safe to the perpetrator by accident of position.[3] 'The thing that impressed me, in reading that review was,—how ingenious men are in seeking how to

---

[1]   Possibly John Chapman, who published the book and was Martineau's longtime friend.

[2]   Atkinson had published "Mesmeric Phrenology" and other letters and essays in *The Zoist: A Journal of Cerebral Physiology and Mesmerism* 1 (1844), 134–44. James Martineau quotes from these articles in his *Prospective Review* article to show Atkinson's poor grammar and style.

[3]   That is, the reviewer's position as her brother.

poison their neighbours, and how men themselves do just what they accuse others of doing. Honest scorn I don't at all mind: but I don't like a wrong or undue advantage being taken. I don't like a cabman to charge a shilling extra when one is with ladies, thinking you won't dispute it. All our principles of honour and justice and benevolence seem to me to be implicated in questions of truth; and in this, I certainly feel firm as a rock, and with the courage of the lion:—that the position is to be maintained, and the thing to be done, and there's an end of it,—be the consequences what they may.' Then came a letter to him, 'candidly advising' him to do himself justice, as speedily as might be, by publishing something alone, to repair the disadvantage of having let a woman speak under the same cover: and on the same day, came a letter to me, gently reproving my good-nature in lending my literary experience to any man's objects. Sometimes the volume was all mine, and sometimes all his,—each taking the advantage of the other's name. There was a good deal of talk to the same purpose; and Mr. Atkinson's comment on this policy was,—'the aim is evident,—to stir up jealousy between us. But it won't do. They don't know the man,—nor the woman either.'

The following morsel may serve to show our view of the large class of censors who, believing nothing themselves, of theology or any thing else, were scandalised at our 'shaking the faith' of other people. A lawyer of this class, avowing that he had not read the book, launched 'a thunderbolt' at me,—possibly forgetting how many 'thunderbolts' I had seen him launch at superstitions, like that of a future life, and at those who teach them.[1] Mr. Atkinson's remark on this will not take up much space. 'Bravo —! A pretty lawyer he, to give judgment before he has read his brief! What a Scribe it is! lawyer to the backbone! I wish he would tell us what truths we may be allowed to utter, and when. Certainly it seems a pity to hurt any one's feelings: but Christianity was not so tender about that: nor does Nature seem very particular. It is all very fine, talking about people's religious convictions; but what is to become of those who have no such convictions, —that increasing crowd filling up the spaces between the schisms of the churches? The Church is rotting away daily. Convictions are losing their stability. Men are being scattered in the wilderness. Shall we not hold up a light in the distance, and prepare them a shelter from the storm? The religious people, you will see, will respect us more than the infidels, who have no faith in truth, no light but law, no hope for Man but his fancies

---

[1]   Lord John Campbell, referred to below by name; see p. 580, n. 3.

("convictions"). No, I don't feel any thing at "thunderbolts" of this kind, I assure you. I think it more like the squash of a rotten apple. Let such thunderbolts come as thick as rain; and they will not stir a blade of grass.' On April eleventh,[1] my friend wrote, in reply to some accounts of excursions with two nieces, who were staying with me:

'Here is a nice packet of letters from you. It is delightful to read your account of your doings. You have no time to be miserable and repent,—have you? no time to be thinking of your reputation or your soul. Your cheerful front to the storm and active exertions will make you respected; and remember, the Cause requires it. It would be hard for a Christian to be brave and cheerful in a Mahomedan country, with any amount of pitying and abusing; and so you have not a fair chance of the effect of your faith on your happiness in life,—as it will be for all when the community think as you do, and each supports each, and sympathy abounds. ... ... As for Dr. B. and the rest,[2]—when men don't like the end, of course they find fault with the means. How *could* it be logical and scientific if it leads to a different conclusion from them:—*them*—yes, all of them thinking differently! F. in "Fraser" does not think any thing of a future life from instinct, or a God from design: but these points are just what the others insist on. To my mind F.'s article and the one in the "Westminster" are full of sheer assertion and error and bad taste.[3] I think *they* want logic, science, or whatever they may term it. If I am wrong and unscientific, why do they not put me right?—taking the "Letters" as a mere sketch, of course, and presenting only a few points of the subject. It is but a slight sketch of the head, leaving the whole figure to be completed. The fact is, these reviewers skip over the science to the theology, and talk nonsense when they *feel* uncomfortably opposed, —perhaps insulted. I don't mean in the least to argue that I am not wrong; only, those who think so ought to show how and why. Mr. F. reasons from analogy when my chief argument is in opposition to those analogical reasonings. The *analogy* with Christ is curious, as showing how minds are impressed with resemblances. Some see a man with the slightest curve of the nose, and say, "How like the Duke of Wellington!" or with a club-foot, and say, "How like Byron!" I am

---

[1] 1851.

[2] Dr. B— is unidentified; F— is James Anthony Froude (1818–94), who wrote the review "Materialism: Miss Martineau and Mr. Atkinson," in *Fraser's Magazine* 43 (April 1851), 418–34. Other reviewers were John Campbell in the *Athæneum* (March 1, 1851) and George Eliot in *The Leader* (March 1 & 8, 1851).

[3] The article in the *Westminster Review*, "Martineau and Atkinson," 55 (April 1851), 83–92, is signed N.N.

certainly well contented with F.'s praise; for one reason only; that people won't think you so foolish in bringing me forward in the way you have. As for the book, it is left by the critics just where it was; nothing disproved,—neither the facts nor the method, nor Bacon; and after all, if mine is "a careless sketch"[1] (and I dare say it is), the question is the truth of what it contains. If these men are such good artists, they will read the fact out of a rough sketch. F. throws out that idea about Bacon again, and calls it a *moral* fault in me. I cannot see it, especially as I am supported by others well acquainted with Bacon. The sin was of a piece with the rest of his doings, —in a measure essential at the time for getting a hearing at all for his philosophy: and F. forgets that if Bacon was an atheist, there was no offence against sacred matters, seeing that he did not consider them sacred, but "the delirium of phrenetics;" and thus it was rather a showing of respect and yielding. I do not see that this can spoil him as an author-ity, any more than Macaulay spoils him:[2] and if it did, he had better be no authority at all than an authority *against* science. Lord Campbell says Bacon was accustomed in his youth to ridicule religion, thinks the Paradoxes were his, but that in riper years he probably changed his opinion; the only reason given for which is a sentence in the Advancement of Learning,—his *earli-est* great work. The passage there is, "A little or superficial knowledge of philosophy may incline the mind of man to atheism, &c.;" which is absurd, if it were insisted on by Campbell.[3] (I suppose Pope's "A little learning is a dangerous thing,"[4] is taken from this passage.) Of course, people will say

---

1 The phrase, "a careless sketch," does not appear in James Martineau's review, but he repeat-edly points to lapses in logic and rhetoric in Atkinson's prose, as in "The coherent thinker may take his choice between the two [Unconditional Necessity or Alternative Power]: but Mr. Atkinson freely rambles from the one to the other, quite unconscious of self-contradiction" (240).

2 Thomas Babington Macaulay (1800–59) wrote an influential account of Francis Bacon's life and work for the *Edinburgh Review* (1837), later included in his collection, *Critical and Historical Essays Contributed to the Edinburgh Review* (London: Longman, Brown, Green and Longmans, 1843). He treats Bacon as a self-seeker, duplicitous and dishonorable, ascribing to Bacon a betrayal of his patron, the Earl of Essex, and corruption during his tenure as lord chancellor.

3 John Campbell (1779–1861), 1st Baron Campbell of St. Andrews, was a lawyer and Whig M.P. The passage quoted comes from Bacon's *Advancement of Learning* (1605), but is only partially quoted by Atkinson: "But farther, it is an assured truth, and a conclusion of experience, that a little or superficial knowledge of Philosophy may incline the mind of man towards Atheism, but a farther proceeding therein doth bring the mind back again to Religion." Atkinson argues that Campbell (wrongly) uses an early work to support an argument about Bacon's mature views, but Atkinson tellingly omits to comment on the full quotation.

4 Alexander Pope (1688–1744), *An Essay on Criticism* (1711): "A little learning is a danger-ous thing; / Drink deep, or taste not the Pierian spring: / There shallow draughts intox-icate the brain, / And drinking largely sobers us again."

I am wrong; *but let them show it*, with all their logic; and we shall see who has the best of it.—So you think the storm is at its height. It shows how little I know of it,—I thought it was all over. The organ now playing a wretched tune before my windows is more annoyance than all their articles put together. If they generally speak so of it, methinks there must be something in it, and they are not indifferent to it. Your American correspondent is quite a mystic.[1] What curious turns and twists the human mind takes, before it gets into the clear road of true philosophy, walking through the midst of the facts of Nature, the view widening and clearing at every step! Men like — and — don't like our book because it makes so little of theirs and all their study, by taking a more direct line to the results. I can't think what—can have to say that has not been said. So he is reading Comte, is he? I hope it will do him good.—Make Dr. — understand that repetition of the general fact was not the thing required or intended. I had other things to say, and to press into a mere notice. It is this very fact of incompleteness, &c., &c., that I believe Bacon would have praised. There is nothing cut and dried. There are facts; and in a certain order; a form for thinking men to work upon,—not to satisfy superficial men with a show of completeness. There are "particulars not known before for the use of man,"[2] which is better than all their logic: the one is mere measure and music,—the other "for future ages,"—the grain of mustard seed only, perhaps, but a germ full of life. The first letters are a sketch expository of my views on mental science and the means of discovery; and the following letters merely an *example* (like Bacon's Natural History) of the kind of fact that will throw light on the nature of the mind's action, out of which, when *extended and arranged in order*, inductions are to be made of the laws of action. The rest is little more than conversational replies to your questions.'

Another of these letters was written when I was ill under an attack of influenza, which disabled me from duly enjoying a visit I was paying in the north of the district, and from getting on with my next great scheme. After telling me how ill every body was at that time, he says:

'It is sad to be making your visit now. As to our concerns,—there is no saying how the next post may alter every thing. There really is no place for an ill feeling, or a disturbed one, if we could but keep it so in view. It seems to me that life is either too holy, or a matter too indifferent to be moved by every silly thought or angry feeling. With regard

---

[1]   Probably Ralph Waldo Emerson, with whom Martineau corresponded about the book,
      Margaret Fuller's *Memoirs*, and his own *Essays*; see *Letters*, ed. Sanders, pp. 121–24.
[2]   Quotation untraced.

to what they say about us, it is only precisely what you anticipated they would say: and it seems to me that after all is said, our facts and position remain untouched. It seems that we ought to have something to bear. I value this more every day. If I can be safe from flatterers and induce-ments to indulgence, I will be thankful for all the rest, and smile at all their scandal, and their great discovery that I am not allwise. It all pres-ents some new matter for contemplation; and if we cannot absolutely love our enemies, at least we may thank them for showing us our faults, which flattering friends hide from us. It seems all kinds of things must happen to us before we can become at all wise. First, we must become disenchanted of many delusions, that we may discover the pure gold through all the alloy which passes with it in the current coin of life. The Idols of the Market[1] are inveterate; but down they must go, if we would be in the least wise: and the process must be healthful when one does not become soured, but feels one's heart rather expanding and warming than cooling with years; and more thankful for every kindness, and not exacting as formerly.—I have been staying a few days in the country. We went over to a charming place, one day. Such a common! Perfectly beau-tiful! Acres of cherry-blossom, and splendid furze, like heaps of living gold; and the dark pine-trees rising from the midst! But one can't describe such things. I walked about there alone while the others were shooting young rooks,—the parson at the head of them. I had a little volume which pleased me much. It was never published ... ...

There does not seem to be any chance of my having got at Comte's ideas through any indirect channel; and I know nothing of him directly. Knight's volume by Lewes is the whole of my acquaintance with him.[2] What I do think is by labour in the fields or wild commons, and on the bench in the Regent's Park.—That unqualified condemnation of us in regard to Bacon looks rather like a condemnation by prejudiced and ignorant divines which Bacon grieves over. The whole matter is not

---

[1]   The third of the "idols" in Francis Bacon's *Novum Organum* (*The New Organon, Or True Directions Concerning the Interpretation of Nature*, 1620), by which is meant (taking *idol* from the Greek) "a species of illusion, or false appearance." Atkinson may have had in mind the passage in which Bacon explains that these idols are "formed by the reciprocal intercourses and society of man with man. ... For it is by discourse that men associate; and words are imposed according to the apprehension of the vulgar. And therefore the ill and unfit choice of words wonderfully obstructs the understanding."

[2]   When they published their *Letters* (1851), Martineau and Atkinson knew little of Auguste Comte (1798–1857) or his *Cours de philosophie positive* (*Course in Positive Philosophy*, 1830–42), except what they had read in G.H. Lewes's *Biographical History of Philosophy* (1845), which contained a chapter on Comte written by his disciple Emile Littré (1801–81).

worth wasting good feelings upon: but it should rather bring them forth, not injured, but strengthened. If, from being ill, we cannot depend on our forces, we can only make the best of it. I will soon tell you what I think I can best do now, in furtherance of our subject. All before us seems clear and sure, and the prospect even full of gaiety, if only I knew that you were quite well again. We must have our sad moments that we may have our wise ones.'

Here is his Good Friday letter, written amidst the ringing of church bells. It begins with a comment on an unhappy aged person,[1]—of whom we have been speaking:

'Age is a sad affair. If men went out of life in the very fulness of their powers, in a flash of lightning, one might imagine them transferred to heaven: but when the fruit fails, and then the flower and leaf, and branch after branch rots by our side while we yet live, we can hardly wish for a better thing than early death. Yes; it is true;—we do good to those to whom we have done good: we insult those we have insulted. Goodness is twice blessed; but hatred cankers the soul; and there is no relief, no unction, but in hating on. But of all the sad effects of age, the saddest is when as in this case a person reverses the noble principle of his life,— like the insane mother who detests the child she has so tenderly nurtured and loved. Every thing is flimsy, wrong, illogical, which does not confirm such an one in his own opinions: as a lady declared last evening who had been accusing *me* of not giving a fair consideration to the other side of the question, while I was recommending *her* to read so and so. "Well," said she, "it does not signify talking: in plain truth, I do not care to know about any body's views or reasons which will not confirm me in my own faith." This was a sudden burst of honest pride, and eagerness, in the midst of the confusion, to hold tight where she had got footing. Notions are worth nothing which are uttered in irritation partly, and in ignorance greatly, and in the spirit of old age,—not of Christ or of Paul. If what I have said is wrong in logic or in fact, it is no use abusing us: the thing is to exhibit the error; and I am sure none will be more thankful for the correction than I. F — [2] is the only one who has tried to do this; and I thank him for it, though I think him wholly wrong on matters of fact.—The book is objected to on religious grounds. Now, what is the use of all the millions spent, of all the learning of the colleges, and of all the parsons,—as thick as crows over the land,—if they cannot

---

[1]   Unidentified.

[2]   James Anthony Froude, Oxford historian and author of the novel *The Nemesis of Faith* (1849), reviewed their book in *Fraser's Magazine*; see p. 579, n. 2.

correct what is "shallow" and "superficial?" No; they feel otherwise than as they assert. They fear that however arrogant or superficial the book may be, there is substance in the midst of it; there is danger to the existing state of things; and they dare not honestly face the facts, and meet the argument which they declare to be too superficial to deceive any one. They dare not honestly and fairly do it. Shame upon the land! With that skulking phantom of a dressed-up faith that dares not face the light in broad day: with God upon their lips, and preaching Christ crucified, they fear to encounter God's truth by the way side! Why does Gavazzi waste his breath upon the Pope?[1] Let him face the wide world, and denounce its false faith, and show them how God walks with them in Nature as he did by Adam in Eden, and they hide away in shame, worship the Devil, and feed on the apple of sin every day of their lives. Men are subdued by *fear*. There is no faith in change, in progress, in truth, in virtue, in holiness. It is a terror-stricken age; and men fly to God to save them, and God gives them truth in his own way; and they receive it not. There is every kind of stupid terror got up about the Great Exhibition. F. is in terror about phreno-mesmerism: he would drown himself,—go out of the world if the thing were true. They like "Deerbrook"—yes, as a picture: but the spirit of "Deerbrook" is not in them, or they would love the spirit of the author of "Deerbrook." Well! it is not so bad as Basil Montagu used to say,[2] "My dear Atkinson, they will tear you to pieces." It is something then to say what we have said, and remain in a whole skin. ... ... The world is ripe if there were but the towering genius that would speak to it. We are all dead asleep. We want rousing from a lethargy, that we may listen to the God of Heaven and of earth who speaks to us in our hearts. The word of God is in every man, if he will listen. God is with us in all Nature, if we will but read the written law; written not on tables of stone, but on the wide expanse of nature. Yes, the savage is more right. God is in the clouds, and we hear him in the wind. Yes: and in the curse of ignorance, and the voice of reprobation, there too is God,—warning us of ignorance,—of unbelief of temper,—putting another law in our way, that we may read

---

[1] Alessandro Gavazzi (1809–89), professor at the University of Naples, joined Garibaldi to fight on the walls of Rome during the revolution of 1848. When Pope Pius IX fled in November 1848, Garibaldi declared a republic, but the Pope marshaled four armies to destroy it and re-take Rome. Garibaldi defended the besieged city from April 30, 1849 to July 3, 1849, when he and his forces could no longer hold out. Gavazzi fled to London, where he began lecturing on the cause of Italian freedom.

[2] Basil Montagu (1770–1851), a mutual friend who had arranged for Martineau's mesmeric treatment by Mrs. Wynard; he had recently died.

and interpret the book of fate. O! that some great teacher would arise, and make himself heard from the mountain top! The man whom they crucified on this day gave a Sermon on a mount. It is in every house, in every head; it is known, passage after passage: but in how few has it touched the heart, and opened the understanding! Men are but slowly led by pure virtue or by pure reason. They require eloquence and powerful persuasion; deep, solemn, unceasing persuasion. The Bible is a dead letter. Men worship the air and call it God. God is truth, law, morals, noble deeds of heroism, conscience, self-sacrifice, love, freedom, and cheerfulness. Men have no God. It is yet to be given them. They have but a log, and are croaking and unsatisfied;[1] and to-morrow they try King Hudson[2] or the Devil.'

The looking over these letters has revived my recollection of the really critical time at which they were written,—the trials of which I had forgotten as completely as the fatigues of the outside, and the gloomy horror of the inside of the pyramid.—I shall say nothing of the counter-part of the experience; of the vast discoveries of sympathy, the new connexions, the pleasant friendships, and the gratitude of disciples which have accrued to us, from that time to the present hour. The act was what I had to give an account of, and not its consequences. The same reasons which have deterred me from exhibiting the praises awarded to other works are operative here. I will conclude the whole subject with observing that time shows us more and more the need there is of such testi-mony as any of us can give to the value of philosophy, and of science as its basis. Those who praised us and our book, in print or in conversation, seem to have no more notion than those who condemned us of the infi-nite importance of philosophy,—not only to intellectual wisdom, but to goodness and happiness; and, again, that, in my comrade's words, 'the only method of arriving at a true philosophy of Mind is by the contemplation of Man as a whole,—as a creature endowed with definite properties, capable of being observed and classified like other phenomena resulting from any other portion of Nature.' The day when we agreed upon bear-ing our testimony, (in however imperfect a form) to these great truths

---

[1] An allusion to Aesop's fable "The Frogs Desiring a King," in which Jupiter answers the frogs' plea for a god by throwing a log into their lake.

[2] George Hudson (1800–71), the English financier known as the "Railway King," had obtained passage of a parliamentary act to raise capital for the York and North Midland Railway, of which he subsequently became chairman, and controlled more than 1,000 miles of railway. In "Hudson's Statue," in the *Latter-Day Pamphlets* (1851), Carlyle ridiculed the proposed erecting of a monument to Hudson as a wrong-headed "oblation" offered "by the Hero-worshippers of England to their Ideal of a Man."

was a great day for me, in regard both to my social duty and my private relations. Humble as was my share in the book, it served to bring me into a wide new sphere of duty; and, as to my private connexions, it did what I have said before; it dissolved all false relations, and confirmed all true ones. Its great importance to me may excuse, as well as account for, the length to which this chapter of my life has extended.

SECTION VII

IT appears, from two or three notices above, that Comte's philosophy was at this time a matter of interest to me. For many months after, his great work was indeed a means of singular enjoyment to me. After hearing Comte's name for many years, and having a vague notion of the relation of his philosophy to the intellectual and social needs of the time, I obtained something like a clear preparatory view, at second-hand, from a friend, at whose house in Yorkshire I was staying, before going to Bolton, in 1850.[1] What I learned then and there impelled me to study the great book for myself; and in the spring of 1851, when the 'Atkinson Letters' were out, and the History was finished, and I intended to make holiday from the pen for awhile, I got the book, and set to work. I had meantime looked at Lewes's chapter on Comte in Mr. Knight's Weekly Volume, and at Littré's epitome;[2] and I could thus, in a manner, see the end from the beginning of the complete and extended work. This must be my excuse for the early date at which I conceived the scheme of translating the *Philosophie Positive*.[3]

My course of lectures on English History finished on the first of April: and on the eighth, I sent off the last proof-sheet of my history. On the fourteenth, my nieces left me; and there was an interval before

---

[1] Dr. and Mrs. Stolterfoth; see p. 587, n. 2.

[2] G.H. Lewes's *Biographical History of Philosophy* (London: Charles Knight, 1845–46) included a summary by Emile Littré (1801–81).

[3] Despite this dream of April, 1851, she began translating in June, 1852. Another translation was already underway by the Rev. W. M.W. Call, and John Chapman, the publisher, had to decide whose translation would best serve. Martineau was given £500 by Edward Lombe, a Norfolk philanthropist, for the project, but took only £200 for herself and gave Chapman the rest to underwrite the cost of publishing the book; see R.K. Webb, *Harriet Martineau: A Radical Victorian* (New York: Columbia UP, 1960), p. 303.

my spring visits which I employed in a close study of the first volume of Comte's work. On the twenty-fourth, the book arrived from London; and I am amazed, and somewhat ashamed to see by my Diary, that, on the twenty-sixth, I began to 'dream' of translating it; and on the next night (Sunday the twenty-seventh) sat up late,—not dreaming, but planning it. On the second of May, I was in such enthusiasm that I wrote to one of the best-informed men on this matter in the kingdom, (an old friend) to ask his opinion on my scheme.[1] He emphatically approved my design,—of introducing the work to the notice of a wide portion of the English public who could never read it in the original; but he proposed a different method of doing it. He said that no results could compensate to me for the toil of translating six volumes in a style like Comte's, and in the form of lectures, whereby much recapitulation was inevitable. He proposed that I should give an abstract of Comte's philosophy, with illustrations of my own devising, in one volume; or, at most, in two of a moderate size. I was fully disposed to do this; and I immediately began an analysis, which would, I thought, be useful in whatever form I might decide to put forth the substance. I know no greater luxury, after months of writing, than reading, and making an analysis as one goes. This work I pursued while making my spring visits. On the eighth of May, I went for a fortnight to stay with some friends, between whom and myself there was cordial affection, though they were Swedenborgians,[2] of no ordinary degree of *possession* (for I will not call it fanaticism in people so gentle and kind). Their curiosity about Comte rather distressed me; and certainly it is not in the power of the most elastic mind to entertain at once Swedenborg and Comte. They soon settled the matter, however. My host kept aloof,—going out to his fishing every morning, while I was at work, and having very different matters to talk about in the evenings. It was his lady who took

---

[1] Possibly George Jacob Holyoake (1817–1906), editor of the secularist journal *The Reasoner*, which had favorably reviewed the *Atkinson Letters* and with whom she corresponded about Comte. She also asked her friend J. P Nichol (1804–59), Regius Professor of Astronomy at the University of Glasgow, to review the early sections on mathematics, physics, and astronomy.

[2] Dr. and Mrs. Stolterfoth, who lived at Armathwaite, near Carlisle, were followers of Emanuel Swedenborg (1688–1772), the philosopher and mystic who sought a comprehensive explanation of the universe, believing that it had an essentially spiritual structure. Blake was deeply influenced by him, as was Elizabeth Barrett Browning. In a letter to Fanny Wedgwood of May 15, 1851, Martineau characterizes them as "full of wonderful visions on the one hand, and the wisest and most active practical benevolence" (see *Letters*, ed. Arbuckle, p. 114).

up the matter; and I was amused to see how. She came to my writing-table, to beg the loan of the first volume, when I was going out for a walk. When her daughter and I returned from our walk, we met her in the wood; and the whole affair was settled. She knew 'all about it,' and had decided that Comte knew nothing. I inquired in amazement the grounds of this decision. She had glanced over the first chapter, and could venture to say she now 'knew all about it.' There was mere human science (which, for that matter, Swedenborg had also); and such science bears no relation to the realities which concern men most. This was all very well: and I was rejoiced that the thing had passed over so easily, though marvelling at the presumption of the judgment in one whom I consider nearly the humblest of women where her own qualities are concerned. A year later, however, she sent me a letter of rebuke about my work, which had less of the modesty, and more of the presumption, than I should have expected. I reminded her of what we had often agreed upon, with remarkable satisfaction,—the superiority of the Swedenborgian to all other religious sects in liberality. Not only does their doctrine in a manner necessitate this liberality, but the temper of its professors responds to the doctrine more faithfully than that of religious professors in general. I was sorry, as I told my friend, to see this liberality fail, on a mere change of the ground,—from that of religious controversy to that of the opposition between science and theology. I claimed my liberty to do the work which I thought best for the truth, for the same reason that I rejoiced in seeing her and her excellent family doing what they thought best for what they regarded as truth. I have had no more censure or remonstrance from any of the family, and much kindness,—the eldest daughter even desiring to come and nurse me, when she heard of my present illness: but I have no doubt that all the heresy I have ever spoken and written is tolerable in their eyes, in comparison with the furtherance given to science by the rendering of Comte's work into a tongue which the multitude can read; and which they will read, while the young men should be seeing visions and the old men dreaming dreams.

During other visits, and a great press of business about cottage-building, and of writing for 'Household Words' and elsewhere, I persevered in my study and analysis, —spending the evenings in collateral reading,—the lives and the history of the works of eminent mathematicians, and other scientific men. This went on till the twenty-sixth of June, when tourists began to fill the place and every body's time, and I must be off to London and into Norfolk, and leave my house to my tenant for three months. My first visit was to some beloved American friends in London, by whom I was introduced to the Great Exhibition.[1] I attended the last of Mr. Thackeray's lectures of that season, and paid evening visits, and saw many old friends.[2] But I was now convinced that I had lost my former keen relish for London pleasures. The quiet talks late at night with my hostesses were charming; and there was great pleasure in meeting old acquaintances: but the heat, and the glare, and the noise, and the superficial bustle, so unlike my quiet life of grave pursuit and prevailing solitude at home, showed me that my knoll had in truth spoiled me for every other abode.

The mention of Mr. Thackeray's name here reminds me that it does not occur in my notes of literary London twenty years ago. At that time I saw him, if I remember right, only once. It was at Mr. Buller's, at dinner;—at a dinner which was partly ludicrous and partly painful.[3] Mrs. Buller did not excel in tact; and her party was singularly arranged at the dinner-table. I was placed at the bottom of the table, at its square end, with an empty chair on the one hand, and Mr. Buller on the other,— he being so excessively deaf that no trumpet was of much use to him. There we sat with our trumpets,—an empty chair on the one hand, and on the other, Mr. J.S. Mill, whose singularly feeble voice cut us off from conversation in that direction. As if to make another pair, Mrs. Buller placed on either side of her a gentleman with a flattened nose,—Mr. Thackeray on her right, and her son Charles on the left. It was on this day only that I met either Mr. Dickens or Mr. Thackeray during my London life. About Mr. Thackeray I had no clear notion in any way, except that he seemed cynical; and my first real interest in him arose from reading M.A. Titmarsh in Ireland,[4] during my Tynemouth illness. I confess to being unable to read 'Vanity Fair,' from the moral disgust it occasions; and this was my immediate association with the writer's name when I next met him, during the visit to London in 1851. I could not

---

[1]   Maria Chapman, her literary executor, was in London with her daughters to see the Great Exhibition; also present were Eliza Follen and her son Charles, who had graduated from Harvard in 1849.

[2]   William Makepeace Thackeray (1811–63), then writing for *Punch*, gave lectures on *The English Humourists of the Eighteenth Century* in 1851.

[3]   Charles Buller, Sr. (d. 1848) served as M.P. for West Looe, Cornwall. His son Charles Buller (1806–48), Radical M.P. for Liskeard, and William Thackeray, the novelist, both had noses broken in fights.

[4]   Thackeray's most familiar pseudonym was Angelo Titmarsh, used for *The Paris Sketch Book* (1840) and *The Great Hoggarty Diamond* (1841). *The Irish Sketch Book* (1843) had a preface signed, for the first time, with Thackeray's name.

follow his lead into the subject of the Bullers (then all dead), so strong was my doubt of his real feeling. I was, I fear, rather rough and hard when we talked of 'Vanity Fair;' but a sudden and most genuine change of tone,—of voice, face, and feeling,—that occurred on my alluding to Dobbin's admirable turning of the tables on Amelia, won my trust and regard more than any thing he had said yet. 'Pendennis' much increased my respect and admiration; and 'Esmond' appears to me *the* book of the century, in its department.[1] I have read it three times; and each time with new wonder at its rich ripe wisdom, and at the singular charm of Esmond's own character. The power that astonishes me the most in Thackeray is his fertility, shown in the way in which he opens glimpses into a multitudinous world as he proceeds. The chief moral charm is in the paternal vigilance and sympathy which constitute the spirit of his narration. The first drawback in his books, as in his manners, is the impression conveyed by both that he never can have known a good and sensible woman. I do not believe he has any idea whatever of such women as abound among the matronage of England,—women of excellent capacity and cultivation applied to the natural business of life. It is perhaps not changing the subject to say next what the other drawback is. Mr. Thackeray has said more, and more effectually, about snobs and snobbism than any other man;[2] and yet his frittered life, and his obedience to the call of the great are the observed of all observers. As it is so, so it must be; but 'O! the pity of it! the pity of it!' Great and unusual allowance is to be made in his case, I am aware; but this does not lessen the concern occasioned by the spectacle of one after another of the aristocracy of nature making the ko-tow to the aristocracy of accident. If society does not owe all it would be thankful to owe to Mr. Thackeray, yet it is under deep and large obligations to him; and if he should even yet be seen to be as wise and happy in his life and temper as he might be any day, he may do much that would far transcend all his great and rising achievements thus far; and I who shall not see it would fain persuade myself that I foresee it. He who stands before the world as a sage *de jure* must surely have impulses to be a sage *de facto*.

---

[1]   The novels mentioned include *Vanity Fair* (1847–48), Thackeray's great satirical novel of English society set during the Napoleonic Wars; *The History of Pendennis* (1848–50), a semi-autobiographical novel with an author-protagonist; and *The History of Henry Esmond* (1852), a historical novel set in the seventeenth century. Martineau must have disliked the cynicism of the first, and admired the faithfulness in love and duty of the third.

[2]   In 1846–47 Thackeray published a 53–part series, *The Snobs of England*, in *Punch*, later republished as *The Book of Snobs* (1848).

Of Mr. Dickens I have seen but little in face-to-face intercourse; but I am glad to have enjoyed that little. There may be, and I believe there are, many who go beyond me in admiration of his works,—high and strong as is my delight in some of them. Many can more keenly enjoy his peculiar humour,—delightful as it is to me; and few seem to miss as I do the pure plain daylight in the atmosphere of his scenery. So many fine painters have been mannerists as to atmosphere and colour that it maybe unreasonable to object to one more: but the very excellence and diversity of Mr. Dickens's powers makes one long that they should exercise their full force under the broad open sky of nature, instead of in the most brilliant palace of art. While he tells us a world of things that are natural and even true, his personages are generally, as I suppose is undeniable, profoundly unreal. It is a curious speculation what effect his universally read works will have on the foreign conception of English character. Washington Irving came here expecting to find the English life of Queen Anne's days, as his 'Sketchbook' shows; and very unlike his preconception was the England he found.[1] And thus it must be with Germans, Americans, and French who take Mr. Dickens's books to be pictures of our real life.— Another vexation is his vigorous erroneousness about matters of science, as shown in 'Oliver Twist' about the new poor-law (which he confounds with the abrogated old one) and in 'Hard Times,' about the controversies of employers.[2] Nobody wants to make Mr. Dickens a Political economist; but there are many who wish that he would abstain from a set of difficult subjects, on which all true sentiment must be underlain by a sort of knowledge which he has not. The more fervent and inexhaustible his kindliness (and it is fervent and inexhaustible), the more important it is that it should be well-informed and well-directed, that no errors of his may mislead his readers on the one hand, nor lessen his own genial influence on the other.

The finest thing in Mr. Dickens's case is that he, from time to time, proves himself capable of progress,—however vast his preceding achievements had been. In humour, he will hardly surpass 'Pickwick,'

---

[1]   Washington Irving (1783–1859) published the essays and stories of *The Sketch Book* serially (1819–20) after his first tour of England; he returned to London in 1829–32 as the secretary to the U.S. legation.

[2]   For other comments on *Oliver Twist* (1837), see Period IV, sec. i, p. 180, n. 1. *Hard Times* (1854) satirizes Utilitarianism in the characters of Josiah Bounderby, a heartless manufacturer, and Thomas Gradgrind, who puts his trust solely in facts and statistics, even in the education of his children.

simply because 'Pickwick' is scarcely surpassable in humour: but in several crises, as it were, of his fame, when every body was disappointed, and his faults seemed running his graces down, there has appeared something so prodigiously fine as to make us all joyfully exclaim that Dickens can never permanently fail. It was so with 'Copperfield:' and I hope it may be so again with the new work which my survivors will soon have in their hands.[1]—Meantime, every indication seems to show that the man himself is rising. He is a virtuous and happy family man, in the first place. His glowing and generous heart is kept steady by the best domestic influences;[2] and we may fairly hope now that he will fulfil the natural purpose of his life, and stand by literature to the last; and again, that he will be an honour to the high vocation by prudence as well as by power: so that the graces of genius and generosity may rest on the finest basis of probity and prudence; and that his old age may be honoured as heartily as his youth and manhood have been admired.— Nothing could exceed the frank kindness and consideration shown by him in the correspondence and personal intercourse we have had; and my cordial regard has grown with my knowledge of him.

When I left London, it was for the singular contrast of spending the next night in a workhouse. Two of my servants (brother and sister) had been sent to me from Norfolk, —the maid by my own family, and the man by the excellent master of the Union Workhouse near Harling.[3] The girl (now married to the master of the Ragged School at Bristol) had a strong inclination to school-keeping, and had pursued it in this workhouse and elsewhere with such assiduity as to lose her health. During the five years that she lived with me (beloved like a daughter by me, and honoured by all who knew her) she in a great measure recovered her health; and when she married from my house, at Christmas 1852, she went to resume her vocation, in which she is now leading the most useful life conceivable. We went to Harling, she and I, in this July 1851, to see her old friends, and the old school, and her old parents, and the success of the agricultural part of the management

---

[1]   *Pickwick Papers* (1836–37) included the comic Mr. Samuel Pickwick; his devoted servant, Sam Weller; and Sam's father Tony, the coachman; *David Copperfield* (1849–50), a veiled autobiography with its scenes in the blacking warehouse, was then (as now) a favorite; and *Little Dorrit* (1855–57), set in the Marshalsea prison, followed *Hard Times* (1854).

[2]   This was written before Dickens's separation from his wife Catherine in 1858.

[3]   Robert and Martha Fulcher. Harling is twenty miles from Norwich, Martineau's hometown. Martha Fulcher married a Mr. Andrews, teacher at a school founded by the educator and reformer Mary Carpenter (1807–77). They were married by the Rev. Philip Carpenter (1819–77), Mary's brother, and a regular correspondent of Martineau's.

of this Guiltcross Union. Thus it was that I went from London to sleep in a workhouse. Very comfortable and agreeable I found it.

The next weeks were spent in the neighbourhood of Norwich, and at Cromer,[1] where I was joined by my younger sister and her children. It was at Cromer that a strange impulse on my part,—an impulse of yielding chiefly,—caused me to go into an enterprise which had no result. It put me, for a time, in the difficulty of having too many irons in the fire; but that was not my fault; for I could have no conception of the news which was awaiting me in London, on my return. While at Cromer, I was justified in feeling that I might take as much time as I pleased about Comte. It depended wholly on myself: but before I got home, the case was changed, as I shall presently have to tell. The intervening anecdote has been hitherto a profound secret, by my own desire;—perhaps the only secret of my own that I ever had: and this was part of the amusement. One reason why I tell it now is because it affords a confirmation out of my own experience of what many of my friends have wondered to hear me say;—that one cannot write fiction, after having written (*con amore*, at least) history and philosophy.

Ever since the 'Deerbrook' days, my friends had urged me to write more novels. When 'Currer Bell' was staying with me, the winter before the time I have arrived at, she had spoken earnestly to me about it, and, as it appeared to us both, wholly in vain. While at Cromer, however, I read 'Pendennis' with such intense enjoyment, and it seemed so much the richer from its contrast with 'The Ogilvies,'[2] and some other metaphysical, sentimental novels that had fallen in my way, that the notion of trying my hand once more at a novel seized upon me; and I wrote to Charlotte Brontë, to consult her as to the possibility of doing it secretly, and getting it out anonymously, and quite unsuspected, —as a curious experiment. She wrote joyously about it, and at once engaged her publisher's[3] interest in the scheme. She showed the most earnest friendliness throughout. She sent me a packet of envelopes directed by herself to her publisher; and she allowed his letters to me to come through her hands. When I reached home, on the first of October, I was somewhat scared at what I had undertaken,—the case of Comte

---

1   Seaside resort north of Norwich on the North Sea coast, where the Martineau family had gone in Harriet's childhood; see Period II, sec. i.

2   Dinah Mulock (later Craik, 1826–87), *The Ogilvies* (London: Chapman and Hall, 1849). This first novel turned on the problems of a marriage choice—not the sort of subject that Martineau admired.

3   Mr. G. Smith, of the firm of Smith, Elder, & Co. [Martineau's note]

having so changed, as I will tell; and the matter was not made easier by my inability to tell Mr. Chapman, who was to publish Comte, or Mr. Atkinson, who was in almost daily correspondence with me, what was delaying the progress of the philosophical half of my work. The difficulty was at an end before Christmas by the scheme of the novel being at an end. It was on an odd plan. It was no oddness in the plan, however, which discouraged me; but I doubted from the first whether I could ever again succeed in fiction, after having completely passed out of the state of mind in which I used to write it. In old days, I had caught myself quoting the sayings of my own personages, so strong was the impression of reality on myself; and I let my pen go as it would when the general plan of the story, and the principal scenes, were once laid down. Now I read and pondered, and arranged, and sifted, and satisfied myself, before I entered upon any chapter, or while doing it:—carrying, in fact, the methods and habits of historical composition into tale-telling. I had many misgivings about this; but, on the whole, I thought that the original principle of the work, and some particular scenes, would carry it through. At Christmas, I sent the first volume to Charlotte Brontë, who read it before forwarding it to the publisher. She wrote gloriously about it: and three days after came a pathetic letter from the publisher. He dared not publish it on account of some favourable representations and auguries on behalf of the Catholics.[1] That was a matter on which C. Brontë and I had perpetual controversy,—her opinion being one in which I could by no means agree; and thus expressed, after I had claimed credit for the Catholics, as for every body else, as far as their good works extended: 'Their good deeds I don't dispute; but I regard them as the hectic bloom on the cheek of disease. I believe the Catholics, in short, to be always doing evil that good may come, or doing good that evil may come.' Yet did my representation of the Catholics in no way shake her faith in the success of my novel; and her opinion, reaching the publisher the day after he had written his apprehensions to me, aggravated, as he said, his embarrassment and distress. He implored me to lay aside this scheme, and send him a novel 'like "Deerbrook."' That was no more in my power now than to go back to thirty years of age. C. Brontë entreated me merely to lay aside my novel, if I would not finish it on speculation, saying that some things in it were equal to, or beyond, any thing I had ever writ-

---

[1] George Smith of Smith & Elder declined to publish *Oliver Weld*, as she called this novel, but agreed to re-issue *Deerbrook* and immediately sent her £50 for a third edition. Smith, Elder re-issued the novel frequently throughout the rest of the century.

ten. I did intend at first to finish it: but other works pressed; the stimulus, and even the conception, passed away; and I burned the MS. and memoranda, a few months since, not wishing to leave to my survivors the trouble of an unfinished MS. which they could make no use of, and might scruple to burn. I told Mr. Atkinson and my Executor the facts when the scheme was at an end; and I hereby record the only failure of the sort I had experienced since the misleading I underwent about the Life of Howard,[1] at the outset of my career. I may add that the publisher behaved as well as possible, under the circumstances. He showed me civility in various ways, was at all times ready to negotiate for another novel 'like "Deerbrook,"' and purchased the copy-right of 'Deerbrook' itself, in order to bring it out in a cheap series, with the novels of Mr. Thackeray and 'Currer Bell.'

While I write, I recal, with some wonder, the fact that I had another literary engagement on my hands, at that very time. On recurring to my Diary, I find it was even so; and I wonder how I could justify it to myself. It was at Cromer, as I have said, that this scheme of the novel was framed, after I had consulted Mr. Chapman in London about publishing Comte's 'Positive Philosophy.' We had a clear understanding that it was to be done; but I was then wholly free in regard to time. On my return, I spent a week in London (then 'empty,' according to the London use of the word) with a cousin, in a lodging, for the sole object of seeing the Exhibition in our own way, and in peace and quiet. On the last day, Mr. Chapman, who had been trying to track me,[2] overtook me with a wonderful piece of news. Mr. Lombe, a Norfolk country gentleman, and late High Sheriff of the county,[3] had for many years been a disciple of Comte, and had earnestly wished to translate the 'Positive Philosophy,' but had been prevented by ill health. He was a perfect stranger to me, and residing in Florence; but, hearing from Mr. Chapman what I was doing, he sent me, by him, a draft on his bankers for 500*l*. His obvious intention was to give me the money, in recompense for the work; but I preferred paying the expenses of paper, print, and publication out of it, taking 200*l*. for my own remuneration. To finish now about the money part of the affair,—I took

---

[1]   See Period III, sec. iii, p. 127, for the unpublished life of Howard. Her executor at this time was her nephew Thomas Martineau, Robert's eldest son; she later added Robert Francis Martineau, another nephew, as a second executor; both Thomas and Robert Francis are named in her will.

[2]   Despite this account, a letter to Fanny Wedgwood on June 22, 1851, makes it clear that Martineau had arranged in advance to stay two days with the Chapmans at their home, 39 Devonshire Street, Portland Place (see *Letters*, ed. Arbuckle, p. 118).

[3]   Edward Lombe (d. 1852), a philanthropist who sponsored writing on serious subjects.

advice how to act, in regard to so important a trust; and, in accordance with that advice, I immediately invested the whole amount in the Three per Cents., and, on the death of Mr. Lombe, in the next winter, I added a codicil to my will, appointing two trustees to the charge and application of the money, in case of my dying before the work was completed and published. Just when Mr. Lombe died, I was proposing to send him a portion of my MS., to see whether my method and execution satisfied him. When the whole sum was distributed, and the work out, I submitted the accounts and vouchers to two intimate friends of Mr. Lombe, both men of business, and obtained their written assurance of their entire approbation of what I had done,—with the one exception that they thought I ought to have taken more of the money myself. As to the profits of the sale,—it seemed to me fair that M. Comte should have a portion; and also Mr. Chapman, through whom Mr. Lombe had become interested in the scheme. The profits have therefore been, up to this time, and will be henceforward, divided among the three,—M. Comte, Mr. Chapman and myself or my legatees.—My engagement to Mr. Chapman was to deliver the MS. entire within two years of my return home; that is, in October, 1853; and this was precisely the date at which I delivered the last sheets. The printing had been proceeding during the summer; so that the work appeared at the beginning of November 1853.

The additional work to which I have referred, as upon my hands at the same time, was this. I returned home, in the autumn of 1851, by Birmingham, where I spent a month at my brother Robert's house, at Edgbaston. The proprietors of 'Household Words' had all this time been urgent with me to write stories for them. I found myself really unable to do this with any satisfaction,—not only because of the absurdity of sending fiction to Mr. Dickens, but because I felt more and more that I had passed out of that stage of mind in which I could write stories well.[1] It struck me that a full, but picturesque account of manufactures and other productive processes might be valuable, both for instruction and entertainment: and I proposed to try my hand on two or three of the Birmingham manufactures, under the advantage of my brother's introduction, in the first place, and, in the next, of his correction, if I should fall into any technical mistakes. The proposal was eagerly accepted and I then wrote the papers on Electro-plating, Papier-mâché and the Nail and Screw manufacture,—which stand in 'Household Words' under the titles

---

[1]   Nonetheless, she did contribute stories to *Household Words*, including "A Real Sister of Charity" 3 (1851), 291–98; "The Highest House in Wathendale" 3 (1851), 389–96; and "The Fortunes of the Reverend Caleb Ellison" 3 (1851), 533–39.

of 'Magic Troughs at Birmingham,' 'Flower-shows in a Birmingham Hot-house,' and 'Wonders of Nails and Screws.'[1] These succeeded so well that I went on at home with such materials as the neighbourhood afforded,—the next papers which appeared being 'Kendal Weavers,' and 'The Bobbin-mill at Ambleside.'[2] Moreover, it was presently settled that I should spend a month at Birmingham after Christmas, to do another batch. Thereby hangs a pretty little tale:—at least, so it appears to me. My brother and sister having taken for granted that I should go to their house, I begged them not to take it amiss if I preferred going to a lodging, with my maid. My reasons were that I was going for business purposes, which would occupy all the daylight hours at that time of year; that I must therefore dine late; that I should be going about among the manufactories, with my maid to *hear* for me; and that I really thought my family and I should enjoy most of one another's society by my lodging near enough to go to tea with them every evening, and spend the Sundays at their house. They appeared to acquiesce at once,—saying, however, that I ought to be very near, on account of the highway robberies, with violence, which were at that time taking place at Edgbaston almost every evening. My sister wrote me an account of the rooms she had secured. I was rather struck by her recommendations about leaving terms and arrangements to my landlady, and by an odd bit of deprecation about not expecting the charms of my beautiful home. The next letter from one of my nephews at first dispersed a nascent doubt whether they were not intending to take me in,—in both senses. He wrote, 'Your rooms are in one of those houses near Mrs. F —'s, in the Highfield Road; so that you will not have so far to go to our tea-table but that you will be very safe from thieves. Your landlady is a very trustworthy person. She lived with us when we lived in the Bristol road; and she left that place, not for any fault, but for a better situation.' On a second reading, it struck me that this was all true of his mother, and of their house; and I was not therefore wholly surprised when the nephew who met us at the station directed the car to my brother's house. I was surprised, however, when I saw what preparation they had made for me and my work. They had taken down a bed in one of the prettiest rooms in the house, and had put in a writing-table, a sofa, a lamp, and all possible conveniences.—As one of my nephews had to dine late, there was no difficulty about that; and my sister and nieces went every where with me, one at a time, to listen

---

[1]   *Household Words* 4 (1851), 82–85, 113–17, 138–42.

[2]   *Household Words* 4 (1851), 183–89, 224–28.

with and for me, make notes, and render all easy. It really was charming. I then wrote ten more papers, as follows:

'The Miller and his Men,'—The Birmingham Flour-mills.

'Account of some treatment of Gold and Gems,'—Gold refining, Gold Chains and Jewellery.

'Rainbow-Making,'—Coventry Ribbons.

'Needles,'—the Redditch Manufacture.

'Time and the Hour,'—Coventry Watches.

'Guns and Pistols,'—Birmingham Gun-manufacture.

'Birmingham Glass-works,'—Messrs. Chances and Messrs. Oslers.

'What there is in a Button,'—Birmingham buttons.

'Tubal Cain,'—Brass-founding.

'New School for Wives,'—Evening School for Women.[1]

Invitations were sent me, when the authorship of these papers got abroad, from various seats of manufacture; but the editors and I agreed that our chief textile manufactures were already familiar to every body's knowledge; and I therefore omitted all of that kind except Kendal carpets, Coventry ribbons, and Paisley shawls. This last was done the next summer, when I was in Scotland, at the same time with Paper-hangings ('Household Scenery') and 'News of an old Place,'— the Lead works at 'Leadhills.'[2] From Scotland, my niece and I passed into Ireland, as I shall have to tell; and there I wrote, at the Giant's Causeway, 'the Life of a Salmon;' and afterwards 'Peatal Aggression,'— the Peat Works near Athy: the 'English Passport System,'—Railway ticket manufacture; 'Triumphant Carriages,'—Messrs. Hutton's Coach factory at Dublin: 'Hope with a Slate Anchor,'—the slate quarries in Valentia: 'Butter,' 'the Irish Union,' a workhouse picture; and 'Famine-time,' a true picture of one of the worst districts, at the worst time of the visitation.[3] I have done only two more of the same character,—of the productive processes;—'Cheshire Cheese,' and 'How to get Paper,'—both last year, (1854).[4]—It will be seen that I need have entertained no apprehension of enforced idleness in consequence of the publication of the 'Atkinson Letters.' It appears that, at the close of the same year, I was over-burdened with work; and I will add, for truth's sake, that I was uneasy, and dissatisfied with myself for having under-

[1]   *Household Words* 4 (1852), 415–20, 449–55, 485–90, 540–46, 555–59, 580–85; 5 (1852), 32–38, 84–89, 106–12, 192–97.

[2]   *Household Words* 5 (1852), 513–19, 537–42, 552–56.

[3]   *Household Words* 5 (1852), 606–10; 6 (1852), 13–18, 31–34, 121–25, 156–61, 169–75, 214–16.

[4]   *Household Words* 6 (1852), 344–50; 10 (1854), 52–56.

taken so much. The last entry in my Diary (a mere note-book) for 1851 is on the thirtieth of December. 'As I shall be travelling to Birmingham to-morrow, I here close my journal of this remarkable year: —an improving and happy one, little as the large world would believe it. I have found it full of blessings.'

All this time, my study of Comte was going on; and I continued the analysis for some weeks; but at length I found that I had attained sufficient insight and familiarity to render that work unnecessary. The first day on which I actually embodied my study of it in writing,—the first day on which I wrote what was to stand,—was June 1st. 1852: and a month before that, the greatest literary engagement of my life had been entered upon, of which I shall have to speak presently. After my return from Birmingham, I had had to give my annual course of lectures to the Mechanics; and my subject, the History of the United States, from Columbus to Washington, required some study. Before I left home for the tourist season, I had got into the thick of the mathematical portion of Comte: and there I had to stop till my return in the middle of October. I had then to write an article on Ireland for the 'Westminster Review,'[1] and other matters; so that it was the first of December before I opened Comte again, and Christmas day when I finished the first of the six volumes. After that, the work went on swimmingly. All the rest was easy. I finished Astronomy in the middle of January, and Biology on the twenty-third of April; so that I had five months for the last three volumes, which were by far the easiest to do, though half as long again as the first three.[2] I had a perpetual succession of guests, from April till the end of September; but I did not stop work for them; nor did I choose to leave home till I had fulfilled my engagement. It was on the eighth of October that I put the finishing stroke to the version: on the ninth I wrote the Preface; and on the tenth, I had the pleasure of carrying the last packet of MS. to the post. Some cousins who were staying with me at the time went on an excursion for the day; and when they returned, they sympathised with me on the close of so long and so arduous a task. I was much exhausted,—after a summer of abundant authorship in other ways, as well as of social engagement from the number and variety of guests, and the

---

[1]   "Condition and Prospects of Ireland," *Westminster Review* 3 N.S. (1852–3), 35–62.

[2]   Martineau's translation and redaction, *The Positive Philosophy of Auguste Comte*, 2 vols. (London: John Chapman, 1852), follows this arrangement: Introduction; Book I, Mathematics; Book II, Astronomy; Book III, Physics; Book IV, Chemistry; Book V, Biology; Book VI, Social Physics. The last book is by far the longest because it introduces the new science of sociology and its relation to other departments of positive philosophy.

absence of my usual autumn retirement to the sea, or some other quiet place: but the gain was well worth the toil. I find in my Diary some very strong expressions of rapture about my task; and I often said to myself and others, in the course of it, that I should never enjoy any thing so much again. And I believe that if I were now to live and work for twenty years, I could never enjoy any thing more. The vast range of knowledge, through which one is carried so easily, is a prodigious treat; and yet more, the clear enunciation, and incessant application of principles. The weak part of the book,—the sacrifices made to system and order,—happens just to fall in with my weak tendency in that direction; so that it required some warning from others, and more from within, to prevent my being carried away altogether by my author. After all deductions made, on the score of his faults as a teacher, and my weakness as a learner, the relation was a blessed one. I became 'strengthened, stablished, settled'[1] on many a great point; I learned much that I should never otherwise have known, and revived a great deal of early knowledge which I might never other-wise have recalled: and the subdued enthusiasm of my author, his philo-sophical sensibility, and honest earnestness, and evident enjoyment of his own wide range of views and deep human sympathy, kept the mind of his pupil in a perpetual and delightful glow. Many a passage of my version did I write with tears falling into my lap; and many a time did I feel almost stifled for want of the presence of some genial disciple of my instructor, to whom I might speak of his achievement, with some chance of being understood.

As for my method of working at my version, about which I have often been questioned,—it was simple enough.—I studied as I went along, (in the evenings, for the most part) the subjects of my author, reviving all I had ever known about them, and learning much more. Being thus secure of what I was about, I simply set up the volume on a little desk before me, glanced over a page or a paragraph, and set down its meaning in the briefest and simplest way I could. Thus, my work was not mere transla-tion: it involved quite a different kind of intellectual exercise; and, much as I enjoy translating, —pleasant as is the finding of equivalent terms, and arranging them harmoniously,—it is pleasanter still to combine with this the work of condensation.[2] To me, in truth, nothing was ever pleasanter:

---

[1]   Quoting I Peter 5:10 (KJV): "The God of all grace, who hath called us unto his eternal glory, by Christ Jesus, after that we have suffered awhile, make you perfect, stablish, strengthen, settle you."

[2]   Martineau's version condensed six volumes into two; it had the full endorsement of Comte, who authorized the translation of her English version back into French.

and I had no sympathy with the friends who hoped, as I proceeded, that I should not again occupy myself with translation. I told them that it was like going to school again while doing the useful work of mature age; and that I should relish nothing better than to go on with it as long as I lived. As for the average amount of my daily work, (four or five days in the week) I was discontented if it was under twenty pages of my author, and satis- fied if it was any where from twenty-five to thirty. The largest day's work, in the whole course of the business, was forty-eight pages: but that was when I had breakfasted before seven, to dismiss a guest; and on a Saturday, when there was no post to London, and I had set my mind on finishing a volume. I worked nearly all day, and finished after midnight. I find fifty pages set down on another occasion; but in that case there was an omis- sion of a recapitulatory portion. In saying what was the daily amount done, I ought to observe that it was really *done*. I finished as I went along; and I looked at my work no more till it came in the shape of proof-sheets.—I have stated in my Preface to the work that, on my expressing my inten- tion to obtain a revision of the three first Books, (Mathematics, Astronomy and Physics) by a scientific man, Professor Nichol kindly offered his serv- ices.[1] His revision of that portion (in which he found, he said, no mistakes) and the few notes and observations which he inserted, made me easy about the correctness of what I was putting forth; and I did not run the risk of spoiling the freshness of what I had done so enjoyably by any retouching. It came out precisely as I wrote it, day by day.

One part of my enjoyment was from the hope that the appearance of a readable English version would put a stop to the mischievous, though ludicrous, mistakes about Comte's doctrine and work put forth by men who assumed, and might be expected, to know better. The mistakes were repeated, it is true; but they were more harmless after my version had appeared. When I was studying the work I was really aston- ished to see a very able review article open with a false statement about Comte, not only altogether gratuitous, but so ignorant that it is a curi- ous thing that it could have passed the press.[2] It alleged that a man called Auguste Comte, who assumed in 1822 to be a social prophet, had

[1]   J.P. Nichol (1804–59), Regius Professor of Astronomy at the University of Glasgow.

[2]   Untraced. The most likely reviews for Martineau to have read were W.A. Butler, "M. Compte [sic]: The System of Positive Philosophy," *Dublin University Magazine* 25 (April 1845), 452–63, and David Brewster, "M. Comte's Course of Positive Philosophy," *Edinburgh Review* 67 (July 1838), 271–308. Both were published anonymously, though Martineau may have known their authors; Butler was a Professor of Moral Philosophy at Trinity College, Dublin, and Brewster, a natural philosopher appointed at the University of St. Andrews and a friend of Henry, Lord Brougham.

declared the belief and interest in theology to be at an end; whereas, here was the whole kingdom, thirty years later, convulsed with theological passion, about Papal aggression and the Gorham controversy.[1] Now, this was a treble blunder. In the first place, Comte has never said that theology and the popular interest in it are over. In the next, he has written largely on the social turmoil which this generation is in, and generations to come will be in, from the collision between the theological passion of one social period, and the metaphysical rage of another, with the advance of the positive philosophy which is to supersede them both. If there is one thing rather than another reiterated to weariness in Comte's work, it is the state of turmoil, and its causes, of which the Gorham controversy was an admirable exemplification. In the third place, Comte's doctrine is that theology can be extinguished only by a true Science of Human Nature; that this science is as yet barely initiated; and that therefore theology is very far from being yet popularly superseded.

At a later time, in October 1851, when an eminent philosopher from Scotland was my guest for a few days,[2] I invited to meet him at dinner a friend of his, who was in the neighbourhood, and that friend's lady, and another guest or two. I was before slightly acquainted with this couple, and knew that the gentleman was highly thought of, by himself and others (by the late Dr. Arnold, among the rest) as a scholar and writer. When he was taking me in to dinner, he asked me whether I had heard that M. Comte was insane. I replied that it was not true,— M. Comte being perfectly well the week before; and I told him that I was engaged on his work. My guest replied that he had heard the whole story,—about Mr. Lombe's gift and all,—from another gentleman, then present. He asked me an insulting question or two about the work, and made objections to my handling it, which I answered shortly, (the servants being present) and put down my trumpet, to help the fish.[3] While I was so engaged, he asked questions which I could not hear,

---

[1] The Gorham controversy erupted when Henry Phillpotts, the Bishop of Exeter, refused to induct George Gorham as clergyman of the parish of Brampton Speake because Gorham rejected the teaching of unconditional regeneration in baptism as taught by the Church of England—i.e., that infants are regenerated by the sprinkling of holy water called "baptism." Gorham won an appeal at the Court of Arches, a decision implying that it was possible to be an Anglican clergyman in good standing while denying the standard doctrine of Baptismal Regeneration. The reviewer's point was that Englishmen and women were still deeply concerned with matters of theological belief.

[2] Dr. Samuel Brown (1817–56), Scottish chemist, philosopher, and historian of science. The rude guest has not been identified.

[3] I.e., serve the fish.

across me, of my philosopher guest; and then, with triumph and glee, reported to me my friend's replies, as if they were spontaneous remarks, and with gross exaggeration. During the whole of dinner, and in the presence of my servants, he continued his aspersions of Comte, and his insults to me as his translator; so that, as it came to my knowledge long afterwards, my other guest wondered that I put up with it, and did not request him to leave the house. I saw, however, that he knew nothing of what he was talking about; and I then merely asked him if he had read the portion of the work that he was abusing. Being pressed, he reluctantly answered—No; but he knew all about it. When the dessert was on the table, and the servants were gone, he still continued his criticisms. I looked him full in the face, and again inquired if he had read that portion of the *Philosophie Positive:*—'No—n—o:' but he knew all about it. I said I doubted it; and asked if he had read the book at all. 'N—o—o:' but he knew all about it. 'Come,' said I, 'tell me,—have you ever seen the book?'—'No: I can't say I have;' he replied, 'but I know all about it.' 'Now,' said I, 'look at the bookshelves behind you. You see those six volumes in green paper? Now you can say that you have seen the book.' I need not say that this was the last invitation that this *gentleman* would ever have from me.

Again,—a lady, younger than myself,[1] who shrinks from the uncomfortable notion that there is any subject which she is not qualified to lay down the law upon, folded her hands on her knees, and began in an orderly way to reprehend me for translating a book which had such shocking things in it as Comte's work. I made the usual inquiry,— whether she had read it. She could not say she had; but she too 'knew all about it,' from a very clever man; a *very* clever man, who was a great admirer of Comte, and on my 'side.' She was sorry I could introduce into England the work of a man who said in it that he could have made a better solar system than the real one;—who declared that he would have made it always moonshine at night. I laughed, and told her she was the victim of her clever friend's moonshine. She ended, however, with a firm faith in her clever friend, in preference to reading the book for herself. She will go on to the end of her days, no doubt, regarding the 'Positive Philosophy' as a receipt for making permanent moonshine, in opposition to the nineteenth Psalm.

Once more, (and only once, though I might fill many pages with anecdotes of the blunders about Comte made by critics who assume to

---

[1]   Untraced.

understand their subject:)—a professor of Mental Philosophy has, even since the publication of my version, asserted, both in print, and repeatedly in his lectures in London,[1] that Positive philosophers declare that 'we *can* know nothing but phenomena:' and the lecturer fancies that he has confuted the doctrine by saying that the knowledge of phenomena would occupy Man's observing faculties only, and leave the reasoning and other faculties without exercise. In this case, the lecturer has taken half Comte's assertion, and dropped the other half,—'*and their laws.*' This restoration, of course, overthrows the lecturer's argument, even if it were not otherwise assailable. It is true that Mr. Atkinson and I, and many others, have made the assertion as the lecturer gives it;–that 'we *can* know nothing but phenomena,'—the laws being themselves phenomena: but in that view, as in the case of the restoration of Comte's text, the lecturer's argument about the partial use of the human faculties is stultified. Some of his pupils should have asked him what we can know but phenomena. The *onus* of showing that certainly rests with him. Such are, at present, the opponents of Comte among us, while his work is heartily and profitably studied by wiser men, who choose to read and think and understand before they scoff and upbraid.

A letter of Mr. Atkinson's in my possession seems to me to give so distinct an account of what Man 'can know,' and of the true way of obtaining the knowledge, that I am tempted to insert a part of it here as settling the question with our incompetent critics, as to what we declare that we can and cannot know.

'Man cannot know more than has been observed of the order of Nature,—he himself being a part of that nature, and, like all other bodies in nature, exhibiting clear individual effects according to particular laws. The infinite character and subtlety of Nature are beyond his power of comprehension; for the mind of Man is no more than (as it were) a conscious mirror, possessing a certain extent of interreflexion. In a rude state, as before it has become reduced to a proper focus, and cleansed and purified by knowledge, it is subject to all manner of spectral illusions, presumptuous and vain conceits, which may be well termed a kind of normal or infantine madness; a kind of disease like the small-pox or the measles: conditions to which all children are subject; and it is well if the child can be helped through these strange

---

[1]   A likely candidate is H.R. Reynolds, President of Chesthunt College and a regular contributor to the *British Quarterly Review* on theology and philosophy, who published "Auguste Comte—His Religion and His Philosophy" in the *British Quarterly Review* 19 (April 1854), 297–376, shortly after Martineau's translation appeared. See also p. 601, n. 2.

malignant conditions in early youth, and be then and there cleansed from them for ever.

'If we study the formation of the globe, and the history of nations or of individuals, or glance at the progress of knowledge in the human mind, we shall perceive that difficulties have been overcome and advances achieved in the early stages through violent means; that that which we call evil has always in effect been working for the general good; and that, in the very nature of things, that good could not have come about by any other means: and thus, whatever is is good, in its place and season. Concluding thus, I think we may henceforth dispense with that very popular gentleman in black, the Devil. Indeed, once for all, we may sign ourselves Naturalists, as having no knowledge, or having no means of knowing any thing, beyond Nature. To advance by the acquiring of knowledge and by reason is the high privilege and prerogative of Man: for, as glorious as it is to possess a just, candid, and truth-loving nature, essential as it is that we know what is true,—yet must we be content that in the first instance, and for some short space, the progress should be slow and devious: for the errors and imperfections of the mind itself prevent men from attaining that knowledge which is almost essential to the cure of those very errors, imperfections and impediments. Thus, mankind have had to rely upon a genius springing up here and there,—great men who have had the strength to overleap the difficulties, and the sense to see what was before them and the honesty to declare what they have seen.

'The power of knowledge is in the knowledge of causes; that is, of the material conditions and circumstances under which any given effect takes place. These conditions we have termed Second Causes: but of the primitive matter which is *sui generis* we know nothing: for knowledge is limited by the senses. The knowledge of a thing includes a sense of its material cause or conditions,—its relative or distinguishing qualities,—the laws of form and quantity implicated in the case, and the laws of action in sequence and duration.—The higher laws are discovered in the analogy of knowledge: but of the primitive or fundamental cause or matter,—that "cause of causes itself without a cause,"—we know and can know absolutely nothing. We judge it to be something positive: to so much the nature of the mind compels assent: but we do not know what this positive something is in itself, in its absolute and real being and presence. We must rest content to take it as we find it, and suppose it inherently capable of performing or flowing into all those effects exhibited throughout nature. We only recognise a primitive matter as a required cause and necessary existence implied in the sensational phenomena which appear to include it in their embraces. But the existence of matter cannot be proved; nor can we form any conception of its real nature, because we can only divine by similitudes; and our similitudes cannot press beyond sensational phenomena and the simple inference. "So that all the specious meditations, speculations, and theories of mankind (in regard to the nature of nature) are but a kind of insanity." "But those who resolve not to conjecture and divine, but to discover and know; not to invent buffooneries and fables about worlds, but to inspect, and, as it were, dissect the nature of this real world, must derive all from things themselves: nor can any substitution or compensation of wit, meditation, or argument (were the whole wit of all combined in one) supply the place of this labour, investigation, and personal examination of the world; our method then must necessarily be pursued, or the whole for ever abandoned."[1]

'The intellect, in a general sense, is simply an observing faculty. The highest efforts of reason and of imagination are but an extension of observation. A law is but the observed form of a fact; and, in truth, the entire conscious mind may be termed a faculty of observation. To deny this is only to make a quibble about distinctions not really essential. The most important fact which the experienced mind observes is the fixed order in nature: and the trained philosopher instinctively concludes, and I may say perceives, the necessity of this order, just as he acknowledges the existence of objects in their objective or material appearance: (and this in spite of all that Bishop Berkeley[2] and others have said). The human mind by the constitution of its nature recognises the necessity of a determinate order in nature,—dependence in causes, and form or law in effects; and on this faith we build all our confidence that similar results will always flow, as a necessary consequence, from similar causes. In this fact we have the reason of reason, and the power of knowledge over nature, applying the principles of nature by art to the wants of Man. The instinct or sense of Man acknowledges a fundamental cause

---

[1] Both are quotations of Francis Bacon. The first begins, "The subtilty of nature is far beyond that of sense or of the understanding: so that the specious meditations, speculations, and theories of mankind, are but a kind of insanity, only there is no one to stand by and observe it." The second comes from Bacon's *The Great Instauration*, from *The Works of Francis Bacon: A New Edition*, ed. and trans. Basil Montague (London: William Pickering, 1825–34). Montague (1770–1851) had been a friend of both Atkinson and Martineau.

[2] George Berkeley (1685–1753), English philosopher who argued that Spirit is the only real cause or power and that the dualism of spirit and matter in Descartes, Locke, et al. leads logically to skepticism and atheism.

in the primitive matter, and the necessity of a particular form and order in objects and their effects: and that it is absolutely impossible that things should be different from what they are found to be. Now, until a man clears his mind, and abstracts it from all fanciful causes, to rest upon the true and fundamental cause in the primitive matter, perceiving at the same time that this cause must be positive, and capable of producing all the effects and variety of nature, and in a form and order absolutely fixed in "an adamantine chain of necessity"—until, I say, a man is fully and deeply impressed with this law of laws, this form of forms, evolved from the inherent nature of the ultimate fact and cause (this primitive matter and cause being fundamental, neither depending upon nor requiring any other cause) he is not a philosopher, but a dreamer of dreams, a poor wanderer on a false scent, seeking for a cause out of nature, and in a magnified shadow of himself. "If," says Bacon,[1] "any man shall think, by view and inquiry into these sensible and material things, to attain to any light for the revealing of the nature or will of God, he shall dangerously abuse himself."—"And this appeareth sufficiently in that there is no proceeding in invention of knowledge but by similitude; and God is only self-like, having nothing in common with any creature, otherwise than as in shadow and trope."[2] These remarks of Bacon in regard to the "invention" of a cause out of nature apply equally to the "invention" of the nature of the cause in nature: for all the knowledge we can have of the primitive matter is by way of negatives and exclusions.

'I hold, then, with Democritus, Heraclitus, Empedocles, Anaxagoras, Anaximenes and others,[3] that matter is eternal, possessing an active principle, and being the source of all objects and their effects: for you may as well suppose time and space to have a beginning, and to have been created, as that matter should have been brought out of nothing, and have had a beginning. The active principle and the properties of matter are essential to our very conception of matter: and the necessary form of the effects we term Laws:—laws, not to be considered in

---

1   Interpretation of Nature. Chapter I. [Martineau's note]
2   Interpretation of Nature. Chapter I. [Martineau's note]
3   All are Greek materialist philosophers, though of different sorts—Democritus (460–357 B.C.), a founder of atomic theory; Heraclitus (c.540–c.480 B.C.), author of "On Nature" and proponent of fire as the essential stuff of the universe; Empedocles (c.495–c.435 B.C.), whose philosophy is founded on the four persisting elements of earth, air, fire, and water; Anaxagoras (c.500–c.428 B.C.), whose book "On Nature" proposes "seeds" as the basis of the cosmos; and Anaximenes (mid-sixth century B.C.), whose originative principle of the cosmos was air, which was rarified as fire or condensed as water or earth.

a political sense, as rules laid down by a ruler, and capable of alteration and change; but the rule of rules;—the essential and necessary form and life and mind, so to speak, of what is in fact not a ruling power at all, but simply the principle or form of the result,—just as grammar exhibits the form of language.

'The belief in the freedom of the will, or that any thing is free in any other way than as being unimpeded and at liberty to move according as it is impelled by that which determines its motion or choice, is absolutely nonsense: and the doctrine of chance is as absurd as would be the belief that Nature arose from a rude mob of lawless atoms, arranging themselves by chance; a notion which is clearly nonsense,— a weak and unmitigated atheism, to escape from which men impose upon themselves a despotism in the shape of a King Log or a King Stork,[1] as the case may be. That which they suppose to be divine and most holy is but a presumptuous, shallow, and ridiculous assumption. It is a folly built upon a shifting sand-bank, which the tide will presently carry away, exhibiting the true stronghold of the understanding built upon the solid granite rock of Nature:—that Nature which is no despotism, but a pure and free republic, and a law unto itself,—an eternal, unalterable law unto itself: for two and two will never become five; nor will the three angles of a triangle ever be less than two right angles; nor will the great law of gravity be changed, nor the Atomic rule in chemical effects; nor the material conditions essential to thought and feeling be reversed. The world may come to an end,—become worn out, and dissolve away, or explode; but the nature of the particles of matter cannot change: the principles of truth will hold the same, and a new world will rise out of the dust.

'With regard to the origin of the mind itself,—it is clearly a consequence or result of the body evolved under particular laws:—as much so as a flower is a consequence of the growth of a tree,—instinct of the lower animal body,—light of a tallow candle. The light and heat of a candle may set light to other candles, or react upon its own body, as mental conditions may, when they cause the heart to beat, and the face to flush, and tears to flow, and the whole frame to be convulsed by laughter. So may the bile, or any other secretion, react on the body: but not the less is the mind the effect and consequent of the body, dependent on the condition

---

[1]   Another of Atkinson's allusions to Aesop's fable "The Frogs Desiring a King," in which Jupiter answers the frogs' plea for a god by throwing a log into their lake; when the frogs realize the powerlessness of the log and ask for a real king, Jupiter sends them a stork, who gobbles them up.

of the body, and the proper supply of air and food. To suppose otherwise is to give up all hope and all philosophy, and to desert common sense and universal experience. The mind proper is simply the conscious phenomenon which is not a power at all, but the representative or expression of an unconscious power and condition of which it is a concomitant. Strictly speaking, there are but two conditions in nature; matter the *physique*, and the conscious mind, or the *metaphysique*,—the positive and the negative. The conscious mind is purely phenomenal: it is not therefore the mind proper which acts upon the body, but that force which underlies the mind, of which the mind is simply the result, expression or exponent. The mind's unconscious working power or sphere is evident in almost every act of the body, as well as in almost every fact of the mind. It may be studied in the higher phenomena of *clairvoyance* and prophecy,— higher, only as an extending of experience by another and a clearer sense. We spring up from the earth like a flower. We live, love, and look abroad on the wide expanse of heaven, wondering at the night which lies behind, and at the dim shadows and flickering lights which coming events cast before them: and then we expire, and give place, as others have given place to us. We have but a glance at existence; yet the laws we discover are eternal truths. Knowledge is not infinite. A few simple principles or elements are fundamental to the whole; as a few simple primitive sounds form into glorious music, and all the languages which exist: and therefore knowledge is not infinite, and progress has its limit. ... ...
Still, "the mighty ocean of truth lies before us,"[1] and its advance is irresistible; and it will be well to remember King Canute,[2] and take the hint in time;—to look abroad upon the expanse, and up to the multitude of stars; and to listen to the deep-speaking truths which are now making themselves heard in society; and not to seek to resist what is inevitable. That the new day will be bright and glorious when Man will know his own power and nature, and rise into his new dignity as a rational human being, is enough for us now to prophesy.'

---

[1]   A slight misquotation of Isaac Newton (1642–1727): "I do not know what I may appear to the world; but to myself I seem to have been only like a boy playing on the seashore, and diverting myself in now and then finding a smoother pebble or a prettier shell than ordinary, whilst the great ocean of truth lay all undiscovered before me."

[2]   King Canute, Danish king of England (1016–35) who tried—and failed—to repel the sea.

SECTION VIII

I HAVE referred, some pages back, to a great opening for work, of a delightful kind, which offered while I was busy about Comte. As I have explained, the whole version, except half of Comte's first volume (that is, about a sixteenth part) was done between Christmas 1852 and the following October: and it remains to be told what else I had to do while engaged on that version. In April 1852 I received a letter from a literary friend in London, asking me, by desire of the Editor of 'Daily News,' whether I would 'send him a "leader" occasionally.' I did not know who this editor was; had hardly seen a number of the paper, and had not the remotest idea whether I could write 'leaders:'[1] and this was my reply. I saw that this might be an opening to greater usefulness than was likely to be equalled by anything else that I could undertake; so I was not sorry to be urgently invited to try. The editor, my now deeply-mourned friend, Mr. Frederick Knight Hunt,[2] and I wrote frank and copious letters, to see how far our views and principles agreed; and his letters gave me the impression which all my subsequent knowledge of him confirmed, that he was one of the most upright and rational of men, and a thorough gentleman in mind and manners. I sent him two or three articles, the second of which (I think it was) made such a noise that I found that there would be no little amusement in my new work, if I found I could do it. It was attributed to almost every possible writer but the real one. This 'hit' sent me forward cheerily: and I immediately promised to do a 'leader' per week, while engaged on Comte. Mr. Hunt begged for two; and to this I agreed when I found that each required only two or three hours in an evening, and that topics abounded. I had sufficient misgiving and uncertainty to desire very earnestly to have some conversation with Mr. Hunt; and I offered to go to London (on my way to Scotland) for the purpose. He would not hear of this, but said he would come to me, if public affairs would allow of his leaving the office. Then Parliament was dissolved; and the elections kept him

---

[1] "Leader" or "leader-column," the first article of a newspaper, usually expressing editorial opinion.

[2] Frederick Knight Hunt (1814–54), editor of the *Daily News*.

at home; so that I looked for him in vain by every train for ten days before my niece and I started for Edinburgh.[1] He came to us at Portobello;[2] and for two half days he poured out so rich a stream of conversation that my niece could not stand the excitement. She went out upon the shore, to recover her mind's breath, and came in to enjoy more. It was indeed an unequalled treat; and when we parted, I felt that a bright new career was indeed opened to me. He had before desired that I should write him letters from Ireland; and he now bespoke three per week during our travels there.[3] This I accomplished; and the letters were afterwards, by his advice and the desire of Mr. Chapman, published in a volume.[4] It was on occasion of that long journey, which extended from the Giant's Causeway to Bantry Bay, and from the Mullet to Wexford,[5] that I first felt the signs of failure in bodily strength which I now believe to have been a warning of my present fatal malady. My companion was an incomparable help. It was impossible to be more extensively and effectually aided than I was by her. She took upon herself all the fatigue that it was possible to avert from me; and I reposed upon her sense and spirit and watchfulness like a spoiled child. Yet I found, and said at the time, that this must be my last arduous journey. The writing those Letters was a pure pleasure, whether they were penned in a quiet chamber at a friend's house, or amidst a host of tourists, and to the sound of the harp, in a *salon* at Killarney; but, in addition to the fatigue of travelling and of introductions to strangers, they were too much for me. I had some domestic griefs on my mind, it is true. During the spring, my neighbours had requested me to deliver two or three lectures on Australia; and one consequence of my doing so was that my dear servant Jane resolved to emigrate (for reasons which I thought sound), and she was to sail in November: and now at Cork, the news met me that the other servant, no less beloved, was going to

---

1   Maria Martineau (1827–64) accompanied her aunt to Scotland and Ireland in the summer of 1852; she became an indispensable part of the household when Martineau was diagnosed with a fatal illness in 1855.

2   Outside of Edinburgh, with a mile-long sandy beach.

3   After Portobello, Martineau and her niece traveled west in Scotland to Loch Katrine and Loch Lomond; then they crossed to Ireland, landing at Derry via Lough Foyle in the north and traveling as far as Valencia Island in the southwest.

4   *Letters from Ireland* (London: John Chapman, 1852).

5   The Giant's Causeway, a formation of columnar basalt extending across the North Channel to Scotland, is in the northeast; Bantry Bay, the southwest. The Mullet is a wild peninsula in the northwest; Wexford, a city in the southeast. In other words, Martineau criss-crossed Ireland in her travels.

marry the Master of the Ragged School at Bristol, who had been her coadjutor in the Norfolk Workhouse School before mentioned. I wrote to advise their marriage at Christmas; but it was with the sense of a heavy misfortune having befallen me.[1] I did not believe that my little household could ever again be what it had been since I built my house: and I should have been thankful to have foreseen how well I should settle again,—to change no more. I did not fully recover my strength till our pretty wedding was over, and I was fairly settled down, in winter quiet, to Comte and my weekly work for 'Daily News.'—The wedding was truly a charming one. My dear girl had the honour of having Miss Carpenter for her bridesmaid, and the Revd. Philip P. Carpenter to perform the ceremony,—the Bristol Ragged School being, as every body knows, the special care of Miss Carpenter.[2] I told the bride, the week before the bridegroom and guests arrived, that, as I could not think of sending the former to the kitchen table, nor yet of separating them, it would be a convenience and pleasure to me if she would be my guest in the sitting-rooms for the few days before the marriage. She did it with the best possible grace. She had worked hard at her wedding clothes during my absence, that she might be free for my service after my return: and now, after instructing her young successor, she dressed herself well, and dined with us, conversing freely, and, best of all, making a good dinner, while watching that every body was well served. A more graceful lady I never saw. She presented me with a pretty cap of her own making for the wedding morning; and would let nobody else dress me. The evening before, when Mr. Carpenter delivered a Temperance lecture, Miss Carpenter and I sent the entire household to the lecture; and we set out the long table for the morning, dressed the flowers (which came in from neighbouring conservatories) and put on all the cold dishes; covered up the whole, and shut up the cat. The kitchen was the only room large enough for the party; and there, after the ceremony, we had a capital breakfast, with good speaking, and all manner of good feeling. When all were gone and my new maids had dried their sympathetic tears, and removed the tables, and given away the good things which that year served my usual Christmas day guests for dinner at home instead of here; and when I had put off my finery, and sat down, with a bursting headache, to write the story to the bride's family, and

---

[1] Jane Arrowsmith emigrated in November, 1852; Martha Fulcher married in December, 1852.

[2] Mary (1807–77) and Philip (1819–77) Carpenter were the children of Martineau's former teacher and mentor, Lant Carpenter of Bristol; see Period II, sec. iii.

the Carpenters' and my own, I felt more thoroughly down-hearted than for many a year.—All went well, however. The good couple are in their right place, honoured and useful; and 'our darling,' as Miss Carpenter called my good girl, is beloved by others as by me. There have been no more changes in my household; and, as for me, I soon recovered entirely from my griefs in my delectable work.

When summer was coming on, and Comte was advancing well, I agreed to do three leaders per week for Mr. Hunt. All the early attempts at secrecy were over. Within the first month, I had been taxed with almost every article by somebody or other, who 'knew me by my style,' or had heard it in omnibuses, or somehow; and, after some Galway priests had pointed me out by guess, in the Irish papers, as the writer of one of the Irish Letters, and this got copied into the English papers, Mr. Hunt wrote me that all concealment was wholly out of the question, and that I need not trouble myself further about it. In the summer he came to see me; and we settled that I should send him four articles per week when Comte was out of my hands. During that visit of his, we went by the lake one day, to pay a visit a few miles off,—he rowing me in one of the lake skiffs. A windy rain overtook us on our return. I had no serious idea of danger, or I should not have talked as I did, about drowning being an easy death, and my affairs being always settled, even to the arrangement of my papers, &c. We came home to dinner without his giving me (experienced boatman as he was) any idea of our having had a serious adventure. I found afterwards that he had told his friends in London that we had been in extreme danger from the swell on the lake; and that when I was talking of the ease of drowning, in comparison with other deaths, he was thinking of his wife and children. He requested me to write an article, at the opening of the next season, on the criminal carelessness of our boat-keepers in letting those little skiffs to strangers, on a lake subject to gusts and sudden storms: and this I did. How little did he imagine that before the beginning of yet another season, he would have been months in his grave,[1] and I standing on the verge of mine!

Immediately on the publication of my 'Positive Philosophy,' I went to London and Birmingham for nearly three months. I visited so many hosts, and saw so much society that I became fully and finally satisfied that my settling myself at Ambleside was, as Wordsworth had said, the wisest step of my life. It is true, I was at work the whole time. Besides the plentiful assistance which I desired to give the 'Daily News,' while

---

[1] Hunt died suddenly late in 1854; see below for Martineau's account of his death.

on the spot, and some papers for 'Household Words,' a serious piece of business required my attention.[1] The impending war rendered desirable an earnest and well-studied article on England's Foreign Policy, for the 'Westminster Review;' and I agreed to do it. I went to the Editor's house, for the purpose, and enjoyed both my visit and my work.[2]—On taking possession of my room there, and finding a capital desk on my table, with a singularly convenient slope, and of an admirable height for writing without fatigue, it struck me that, during my whole course of literary labour,—of nearly five-and-thirty years, it had never once occurred to me to provide myself with a proper, business-like desk. I had always written on blotting-paper, on a flat table, except when, in a lazy mood in winter, I had written as short-sighted people do (as Mrs. Somerville and 'Currer Bell' always did) on a board, or something stiff, held in the left hand. I wrote a good deal of the 'Political Economy' in that way, and with steel pens; and the method had the effect, advantageous or not, of making the writing more upright, and thereby increasing the quantity in a page. But it was radically uncomfortable; and I have ever since written on a table, and with quill pens. Now, on occasion of this visit at my friend's, Mr. Chapman's, I was to begin on a new and most luxurious method,—just, as it happens, at the close of my life's work. Mr. Chapman obtained for me a first-rate regular Chancery-lane desk,[3] with all manner of conveniences, and of a proper sanitary form: and, moreover, some French paper of various sizes, which has spoiled me for all other paper: ink to correspond; and a pen-maker, of French workmanship, suitable to eyes which were now feeling the effects of years and over-work. I had before me the prospect of more moderate work than for a quarter of century past, with sure and sufficient gain from it; work pleasant in itself, and recommended by all agreeable appliances. Never was I more home-sick, even in the wilds of Arabia, than I now was, amidst the high civilisation of literary society in London.— I came home very happy; and well I might.

Mr. Hunt escorted me part of the way to my host's, on our last meeting for that time, for the sake of some conversation which he, very properly, called serious. He told me that he had something to say which

---

[1] Martineau went to London in mid-summer, 1854, to stay at the home of Frederick Knight Hunt, and then at lodgings opposite the Crystal Palace. She also conferred with John Chapman, who had purchased the *Westminster Review* in 1851, about his financial difficulties with the periodical and the demands of his creditors.

[2] "England's Foreign Policy," *Westminster Review* 5 N.S. (January 1854), 190–232.

[3] Chancery Lane is a street in the legal district, passing the Inns of Court.

he begged me to consider well. He told me that he had been looking back through my connexion with 'Daily News;' and he found that of nearly 300 articles that I had sent him, only eight had not been used; and that (I think) six of those eight had been sent during the first few weeks, before I had got into the ways of the paper. I had now written four or five per week for a considerable time, without one rejection. His advice was that I should henceforth do six per week,—under the liability, of course, of a few more being unused, from the enhanced chances of being intercepted by recent news, when my communications were daily. If I should agree to this, and continue my other literary connexion, he thought I ought to lay out money freely in books, and in frequent visits to London, to keep up with the times. This scheme suited me exactly; for my work, under his guidance, had become thoroughly delightful.

His recourse to me was avowedly on account of the 'History of the Peace;' and now that war was beginning, my recent study of the politics of the last half-century *was* a fair qualification. We were precisely agreed as to the principle of the war, as to the character of the Aberdeen Ministry, as to the fallaciousness and mischievousness of the negotiations for the Austrian alliance, and as to the vicious absurdity of Prussia, and the mode and degree in which Louis Napoleon was to be regarded as the representative of the French nation.[1] For some time past, the historical and geographical articles had been my charge; together with the descriptive and speculative ones, in relation to foreign personages and states. At home, the agricultural and educational articles were usually consigned to me; and I had the fullest liberty about the treatment of special topics, arising anywhere. With party contests, and the treatment of 'hot and hot' news, I never had any concern,—being several hundred miles out of the way of the latest intelligence. Mr. Hunt thought my distance from London no disadvantage; and he was quite plain-spoken about the inferiority of the articles I wrote in London and Birmingham to those I sent him from home.—I followed his suggestions with great satisfaction,—his wife and family having already made a compact with me for an exchange of visits when I wanted London news, and they needed country refreshment. So I bought books to the amount of above £100, under his guidance, and came home exceedingly happy,—little dreaming that in one year from that time, he would be in his grave, his wife a broken-spirited widow, and I myself

---

[1]   Martineau comments on these issues in her *History of the Peace*, v. 4, ch. 12.

under sentence of death, and compelled to tell her that we should never meet again.

That eventful year, 1854, began most cheerily to us all. Mr. Hunt had raised the paper to a condition of high honour and prosperity. He enjoyed his work and his position, and was at ease about his affairs and his beloved family, after years of heroic struggle, and the glorious self-denial of a man of sensitive conscience and thoroughly domestic heart. He had to bear the wear and tear which a man of his order of conscience has to endure in a post of such responsibility as his; and this, we all believe, was a predisposing cause of his inability to resist an attack of disease. But at the opening of the year, he was in his usual health, and had every reason to be very happy. As for me,—my life was now like nothing that I had ever experienced. I had all the benefits of work, and of complete success, without any of the responsibility, the sense of which has always been the great drawback on my literary satisfactions, and especially in historical writing,—in which I could have no comfort but by directing my readers to my authorities, in all matters of any importance. Now, while exercising the same anxious care as to correctness, and always referring Mr. Hunt to my sources of information, I was free from the responsibility of publication altogether. My continued contributions to the 'Westminster Review'[1] and elsewhere preserved me from being engrossed in political studies; and I had more leisure for philosophical and literary pursuits than at any time since my youth. Two or three hours, after the arrival of the post (at breakfast time now) usually served me for my work; and when my correspondence was done, there was time for exercise, and the discharge of neighbourly business before dinner. Then,—I have always had some piece of fancy-work on hand,— usually for the benefit of the Abolition fund in America; and I have a thoroughly womanish love of needle-work,—yes, even ('I own the soft impeachment')[2] of wool-work, many a square yard of which is all invisibly embossed with thoughts of mine wrought in, under the various moods and experiences of a long series of years. It is with singular alacrity that, in winter evenings, I light the lamp, and unroll my wool-work, and meditate or dream till the arrival of the newspaper tells me that the tea has stood long enough. Before Mr. Rowland Hill gave us a

---

[1] Martineau's contributions to the *Westminster Review* in the 1850s included articles on "Rajah Brooke," "The Crystal Palace," "The Anglo-French Alliance," "Christian Missions," and "'Manifest Destiny' of the American Union," as well as those specifically noted in the text.

[2] Quotation from Richard Brinsley Sheridan's *The Rivals*, Act V, scene iii.

second post delivery at Ambleside,[1] Mr. Hunt had made arrangements by which I received the paper of the day at tea time. After tea, if there was news from the seat of war, I called in my maids, who brought down the great atlas, and studied the chances of the campaign with me. Then there was an hour or two for Montaigne, or Bacon, or Shakspere, or Tennyson, or some dear old biography, or last new book from London,—historical, moral or political. Then, when the house and neighbourhood were asleep, there was the half-hour on the terrace, or, if the weather was too bad for that, in the porch,—whence I seldom or never came in without a clear purpose for my next morning's work. I believe that, but for my country life, much of the benefit and enjoyment of my travels, and also of my studies, would have been lost to me. On my terrace, there were two worlds extended bright before me, even when the midnight darkness hid from my bodily eyes all but the outlines of the solemn mountains that surround our valley on three sides, and the clear opening to the lake on the south. In the one of those worlds, I saw now the magnificent coast of Massachusetts in autumn, or the flowery swamps of Louisiana, or the forests of Georgia in spring, or the Illinois prairie in summer; or the blue Nile, or the brown Sinai, or the gorgeous Petra, or the view of Damascus from the Salahiey; or the Grand Canal under a Venetian sunset, or the Black Forest in twilight, or Malta in the glare of noon, or the broad desert stretching away under the stars, or the Red Sea tossing its superb shells on shore, in the pale dawn. That is one world, all comprehended within my terrace wall, and coming up into the light at my call.—The other and finer scenery is of that world, only beginning to be explored, of Science. The long study of Comte had deeply impressed on me the imagery of the glorious hierarchy of the sciences which he has exhibited. The time was gone by when I could look at objects as mere surface, or separate existences; and since that late labour of love, I had more than ever seen the alliance and concert of the heavenly bodies, and the mutual action and interior composition of the substances which I used to regard as one in themselves, and unconnected in respect to each other. It is truly an exquisite pleasure to dream, after the toil of study, on the sublime abstractions of mathematics; the transcendent scenery unrolled by astronomy; the mysterious, invisible forces dimly hinted to us by Physics; the new conception of the constitution of Matter originated

---

[1]   Rowland Hill (1795–1879) proposed improved postal service in his pamphlet, *Post Office Reform: Its Importance and Practicability* (1837), which argued the need for pre-printed envelopes and adhesive postage. He is credited with the introduction of uniform penny postage (one penny per half-ounce letter to anywhere in the British Isles), and regular, frequent delivery of the mail.

by Chemistry; and then, the inestimable glimpses opened to us, in regard to the nature and destiny of Man, by the researches into vegetable and animal organisation, which are at length perceived to be the right path of inquiry into the highest subjects of thought. All the grandeur and all the beauty of this series of spectacles is deepened by the ever-present sense of the smallness of the amount of discovery achieved. In the scenery of our travels, it is otherwise. The forest, the steppe, the lake, the city, each filled and sufficed the sense of the observer in the old days when, instead of the Western Continents, there were dreams of far Cathay; and we of this day are occupied for the moment with any single scene, without caring whether the whole globe is explored. But it is different in the sphere of science. Wondrous beyond the comprehension of any one mind is the mass of glorious facts, and the series of mighty conceptions laid open; but the shadow of the surrounding darkness rests upon it all. The unknown always engrosses the greater part of the field of vision; and the awe of infinity sanctifies both the study and the dream. Between these worlds, and other interests, literary and political, were my evenings passed a short year ago. Perhaps no one has had a much more vivid enjoyment than myself of London society of a very high order; and few, I believe, are of a more radically social nature than myself: yet, I may say that there has never been, since I had a home of my own, an evening spent in the most charming intercourse that I would not have exchanged (as far as the mere pleasure was concerned) for one of my ordinary evenings under the lamp within, and the lights of heaven without.

I did not at once, however, sit down in comparative leisure on my return. I had before promised, most unwillingly, and merely for neighbourly reasons, to write a guide to Windermere and the neighbourhood; and this, and an article on the Census (requiring much care) for the 'Westminster Review' for April, were pressing to be done, as soon as I could sit down on my return home.[1] Then there was a series of articles (on Personal Infirmities,—the treatment of Blindness, Deafness, Idiotcy, &c.) promised for 'Household Words.'[2]

---

[1]   As Martineau explains below, this project became *A Guide to the English Lakes* (Windermere: John Garnett, 1855). She wrote "Results of the Census" for the *Westminster Review* 5 N.S. (April 1854), 323–57.

[2]   Martineau's last contributions to Dickens's periodical include the three articles on personal disabilities (*Household Words* 9 [1854], 134–38, 197–200, 421–25), as well as two on "Freedom, or Slavery?" and "How to Get Paper," *Household Words* 9 (1854), 537–42, 241–45. Another article, "The Rampshire Militia," *Household Words* 10 (1855), 505–11, has been attributed to Martineau, but more likely was written by James Payn (1830–98), another contributor, especially given Martineau's letter (below) withdrawing her support.

I must pause a moment here to relate that these papers were the last I sent to 'Household Words,' except two or three which filled up previous schemes. I have observed above that Magazine writing is quite out of my way: and that I accepted Mr. Dickens's invitation to write for his, simply because its wide circulation went far to compensate for the ordinary objections to that mode of authorship. I did not hesitate on the ground on which some of my relations and friends disapproved the connexion; on the ground of its being *infra dig.*: for, in the first place, I have never stopped to consider my own dignity in matters of business; and in the next, Mr. Dickens himself being a contributor disposed of the objection abundantly. But some time before the present date, I had become uneasy about the way in which 'Household Words' was going on, and more and more doubtful about allowing my name to be in any way connected with it: and I have lately finally declined Mr. Wills's invitation to send him more papers. As there is no quarrel concerned in the case, I think it is right to explain the grounds of my secession. My disapproval of the principles, or want of principles, on which the Magazine is carried on is a part of my own history; and it may be easily understood that feelings of personal friendliness may remain unaffected by opposition of views, even in a matter so serious as this. I think the proprietors of 'Household Words' grievously inadequate to their function, philosophically and morally; and they, no doubt, regard me as extravagant, presumptuous and impertinent. I have offered my objections as a reply to a direct request for a contribution; and Mr. Wills has closed the subject. But on all other ground, we are friends.

In the autumn of 1849, my misgivings first became serious. Mr. Wills proposed my doing some articles on the Employments of Women (especially in connexion with the Schools of Design and branches of Fine-Art manufacture),[1] and was quite unable to see that every contribution of the kind was necessarily excluded by Mr. Dickens's prior articles on behalf of his view of Woman's position; articles in which he ignored the fact that nineteen-twentieths of the women of England earn their bread, and in which he prescribes the function of Women; viz., to dress well and look pretty, as an adornment to the homes of men. I was startled by

---

[1] At this period Schools of Design were established throughout Britain to train men and women in the skills and aesthetic principles necessary to good industrial design and manufactured products; as Joseph Bizup explains in *Manufacturing Culture* (Charlottesville: U of Virginia P, 2003), pp. 131–40, the period 1849 to 1852 witnessed intense debate in the *Art Journal* and the *Journal of Design and Manufactures* over the kind of education such designers should receive.

this; and at the same time, and for many weeks after, by Mr. Dickens's treatment in his Magazine of the Preston Strike, then existing, and of the Factory and Wages controversy, in his tale of 'Hard Times.' A more serious incident still occurred in the same autumn.[1] In consequence of a request from Mr. Dickens that I would send him a tale for his Christmas Number, I looked about for material in real life; for, as I had told him, and as I have told every body else, I have a profound contempt of myself as a writer of fiction, and the strongest disinclination to attempt that order of writing. I selected a historical fact, and wrote the story which appears under the title of 'The Missionary' in my volume of 'Sketches from Life.'[2] I carried it with me to Mr. Wills's house; and he spoke in the strongest terms of approbation of it to me, but requested to have also 'a tale of more domestic interest,' which I wrote on his selection of the groundwork (also fact). Some weeks afterwards, my friends told me, with renewed praises of the story, that they mourned the impossibility of publishing it—Mrs. Wills said, because the public would say that Mr. Dickens was turning Catholic; and Mr. Wills and Mr. Dickens, because they never would publish any thing, fact or fiction, which gave a favourable view of any one under the influence of the Catholic faith. This appeared to me so incredible that Mr. Dickens gave me his 'ground' three times over, with all possible distinctness, lest there should be any mistake:—he would print nothing which could possibly dispose any mind whatever in favour of Romanism, even by the example of real good men. In vain I asked him whether he really meant to ignore all the good men who had lived from the Christian era to three centuries ago: and in vain I pointed out that Père d'Estélan was a hero as a man, and not as a Jesuit, at a date and in a region where Romanism was the only Christianity. Mr. Dickens *would* ignore, in any publication of his, all good Catholics; and insisted that Père d'Estélan was what he was as a Jesuit and not as a man;—which was, as I told him, the greatest eulogium I had ever heard passed upon Jesuitism. I told him that his way of going to work,—suppressing facts advantageous to the Catholics,—was the very way to rouse all fair minds in their defence; and that I had never before felt so disposed to make popularly known all historical facts in their favour. I hope I need not add that the editors never for a moment supposed that my remonstrance had any connexion with the story in question being written by me. They knew me too well to suppose that

---

[1]   1854. *Hard Times* had been published serially in *Household Words* from April to August, and appeared in book form at the end of the year.

[2]   "The Missionary," *Sketches from Life* (Windermere: John Garnett; London: Whittaker, 1856).

such a trifle as my personal interest in the acceptance or rejection of the story had anything to do with my final declaration that my confidence and comfort in regard to 'Household Words' were gone, and that I could never again write fiction for them, nor any thing in which principle or feeling were concerned. Mr. Dickens hoped I should 'think better of it'; and this proof of utter insensibility to the nature of the difficulty, and his and his partner's hint that the real illiberality lay in not admitting that they were doing their duty in keeping Catholic good deeds out of the sight of the public, showed me that the case was hopeless. To a descendant of Huguenots,[1] such total darkness of conscience on the morality of opinion is difficult to believe in when it is before one's very eyes.

I need not add that my hopes from the influence of 'Household Words' were pretty nearly annihilated from that time (the end of 1853) forwards: but there was worse to come. I had supposed that the editors would of course abstain from publishing any harm of Catholic priests and professors, if they would admit no good; but in this I have recently found myself mistaken: and great is my concern. I had just been reading in an American advertisement a short account of the tale called the 'Yellow Mask,' with its wicked priest, when I received from the editor of 'Household Words' another request for an article. I had not read 'The Yellow Mask'; but a guest then with me related the story so fully as to put me in complete possession of it. I will cite the portion of my letter to Mr. Wills which contains my reply to his request. It is abundantly plain-spoken; but we were plain-spoken throughout the controversy; and never did occasion more stringently require the utmost plainness of remonstrance on the side of the advocate of religious liberty and social justice, and any clearness of reply that might be possible on the opposite side.—Here is my letter, as far as relates to Mr. Wills's petition:—

' ... ... Another paper from me? you ask. No—not if I were to live twenty years,—if the enclosed paragraph from an American paper be no mistake; and except, of course, in case of repentance and amendment.

'"The 'Yellow Mask,' in Twelve Chapters: Philadelphia. [2]

'"This pamphlet is a reprint from Dickens's 'Household Words.' The story is ingenious, and fraught with considerable interest. The despicable

---

[1] As Martineau explains in the preface to the *Autobiography*, her ancestors were Protestants who left France after the Revocation of the Edict of Nantes and settled in England to obtain liberty of conscience.

[2] "The Yellow Mask," by Wilkie Collins, appeared in four installments of *Household Words*, 11 (1855), 529–39, 565–73, 587–98, 601–19.

course of 'Father Rocco' pursued so stealthily for the pecuniary benefit of 'holy mother church' shows of what stuff priestcraft is made."

'The last thing I am likely to do is to write for an anti-catholic publication; and least of all when it is anti-catholic on the sly. I have had little hope of "Household Words" since the proprietors refused to print a historical fact (otherwise approved of) on the ground that the hero was a Jesuit: and now that they follow up this suppression of an honourable truth by the insertion of a dishonouring fiction (or fact,—no matter which) they can expect no support from advocates of religious liberty or lovers of fair-play: and so fond are English people of fair-play, that if they knew this fact, you would soon find your course in this matter ruinous to your publication.—As for my writing for it,—I might as well write for the "Record" newspaper; and, indeed, so far better, that the "Record" avows its anti-catholic course. No one wants "Household Words" to enter into any theological implication whatever:—but you choose to do it, and must accept accordingly the opinions you thereby excite. I do not forget that you plead duty; and I give you credit for it,—precisely as I do to the Grand Inquisitor. He consecrates his treatment of heretics by the plea of the dangers of Protestantism: and you justify your treatment of Catholics by the plea of the dangers of Romanism. The one difference that there is, is in his favour;—that *he* does not profess Protestant principles while pursuing the practices of Jesuitry.—No, I have no more to say to "Household Words"; and you will prefer my telling you plainly why, and giving you this much light on the views your course has occasioned in one who was a hearty well-wisher to "Household Words," as long as possible. ... ...
... ...'H. MARTINEAU.'

Mr. Wills replied that he felt justified in what he had done; that we should never agree on the matter; and that, agreeing to differ, we would drop the subject.—Such are the grounds, and such was the process, of my secession from the corps of Mr. Dickens's contributors.

When I fancied I was going to do what I pleased till I left home in July 1854, the proprietor of the Windermere Guide made an irresistible appeal to me to do the whole district, under the form of a 'Complete Guide to the Lakes.' Still in hope that leisure would come at last, and feeling that I should enjoy it the more for having omitted no duty, I gave up my holiday evenings now. I made the tour of the district once more with a delightful party of friends,—reviving impressions and noting facts, and then came home, resigned to work 'double tides' for the remaining weeks before my summer absence,—dining early, after my morning's work, and writing topography in the evenings. I received much aid in the collection of materials from the publisher, and from the accomplished artist, Mr. Lindsey Aspland,[1] who illustrated the volume: and I finished my work, and went forth on a series of visits which were to occupy the tourist season,—my house being let for that time. I little imagined when I left my own gate, that the ease and light-hearted pleasure of my life,—I might almost say my life itself,—were left behind me;—that I was going to meet sickness and sorrow, and should return to sorrow, sickness, and death.

If I had been duly attentive to my health, I might have become aware already that there was something wrong. Long after, I remembered that, from about March, I had been kept awake for some little time at night by odd sensations at the heart, followed by hurried and difficult breath-ing: and once, I had been surprised, while reading, to find myself unable to see more than the upper half of the letters, or more of that than the word I was reading. I laid aside my book; and if I thought at all of the matter it was to suppose it to be a passing fit of indigestion, though I had no other sign of indigestion. While at Liverpool, I found myself far less strong than I had supposed; and again in Wales and at Shrewsbury; but I attributed this to the heat.[2] Mr. Hunt met me and my maid at the station in London, and took us over to his house at Sydenham,[3] giving us bad news by the way of the spread of cholera. A poor carpenter had, the week before, died of cholera while at work in Mr. Hunt's house,— the seizure being too sudden to admit of his removal to his own unhealthy home,—from whence, no doubt, he brought the disease. On our way from the Sydenham station to Mr. Hunt's house, he pointed out to me an abominable pond, covered with slime and duckweed, which he had tried in vain to draw official attention to. During my short visit, and just after it, almost all of us were ill,—my host and host-ess, some of the children, a servant, and myself: and after my removal to an airy lodging at Upper Norwood, opposite the Crystal Palace fence, I had repeated attacks of illness, and was, in fact, never well during the five weeks of my residence there.—It was a time of anxiety and sorrow. My good friend and publisher, Mr. Chapman, had just failed,—in consequence of misfortunes which came thick upon him, from the time of Mr. Lombe's death, which was a serious blow to the 'Westminster

---

1   Lindsey Aspland (1807–90), landscape painter who lived on Esthwaite Water in the Lake District.
2   Martineau had visited family members in Liverpool, then continued south into Wales.
3   Suburban village south of the Thames, near the Crystal Palace.

Review.'[1] Mr. Chapman, never in all our intercourse, asked me to lend him money; yet the 'Westminster Review' was by this time mortgaged to me. It was entirely my own doing; and I am anxious, for Mr. Chapman's sake, that this should be understood. The truth of the case is that I had long felt, as many others had professed to do, that the cause of free-thought and free-speech was under great obligations to Mr. Chapman; and it naturally occurred to me that it was therefore a duty incumbent on the advocates of free-thought and speech to support and aid one by whom they had been enabled to address society. Thinking, in the preceding winter, that I saw that Mr. Chapman was hampered by certain liabilities that the Review was under, I offered to assume the mortgage,—knowing the uncertain nature of that kind of investment, but regarding the danger of loss as my contribution to the cause. At first, after the failure, there was every probability, apparently, that Mr. Chapman's affairs would be speedily settled,—so satisfied were all his creditors who were present with his conduct under examination, and the accounts he rendered. A few generous friends and creditors made all smooth, as it was hoped; but two absent discontented creditors pursued their debtor with (as some men of business among the credi-tors said) 'a cruelty unequalled in all their experience.' One of their endeavours was to get the Review out of Mr. Chapman's hands; and one feature of the enterprise was an attempt to upset the mortgage, and to drive Mr. Chapman to bankruptcy, in order to throw the Review into the market, at the most disadvantageous season, when London was empty, and cholera prevalent,—that these personages might get it cheap. One of them made no secret of his having raised a subscription for the purpose. It was the will of the great body of the creditors, however, that Mr. Chapman should keep the Review, which he had edited thus far with great and rising success; and his two foes were got rid of by the generosity of Mr. Chapman's guaranteeing supporters. The attempt to upset the mortgage failed, of course. I had an intimation in twenty-four hours that I was 'not to be swindled out of the Review': but the whole anxiety, aggravated by indignation and pain at such conduct on the part

---

[1]   Martineau summarizes the problems facing the *Westminster Review*, but omits personal details. She had loaned Chapman £500 in April, 1854 as security. Just when the financial matters seemed settled, one creditor, William B. Hodgson (1815–94), began legal proceed-ings with the intention of buying it at a low cost, amalgamating it with the *Prospective Review*, and giving James Martineau, Harriet's brother, the editorship. Harriet knew that James was behind this action—thus she refers to "two absent discontented creditors," not just Hodgson. In a letter to Fanny Wedgwood of September 17, 1854, she explains that "Mr Courtauld paid off Dr Hodgson; and I pay off James" (see *Letters*, ed. Arbuckle, p. 128).

of men who had professed a sense of obligation to Mr. Chapman, extended over many weeks. The whole body of the creditors were kept waiting, and the estate was deteriorating for those weeks, during which the two persecutors were canvassing for subscriptions for the Review which one of them endeavoured to drive into a bad market, at my expense, and to the ruin of its proprietor. The business extended over my residence at Sydenham. I had long before promised an article, involving no small labour, for the next number of the Review ('Rajah Brooke'); and, when I was reckoning on my return home, two misfortunes occurred which determined me to stay another week, and work. A relative of Mr. Chapman's, his most valued friend and contributor, was struck down by cholera in the very act of writing an article of first-rate consequence for the forthcoming number: and, while my poor friend was suffering under the first anguish of this loss, another contributor, wrought on by evil influences, disappointed the editor of a promised article at the time it ought to have been at press.[1] I could not but stay and write another; and I did so,—being bound, however, to be at home on the nineteenth of September, to receive the first of a series of autumn guests. On the night of my arrival at home, after a too arduous journey for one day, I was again taken ill; and next morning, the post brought the news of the death of another of my dear aunts,—one having died during my absence from home.[2] I had left Mr. Hunt in a very poor state of health—as, indeed, everybody seemed to be during those melancholy months; but we hoped that a shooting excursion would restore him to business in his usual vigour. It appeared to do so; but cholera was making such ravage among the corps of the paper that those who could work were compelled to over-work; and the editor slept at the office during the most critical time. Every circumstance was against him; and we began to be uneasy, without having any serious apprehension of what was about to befal.

There was great enjoyment in that Sydenham sojourn, through all its anxieties. During the first half of the time that I was in lodgings, a

---

[1]   William R. Greg (1809–81), a well-known essayist and neighbor in the Lake District, failed to produce an article he had promised, and then Chapman's cousin (also a John Chapman) died of cholera on September 11, 1854. The articles Martineau contributed were "Rajah Brooke," *Westminster Review* 6 N.S. (October 1854), 381–419, an account of the life and achievements of James Brooke (1803–68), the developer of Sarawak in Malaysia, and "The Crystal Palace," *Westminster Review* 6 N.S. (October 1854), 534–50, an overview of the Great Exhibition.

[2]   Probably Martineau's maternal aunts, Mary (b. 1783) and Georgina Alice (b. 1787) Rankin, as the recorded death dates of other aunts do not correspond with this year.

dear young niece was with me; and for the other half, a beloved cousin—my faithful friend for forty years.[1] Some whole days, and many half holidays, I spent with them in the Crystal Palace, with great joy and delight.[2] I dwell upon those days now with as much pleasure as ever,—the fresh beauty of the summer morning, when we were almost the first to enter, and found the floors sprinkled, and the vegetation revived, and the tables covered with cool-looking viands, and the rustics coming in and venting their first amazement in a very interesting way:—and again, our steady duties in the courts in the middle of the day; and again, the walk on the terrace, or the lingering in the nave when the last train was gone, and the exhibitors were shutting up for the day. There were also merry parties, and merry plans at Mr. Hunt's. We went, a carriage-full, to the prorogation of parliament,[3] when I had a ticket to the peeresses' gallery, where, however, we were met by the news (which encountered us everywhere) of a mournful death from cholera,—Lord Jocelyn having died that afternoon.[4] We had a plan for going, a party of fifteen, in the next April to Paris, for the opening of the Exhibition on May-day. May-day has passed without the opening of the Exhibition: Mr. Hunt has been above five months in his grave; and I have been above three months in daily expectation of death. In November, when Mr. Hunt was ill, but we knew not how ill, I wrote to him that, on consideration, it seemed to me that the party to Paris would be better without me (for political reasons): and Mr. Hunt's message (the last to me) was that it would be time enough to settle that when April came. I suspect that he foresaw his fate.—In November, my correspondence was with the sub-editor, because Mr. Hunt was ill. The cashier told me next of his 'alarm' about his beloved friend: but the sub-editor wrote that *he* was not alarmed like the rest. Then the accounts were worse; there was one almost hopeless: and then, he was dead. I did not think that such capacity for sorrow was left in me. He was so happy in life; and the happiness of so many was bound up in him! He was only forty; and he had fairly entered on a career of unsurpassed usefulness and honour, and was

---

[1]   Maria Martineau and Isabella Rankin.

[2]   The Crystal Palace, built for the Great Exhibition of 1851, had been moved from Hyde Park to Sydenham in south London, where it re-opened in June, 1854. It housed some of the original 13,000 exhibits of British industrial and social progress, but also became a site for concerts, plays, and other amusements.

[3]   I.e., the formal end of the parliamentary session, usually via an announcement on behalf of the monarch made in the House of Lords.

[4]   Robert Jocelyn (1816–54) died on August 12, 1854, of Asiatic cholera.

beginning to reap the natural reward of many years of glorious effort! But he was gone; and I had not known such a personal sorrow since the loss of Dr. Follen, in 1840, by the burning of a steamer at sea.[1] I certainly felt very ill; and I told my family so; but I thought I could go to London, and work at the office during the interval till his place could be filled. I offered to do so; but the proprietors assured me that I could help them best by working daily at home. The cousin, who had been my companion at Sydenham, wrote that she was glad I had not gone: for she believed, after what she had seen in September, that it would have killed me. I believe she was right, though it seemed rather extravagant at the time.

SECTION IX

By December I felt somewhat better; but I was not able to write my usual New Year's letters to my family. The odd obliteration of words and half letters when I read returned once or twice when there was certainly no indigestion to account for it; and a symptom which had perplexed me for months grew upon me,—an occasional uncertainty about the spelling of even common words. I had mentioned this, as an odd circumstance, to a Professor of Mental Philosophy, when he was my guest in October: and his reply was, 'there is some little screw loose somewhere': and so indeed it proved.[2] Throughout December and the early part of January, the disturbance on lying down increased, night by night. There was a *creaking* sensation at the heart (the beating of which was no longer to be felt externally); and, after the creak, there was an intermission, and then a throb. When this had gone on a few minutes, breathing became perturbed and difficult; and I lay till two, three, or four o'clock, struggling for breath. When this process began to spread back into the evening, and then forward into the morning, I was convinced that there was something seriously wrong; and with the approbation of my family, I wrote to consult Dr. Latham; and soon after,

---

[1]   Her American friend Charles Follen had died in an explosion of the steamboat *Lexington* on January 13, 1840; see Period V, sec. ii.

[2]   Dr. Samuel Brown; see p. 602, n. 2.

went to London to be examined by him.[1] That honest and excellent physician knew beforehand that I desired, for reasons which concerned others more than myself, to know the exact truth; and he fulfilled my wish.—I felt it so probable that I might die in the night, and any night, that I would not go to the house of any of my nearest friends, or of any aged or delicate hostess: and I therefore declined all invitations, and took rooms at Mr. Chapman's, where all possible care would be taken of me, without risk to any one. There Dr. Latham visited and examined me, the day after my arrival, and frankly told me his 'impression,'—observing that it could not yet be called an opinion. The impression soon became an opinion, as I knew it would, because he would not have told me of such an impression without the strongest ground for it. He requested me to see another physician; and Dr. Watson's opinion, formed on examination, without prior information from Dr. Latham or me, was the same as Dr. Latham's. Indeed the case appears to be as plain as can well be. It appears that the substance of the heart is deteriorated, so that 'it is too feeble for its work'; there is more or less dilatation; and the organ is very much enlarged. Before I left London, the sinking-fits which are characteristic of the disease began to occur; and it has since been perfectly understood by us all that the alternative lies between death at any hour in one of these sinking-fits, or by dropsy, if I live for the disease to run its course.

Though I expected some such account of the case, I was rather surprised that it caused so little emotion in me. I went out, in a friend's carriage, to tell her the result of Dr. Latham's visit; and I also told a cousin who had been my friend since our school-days. When I returned to my lodgings, and was preparing for dinner, a momentary thrill of something like painful emotion passed through me,—not at all because I was going to die, but at the thought that I should never feel health again. It was merely momentary; and I joined the family and Mr. Atkinson, who dined with us, without any indisposition to the merriment which went on during dinner,—no one but my hostess being aware of what had passed since breakfast. In the course of the evening, I told them; and I saw at once what support I might depend on from my friend. I did not sleep at all that night; and many were the things I had to think over; but I never passed a

---

[1]   Dr. Peter Mere Latham (1789–1875), physician extraordinary to Queen Victoria. She also consulted Dr. Thomas Watson (1792–1882), who suggested that her tumor had shifted location with her mesmeric "cure" and was again the source of her symptoms. This public presentation of her illness as a heart complaint allowed Martineau to avoid renewed discussion of the efficacy of the mesmeric treatment.

more tranquil and easy night. As soon as my family heard the news, a beloved niece, who had repeatedly requested to be allowed to come to me, joined me in London, and gave me to understand, with her parents' free consent, that she would not leave me again.[1] I sent for my executor, made a new will, and put him in possession of my affairs, my designs and wishes, as fully as possible, and accepted his escort home to Ambleside. As there was but one possible mode of treatment, and as that could be pursued in one place as well as another, I was eager to get home to the repose and freshness of my own sweet place. It was not only for the pleasure of it, but for the sake of my servants; and, because, while prepared, in regard to my affairs, to go at any time, there were things to be done, if I could do them, to which the quiet of home was almost indispensable. The weather was at that time the worst of a very bad winter; and it was a very doubtful matter whether I could perform the journey. By the kindness of a friend,[2] however, the invalid carriage of the North Western Railway was placed at my disposal; and we four,—my niece, my executor, my maid and myself,—travelled in all possible comfort. The first thing I saw in my own house,—the pale, shrunk countenance of the servant I had left at home,—made me rejoice that I had returned without further delay. I found afterwards that she had cried more than she had slept from the time that she had heard how ill I was, and what was to happen.—That was three months ago: and during those three months, I have been visited by my family, one by one, and by some dear friends,[3] while my niece has been so constantly with me as to have, in my opinion, prolonged my life by her incomparable nursing. The interval has been employed in writing this Memoir,[4] and in closing all my engagements, so that no interest of any kind may suffer by my departure at any moment. The winter, after long lingering, is gone, and I am still here,—sitting in the sun on my terrace, and at night going

---

1   Maria Martineau, daughter of her brother Robert. Thomas, Maria's brother, was an executor of his aunt's estate.

2   Emma Sargant, Maria's friend, with whom she spent a week each year.

3   Among those who visited were her nieces Maria, Jenny, and Susan, Robert's daughters; her cousin and long-time friend, Catherine Turner; her old friend, Mrs. Elisabeth Reid; various abolitionists, including Parker Pillsbury and Mary Estlin; and her maternal aunt, Margaret Rankin of Newcastle. Notably, her brother James and his family did not visit, despite the fact that they were in the Lake District for six weeks.

4   Martineau wrote to Fanny Wedgwood on August 29, 1855, "On Monday I finished my autobiography, which spread out to two thick vols, leaving one for Mrs Chapman and Mr Atkinson to say what they wish. There is a good press and a devoted printer at Windermere, so I am printing my portion,—to save my Exr all responsibility, and from all interference." See *Letters*, ed. Arbuckle, p. 132.

out, according to old custom, to look abroad in the moon or star-light. We are surrounded by bouquets and flowering plants. Never was a dying person more nobly 'friended,' as the Scotch have it. My days are filled with pleasures, and I have no cares; so that the only thing I have to fear is that, after all the discipline of my life, I should be spoiled at the end of it.

When I learned what my state is, it was my wish (as far as I wish anything, which is indeed very slightly and superficially) that my death might take place before long, and by the quicker process: and such is, in an easy sort of way, my wish still. The last is for the sake of my nurse, and of all about me; and the first is mainly because I do not want to deteriorate and get spoiled in the final stage of my life, by ceasing to hear the truth, and the whole truth: and nobody ventures to utter any unpleasant truth to a person with 'a heart-complaint.' I must take my chance for this; and I have a better chance than most, because my nurse and constant companion knows that I do not desire that anybody should 'make things pleasant' because I am ill. I should wish, as she knows, to live under complete and healthy moral conditions to the last, if these can be accommodated, by courage and mutual trust, with the physical conditions.—As to the spoiling process,—I have been doubt-ing, for some years past, whether I was not undergoing it. I have lived too long to think of making myself anxious about my state and prospects in any way; but it has occurred to me occasionally, of late years, whether I could endure as I formerly did. I had become so accus-tomed to ease of body and mind, that it seemed to me doubtful how I might bear pain, or any change;—for it seemed as if any change must be for the worse, as to enjoyment. I remember being struck with a saying of Mrs. Wordsworth's, uttered ten years ago, when she was seventy-six,—that the beauty of our valley made us too fond of life,—too little ready to leave it. Her domestic bereavements since that time have doubtless altered this feeling entirely; but, in many an hour of intense enjoyment on the hills, I have recalled that saying; and, in wonder at my freedom from care, have speculated on whether I should think it an evil to die, then and there. I have now had three months' experience of the fact of constant expectation of death; and the result is, as much regret as a rational person can admit at the absurd waste of time, thought, and energy that I have been guilty of in the course of my life in dwelling on the subject of death. It is really melancholy that young people (and, for that matter, middle-aged and old people) are exhorted and encouraged as they are to such waste of all manner of power. I romanced internally about early death till it was too late to die early; and, even in the midst of work and the busiest engagements of my life, I used to be always thinking about death,—partly from taste, and partly as a duty. And now that I am waiting it at any hour, the whole thing seems so easy, simple and natural that I cannot but wonder how I could keep my thoughts fixed upon it when it was far off. I cannot do it now. Night after night since I have known that I am mortally ill, I have tried to conceive, with the help of the sensations of my sinking-fits, the act of dying, and its attendant feelings; and thus far I have always gone to sleep in the middle of it. And this is after really knowing something about it; for I have been frequently in extreme danger of immediate death within the last five months, and have felt as if I were dying, and should never draw another breath. Under this close experience, I find death in prospect the simplest thing in the world,— a thing not to be feared or regretted, or to get excited about in any way.—I attribute this very much, however, to the nature of my views of death. The case must be much otherwise with Christians,—even independently of the selfish and perturbing emotions connected with an expectation of rewards and punishments in the next world. They can never be quite secure from the danger that their air-built castle shall dissolve at the last moment, and that they may vividly perceive on what imperfect evidence and delusive grounds their expectation of immortality or resurrection reposes. The mere perception of the incompatibility of immortality and resurrection may be, and often is deferred till that time; and that is no time for such questions. But, if the intellect be ever so accommodating, there is the heart,—steady to its domestic affections. I, for one, should be heavy-hearted if I were now about to go to the antipodes,—to leave all whom I love, and who are bound up with my daily life,—however certain might be the prospect of meeting them again twenty or thirty years hence; and it is no credit to any Christian to be 'joyful,' 'triumphant' and so forth, in going to 'glory,' while leaving any loved ones behind,—whether or not there may be loved ones 'gone before.' An unselfish and magnanimous person cannot be solaced, in parting with mortal companions and human sufferers, by personal rewards, glory, bliss, or anything of the sort. I used to think and feel all this before I became emancipated from the superstition; and I could only submit, and suppose it all right because it was ordained. But now, the release is an inexpressible comfort; and the simplifying of the whole matter has a most tranquillising effect. I see that the dying (others than the aged) naturally and regularly, unless disturbed, desire and sink into death as into sleep. Where no artificial state is induced, they feel

no care about dying, or about living again. The state of their organisation disposes them to rest; and rest is all they think about. We know, by
all testimony, that persons who are brought face to face with death by
an accident which seems to leave no chance of escape, have no religious
ideas or emotions whatever. Where the issue is doubtful, the feeble and
helpless cry out to God for mercy, and are in perturbation or calmness
according to organisation, training, and other circumstances: but, where
escape appears wholly impossible, the most religious men think and feel
nothing religious at all,—as those of them who have escaped tell their
intimate friends. And again, soldiers rush upon death in battle with utter
carelessness—engrossed in other emotions, in the presence of which
death appears as easy and simple a matter as it does to me now.—
Conscious as I am of what my anxiety would be if I were exiled to the
antipodes,—or to the garden of Eden, if you will,—for twenty or thirty
years, I feel no sort of solicitude about a parting which will bring no
pain. Sympathy with those who will miss me, I do feel of course: yet
not very painfully, because their sorrow cannot, in the nature of things,
long interfere with their daily peace; but to me there is no sacrifice, no
sense of loss, nothing to fear, nothing to regret. Under the eternal laws
of the universe, I came into being, and, under them, I have lived a life
so full that its fulness is equivalent to length. The age in which I have
lived is an infant one in the history of our globe and of Man; and the
consequence is, a great waste in the years and the powers of the wisest
of us; and, in the case of one so limited in powers, and so circumscribed
by early unfavourable influences as myself, the waste is something
deplorable. But we have only to accept the conditions in which we find
ourselves, and to make the best of them; and my last days are cheered
by the sense of how much better my later years have been than the
earlier; or than, in the earlier, I ever could have anticipated. Some of the
terrible faults of my character which religion failed to ameliorate, and
others which superstition bred in me, have given way, more or less, since
I attained a truer point of view: and the relief from old burdens, the
uprising of new satisfactions, and the opening of new clearness,—the
fresh air of Nature, in short, after imprisonment in the ghost-peopled
cavern of superstition,—has been as favourable to my moral nature as
to intellectual progress and general enjoyment. Thus, there has been
much in life that I am glad to have enjoyed; and much that generates a
mood of contentment at the close. Besides that I never dream of wishing that any thing were otherwise than as it is, I am frankly satisfied to
have done with life. I have had a noble share of it, and I desire no more.

I neither wish to live longer here, nor to find life again elsewhere. It seems to me simply absurd to expect it, and a mere act of restricted human imagination and morality to conceive of it. It seems to me that there is, not only a total absence of evidence of a renewed life for human beings, but so clear a way of accounting for the conception, in the immaturity of the human mind, that I myself utterly disbelieve in a future life. If I should find myself mistaken, it will certainly not be in discovering any existing faith in that doctrine to be true. If I am mistaken in supposing that I am now vacating my place in the universe, which is to be filled by another,—if I find myself conscious after the lapse of life,—it will be all right, of course; but, as I said, the supposition appears to me absurd. Nor can I understand why any body should expect me to desire any thing else than this yielding up my place. If we may venture to speak, limited as we are, of any thing whatever being important, we may say that the important thing is that the universe should be full of life, as we suppose it to be, under the eternal laws of the universe: and, if the universe be full of life, I cannot see how it can signify whether the one human faculty of consciousness of identity be preserved and carried forward, when all the rest of the organisation is gone to dust, or so changed as to be in no respect properly the same. In brief, I cannot see how it matters whether my successor be called H.M. or A.B. or Y.Z. I am satisfied that there will always be as much conscious life in the universe as its laws provide for; and that certainty is enough, even for my narrow human conception, which, however, can discern that caring about it at all is a mere human view and emotion. The real and justifiable and honourable subject of interest to human beings, living and dying, is the welfare of their fellows, surrounding them, or surviving them. About this, I do care, and supremely; in what way I will tell presently.

Meantime, as to my own position at this moment, I have a word or two more to say.—I had no previous conception of the singular interest of watching human affairs, and one's own among the rest, and acting in them, when on the verge of leaving them. It is an interest which is full even of amusement. It has been my chief amusement, this spring, to set my house and field in complete order for my beloved successor;—to put up a handsome new garden fence, and paint the farming man's cottage, and restore the ceilings of the house, and plan the crops which I do not expect to see gathered. The mournful perplexity of my good farm-servant has something in it amusing as well as touching;— the necessity he is under of consulting me about his sowings, and his plans for the cows,—relating to distant autumn months, and even to another spring,—the embarrassing necessity that this is to him, while his mind is full of the expectation that I shall then be in my grave. In the midst of every consultation about this or that crop, he interposes a hope that I may live to see his hay, and to eat his celery and artichokes and vegetable marrow, and to admire the autumn calf; and his zeal for my service, checked by the thought that his services are in fact for others, has something in it as curious as touching.—And so it is, more or less, with all my intercourses—that a curious new interest is involved in them. Mere acquaintances are shocked that the newspapers should tell that I am 'in a hopeless state,' that 'recovery is impossible,' &c., while my own family and household have no sort of scruple in talking about it as freely as I do. A good many people start at hearing what a cheerful,—even merry,—little party we are at home here, and that we sometimes play a rubber in the evenings, and sometimes laugh till I, for one, can laugh no more. To such wonder, we answer—why not? If we feel as usual, why not do as usual? Others, again, cannot conceive how, with my 'opinions,' I am not miserable about dying; and declare that they should be so; and this makes me wonder, in my turn, that it does not strike them that perhaps they do not comprehend my views and feelings, and that there may be something in the matters more than they see or understand. There is something very interesting to me in the evidences of different states of mind among friends and strangers in regard to my 'good' or 'bad spirits,'—a matter which appears to me hardly worth a thought. As it happens, my spirits are good; and I find good spirits a great blessing; but the solicitude about them, and the evident readiness to make much of bad spirits, if I had them, are curious features in my intercourse with acquaintance or strangers who are kind enough to interest themselves in my affairs. One sends me a New Testament (as if I had never seen one before) with the usual hopes of grace &c., though aware that the bible is no authority with me; and, having been assured that I am 'happy,' this correspondent has the modesty to intimate that I ought not to be happy, and that people sometimes are so 'without grounds.' It is useless to reply that, as I have not pursued happiness as an aim, all this kind of speculation is nothing to me. There is the fact; and that is enough.—Others, again, who ought, by their professions, to know better, are very glad about this 'happiness,' and settle it in their own minds that Christian consolations are administered to me by God without my knowing it. If so, I can only say it is a bounty not only gratuitous, but undesired. Christian consolations would certainly make me any thing but happy, after my experience of them in contrast with the higher state of freedom, and the wider sympathies opened by my later views.

The lesson taught us by these kindly commentators on my present experience is that dogmatic faith compels the best minds and hearts to narrowness and insolence. Even such as these cannot conceive of my being happy in any way but theirs, or that there may be views whose operation they do not understand. In a letter just received, a dear friend says 'I have seen no one since I left you who is "sorry" about you (about my "opinions"). Still I see that the next row, and the next, still more so, are "very sorry" and "very, very sorry."' The unconscious insolence revealed in this 'sorrow' is rebuked by the more rational view of others who are no nearer agreeing with me than the second and third 'row.' 'Not agreeing,' says my friend, 'they still see no more reason for lamentation over you than for you to lament over them. *"Il y a aussi loin de chez toi chez moi que de chez moi chez toi,"* is the perfectly applicable French proverb.'[1] Another, who professes to venerate martyrs and reformers (if only they are dead) is 'sorry' again because this, that, or the other Cause suffers by my loss of influence. The mingled weakness and unconscious insolence of this affords a curious insight. First, there is the dereliction of principle shown in supposing that any 'Cause' can be of so much importance as fidelity to truth, or can be important at all otherwise than in its relation to truth which wants vindicating. It reminds me of an incident which happened when I was in America, at the time of the severest trials of the Abolitionists. A pastor from the Southern States lamented to a brother clergyman in the North the introduction of the Anti-slavery question, because the views of their sect were 'getting on so well before!' 'Getting on!' cried the Northern minister. 'What is the use of getting your vessel on when you have thrown both captain and cargo overboard?' Thus, what signifies the pursuit of any one reform, like those specified,—Anti-slavery and the Woman question,—when the freedom which is the very soul of the controversy, the very principle of the movement,—is mourned over in any other of its many manifestations? The only effectual advocates of such reforms as those are people who follow truth wherever it leads. The assumption that I have lost influence on the whole exposes itself. Nobody can know that I have lost influence on the whole, either in regard to ordinary social intercourse or to subjects of social controversy;

---

[1] Loosely translated, "You are just as far from me as I am from you."

and I have reason to believe that I have (without at all intending it) gained influence in proportion to the majority that the free-thinkers of our country constitute to the minority existing in the form of the sect in which I was reared, or any other.

As to the curious assortment of religious books and tracts sent me by post, they are much what I have been accustomed to receive on the publication of each of my books which involved religious or philosophical subjects. They are too bad in matter and spirit to be safe reading for my servants; so, instead of the waste-basket, they go into the fire. I have not so many anonymous letters now as on occasions of publication; but some which are not anonymous are scarcely wiser or purer. After the publication of 'Eastern Life,' I had one which was too curious to be forgotten with the rest. It was dated 'Cheltenham,' and signed 'Charlotte'; and it was so inviting to a reply that, if it had borne an address, I should have been tempted to break through my custom of silence in such cases. 'Charlotte' wrote to make the modest demand that I would call in and destroy all my writings, 'because they give pain to the pious.' It would have been amusing to see what she would think of a proposal that 'the pious' should withdraw all their writings, because they give pain to the philosophical. It might have been of service to suggest the simple expedient, in relief of the pious, that they should not read books which offend them. After the publication of the 'Atkinson Letters,' anonymous notes came in elegant clerical hand-writing, informing me that prayers would be offered up throughout the kingdom, for my rescue from my awful condition, 'denying the Lord that bought me,' &c. Now, the concern seems to be of a gentler sort, and to relate more to my state of spirit at present than to my destiny hereafter.—But enough of this. I have referred to these things, not because they relate to myself, but because the condition of opinion in English society at present affords material for profitable study; and my own position at this moment supplies a favourable opportunity. In the midst of the meddlesomeness, I do not overlook the humanity thus evidenced. My only feeling of concern arises from seeing how much moral injury and suffering is created by the superstitions of the Christian mythology; and again from the chaotic state of opinion among Christians themselves, and among those who would fain retain the name, while giving up all the essentials, and unfurnished with a basis of conviction, while striving to make the fabrics of the imagination serve the purpose.—As for me, who unexpectedly find myself on the side of the majority of thoughtful persons on these questions, I am of course abundantly solaced with sympathy which I can accept; and I am more and more sensible, as I recede from the active scenes of life, of the surpassing value of a philosophy which is the natural growth of the experience and study,—perhaps I may be allowed to say,—the progression of a life. While conscious, as I have ever been, of being encompassed by ignorance on every side, I cannot but acknowledge that philosophy has opened my way before me, and given a staff into my hand, and thrown a light upon my path,[1] so as to have long delivered me from doubt and fear. It has, moreover, been the joy of my life, harmonising and animating all its details, and making existence itself a festival. Day by day do I feel that it is indeed

> Not harsh and crabbed as dull fools suppose;
> But musical as is Apollo's lute.

A state like mine of late has its peculiar privileges,—the first felt of which is its freedom from cares and responsibilities. I have hitherto loved solitude perhaps unduly; partly, no doubt, on account of my deafness, which, from its attendant fatigues, has rendered solitude necessary, to husband my strength,—(always, I now suspect, below the average) for my work; but partly also from the unusual amount of intellectual labour which it has been my duty to undertake. Now, when my work is done, I am enjoying genuine holiday, for the first time for a quarter of a century. I relish, very keenly, the tending of affection, and the lawful transference of my responsibilities to the young and strong, and those who have a tract of life before them, and who are pausing on their way to give me the help I need. I am now free for intellectual luxury,—to read what charms me most, without the feeling that I am playing truant from the school of technical knowledge, for which I shall have no further occasion. Again, I enjoy the free expenditure of my resources. It is something pleasant not to have to consider money—the money which I have earned, and laid up to meet such an occasion. But it is more and better not to grudge my time. My hours are now best spent in affectionate intercourses, and in giving a free flow to every passing day. I need not spare my eyes, nor husband my remaining hearing. I may, in short, make a free and lavish holiday before I go.

Such is the selfish aspect of the case; and I am bound, having begun,

---

[1]   The language here paraphrases Psalm 119:105 (KJV): "Thy word is a lamp unto my feet, and a light unto my path."

to tell the whole case.—Far greater are the privileges I enjoy in regard to the world outside my home. I need not say that one's interests in regard to one's race, and to human life in the abstract, deepen in proportion to the withdrawal of one's own personal implication with them. Judging by my own experience, one's hopes rise, and one's fears decline as one recedes from the action and personal solicitude which are necessary in the midst of life, but which have a more or less blinding and perturbing influence on one's perception and judgment. When at the zenith, clouds are apt to come between one's particular star and the wide world; whereas, on the clear horizon, at the moment of the star's sinking, nothing intervenes to shroud or distort the glorious scene. I was always hopeful for the world; but never so much so as now, when I am at full leisure to see things as they are, and placed apart where the relation of the past and the future become clear, and the meeting-point of the present is seen in something like its due proportion. It appears to me now that, while I see much more of human difficulty from ignorance, and from the slow working (as we weak and transitory beings consider it) of the law of Progress, I discern the working of that great law with far more clearness, and therefore with a far stronger confidence, than I ever did before.

When I look at my own country, and observe the nature of the changes which have taken place even within my own time, I have far more hope than I once had that the inevitable political reconstitution of our state may take place in a peaceable and prosperous manner. There have been times in my life when, having a far obscurer view than I now entertain of the necessity of a total change in the form of government, I yet apprehended a revolution in the fearful sense in which the word was understood in my childhood, when the great French Revolution was the only pattern of that sort of enterprise. I now strongly hope that, whenever our far-famed British Constitution gives place to a new form of government, it may be through the ripened will of the people, and therefore in all good will and prudence. That the change must be made, sooner or later, was certain from the time when the preponderance of the aristocratic over the regal element in our state became a fact. From the natural alliance between king and people, and the natural antagonism of aristocracy and people, the occurrence of a revolution is always, in such a case, a question merely of time. In our case, the question of time is less obscure than it was in my childhood. The opponents of the Reform Bill were right enough, as every body now sees, in saying that the Constitution was destroyed by that act; though wrong, of course, in supposing that they could have preserved the balance by preventing the act of reform. A constitution of checks and balances, made out of old materials, can never be more than a provisional expedient; and, when the balance is destroyed,—when the power of the Crown is a mere lingering sentiment, and the Commons hold the Lords in the hollow of their hand, while no recent House of Commons has been in any degree worthy of such a trust, the alternative is simply between a speedy revolution with an unworthy House of Commons, or a remoter one, with a better legislature in the mean time. The circumstances of the hour in which I write seem to show that so much social change is near as may be caused by the exposure of administrative incompetence under the stress of the war.[1] It may be this, or it may be something else which will rouse the people to improve the House of Commons: and under an improved House of Commons, the establishment of a new method of government may be long delayed. From the general state of prosperity and contentment at home, the retrieval of Ireland, the rapid advance of many good popular objects, and the raising of the general tone of the popular mind, we may hope that what has to be done will be done well.—Meantime, the thing that causes me most anxiety, in regard to our political condition, is the universal ignorance or carelessness about the true sphere of legislation. Before the people can be in any degree fit for the improved institutions, it is highly necessary that they should understand, and be agreed upon, the true function of legislation and government; and this is precisely what even our best men, in and out of parliament, seem to know nothing about. I regard this as a most painful and perilous symptom of our condition,—though it has been brought to light by beneficent action which is, in another view, altogether encouraging. Our benevolence towards the helpless, and our interest in personal morality, have grown into a sort of public pursuit; and they have taken such a hold on us that we may fairly hope that the wretched and the wronged will never more be thrust out of sight. But, in the pursuit of our new objects, we have fallen back,—far further than 1688,—in the principle of our legislative proposals, —undertaking to provide by law against personal vices, and certain special social contracts, while refusing that legitimate legislative boon,—a system of national education,—which would supersede the vices and abuses complained of by intelligence more effectually than acts of parliament

---

[1]   The bungling of the Crimean War, including the lack of supplies and inadequate medical treatment for wounded soldiers, caused the fall of Lord Aberdeen's ministry in 1855.

can ever obviate them by penalty. If I were to form one hope rather than another in relation to the political condition of England, it would be that my countrymen should rise to the level of their time, and of their intelligence in other respects, in regard to the true aims of government and legitimate function of legislation.

As to the wider political prospects outside our own empire, I am of much the same opinion now as when I wrote a certain letter to an anti-slavery friend in America in 1849, which I will subjoin. That letter was published in the newspapers at the time by my correspondent,[1] and it has been republished in England since the outbreak of the war with Russia:—

'October 18th, 1849.

'My dear—; We can think of little else at present than of that which should draw you and us into closer sympathy than even that which has so long existed between us. We, on our side the water, have watched with keen interest the progress of your War of Opinion,—the spread of the great controversy which cannot but revolutionize your social principles and renovate your social morals. For fifteen years past, we have seen that you are "in for it," and that you must stand firm amidst the subversion of Ideas, Customs and Institutions, till you find yourselves encompassed by "the new heavens and the new earth"[2] of which you have the sure promise and foresight.

'We,—the whole population of Europe,—are now evidently entering upon a stage of conflict no less important in its issues, and probably more painful in its course. You remember how soon after the conclusion of the Napoleonic wars our great Peace Minister, Canning,[3] intimated the advent, sooner or later, of a War of Opinion in Europe; a war of deeper significance than Napoleon could conceive of, and of a wider spread than the most mischievous of his quarrels. The war of Opinion which Canning foresaw was in fact a war between the further

---

[1]   Maria Chapman. According to Deborah Logan, editor of *The Collected Letters of Harriet Martineau* (London: Pickering and Chatto, 2007), the letter appeared in the *Liberty Bell*, an abolitionist periodical.

[2]   A prophetic phrase from Isaiah 65:17, repeated in Revelation 21:1: "For behold I create new heavens and a new earth."

[3]   George Canning (1770–1827), Tory M.P., foreign secretary from 1807–09 and 1822–27, and briefly prime minister in 1827. A progressive Tory, Canning pursued liberal policies at home and abroad; after the Napoleonic Wars, he refused to support the European governments that sought to suppress liberal and revolutionary movements.

and nearer centuries,—between Asia and Europe,—between despotism and self-government. The preparations were begun long ago. The Barons at Runnymede beat up for recruits when they hailed the signature of Magna Charta; and the princes of York and Lancaster did their best to clear the field for us and those who are to come after us. The Italian Republics wrought well for us, and so did the French Revolutions, one after the other, as hints and warnings; and so did the voyage of your Mayflower,—and the Swiss League, and German Zollverein,[1] and in short, everything that has happened for several hundreds of years. Everything has tended to bring our continent and its resident nations to the knowledge that the first principles of social liberty have now to be asserted and contended for, and to prepare the assertors for the greatest conflict that the human race has yet witnessed. It is my belief that the war has actually begun, and that, though there may be occasional lulls, no man now living will see the end of it.

'Russia is more Asiatic than European. It is obscure to us who live nearest to her where her power resides. We know only that it is not with the Emperor nor yet with the people. The Emperor is evidently a mere show,—being nothing except while he fulfils the policy or pleasure of the unnamed power which we cannot discern. But, though the ruling power is obscure, the policy is clear enough. The aim is to maintain and extend despotism; and the means chosen are the repression of mind, the corruption of conscience, and the reduction of the whole composite population of Russia to a brute machine. For a great lapse of time, no quarter of a century has passed without some country and nation having fallen in, and become a compartment of the great machine; and, the fact being so, the most peace-loving of us can hardly be sorry that the time has come for deciding whether this is to go on,— whether the Asiatic principle and method of social life are to dominate or succumb. The struggle will be no contemptible one. The great tarantula has its spider-claws out and fixed at inconceivable distances. The people of Russia, wretched at home, are better qualified for foreign aggression than for anything else. And if, within her own empire, Russia

---

[1]   The Swiss League, formed in 1291 among three cantons, became the basis of the Swiss confederation of 22 cantons in 1815; a civil war in 1847 produced a new constitution and more centralized federal state. The Prussian Zollverein, a union established in 1818 to eliminate tariff barriers, became the German Zollverein in 1834 when it combined with the South German Zollverein and the Central German Trade Union. By a series of treaties in 1851–54, it joined with the Steuerverein of Central Germany, and thus united most of the German states. Martineau praises the Zollverein in *A History of the Peace* (III, 422) for its enlightened free trade agreement.

knows all to be loose and precarious, poor and unsound, and with none but a military organisation, she knows that she has for allies, avowed or concealed, all the despotic tempers that exist among men. Not only such Governments as those of Spain, Portugal, Rome and Austria are in reality the allies of Eastern barbarism; but all aristocracies,—all self-seekers,—be they who and where they may. It is a significant sign of the times that territorial alliances are giving way before political affini-ties,—the mechanical before the essential union: and, if Russia has not for allies the nations that live near her frontier, she has those men of every nation who prefer self-will to freedom.

'This corrupted 'patriarchal' system of society, (but little superior to that which exists in your slave States) occupies one-half of the great battle-field where the hosts are gathering for the fight. On the other, the forces are ill-assorted, ill-organised, too little prepared; but still, as having the better cause, sure, I trust, of final victory. The conflict must be long, because our constitutions are, like yours, compromises, our governments as yet a mere patch-work, our popular liberties scanty and adulterated, and great masses of our brethren hungry and discontented. We have not a little to struggle for among ourselves, when our whole force is needed against the enemy. In no country of Europe is the representative system of government more than a mere beginning. In no country of Europe is human brotherhood practically asserted. Nowhere are the principles of civilisation of Western Europe determined and declared, and made the ground-work of organised action, as happily your principles are as against those of your slave-holding opponents. But, raw and ill-organ-ised as are our forces, they will be strong, sooner or later, against the serried armies of the Asiatic policy. If, on the one side, the soul comes up to battle with an imperfect and ill-defended body, on the other, the body is wholly without a soul, and must, in the end, fall to pieces. The best part of the mind of Western Europe will make itself a body by dint of action, and the pressure which must bring out its forces; and it may be doubted whether it could become duly embodied in any other way. What forms of society may arise as features of this new growth, neither you nor I can say. We can only ask each other whether, witnessing as we do the spread of Communist ideas in every free nation of Europe, and the admission by some of the most cautious and old-fashioned observers of social movements that we in England cannot now stop short of 'a modified communism,' the result is not likely to be a wholly new social state, if not a yet undreamed-of social idea.

'However this may be,—while your slave question is dominant in

Congress, and the Dissolution of your Union is becoming a familiar idea, and an avowed aspiration, our crisis is no less evidently approaching. Russia has Austria under her foot, and she is casting a corner of her wide pall over Turkey. England and France are awake and watchful; and so many men of every country are astir, that we may rely upon it that not only are territorial alliances giving way before political affinities, but national ties will give way almost as readily, if the principles of social liberty should demand the disintegration of nations. Let us not say, even to ourselves, whether we regard such an issue with hope or fear. It is a possibility too vast to be regarded but with simple faith and patience. In this spirit let us contemplate what is proceeding, and what is coming, doing the little we can by a constant assertion of the principles of social liberty, and a perpetual watch for opportunities to stimulate human progress.

'Whether your conflict will be merely a moral one, you can form a better idea than I. Ours will consist in a long and bloody warfare—possibly the last, but inevitable now. The empire of brute force can conduct its final struggle only by brute force; and there are but few yet on the other side who have any other notion or desire. While I sympathise wholly with you as to your means as well as your end, you will not withhold your sympathy from us because our heroes still assert their views and wills by exposing themselves to wounds and death in the field, and assenting once more to the old *non sequitur* about Might and Right. Let them this time obtain the lower sort of Might by the inspiration of their Right, and in another age they will aim higher. But I need not thus petition you; for I well know that where there is most of Right, there will your sympathies surely rest.

'Believe me your friend,
'HARRIET MARTINEAU.'

I have no doubt whatever of the power of France and England to chastise Russia, without the aid of any other power. I should have no doubt of the power of England alone (if that power were well administered) to humble Russia, provided the case remained a simple one. But that is precisely what appears impossible, under the existing European dynasties. I now expect, as I have anticipated for many years, a war in Europe which may even outlast the century,—with occasional lulls; and I suppose the result must be, after a dreary chaotic interval, a discarding of the existing worn-out methods of government, and probably the establishment of society under a wholly new idea. Of course, none but a prophet could be expected to declare what that new idea will be. It would be rational, but it is not necessary here, to foretell what it would *not* be or include. But all that I feel called on to say now, when I am not writing a political essay, is that the leading feature of any such radical change must be a deep modification of the institution of Property;—certainly in regard to land, and probably in regard to much else. Before any effectual social renovation can take place, men must efface the abuse which has grown up out of the transition from the feudal to the more modern state; the abuse of land being held as absolute property; whereas in feudal times land was in a manner held in trust, inasmuch as every land-holder was charged with the subsistence of all who lived within his bounds. The old practice of Man holding Man as property is nearly exploded among civilised nations; and the analogous barbarism of Man holding the surface of the globe as property cannot long survive. The idea of this being a barbarism is now fairly formed, admitted, and established among some of the best minds of the time; and the result is, as in all such cases, ultimately secure.

These considerations lead my thoughts to America; and I must say that I regard the prospects of the republic of the United States with more pain and apprehension than those of any other people in the civilised world. It is the only instance, I believe, of a nation being inferior to its institutions; and the result will be, I fear, a mournful spectacle to the world. I am not thinking chiefly, at this moment, of American slavery. I have shown elsewhere what I think and expect about that. Negro slavery in the United States, as regards the existing Union, is near its end, I have no doubt. I regard with a deeper concern the manifest retrogression of the American people, in their political and social character. They seem to be lapsing from national manliness into childhood,—retrograding from the aims and interests of the nineteenth century into those of the fifteenth and sixteenth. Their passion for territorial aggrandisement, for gold, for buccaneering adventure, and for vulgar praise,[1] are seen miserably united with the pious pretensions and fraudulent ingenuity which were, in Europe, old-fashioned three centuries ago, and which are now kept alive only in a few petty or despised States, where dynasty is on its last legs. I know that there are better men, and plenty of them, in America than those who represent the nation in the view of Europe; but those better men are silent and inactive; and the national retrogression is not visibly retarded by them. I fear it cannot be. I fear that when the bulk of a nation is below its institutions,—whether by merely wanting the requisite

---

[1]   Martineau wrote critically in these terms of American militarism and expansionism in *Daily News* "leaders" of September 9 and 15, October 30, and November 1, 1855.

knowledge, or by being in an immature moral condition, —it is not the intelligence and virtue of a small, despairing, inactive minority that can save it from lapse into barbarism. I fear that the American nation is composed almost entirely of the vast majority who coarsely boast, and the small minority who timidly despair, of the Republic. It appears but too probable that the law of progression may hold good with regard to the world at large without preventing the retrogression of particular portions of the race. But the American case is not exactly of this kind. I rather take it to be that a few wise men, under solemn and inspiring influences, laid down a loftier political programme than their successors were able to fulfil. If so, there is, whatever disappointment, no retrogression, properly speaking. We supposed the American character and policy to be represented by the chiefs of the revolution, and their Declaration of Independence and republican constitution; and now we find ourselves mistaken in our supposition. It is a disappointment; but we had rather admit a disappointment than have to witness an actual retrogression.

Effacing these national distinctions, in regarding the peoples as the human race, the condition of humanity appears to one who is taking leave of it very hopeful, though as yet exceedingly infantine. It is my deliberate opinion that the one essential requisite of human welfare in all ways is scientific knowledge of human nature. It is my belief that we can in no way but by sound knowledge of Man learn, fully and truly, any thing else; and that it is only when glimpses of that knowledge were opened,— however scantily and obscurely,—that men *have* effectually learned any thing else. I believe that this science is fairly initiated; and it follows of course that I anticipate for the race amelioration and progression at a perpetually accelerated rate. Attention is fully fixed now on the nature and mode of development of the human being; and the key to his mental and moral organisation is found. The old scoff of divines against philosophers must now soon be dropped,—the reproach that they have made no advance for a thousand years;—that there were philosophers preaching two thousand years ago, who have hardly a disciple at this day. In a little while this can never more be said; nor could it be said now by any one who understood the minds of the people among whom he lives. The glorious aims and spirit of philosophy have wrought for good in every age since those ancient sages lived; and the name and image of each is the morning star of the day in which each lived. In this way were the old philosophers truly our masters; and they may yet claim, in a future age, the discipleship of the whole human race. But to them scientific fact was wanting: by them it was unattainable. Their aim and their spirit have led recent generations to the discovery of the element wanting,—the scientific fact; and, now that is done, the progression of philosophy is secure. The philosophy of human nature is placed on a scientific basis; and it, and all other departments of philosophy, (for all depend mainly on this one) are already springing forward so as to be wholly incomparable with those of a thousand years ago. There is no need to retort the scoff of divines, as facts are against them. There is no need to inquire of them what is the state of Christianity at the end of 1800 years, nor what it has done in regenerating human nature, and establishing peace on earth and goodwill among men, according to its promise. Leaving divines on one side, as professionally disqualified for judging of the function and prospects of philosophy, and looking at the matter in a speculative, and not an antagonistic way, I should say that the time cannot be far off when, throughout the civilised world, theology must go out before the light of philosophy. As to the fact, the civilised world is now nearly divided between gross Latin or Greek Catholicism and disbelief of Christianity in any form. Protestantism seems to be going out as fast as possible. In Germany the Christian faith is confessedly extinct; and in France it is not far otherwise. The Lutheranism of Sweden is, in its effects, precisely like the Catholicism of Spain or Italy, and will issue in 'infidelity' in the one country as surely as in the others. In England the lamentations of the religious world, and the disclosures of the recent Census, show how even outward adhesion to Christianity is on the decline: and if they did not, the chaotic state of religious opinion would indicate the fact no less reliably. In America we see Protestantism run wild,—each man being his own creed-maker; and the result,—a seeking ere long for something true and stable,—is secure.— Not only is such the state of the civilised world, but it must be so. Precisely in proportion to Man's ignorance of his own nature, as well as of other things, is the tendency of his imagination to inform the outward world with his own consciousness. The fetish worshipper attributes a consciousness like his own to everything about him; the imputation becomes more select and rare through every rising grade of theology, till the Christian makes his reflex of himself invisible and intangible, or, as he says, 'spiritual.' His God is an invisible idol, fading away into a faint abstraction, exactly according to the enlightenment of the worshipper, till he who does justice to his own faculties gives up the human attributes, and the personality of that First Cause which the form of his intellect requires him to suppose, and is called an Atheist by the idolaters he has left behind him. By the verification and spread of the science of human nature, the conflict which has hitherto attended such attainment as this will be spared to our successors.

When scientific facts are established, and self-evident truths are brought out of them, there is an end of conflict;—or it passes on to administer discipline to adventurers in fresh fields of knowledge. About this matter, of the extinction of theology by a true science of human nature, I cannot but say that my expectation amounts to absolute assurance; and that I believe that the worst of the conflict is over. I am confident that a bright day is coming for future generations. Our race has been as Adam created at nightfall. The solid earth has been but dark, or dimly visible, while the eye was inevitably drawn to the mysterious heavens above. There, the successive mythologies have arisen in the east, each a constellation of truths, each glorious and fervently worshipped in its course; but the last and noblest, the Christian, is now not only sinking to the horizon, but paling in the dawn of a brighter time. The dawn is unmistakeable; and the sun will not be long in coming up. The last of the mythologies is about to vanish before the flood of a brighter light.

With the last of the mythologies will pass away, after some lingering, the immoralities which have attended all mythologies. Now, while the state of our race is such as to need all our mutual devotedness, all our aspiration, all our resources of courage, hope, faith and good cheer, the disciples of the Christian creed and morality are called upon, day by day, to 'work out *their own* salvation with fear and trembling,'[1] and so forth. Such exhortations are too low for even the wavering mood and quacked morality of a time of theological suspense and uncertainty. In the extinction of that suspense, and the discrediting of that selfish quackery, I see the prospect, for future generations, of a purer and loftier virtue, and a truer and sweeter heroism than divines who preach such self-seeking can conceive of. When our race is trained in the morality which belongs to ascertained truth, all 'fear and trembling' will be left to children; and men will have risen to a capacity for higher work than saving themselves,—to that of 'working out' the welfare of their race, not in 'fear and trembling,' but with serene hope and joyful assurance.

The world as it is is growing somewhat dim before my eyes; but the world as it is to be looks brighter every day.

END OF THE AUTOBIOGRAPHY

---

[1]   Philippians 2:12–13 (KJV): "Wherefore, my beloved, as ye have always obeyed, not as in my presence only but now much more in my absence, work out your own salvation in fear and trembling. For it is God who worketh in you both to will and to do of his good pleasure."

Appendix A: Illustrations from the Autobiography *(1877)*

[Nineteenth-century autobiographies usually included a portrait of the author, and often added an illustration of a birthplace, adult home, or favorite "haunt." Martineau's *Autobiography* includes engravings of two portraits by George Richmond: one painted in 1833 at the height of her fame, now owned by the Armitt Trust; the second by George Richmond, drawn in 1849 in Martineau's middle age, engraved in 1850 by Francis Holl, and now owned by the National Portrait Gallery, London. Through its illustrations, the *Autobiography* particularly emphasizes Martineau's homes—her birthplace in Norwich, her lodgings during her five-year invalidism in Tynemouth, and two views of the home she built, The Knoll, in Ambleside in the Lake District and where she died in 1876.]

Harriet Martineau

1833.

Portrait of Harriet Martineau, 1833

House in which Harriet Martineau was born

G. Richmond.   Francis Holl.

Harriet Martineau

1850.

Portrait of Harriet Martineau, 1850

Tynemouth from the Sick-Room Window

The Knoll
Ambleside
as it appeared in 1846.
Sketched by Hammersley; drawn on wood by Harvey,
and engraved by Harriet L. Clarke.

The Knoll, Ambleside, as it appeared in 1846

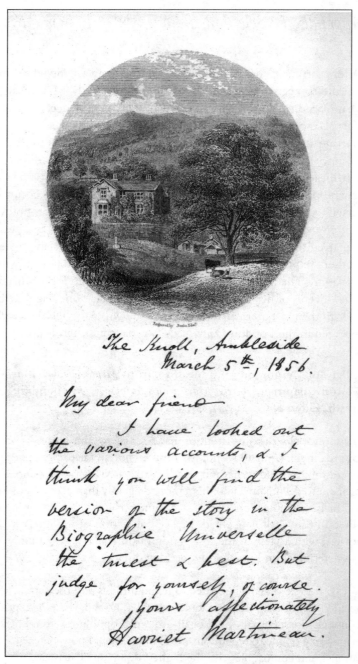

The Knoll, Ambleside, with Autograph Letter

Appendix B: Selections from the Memorials *(1877)*

[After Martineau's death, Maria Weston Chapman assembled a third volume to accompany the *Autobiography*, entitled "Memorials." Chapman drew on Martineau's private correspondence, a private journal, and personal recollections to expand the life narrative that Martineau completed in 1855. The following selections from the "Memorials" represent alternative or supplementary accounts of Martineau's life, written at different points in her career. The first, a private memorandum of 1829, records her decision to commit herself to professional authorship. The second, a letter to her mother written in 1830, expresses her desire to move to London as a periodical editor and woman of letters, but also acquiesces in her mother's request that she return home to Norwich and remain with her family. The third, a letter of correction written to John Murray, fills in details of her family background and education. The fourth, perhaps the most unusual, is an obituary she wrote for herself, which appeared in the London *Daily News* two days after her death.]

1. Private Memorandum, June 1829, from *Memorials*, ed. Maria Weston Chapman, *Harriet Martineau's Autobiography* (London: Smith, Elder, & Co., 1877), III, 32-34

For some years past my attention has been more and more directed towards literary pursuits; and, if I mistake not, my capacity for their successful prosecution has increased, so that I have now fair encouragement to devote myself to them more diligently than ever. After long and mature deliberation, I have determined that my chief subordinate object in life shall henceforth be the cultivation of my intellectual powers, with a view to the instruction of others by my writings. On this determination I pray for the blessing of God.

I wish to hold myself prepared to relinquish this purpose, should any decided call of duty interfere; but I pray that no indolence or caprice in myself, no discouragement or ill-grounded opposition from others, may prevail on me to relinquish a resolution which I now believe to be rational, and compatible with the highest desire of a Christian.

I am now just twenty-seven years of age. It is my wish to ascertain (should life and health be spared) how much may be accomplished by diligent but temperate exertion in pursuit of this object for ten years.

I believe myself possessed of no uncommon talents, and of not an atom of genius; but as various circumstances have led me to think more accurately and read more extensively than some women, I believe that I may so write on subjects of universal concern as to inform some minds and stir up others. My aim is to become a forcible and elegant writer on religious and moral subjects, so as to be useful to refined as well as unenlightened minds. But, as I see how much remains to be done before this aim can be attained, I wish to be content with a much lower degree of usefulness, should the Father of my spirit see fit to set narrow bounds to my exertions. Of posthumous fame I have not the slightest expectation or desire. To be useful in my day and generation is enough for me. To this I henceforth devote myself, and desire to keep in mind the following rules. (A frequent reference to them is necessary.)

I. To improve my moral constitution by every means; to cultivate my moral sense; to keep ever in view the subordination of intellectual to moral objects; by the practice of piety and benevolence, by entertaining the freedom and cheerfulness of spirit which results from dependence on God, to promote the perfection of the intellectual powers.

II. To seek the assistance of God in my intellectual exertions, and his blessing on their results.

III. To impart full confidence to my family respecting my pursuits, but to be careful not to weary them with too frequent a reference to myself; and to be as nearly as possible silent on the subject to all the world besides.

IV. To study diligently, 1. The Scriptures, good commentators, works of religious philosophy and practice,—*for moral improvement;* 2. Mental philosophy,—*for intellectual improvement;* 3. Natural philosophy and natural history, languages and history,—*for improvement in knowledge;* 4. Criticism, belles-lettres, and poetry,—*for improvement in style.* Each in turn, and something every day.

V. While I have my intellectual improvement ever in view, to dismiss from my thoughts the particular subject on which I have written in the morning for the rest of the day, i.e. to be temperate in my attention to an object.

VI. By *early rising*, and all due economy of time, and especially by a careful government of the thoughts, to employ my life to better purpose than heretofore.

VII. To exalt, enlarge, and refresh my mind by social intercourse, observation of external nature, of the fine arts, and of the varieties of human life.

VIII. To bear in mind that as my determination is deliberately formed and now allowed to be rational, disappointments should not be lightly permitted to relax my exertions. If my object is conscientiously adopted, mortifications of vanity should prove stimulants, rather than discouragements. The same consideration should induce patience under *painful labour, delay,* and *disappointment,* and guard me against heat and precipitation.

IX. To consider my own interests as little as possible, and to write with a view to the good of others; therefore to entertain no distaste to the humblest literary task which affords a prospect of usefulness.

X. Should my exertions ultimately prove fruitless, to preserve my cheerfulness, remembering that God only knows how his work may be best performed, and that I have no right to expect the privilege of eminent usefulness, though permitted to seek it. Should success be granted, to take no honour to myself, remembering that I possess no original power or intrinsic merit, and that I can receive and accomplish nothing, except it be given me from Heaven.

2. Letter from Harriet Martineau to her Mother, 22 January 1830, from the *Memorials*, ed. Chapman, III, 43-45

MY DEAR MOTHER,—I received your letter yesterday, and the purpose of my answering it already is to prevent —'s having the trouble of writing. He knows how I like hearing from him, but his time is very fully occupied, and I shall be glad to save him trouble. I have read yours to my dear aunt, who has been my confidante in the business, and we agree in seeing that there is not a shadow of a doubt as to what I am to do. We chiefly regret that such painful feelings should have been excited, where my sole intention was to offer a confidence which is your due. I could not but let you know how entirely my prospects are declared to depend on certain circumstances; but once knowing your wishes, I have no other desire than to comply with them, reserving to myself, however, the liberty of changing my plans when I find my resources fail, as Mr. Fox says they inevitably will, if I remain at a distance from town. There is no periodical work ever sent into the country, and my choice lies between the little stories for Houlston and Darton, and original works, which I have neither capital nor courage to undertake. Mr. Fox is exceedingly sorry that I am to decline the three offers which have been made me,— the Westminster, the larger engagement for the M. R., and Mr. Hill's assistance. If Mr. Fox can get his work done under his own eye, I cannot expect him to send it to a distance, and he declines doing so. Mr. Hill has asked the essential question, whether I have continual access to the Museum and other libraries, and literary society here; and finding that I live in the country, can do nothing for me, and "Pemberton"[1] is coming back to me. I must try if Baldwin or somebody else will take it. Mr. Fox will keep his eye upon my interests, and, if anything offers, I shall be sure to have the benefit of it. A better and kinder friend I cannot have; and he shows his kindness in not puffing me up with false hopes. He says 100*l.* or 150*l.* per year is as much as most successful writers usually make, with all the advantages of town: and I must not expect any such thing except in particularly lucky years. Neither he nor I dreamed of writing to dispel *selfish* doubts in you, my dear mother, but only to show that my change of views arose from no fancy of my own. When I came, I believed as firmly as you do that my means of subsistence were in my own power at home. Now I see that they will probably not be so; but I am not anxious, while I have any prospect at all of useful employment. I have given up Derby. We see no use in going to Bristol, as there are no literary people but Sydney Smith, who is but a slight acquaintance of Aunt K.'s and has little literary influence, and there I should not have the leisure for writing which I should enjoy at Derby. So, if you please, I will remain here for a few weeks, and make the most of my time and opportunities. My aunt insists on my remaining here, as being near Mr. Fox. One thing more,—I never entertained so preposterous an idea for a

---

[1] I think Pemberton and its politics is the "Brook Farm" of the Political Economy series. [Maria Chapman's note.]

moment as that of going alone into lodgings, and must have expressed myself very ill if I led you to think so. It would be positively disreputable. I thought of boarding in a family. So the conclusion of the whole matter is that you will see me in two or three months, quite inclined to be happier at home than anywhere else, as long as I can maintain myself there in a useful way; but holding the power of seeking employment elsewhere, should my resources fail. I cannot regret (and here my aunt bears me out) having mentioned to you the proposals I have received; but if the manner has caused you pain, I ask your forgiveness, and beg you to forget the matter as speedily as possible. We know well how far you are from being selfish on such occasions, and this consideration made me the more ready to be perfectly open with you. And here I make an end of the subject entirely.

I have been enjoying myself exceedingly since I last wrote, and some very pleasant things have happened. The thing which was more wanting to my peace than any one circumstance besides has been granted to me. A— W—[1] called on me at Chiswell Street on Monday; and we had a very long and satisfactory explanation of past mysteries, the particulars of which you shall hear when we meet. There is nothing so delightful as coming to a clear understanding in such cases, and a load has been taken off our minds by it. She is a very sensible girl, and talked in a way that I liked very much. She is not in the slightest degree like her brother in countenance, which disappointed me. I think I never before failed to trace a family resemblance.

My aunt is so pleased with the basket making that she has given me two dozen pieces of braid and cord, satin,—lilac, blue, and pink,— paper, etc. How very kind! I have seen a most beautiful new sort of bag, which I find I can imitate; and I have several orders already in this family, and shall probably make two or three guineas by them. ... As I write much and often to you, I am obliged to hurry, which I hope you will pardon.

Farewell. With dear love to all, believe me, dear mother, your very affectionate

H. Martineau

---

[1]   The sister of her betrothed. [Maria Chapman's note.]

3. Letter to the Editor of "Men of the Time," 22 March 1856, from *Memorials*, ed. Chapman, III, 292–94

Sir,—Mr. Murray is always glad to receive information of mistakes in his handbooks; and I presume you wish to be made aware of all such serious errors in your 'Men of the Time' as may discredit a work upon so excellent a plan. The mistakes of fact in the notice of myself are so numerous, and I must say so inexcusable, considering the means of information that exist in print, that you ought to be informed of them on authority, in order to their rectification. If allowed to remain, such mistakes discredit the whole work, as is the case already with my family and friends, who ask how they can trust any part of the book, when any one memoir is so *unnecessarily* full of errors.

1. My forefathers were not manufacturers, but surgeons. It was that profession which descended from generation to generation.

2. There was no silk manufacturer in Norwich till after my father's death, and the removal of the family from the city. My father (the first manufacturer of the family) was a bombazine and camlet manufacturer.

3. This is the most important mistake of all, because it deprives my parents of honour due to them. My education was not of the "limited character" imputed. On the contrary, my parents gave their children, girls as well as boys, an education of a very high order, including sound classical instruction and training. What the family have *done* is sufficient evidence that their education was not of a "limited character."

4. It was in 1834 that I went to America.

5. "Deerbrook" has been more popular than almost any of my works, and has gained a higher reputation than any other. It has gone through two large editions (a rare thing for a novel) and I have disposed of it for a third.

6. Lord Grey never offered me a pension. The one which was at first proposed was not £150, but £300.

7. It was at the end of 1842, and not 1853, that my medical men declared me incurably ill.

8. Rev. James Martineau was not of the party to the East, or ever in the East at all. The names of the party are given in my "Eastern Life."

9. Mr. Atkinson is not a "Mesmerist," but a philosophical student, and a gentleman of independent fortune. The standing of the "Letters on Man's Nature and Development" is, in point of fact, as different as possible from that groundlessly asserted in the memoir.

10. My version of Comte does not close the list of my labours.

11. One of the best received and most important of my books is not mentioned, —"Household Education."

12. Nobody has witnessed "flashes of wit" from me. The giving me credit for wit shows that the writer is wholly unacquainted with me. . . .

Now, what will you do? Of course, you will not allow proved errors to continue to circulate uncontradicted. Will you cancel these notices, or print this letter, or what will you do?

You are probably aware that I am mortally ill. I have written and got printed an Autobiography, which will be published immediately after my death. But this does not affect the case, as your notice will then be withdrawn. It is the interval between this time and that, that you have to provide for: and I hope to hear, before I decide on a polite contradiction, what course you propose to take.

Yours obediently,
HARRIET MARTINEAU

4. Obituary, London *Daily News*, 29 June 1876; reprinted in the *Memorials*, ed. Chapman, III, 459-70

"We regret to announce the death of Harriet Martineau. The following memoir, though written in the third person, was from her own pen. The frankness of its self-criticism makes it necessary to guard the reader against confounding her own strict and sometimes disparaging judgment of herself with the impressions made by her upon others."

Harriet Martineau was born in 1802, in the city of Norwich, where the first of the name settled in 1688. David Martineau, the earliest of whom any record remains, was a French Protestant, who came over on the revocation of the Edict of Nantes. He married a French lady, whose family emigrated in the same ship, and pursued his profession as a surgeon in Norwich, where a succession of surgeons of the name existed, till the death of the most eminent of them, Philip Meadows Martineau (the uncle of Harriet), in 1828. He was considered the most eminent provincial surgeon of his day. The eldest brother of Harriet— a man of qualifications so high as to promise to sustain the honour of his name and profession in the old city—died before the age of thirty, and only one member of the family now remains in the city where many generations grew up. Harriet was the third daughter, and the sixth of eight children of Thomas Martineau, who was a manufacturer of the Norwich staples,—bombazine and camlet. His acquaintance with Dr.

Parr was kept up and signalized by the gift of a black camlet study-gown every year or so, a piece of the right length being woven expressly for the doctor and dyed with due care.

There was nothing remarkable about the childhood and youth of any of Thomas Martineau's children, unless in the case of Thomas, the eldest son, already referred to. His scholarship was of a high quality, and his mind was altogether of the rare ripeness and richness which comes of the equable cultivation of the intellectual and moral nature. The remarkable feature of the family story, in those days, was the steady self-denial, and clear, inflexible purpose with which the parents gave their children the best education which they could, by all honourable means, command. In those times of war and middle-class adversity, the parents understood their position, and took care that their children should understand it, telling them that there was no chance of wealth for them, and about an equal probability of a competence or of poverty; and that they must, therefore, regard their education as their only secure portion. Harriet came in for her share of this advantage, being well furnished with Latin and French (to which in due time she added Italian and German), and exercised in composition as well as reading in her own language and others. The whole family, trained by parental example, were steady and conscientious workers; but there were no tokens of unusual ability in Harriet during any part of her childhood or youth. Her health was bad, her tone of spirits low, her habit of mind anxious, and her habits of life silent, and as independent as they could be under the old-fashioned family rule of strictness and the strong hand. At her entrance upon womanhood a deafness, unperceived during her child-hood and slight in youth, was aggravated by a kind of accident, and became so severe as to compel (for other people's accommodation as well as her own) the use of a trumpet for the rest of her life. This misfor-tune, no doubt, strengthened her habits of study, and had much to do with the marking out of her career. What other effects it produced upon her she has shown in her "Letter to the Deaf."

Her first appearance in print was before she was out of her teens, in a religious periodical; the same in which the late Judge Talfourd had made his early attempts not very long before. Not only her contributions to the "Monthly Repository," but her first books were of a religious character, her cast of mind being more decidedly of the religious order than any other during the whole of her life, whatever might be the basis and scope of her ultimate opinions. Her latest opinions were, in her own view, the most religious,—the most congenial with the emotional as well as the rational department of human nature. In her youth she naturally wrote what she had been brought up to believe, and her first work, "Devotional Exercises," was thoroughly Unitarian. Of this class, and indeed of all her early writings, the only one worth mention is the little volume "Traditions of Palestine," which first fixed attention upon her, and made her name known in the reviews. There are some even now who prefer that little volume to all her other writings. Before it was out its writer had formed the conception of the very different kind of work which at once and completely opened her career, her "Illustrations of Political Economy." Her stimulus in all she wrote, from first to last, was simply the need of utterance. This need she had gratified early; and those who knew her best were always aware that she was not ambitious, though she enjoyed success, and had pride enough to have suffered keenly under failure. When, in 1829, she and her sisters lost their small fortunes by the failure of the house in which their money was placed, Harriet continued to write as she had written before, though under the new liability of having no money to spend upon ventures. Without capital, without any literary connections (except the editor of the "Monthly Repository"), without any visible means of accomplishing her object, she resolved to bring out a series of "Illustrations of Political Economy," confident that the work was at that time (1831) very much needed by the working-classes, to say nothing of other persons who had influence in the community, agitated as it then was by the Reform struggle. That Reform struggle and the approach of the cholera on its first visit made the booksellers disinclined to publish any thing. Messrs. Baldwin and Cradock had all but consented to the scheme, and had in fact engaged a stitcher for the monthly volumes, when they took fright and drew back. Harriet Martineau's forthcoming Autobiography will of course tell the story of the struggle she passed through to get her work published in any manner and on any terms. Almost every considerable publisher had refused it; the Diffusion Society had declined it, on the report of their sub-committee against it. It appeared, however, at the beginning of 1832, when its writer was worn out with anxiety and fatigue, and had met with uniform discouragement, except in her own home, where her own confidence that the book would succeed, because it was wanted, commanded the sympathy of her family. In a fortnight after the day of publication her way was open before her for life. The work reached a circulation of about ten thousand in the next few years. The difficulties under which it appeared prevented her being enriched by it; and her own unalterable view of what it could and what it could not effect prevented her expecting too much from it, either in regard to its social operation or its influence on her own fame. The original idea of exhibiting the great natural laws of society by a series of pictures of selected social action was a fortunate one; and her tales initiated a multitude of minds into the conception of what political economy is, and of how it concerns every body living in society. Beyond this, there is no merit of a high order in the work. It did not pretend to offer discoveries, or new applications or elucidations of prior discoveries. It popularized, in a fresh form, some doctrines and many truths long before made public by others. Those were the days of her success in narrative, in fiction. In about ten years from that time she had nearly ceased to write fiction, from simple inability to do it well. On the whole, perhaps, her novel of "Deerbrook" has been the most popular of her works of fiction, though some prefer her history (in the form of a romance) of Toussaint L'Ouverture ("The Hour and the Man"), and others again her story-book for children, written in illness,—"The Playfellow." But none of her novels or tales have, or ever had, in the eyes of good judges or in her own, any character of permanence. The artistic aim and qualifications were absent; she had no power of dramatic construction; nor the poetic inspiration on the one hand, nor critical cultivation on the other, without which no work of the imagination can be worthy to live. Two or three of her Political Economy Tales, are, perhaps, her best achievement in fiction,—her doctrine furnishing the plot which she was unable to create, and the brevity of space duly restricting the indulgence in detail which injured her longer narratives, and at last warned her to leave off writing them. It was fortunate for her that her own condemnation anticipated that of the public. To the end of her life she was subject to solicitations to write more novels and more tales; but she for the most part remained steady in her refusal. Her three volumes of "Forest and Game Law Tales" and a few stories in "Household Words," written at the express and earnest request of Mr. Dickens, and with little satisfaction to herself, are her latest efforts in that direction.

Her popularity was, however, something extraordinary during the appearance of her "Illustrations of Political Economy." It was presently necessary for her to remove to London, to be within reach of the sources of information rendered indispensable by the success of her scheme and the extension of her influence. She lived in a lodging in Conduit Street for some months, till her mother joined her in London. Their house was in Fludyer Street, Westminster; and there they lived till a serious and long illness compelled Harriet Martineau to leave London, to which she never returned as a resident. On her first taking up her abode there many foolish stories were afloat about the origin of her series, and the aid she received in it from Lord Brougham and others. The facts were that the enterprise was wholly her own, and the execution of it also; and that Lord Brougham in particular knew nothing whatever about her or her work till his secretary sent him the first five numbers half a year after the publication began. His lordship's first thought was to engage her assistance in illustrating the evils of the old poor-law and the intended provisions of the new; and her four little volumes on the poor-laws appeared during the publication of her larger work. The two years which followed her first great success were the busiest of a busy life. All advocates of all schemes applied to her for cooperation. She was plunged at once into such a social whirl that she dined out every day but Sundays. New material for her work was always accumulating on her hands; and besides the production of one number, and occasionally two, of her little volumes per month, she had an unmanageable amount of correspondence always pressing upon her. It was at that time that she formed the habit which she continued for the rest of her life,—of sitting up late, while going on to rise early. She took, on an average, five hours or five and a half of sleep, going to bed at one in the morning, and being at her breakfast at half past seven, to save the precious morning hours for her most serious business. Such was her practice, with few intervals, to the date of her last illness.

Before the publication of her work was completed she had sailed for America. At first her object was simply to travel for the sake of recreation and repose; but, at the suggestion of the late Lord Henley, she turned her face in the direction of the United States, in order to examine some points of social policy and morals, honourable to the Americans and worthy of our emulation, but generally overlooked by European travellers who go to amuse themselves and return to quiz. She hoped to learn some secrets of success in the treatment of criminals, the insane, and other unhappy classes, and in the diffusion of education. She succeeded in her aims in some measure; but the interest of the anti-slavery question just at that time absorbed every other. She arrived just at the culmination of that reign of terror which she described after her return in the "Westminster Review," in the narrative entitled "The Martyr Age of the United States," which was reprinted as a pamphlet, and by which the nature and significance of the anti-slavery movement in America (where it involved the entire political and personal liberty of every citizen) were first made known in this country. Harriet Martineau, received with unbounded hospitality and unmeasured flatteries, though known to have written an anti-slavery story in her series, was not converted to the American view, as had been hoped and expected. Under circumstances in which she had no choice but to speak out she condemned slavery and its political consequences as before; and, for some months preceding her return, she was subjected to insult and injury, and was even for some weeks in danger of her life while travelling where the tar-barrel, the cowhide, and the pistol were the regimen prescribed for and applied to abolitionists, and threatened especially in her case. In her books upon America she said little or nothing of her personal share in the critical troubles of the time, because her purpose was, not to interest the public in her adventures, but to exhibit, without passion or prejudice, the actual condition of society in the United States. Its treatment of herself is rather a topic for her Autobiography, and there, no doubt, it will be found.

After an absence of two years she returned to England in August, 1836, and early in the next spring she published "Society in America." Her own opinion of that work changed much for the worse before her death. It was written while she was in the full flow of sympathy with the theoretical American statesmen of that time, who were all *à priori* political philosophers to a greater or less degree like the framers of the Declaration of Independence. Her intercourse with these may be traced in the structure and method of observation of her book, and her companionship with the adorers of Thomas Carlyle in her style. Some constitutional lawyers of the United States have declared that there is no error in her account of the political structure and relations of the Federal and State governments of that country; and the book contains the only account we have of the condition of slavery, and of the country under it, at the time of the rise of the abolition movement. But, on the whole, the book is not a favourable specimen of Harriet Martineau's writings, either in regard to moral or artistic taste. It is full of affectations and preachments, and it marks the highest point of the metaphysical period of her mind. Little as she valued the second work on America—"Retrospect of Western Travel"—which she wrote at the request of her publishers, to bring into use her lighter observations on scenery and manners, it was more creditable to her mood, and perhaps to her powers, than the more ambitious work. The American abolitionists, then in the early days of their action, reprinted as a pamphlet the parts of these two works which relate to the slave institutions of their country, and sowed it broadcast over the land. The virulence with which the Southern press denounces her to this day, in company with Mrs. Chapman and Mrs. Stowe, seems to show that her representations were not lost on the American public. If they are operating at the end of so many years, there must be truth in them. Though the customary dispensers of hospitality in the United States passed from the extreme of courtesy to that of rudeness to the traveller, she formed valuable friendships in that country which lasted as long as her life. Her connection with the interests of America remained a close one, and its political course was a subject of action to a late period, and of study to the last.

In the interval between her return from America and her leaving London—somewhat less than three years—she wrote "How to Observe Morals and Manners," a volume of a series published by Mr. Knight, of which Sir Henry Delabêche's "How to Observe Geology" was the opening volume; a few of the volumes of the "Guide to Service," issued also by Mr. Knight; and her novel "Deerbrook." The "Guides to Service" were originated by the Poor-law Commissioners, with the object chiefly of training the ideas of children, especially in the workhouse schools, for the occupation of their lives. Harriet Martineau agreed to write the model number, provided she might take the "Maid-of-all-Work" for her subject; which she did, with the amusing result that at various turns of her life afterwards she was met by the popular belief that she had herself been a maid-of-all-work; a mistake which she regarded with some complacency whenever she encountered it. The other volumes of the Series written by her are the "Dressmaker" (in which she had some technical assistance from a professional person), the "Housemaid," and the "Lady's Maid."

On the publication of "Deerbrook," in April, 1839, she went abroad with a party of friends, partly to escort an invalid cousin, and partly for rest and refreshment to herself. She was not aware of the extent of her own illness; and she was brought home on a couch from Venice in June, in a state of health so hopeless that she left London and settled herself at Tynemouth, on the Northumberland coast, within reach of family care and tendance. There she remained, a prisoner to the couch, till the close of 1844. During her illness she wrote her second novel ("The Hour and the Man"), the four volumes of children's tales called "The Playfellow," and "Life in the Sick-Room," originating also, in concert with the present Countess of Elgin and Mr. Knight, the series since so well known as "The Weekly Volume." Of her recovery the public heard at the time much more than she desired and approved. At the instigation of several of her friends, and especially of her medical attendant, she made trial of mesmerism, for the purpose of obtaining some release from the use of opiates. To her own surprise and that of others, the treatment procured her a release from the disease itself, from which several eminent medical men had declared recovery to be impossible. In five months she was perfectly well. Meantime, doctors and strangers in various parts of the kingdom had rushed into print, without her countenance or her knowledge; and the amount of misrepresentation and mischief soon became so great as to compel her to tell the story as it really happened. The commotion was just what might have been anticipated from the usual reception of new truths in science and the medical art. That she recovered when she ought to have died was an unpardonable offence. According to the doctors who saw her enter society again from the beginning of 1845, she was in a state of infatuation, and, being as ill as ever in reality, would sink down in six months. When, instead of so sinking down, she rode on a camel to Mount Sinai and Petra, and on horseback to Damascus, they said she had never been ill. To the charge that it had been "all imagination," her reply was that, in that case, it was the doctor's imagination and not hers that was involved; for they had told her, and not she them, what and how serious her illness was. To the friends who blamed her for publishing her experience before the world was ripe for it, her reply was, first, that she had no option; and next, that it is hard to see how the world is to get ripened if experimenters in new departments of natural philosophy conceal their experience. The immediate consequence of the whole business—the extension of the practice of mesmerism as a curative agent, and especially the restoration of several cases like her own—abundantly compensated Harriet Martineau for an amount of insult and ridicule which would have been a somewhat unreasonable penalty on any sin or folly which she could have committed. As a penalty on simply getting well when she was expected to die, the infliction was a curious sign of the times.

Being free to choose her place of abode, on her recovery, her friends universally supposed she would return to London and its literary advantages and enjoyment. But literature, though a precious luxury, was not, and never had been, the daily bread of her life. She felt that she could not be happy, or in the best way useful, if the declining years of her life were spent in lodgings in the morning and drawing-rooms in the evening. A quiet home of her own, and some few dependent on her for their domestic welfare, she believed to be essential to every true woman's peace of mind; and she chose her plan of life accordingly. Meaning to live in the country, she chose the most beautiful, and settled at the Lakes. She bought a field near Ambleside, opposite Fox How, and about a mile from Rydal Mount. She built a house, and tried her hand successfully on the smallest of farms,—a farm of two acres. She set on foot some remedial schemes applicable to local mischiefs; and by degrees found herself pledged to a practice of delivering a series of lectures every winter to the mechanics of the little town and their families. She and they were so well acquainted, that there was nothing odd in this in their view, and no strangers were admitted, nor even the gentry of the place, for want of room. Her subjects were Sanitary Principles and Practice, the History of England, the History of North America, and the Scenes of her Eastern Travel. In her Ambleside home she lived for ten years of health and happiness, which, as she was wont to say, was worth all the rest of her life.

At various times since 1832 she had been sounded about accepting a pension on the Civil List; and she had repeatedly replied by objecting to receive one. Her objections remained in full force when Lord Melbourne made an express offer to her of a pension of £150,[1] to be increased as circumstances permitted, as his last act before going out of power in 1841. Lord Melbourne was aware that she had invested her spare earnings in a deferred annuity, and that while hopelessly ill she was very poor. Her objections, however, bore no relation to this class of considerations. Her letter to Lord Melbourne found its way into the newspapers without her knowledge, and it speaks for itself. Not the less for this was she misunderstood. Nothing was further from her thoughts than passing condemnation on the literary pensioners of the time. They must judge for themselves, and their position was different. It was a matter of feeling with her quite as much as of principle; and she would have thankfully received any acknowledgment of past labours which might have been decreed, otherwise than through a method of favouritism. She felt that, once under pecuniary obligation to the sovereign and the minister, she could never again feel perfectly free on political questions, though Lord Melbourne generously deprecated any such conclusion. As it happened, she did very well without the money, and she wrote the "History of the Thirty Years' Peace," which she could hardly have done while in receipt of a pension.

This, the bulkiest of her works and the most laborious, was undertaken at the request of Mr. Charles Knight, who had himself written the first few chapters, then deputed the work to another, and presently found it at a stand. Harriet Martineau had no idea whatever whether

---

[1]   Cf. Martineau's statement in the letter to the editor of "Men of the Time," March 22, 1856 (Appendix B.3): "Lord Grey never offered me a pension. The one which was at first proposed was not £150, but £300."

she could write history; but, on Mr. Knight's pressing his request, she went to work in August, 1848, and completed the work (after an interval of a few weeks) in the autumn of 1849. The introductory volume was written in 1850, also at Mr. Knight's solicitation. Without taking the chronicle form this history could not, from the nature of the case, be cast in the ultimate form of perfected history. All that can be done with contemporary history is to collect and methodize the greatest amount of reliable facts and distinct impressions, to amass sound material for the veritable historian of a future day,—so consolidating, assimilating, and vivifying the structure as to do for the future writer precisely that which the lapse of time and the oblivion which creeps over all transactions must prevent his doing for himself. This auxiliary usefulness is the aim of Harriet Martineau's history; and she was probably not mistaken in hoping for that much result from her labour. It rendered her a personal service which she had not anticipated. There was an impression abroad of her being a sort of demagogue or dangerous Radical, though it is hard to say which of her writings could have originated such an impression. The history dispelled it thoroughly; and if it proved that she belonged to no party, it showed that it was not because she transcended the extremes of all.

The work which she published on her return from her Eastern travels, which she enjoyed as the guest of Mr. and Mrs. Richard V. Yates, of Liverpool, had shown that she was no longer a Unitarian nor a believer in revelation at all. "Eastern Life, Present and Past," exhibits the history and generation of the four great faiths—the Egyptian, the Jewish, the Christian, and the Mohammedan—as they appear when their birthplaces are visited in succession. She had passed from the Nile to Sinai; and thence to Jerusalem, Damascus, and Lebanon. The work in which she gave out her views on her return ranks, on the whole, as the best of her writings; and her reputation assumed a new, a graver, and a broader character after its appearance. It was followed in 1851 by a volume which, though not for the most part written by her, was of her procuring and devising. She took the responsibility of the "Letters on the Laws of Man's Nature and Development," which were for the greater part written by her friend, Mr. Atkinson, in reply to the short letters of her own which occupy a small proportion of the book. This book brought upon its writers, as was inevitable, the imputation of atheism from the multitude who cannot distinguish between the popular and the philosophical sense of the word,—between the disbelief in the popular theology which has caused a long series of religious men to be called atheists, and the disbelief in a First Cause,—a disbelief which is expressly disclaimed in the book. A full account of Harriet Martineau's faith and philosophy will of course be found in her forthcoming Autobiography, where it is more in place than here. As to the consequences of such an expression of them, they were somewhat different from what might have been expected. The reception of the volume disclosed some curious social facts, revealing to its authors an altogether unexpected proportion between the receivers and repudiators of dogmatic theology in this country. What is called "the entire periodical press" condemned the book, without, however, in any one case meeting its argument or recognizing its main subject; and yet was it excellently received and widely sympathized with. Everybody supposed that its authors would be ruined, excluded from society, stopped in their work, and so forth. But the actual result was that this open avowal of heretical opinion made all the relations of life sounder than they had ever been. As Harriet Martineau declared, it dissolved all false relations and confirmed all true ones. At no time of her life was she more occupied, more prosperous, so cheered by sympathy, or so thoroughly happy, as during the interval between the publication of that book and the close of her labours.

Besides some small works, such as "Guide to the Lakes," it remained for her to bring out two of more general importance,—her volume on "Household Education," which is more popular than almost any of her works, and her condensation of Comte's "Positive Philosophy." The story of the intention and achievement of that work is told in its prefaces. Begun in 1852, it occupied the greater part of the year 1853, and appeared in November of that year. It was her last considerable work; and there is no other, perhaps, which so well manifests the real character of her ability and proper direction of her influence,—as far as each went. Her original power was nothing more than was due to earnestness and intellectual clearness within a certain range. With small imaginative and suggestive powers, and therefore nothing approaching to genius, she could see clearly what she did see, and give a clear expression to what she had to say. In short, she could popularize, while she could neither discover nor invent. She could sympathize in other people's views, and was too facile in doing so; and she could obtain and keep a firm grasp of her own, and, moreover, she could make them understood. The function of her life was to do this, and, in as far as it was done diligently and honestly, her life was of use, however far its achievements may have fallen short of expectations less moderate than her own. Her duties and her business were sufficient for the peace and the desires of her mind. She saw the human race, as she believed, advancing under the law of progress; she enjoyed her share of the experience, and had no ambition for a larger endowment, or reluctance or anxiety about leaving the enjoyment of such as she had.

From the early part of 1852 she had contributed largely to the "Daily News," and her "Letters from Ireland" in the summer of that year were written for this paper. As her other works left her hands the connection with the paper became closer, and it was never interrupted except for a few months at the beginning of her last illness, when all her strength was needed for her Autobiography. When she had finished that task she had the work printed, and the engravings prepared for it under her own supervision, partly to avoid delay in its appearance (because any good that it could do would be best done immediately after her death), but chiefly to spare her executors all responsibility about publishing whatever may be found in the Memoir. Her last illness was a time of quiet enjoyment to her, soothed as it was by family and social love, and care, and sympathy, and, except for one heart-grief,—the loss in 1864 of her niece Maria, who was to her as a daughter,—free from anxiety of every kind, and amused by the constant interest of regarding life and its affairs from the verge of the horizon of existence. Her disease was deterioration and enlargement of the heart, the fatal character of which was discovered in January, 1855. She declined throughout that and subsequent years, and died—

—And died in the summer sunset of her home amid the Westmoreland mountains, on the 27th of June, 1876, after twenty-one more diligent, devoted, suffering, joyful years,—by the family friends she most loved, and in possession of all her mental powers up to the last expiring day; aged seventy-four years.[1]

---

[1]   This paragraph was added by Maria Weston Chapman in the *Memorials*.

Appendix C: Contemporary Reviews

[The first "review" of Harriet Martineau's life and work was the self-composed obituary that appeared on June 29, 1876, two days after her death, in the London *Daily News* (see Appendix B). As soon as the *Autobiography* was released in 1877, the full-scale reviews of her career began to appear in the major periodicals, most of them between April and July, 1877. All provided assessments of Martineau's achievement as a writer, but they also debated issues of life writing: Should autobiographers include negative accounts of family life or negative judgments of friends, as Martineau did? Should readers of autobiography expect (and accept) a certain amount of egotism, or should they read skeptically, in effect judging any self-praise as grounds for doubt of the autobiographer's veracity?

The three reviews included here, all written by major Victorian essayists, appeared in periodicals with different political and literary emphases. Margaret Oliphant's review, published anonymously, reveals the politically conservative perspective of *Blackwood's*, firmly Tory at the time of the British Reform Act of 1832 when Martineau aided the cause of reform with her *Illustrations of Political Economy*; it also reveals the bemusement (and perhaps envy) of a younger woman writer at the public acclaim achieved by Martineau in an earlier generation. John Morley, writing for *Macmillan's Magazine*, gives the most literary of the assessments, comparing Martineau's work with that of fellow women writers, such as Charlotte Brontë and George Eliot, and her views on literary life with a wide range of British and European writers, from Jean-Jacques Rousseau to Arthur Schopenhauer; a journalist thirty-five years younger than Martineau, Morley is more generous than Oliphant in his assessment of Martineau's achievement, no doubt because he, like Martineau, underwent a de-conversion and was associated with the English positivists, the disciples of the French sociologist Auguste Comte whose work Martineau translated in the 1850s. William Rathbone Greg, reviewing for *The Nineteenth Century*, knew Martineau well as a neighbor in the Lake District and an associate on the liberal *Westminster Review*; he writes in part to redeem the reputation of Whig friends whom Martineau deprecates in the *Autobiography*, in part to redeem her own reputation as unamiable in harshly criticizing her former literary and political associates. I have included the full reviews, except for long passages of quotation from the *Autobiography*, for which I have provided page numbers in square brackets.]

1. Margaret Oliphant, "Harriet Martineau," *Blackwood's Edinburgh Magazine* 121 (April 1877), 472–96

It is a dangerous thing to have your life written when you are dead and helpless, and can do nothing to protest against the judgment. Either your biographer will be partial, and so load you with panegyric that your wisest acts will look foolish, and the public will be tempted to hate you out of mere human contradictoriness, to break the monotony of praise; or else your biographer will be nobly *im*partial, picking out the holes in your coat, and kindly accounting for and explaining them by the follies of your parents, the wickedness of your family, or your own defective education and moral weakness. These are well-understood and often-practised arts; and it is a proof of the enormous interest we take in the records of humanity that neither pity nor justice interferes to prevent the habitual desecration of the homes and secrets of the dead. But if biography is thus dangerous, there is still more fatal art, more radical in its operation, and infinitely more murderous, against which nothing can defend the predestined victim. This terrible instrument of self-murder is called autobiography; and no kind interpreter, no gentle critic, no effacing tear from any angel of the eternal records, can diminish its damning power. When a stranger hand lifts the curtain which shrouds every individual soul from its neighbours, and often from itself, we can always hope and believe that the revelations it makes may be more or less mistaken, that the stains it exhibits might disappear on closer inspection, and that the victim who is thus judged in his absence might have had much to say for himself had he been present. But these reflections do not help us when it is a self-revelation upon which we look; for nobody can be so thoroughly acquainted with the pettinesses of character, the solemnities of self-importance, the unkind thoughts and harsh judgments which blemish the memory, as he or she whose personal peculiarities are in question. Nor is this all. The right of libeling himself is a right which cannot be taken from any human creature, living or dead; but a posthumous assault on his fellow-creatures is one of the worst and most cowardly, as it is the last sin of which a man is capable. Some dismal examples have been lately given to the world of the enduring rancour which could hoard up the records of past scandal, or the ill-natured gossip of the moment, to secure a far-off vengeance, and inflict wounds and do mischief without any fear of being called upon to answer for the consequences; and it is to be supposed that the cruel cowards who thus take shelter under the very shadow of death, and wing their arrows from behind the shield of the king of terrors, forget that in so doing they execute the most complete and sweeping judgment upon themselves. But it ought to be fully understood and acknowledged that there is no meaner and more unpardonable social crime, especially when the persons thus assailed are picked out from the gentle obscurity of private life, and have neither public record nor well-known history to be brought forth in their favour; and worst of all when the assailant has all the intimacy of family knowledge and that embittered recollection which tenacious memories preserve of petty wrong, to give point to the posthumous vengeance.

These observations have been forced upon us by the two volumes of Autobiography which have just been published under the name of Harriet Martineau. This is not the first portrait of herself which this distinguished writer has given to the world. In the end of last summer, at the time of her death, there appeared in the 'Daily News' a short account of her life, character, and works, which we were informed by an editorial note was from her own hand, and upon which the present writer had begun to found an estimate of Miss Martineau's life and labours, when we were stopped by the announcement that another longer and more detailed autobiography was—not only written, but printed, illustrated, and ready for immediate publication. The fact that a woman had thought it fit and becoming to leave her own account of herself in an editor's drawer for some twenty years, ready for the moment when death might overtake her, was of itself a curious evidence of the high weight she attached to it, and her anxiety to make the world aware of her own deliberate judgment upon her own character. But there was the quaint excuse for this that Miss Martineau had already described and estimated in the same columns of the 'Daily News' a great many important persons in her own generation, and that to her cool judgment and impartial mind it might seem natural that her own portrait should hang in the same gallery—an idea which many an able portrait-painter before her has carried out without any breach of modesty. And there was nothing in the concise biography of the 'Daily News'—which was entirely historical and descriptive, and not even written in the first person—to offend the hearer, who might indeed smile at the serene sense of national importance with which the progress of her life was recorded, but who could scarcely complain of a self-estimate which was on the whole just enough, and claimed for

Harriet Martineau no applause beyond that naturally belonging to talent and industry. The limited space prevented at once all undue detail of self-characterisation, and all that disadvantageous contrast of others with herself, which any extended sketch of society is likely to draw an autobiographer into. Had some kind fairy set fire benevolently to the piles of printed paper so easily disposed of in one stage, so indestructible in another, which have now at last made their way into the world, and are unhappily no longer within the reach of burning, the reputation of Miss Martineau would have settled down into that mellow glow of universal acceptance which lasts longer than more special crowns. We might not have known exactly why it was, but we should no less have acknowledged it as having become her property by possession and prescriptive right—which are better title-deeds than any other, at least in the temples of fame.

It takes a long time to reach to this calm of unquestioned, if not very distinctly understood honour; and Miss Martineau had passed like other people through many clouds and discouragements on the way. There can be no doubt that she was during her life, in the earlier portion of her career, as well abused as most political persons were in that lively and plain-spoken period. The difference between her and most other women who wrote, was, that her topics, even when treated under the disguise of what we must call fiction, we suppose, since her generation enthusiastically accepted it as such—were almost entirely of a political, or at least politico-philosophical, character; and accordingly, the same means then in vogue to bring down political opponents of all kinds, were used freely upon her. These means have fortunately for the moment gone out of fashion, and notwithstanding the recent creation of gossip-newspapers, will, we trust, continue out of fashion. It is no longer a matter of much value in criticism whether an author is deaf and a Unitarian, or orthodox and possessed of ears as keen as his who heard the grass growing. We cannot go the length of saying yet that it is immaterial whether the writer be man or woman, for on this point it must be allowed all critics are fallible, and there is no female writer existing who is not benevolently or contemptuously reminded of her sex, except, indeed, George Eliot, whose supremacy is characteristically acknowledged by the absence of this favourite accusation. In this respect Harriet Martineau fared a little worse than most people did in her day, as uniting in her own person the characteristic reproaches addressed habitually to literary women and those addressed habitually to political opponents. The conjunction produced some sharp and violent talk and many biting gibes; but, on the other hand, it was conjoined with, according to her own showing, a most superlative and extraordinary fame and influence, which ought to have neutralized the evil. Both had long ago dropped—or so at least it seemed to the younger generation—into dimness, if not into peaceable oblivion. Abuse dies early, and fame requires a more solid foundation than that upon which hers was based, to resist the wear and tear even of five-and-twenty years. And when she died, not yet a year ago, most people were ready to recognize in Miss Martineau an eminent person, who had played a considerable part in her time, though it was beginning to be doubtful in what way she had been so eminent. That she had written much on philosophical and political subjects people were vaguely aware; and she had produced one clever book, 'Deerbrook,' and one little story more than clever, the 'Feats on the Fiord,' and had written many good newspaper biographies and other articles. These things were scarcely enough to account for the tradition of fame which hung about her; but most people have been born or at least have grown up, since the time when the Reviews snarled at the young lady who was a Malthusian, and angry politicians fought over her in abuse or in praise; and we were willing to be respectful and friendly to her memory without entering too closely into the foundation of our faith. For our own part, we avow, we were about to discuss her literary work calmly, on that level of honest mediocrity to which it seemed to belong, with no more notion that she was one of the greatest of national reformers and authorities—in a way the saviour of her country, the inspirer of laws and instructor of lawgivers—than we have of the undeveloped capacities for government of the child at our knee. Whether this was mere ignorance on our part, the reader has now full power of judging; and we will try to put the materials as well as we can before him. There is not one only, but two autobiographies to decide by: one, the concise record of the newspapers; the other, the diffusive narrative which fills two octavo volumes—the slow and gradual accumulation of her later years.

We scarcely remember any one who has taken so much trouble to set himself right with the world. No literary person, poet or prose writer, of Miss Martineau's period, has had so much care for his or her reputation; and even of the statesmen, only her favourite aversion, Lord Brougham, has taken any steps in his own person to make us aware what he thought of himself, and what of his contemporaries. The mass of human creatures, small and great, are content to leave themselves with no better appeal to recollection than the pathos of a tombstone, and no surer foundation that their own works, good or bad, at the mercy or to the kindness of their fellows. And this confidence in the justice, on the whole, of human nature, is not undeserved. Posterity, if severe, is often kind; and so, notwithstanding all private spites and enmities, are a man's contemporaries. Even in the private retirement of the poor queen whom he had helped to wrong, there is found a Griffith to do justice to the fallen Wolsey. Death of itself does much by the mere fact of the isolation and separation it brings; and with death comes gentle charity, indulgence, sometimes understanding and sympathy, such as the living were never able to gain.

But all these gentle influences are neutralized, when, almost before the echo of the living voice is over, we are startled by a postscriptal harangue from the tomb. The grave has all the worst qualities of the pulpit, heightened to almost an infinite degree, in so far as the difficulties of reply are increased: for whereas it may be possible to make the occupant of the latter hear reason when he descends from that point of vantage, or at least to let him know our mind on the subject, the inmate of the first is entirely beyond either conviction or compunction—the one irresponsible, unpunishable moral assailant whom neither complaint, nor protest, nor contradiction can touch, and even in whose favour a certain natural human prejudice is always enlisted. There is a natural presumption that what a dying man says must be true, which gives an indescribable sting to posthumous slander. What good could it do *them* to lie? Their vengeance, if not righteous, is too diabolical to be consistent with our tremulous instinctive apprehension of them, as beings passed into a region where only truth can reign, and all subterfuges, and even defects of vision, must be done away with. Even the most heedless deathbed utterance takes a certain sacredness—and a letter from a dead hand becomes a supplementary testament, holy and binding to all persons of deep feeling. Posthumous books, however, it must be said, have not done much to keep up this good character of the dead. The sense of immunity from all reprisals—the knowledge that all ordinary bonds of affection, of gratitude, of courtesy, are, as it were, abrogated for the benefit of the writer, who can smile in anticipation at the tumult he will cause, while sure of never being brought to book for what he has said, never called upon to substantiate any accusation or account for any spiteful saying—seems often to inspire a malign pleasure; and it is even possible that a distorted sense of the advantages of making known "the truth" may obscure the eyes, to all the baseness of confidence betrayed and injured reputation. That this should be the case even in respect to the home, doubly screened by the obscurity of private life and the lapse of time from public knowledge, which a writer may enhance his own character by traducing and exposing, is a wonderful and horrible thought; yet we suppose it is not without precedent. Often enough the experiences of life steal from us our primitive belief in the authorities which were infallible to our early years; and the best of sons and daughters must often perceive the defects of their own education, even the mistakes made in their training—the little injustices and petty wrongs of the nursery, the hasty judgment, or perhaps too great severity, of father or mother—and by perceiving imply a gentle censure. Nothing can be more common than to record our tacit disapproval of the principles on which we were ourselves brought up, by a total change of system in respect to our children—to be by them reversed again in their day, in all probability, in proof of the fact that no human systems are infallible. But this natural sentiment may exist along with the most tender piety and loyalty to the home, which, at its least, is more to us, and at its worst, better than any strange place. When it leads to the desecration of that home, and the holding up of the chief figure in it to deliberate blame and insult, what can any one say? The writer who does this in the safety of declining years, going back over half a century to impress upon our minds an unfavourable estimate of her mother, revolts us by the very key-note thus struck with determined iteration, as the first thing to be insisted upon in the account of her life. That this could be no fault of accident or inadvertence is clearly apparent by the importance which Miss Martineau attached to her autobiography. "From my youth upward," she says, "I have felt that it was one of the duties of my life to write my autobiography:" and she adds, "for thirteen or fourteen years it has been more or less a weight on my mind that the thing was not done." It was thus with the determination of setting herself right in every respect from her childhood up, that this book was written; and the writer brooded over it for the last twenty years of her life; there can be little doubt, in such a case, that everything said was fully meant.

The tone of the autobiography is all the more remarkable in this respect, from the moderation and good sense of the biographies published by Miss Martineau in her lifetime, and concluding with the article upon herself, which, written in 1855, was published only six months ago. In these sketches there is a prevailing sobriety and justice, and absence of rancour even in respect to those whom she might reasonably have considered her enemies, which is worthy of all praise, and which is admirably carried out in the curiously honest self-estimate which concludes them. All is straightforward, moderate, modest, and sensible in those brief histories, spoken as it were face to face with her audience in the light of day. But the very atmosphere is changed when we get to the detailed and elaborate narrative written in her seclusion, in her weakness, when the clouds were already shadowing over her, and which was not intended to be made public until she had, as she believed, entirely ceased and been made an end of, at once and for ever.

The first scene brings before us the morbid sense of wrong and unreal misery of a child *incomprise*[1]—an unhappy little being, to whom every rebuff was tragical, and who feels herself to have been bitterly oppressed by the "taking down" system, the hardness of her parents, the gibes of elder brothers and sisters. "My temper might have been made a thoroughly good one," she says, "by the slightest regard shown to my natural affections, and any rational dealing with my faults; but I was almost the youngest of a large family, and subject not only to the rule of severity to which all were liable, but also to the rough and contemptuous treatment of the elder children, who meant no harm, but injured me irreparably." "Justice was precisely what was least understood in our house," she goes on to say. "The duties preached were those of inferiors to superiors; while the *per contra* was not insisted upon with any equality of treatment at all. Parents were to bring up their children 'in the nurture and admonition of the Lord,' and to pay servants due wages; but not a word was ever preached about the justice due from the stronger to the weaker. I used to thirst to hear some notice of the oppression which servants and children had (as I supposed universally) to endure in respect to their feelings, while duly clothed, fed, and taught." "One of my chief miseries," she continues, "was being sent with insulting messages to the maids—*e.g.*, to bid them not to be so like cart-horses overhead, and the like. On the one hand, it was a fearful sin to alter a message; and on the other, it was impossible to give such a one as that." These were the kind of distresses which made her "usually very unhappy," often planning suicide, never passing a day without crying. Miss Martineau's imagination, however, was not lively enough to make her aware that imaginative children are full of such wretchedness, even without any particular sin on the part of their fathers and mothers. Here is rather a horrible picture—yet not so horrible as it looks—of the little, lonely, miserable creature, who was not so much petted and taken notice of as she believed her merits to require:—

---

[1]   Misunderstood (French).

"Now and then I desperately poured forth my complaints; but, in general, I brooded over my injuries, and those of others who dared not speak, and then the temptation to suicide was very strong. No doubt there was much vindictiveness in it. I gloated over the thought that I would make somebody care about me in some sort of way at last; and as to my reception in the other world, I felt sure that God would not be very angry with me for making haste to Him when nobody else cared for me, and so many people plagued me."

This sounds very serious and terrible as reported by a mature woman with great gravity fifty years or so after; but which of us does not remember that half-wretched, half-delightful sense of injury, and the tragic innocent idea of "making somebody care about me in some sort of way at last"—rousing the whole house into excitement and anxiety about that one small, at present much misunderstood and unconsidered member of it, whom then *they* would finally discover to have been, not a naughty child, but a great hero or heroine, and for whom everybody would weep ever after with remorse and passion? What a constriction of delicious anguish would come into our inno-cent bosom, what a sob of satisfaction move our throat, at thought of the flowers to be put on our grave, and the everlasting first place to be accorded to us ever after! That Miss Martineau should have made the curious mistake of supposing this mood, so common to the fanciful child, to have belonged to herself alone—to have been caused by the injustice or cruelty of her family—and to have been worthy of solemn note so long after, and still more solemn, not to say bitter censure of her nearest relations,—is a curious token of the limitation and ungra-ciousness of her imagination. Most of us, after we are full-grown, laugh at the tragical little humbug with its innocent complacence and profound unconscious self-importance, which was ourself. It must be added, that whenever the picture expands a little, and we are permit-ted to see the homely house in Norwich in which this child brooded and felt herself misunderstood, these good Martineaus seem very kindly sort of people, caressing their sulky little Harriet out of her troubles, and taking her complaints of their partiality with much greater patience than many parents would have done. They "exercised every kind of self-denial to bring us up qualified to take care of ourselves," their daughter admits; "they pinched themselves in luxu-ries to provide their girls as well as their boys with masters and school-ing;" and they gave to both a thoroughly good education, training the girls not only in the old-fashioned way of domestic usefulness, but with a classic foundation of Latin for their English,—a plan which is supposed to be an innovation of the present day, but is in reality as old as English society in its best development. This being the case, the persistent attack made upon these good parents, especially the mother, which is carried on into the more serious records of maturer life, is especially painful. "To one person I was habitually untruthful from fear," says this unkind and thankless child. "To my mother I would in my childhood assert or deny anything that would bring me through most easily.... When I left home all temptation to untruth ceased." A more cruel accusation against a person unable to defend herself could not be. "I knew thee that thou wert an austere man, ... therefore I was afraid." The reader is not apt to sympathise in this case with the ungenerous churl who makes the statement, but with the master whose higher purpose is thus balked. A page or two further on Miss Martineau allows herself to have been "deeply and effectually moved by my mother's consideration for my feelings;" but this does not operate upon her mind in the way of altering the cruel and persistent indictment. Many years later, after an appearance of the kindest union and sympathy between the mother and grown-up daughter, when Mrs Martineau joined Harriet in London, the old opposition comes out under a new form, and we are given to understand that the mother was jealous of her child's eminence. "To pass it over as lightly as possible," says Miss Martineau, "my mother, who loved power and had always been in the habit of exercising it, was hurt at confidence reposed in me, and distinctions shown, and visits paid to me; and I, with every desire to be passive, and being in fact wholly passive in the matter, was kept in a state of constant agitation at the influx of distinctions which I never sought, and which it was impossible to impart." If this were true to the strictest letter, it would not in the least diminish the offence against good taste, as well as against all family loyalty and the needful and graceful restraints of private life, which every right-thinking person must find in it. Nor is this all; the autobiographer has done a still greater wrong by leaving such a suggestion to the vulgar hand of her American editress, who pounces upon so delightful a piece of personality, and adds her own rude daub of the domineering mother, to add effect to the ludicrous picture of the great authoress, with which she has favoured the reader. Perhaps Mrs Chapman may be allowed to be revenge enough for Mrs Martineau. For our serious judgment upon a woman who, for good or evil, certainly occupied a large place in the public estimation, evaporates in disgust or laughter, when we come to the *résumé*[1] of the third volume, in which Miss Martineau's chosen literary executrix exerts all her powers, with the finest effect, to make Miss Martineau absurd. But what can be thought of the daughter who leaves it within the power of so foolish a commentator as Mrs Chapman to insult and outrage the memory of her own mother? It is time that the abominable practice of magnifying notable persons by abuse of all their nearest relations should be treated as it deserves. We can forgive Miss Martineau many chapters in her life which evoked public criticism, sooner than we can forgive her this unfavourable representation and exposure of her home. But Mrs Chapman is poetic justice embodied; and if unkindness to one's mother were always to be punished by judicial blindness in the choice of one's representative, as in the present case, we cannot but allow that all the ends of justice would be attained.

There are features, however, in the gloomy, ill-tempered, and self-absorbed girl, which soften the heart of the reader towards her. Her adoration of the children who come after her in the household, atones for her jealousy and doubt of those who came before. When she pinches "James's pink toes" to wake him, and drags the baby out of his crib to show to him that early glory of the summer morning when all the world is asleep, which is so entrancing to a child; and finds "a new life" in her little sister, the darkness seems to clear away from the hitherto morbid picture. "When I first saw her, it was as she was lifted out of her crib at a fortnight old, asleep, to be shown to my late hostess who had brought Rachel and me home. The passionate fondness I felt for her from that moment has been unlike anything else I have felt in life—though I have made idols of not a few nephews and nieces," she tells us, looking back, after "our close friendship of forty years," with affection undiminished. "When I am among little children, it frightens me to think what my idolatry of my own children would have been," she says, suddenly, with startling vehemence and the simplicity of real feeling, notwithstanding that she was a supporter of Mr Malthus, and got into trouble enough afterwards on that account. These words soften our idea of the woman who, being a born lecturer and politician, was less distinctively affected by sex than perhaps any other, male or female, of her generation. Yet she adored babies, and loved needlework,—than which no two tastes can be

---

[1]   Recapitulation (French). Maria Chapman, the editor, reviewed Martineau's life chronologically in a third volume of "Memorials," repeating and amplifying its history with further documents.

more feminine. And it would perhaps be difficult to overestimate the external disadvantages of a plain girl, without any apparent attractiveness, growing deaf, and conscious of no special power to please. "She was grave, and laughed more rarely than any young person I ever knew," says a school friend, describing her as she appeared at sixteen. "Her face was plain, and (you will scarcely believe it) she had no light in the countenance, no expression, to redeem the features. Her low brow and rather large under lip increased the effect of her natural seriousness of look, and did her much injustice. I used to be asked occasionally, 'What has offended Harriet?' I, who understood her, used to answer, 'Nothing: she is not offended; it is only her look.'" Miss Martineau herself adds, "When I left Bristol I was as pale as a ghost, and as thin as possible, and still very frowning and repulsive-looking." This fact is not without interest as affecting both her character and habits of thought. The prejudices of life and of literature are, no doubt, in favour of pretty persons; but the effect upon the mind of this consciousness of the absence of beauty is worth consideration too.

Miss Martineau had the great fundamental misfortune of being brought up a Unitarian. By nature and circumstance religion was her great refuge at this period of her life, the only thing which could give her any effectual support amid all the discouragements of her gloomy temper, and sense of cruelty and injustice surrounding her; but she was too clear-headed not to be early awakened to the absence of any mystic sanction or inherent sacredness in what she was trained to believe. The logical mistake common to her sect of "appropriating all the Christian promises without troubling themselves with the clearly specified condition of faith in Christ as a Redeemer," became, she tells us, very soon clear to her. Of the mode of argument commonly used by her early teachers she gives the following striking example: "One evening," she says, "I was in the parlour, when our Unitarian minister, Mr Madge, was convicting of error (and what he called idiotcy) an orthodox schoolmaster. 'Look here,' said Mr Madge, seizing three wineglasses and placing them in a row; 'here is the Father, here the Son, and here the Holy Ghost. Do you mean to tell me that these three glasses can in any case be one? 'Tis mere nonsense.' And so were we children taught that it was mere nonsense." Another point upon which she remarks is "the practice, necessarily universal among Unitarians, of taking any liberties they please with the revelation they profess to receive." This opened the doors to all after-changes; but at first, in her imperfect and unhappy youth, religion was everything to her. It was her refuge from herself and all the evils round her. She took notes of sermons, and attended Bible classes, and studied Scriptural illustrations, and Eastern life, like the most pious of evangelical maidens. She made herself a little paper book, in which she wrote down "Scripture instructions under the heads of the virtues and vices, to have encouragement or rebuke always ready at hand, while she was still a child;" and when her mind turned to authorship, it was entirely in the religious vein. There is a pretty account of her first publication, which, by way of bringing the reader once more into charity with the sulky, deafish, ugly girl, all throbbing with pains and dormant capabilities, we may quote here. The idol of her youth was her younger brother James, between whom and herself there was destined to be a great gulf afterwards, but to whom in her young days she was devoted with all a sister's adoring faith and admiration. His return to college after the vacation made Harriet miserable; and to console herself she began to write, as he had advised. The subject she chose was an odd one, yet quite likely to take the fancy of a girl brought up in a little Dissenting community. It was, "Female writers on practical divinity." Half alarmed, half contemptuous of herself as attempting something much too great for her, she sent this production to the 'Monthly Repository,' a little Unitarian magazine, the organ of the sect. The next number was sent in "before service-time on a Sunday morning."

"My heart may have been beating when I laid hands on it; but it thumped prodigiously when I saw my article there, and in the notices to correspondents a request to hear more from V. of Norwich. There is certainly something entirely peculiar in the sensation of seeing one's self in print for the first time—the lines burn themselves in upon the brain in a way of which black ink is incapable in any other mode. So I felt that day when I went about with my secret. I have said what my eldest brother was to us, in what reverence we held him. He was just married, and he and his bride asked me to return from chapel with them to tea. After tea he said, 'Come now, we have had plenty of talk; I will read you something'; and he held out his hand for the new 'Repository.' After glancing at it, he exclaimed, 'They have got a new hand here. Listen.' After a paragraph, he repeated, 'Ah! this is a new hand; they have had nothing so good as this for a long while.' (It would be impossible to convey to any who do not know the 'Monthly Repository' of that day how very small a compliment this was.) I was silent, of course. At the end of the first column he exclaimed about the style, looking at me in some wonder at my being as still as a mouse. Next (and well I remember his tone and thrill to it still) his words were—'What a fine sentence that is! Why, do you not think so?' I mumbled out sillily enough that it did not seem anything particular. 'Then' said he, 'you were not listening; I will read it again. There now!' As he still got nothing out of me, he turned round upon me, as we sat side by side on the sofa, with 'Harriet, what is the matter with you? I never knew you so slow to praise anything before.' I replied, in utter confusion, 'I never could baffle anybody. The truth is, that paper is mine.' He made no reply; read on in silence, and spoke no more till I was on my feet to go away. He then laid his hand on my shoulder and said gravely (calling me 'dear' for the first time), 'Now, dear, leave it to other women to make shirts and darn stockings; and do you devote yourself to this.' I went home in a sort of dream, so that the squares of the pavement seemed to float before my eyes."

This is a pretty story enough, with the pleasant atmosphere of family life in it. After this she wrote a volume of 'Devotional Exercises,' not a kind of composition in which a mind like hers might be supposed likely to excel; and then came to a pause apparently, being overtaken by that rush of life which now and then swells the calm tide of family affairs. Misfortune came, and death. Her elder brother above referred to went to Madeira to die; and there is a touching page about his departure—the manner in which the newly-born baby kept up a kind of forlorn courage in the household which was parting with the child's father for ever. "I was the last who held the dear baby, even to the moment of his being put into the carriage," she says; and the child, too, never came back. Then the elder Mr Martineau, Harriet's father, died, leaving them in reduced circumstances; and then, crown of all the sufferings thus crushed into one brief space, her betrothed lover "became suddenly insane, and after months of illness of body and mind, died." So briefly is the incident, to which we are apt to give the chief place in early life, recorded; and it can scarcely be supposed that there was any very profound feeling involved, at least on the lady's side. "I dared not refuse, because I saw it would be his death-blow," she says. "I have never since been tempted, nor have suffered anything at all in relation to that matter which is held to be all-important to women—love and marriage—nothing, I mean, beyond occasional annoyances, presently disposed of. Every literary woman, no doubt, has plenty of importunity of that sort to deal with." This last sentence will perplex the general mind, which has not, we fear, come to look upon literature, at least on the woman's side, as a great inducement to matrimony. But, of course, Miss Martineau ought to know.

The romance of life being thus summarily disposed of, the heroic period soon ensues. Mr Martineau had suffered greatly in the commercial crisis of 1826; and his daughters were, contrary to his hopes, left dependent upon their own exertions. The natural resource of teaching, or even of needlework, was thought of instantly; and one of them at least seems to have taken up the former universal trade. Harriet's occupation seemed plain enough before her; but some objections very naturally raised by her mother against her going to London alone, under the idea that literature could only be profitably pursued there, are represented by Miss Martineau herself as tyrannical interference, and construed by Mrs Chapman into a decision "that her daughter's hopes of a literary career should be crushed." The next enterprise in which we find her engaged, is probably the most strange that ever occupied a person of talent or commenced a considerable career. The Unitarian body, not generally much given to proselytising, suddenly offered prizes for three essays "by which Unitarianism was to be presented to the notice of Catholics, Jews, and Mahommedans." It seems almost impossible to think of any scheme so solemnly grotesque issuing from a sect so calm, genteel, and cultivated; but such was the case. "The prizes were ten guineas for the Catholic, fifteen for the Jewish, and twenty for the Mahommedan essay;" the value rising in proportion to the difficulty of the work. Harriet competed for all three, and won them in succession one after the other. In one of her letters to her mother she gives an account of a meeting, the May meeting of the Unitarian body, in which the quaint excitement of the little community all aglow with its fit of missionary energy is made curiously apparent. A certain Rammohun Roy, a Hindoo convert, shared the honours of this assembly with Miss Harriet Martineau of Norwich; and she writes of him with all the gentle enthusiasm appropriate to the time and occasion. "His upward look, the meek expression of his countenance, his majestic bending figure, and the peculiarities of his costume and complexion, made it such a picture as I shall never again behold." All this is amusing enough when we think of the after life and work of this young lady, modestly hearing her own distinctions celebrated, in the midst of her sect. Another convert, a Catholic priest, who had "nobly renounced his office and avowed himself a Unitarian," though he had only five pounds in the world, fills her with equal enthusiasm. This outburst of zeal, however, was the last. "I had already ceased to be a Unitarian in the technical sense," she tells us, though she was their chosen expositor. If the essays were published, we are not informed; but Miss Martineau herself does not hesitate to say, that "if either Mahommedans or Jews have ever been converted by them, such converts can hardly be rational enough to be worth having." Altogether this is as amusing a chapter as could be imagined, and rather more unlike nature than any one could venture to imagine in the history of so sober a sect.

Miss Martineau was now on the verge of her great effort. A year or two before the period of the missionary essays, Mrs Marcet's 'Conversations on Political Economy' had fallen into her hands. This set her brain working, and she immediately determined to embody the principles of the science which formally she was little acquainted with, yet which already gave their favourite direction to her thoughts, in a series of stories. "I mentioned my notion," she tells us, "when we were sitting at work one bright afternoon at home. Brother James nodded assent; my mother said, 'Do it;' and we went to tea unconscious what a great thing we had done since dinner." This is the first intimation we have of "the great thing" which Mrs Chapman announces in a much more splendid manner. England was in a very bad way at this time, the American lady tells us. "The condition of the country was terrible to think of. There were twenty-five millions of people shut up to starve in the small area of the British Isles, exhausted by war, and taxed to the war point.... They were dying for want of bread, while hindered alike from producing and importing grain, as well as from going to live where it grew." (We were not aware that there had been any laws against emigration, or against the production of grain in England; but that was our ignorance, no doubt.) "Men in power saw no cure but in killing," Mrs Chapman adds. "The hangman had a fearful work to do." The gallows and the bayonet were the chief weapons of Government; Government itself was considered a curse; and all the departments were at their wits' end. "In such a crisis it was," says our instructor, "that Harriet Martineau set herself to consider the Crisis." The country was perishing visibly before the eyes of a much-interested world; when lo! on that bright afternoon, over the needlework, brother James nodded assent, the mother said "Do it," and before the tea was poured out England's salvation was secured, and the great thing as good as done.

This was in the year 1831. It would require more labour than the subject is worthy of to go back upon the daily records of the time, and ascertain beyond question, as no doubt might be done, the real effect of the little books which were the produce of the "great" plan thus made up; but it is very wonderful and incredible that they should have had the results recorded here. They have fallen out of knowledge altogether by this time, and are to the present generation as if they had never existed. To ourselves, we confess, they read now like Sunday school stories twisted aside out of the religious channel, and made to teach political instead of spiritual doctrine. They are framed on the broadest elementary principles, as simple as Hogarth's Idle Apprentice—the good people doing well, and the naughty people doing badly—and life reduced to a geometrical diagram, the easiest and most commonplace affair in the world. We can remember nothing that is even objectionable in the simple-minded but rigidly-constructed tale, which is supposed to have set all England by the ears on the Malthusian question. If England was set by the ears so easily, and excited out of her propriety by such simple means, how much stronger in digestion, and more tranquil in temper, must England have become since then. We read with amazement of the commotion of society—the agitation in the highest circles—the statesmen who crowded to Harriet's humble lodging to ask her advice and adopt her suggestions, as well as to request her support. Could all this be true, we ask ourselves with amazement? And it is not to be believed that it was other than true, more or less. Miss Martineau might unconsciously exaggerate—she might unawares add a little, as is natural enough, to the glory of her own success. She might take in solemn earnest a question asked half in joke, half in compliment; but she could not altogether deceive herself on the broader question: and the fact is evident that she did gain for herself an important, and indeed exceptional, position in society—a position more distinct and certain than the best that is attained by writers much surpassing her in genius—all on account of these little Sunday-school stories. The only explanation of this astonishing fact that we can attain to is, that they suited, or were supposed to suit, a want of the time. Didactic fiction seldom recommends itself to educated readers, but it is almost always popular with the simple-minded; and these tales were a kind of "reading made easy" of that social science which had begun to take hold upon the popular mind, and to claim an occult power of controlling the tides of human action, though nobody quite knew how. To tell the why and wherefore, to show that non-producers were useless in the early stages of society, and not much good at any time; that industry and thrift were the most potent of all forces in the regulation of family affairs, but that even prosperity would not tempt any one to overestimate the hopes of the future; that machinery was not evil, but the destruction of it a great one; —all these cut-and-dry lessons were, it is to be supposed, desired by the public in a portable and easily-managed form. We confess that this is to ourselves a weak and lame explanation of so great a success; but we have no other to offer: and though much higher pretensions are set forth in the Autobiography now in our hands, the account given in the smaller autobiography of the 'Daily News,' which is so much more sensible and dignified than the expanded record, is entirely in agreement with our view. "The original idea of exhibiting the great natural laws of society by a series of pictures of selected social action," says Miss Martineau, "was a fortunate one; and her tales initiated a multitude of minds into the conception of what political economy is, and of how it concerns everybody living in society. Beyond this, there is no merit of a high order in the work."

This is simply true, and it says much for the judgment and excellent sense of the author, as well as for her candour and humility, that she shows herself so well able to estimate her own work at its right value. So discriminating and modest a statement, indeed, might well neutralise the more vaporous assertions of the present volumes, which are neither so modest nor so sensible. The Political Economy Tales went on for about two years; and though the interest has gone out of them, the struggles of the young author, unknown and unfriended as she was, with nothing to help her but her own stout heart, and unfailing resolution, and confidence in her project, form a chapter in literature much more interesting than a dozen mediocre stories like Ella of Garveloch. From the time when the "great thing was done" between dinner and tea, the mind of Harriet Martineau had been possessed by it. If the story is told with a certain solemnity, and the project announced as if no such serious enterprise had ever occurred to any one before, it must be recollected that in most undertakings of the kind the author is insensibly led into his work, and is not called upon to invent at once the work, and the need for it, and the means of publication altogether, which was the case in this. A series of magazine articles, or the successive numbers of a serial story, involve perhaps as much risk, at least of a literary kind, and quite as much labour, as the undertaking of Miss Martineau; but no one thinks of leaping suddenly upon an unprepared public in the monthly numbers which only the most popular of authors, even in our own days, dare venture upon. And here was a young woman quite unknown who insisted upon trying it. No wonder that London publishers shrank and trembled at the bold suggestion, and she herself felt through and through the gravity and risk of the undertaking. "I was resolved that the thing should be done. The people wanted the book, and they should have it. I staked my all upon this project. I strengthened myself in certain resolutions, from which I promised myself no power on earth should draw me away." This is how she speaks of her beginning. And publisher after publisher declined the risk. If England was not quite, as according to Mrs Chapman, on the eve of destruction, and waiting for her saviour, yet men's minds were very much occupied by the Reform Bill and cholera, two great subjects of popular commotion, and nobody seemed to have any leisure for Miss Martineau. She wrote to one after another, "stifled my sighs, swallowed my tears," and persevered with indomitable resolution. At last Mr Fox, the editor of that little Unitarian Monthly Repository, to which Harriet had given a great deal of unre-munerated work, suggested a possibility of publication; and the eager young woman, getting with some difficulty her mother's consent to her sudden journey to London, started by the early coach to look after it. She had fortunately a home to go to in the house of a cousin, "a great Brewery house;" and here arriving suddenly, she found the family on the eve of a temporary absence, but was almost relieved to find herself alone for the last struggle.

"My first step on Monday was seeing the publisher mentioned by Mr Fox. He shook his head.... I need not detail, even if I could remember, the many applications I made in the next few days. Suffice it that they were all unsuccessful, and for the same alleged reasons. Day after day I came home weary with disappointment, and with trudging many miles through the clay of the streets, and through the fog of the gloomi-est December I ever saw. I came home only to work, for I must be ready with two first numbers, in case of a publisher turning up any day. All the while, too, I was as determined as ever that my scheme should be fulfilled. Night after night the brewery clock struck twelve while the pen was still pushing on in my trembling hand. I had promised to take one day's rest, and dine and sleep at the Foxes'. Then, for the first time I gave way, in spite of all my efforts. Some trifle having touched my feel-ings before saying good-night, the sluices burst open, and I cried all night. In the morning Mr Fox looked at me with great concern, stepped into the next room, and brought a folded paper to the breakfast-table, saying, 'Don't read this now. I can't bear it. These are what may be called terms from my brother' (a young bookseller who did not pretend to have any business at that time). 'I do not ask you even to consider them; but they will enable you to tell publishers that you hold in your hand terms offered by a publisher, and this may at least procure attention to your scheme.' These were, to the subsequent regret of half a score of publishers, the terms on which my book was issued at last."

These terms, however, proved most unsatisfactory, requiring a subscription, which was very disagreeable to the author, and exacting many other conditions painful to her; but finally she had to yield, nothing else being practicable. Here is the conclusion of the struggle: —

"I set out to walk the four miles and a half to the brewery. I could not afford to ride, more or less; but, weary already, I now felt almost too ill to walk at all. On the road, not far from Shoreditch, I became too giddy to stand without support; and I leaned over some dirty palings, pretending to look at a cabbage-bed, but saying to myself, as I stood with closed eyes, 'My book will do yet.' I moved on as soon as I could, apprehending that the passers-by took me to be drunk; but the pavement swam before my eyes, so that I was glad to get to the Brewery. I tried to eat some dinner; but the vast rooms, the plate, and the liveried servant, were too touching a contrast to my present condition, and I was glad to go to work to drown my disappointment in a flow of ideas. Perhaps the piece of work that I did may show that I succeeded. I wrote the preface to my 'Illustrations of Political Economy' that evening; and I hardly think that any one would discover from it that I had that day sunk to the lowest point of discouragement about my scheme. At eleven o'clock I sent the servants to bed. I finished the preface just after the brewery clock had struck two. I was chilly and hungry: the lamp burned low and the fire was small. I knew it would not do to go to bed to dream over again the bitter disappointment of the morning. I began now, at last, to doubt whether my work would ever see the light. I thought of the multitudes who needed it—and especially of the poor—to assist them in managing their own welfare. I thought, too, of my own conscious power of doing this very thing. Here was the thing wanting to be done, and I wanting to do it; and the one person who had seemed best to understand the whole affair, now urged me to give up either the whole scheme, or, what was worse, its main principle! It was an inferior consideration, but still no small matter to me, that I had no hope or prospect of usefulness or independence if this project failed; and I did not feel that night I could put my heart into any that might arise. As the fire crumbled, I put it together till nothing but dust and ashes remained; and when the lamp went out I lighted the chamber candle: but at last it was necessary to go to bed; and at four o'clock I went, after crying for two hours with my feet on the fender. I cried in bed till six, when I fell asleep; but I was at the breakfast-table by half-past eight, and ready for the work of the day."

There is nothing in all the stories which, in the twinkling of an eye, made this stout-hearted young woman a prosperous and popular writer, which is half so interesting as this plain but touching narrative.

The first edition consisted of fifteen hundred copies; and came into the world gloomily, only some three hundred being subscribed. The publisher wrote "always gloomily, sometimes rudely," with the parcel of proofs, which arrived weekly (there was no penny post in those days), and the prospects were discouraging enough.

"To the best of my recollection I waited ten days from the day of publication before I had another line from the publisher. My mother, judging from his ill-humour, inferred that he had good news to tell; whereas I supposed the contrary. My mother was right; and I could now be amused at his last attempts to be discouraging in the midst of splendid success. At the end of these ten days he sent with his letter a copy of my first number, desiring me to make with all speed any corrections I might wish to make, as he had scarcely any copies left. He added that the demand led him to propose that we should now print two thousand. A postscript informed me that since he wrote the above he had found we should want three thousand. A second postscript proposed four thousand, and a third five thousand. The letter was worth having, now it had come. There was immense relief in this; but I remember nothing like intoxication—like any painful reaction whatever. I remember walking up and down the grass-plot in the garden (I think it was on the 10th of February) feeling that my cares were over. And so they were. From that hour I have never had any other anxiety about employment than what to choose, nor any real care about money.... The entire periodical press—daily, weekly, and as soon as possible, monthly—came out in my favour, and I was overwhelmed with newspapers and letters containing every sort of flattery. The Diffusion Society wanted to have the series now; and Mr Hume offered, on behalf of a new Society of which he was the head, any price I would name for the purchase of the whole. I cannot precisely answer for the date of these and other applications, the meanest of which I should have clutched at a few weeks before. Members of Parliament sent down Blue-books through the post-office, to the astonishment of the postmaster, who one day sent word that I must send for my own share of the mail, for it could not be carried without a barrow—an announcement which, spreading in the town, caused me to he stared at in the streets. Thus began that sort of experience. Half the hobbies of the House of Commons, and numberless notions of individuals, anonymous and other, were commended to me for treatment in my series, with which some of them had no more to do than geometry or the atomic theory."

The success thus attained necessitated the removal to London, which Miss Martineau had so long desired, and which for the time she seems to have supposed imperative for her work, though she afterwards found that even the career of a journalist might be well enough followed out in the depths of Westmoreland. However, to London she went, living for nearly a year alone in lodgings, a young woman of thirty, with her ear-trumpet, shy, grave, and indomitable, in all the simplicity of a lodging in Conduit Street, up two pair of stairs. "I became the fashion," she says, "and I might have been the lion of several seasons if I had chosen to permit it." As it was, she entered a great deal into society; and her account of the manner in which she was oppressed by invitations and admiring friends, specially as described in the article on 'Literary Lionism,' which is reprinted in the appendix, will be amusing and amazing to many quiet literary persons of the present day, who know that the world is very willing to let authors follow their occupation in as much obscurity as if they were carpenters or ploughmen. Great fortune, however, came to the young lady from Norwich, who naturally, finding that everybody round proclaimed and celebrated the importance of her work, did so too, as it would have been very singular if she had not. The amount of the labour involved she speaks of as enormous—so great as to keep her always aware "of the strong probability that my life would end as the lives of hard literary workers usually end in paralysis, with months or years of imbecility;" but she adds, with a calm complacence of self-esteem, mingled with the conscious rectitude of duty, "I could not have written a volume the less if I had foreknown that, at a certain future day and hour, I should be struck down like Scott and Southey." Happily the little stories illustrative of Political Economy did not quite represent the same strain of misfortune and heroic toil as filled the last years of Sir Walter, and made them tragical; and many a "hard literary worker" will smile at these tremendous prognostications. Somebody informed her that "no author or authoress was free from the habit of taking some pernicious stimulant—either strong green tea or strong coffee at night, or wine, or spirits, or laudanum. The amount of opium taken to relieve the wear and tear of authorship was, he said, greater than most people had any conception of—and *all* literary workers took something." With such an assurance (how completely unfounded it is not necessary to say), Miss Martineau contrasts her own stimulants of "fresh air and cold water" with much satisfaction; but informs us that a physician advised her to keep, like Mrs Gamp, a bottle on the chimney-piece, to which she might put her lips when necessary. The refreshment was to be hock, indeed, instead of the stronger cordial which kept Mrs Gamp comfortable.

All these snares, however, Harriet successfully resisted. Never was such a busy or such a courted woman. Society besieged her on every side. Some fine person or other sent a carriage for her to take her out to dinner, and to a party or two afterwards, every evening. Great and small contended for the honour of breathing a word into the flexible tube of her ear-trumpet, though this was a process which made even statesmen nervous. She sat for five portraits in the year and half before she went to America. Great and small asked her advice in matters both private and public. Her correspondence "threatened to become infinite." And while all this was going on to exalt her to the skies, the powers of darkness were moved on the other hand to crush this prophetess, whose beneficent work was throwing too much light upon the strongholds of ignorance. Messrs Croker and Lockhart put their heads together to crush her in the 'Quarterly Review,' the latter gentleman, we are told, having vowed to "destroy Miss Martineau." All these great things are as completely over and gone as if they had happened in the ninth instead of the nineteenth century. We receive the narrative, both of the glory and the opposition, with a certain respectful awe, yet with a sigh of envy. Nobody nowadays mobs the professors of literature when they take their walks abroad, follows them reverentially, listens to them humbly, takes their portraits. We are not subject to be conspired against by one great Review, and defended by the other. Society does not echo with our names. We are permitted to live just as we like, and nobody minds. What a falling off is here! and why were we not born in those better days? The climax of all this fame and splendour is in the following extraordinary story, which we cannot but accept as somehow or other true, since Miss Martineau says it, though almost too wonderful to be believed. She was about publishing those of her Tales which were intended as "Illustrations of Taxation."

"Just at this time Mr Drummond called upon me with a private message from Lords Grey and Althorp, to ask whether it would suit my purpose to treat of tithes at once instead of later, the reason for such inquiry being quite at my service. As the principles of taxation involve no inexorable order like those of political economy at large, I had no objection to take any topic first which might be most useful. When I had said so, Mr Drummond explained that a tithe measure was prepared by the Cabinet, which Ministers would like to have introduced to the people by my number on the subject before they themselves introduced it into Parliament. Of course this proceeded on the supposition that the measure would be approved by me. Mr Drummond said he would bring the document on my promising that no eye but my own should see it, and that I would not speak of the affair till it was settled; and especially not to any member of any of the Royal Commissions, then so fashionable. It was a thing unheard of, Mr Drummond said, to commit any Cabinet measure to the knowledge of anybody out of the Cabinet before it was offered to Parliament. Finally, the secretary intimated that Lord Althorp *would be obliged by any suggestion in regard to the principles and methods of taxation.*

"Mr Drummond had not been gone five minutes before the chairman of the Excise Commission called to ask in the name of the Commissioners whether it would suit my purpose to write immediately on the excise, offering on the part of Lord Congleton (then Sir Henry Parnell) and others to supply me with the most extraordinary materials, by my exhibition of which the people might be enlightened and prepared on the subject before it should be brought forward in Parliament. The chairman, Mr Henry Wickham, required a promise that no eye but my own should see the evidence; and that the secret should be kept with especial care from the Chancellor of the Exchequer and his secretary, as it was a thing unheard of that any party unconcerned should be made acquainted with this evidence before it reached the Chancellor of the Exchequer. I could hardly help laughing in his face, and wondered what would have happened if he and Mr Drummond had met on the steps, as they very nearly did. Of course I was glad of the information offered, but I took leave to make my own choice among the materials lent."

Thus two departments of the imperial government appealed to Miss Martineau's aid and counsel on the same day, for the highest purposes of legislation. Such a story was probably never told before, or such an honour paid to a purely literary person, not to say a woman. But whether it is most wonderful as a tribute to her unrivalled powers, or the strangest demonstration of the legislative weakness and confusion of mind, we could not venture to pronounce. In either case, a more startling incident could not be.

We may conclude the splendid period of Miss Martineau's life with this incomparable honour. If Lord Althorp's political adversaries twitted him afterwards with acting on the advice "of a young lady in Fludyer Street," the accusation apparently was not undeserved. How it was after this profoundest flattery that Miss Martineau should have so thoroughly hated the Whigs, it is hard to say. Certainly it was an odd way of showing their talent for government, but such deference for her opinion ought to have pleased her at least. Her series, the occasion of all this greatness, lasted for two years, and never lost its popularity. The supplementary numbers on the Corn Laws, &c., do not seem to have had the same success; but nothing impaired the popularity of the first series. There were some twenty-eight in all, and she made, she tells us, about two thousand pounds by them—a remuneration which does not seem great considering the excitement they caused; but she was very determined at all times that her work was not to be done for money, but more or less for love, by a spontaneous impulse. When the two years were over, her health began to break down, and her household life does not seem to have been successful, whether the fault was hers or that of the mother and aunt, whom she describes somewhat unceremoniously as her "two old ladies." One would have supposed that the protection of their presence alone would have been an apparent advantage to the sensible young woman; but the freedom of her first spell of bachelor life, so to speak, seems to have suited her best. It would appear to have been as much with the intention of breaking up the uncomfortable household life as from any other cause that Harriet decided on going to America, where she passed two years in such a maze of compliment, homage, and adoration as might have turned any head, though by times in danger of her life; for she had been betrayed (she intimates this point very distinctly) into a public adhesion to the cause of the Abolitionists, then a cruelly persecuted and small minority in the United States. This act gave her immense glory among the party of agitators, and does not seem, except for the fright, to have done herself much harm; for she was a courageous woman, cool and firm, and did not dislike the importance of being regarded as a possible martyr in the cause of freedom. How far it was in good taste to commit a visitor, who had been received with unbounded hospitality on both sides, to a decided and violent partisanship, we need not inquire now. At the moment it was done she evidently felt that an advantage had been taken of her; and in this we fully agree. It seems about the only time in her life that Harriet Martineau allowed herself to be half forced to take a step which she had not intended. Let us say no more, however, about this ill-fated visit to America, which has brought its own punishment in the shape of Mrs Chapman. If there remain any pro-slavery champions who were disgusted by the part she took in the controversy, they have but to look at the third volume of this publication and they will forgive her all.

We have not space to enter upon the books, two of them, the 'Retrospect of Western Travel,' and 'Society in America,' which followed. So far as our recollection of them goes, they are not very remarkable books; but the world has changed so completely since then, that the interest has, of course, very nearly gone out of them. Miss Martineau herself informs us that the latter work was too abstract and metaphysical, though containing much truth. But a great many people "took the truth to heart very earnestly," pouring forth floods of letters upon the author for years after the publication. "The applications made to me for guidance and counsel—applications which even put into my hand the disposal of a whole life in various instances, arose not from agreement in political opinions, nor in discontent with things at home, but from my hearty conviction that social affairs are the duty of every individual, and from my freedom in saying what I thought." One wonders whether there is a class of people which spends its time in asking "guidance and counsel" from the writers of its day. It is not long since we had occasion to note the same phenomena in the experience of Charles Kingsley, who also was a devout believer in his own influence. It is a curious question what kind of persons they could be who put "the disposal of a whole life" into the hands of Harriet Martineau.

Her next piece of work was 'Deerbrook,' which is now one of the best known of her productions, and has been what we may call shouldered into a kind of galvanic fame by the otherwise remarkable reputation of its author. 'Deerbrook' is a much more worthy production as a work of art than the Political Economy series; yet but for the Political Economy series it would have lasted its year or two, as many a work as deserving has done, and then dropped into the limbo where a great many works of art, good, but not great, are *sospesi*,[1] like the great heathen world in the Inferno. It has not a single feature of greatness in it. The character of the hero, Miss Martineau herself informs us, was "drawn from" an American friend—which is of itself an infallible guarantee of mediocrity; and the story is that of another friend. It is the history of one of those mistakes occurring rarely in life, and very disagreeable to meet with in fiction, which, however, are tempting enough to some imaginations. The hero of a village circle, a young doctor, falls in love with the younger of two sisters who come suddenly into the little place; but by force of representation on the part of friends, and certain signs of preference shown by the young lady herself, proposes to, and marries the elder, while still passionately attached to her sister, who, however, knows

---

[1] Suspended (Italian), referring to Dante Alighieri's depiction in the *Inferno* of souls suspended in limbo.

nothing of this, and continues to live with the married pair. This situation, however, affords but little of the play of the story, being too evidently dangerous ground for the treatment of a writer so little experienced in passion. And the chief dramatic action is occasioned by a perfectly causeless persecution got up against the doctor, who, there being no possible foundation for it, lives through it triumphantly, learns to love his wife, and becomes eventually as happy as so high principled and well-balanced a man has a right to expect to be. The curious unnecessariness of the whole, the feebleness of the arguments which induce Hope to run the risk of breaking his own heart to make Hester happy, and the mere nothings which move the other lover to wring the heart of the exemplary Margaret, are quite remarkable evidences of the weakness of fiction when it is, as in this case, an elaborate manufacture—the only *raison d'être*[1] of the party of people thus exhibited being that Miss Martineau wished to write a novel, not that her imagination naturally framed itself into those everlasting variations of the story of human life which genius has in its own heart. The novel called the 'Man and the Hour,' and embodying the story of Toussaint l'Ouverture, the black hero of St Domingo, we have not read—and the author herself seems to have considered it the better of the two; but it made less impression upon the public. Infinitely better and finer is the little story which was written after Miss Martineau fell ill, and which is, in our judgment, the only one of her productions which specially deserves to live, the beautiful little idyll, of the north, called 'Feats on the Fiord.' It adds, of course, to the wonder of this little book that its author never was in the country which she describes with so much freshness and power; but this is but a vulgar wonder after all, and the book itself requires no such adventitious recommendation. It has its "object," for it was impossible for Miss Martineau to write without one; but as this is the vaporous object of discouraging superstition, it does no particular harm to the tale, which, with its salt fiords and grassy mountains, the breath of the cows, and the glimmer of the sea, is really beautiful. The other works of the same little series, which was called the "Playfellow," are very inferior, though children still like 'The Crofton Boys' and the 'Settlers at Home.' For the first and only time in her life, a spark of genius seems by some charm of wandering reflection to have communicated itself to the steady good workmanship and well-selected material, lighting up this one little volume as nothing else from the same hand had ever been lighted up; but the author seems

---

[1]   Reason for being, justification (French).

completely unaware of the difference. She is pleased that people were so much impressed by it as to wonder and hold up their hands in amazement when they heard she had never been in Norway; but of the other wonder, which seems to us so much greater, she knows nothing at all.

She remained for two years longer in London, apparently making an effort to "get on with" her companions. During all this time her fame and prosperity, if not at the top-gallant height of the first outburst, continued with little diminution. Unfortunately, however, the use she makes of this in the Autobiography is to leave behind her an unkindly criticism of most people she encountered. From the young queen, surely in a position to claim all tenderness and sympathy, to the most harmless journalist (mentioned by name), there is nobody who does not get a stab. The Kemble sisters, for example, are discussed as in the gossip of a drawing-room and so are various other ladies, still living, or recently dead. Lord Lytton is described as "a woman of genius enclosed by misadventure in a man's form," "Poor Campbell, obtruding his sentimentalities," obtains another niche. Macaulay is announced as having made "signal failure" in politics, in legislation, and pretty nearly in literature, "that alone remaining open to him." Of Thackeray, it is noted that "his frittered life, and obedience to the call of the great, are the observed of all observers." Wordsworth is represented as a pottering and shabby old man and so on. There is a whole page given to the presumption of "the Howitts," in having claimed to know Miss Martineau, and an elaborate refutation of that claim; while still greater space is occupied in vituperating poor Miss Margaret Gillies, for the venial and flattering offence of having painted a number of likenesses of her, not one good. Had all this been in a grandmother's querulous recollections of her own time for the amusement of her children, it would have been comprehensible; and all that a virtuous critic could have been called upon to do would have been to execute sharp justice upon the grasping nephew or worldly executor who had thus taken advantage of the old lady's notes. But that these trifling depreciations of her acquaintances should have been carefully prepared, printed under her own eye, and kept for years ready for publication by a really sensible and not rancorous woman, is as strange an exhibition as we ever remember to have met with. The greater censures might pass; Lockhart, for instance, was her enemy; Brougham she had lost by, and frankly hated. The throwing even of a poisoned javelin in fair fight may be overlooked; but the deliberate pin-pricks are unpardonable.

We must hasten, however, to a conclusion. Miss Martineau fell ill, and retired to a lodging in Tynemouth, in order to be near her doctor, who was her brother-in-law, and lived at Newcastle. Here she remained, chiefly on a sofa in a room commanding a view of the sea, for nearly six years, alone, except at intervals. The fact that she was at length cured by mesmerism, and published the cure, brought upon her, she tells us, universal odium and a breach with several members of her family. The case made a great noise at the time, and it seems extremely unreasonable that a sick person should not be permitted to cure herself or achieve a cure in any way that is practicable. Any treatment in the world which made a sufferer well, and restored an invalid to active life, must have had an excellent claim upon the belief of that invalid, if of no one else, and the assaults upon her in this case seem most foolish and unreasonable. She was so completely cured, that she undertook a journey to the East, an account of which she afterwards published. While ill at Tynemouth, one of the most noticeable events in her life occurred; the offer of a pension from the Whig Government in 1841. This had been spoken of once or twice before, and had come to nothing. Miss Martineau, without hesitation, refused the offer, believing that it would curb her independence, and pledge her to support the Government which thus offered her what she seems to have regarded as a kind of retaining fee. Very great praise has been given to her disinterestedness and pride of independence in this respect; but, after all, it turns out to be more a question of taste than of independence. Shortly after, a subscription was raised among Miss Martineau's friends, which provided for her some equivalent—we are not told how much less than the pension offered. The refusal was publicly known, but not, we think, this compensation, which somewhat changes the matter. To many writers, who consider a pension, conferred not by a party but by the nation, as an honour, a private subscription would be an intolerable kindness. We do not say which weakness is best, but neither is such a supreme virtue, perhaps, as has been hitherto attributed to Miss Martineau.

In the year 1845, being over forty, and having apparently shaken off all family ties, Miss Martineau settled at Ambleside, building a house for herself, which pleased her in every respect within and without; and here she began a happy and quiet life, which only terminated last year. During this long period she was full of occupation, full of cheerful activity—visited by crowds of visitors from England and America, admired and evidently beloved by a large circle. Her religious ideas had been gradually changing during these years, and her beliefs growing fewer and fewer. The emotional religiousness which had been her early characteristic had disappeared long before this, and there was no logic (as she herself tells us) in the Unitarianism of her youth to hold her to that compromise of doctrine, when the unreal and uncharacteristic atmosphere of devotion had been dispelled. It was not, however, till this year, just before her settlement in Westmoreland, that she met with the apostle of her later life. We have made some feeble attempts to find out who Mr H. G. Atkinson is. A man occupying so great and important a position in the world as is allotted to this gentleman by a sensible and intellectual woman like Miss Martineau, herself so eminent and so famous, the admired of two hemispheres, ought to have been heard of, one cannot but suppose, or to have left some trace of himself other than that which we find in her narrative. But our researches have not been attended with any success, and except the mere fact that he is "a gentleman of independent fortune," certified by Miss Martineau and Mrs Chapman, we are sorry to say we can discover nothing about him. But perhaps the reader would like to see him as he appeared to Miss Martineau on the blissful occasion of their first meeting.

"I saw him turn the corner into the lawn, talking with the gardener, who was carrying his carpet-bag. He also carried a bag on his shoulder. He looked younger than I expected, and than I knew he was. His perfect gentlemanliness is his most immediately striking and uncontested attribute. We were struck with this; and also with a certain dryness in his mode of conversation which showed us at once that he was no sentimentalist; a conviction which was confirmed in proportion as we became acquainted with his habit of thought. We could not exactly call him reserved; for he was willing to converse and ready to communicate his thoughts; yet we felt it difficult to know him."

This was, no doubt, only the proper atmosphere of mystery which ought always to surround an oracle. Mr Atkinson had been the adviser, though at a distance, of the mesmeric treatment which cured Miss Martineau, and had therefore a claim upon her gratitude to start with. He became from this time the guide and glory of her future life. How it was that so hard-headed a woman should have given herself up to the almost servile subjection which subsequent events proved, is as curious as anything in the history of the mind—that standing paradox and ever-lasting mystery. Harriet Martineau, the philosopher and politician—she whom Secretaries of State had asked counsel from, and all America had raged and stormed about, the mature woman of the world, and veteran writer— suddenly disappears from the scene; and in her place we find the guileless

Harriet Martineau who took notes of Dr Carpenter's sermons, and lived upon the instructions of his Bible class, and adored the good Unitarian minister as the epitome of eloquence and wisdom, nearly thirty years before. The transformation is wonderful, laughable to those who like to see the respectable made ridiculous and intellect behave itself like folly, but not to those whose sympathy is greater than their cynicism. Miss Martineau's opinions were her own affair. The disciples of M. Comte seem to the ordinary spectator capable of swallowing any amount of nonsense with their belief (as witness the sermons of Mr Congreve) which would be past credit, if they did not ingenuously reveal it to us; but yet there are a great many able persons in that small and persecuting remnant. Indeed we rather think they are all able persons, with scarce even Falstaff's poor ha'porth of bread to the strong wine of talent which floats them. And nobody had the slightest right to interfere with Miss Martineau for attaching herself to this sect. It is entirely a different sentiment from that of religious disapproval, which moves us when we come to the 'Letters on Man's Nature and Development,' which appeared five years later, and in which was revealed Miss Martineau's final conversion to the creed (if it can be justly called a creed) which is now, we believe, known as "Agnosticism"— the religion of unknowableness. These letters are the productions of the catechumen Harriet and her master, in which the instructed, with all the fulness of innocent emotion, glows and thrills over every fresh revelation of wisdom and truth from the instructor's lips. Never was a more unlovely spectacle. Mr Atkinson's share of the performance reminds us irresistibly of a story told of an Oxford undergraduate, who took an essay, after the manner of a certain college, to read to its head. The story may be an old one, but this is how it is fathered in the present generation. The subject was the immortality of the soul—just the kind of easy subject calculated to call forth an undergraduate's eloquence. The young man began, "This now exploded theory—." The system of philosophy which Mr Atkinson disclosed to Miss Martineau was entirely in this tone, "I have fully proved," or, "It is fully proved," he says—that all such pernicious systems as Christianity, and all such insane theories as an immortal state, are absolutely false, and beneath the discussion of reasonable persons. And his pupil replies, How beautiful! how interesting! how instructive! Miss Martineau flatters herself that it was the importance of the revelation of her views, and of Him who inspired them, which produced so much commotion in the world; but in reality it was something still more unpleasant,—the exposition of an infallible popedom much more than Catholic, and of a devotion as blind as that inspired by any fetish. Most people laughed, being glad to see a "superior" woman, a female philosopher, an incarnation of strong-mindedness, prove herself as silly as any poor evangelical sister worshipping a doubtful "shepherd;" but there were many to whom the laughter was not pleasant, and whose feelings were those of distress and shame. The result, however, so far as concerned Miss Martineau herself, was not of much importance. It moved her to translate and condense the writings of Comte, so well, we are told, that he had the volumes retranslated, as being more handy and readable than the original works; and it made her still more fully and cheerfully convinced in her own mind that this world was the entire sphere of human existence, and that death was a final and complete cessation of being. This belief, of course, was a thing with which nobody had any right to interfere. The publication of the translation of Comte, by the way, was aided by a gift of £500, given by a Mr Lombe for the purpose, and sent by him, an entire stranger, to Miss Martineau, through her publisher.

After this era in her life, which brought her some annoyance, but no active trouble—since she informs us that she made more money, and acquired more reputation, after than before the publication of the letters—Miss Martineau became a large contributor to the 'Daily News,' writing not only the biographical sketches, which have been republished, but a great number of leading articles, as many sometimes as six in the week: and wrote her sober and sensible "History of the Peace," besides many stray articles of various descriptions for 'Household Words' and other periodicals. In the year 1854, after some interval of partial illness, she went to London for the purpose of consulting a physician, and was informed that she had disease of heart, and might die at any moment. A more solemn intimation could not be made to any one; and Miss Martineau, who had suspected the state of affairs, took it with her usual courage. She dined with a merry family party on the evening of the day and was as gay as any. Then she took all necessary steps for the arrangement of her affairs, and returned home with a certain, not unpleasing, solemnity and cheerfulness. It is in this condition that we leave her—for here the Autobiography ends. "In sure and certain hope" of a tranquil annihilation, resigning all life or thought of life for ever, she yet lived on for years; and into the record as it approaches the end, there steals a sense of her own specially important and interesting position as a dying person, which is natural enough. Perhaps the consciousness of this pedestal upon which she is standing has, more or less, inflated the self-applauses of the work throughout, and given a heightening touch to all the incidents of the past as they filed before her in a silent round. And there is a certain excuse in this which the reader will be glad to admit. The hopes of another life, the visions with which most of us beguile the twilight darkness, of light and home and heaven beyond, Harriet Martineau had put aside as vain delusions. And it was very comprehensible that her heart within her, having no outlet of this kind, should concentrate all its last efforts on the monument which she meant to leave of herself within "the warm precincts of the cheerful day." This is the kind of everlasting life which Comte teaches his disciples to desire. Perhaps a month may some time be called after her, and her fellow-believers date their letters from the 10th day of Harriet Martineau. We can fancy that she would not have disliked this curious kind of fame. As it was, however, she lived more than twenty years after her death-warrant was given out. At once, and to save time, she wrote, it is evident, the little autobiography of the 'Daily News,' with all the moderation and good sense which distinguished her biographies of other people; but having thus secured an immediate notice to her mind, set to work in her long leisure to work it out in detail. This curious sense of human importance and dignity which comes upon her when she knows that her days are numbered is very significant, and one of the most touching things in the book.

We will not spoil the effect of this last apology by any reference to the volume of Mrs Chapman, a muddle of folly, false enthusiasm, and still more false sentimentality from beginning to end. Miss Martineau does not seem to have had much discrimination in the choice of her friends. It is evident that she could swallow a good deal of praise, especially from America; but we think the detailed comparison between herself and Joan of Arc, which seems to her biographer so happy, must have roused the instinct of British laughter in the sensible Harriet. The verdict of the world upon her will not, we think, be so high. She was a very sensible woman; yet not very much of a woman at all, notwithstanding her innocent and honest love of Berlin wool. She was a very clever writer, with a most useful, serviceable, working faculty, and as little nonsense about her as could be desired. She was kind, friendly, and reasonable, yet hard in her judgments, and intolerant of opposition; more affectionate to those who depended upon and were subject to her, than to those who were independent and liked their own way. Thus her relations to the elder generation seemed all wrong, false, and jarring; while her relations to her inferiors in the succession of life are all sweet and harmonious. This is perhaps not an unusual characteristic of a strong, somewhat harsh, self-sufficing nature, which can acknowledge the loveliness of voluntary services, but kicks at that which has the claim of a right. We cannot but think she has been very much overrated as a writer; and indeed except for the single fact that her Political Economy really met a public need, we find it very difficult to understand on what her great reputation was founded. And unfortunately it will not be increased by her Autobiography, when that solid, sound sense, which is her strongest point, shows less strong than ever before without any increase of power or human interest to set the balance right.

2. John Morley, "Harriet Martineau," *Macmillan's Magazine* 36 (May 1877), 47–60

IN 1850 Charlotte Brontë paid a visit to Harriet Martineau at Ambleside, and she wrote to her friends various emphatic accounts of her hostess. "Without adopting her theories," Miss Brontë said, "I yet find a worth and greatness in herself, and a consistency, benevolence, perseverance in her practice, such as wins the sincerest esteem and affection. She is not a person to be judged by her writings alone, but rather by her own deeds and life, than which nothing can be more exemplary or noble."

The division which Miss Brontë thus makes between opinions and character, and again between literary production and character, is at the root of any just criticism of the two volumes of autobiography which have just been given to the public. Of the third volume, *The Memorials*, by Mrs. Chapman, it is impossible to say anything serious. Mrs. Chapman fought an admirable fight in the dark times of American history for the abolition of slavery, but unhappily she is without literary gifts; and this third volume is one more illustration of the folly of intrusting the composition of biography to persons who have only the wholly irrelevant claim of intimate friendship, or kinship, or sympathy in public causes. The qualification for a biographer is not in the least that he is a virtuous person, or a second cousin, or a dear friend, or a trusty colleague; but that he knows how to write a book, has tact, style, taste, considerateness, senses of proportion, and a good eye for the beginnings and ends of things. The third volume, then, tells us little about the person to whom they relate. The two volumes of autobiography tell all that we can seek to know, and the reader who judges them in an equitable spirit will be ready to allow that, when all is said that can be said of her hardness, arbitrariness, and insularity, Harriet Martineau is still a singular and worthy figure among the conspicuous personages of a generation that has now almost vanished. Some will wonder how it was that her literary performances acquired so little of permanent value. Others will be pained by the distinct repudiation of all theology, avowed by her with a simple and courageous directness that can scarcely be counted other than honourable to her. But everybody will admit, as Charlotte Brontë did, that though her books are not of the first nor of the second rank, and though her anti-theological opinions are to many repugnant, yet behind books and opinions was a remarkable personality, a sure eye for social realities, a moral courage that never flinched; a strong judgment, within its limits; a vigorous self-reliance both in opinion and act, which yet did not prevent a habit of the most neutral self-judgment; the commonplace virtues of industry and energy devoted to aims too elevated, and too large and generous, to be commonplace; a splendid sincerity, a magnificent love of truth. And that all these fine qualities, which would mostly be described as manly, should exist not in a man but a woman, and in a woman who discharged admirably such feminine duties as fell to her, fills up the measure of our interest in such a character.

Harriet Martineau was born at Norwich in 1802, and she died, as we all remember, in the course of last summer (1876). Few people have lived so long as three-quarters of a century, and undergone so little substantial change of character, amid some very important changes of opinion. Her family was Unitarian, and family life was in her case marked by some of that stiffness, that severity, that chilly rigour, with which Unitarians are sometimes taxed by religionists of a more ecstatic doctrine. Her childhood was very unhappy; the household seems to have been unamiable, and she was treated with none of that tenderness and sympathy, for which firm and defiant natures are apt to yearn as strongly as others that get the credit of greater sensibility. With that singular impulse to suicide which is frequent among children, though rarer with girls than boys, she went one day into the kitchen for the carving knife, that she might cut her throat; luckily the servants were at dinner, and the child retreated. Deafness, which proved incurable, began to afflict her before she was sixteen. A severe, harsh, and mournful kind of religiosity seized her, and this "abominable spiritual rigidity," as she calls it, confirmed all the gloomy predispositions of her mind. She learned a good deal, mastering Latin, French, and Italian in good time; and reading much in her own tongue, including constant attention to the Bible, with all sorts of commentaries and explanations, such as those of us who were brought up in a certain spiritual atmosphere, have only too good reasons never to forget. This expansion of intellectual interest, however, did not make her less silent, less low in her spirits, less full of vague and anxious presentiment. The reader is glad when these ungracious years of youth are at an end, and the demands of active life stirred Harriet Martineau's energies into vigorous work.

In 1822 her father died, and seven years later his widow and his daughters lost at a single blow nearly all that they had in the world. Before this event, which really proved to be a blessing in the disguise of a catastrophe, Harriet Martineau had written a number of slight pieces. They had been printed, and received a certain amount of recognition. They were of a religious cast, as was natural in one with whom religious literature, and religious life and observance, had hitherto taken in the whole sphere of her continual experience. *Traditions of Palestine* and *Devotional Exercises* are titles that tell their own tale, and we may be sure that their authoress was still at the antipodean point of the positive philosophy in which she ended her speculative journey. She still clung undoubtingly to what she had been brought up to believe, when she won three prizes for essays intended to present Unitarianism to the notice of Jews, of Catholics, and of Mahometans. Her success in these and similar efforts, turned her mind more decidedly towards literature as a profession.

Miss Martineau is at some pains to assure us on several occasions that it was the need of utterance now and always that drove her to write, and that money, although welcome when it came, was never her motive. This perhaps a little savours of affectation. Nobody would dream of suspecting Miss Martineau of writing anything that she did not believe to be true or useful, merely for the sake of money. But there is plenty of evidence that the prospect of payment stirred her to true and useful work, as it does many other authors by profession, and as it does the followers of all professions whatever. She puts the case fairly enough in another place (i. 422):—"Every author is in a manner an adventurer; and no one was ever more decidedly so than myself; but the difference between one kind of adventurer and another is, I believe, simply this—that the one has something to say which presses for utterance, and is uttered at length without a view to future fortunes; while the other has a sort of general inclination towards literature, without any specific need of utterance, and a very definite desire for the honours and rewards of the literary career." Even in the latter case, however, honest journeyman's work enough is done in literature by men and women who seek nothing higher than a reputable source of income. Miss Martineau did, no doubt, seek objects far higher and more generous than income, but she lived on the income which literature brought to her; and there seems a certain failure of her usually admirable common sense in making any ado about so simple a matter. When doctors and counsel refuse their guineas, and the parson declines a stipend, it will be quite soon enough for the author to be especially anxious to show that he has a right to regard money much as the rest of the human race regard it.

Miss Martineau underwent the harsh ordeal which awaits most literary aspirants. She had a scheme in her head for a long series of short tales to illustrate some of the propositions of political economy. She trudged about London day after day, through mud and fog, with weary limbs and anxious heart, as many an author has done before and since. The times were bad; cholera was abroad; people were full of apprehension and concern about the Reform Bill; and the publishers looked coldly on a doubtful venture. Miss Martineau talks none of the conventional nonsense about the cruelty and stupidity of publishers. What she says is this:—"I have always been anxious to extend to young or struggling authors the sort of aid which would have been so precious to me in that winter of 1829-30, and I know that, in above twenty years, I have never succeeded but once." One of the most distinguished editors in London, who had charge of a periodical for many years, told us what comes to the same thing, namely, that in no single case during all these years did a volunteer contributor of real quality, or with any promise of eminence, present himself or herself. So many hundreds think themselves called, so few are chosen. In Miss Martineau's case, however, the trade made a mistake. When at length she found some one to go halves with her in the enterprise, on terms extremely disadvantageous to herself, the first of her tales was published (1832), and instantly had a prodigious success. The sale ran up to more than ten thousand of each monthly volume. In that singular autobiographical sketch of herself which Miss Martineau prepared for the *Daily News*, to be printed as her obituary notice, she pronounced a judgment upon this work which more disinterested, though not more impartial, critics will confirm. Her own unalterable view, she says, of what the work could and could not effect, "prevented her from expecting too much from it, either in regard to its social operations or its influence on her own fame. The original idea of exhibiting the great natural laws of society by a series of pictures of selected social action was a fortunate one; and her tales initiated a multitude of minds into the conception of what political economy is, and how it concerns everybody living in society. Beyond this there is no merit of a high order in the work. It popularised in a fresh form some doctrines and many truths long before made public by others." James Mill, one of the acutest economists of the day, and one of the most vigorous and original characters of that or any other day, had foretold failure; but when the time came he very handsomely admitted that his prophecy had been rash. In after years, when Miss Martineau had acquired from Comté a conception of the growth and movement of societies as a whole, with their economic conditions controlled and constantly modified by a multitude of other conditions of various kinds, she rated the science of her earlier days very low. Even in those days, however, she says, "I believe I should not have been greatly surprised or displeased to have perceived, even then that the pretended science is no science at all, strictly speaking; and that so many of its parts must undergo essential change, that it may be a question whether future generations will owe much more to it than the benefit (inestimable, to be sure) of establishing the grand truth that social affairs proceed according to general laws, no less than natural phenomena of every kind" (*Autob.* ii. 24).

Harriet Martineau was not of the class of writers, most of them terribly unprofitable, who merely say literary things about social organisation, its institutions, and their improvement. Her feeling about society was less literary than scientific: it was not sentimental, but the business-like quality of a good administrator. She was moved less by pity or by any sense of the pathos and the hardness of the world, than by a sensible and energetic interest in good government and in the rational and convenient ordering of things. Her tales to illustrate the truths of political economy are what might be expected from a writer of this character. They are far from being wanting—many of them—in the genuine interest of good story-telling. They are rapid, definite, and without a trace of either slovenliness or fatigue. We are amazed as we think of the speed and prompt regularity with which they were produced; and the fertile ingenuity with which the pill of political economy is wrapped up in the confectionery of a tale, may stand as a marvel of true cleverness and inventive dexterity. Of course, of imagination or invention in a high sense there is not a trace. Such a quality was not in the gifts of the writer, nor could it in any case have worked within such limitations as those set by the matter and the object of the series.

Literary success was followed in the usual order by social temptation. Miss Martineau removed from Norwich to London, and she had good reasons for making the change. Her work dealt with matters of a political kind, and she could only secure a real knowledge of what was best worth saying by intercourse with those who had a better point of view for a survey of the social state of England than could be found in a provincial town like Norwich. So far as evening parties went, Miss Martineau soon perceived how little "essential difference there is between the extreme case of a cathedral city and that of literary London, or any other place, where dissipation takes the turn of book-talk instead of dancing or masquerading." She went out to dinner every night except Sundays, and saw all the most interesting people of the London of five-and-forty years ago. While she was free from presumptuousness in her judgments, she was just as free from a foolish willingness to take the reputations of the hour on trust. Her attitude was friendly and sensible, but it was at the same time critical and independent; and that is what every frank, upright, and sterling character naturally becomes in face of an unfamiliar society. Harriet Martineau was too keen-sighted, too aware of the folly and incompetent pretension of half the world, too consciously self-respecting and proud, to take society and its ways with any diffidence or ingenuous simplicity. On the importance of the small *littérateur*[1] who unreasonably thinks himself a great one, on the airs and graces of the gushing blue-stockings who were in vogue in that day, on the detestable vulgarity of literary lionising, she had no mercy. She recounts with caustic relish the story about a certain pedantical lady, of whom Tierney had said that there was not another head in England that could encounter hers on the subject of Cause and Effect. The story was that when in a country house one fine day she took her seat in a window, saying, in a business-like manner (to David Ricardo), "Come now, let us have a little discussion about Space." We remember a story about a certain Mademoiselle de Launay, afterwards well known to the Paris of the eighteenth century, being introduced at Versailles by a silly great lady who had an infatuation for her. "This," the great lady kept saying, "is the young person whom I have told you about, who is so wonderfully intelligent, who knows so much. Come, Mademoiselle, pray talk. Now Madame, you will see how she talks. Well, first of all, now, talk a little about religion; then you can tell us about something else."

We cannot wonder that Miss Martineau did not go a second time to the house where Space might be the unprovoked theme of a casual chat. Pretension in every shape she hated most heartily. Her judgments in most cases were thoroughly just—at this period of her life at any rate—and sometimes even unexpectedly kindly, and the reason is that

---

[1]   Literary writer, person professionally involved with literature (French).

she looked at society through the medium of a strong and penetrating kind of common sense, which is more often the gift of clever women than of clever men. If she is masculine, she is, like Mrs. Colonel Poyntz, in one of Bulwer's novels, "masculine in a womanly way." There is a real spirit of ethical divination in some of her criticism of character. Take the distinguished man whose name we have just written. "There was Bulwer on a sofa," she says, "sparkling and languishing among a set of female votaries—he and they dizened out, perfumed, and presenting the nearest picture to a seraglio to be seen on British ground—only the indifference or hauteur of the lord of the harem being absent." Yet this disagreeable sight does not prevent her from feeling a cordial interest in him, amidst any amount of vexation and pity for his weakness. "He seems to be a woman of genius inclosed by misadventure in a man's form. He has insight, experience, sympathy, letters, power and grace of expression, and an irrepressible impulse to utterance, and industry which should have produced works of the noblest quality and these have been intercepted by mischiefs which may be called misfortune rather than fault. His friendly temper, his generous heart, his excellent conversation (at his best), and his simple manners (when he forgot himself), have many a time 'left me mourning' that such a being should allow himself to sport with perdition." Those who knew most about Bulwer, and who were most repelled by his terrible faults, will feel in this page of Miss Martineau's the breath of social equity in which charity is not allowed to blur judgment, nor moral disapproval to narrow, starve, and discolour vision into lost possibilities of character. And we may note in passing how even here, in the mere story of the men and women whom she met in London drawing-rooms, Harriet Martineau does not lose herself in gossip about individuals looked at merely in their individual relations. It is not merely the "blighting of promise nor the forfeiture of a career" that she deplores in the case of a Bulwer or a Brougham; it is "the intercepting of national blessings." If this view of natural gifts as a source of blessing to society, and not merely of power or fame to their privileged possessor, were more common than it is, the impression which such a thought is calculated to make would be the highest available protection against those blighted promises and forfeited careers of which Brougham and Bulwer were only two out of a too vast host of examples.

It is the very fulness with which she is possessed by this large way of conceiving a life in its manifold relations to the service of the world, that is the secret of Harriet Martineau's firm, clear, calm, and almost neutral way of judging both her own work and character and those of others. By calm we do not mean that she was incapable of strong and direct censure. Many of her judgments, both here and in her *Biographic Sketches*, are stern; and some—like that on Macaulay, for instance—may even pass for harsh. But they are never the product of mere anger or heatedness, and it is a great blunder to suppose that reasoned severity is incompatible with perfect composure, or that calm is another name for amiable vapidity.

"Thöricht ist's
In allen Stücken billig sein; es heißt,
Sein eigen Selbst zerstören."[1]

Her condemnation of the Whigs, for example, is as stringent and outspoken as condemnation can be; yet it is a deliberate and reasoned judgment, not a mere bitterness or prejudice. The Whigs were at that moment, between 1832 and 1834, at the height of their authority, political, literary, and social. After a generation of misgovernment they had been borne to power on the tide of national enthusiasm for parliamentary reform, and for all those improvements in our national life to which parliamentary reform was no more than the first step. The harshness and darkness of the past generation were the measure of the hopes of the new time. These hopes, which were at least as strong in Harriet Martineau as in anybody then living, the Whigs were soon felt to have cheated. She cannot forgive them. Speaking of John and Edward Romilly, "they had virtuous projects," she says, "and had every hope of achieving service worthy of their father's fame; but their aspirations were speedily tamed down—as all high aspirations *are* lowered by Whig influences." A certain peer is described as "agreeable enough in society to those who are not very particular in regard to sincerity; and was, as Chancellor of the Exchequer or anything else, as good a representative as could be found of the flippancy, conceit, and official helplessness and ignorance of the Whig administration." Charles Knight started a new periodical for the people under the patronage of the official Whigs. "But the poverty and perverseness of their ideas, and the insolence of their feelings, were precisely what might be expected by all who really knew that remarkably vulgar class of men. They purposed to lecture the working classes, who were by far the wiser party of the two, in a

---

[1] Lines from Wolfgang von Goethe's *Torquato Tasso*: "It is foolish / to be cheap in all things; that means / destroying one's own self."

jejune, coaxing, dull, religious-tract sort of tone, and criticised and deprecated everything like vigour, and a manly and genial tone of address in the new publication, while trying to push in as contributors effete and exhausted writers and friends of their own, who knew about as much of the working classes of England as of those of Turkey." This energetic description, which belongs to the year 1848, gives us an interesting measure of the distance that has been traversed during the last thirty years. The workmen have acquired direct political power; they have organised themselves into effective groups for industrial purposes; they have produced leaders of ability and sound judgment; and the Whig who seeks their support must stoop or rise to talk a Radicalism that would have amply satisfied even Harriet Martineau herself.

The source of this improvement in the society to which she bade farewell, over that into which she had been born, is set down by Miss Martineau to the most remarkable literary genius with whom, during her residence in London, she was brought into contact. "What Wordsworth did for poetry," she says, "in bringing us out of a conventional idea and method to a true and simple one, Carlyle has done for morality. He may be himself the most curious opposition to himself,—he may be the greatest mannerist of his age while denouncing conventionalism,—the greatest talker while eulogising silence,—the most woeful complainer while glorifying fortitude,—the most uncertain and stormy in mood, while holding forth serenity as the greatest good within the reach of man; but he has nevertheless infused into the mind of the English nation a sincerity, earnestness, healthfulness, and courage which can be appreciated only by those who are old enough to tell what was our morbid state when Byron was the representative of our temper, the Clapham church of our religion, and the rotten-borough system of our political morality." We have no quarrel with this account of the greatest man of letters of our generation. But Carlyle has only been one influence among others. It is a far cry indeed from *Sartor Resartus* to the *Tracts for the Times*, yet they were both of them protests against the same thing, both of them attempted answers to the same problem, and the *Tracts* perhaps did more than *Sartor* to quicken spiritual life, to shatter "the Clapham church," and to substitute a mystic faith and not unlovely hope for the frigid, hard, and mechanical lines of official orthodoxy on the one hand, and the egotism and sentimental despair of Byronism on the other. There is a third school, too, and Harriet Martineau herself was no insignificant member of it, to which both the temper and the political morality of our time have owed a deep debt; the school of those utilitarian political thinkers who gave light rather than heat, and yet by the intellectual force with which they insisted on the right direction of social reform, also stirred the very impulse which made men desire social reform. The most illustrious of this body was undoubtedly John Mill, because to accurate political science he added a fervid and vibrating social sympathy, and a power of quickening it in the best minds of a scientific turn. It is odd, by the way, that Miss Martineau, while so lavish in deserved panegyric on Carlyle, should be so grudging and disparaging in the case of Mill, with whom her intellectual affinities must have been closer than with any other of her contemporaries. The translator of Comte's *Positive Philosophy* had better reasons than most people for thinking well of the services of the author of the *System of Logic*: it was certainly the latter book which did more than any other to prepare the minds of the English philosophic public for the former.

It is creditable to Miss Martineau's breadth of sympathy that she should have left on record the tribute of her admiration for Carlyle, for nobody has written so harshly as Carlyle on the subject which interested Harriet Martineau more passionately than any other events of her time. In 1834 she had finished her series of illustrations of political economy; her domestic life was fretted by the unreasonable exigences of her mother; London society had perhaps begun to weary her, and she felt the need of a change of scene. The United States, with the old European institutions placed amid new conditions, were then as now a natural object of interest to everybody with a keen feeling for social improvement. So to the Western Republic Miss Martineau turned her face. She had not been long in the States before she began to feel that the Abolitionists, at that moment a despised and persecuted handful of men and women, were the truly moral and regenerating party in the country. Harriet Martineau no sooner felt this conviction driving out her former prejudice against them as fanatical and impracticable, than she at once bore public testimony, at serious risk of every kind to herself, in favour of the extreme Anti-Slavery agitators. And for thirty years she never slackened her sympathy nor her energetic action on English public opinion, in this most vital matter of her time. She was guided not merely by humanitarian disgust at the cruel and brutal abominations of slavery,—though we know no reason why this alone should not be a sufficient ground for turning Abolitionist,—but also on the more purely political ground of the cowardice, silence, corruption, and hypocrisy that were engendered in the Free States by purchased connivance at the peculiar institution of the Slave States. Nobody has yet traced out the full effect upon the national character of the Americans of all those years of conscious complicity in slavery, after the moral iniquity of slavery had become clear to the inner conscience of the very men who ignobly sanctioned the mobbing of Abolitionists.

In the summer of 1836 Miss Martineau returned to England, having added this great question to the stock of her foremost objects of interest and concern. Such additions, whether literary or social, are the best kind of refreshment that travel supplies. She published two books on America: one of them abstract and quasi-scientific, *Society in America*; the other, *A Retrospect of Western Travel*, of a lighter and more purely descriptive quality. Their success with the public was moderate, and in after years she condemned them in very plain language, the first of them especially as "full of affectations and preachments." Their only service, and it was not inconsiderable, was the information which they circulated as to the condition of slavery and of the country under it. We do not suppose that they are worth reading at the present day, except from a historical point of view. But they are really good specimens of a kind of literature which is not abundant, and yet which is of the utmost value—we mean the record of the sociological observation of a country by a competent traveller, who stays long enough in the country, has access to the right persons of all kinds, and will take pains enough to mature his judgments. It was a happy idea of O'Connell's to suggest that she should go over to Ireland, and write such an account of that country as she had written of the United States. And we wish at this very hour that some one as competent as Miss Martineau would do what O'Connell wished her to do. A similar request came to her from Milan: why should she not visit Lombardy, and then tell Europe the true tale of Austrian rule?

But after her American journey Miss Martineau felt a very easily intelligible desire to change the literary field. For many years she had been writing almost entirely about fact: and the constraint of the effort to be always correct, and to bear without solicitude the questioning of her correctness, had become burdensome. She felt the danger of losing nerve and becoming morbidly fearful of criticism on the one hand, and of growing narrow and mechanical about accuracy on the other. "I longed inexpressibly," she says, "for the liberty of fiction, while occasionally doubting whether I had the power to use that freedom as I could have done ten years before." The product of this new mental phase was *Deerbrook*, which was published in the spring of 1839. *Deerbrook* is a story of an English country village, its petty feuds, its gentilities, its chances and changes of fortune. The influence of Jane Austen's stories is seen in every chapter; but Harriet Martineau had none of the easy flow, the pleasant humour, the light-handed irony of her model, any more than she had the energetic and sustained imaginative power of Charlotte or Emily Brontë. There is playfulness enough in *Deerbrook,* but it is too deliberate to remind us of the crooning involuntary playfulness of *Pride and Prejudice* or *Sense and Sensibility. Deerbrook* is not in the least a story with a moral; it is truly and purely a piece of art; yet we are conscious of the serious spirit of the social reformer as haunting the background, and only surrendering the scene for reasons of its own. On the other hand, there is in *Deerbrook* a gravity of moral reflection that Jane Austen, whether wisely or unwisely, seldom or never attempts. In this respect *Deerbrook* is the distant forerunner of some of George Eliot's most characteristic work. Distant, because George Eliot's moralising is constantly suffused by the broad light of a highly poetic imagination, and this was in no degree among Miss Martineau's gifts. Still there is something above the flat touch of the common didactic in such a page as that in which (chapter xix) she describes the case of "the unamiable—the only order of evil ones who suffer hell without seeing and knowing that it is hell: nay, they are under a heavier curse than even this, they inflict torments second only to their own, with an unconsciousness worthy of spirits of light." However, when all is said, we may agree that this is one of the books that give a rational person pleasure once, but which we hardly look forward to reading again.

Shortly after the publication of her first novel, Miss Martineau was seized by a serious internal malady, from which recovery seemed hopeless. According to her usual practice of taking her life deliberately in her hands, and settling its conditions for herself instead of letting things drift as they might, she insisted on declining the hospitable shelter pressed upon her by a near relative, on the excellent ground that it is wrong for an invalid to impose restraints upon a healthy household. She proceeded to establish herself in lodgings at Tynemouth, on the coast of Northumberland. Here she lay on a couch for nearly five years, seeing as few persons as might be, and working at such literary matters as came into her head with steadfast industry and fortitude. The ordeal was hard, but the little book that came of it, *Life in a Sickroom,* remains to show the moods in which the ordeal was borne.

At length Miss Martineau was induced to try mesmerism as a possible cure for her disease, and what is certain is, that after trying mesmeric treatment, the invalid whom the doctors had declared incurable shortly recovered as perfect health as she had ever known. A virulent controversy arose upon the case, for by some curious law, physicians are apt to import into professional disputes a heat and bitterness at least as marked as that of their old enemies, the theologians. It was said that Miss Martineau had begun to improve before she was mesmerised, and what was still more to the point, that she had been taking heavy doses of iodine. "It is beyond all question or dispute," as Voltaire said, "that magic words and ceremonies are quite capable of most effectually destroying a whole flock of sheep, if the words be accompanied by a sufficient quantity of arsenic."

Mesmerism was indirectly the means of bringing Miss Martineau into an intimate acquaintance with a gentleman who soon began to exert a decisive influence upon the most important of her opinions. Mr. Atkinson is still alive, and we need not say much about him. He seems to have been a grave and sincere person, using his mind with courageous independence upon the great speculative problems which were not in 1844, as they are in 1877, the common topics of everyday discourse among educated people. This is not the place for an examination of the philosophy in which Miss Martineau was finally landed by Mr. Atkinson's influence. That philosophy was given to the world in 1851 in a volume called *Letters on the Laws of Man's Nature and Development*. The greater part of it was written by Mr. Atkinson in reply to short letters, in which Miss Martineau stated objections and propounded questions. The book points in the direction of that explanation of the facts of the universe which is now so familiar under the name of Evolution. But it points in this way only as the once famous *Vestiges of Creation* pointed towards the scientific hypotheses of Darwin and Wallace; or as Buckle's crude and superficial notions about the history of civilisation pointed towards a true and complete conception of sociology. That is to say, the Atkinson Letters state some of the difficulties in the way of the explanations of life and motion hitherto received as satisfactory; they insist upon approaching the facts exclusively by the positive, Baconian, or inductive method; and then they hurry to an explanation of their own, which may be as plausible as that which they intend it to replace, but which they leave equally without ordered proof and strict verification.

The only point to which we are called upon to refer is that this way of thinking about man and the rest of nature led to repudiation by Miss Martineau of the whole structure of dogmatic theology. For one thing, she ceased to hold the conception of a God with any human attributes

whatever; also of any principle or practice of Design; "of an administration of life according to human wishes, or of the affairs of the world
by the principles of human morals." All these became to her as mere
visions; beliefs necessary in their day, but not philosophically nor permanently true. Miss Martineau was not an Atheist in the philosophic sense;
she never denied a First Cause, but only that this Cause is within the
sphere of human attributes, or can be defined in their terms.

Then, for another thing, she ceased to believe in the probability of
there being a continuance of conscious individual life after the dissolution of the body. With this, of course, fell all expectation of a state of
personal rewards and punishments. "The real and justifiable and
honourable subject of interest," she said, "to human beings, living and
dying, is the welfare of their fellows surrounding them or surviving
them." About that she cared supremely, and about nothing else did she
bring herself to care at all.

It is painful to many people even to hear of a person holding such
beliefs as these. Yet it would plainly be the worst kind of spiritual vale-
tudinarianism to insist on the omission from even the shortest account
of this remarkable woman, of what became the very basis and foundation of her life for those thirty years of it, which she herself always
counted the happiest part of the whole.

Although it was Mr. Atkinson who finally provided her with a positive substitute for her older beliefs, yet a journey which Miss Martineau
made in the East shortly after her restoration to health (1846) had done
much to build up in her mind a historic conception of the origin and
order of the great faiths of mankind—the Christian, the Hebrew, the
Mahometan, the old Egyptian. We need not say more on this subject.
The work in which she published the experiences of the journey which
was always so memorable to her deserves a word. There are few more
delightful books of travel than *Eastern Life, Past and Present*. The descriptions are admirably graphic, and they have the attraction of making their
effect by a few direct strokes, without any of the wordy elaboration of
our modern picturesque. The writer shows a true feeling for nature, and
she shows a vigorous sense, which is not merely pretty sentiment, like
Chateaubriand's, for the vast historic associations of those old lands and
dim cradles of the race. All is sterling and real; we are aware that the
elevated reflection and the meditative stroke are not due to more
composition, but did actually pass through her mind as the suggestive
wonders passed before her eyes. And hence there is no jar as we find a
little homily on the advantage of being able to iron your own linen on

a Nile boat, followed by a lofty page on the mighty pair of solemn figures that gaze as from eternity on time amid the sand at Thebes. The whole, one may say again, is sterling and real, both the elevation and the homeliness. The student of the history of opinion may find some interest in comparing Miss Martineau's work with the famous book, *Ruins; or, Meditations on the Revolutions of Empires*, in which Volney, between fifty and sixty years before, had drawn equally dissolvent conclusions with her own, from the same panorama of the dead ages. Perhaps Miss Martineau's history is not much better than Volney's, but her brisk sense is preferable to Volney's high *à priori* declamation and artificial rhetoric.

Before starting for the East, Miss Martineau had settled a new plan of life for herself, and built a little house where she thought she could best carry her plan out. To this little house she returned, and it became her cherished home for the long remainder of her days. London, during the years of her first success, had not been without its usual attractions to the new-comer, but she had always been alive to the essential incompleteness, the dispersion, the want of steadfast self-collection, in a life much passed in London society. And we may believe that the five austere and lonely years at Tynemouth, with their evening outlook over the busy waters of the harbour-bar into the stern far off sea, may have slowly bred in her an unwillingness to plunge again into the bustling triviality, the gossip, the distracting lightness of the world of splendid fire-flies. To have discerned the Pale Horse so near and for so long a space awakens new moods, and strangely alters the old perspectives of our life. Yet it would imply a misunderstanding of Harriet Martineau's character to suppose that she turned her back upon London, and built her pretty hermitage at Ambleside, in anything like the temper of Jean Jacques Rousseau. She was far too positive a spirit for that, and far too full of vivid and concentrated interest in men and their doings. It would be unjust to think of Harriet Martineau as having no ear for the inner voices, yet her whole nature was objective; it turned to practice and not to reverie. She had her imaginative visions, as we know, and as all truly superior minds have them, even though their main superiority happens to be in the practical order. But her visions were limited as a landscape set in a rigid frame; they had not the wings that soar and poise in the vague unbounded empyrean. And she was much too sensible to think that these moods were strong, or constant, or absorbing enough in her case to furnish material and companionship for a life from day to day and year to year. Nor again was it for the sake of undisturbed acquisition of knowledge, nor cultivation of her finer faculties that she sought a hermitage. She was not moved by thought of the famous maxim which Goethe puts into the mouth of Leonore—

"Es bildet em Talent sich in der Stille,
Sich ein Charakter in dem Strom der Welt."[1]

Though an intense egotist, in the good and respectable sense of insisting on her own way of doing things, of settling for herself what it was that she was living for, and of treading the path with a firm and self-reliant step, yet Harriet Martineau was as little of an egotist as ever lived, in the poor and stifling sense of thinking of the perfecting of her own culture as in the least degree worthy of ranking among Ends-in themselves. She settled in the Lake district because she thought that there she would be most favourably placed for satisfying the various conditions which she had fixed as necessary to her scheme of life. "My own idea of an innocent and happy life," she says, "was a house of my own among poor improvable neighbours, with young servants whom I might train and attach to myself, with pure air, a garden, leisure, solitude at command, and freedom to work in peace and quietness."

"It is the wisest step in her life," Wordsworth said, when he heard that she had bought a piece of land and built a pretty house upon it; and then he added the strangely unpoetic reason—"because the value of the property will be doubled in ten years." Her poetic neighbour gave her a characteristic piece of advice in the same prudential vein. He warned her that she would find visitors a great expense. "When you have a visitor," he said, "you must do as we did; you must say, 'If you like to have a cup of tea with us, you are very welcome; but if you want any meat, you must pay for your board.'" Miss Martineau declined to carry thrift to this ungracious extremity. She constantly had guests in her house, and, if they were all like Charlotte Brontë, they enjoyed their visits in spite of the arbitrary ways of their energetic hostess.

Her manner of life during these years is pleasant to contemplate; cheerful, active, thoroughly wholesome. "My habit," she says, "was to rise at six and to take a walk, returning to my solitary breakfast at half-past seven. My household orders were given for the day, and all affairs settled out of doors and in by a quarter or half-past eight, when I went to work, which I continued without interruption, except from the post, till three

---

[1] Lines from Wolfgang von Goethe's *Torquato Tasso*: "Talent develops (is formed) in stillness (in solitude), character in the full current of the world."

o'clock or later, when alone. While my friend was with me we dined at two, and that was of course the limit of my day's work." De Tocqueville, if we remember, never saw his guests until after he had finished his morning's work, of which he had done six hours by eleven o'clock. Schopenhauer was still more sensitive to the jar of external interruption on that finely-tuned instrument, the brain, after a night's repose, for it was as much as his housekeeper's place was worth to allow either herself or any one else to appear to the philosopher before mid-day. After the early dinner at the Ambleside cottage came little bits of neighbourly business, exercise and so forth. "It is with singular alacrity that in winter evenings I light the lamp and unroll my wool-work, and meditate or dream till the arrival of the newspaper tells me that the tea has stood long enough. After tea, if there was news from the seat of war, I called in my maids, who brought down the great atlas and studied the chances of the campaign with me. Then there was an hour or two for Montaigne, or Bacon, or Shakespeare, or Tennyson, or some dear old biography."

The only productions of this time worth mentioning are the *History of the Thirty Years' Peace* (1849) and the condensed version of Comte's *Positive Philosophy* (1853), both of them meritorious and useful pieces of work, and both of them undertaken, as nearly all Miss Martineau's work was, not from merely literary motives, but because she thought that they would be meritorious and useful, and because nothing more useful came into her head or under her hand at the moment. The condensation of Comte is easy and rapid, and it is said by those who have looked very closely into it, to be hardly free from some too hasty renderings. It must, however, on the whole be pronounced a singularly intelligent and able performance. The pace at which Comte was able to compose is a standing marvel to all who have pondered the great and difficult art of composition. It must be admitted that the author of the English version of him was in this respect no unworthy match for her original. Miss Martineau tells us that she despatched the last three volumes, which number over 1,800 pages, in some five months. She thought the rendering of thirty pages of Comte a fair morning's work. If we consider the abstract and difficult nature of the matter, this must be pronounced something of a feat. We have not space to describe her method, but any reader who happens to be interested in the mechanism of literary productions, will find the passage in vol. ii, p. 391. The *History of the Thirty Years' Peace* is no less astonishing an example of rapid industry. From the first opening of the books to study for the history, to the depositing of the MS. of the first volume at press, was exactly six months. The second volume took six months to do, with an interval of some weeks of holiday and other work!

We think all this worth mentioning, because it is an illustration of what is a highly important maxim; namely, that it is a great mistake to expend more time and labour on a piece of composition than is enough to make it serve the purpose in hand. The immeasurable moment and far-reachingness of the very highest kinds of literature are apt to make men who play at being students forget that there are many other kinds of literature, which are not in the least immeasurably far-reaching, but which, for all that, are extremely useful in their own day and generation. Those highly fastidious and indolent people, who sometimes live at Oxford and Cambridge, with whom indeed for the most part their high fastidiousness is only a fine name for impotence and lack of will, forget that the less immortal kinds of literature are the only kinds within their own reach. Literature is no doubt a fine art—the finest of the arts—but it is also a practical art, and it is deplorable to think how much stout, instructive work might and ought to be done by people who in dreaming of ideals in prose or verse beyond their attainment, end, like the poor Casaubon of fiction, in a little pamphlet on a particle, or else in mediocre poetry, or else in nothing. By insisting on rearing nothing short of a great monument more durable than brass, they are cutting themselves off from building the useful little mud-hut, or some of the other modest performances, by which only . they are capable of serving their age. It is only one volume in a million that is not meant to perish, and to perish soon, as flowers, sunbeams, and all the other brightnesses of the earth are meant to perish. There are some forms of composition in which perfection is not only good but indispensable. But the most are designed for the purpose of a day, and if they have the degree of elaboration, accuracy, grasp, and faithfulness that suffice for the given purpose, then we may say that it is enough. There is literature proper, for which only two or three men and women in a generation have the true gift. This cannot be too good. But besides this there is a mass of honest and needful work to be done with the pen, to which literary form is only accidental, and in which consummate literary finish or depth is a sheer work of supererogation. If Miss Martineau had given twice as many years as she gave months to the condensation of Comte, the book would not have been a whit more useful in any possible respect—indeed, over-elaboration might easily have made it much less so—and the world would have lost many other excellent, if not dazzling or stupendous services.

"Her original power," she wrote of herself in that manly and outspoken obituary notice to which we have already referred, "was nothing more than was due to earnestness and intellectual clearness within a certain range. With small imaginative and suggestive powers, and therefore nothing approaching to genius, she could see clearly what she did see, and give a clear expression to what she had to say. In short, she could popularise, while she could neither discover nor invent.... She could obtain and keep a firm grasp of her own views, and moreover she could make them understood. The function of her life was to do this, and in as far as it was done diligently and honestly, her life was of use." All this is precisely true, and her life was of great use; and that makes what she says not only true, but an example worth much weighing by many of those who meddle with literature.

Miss Martineau was never tired of trying to be useful in directing and improving opinion. She did not disdain the poor neighbours at her gates. She got them to establish a Building Society, she set them an example of thrifty and profitable management by her little farm of two acres, and she gave them interesting and cheerful courses of lectures in the winter evenings. All this time her eye was vigilant for the great affairs of the world. In 1852 she began to write leading articles for the *Daily News*, and in this department her industry and her aptitude were such that at times she wrote as many as six leading articles in a week. When she died, it was computed that she had written sixteen hundred. They are now all dead enough, as they were meant to die, but they made an impression that is still alive in its consequences upon some of the most important social, political, and economical matters of five and twenty important years. In what was by far the greatest of all the issues of those years, the Civil War in the United States, Harriet Martineau's influence was of the most inestimable value in keeping public opinion right against the strong tide of ignorant Southern sympathies in this country. If she may seem to some to have been less right in her views of the Crimean War, we must admit that the issues were very complex, and that complete assurance on that struggle is not easy even at this distance of time.

To this period belong the Biographic Sketches which she contributed to a London newspaper. They have since been collected in a single volume, now in its fourth edition. They are masterpieces in the style of the vignette. Their conciseness, their clearness in fact, their definiteness in judgment, and above all the rightly-graduated impression of the writer's own personality in the background make them perfect in their kind. There is no fretting away of the portrait in over-multiplicity of lines and strokes. Here more than anywhere else, Miss Martineau shows the true quality of the writer, the true mark of literature, the sense of proportion, the modulated sentence, the compact and suggestive phrase. There is a happy precision, a pithy brevity, a condensed argumentativeness. And this literary skill is made more telling by the writer's own evident interest and sincerity about the real lives and characters of the various conspicuous people with whom she deals. It may be said that she has no subtle insight into the complexities of human nature, and that her philosophy of character is rather too little analytical, too downright, too content with averages of motive, and too external. This is so in a general way, but it does not spoil the charm of these sketches, because the personages concerned, though all of them conspicuous, were for the most part commonplace in motive, though more than commonplace in strength of faculty. Subtle analysis is wholly unreasonable in the case of Miss Martineau herself, and she would probably have been unable to use that difficult instrument in criticising characters less downright and objective than her own.

The moment of the Crimean War marked an alarming event in her own life. The doctors warned her that she had a heart disease which would end her days suddenly and soon. Miss Martineau at once set her affairs in order, and sat down to write her Autobiography. She had the manuscript put into type, and the sheets finally printed off, just as we now possess them. But the hour was not yet. The doctors had exaggerated the peril, and the strong woman lived for twenty years after she had been given up. She used up the stuff of her life to the very end, and left no dreary remnant nor morbid waste of days. She was like herself to the last—English, practical, positive. Yet she had thoughts and visions which were more than this. We like to think of this faithful woman and veteran worker in good causes, in the stroll which she always took on her terrace before retiring to rest for the night:—

"On my terrace there were two worlds extended bright before me, even when the midnight darkness hid from my bodily eyes all but the outlines of the solemn mountains that surround our valley on three sides, and the clear opening to the lake on the south. In the one of those worlds I saw now the magnificent coast of Massachusetts in autumn, or the flowery swamps of Louisiana, or the forests of Georgia in spring, or the Illinois prairie in summer; or the blue Nile, or the brown Sinai, or the gorgeous Petra, or the view of Damascus from the Salahiey; or the Grand Canal under a Venetian sunset, or the Black Forest in twilight, or Malta in the glare of noon, or the broad desert stretching away under the stars, or the Red Sea tossing its superb shells on shore in the pale dawn. That is one world, all comprehended within my terrace wall, and coming up into the light at my call. The other and finer scenery is of that world, only beginning to be explored, of Science.... It is truly an exquisite pleasure to dream, after the toil of study, on the sublime abstractions of mathematics; the transcendent scenery unrolled by astronomy; the mysterious, invisible forces dimly hinted to us by physics; the new conception of the constitution of matter originated by chemistry; and then, the inestimable glimpses opened to us, in regard to the nature and destiny of man, by the researches into vegetable and animal organisation, which are at length perceived to be the right path of inquiry into the highest subjects of thought.... Wondrous beyond the comprehension of any one mind is the mass of glorious facts and the series of mighty conceptions laid open; but the shadow of the surrounding darkness rests upon it all. The unknown always engrosses the greater part of the field of vision, and the awe of infinity sanctifies both the study and the dream."

It would be a pity if differences of opinion upon subjects of profound difficulty, remoteness, and manifold perplexity, were to prevent any one from recognising in such words and such moods as these what was, in spite of some infirmities, a character of many large thoughts and much generous purpose. And with this feeling we may part from her.

J.M.

3. W.R. Greg, "Harriet Martineau," *The Nineteenth Century* 2 (August 1877), 97–112

THE biography of this remarkable woman has been received by the public with the eagerness and interest which her fame and her works were pretty sure to command, and has been so widely read that all who see this notice may be confidently assumed to be familiar with the book itself. We can, therefore, dispense with the task of following the narrative step by step, or in any material detail. At the same time the reviews of it which have appeared have, with scarcely an exception, been so discriminating and appreciative, and on the whole so kind and just, that little is left to correct and not a great deal to supply.

But, deeply interesting as the work is, it is impossible to deny that it has given more pain than pleasure to large numbers of those friends who knew her best and valued her most truly. Her own autobiography does her so much less than justice, and the needless, tasteless, and ill-conditioned memorials of the lady to whom she injudiciously entrusted the duties of editor, have managed to convey such an unsound and disfiguring impression of her friend, that the testimony of one who enjoyed her intimacy for many years, and entertained a sincere regard for her throughout, seems wanted to rectify the picture.

It is idle to criticise the egotism of autobiographies, however pervading and intense. Their egotism is their *raison d'être*.[1] It is certain that all persons know much about themselves which no one else can know, look and must look at themselves from a special standpoint, and from one which has, if exceptional dangers, exceptional advantages as well; and the more thoroughly searching and self-observing—that is, the more egotistical—their narrative is, the more valuable is it likely to prove. All that we are entitled to require is that it shall be unflinchingly honest and sincere according to the writers' light. Self-knowledge, humility, just and moderate appreciation of their qualities and achievements, we may desiderate, but we have no right to demand. The very absence of these mental or moral gifts may be among the most salient characteristics which it is the worth of autobiography that it reveals to us. We cannot claim from the painters of their own portraits, or the writers of their own lives, that they shall tell us truly what they were— only that they shall tell us truthfully what they appeared to themselves to be—and this requisite of biography Miss Martineau rigidly fulfils. Writing invariably with the most patent candour and courage, she tells the truth wherever and so far as she could see it, and betrays it almost as plainly where it was obviously hidden from her eyes.

But not only is the book preponderatingly full of herself, as it was quite right that it should be; not only does it describe everything exclusively and unquestioningly from her own point of view, as was inevitable: it will appear to most readers to paint the world itself as also extravagantly full of her, and to represent herself as occupying a larger space in its horizon, and making a more prominent figure in its drama, than was really the case. She describes herself, from her first sudden plunge into publicity and fame in 1832 (when the extraordinary success of her *Political Economy Tales* took the world by surprise), as run after, fêted, flattered, beset with admirers, haunted and beleaguered by politicians who wanted to use her, publishers who wanted to secure her services, worshippers of celebrity who wanted her presence in their saloons, real adorers of talent and worth, who out of simple kindliness and interest wished to know and to befriend a writer of such rare promise;— and she narrates all this with a certain natural excitement and vividness

---

[1]   The reason or justification for its being (French).

of colouring which irresistibly convey the impression of exaggeration. The answer is that all this was true. The London world did run after her in a fashion to which it is often prone. Her advent created a sensation which was extraordinary, which, looking back upon the circumstances, seems now somewhat disproportionate to its cause, and which continued for a longer period than is usual with sudden enthusiasms of that nature. The *digito monstrari et dicier hæc est*[1] haunted her steps for many years and in far-distant scenes. 'The United States,' says Mrs. Chapman, 'seemed for the moment a mere whispering gallery for the transmission of her opinions.' Fussy patriots of several lands applied to her to make constitutions for them, and to plead their cause before the world's tribunal. Small blame to her if she took herself at the world's estimation, and believed, what hosts of people assured her, hour by hour—namely, that she was a rising star, a new power come upon the stage, gifted with astonishing capacities and destined to an exceptional career. She was not exactly spoiled by her metropolitan reception, novel and stimulating as it was; but it developed the seeds of already existing faults into a singularly rapid growth. She was suspiciously on her guard against its dangers; she resented the bare notion of being 'lionised,' and constantly fancied she was being lionised in circles whose tone, if she had understood it, would have secured her from anything of the sort. She accepted the homage readily enough, and enjoyed it thoroughly, though scarcely simply; for she took up the absurd position of refusing to be sought for her eminent talent and success, 'would not be visited or invited as a blue-stocking, but as a lady, &c.'—forgetting that, as a mere unknown lady and apart from her literary powers, she had no claim to be visited at all; so that no wonder her genial and experienced friend, Mr. Hallam, thought her conceited and presuming. There is scarcely an indication of simple gratification at having obtained entrance and cordial greeting into a class of society incomparably superior, intellectually and politically, to that she had been used to—no trace of a perception that it was in any way superior—no attitude of mind towards it except the critical one; and her criticisms were, in the vast majority of instances, depreciating even to unseemliness.

The tone in which she speaks of at least half her London acquaintances, her sketches of friends and foes alike, the sovereign contempt in the one set of portraits, the rancorous animosity in the other, and the

---

[1]   Roughly, to be pointed out and to have it said—"This be he" (Latin). From the proverbs of Persius (34–62 A.D.): "It is a pleasant thing to be pointed at with the finger, and to hear it said, 'That is he.'"

utter injustice and almost libellous character of many, are probably the features of her book which will leave the most painful impression. The Whigs, as a body, though the party to whose gallant efforts the wonderful progress of the nation in those days was incontestably due, were, for some reason or other, the objects of her vehement detestation.

'The young Romillys had virtuous projects when they entered political life, and had every hope of achieving service worthy of their father's fame; but their aspirations were speedily tamed down, *as all high aspirations are lowered by Whig influences.*' The Whig touch perished it (the voice of the people) at once; the poverty and perverseness of their ideas and the insolence of their feelings were precisely what might have been expected from *that remarkably vulgar class of men.*' There was nothing to be expected from the official Whigs now (1848) that they were spoiled by the possession of place and power. [They had been her earliest admirers and most eager assistants, but they had made the mistake of offering advice.] I had seen that they had learned nothing by their opportunities; that they were hardened in their conceit and prejudices, and as blind as bats to the new lights which time was introducing into society.... I have seen a good deal of life, and many varieties of manners; and it now appears to me (1855) that *the broadest vulgarity I have encountered is in the families of official Whigs,* who conceive themselves the cream of society, and the lights and rulers of the empire.'

Her abuse of Brougham we shall not contest, and there may have been excuse enough for her remarks on Lockhart and Croker. But her *de-haut-en-bas* [1] judgment of Macaulay is perhaps widest of the mark. He was all blossom and no fruit; 'he wants heart;' his speeches 'were fundamentally *weak*;' 'he has never (1855) achieved any complete success. As a politician his failure has been signal,' &c. &c.

Her sketch of Bishop Stanley is ludicrously astray; he, remarkable for pluck and spirit, and liberal in days when liberality was rare, 'had no courage or dignity under the bad manners of his Tory clergy; and he repeatedly talked to me about it in such a style as to compel me to tell him plainly that dissenters like myself are not only accustomed to ill-usage for difference of opinion, but are brought up to regard that trial as one belonging to all honest avowal of convictions, and to be borne with courage and patience like other trials!'

---

[1] Top-to-bottom (French).

But 'good Mr. Porter, of the Board of Trade,' an intimate friend of her own, the eminent publicist and statistician, perhaps fares the worst. He was 'amiable and friendly, industrious and devoted to his business, but sadly weak and inaccurate, prejudiced and *borné* in ability.' 'Nothing could be more untrustworthy and delusive than his statistics.' His great book, still an authority, on the *Progress of the Nation*, is declared to be full of the shallowest and most ludicrous blunders. 'Not his innocent vanity, which was far from immoderate, but his deficiency in sense and intellectual range, together with his confidence in himself and his want of confidence in all public men, was an insuperable disqualification for the sound discharge of his functions,' &c. &c.

Now it is difficult for those who read this gallery of portraits—shallow, contemptuous, condemnatory, and curiously astray as, in spite of occasional shrewdness, they for the most part are—who remember, too, that they are the judicial sentences delivered posthumously upon a number of eminent contemporaries by a writer whose most marked characteristic it was that she would neither endure nor pardon the faintest censure on herself, nor admit for a moment that any human being had the slightest claim to sit in judgment on her, far less to express an opinion or pronounce a verdict—and who find that these depreciating pictures were painted, laid by in closets, embalmed for the enlightenment of posterity, for twenty years before the painter's death without any dream of revision—it is difficult for readers not to receive the impression that Miss Martineau was essentially ill-natured and given to bitterness and depreciation. In conveying this impression she does herself grievous injustice. There has seldom been a more kindly-hearted or affectionate person, or even one more given to an over-estimate of her friends, perhaps even more prone to make idols out of not quite the finest clay, more watchfully considerate to all dependent upon her, more steadfastly devoted to those who had once got hold of her imagination or attachment, unless they tried her constancy too hardly by criticism, opposition, or condemnation. All her geese were swans. All her servants and junior relatives were devoted to her, and with good reason, for there was a vast element of geniality about her. In spite of the painful description she gives of her early life (which we believe her connections scarcely recognise as faithful), she was, we should pronounce, from the time she had once found her work and made her mark, a singularly happy person; and continued to grow happier and happier, illness notwithstanding, till near the end. Her unflinching belief in herself, her singular exemption from the sore torment of doubt or hesitation, helped to make her so.

Now, happy people, where really good-hearted and sociable, *are* genial; their enjoyment is so simple and genuine, and their confidence in the prompt cordial sympathy of those around them is so undoubting and so provocative of response. The charm of Harriet Martineau's intercourse (passing over the fits of indignation her dogmatic damnation of your bosom friends would often rouse) may be understood by those who read the 'Sixth Period' of her autobiography,—especially the description of the joyous epoch when, in the midst of rest, and health, and vigour, she settled among the lakes and mountains of Westmoreland, built her Windermere home, and reorganised her recovered life for a fresh burst of animation and productiveness.

Her character was easy to read, for in one sense it was consistent enough and presented no mysteries or depths; and her faults, which were neither few nor small, were readily forgiven her, for she loved much and laboured hard for the happiness of others. In an unusual degree it was to be said of Harriet Martineau *qu'elle avait les défauts de ses qualités.*[1] It would indeed have been difficult for her to have had the mental and moral gifts which distinguished her so signally without the analogous errors, in the way of deficiency or excess, which impaired their perfection and detracted from their value. 'Authors,' says Southey, 'may be divided into two classes, spiders and silk-worms—those who spin because they are empty, and those who spin because they are full.' Miss Martineau was one of the latter. She never, after her very youthful years, wrote either for money or for fame. She wrote because the matter was borne in upon her, because the idea or the subject had taken possession of her, because the thing in her conception 'wanted saying,' and it was in her to say it, and was not open to her to withhold it. With the promptitude and force of irresistible conviction the work assumed in her mind the position of a duty to be done—almost of an inspired utterance that *must* be given forth. Hence the curious arrogance with which she resented the slightest approaches towards suggestion, remonstrance, or advice, the *noli me tangere*[2] vehemence with which she insisted that no other mind should ever be permitted to interfere with the operations or visions of her own. Hence also the extraordinarily rapid imaginations she poured out, and the unhesitating confidence with which, when once written, she hurried them to the press. She not only would not alter at the suggestion of others; she would rarely if ever

---

[1]   That she had the defects (or faults) of her qualities (French).

[2]   Do not touch me (Latin), originally said by Jesus to Mary Magdalene after his resurrection.

revise or correct in consequence of any caution or misgiving of her own. Misgiving seems, indeed, to have been a sensation that was alien to her constitution. Like Balaam, the word that the Lord put into her mouth, that she must speak. Her marvellous productiveness, the unequalled rapidity with which she turned out her admirable stories, might well cultivate her self-confidence to an extravagant degree. No one who worked so quickly or so hard ever worked so well. It seemed almost—quite so to herself—'as if it were given her in that same hour what she should say.' There was no long brooding, no meditation, no slow process of hatching inchoate germs, no painful collection of ample and carefully sifted materials; the plan and the table of contents of her books, as it were, flashed upon her like the intuitions of a poet; the executive efficiency of her intelligence was absolutely unrivalled; her style was always, nearly from the outset, clear, lucid, vigorous, and simple, without a trace of effort, and never, as far as we remember, betraying the faintest lapse into those faults of fine or ambitious writing which are the besetting sin of youth.

Considering, then, these extraordinary powers, her consciousness of abounding energy, the suddenness and brilliancy of her success, and the fame and adulation with which she was surrounded at such exciting times and amid such dazzling circles, the self-confidence which promptly grew upon her, however regrettable, was not only natural, but its absence would have been all but miraculous. The truth is that doubt seems to have been a state of mind unknown to her. She never reconsidered her opinions, or mused over her judgments. They were instantaneous insights, not deliberate or gradual deductions. It scarcely seemed to occur to her that she could be wrong; that thousands of eminent or wise men differed from her never appeared to suggest the probability; we never recollect her views, if once formed, being changed or materially modified during a discussion. And this was the more remarkable because, in the first place, her confidence in her own opinions was not irrational conceit in her own powers; on the contrary, her estimate of these was not at all inordinate, but, as may be seen especially in her last obituary notice of herself in the *Daily News*, rather below the truth, not to say wide of it. And in the second place, she was by no means an unimpressible person, but the reverse. If you spoke to her of men or things before she had formed any judgment of either, you usually found little difficulty in writing your impressions on her mind; but if you were a day too late, if you missed your innings, it was almost hopeless to effect a change—she was

Wax to receive, and marble to retain.[1]

Given, then, a mind of really almost unrivalled innate powers, and, as was inevitable, a strong consciousness of those powers and an irrepressible impulse to use them, a vivid imagination incessantly at work, and—owing partly to her deafness and partly to the early want of exuberant sympathies around her—working usually in solitude; courage, fortitude, and pertinacity of something like the Stoic stamp, a force of conviction akin to that of the fanatic and the martyr, an impatient temperament amounting to a sort of incapacity for doubt, and rendering suspension of judgment an unnatural frame of mind—the fair analyst of character is driven to pronounce that Harriet Martineau could not easily have been less dogmatic, less hasty, or less imperious than she was. One grievous mistake—the parent of countless errors and injustices—she might indeed have escaped, and it is strange that so clear an intelligence as hers should have become so habitually its victim; for the rock was staringly above water. Her deafness absolutely disqualified her either for accurate observation or positive judgments of men—yet she never appears to have dreamed of the disqualification. In society she heard only what was directly intended for her, and moreover only what was specially designed to pass down her trumpet; and comments, sentiments, and statements that must go through this ordeal are inevitably manufactured, or at least modified, for export. A hundred things are dropped or whispered which are never shouted, or pronounced *ore rotundo*[2] or oracularly—and these former are precisely the things which betray character and suggest true conclusions. As Sydney Smith remarked in reference to her, 'she took *au sérieux*[3] half the sayings I meant as mystifications.' Moreover, not only was she not on her guard against this obviously fertile source of blunders—not only did it inspire no sense of misgiving—but she aggravated its unavoidable mischief by a practice, which grew upon her as life went on, of laying down the trumpet before the sentence or the paragraph of her interlocutor was complete, or sometimes, we must add, when she had decided that it would not be worth listening to, or when it was apparently tending in an unwelcome direction. Thus the information or impression conveyed to her by a conversation was often altogether inaccurate or imperfect,

---

[1] Line from George Gordon, Lord Byron's *Beppo* (stanza 34): "His heart was one of those which most enamour us, Wax to receive, and marble to retain."

[2] In well-turned or "rounded" speech (Latin).

[3] Seriously, "as serious" (French).

but never on that account for one instant mistrusted. Those who knew her were fully aware of this peculiarity, and those of her readers who remember the times, and scenes, and people of whom she writes can trace innumerable instances of it, and will be on their guard against too absolute a reliance on narratives and statements written down twenty years after date, then printed and laid up in lavender for another twenty years, and now in many cases out of reach of authoritative correction.

In another point Miss Martineau had *les défauts de ses qualités*. She was conscientious, we may say, in the extreme; her conscience was not only commanding—it had something about it excessive, morbid, or awry. She obeyed it like an oracle, but she rarely took the precaution of requesting it to reconsider its decisions. Now, with all reasonable deference to popular axioms of morality, it is not at all impossible for men and women to have too imperious and impetuous a conscience—in fact, to carry more sail than their ballast will warrant or can bear. Harriet Martineau did this in a signal manner. Having no power of doubt and no sense of fear, she christened all her impulses with the name of Duty, and followed them resolutely and in defiance of remonstrance. Like many of us, only more than most, she abounded in 'views,' which she called 'principles,' and then anointed and enthroned. Conscience was rather her tyrant than her guide, and was installed before it had been anxiously enlightened.

Perhaps the most interesting portion of the autobiography to many will prove to be the narrative of the writer's theological, or, as she names it, anti-theological progress, the gradual movement of a curiously courageous, honest, and inquiring mind—one, too, singularly earnest in tone and religious in temperament—from positive belief to equally 'positive philosophy.' She began as a Unitarian of the dryest and most dogmatic form, and ended life as an enthusiastic Agnostic. She began as a disciple of Belsham, and finished as a disciple of Comte; and of each faith in turn she was, we need scarcely say, an ardent and undoubting proselyting preacher. Her earliest literary success consisted of three prize essays on the arguments for converting Catholics, Mohammedans, and Jews to Unitarian Christianity. Her last book was the *Letters on Man's Nature and Development*, which she undertook in concert with her final 'guide, philosopher, and friend,' Mr. Atkinson, for the conversion of Judaism, Islamism, Christianity, and Deism from all forms of theological belief alike. Her Unitarianism was early discarded, and discarded with what seems to us, according to her own account, irrational and uncharitable contempt. She was first shaken by the necessarian doctrine, then altogether upset by a strong impression of the deep selfishness and almost shocking notions of God which appeared to lie at the root of the whole scheme of damnation and redemption embodied in the popular creed—an impression by no means uncommon with those who either approach Christianity from the outside, or eventually get outside it.

Much that Miss Martineau says about the Atkinson letters seems to us very touching—much curiously blind and almost absurd. Her mind, while marching onward towards unbelief, was very lonely and sometimes sad, and the perhaps scarcely warranted influence obtained over her by Mr. Atkinson was due to the fact that from him she first obtained *full* sympathy in her new and *isolating* views; and neither of them probably was quite able or inclined to recognise how shallow and inconclusive many of the arguments, which seemed to them so decisive, really appeared to profounder and better trained intelligences. Certainly neither of them dreamed how arrogant and irritating the whole tone of the work and scores of the dogmatic and contemptuous expressions must have seemed to the majority of readers, whose tenderest convictions were thus roughly handled. Many of the friends whose anger and antagonism she aroused, no doubt took up a temper and a style of rebuke utterly and often ludicrously inadmissible among devotees of truth, who are not entitled to wonder at differences of opinion or to resent them; but it never seems to have crossed her mind that on the whole her own language was often the unseemlier of the two. On the whole, by the publication of that book, though she gave infinite pain, she suffered little if she ventured much; and considering the vastness and deep gravity of the questions at issue, the space devoted in her autobiography to the purely personal and *sensitive* portion of the subject strikes us as rather below the dignity of Miss Martineau, and we pass on to what interests us far more.

Twice in her life she stood for a long period face to face with death, and *studying that position* day by day with all the courage, sincerity, and solemn earnestness of a deep and very honest nature. There was no doubt of the genuineness of the position, even though both she and her medical advisers may have been in error, or at issue, with regard to the imminence of her danger. And she has left us a singularly plainly drawn portrait of her mental and moral state, analysed with courage, and as she saw it under the influence of two antagonistic creeds. Perhaps such a contrasting and vivid portrait has never been left on record by any equal intellect. It is well worth dwelling on.

The passage we have already quoted, combined with a reference to the 'Sick Room' of which she speaks, will show how she met and regarded her approaching end in the light and under the support of the ordinary views of believers in a future life and a presiding Providence. We will presently quote a passage describing the more genuine confidence and peace with which she prepared to die when convinced that death was the final close of individual or conscious existence, and of the greater comfort as well as *certainty* to her mind of the later faith. For, surprising and startling as it will be to most of her readers, let no man question that these convictions (to most so desolate) were to her positive beliefs and not mere negations, a creed not an atheism, as firmly held as doctrines which take martyrs to the stake, and, moreover, seemingly as joyous as any which ever brightened the last hours of an intelligent and beautiful career. Nothing seems more curiously clear than that her course of thought and sentiment became step by step more enthusiastically cheerful and even glad as, to use her own expression, she exchanged the delusions of theology for the certainties of science, or, as others would describe the same march, as she shook herself gradually free from Christianity, revelation, and dogmatic theism, and took refuge in what some call Agnosticism, and others Knowledge. These views may not be ours; they may be far, indeed, to us from either giving confidence or inspiring joy, but it is simply idle and foolish to deny that they are compatible, at least, with the truest peace and cheerfulness to hundreds with whose intellects we can claim no equality; no one perhaps has explained what comfort they are capable of yielding with such bold and simple nakedness as Harriet Martineau; and it is to lose one of the richest lessons of her book to disbelieve the truthfulness of these pages of self-development. [Quotes from the *Autobiography*, pp. 560–61, 568, 575]

Now, whatever estimate we may form as to the distinctness of the ideas here conveyed, the correctness of the predictions, or the taste and judgment of some of the phraseology employed, no one can doubt the sincerity of the relief expressed; nor can any who knew Miss Martineau question for a moment that the last twenty-five years of her life, the unbelieving portion as it would be termed, were incomparably the happiest and most buoyant. Yet the last twenty of these were passed, in her own conviction at least, under sentence of imminent and probably sudden death. And the following is her deliberate account of her feelings and reflections under the solemn prospect: [Quotes from the *Autobiography*, pp. 630–33]

It is difficult for minds brought up in the conviction of continuous or renewed existence in some altogether different sphere, some world of solved problems and of realised ideals, where every perplexity will be cleared up, every limitation melt away, every corner of space be visited, and every avenue to knowledge opened to our purified vision during eternal years—it is difficult for such minds either to acquiesce in the cessation of conscious being and identity here described, or to thoroughly believe in the cheerfulness of this acquiescence. That so curiously active an intellect should be so content in the prospect of inaction; that one who so thirsted after science should be satisfied, having learned so little, never to learn more; that one so wakeful should thus welcome everlasting sleep; that one who to her last breath felt so intense an interest in the future of the race to which she was to belong no more, should yet be so happy in view of a non-existence in which that future must be absolutely dark, seems all but incredible, would be quite incredible did we not know it to be the case with hundreds who yet calmly submit to the inevitable. But there is something behind yet harder to receive— that those whose blessedness in this world has lain, not in philosophy but in affection, not in the accumulation of knowledge but in the interchange of love, whose joy too has consisted rather in the lastingness than the mere fact of their unitedness, should, out of pure submission not to 'God's will' but to the 'laws of Nature,' be able, when the hour comes to die, willingly and even gratefully to utter the *Vale vale, in æternum vale*,[1] to the sharers of their life on earth. This is unquestionably the harder— may it not also be the higher—form of pious resignation?—the last achievement of the ripened mind? The following is Harriet Martineau's 'last view of the world:'—[Quotes from the *Autobiography*, p. 647]

I am confident that a brighter day is coming for future generations. Our race has been as Adam created at nightfall. The solid earth has been but dark, or dimly visible, while the eye was inevitably drawn to the mysterious heavens above. There, the successive mythologies have arisen in the east, each a constellation of truths, each glorious and fervently worshipped in its course; but the last and noblest, the Christian, is now not only sinking to the horizon, but paling in the dawn of a brighter time. The dawn is unmistakable; and the sun will not be long in coming up. The last of the mythologies is about to vanish before the flood of a brighter light.

With the last of the mythologies will pass away, after some lingering, the immoralities which have attended all mythologies. Now, while the state of our race is such as to need all our mutual devotedness, all our aspiration, all our resources of courage, hope, faith, and

---

[1]   Latin elegiac phrase, "Farewell, farewell, for eternity farewell."

good cheer, the disciples of the Christian creed and morality are called upon, day by day, to 'work out their own salvation with fear and trembling,' and so forth. Such exhortations are too low for even the wavering mood and quacked morality of a time of theological suspense and uncertainty. In the extinction of that suspense, and the discrediting of that selfish quackery, I see the prospect, for future generations, of a purer and loftier virtue and a truer and sweeter heroism than divines who preach such self-seeking can conceive of. When our race is trained in the morality which belongs to ascertained truth, all 'fear and trembling' will be left to children; and men will have risen to a capacity for higher work than saving themselves—to that of 'working out' the welfare of their race, not in 'fear and trembling,' but with serene hope and joyful assurance.

The world as it is is growing somewhat dim before my eyes; but the world as it is to be looks brighter every day.

W.R. GREG.

Works Cited and Recommended Reading

I. Bibliography, Biography, and Letters

Arbuckle, Elisabeth S., ed. *Harriet Martineau's Letters to Fanny Wedgwood.* Stanford, CA: Stanford UP, 1983.

Burchell, R. A., ed. *Harriet Martineau in America: Selected Letters from the Reinhard S. Speck Collection.* Berkeley: Friends of the Bancroft Library, 1995.

Chapman, Maria Weston, ed. *Memorials. Harriet Martineau's Autobiography,* vol. 3. London: Smith, Elder, 1877.

Fielding, Kenneth, and Ian Campbell. "New Letters of Harriet Martineau to Jane Carlyle, 1842–44." *Women's Writing* 9 (2002): 379–94.

Greg, W. R. "Harriet Martineau." *The Nineteenth Century* 2 (August 1877): 97–112.

Horne, R. H. *A New Spirit of the Age,* 2 vols. London: Smith, Elder & Co., 1844.

Logan, Deborah, ed. *The Collected Letters of Harriet Martineau,* 5 vols. London: Pickering & Chatto, 2007.

Maclise, Daniel. "Miss Harriet Martineau." In *Daniel Maclise, 1806–1870: A Gallery of Illustrious Literary Characters.* New York: Scribner and Welford, 1883.

Martineau, James. "The Early Days of Harriet Martineau." *London Daily News,* 30 December 1884.

Miller, Florence Fenwick. *Harriet Martineau.* London: W.H. Allen, 1884. Reprint. Port Washington, NY: Kennikat Press, 1972.

Morley, John. "Harriet Martineau." *Macmillan's Magazine* 36 (May 1877): 47–60.

Oliphant, Margaret. "Harriet Martineau." *Blackwood's Edinburgh Magazine* 121 (1877): 472–96.

Richardson, Betty. "The Wedgwood-Martineau Correspondence." *Papers on Language and Literature* 20 (Fall 1984): 453–57.

Rivlin, Joseph B. *Harriet Martineau: A Bibliography of her Separately Printed Books.* New York: The New York Public Library, 1947.

Sanders, Valerie, ed. *Harriet Martineau: Selected Letters.* Oxford: Clarendon Press, 1990.

Simcox, G.A. "Miss Martineau." *Fortnightly Review* 124 (April 1877): 516–37.

Webb, R.K. *Harriet Martineau: A Radical Victorian.* New York: Columbia UP, 1960.

Yates, Gayle Graham. *Harriet Martineau on Women.* New Brunswick, NJ: Rutgers UP, 1985.

II. Literary History and Criticism

Amigoni, David. "Gendered Authorship, Literary Lionism and the Virtues of Domesticity: Contesting Wordsworth's Fame in the Life and Writings of Harriet Martineau and Thomas Carlyle." *Critical Survey* 13 (2001): 26–41.

Arbuckle, Elisabeth. "Harriet Martineau and her Feminine 'Tail,'" *Women's Writing* 9 (2002): 445–60.

Bohrer, Susan. "Harriet Martineau: Gender, Disability and Liability," *Nineteenth-Century Contexts* 25 (March 2003): 21–37.

Broughton, Trev Lynn. "Making the Most of Martyrdom: Harriet Martineau, Autobiography, and Death." *Literature and History* 2 (1993): 24–45.

David, Deirdre. *Intellectual Women and Victorian Patriarchy: Harriet Martineau, Elizabeth Barrett Browning, George Eliot.* Ithaca: Cornell UP, 1987.

Easley, Alexis. *First-Person Anonymous: Women Writers and Victorian Print Media, 1830–70.* Aldershot, England: Ashgate, 2004.

——. "Authorship, Gender and Power in Victorian Culture: Harriet Martineau and the Periodical Press." *Nineteenth-Century Media and the Construction of Identities.* Ed. Laurel Brake, Bill Bell, and David Finkelstein. New York, NY: Palgrave, 2000. 154–64.

Frawley, Maria. "Harriet Martineau, Health and Journalism." *Women's Writing* 9 (2002): 433–44.

——. "'A Prisoner to the Couch': Harriet Martineau, Invalidism, and Self-Representation." *The Body and Physical Difference: Discourses of Disability.* Ed. David T. Mitchell and Sharon L. Snyder. Ann Arbor, MI: U of Michigan P, 1997. 174–88.

——. "'The Range of Our Vision': Self, Surveillance, and Life in the Sickroom." *Invalidism and Identity in Nineteenth-Century Britain.* Chicago: U of Chicago P, 2004. 200–44.

Freedgood, Elaine. "Banishing Panic: Harriet Martineau and the Popularization of Political Economy." *Victorian Studies* 39 (Autumn 1995): 33–53.

Highfill, Janett K., and William V. Weber. "Harriet Martineau: An Economic View of Victorian Arts and Letters." *Journal of Cultural Economics* 15 (June 1991), 85–92.

Hobart, Ann. "Harriet Martineau's Political Economy of Everyday Life." *Victorian Studies* 37 (Winter 1994): 223–52.

Hoecker-Drysdale, Susan. *Harriet Martineau: First Woman Sociologist.* New York: Berg, 1992.

Hunter, Shelagh. *Harriet Martineau: The Poetics* of *Moralism*. Brookfield, VT: Scolar Press, 1995.

Ketabgian, Tamara. "Martineau, Mesmerism, and the 'Night Side of Nature.'" *Women's Writing* 9 (2002): 351–68.

Logan, Deborah Anna. *The Hour and the Woman: Harriet Martineau's "Somewhat Remarkable" Life*. DeKalb, IL: Northern Illinois UP, 2002.

——, ed. *Harriet Martineau's Writing's on Slavery and the American Civil War*. DeKalb, IL: Northern Illinois UP, 2002.

——, ed. *Illustrations of Political Economy: Selected Tales*. By Harriet Martineau. Peterborough, ON: Broadview Press, 2004.

Logan, Deborah Anna, and Valerie Sanders. *Harriet Martineau*. Special issue of *Women's Writing* 9 (2002): 331–460.

Myers, Mitzi. "Harriet Martineau's Autobiography: The Making of a Female Philosopher." *Women's Autobiography*. Ed. Estelle C. Jelinek. Bloomington, IN: Indiana UP, 1980. 53–70.

——. "Unmothered Daughter and Radical Reformer: Harriet Martineau." *The Lost Tradition: Mothers and Daughters in Literature*. Ed. Cathy Davidson and E. Broner. New York: Frederick Ungar, 1980. 70–80.

Orazem, Claudia. *Political Economy and Fiction in the Early Works of Harriet Martineau*. New York: Peter Lang, 1999.

Pelatson, Timothy. "Life Writing." *A Companion to Victorian Literature and Culture*. Ed. Herbert F. Tucker. Oxford: Blackwell, 1999. 356–72.

Peterson, Linda H. "Harriet Martineau's *Household Education*: Revising the Feminine Tradition." *Culture and Education in Victorian England*. Ed. Patrick Scott and Pauline Fletcher. Lewisburg, PA: Bucknell UP, 1990. 183–94.

——. "Harriet Martineau: Masculine Discourse, Female Sage." *Victorian Sages and Cultural Discourse*. Ed. Thais Morgan. New Brunswick, NJ: Rutgers UP, 1990. 171–86.

——. "The Polemics of Piety: Charlotte Elizabeth Tonna's *Personal Recollections*, Harriet Martineau's *Autobiography*, and the Ideological Uses of Spiritual Autobiography." *Traditions of Victorian Women's Autobiography: The Poetics and Politics of Life Writing*. Charlottesville, VA: UP of Virginia, 1999. 43–79.

——. "(Re)inventing Authorship: Harriet Marinteau in the Literary Marketplace of the 1820s." *Women's Writing* 9 (2002): 337–50.

——. "Sage Writing." *A Companion to Victorian Literature and Culture*. Ed. Herbert E. Tucker. Oxford: Blackwell, 1999. 73–87.

Pichanick, Valerie Kossew. *Harriet Martineau: The Woman and Her Work, 1802–1876*. Ann Arbor: U of Michigan P, 1980.

Postlethwaite, Diana. "Mothering and Mesmerism in the Life of Harriet Martineau." *Signs* 14 (1989): 583–609.

Roberts, Caroline. *The Woman and the Hour: Harriet Martineau and Victorian Ideologies*. Toronto: U of Toronto P, 2002.

Sanders, Valerie. "'Absolutely an Act of Duty': Choice of Profession in Autobiographies by Victorian Women." *Prose Studies* 9 (December 1986): 54–70.

———. "Harriet Martineau in the Bicentenary Year." *Women's Writing* 9 (2002): 331–36.

———. *Reason over Passion: Harriet Martineau and the Victorian Novel*. New York: St. Martin's Press, 1986.

———. "'Meteor Wreaths': Harriet Martineau, 'L. E. L.,' Fame and Fraser's Magazine." *Critical Survey* 13 (2001): 42–60.

Thomas, Gillian. *Harriet Martineau*. Boston: Twayne, 1985.

Wheatley, Vera. *The Life and Work of Harriet Martineau*. Fair Lawn, NJ: Essential Books, 1957.

Winter, Alison. *Mesmerized. Powers of Mind in Victorian Britain*. Chicago: U of Chicago P, 1998.

Weiner, Gaby, ed. "Introduction." *Harriet Martineau's Autobiography*. London: Virago, 1983.

Yates, Jennifer. "A 'Habit of Speculation': Women, Gossip, and Publicity in Harriet Martineau's *Deerbrook*." *Women's Writing* 9 (2002): 369–78.